CHRIST THE LIBERATOR

Jon Sobrino

CHRIST THE LIBERATOR

A View from the Victims

Translated from the Spanish by
Paul Burns

ORBIS BOOKS

Maryknoll, New York 10545

Second printing, October 2003

Founded in 1970, Orbis Books endeavors to publish works that enlighten the mind, nour-ish the spirit, and challenge the conscience. The publishing arm of the Maryknoll Fathers and Brothers, Orbis seeks to explore the global dimensions of the Christian faith and mission, to invite dialogue with diverse cultures and religious traditions, and to serve the cause of reconciliation and peace. The books published reflect the views of their authors and do not represent the official position of the Society. To learn more about Maryknoll and Orbis Books, please visit our website at www.maryknoll.com.

Translation copyright © 2001 by Orbis Books.

This is a translation of *La fe en Jesucristo: Ensayo desde las víctimas*, originally pub-lished in Spanish by Editorial Trotta, Madrid, Spain, copyright © 1999.

Published by Orbis Books, Maryknoll, NY 10545-0308.

Manufactured in the United States of America.

Typesetting by Joan Weber Laflamme.

Library of Congress Cataloging-in-Publication Data

Sobrino, Jon.
    [Fe en Jesucristo. English]
    Christ the Liberator : a view from the victims / Jon Sobrino ; translated from the Spanish
by Paul Burns.
       p. cm.
    Includes bibliographical references.
    ISBN 1-57075-372-5
    1. Jesus Christ—Person and offices. 2. Jesus Christ—Resurrection. 3. Poverty—Religious
aspects—Catholic Church. 4. Liberation theology. 5. Catholic Church—Doctrines. I.
Title.

BT203 .S6413 2001
232—dc21
                                              2001021394

Contents

PART II
CHRISTOLOGICAL TITLES IN THE NEW TESTAMENT
A Rereading from Latin America

PART III
CONCILIAR CHRISTOLOGY

Introduction

This book is the continuation of *Jesus the Liberator: A Historical-Theological Reading of Jesus of Nazareth*.[1] This contained a long introduction on the whys and wherefores of a new book on Jesus Christ, with so many already in existence. Now, in presenting *Christ the Liberator: A View from the Victims*, I should like once more to share with readers the questions I asked myself while writing it, bearing in mind that the seven years that have elapsed between the composition of the first volume and of this one have seen many changes in the concerns, and particularly the approach, of theology. Paradigms have changed, to the point where it might be asked if there is anything so important as not to have changed because it might be called meta-paradigmatic. I shall share the questions I was faced with in the form of short reflections on the book's title, but first let me summarize its contents.

The book is divided into three parts. The first deals with the resurrection of Jesus, the second with the christology of the New Testament as seen in the titles given to Jesus, and the third on the definitions produced by the early councils. In each part I analyze what the biblical and conciliar texts have to say on the reality of Jesus Christ, doing so from specific viewpoints and with a definite aim. So I look at the resurrection of Jesus from *the hope of the victims*—with the correlative revelation of God as God of victims—and from the possibility of *living already as risen beings* in the conditions of historical existence. I examine the christological titles from *the transformation made by God*—and made manifest in Jesus Christ—of what is meant by mediation, messianism, lordship, sonship, to show that the truth of God in Jesus is above all good news. Finally, I analyze the conciliar formulae from their formal dimension: how they present the *totality of reality* and its differentiated unity (its *holism,* one might say, as the term was understood at the time); and how they relate God with humanity, God, and suffering. So I am examining divinity from *the transformation brought about by Jesus*. And I also analyze the definitions as doxological formulae, which require a process of understanding, to which I would add a course through history. This course is the following of Jesus, in such a way that this acquires an epistemological dimension.

This is where the book ends. I do not deal with the history of christologies, those of the Middle Ages, or those that arose in the context of the Reformation, the most important being Luther's. Nor do I analyze present-day systematic christologies, although several of them—above all, what might be called classic ones (those of progressive, political, and liberation theologies)—are incorporated, in one way or another, in my theological discourse. Nor do I examine the new

1

christological essays now issuing from indigenous and African-American con-texts, from gender and ecological concerns, and from interfaith dialogue. As a whole, these essays strike me as both necessary and positive: liberation theology sees them as such because they introduce various forms of *otherness* into christology, not only that generated by *oppression*. To all of them, however, I make only brief allusions.

As the foregoing will have indicated, this book is not designed as a textbook or as a manual setting out and analyzing in a structured manner the sum total of christological understanding proclaimed by the church throughout its history. It is rather an essay in which I try to set out and analyze what strike me as the fundamental points of christology, those that last and recur. I certainly try to write from the *reality of faith*, set in motion by the event of Jesus Christ, and from the *situation of victims* at the present time. Let me say a word about both of these.

1. Faith in Jesus Christ

In this book I am still writing about Jesus Christ, though in a way different from that in the earlier book. The life of Jesus is, of course, written out of faith, but Jesus of Nazareth is all the same an objective fact outside ourselves, a fact that can on principle be analyzed and theologized in itself. The resurrection, however, is not a historical reality in the same way as that of Jesus' life is, but a different reality, historical-eschatological, so that the texts dealing with it express above all the actual experience and faith of the witnesses. And New Testament and conciliar christologies are already clear reflections of faith: they state who Jesus Christ is once one believes in him. In other words, texts about Jesus Christ are of two types: some present *the history of Jesus* (even though this is to be read from faith), while others present *the history of the faith of certain human beings* (though they have a point of reference, Jesus Christ, who originates their faith). This is the basic discontinuity between the two types of books.

This faith is faith in Jesus Christ, obviously, and the texts express, put into words, and theorize on who this Jesus is once he is believed to be the Son of God. Nevertheless, in the New Testament and throughout history, faith in Jesus Christ does not mean just taking an attitude to *his* reality (divine and human) but also expresses, in a novel manner, what is essential to all religious belief: adopting a view on *the totality* of reality. It expresses, specifically, how human beings place their trust in an absolute reality that lends meaning to existence while remaining open and available to the unmanipulable mystery of reality, how they listen to promises and good news while at the same time taking shape in disillusion and cruelty, putting up with reality. Finally, it expresses how human beings live in history exposed to the elements yet cloaked in ineffable mystery.

The texts that speak of Jesus Christ speak of his reality, but at the same time this reality of his places us in relationship with a host of realities. This is why faith in Jesus Christ does not consist solely in adopting a view on *his* reality (whether he is divine or not, whether he is human or not) but in adopting a view (based on him) on reality as a whole. Let us look at an example.

There are texts that speak of Jesus Christ as Lord; faith accepts him as such, and theology (Pauline, in this case) explains what this lordship implies. But in accepting Christ as Lord, believers also adopt a view on a whole constellation of realities beyond the reality of Christ. They recognize, for example, that it is possible to live with freedom and hope in history, since the dominations and powers have already been vanquished, but also with the humility of seeing that God is not yet all in all and with the honesty of an open mind on the question of theodicy—how to reconcile the Lordship of Christ with the suffering of this world. They accept that Christ has to be recognized as Lord in the liturgy, but they add that in history his work of service, abasement, crucifixion has to be reproduced. They recognize that persons and communities can be configured according to the reality of the Son, but without this turning them away from humble following of Jesus. They accept that life flows from the head to the body, but they also see that Christ-the-head has, in a sense, left his embodiment in history, and so his lordship, in our hands. And so on. But the important point to stress is that christological texts do not speak only of Christ, but, in taking a view on him, refer to a constellation of realities on which one also has to take a view. Faith in Jesus Christ is more than faith in him.

The New Testament and conciliar texts, then, also express the *global faith of some human beings*. This is the reason for my method of examining them, relating them to situations of then and now, situations that make up the lives and faith of human beings. Hence my questioning, for example, of the possibility of actual present-day experiences analogous to those of the post-resurrection appearances, of the possibility of living as risen beings in history, meaning the possibility of historical reverberation of the triumph aspect of Jesus' resurrection, so of a "Chalcedonian" reading of the structure of reality. Readers will have to judge the value of such reflections, but the main thing is to refer texts about Jesus Christ (and about God) to something real. Faith certainly comes from hearing, so it has a stage of pure taking in and acceptance without being able to control its content. But it is also certain that faith put into practice is something real, understood by matching it not only to the texts but to real life.

This is why this is not strictly a book of christology, a conceptual analysis of the reality of Jesus Christ, though it does analyze texts in which this reality is expressed. If you like, I am presenting Jesus Christ as an open parable, whose meaning we can accept or not. And as all human beings—not only Christians—are faced with and have to take a view on the realities I have mentioned, discussions such as those in this book may be useful to others, not only to believers. The Christian scheme formulates ultimate questions and gives them a specific response, which, of course, does not have to be accepted by everyone. But I think it can help to formulate the questions common to everyone: what to hope for, what to do with the cross, what to celebrate. . . .

2.   The View of the Victims

The second reflection is on the *where from* of this book. It is true that there is a certain universality both in the believing subject and in the object believed in,

Jesus Christ, but it does not follow from this that reflection can begin with the universal. All thought comes from somewhere and derives from some concern; it has a viewpoint, a "from where" and a "to where," a "why" and a "for whom." This being the case, the "from where" of this book is a *partial, definite, and concerned* viewpoint: the victims of this world. The argument in favor of this viewpoint is, in the final analysis, indefensible, but in the world we live in it is both reasonable and necessary. So, at the risk of stretching the point, and even though it is not usual in a work of christology, I want to start with drawing attention to the plight of victims.

(a) Victims, Poverty, Indifference, Hypocrisy

Let me summarize—though it should not be necessary—the present situation of our world with regard to its victims, the way they are covered over, and the culture of indifference toward this. If I have used the expression *victims* in the subtitle (and elsewhere the stronger one of *crucified peoples*) this is to rescue, at least in language, the challenge that used to be implied by the word *poor*. So let us see what this world of poverty is like today.

Poverty, *first and foremost*, is the situation in which by far the greater part of the human race lives, bowed down under the weight of life. For these people, survival is their greatest problem and death their closest destiny. Poverty means, then, grave difficulty in surviving as the human species, the situation in which, according to the 1996 report of the United Nations Development Program, some three billion human beings find themselves—and their numbers are growing in some places. Eighty-nine countries are now poorer than they were ten years ago, and some of those poorer than thirty years ago. It has become commonplace to talk of people who do not count in the production process. A "subspecies" of the nonexistent, the superfluous, the excluded has made its appearance.

In the second place, the inequality within the species makes it impossible to use the metaphorical—but essential in Christian faith—language of the family to describe it. The same report tells that the gulf between rich and poor is growing. The combined wealth of the 358 individuals whose assets exceed one billion dollars is greater than the combined annual income of 45 percent of the world's population. As for the future, without allowing for disasters, it will take countries like the Ivory Coast sixty-five years to reach the present levels of development of the industrialized countries, while for countries such as Niger and Mozambique it will take more than two centuries. All this indicates that the human "family" has failed. Dives and Lazarus are even farther apart, to the point where the U.N. officer James Gustave Speth can say that we are moving "from the unjust to the inhuman." And this oppression within the human species takes shape and can be seen with ever-mounting crassness at other levels of the human reality: race, culture, religion, gender. . . . The human family, not just the species, is ruined.

In the third place, the deepest roots of this poverty are historical: they lie in structural injustice. The "poor" are impoverished; the "indigenous" are stripped of cultural identity. I mention this because now it is hushed up, and the solutions put forward are based on the same structural injustice. If they were to succeed, such solutions could improve the lives of only some (40 to 50 percent) of the world's people, which means that some authority would have to make the cruel decision as to which peoples would live and which would die. The solution offered is a bad solution, described by Ignacio Ellacuría as "worse than having just problems." The solution offered is impossible because it cannot be universalized, and it is inhuman because, as Adolfo Pérez Esquivel said, "capitalism was born without a heart."

All this was true in 1968—to choose the symbolic date of the Medellín Conference—and is still true today, though its expressions have shifted, but the truth of poverty is so cosmetically overlaid as to be effaced. The 1997 U.N. Development report, for instance, was presented as a message of hope—"It is possible to eradicate poverty in two decades"—which allowed the collective consciousness to cover up its terrifying contents. It also allowed it to ignore the warning of the U.N. special adviser Walter Franco, who, when the report was published, stated, "The international will to cooperate is in decline." The injustice that creates poverty needs to be covered over and forgotten and so has recourse to the "institutionalized lie." Language is used to mask reality—"developing countries," "populations with scant resources"—in order to hide situations of inhuman aberration. It speaks of "wars" in Central America, which is true as far as it goes, but this fails to specify repression and terrorism (including and mostly state terrorism), which should not be subsumed under the more acceptable term *war*, since state terrorism is not so much on the lines of military operation as of holocaust. Also covered over—clumsily, but effectively—is the fact that the agents of this violence and of its originating injustice (repression and war) are organizations and authorities often accepted in the Western world and even put forward as models to the countries of the Third World: governments and local business communities encouraged and supported, in the case of Central America, by the government of the United States, its army, and the C.I.A. When the coverup fails, then we have to have amnesties, for the military above all—"those who are always pardoned," as Mario Benedetti said.

Poverty, *finally*, is the most lasting form of violence and the violence that is committed with the greatest impunity. Holocausts and massacres—sometimes— produce their Nurembergs, but not the depredations on the continent of Latin America or the exploitation of Africa. What court of appeal is there for the thirty-five or forty million people who die annually of hunger or hunger-related diseases? And the most maddening thing is that today it *is* possible to eliminate poverty. . . . This is where the victims view the matter from.

(b) What Is Meta-Paradigmatic in Christology

All this should be impossible to hide and a challenge. But it is not. A few years ago J.-B. Metz said that "there is a spread of a routine post-modernity of hearts that removes poverty to a faceless far distance."[2] At the present time there is a growing psychosocial, cultural, even philosophical atmosphere that, when it comes to the crunch, fails to make victims as such central, even though they are still the "lead story" in the eyes of God. To describe this atmosphere, so characteristic of our time, these words of Pedro Casaldáliga—at least as read from El Salvador—put their finger on the wound:

> Some believe it is now time to change our paradigms. And they even see martyrs as inconvenient in this post-modern or post-military memory. To the tune of this deception, friends and enemies throw out three disturbing questions: What's left of socialism? What's left of liberation theology? What's left of the option for the poor? I hope we won't end up asking ourselves: What's left of the gospel?[3]

I hope, I would add, that we will not end up asking ourselves: What's left of the victims?

For me, this atmosphere always brings back the memory of Ignacio Ellacuría. He asked himself what was *the* sign of the times (that is, what is it that characterizes a *period* and in which *God* is made present), and he replied that this sign is always the crucified people, stripped of life, though the form of their crucifixion may vary. Is this "always" true, the great truth throughout history, or is it an exaggeration, understandable at the outset of the 1980s but now outmoded? This seems to me the basic question, and it is one that is usually left unaddressed at the present time.

We can accept that socialism has fallen, that the revolutions in Latin America have not succeeded, or at least not as many would have liked. Let us also accept that we are a global village, and that globalization has taken over. This, however, still says nothing about whether there is something meta-paradigmatic in Christianity that should be upheld through and against all changes. In other words, we need to ask ourselves whether something exists that, even though it has to respond to changes, has the capacity to put positive values into effect, operate counter-culturally, unmask sin, and find good in any paradigm.

In the New Testament too there is a diversity of views, attributable to different times and places, but something is upheld as central: God's love for and sustaining of the weak, and condemnation of the sin and the oppressors that make people weak. The sin and oppression are characterized as "assassination and lies" by the existing order (John), as "oppressing the truth" and "acting with arrogance before God" (Paul), as "loving money and hating God" and "placing intolerable burdens" (Jesus). What have not changed over the centuries are this arrogance before God (suicide of the spirit) and this oppression, causing the death of others (homicide). Coming back to our world, the changes that have come about have not changed "the weight of the real." This is why it seems to me dangerous to appeal, precipitately, to a change of paradigm.

Let us go back to the question from christology. Does it have something meta-paradigmatic? The reply is a convinced yes, and its central content is the relationship between Jesus and the poor, between Jesus and the victims. This has already been said by others, even if by implication, by asking "how to do theology after Auschwitz." And the reply has been that "it is not possible to do *theo*logy passing over Auschwitz." Auschwitz, is, then, meta-paradigmatic; it is a powerful way of recalling the essential relationship between God and the victims.

We human beings, however, are given to forgetting and capable of spoiling everything. We can even use the memory of Auschwitz to give the impression that, though horrible, it is something that happened in the past, and we can proclaim that in the new paradigm there is no reason for the recent Auschwitzes— our own—always to be centrally present. Auschwitz was the shame of humankind half a century ago. Central America, Bosnia, Kosovo, East Timor, Rwanda, death from hunger, and now the social exclusion of tens of millions of human beings are still the shame of the human race in our day.

These victims, then, are those who provide the perspective for this study. They do not, obviously, provide a mechanical solution for understanding christological texts, but they do bring suspicions, questions, and illuminations that make the texts about Jesus Christ give up more of themselves. This is why, for example, I use them to express my recurrent concern over the devaluation and disappearance of the Kingdom of God. It did not come, but the mediator came, which has led christologies to concentrate on the person of Christ and to ignore the cause of Jesus, which is the Kingdom of God *for the poor*. The Kingdom was reduced to the *person* of Jesus or to his resurrection. Its place was taken, spuriously and sometimes sinfully, by the church. Its beneficiaries were universalized, and the poor lost their centrality in history and in theology.

And from the victims, too, christological reflection became more praxis-based, mystagogical, and existential.

(c) Is It Possible to Adopt the View of the Victims?

The view of the victims is necessary for theology, but is it possible? This is the personal question I have often asked myself, and which I should like to expound. I believe we human beings are divided into two major groups: those who take life for granted, and those for whom life is the one thing they cannot take for granted. In my view one sees things in a different light depending on which of these groups one falls into. How one understands human rights, democracy, freedom, institutions such as banks, legal authorities, armed forces, and so on varies greatly through one's belonging to one or the other group. And I believe this is also substantially true for understanding religion, the church, faith, prayer, hope. . . . It certainly is for life and death.

This difficulty in adopting the view of the victims leads to a paradox that has made me think, and which I should like to set out briefly: Those privileged by God and the primary beneficiaries of God's revelation, the poor and the victims, cannot do theology (in the sense in which this is conventionally understood). And those of us who can do theology are the non-poor, the non-victims. So, can we non-victims do *Christian* theology from the view of the victims?

What can happen is something analogous to *Horizontsverschmelzung* (fusion of horizons) between the faith of victims, peasants, simple men and women, and that of more learned religious leaders, pastors, and thinkers. I believe—and hope— that this has happened in some ways. In the suffering of oppression and the hope of liberation both forms of faith, historically and existentially different, can converge. Then in solidarity with the victims, in mutual support in faith, the eyes of the non-victims are opened to see things differently. Whether this new vision can ever coincide completely with that of the victims is something I do not think we shall ever know. But I do believe that our perspective can change sufficiently for the victims to give us a specific light in which to "see" what we call the objects of theology: God, Christ, grace, sin, justice, hope, incarnation, utopia. The poor and the victims bring theology something more important than contents; they bring light by which we can see the contents properly.

To conclude: The view of the victims helps us to read christological texts and to know Jesus Christ better. Furthermore, this Jesus Christ, known in this way, helps us to understand the victims better and, above all, to work to defend them. A God and a Christ partial to them make theology be done "upholding the victims," which determines the *relevance* of christology in today's world. And it also introduces the poor and the victims into the "theologal" ambit, not merely the ethical one, which determines the *identity* of theology.

This seems to me essential for both theology and faith. In the New Testament sinners are related theologally, leaving the tautology, with God: "God justifies the impious and pardons the sinner through grace," and so theology makes the reality of sin and sinners central. Today we have to insist on another theologal relationship, that between the poor and God: "God loves the poor simply because they are poor," and so theology needs to make the poor and poverty central. In this way the Christian faith is enriched and the task of lowering the crosses of the crucified of history is better carried out.

One final observation: I shall continue to make the victims central in faith and in theology in order to swim against the current that tries to ignore them, as I have already said. Through the values they possess—often—and through what they are—always—the poor and the victims of this world are sacraments of God and the presence of Jesus Christ among us. They offer us light and utopia, the challenge of and need for conversion, welcome, and forgiveness. This is where I finished the previous volume, speaking of the salvation brought by the crucified people, the *historical soteriology* of which Ignacio Ellacuría spoke. And when we call these victims martyrs, we mean that they reproduce the life and death of Jesus and they shed a great light.

In keeping the victims central to theology, I am not seeking to be obstinately old-fashioned or impenitently masochistic. I am seeking to be honest to reality and responsible for it. I want Christians to be those who bring good news: God and his Christ are present in our world, and not just anywhere but where they said they would be—in the poor and the victims of this world. In this way, I think, one can do theology, and christology, as *intellectus amoris*—the work of liberating victims—and as *intellectus gratiae*—from the grace that has been given us in them. To all of this I should like to make a modest contribution, to add a grain of sand.

PART I

THE RESURRECTION OF JESUS

Resurrection and Victims

Chapter 1

Viewpoint

A "Risen" Following and the Hope of the Victims

The resurrection of Jesus is an eschatological event, the irruption of the ultimate into history. It is, then, a sort of overall reality, and as such it is not accessible directly but only from a particular viewpoint, which in fact has changed throughout history. In this chapter I want to make clear, from the situation of the Third World, what my specific viewpoint is. To situate this more clearly among many, I propose to start by summarizing, in broad outline, what recent theology has had to say about the resurrection of Jesus.

Before the Second Vatican Council (1962–65), Catholic theology hardly mentioned the resurrection of Jesus either in christology or in soteriology but relegated it to apologetics as a unique portent.[1] In spirituality it became an anticipation and a reminder of the end of our existence, with the possibility of salvation or condemnation, which led to the devaluation of history.

In a radical change of paradigm, around the time of the Council theology began to take up the subject of Jesus' resurrection as a central reality.[2] This, in principle, overcame various faults: the "sufferingism" of a theology and the cruelty of a (bad) soteriology based on the cross, and the one-sided "sacrificialism" of the liturgy, which from then on became more wholly paschal. Furthermore, biblical research overcame a way of presenting the resurrection as a mythic event and was able to demonstrate its relevance to the needs of modern thought and its anthropology. The raising of Jesus showed, in effect, the values of *corporeality*, since Jesus rose in the wholeness of his being, not in the Greek manner of a soul liberated from the body; *sociability*, since, by rising as the firstborn, he showed the way to the resurrection of all human beings; *cosmicity*, and even evolution to an omega point, in recalling with Isaiah and the Apocalypse the coming of a new heaven and a new earth, which is still more meaningful today when we speak of the cosmic Christ.[3] And above all it revalued the *future* and *hope*, central concerns in the utopic thinking of some decades ago.

These advances in theology are undeniable, but they have not gone far enough.[4] In my view there is now a sort of stagnation in theology of the resurrection, for

11

which there would seem to be—among others—these two reasons. One is that, although the resurrection refers to the future of history, it does not seem to have anything important to say about the *present*, what is with us now. The other is that, although the hope rediscovered by the new theology is important, it is an unduly universal hope and does not recognize the *partiality* essential to it, since Jesus' resurrection is hope, directly, for the victims.

For the resurrection of Jesus to keep its identity and its relevance, I think we need to adopt a new viewpoint, one that, while recognizing the novelty of post-conciliar theology, goes beyond it. It follows from the above that this new viewpoint has to include two things. The first is that Jesus' resurrection should, in some way, be a reality that effectively affects history in its present, which supposes the possibility of living now as risen beings in history and the possibility of re-creating the experience of finality implied in the post-resurrection appearances, with—of course—all the relevant analogies. The second, more fundamental in the Third World, is understanding the resurrection in its essential relationship to the victims, so that the hope it unleashes should, above all, be hope for these victims. Let us look at this in more detail.

1. Living the Following of Jesus as Risen Beings

I should like to begin this reflection with a personal memory. Nearly thirty years ago, at a Mass during which some young Jesuits were making their religious vows, Ignacio Ellacuría spoke of following Jesus but added that we should live as already risen beings. Inclined as he was to historicize the Christian faith, there would have been no surprise in his historicizing the following of Jesus in terms of incarnation, mission, and taking up one's cross. But this "living as risen beings in history" made a profound impression on me, since it related following Jesus with the pleroma and eschatology. The other way around, it meant that the place for verifying—without alienation or self-deception—whether and in what way we are already sharing in the eschatological reality is the following of Jesus and nothing else. In other words, the resurrection of Jesus, in its own reality, can be lived in the present, and within this present, in following Jesus. This, however, is far from clear and involves problems of various sorts that need to be clarified and, as far as possible, answered.

The New Testament presents Jesus' resurrection—and the appearances in which it is manifested—in radical discontinuity from us. In its objective reality, the resurrection is the appearance of the eschatological, and so "*the resurrection is something unique in history.*"[5] With regard to its subjective realization, believers are essentially cast back on the witness of those who had the paschal experience, who "never claimed to make other people enjoy similar visions."[6] And this discontinuity is deepened with the postponement of the parousia: "The fullness that for the disciples began with the appearances of the risen Christ and was palpable for them has once more become promise for us."[7] So, between the reality of the resurrection, including the experience of the appearances, and ourselves, there is an inescapable abyss.

On the other hand, the New Testament makes other sorts of statements that point in a different direction. The resurrection of Jesus, through the outpouring of the Spirit, *already* molds history in the present. Luke's theology examines this action closely and prodigiously, while Paul makes it a daily experience. Looking for the presence of the risen Christ in history is, then, nothing new—though the New Testament also warns of the danger of understanding it only as the work of the Spirit, as shown in the classic example of the Christians of Corinth, whom Paul had to correct severely.

Going beyond critique of this "spirituality of resurrection," however, I see reliance on the Spirit still not expressing the relationship between resurrection and the present as radically as it should so long as this action by the Spirit is not made adequately specific and historical. The basic problem is whether the resurrection is made present, specifically, in the following of Jesus and not just anywhere and anyhow. It is not just a question of the Spirit becoming present in history through showy and powerful (charismatic) actions but—in addition—of building the structure of incarnation, mission, and taking on the burden of history "in a risen manner."

My argument in support of this thesis is not substantially biblical but the product of reflection. It is that if the reality of Jesus' resurrection is not made present in history in some form, then it will remain as something totally extrinsic to us, something that cannot be made historical or verifiable in any way, as the following of Jesus can. It would indeed be paradoxical—not to say absurd—if the eschatological had taken place in history and not marked it in any way.

My viewpoint presupposes, then, that the risen Christ can become victoriously present in the following of the crucified Jesus, so that this following can here and now be shot through with the triumphant aspect of the resurrection of Jesus. I shall go into more detail in the following chapters, but let me say at the outset that the following of Jesus can contain a sort of historical reverberation of his resurrection with two essential elements: (1) what there is of *fullness* in the resurrection, even in the midst of the limitations of history, and (2) what there is of *victory* in the resurrection against the enslavement of history. This is borne out in the following:

> Christianity is the permission, the urgency and the good disposition to live the life of the world to come already here and now. And this means: living the life of the eschatological fullness in a time of lapsing that is not prepared for it; and bearing all the blows and all the disadvantages that such a life involves.[8]

Here the two elements on which I have been insisting are mentioned (fullness and contingency), but to prevent them from remaining bare abstractions we need to specify what "eschatological fullness," "bearing all the blows," and "a time of lapsing" mean.

With regard to *eschatological fullness* we can say, with some daring, that the reverberation in history of the triumph of the resurrection is hope, freedom, and joy in the following of Jesus.[9] With regard to lapsing—in the midst of which fullness comes about—and to what has to be borne, hope comes about *against* resignation, disenchantment, triviality; freedom comes about *against* the bonds history imposes on love (risks, fears, selfishness); joy comes about *against* grief. Fullness, then, comes into being not only *in* times of lapsing but *against* lapsing. More precisely, it becomes present not only against the not-yet of the limited but also against the certainly-not of oppression and dehumanization.

It should be clear that trying to make the presence of the resurrection actual in history is daring, but it seems to me more dangerous to try to understand it as something totally extrinsic to our present condition. This would suppose that the eschatological had come about in history but that it had had no effect on our present life—except in hope.[10]

2. The Resurrection of Jesus and Victims

In the primitive kerygma the resurrection is proclaimed together with the cross of Jesus (cf. 1 Cor 15:3ff.), but not only in the obvious sense of logical-chronological juxtaposition—without death there can be no resurrection—but in a mutually explanatory sense: "This man . . . you crucified. . . . But God raised him up" (Acts 2:23ff.). And this relationship is carried on in the New Testament in the identification of the risen Christ with the crucified Jesus (Jn 20:25–28).

Maintaining this (transcendental) relationship between cross and resurrection is decisive for understanding of the paschal mystery and its content of revelation and salvation. I shall deal with this in subsequent chapters, but bearing this relationship in mind is also important—and perhaps theology does not usually take sufficient account of this—for deciding the proper setting for understanding Jesus' resurrection. If it is right that resurrection (a historical-eschatological reality) bears an essential relationship to death (a historical reality), it does not seen unreasonable to make the latter the setting for understanding the former. And not just this: as the New Testament speaks not only of the death of Jesus but of his cross, the crucified of history will provide the most apt setting from which to understand the resurrection of Jesus; they will be those who introduce the necessary dialectic into it and make it possible for its different dimensions to be displayed.

Something of this appears, if only by way of insinuation, at the end of the (anti-triumphalist) Gospel of Mark. This contains no apparitions but only the command: "But go . . . to Galilee; there you will see him" (16:7). Whatever may have happened geographically and historically, Galilee is the place of the poor and the despised. And there, according to Mark, the risen Christ will be found. It is therefore a theological setting: this is not basically a categorical *ubi* but a substantial *quid*, and depending on which way it is taken, sources of theological understanding automatically produce one thing or another. It is, then, this "Galilee" that allows the resurrection texts to be read in a particular way and provides the reality that directs the most pertinent questions to those texts. This makes it also the setting in which the texts most reveal themselves. In thesis form, the cross is the prime *locus theologicus* for understanding the resurrection, and other *loci* will be so to the extent that they analogously reproduce the reality of the cross.

For me, Galilee is El Salvador, which can well serve as an example of many other places (Rwanda or East Timor, for example, at the time of writing). In this specific situation, and by its very nature, the important questions about the resurrection arise: What possibility is there today of re-creating the experience of the first believers, even if only in analogous form? What possibility is there of living as already risen people in history and how much of the dimension of triumph, as it appears in Jesus' resurrection, can be actualized in history? What hope—and how realistic a hope—has a crucified people of becoming a risen people? How much truth is there in faith that God is a God of life, that God did justice to an innocent victim by raising him from the dead, and that in the end God will be all in all?

These questions about God and justice, and others like them, surface in a world of crosses, not simply the question of whether there is survival after death. It is a matter of the human problem of hope, though not of any hope but the hope of victims. The words of Salvadoran peasants that I am about to quote—which could be multiplied—do not use the language of cross and resurrection, but they point the language of death and life toward it. At a time of crucifixion they ask:

> How many times we tell ourselves that God acts in our history. . . . But, father, if he acts, when is this going to end? And so many years of war and so many thousands of deaths? What's the matter with God?[11]

And they always speak artlessly, theologally, of resurrection. This was said in 1987:

> We are communities abandoned by our diocese. It has never taken any notice of us. But what we are clear about is that God has not abandoned us and will never abandon us. Because we have been able to experience his closeness and his presence with us at the hardest moments we have been through during the course of this war, when the only thing that has been offered us is death. God has offered and given us life.[12]

This chapter has set out the concern that shapes my analysis, that is, being able to live as risen people—in the weakness of history—in following Jesus and to have the victims' hope that God will triumph over injustice. This is my approach. Let me say finally that I have nothing special to offer by way of research into and exegetical debate on the texts. Although I analyze them to some degree, the novelty I have to offer lies in the light shed by this double concern.

I shall first approach the hermeneutical problem provided by the resurrection in that not only is it an event that took place in the past and in a different cultural setting from our own, but it was stated to be the irruption of an eschatological event. It is not clear that an eschatological event can be understood, and therefore one has to try to establish under what conditions it might be, so that, in simple words, we know what we are talking about.

Then I shall tackle the historical problem—what actually happened. Here again I have no exegetical novelty to offer, but I shall make some observations on the evidence of the changes brought about in the disciples and what these mean, then on the need for us to have—and the manner in which we have (or do not have)—an (analogous) experience to that of the post-resurrection appearances.

Finally, I shall deal with the theological question, that is, what Jesus' resurrection has to say about God, about Jesus, and about human beings.

Chapter 2

The Hermeneutical Problem (1)

The Resurrection, a Specific Problem for Hermeneutics

1. The Problematic of Hermeneutics

The resurrection of Jesus is not presented in the New Testament as the return of a dead body to everyday life or as being caught up into heaven but as the action of God by which the eschatological irrupts into history and in which the true reality of Jesus begins to be made plain. In this sense it is narrated in the New Testament as an event without precedent in any other historical event. Therefore, it is not and cannot be described as an *intrahistorical* event, but it is nevertheless described as an event perceived *in history* and one that—decisively—affects history.

If this is the case, we need to ask ourselves how the disciples could understand the resurrection of Jesus. Two dialectically related things need to be said about this. The first is that, according to the New Testament, they were "granted" the capacity to have this experience in the appearances, an experience that is presented in discontinuity with any other, including those of revelations, visions, or callings. And the second, going the opposite way, is that from the mere fact of their having expressed this experience in language or, more precisely, in several languages, of *raising up*, *exalting life*, we have to suppose that what happened to Jesus corresponds in some way, though surpassing it, to some expectation based on the nature of human beings, since without this they could not have understood anything real.

Then we need to ask what has to happen to us today for us to understand what the first disciples said they experienced and what they expressed in terms of *resurrection.* This is a matter of understanding the text, whether or not we then accept the reality. This is the hermeneutical problem. How can we understand a text that is not directly comprehensible in itself, not only for the usual reasons that we are faced with a text from the past, written under cultural presuppositions different and even far removed from our own (such as a language that treats of angels, a dead man appearing, ascension into heaven . . .), all of which brings about the

17

need to overcome *distance in time*, but for the specific reason that this is a text that sets out to express an eschatological reality, which supposes the need to overcome *a metaphysical distance*?

In order to determine what presuppositions are needed today to understand such texts, I believe we have to take three things into account. The first is that in some way these presuppositions should be required by the very texts that speak of the resurrection of Jesus (the need for hope, for example); that is, they have not been arbitrarily selected in advance by us. The second is that the christological dimension should appear in them in some form (that hope should arise because of what happened to Jesus), since the texts essentially relate the irruption of the eschatological into history with what happened to Jesus. And the third is that these presuppositions can somehow be meaningful for readers today (that the history of twenty centuries has not made it impossible to hope that the executioner will not triumph over the victim, for example), since otherwise the text would obviously remain mute.

The hermeneutical circle is already inevitably at work in this selection of presuppositions. That the texts can be read today as requiring something (hope, for example, as we have just seen) can be due, at least in part, simply to the fact of the existence of such texts, which have molded the self-understanding of human beings as beings who hope. So it is clear that in Latin America the tradition of the risen Christ has, at least partly, enabled hope to be generated in commitment, utopias to be formulated, the belief expressed that the last word lies with life, justice, truth, and love. But it is also true—and this is something not often taken into account elsewhere—that actual historical hope, expressed in great love and commitment, helps us at least to understand, if not to accept, the texts of the New Testament. So Juan Luis Segundo, examining the hermeneutical circle within which Latin American theology operates, concludes that the option for the poor is found in the New Testament if it is already present in the situation of the theologian, when it serves as a pre-understanding of the text. With regard to the pre-understanding necessary for grasping the resurrection of Jesus he states that having espoused the same values as Jesus constitutes an indispensable precondition for being able to "see" and "recognize" him as risen.[1]

Investigating what the presuppositions are for being able to understand *today* what is meant when the disciples affirm that Jesus has been raised and that they have met him risen is an important task, but I should like to add that, for believers at least, it is not an optional one. It would be nonsensical to affirm that the resurrection is central to our faith and not even to understand what is meant when we talk about it. Furthermore, in analyzing the presuppositions we are sketching the nucleus of a Christian anthropology. And as these presuppositions refer to central anthropological realities, they become possible mediations of the experience of God. The reflections in these chapters, therefore, refer not only to hermeneutics but ultimately to how to live as Christians.

In this work I want to examine the basic presuppositions seen from the situation of victims, but I shall leave this to the following chapter. Here I want to do two things. The first is to record some basic realities to be borne in mind when analyzing hermeneutics in relation to the resurrection of Jesus. The second is to see how some European theologians—those who can be called classical, both Protestant and Catholic—and some Latin American ones approach the subject,[2] with brief notes on their view of the historicity of the resurrection. I give these different views for their intrinsic value but also so that they can show me how to deal with the subject here.

2. Specifics of the Hermeneutics of the Resurrection

I should like to make three basic points concerning the specific problems for hermeneutics in tackling the resurrection of Jesus.

(a) The Resurrection as Eschatological Action by God

In speaking of the resurrection of Jesus the first thing to stress is that what happened to Jesus is presented as direct action by God. The fact to which the New Testament first and foremost bears witness is that "God raised [Jesus] from the dead" (Rom 10:9).[3] This wording means that the resurrection of Jesus, while essentially affecting Jesus, is above all a theologal reality that directly expresses something new and decisive about God. The resurrection says precisely that God has confirmed Jesus' truth and life, has given him definitiveness forever, and has exalted him.[4] And as this Jesus is an innocent victim—the crucified One—his resurrection expresses not only God's power over death but God's power over the injustice that produces victims. The resurrection, then, applies to Jesus, but it directly reveals and manifests the reality of God: "The ineffable mystery of God who contains all without being contained is made manifest to us in a visible and perceptible manner only in the figure of a human being: the man Jesus."[5] This is the theologal and therefore ultimate dimension, in the face of which every human being has to take some stance. To accept the existence of something ultimate is one thing; that this ultimate should be formulated as "justice toward victims" is, of course, another. But this does not prevent the question of what is ultimate arising some time in the lives of human beings; neither does it prevent us from asking specifically about the future of victims.

   We also need to remember that the New Testament speaks of the resurrection as *the insertion of Jesus in definitive life*—the first effect of God's action—which is never expressed or understood as being caught up into heaven (as in the case of Elijah or Enoch) or as the return of a dead body to everyday life (as the gospel accounts of the raising of Lazarus or of Jairus's daughter might be understood). This is to state that the resurrection of Jesus is an eschatological event; that is, not only God's action but a reality in which "the ultimate" happens, not only or principally in a temporal sense (what happens at the end of history) but primarily in a metaphysical sense (a manifestation of what the ultimate reality is). This, however, also implies that the resurrection cannot and should not be understood as a "miracle" naturally attributable to God. As J. L. Segundo writes: "Everything I have examined concerning the literary genre of the evangelical accounts of the resurrection shows us that, although these seem to contain the most sensational miracle in the story of Jesus, they do not, strictly speaking, relate any miracle at all. The presence of the eschatological comes about without the need to break or replace any natural law."[6]

The conclusion is that, since this is God's action and an action qualitatively different from the other divine actions recounted in scripture, the hermeneutical problem will also present itself in a new and unparalleled form. Trying to understand (and interpret) miracles is not the same as trying to understand (and interpret) the resurrection. Bultmann's existential interpretation of miracles, for example, while it may be correct, cannot be extrapolated to understand the resurrection.

(b) The Language Barrier

There is no adequate language in which to formulate the reality of this event and the experience of it. "The fact of the resurrection . . . cannot be put into words by a language that always proceeds by comparison and universalization."[7] But, even if inadequate, the Bible puts forward various linguistic possibilities on the basis of analogous situations. The Old Testament already speaks of the just man taken by God at the end of his life (Gn 5:24; 2 Kgs 2:11), of the exaltation of the Servant of Yahweh (Is 52:13ff.), and of what has been consecrated: rising up from among the dead (Is 26:19; Dn 12:2).

The New Testament effectively makes use of a plurality of languages: Jesus lives, has been seen, has appeared, and so on—a linguistic model based on *life*; Jesus has been exalted, is seated at the right hand of the Father, will come to judge at the end of time, and so on—a model based on *exaltation*; Jesus has been raised, taken up by God from among the dead, and so on—a model based on the radical change implied by passing from sleeping to waking, *awakening from sleep*.[8]

There is, then, no adequate language in which to express the reality of Jesus' resurrection, which means that a proliferation of languages is natural and inevitable. The importance of the event in itself, though, also has to be stressed. The fact that any one language is really—rather than deservedly—insufficient and cannot be consistent or adequate is one way of pointing to what happened to Jesus as something unique, eschatological, in the sense of what is radically new and cannot, by definition, have an adequate language in which to describe it. Put in terms of what must be denied, it is said that death was not the end of Jesus' life. Put in terms of what must be affirmed, it is said that Jesus goes on possessing a proper entity in the present (not only in the memory of his followers), a reality that is positive, insuperable, and definitive.

All this means that Jesus' resurrection presents the first witnesses—and us today—with a "language barrier."[9] And the reason for this is that we are faced not only with a limit situation—which could apply to love, liberty, evil, grace, and so on—but an eschatological type of limit situation: the disciples state that they have experienced the eschatological in history, and in the face of this all languages are inadequate. (This simple affirmation is already a way of leading us into the message of the resurrection in the manner of negative theology; the impossibility of finding an adequate language brings with it the disposition to a certain not-knowing, which is necessary for knowing the ultimate mystery and the part the resurrection plays in it.)

The variety of languages needed is also an enrichment[10] in that—without them ever meeting—it enables us to understand a little better what happened to Jesus and what the paschal experience is, in the same way that a variety of languages is also necessary to lead us in the same way into the mystery of God. The *language of resurrection* (insofar as it expresses radical change) has the advantage of making us look back and by its nature refers us to the historical life of Jesus and to his cross as a point of reference for what, in its turn, is upheld and overcome in the resurrection: "the risen Christ is none other than the crucified Jesus." The *language of exaltation* has the advantage of recalling something specific to the biblical God: overthrowing reality, putting down the mighty, raising up the oppressed and victims: "He humbled himself and became obedient to the point of death—even death on a cross" (Phil 2:8; cf. Acts 2:22–36; as a more universal attitude, see Lk 1:52, the Magnificat; 6:20–26, the beatitudes and woes). The *language of life* has the advantage of showing that death and denial do not have the last word in history, which belongs to affirmation and life, particularly when Jesus is said not only to live but to live "always" (Heb 7:24ff.).

Usage has made us lose sight of this simple fact, and so today we normally refer to what happened to Jesus in only one of these possible languages, that of resurrection, a hallowed term that I shall also use. Still, we need to remind ourselves at the outset that it is only one among various possible languages and that we need to explain its origin and meaning in a particular tradition, since otherwise it does little to explain what happened to Jesus. For hermeneutics, this means that the language used to describe the event has to be taken into account, since it is the only access we have to understanding its content; it also means that this language is severely limited and has to be complemented with another type of reality if we are to understand what is described as having happened.

(c) A "Trinitarian" Hermeneutical Circle

In the resurrection of Jesus the New Testament not only proclaims a christological event but announces a polyvalent novelty in three dimensions. The first novelty, as we have seen, concerns *God*. The God who raises Jesus is no longer simply Yahweh; this is a new God through the unprecedented eschatological action brought about in Jesus, and—on the basis of this—a God who will be understood in trinitarian terms. The second novelty is that of *Jesus*. From what happened to him, reflection will move on to his actual reality, and this will lead to the proclamation of his indissoluble union with God. The third novelty is about us, *human beings*. In narrative language it will be said that those who lived with Jesus have been given the grace to see him and the mission to witness to him, that they have been given the Spirit to know him and follow him, which in essence constitutes the new being of whom Paul speaks.

If this triple reality belongs to the overall resurrection event, then it also has to be taken into account in hermeneutics, and in a very precise way. As in the whole of the New Testament, the initiative comes from God, and so the (hermeneutical) circle has an origin. But having said this, we need to go back to its circularity: the "new" God makes the reality of the "new" human being possible, and it is this "new" human being who can know the "new" God. Recognizing the novelty in Jesus goes hand in hand with the novelty of being human made possible by the new God.

This novelty of being human should be as far-reaching as possible to accord with the *reality* of Jesus who is raised and of the God who raises him. It not just a question of *Horizontsverchmelszung* (fusion of horizons), in the sense in which cultural horizons come to be blended, but of a fusion of realities. So the following chapters will tackle the hermeneutical problem from the overall reality of human beings (hope, actions, knowledge, and celebration). Put in trinitarian language, the *Father* raises *Jesus* and pours out his Spirit on *us*. This is the total event, and from within it we shall be able to understand God's action in raising Jesus, because the Spirit is in us, making us understand. (Besides this trinitarian circularity there is a dialectical one, which I shall examine later, that is, the circularity between old and new, between discontinuity and continuity. Specifically, this means that we have to understand the risen Christ from the crucified Jesus, and the God who gives life from the silent God on the cross. And vice versa.)

3. Different Hermeneutical Approaches

Before analyzing what type of hermeneutics the victims require and make possible, let us recall the positions of some classical European writers, to which I shall—more briefly—add those of Latin American ones. In its time the pioneering work of European theologians caused a great stir because it delegitimized an ingenuous view of Jesus' resurrection. We can now view their contributions and their limitations more calmly and to greater advantage.

The following analysis may seem long and tedious, especially to those for whom it is familiar ground, but it is still important because these classics teach us two things. One is the need to tackle the subject, and the help they offer us in doing so—in accepting, denying, and transcending. The other is that the hermeneutical presuppositions they elaborate are anthropological realities (seriousness in regard to existence, praxis, hope, and so forth), so that understanding the resurrection is a form of *living.*

I begin with four of the European classics: Bultmann, Marxsen, Pannenberg, and Rahner.

(a) European Protestant Theology

(i) Rudolf Bultmann: The seriousness of existence. Bultmann completely disregards the resurrection as a historical event. As an exegete, he regards the empty tomb as a legend and the narrative traditions of Jesus' bodily appearances as inventions by the communities, of which there is no hint in Paul, whom he furthermore criticizes harshly[11]—improbably—for the apologetic intentions he sees

in 1 Corinthians 15:6: "Then he appeared to more than five hundred brothers and sisters at one time, most of whom are still alive, though some have died." His conclusion is that nothing can be said historically about what happened to Jesus himself: "The paschal event, as the resurrection of Jesus, is not a historical event; as historical event, all that can be known is the Easter faith of the first disciples."[12] The apparitions can be explained by the historian as subjective visions.

This does not mean, as has been thought, that Bultmann does not accept any sense in which Christ has risen.[13] What he insists on is that the important thing for believers is the *meaning* this event has for faith, not its *facticity*. The reason for his insistence, which derives more from his systematic theology than from his exegesis, is this: modern enlightened human beings cannot accept the resurrection or, in general, the worldview put forward by the New Testament. The resurrection of Jesus, formulated as the return of a dead man to life—though Bultmann would not equate it with the raising of Lazarus—is a mythical event, unacceptable in our enlightened times.

Having said all this, however, Bultmann insists that the resurrection of Jesus is essential for Christian faith. As nothing can be known about it historically, we have to accept it simply in faith. But—and here the problem of hermeneutics necessarily arises—this faith is not mere acceptance of a truth but *faith that understands*. But in order to understand, we have to reinterpret the message of the resurrection. As is well known—and where he is the pioneer—Bultmann reinterprets the New Testament and does so *existentially*.

The existential self-understanding of human beings—sinners in that they are closed in on themselves, and saved in that they are open to God—is what makes it possible for the announcement of Jesus' resurrection event to have meaning and to be understood in its true reality. Therefore, Jesus' resurrection has to be essentially related to his cross, and this has to be understood as a possibility of salvation. The reason Bultmann gives for the cross bringing salvation is, simply, that so it is preached. If one asks what then the resurrection adds to the cross, the answer is that "it is true" that the cross brings salvation. From this point of view, the resurrection is nothing other than "the meaning of the cross,"[14] and to accept Jesus' resurrection means believing that the cross has been a saving event. The cross shows human existence as sinful but at the same time accepted by God.

This understanding of Jesus' resurrection is not directly christological but anthropological: "Christ is risen in the kerygma,"[15] that is, "he lives" in that his preached cross and resurrection place us in the unavoidable situation of deciding on the meaning of his existence, either as "sinners-closed" or "as saved-open," and grant us the possibility of open existence.

There have been innumerable discussions on this position of Bultmann's and its implications. Specifically, he has been criticized for reducing the resurrection to the meaning it might have *(geschichtlich)* without recognizing any reality it might possess in itself *(historisch)*. Karl Barth objects that Jesus' resurrection cannot be reduced by simply identifying it with the rise of faith in this resurrection, but that, on the contrary, the resurrection is the foundation of faith.[16] Walter Pannenberg's objection is more radical; he states pragmatically that "whether or not Jesus is risen is a historical question."[17]

Paradoxically, present-day Catholic theologians—after their initial shock—have been more positive toward Bultmann for having directed attention to the *meaning* of the events without becoming stuck in their mere *facticity*, an approach of which Catholic theology had long been starved. But they too make the basic criticism of exaggerated separation of event from meaning. Leonardo Boff questions whether "the relationship of the resurrection to history is as irrelevant to history as he thinks," a postulate that has grave limitations and derives from the Lutheran principle of *sola fides*, with no biblical basis.[18] González Faus's criticism follows the same lines.[19]

What mainly concerns us here is that Bultmann ushered in a new era in understanding of the resurrection, which has produced positive results. One is the insistence of the need for a presupposition from which to understand the narration of Jesus' resurrection; without something previous, the text remains dumb. Another is the content of this "something previous": the existential interpretation of life. This interpretation has an important limitation: the exaggerated separation between event and meaning, between the *historisch* and the *geschichtlich*. But we also need to see how important and even current this existential interpretation is.

With his interpretation Bultmann places the resurrection in a soteriological framework: without a previous interest in salvation (and against condemnation), the text says nothing. And this salvation (or condemnation) is still a present reality. We can still live with authenticity, without which, from the salvific viewpoint, Jesus' resurrection relates only to the end of our lives. There is no doubt that each theology interprets salvation in a specific way (liberation theology would not reduce it to "authentic individual existence" but would understand it in an integral form),[20] but the important thing is to have made an intrinsic connection between Jesus' resurrection and salvation.

Furthermore, the presupposition behind the existential interpretation is acceptance of the seriousness of existence—the possibility that this can be authentic or inauthentic. In this postmodern age, characterized by provisionality and lack of passion and utopias, recovering interest in salvation with the possibility of condemnation seems to me extremely important. With the way things are going in this world, Bultmann's reminder here becomes ever more needed. We have to take existence seriously, together with the possibility of salvation or condemnation, however we understand these. Bultmann formulates this in the language he believes most adequate for responding to the texts of the New Testament, but his basic point remains his reminder of how seriously we have to take existence.

(ii) Willi Marxsen: Carrying on Jesus' cause. Marxsen shares Bultmann's historical scepticism for establishing what really happened and his pastoral concern for making Jesus' resurrection intelligible in modern enlightened society. To do so, however, he concentrates not on demythologizing the texts, with the resulting existential interpretation, but on what they have of call to action and commitment to carrying on Jesus' life and work.[21]

In his analysis of the resurrection Marxsen starts with the appearances, which had a historical character for the disciples and certainly made a great impact on them. The novelty of his analysis lies in finding various possible interpretations—

Interpretament in his technical language—of this fact in the New Testament. One of these interpretations of the appearances is that Jesus rose from the dead; that is, that something happened to Jesus himself before the appearances. What happened is formulated as *resurrection* in the New Testament and in the language of apocalyptic, which is nevertheless only one possible interpretation of what happened to Jesus, facilitated and suggested by the anthropology of Jewish thought, which sees the totality of the human being in unity of spirit and body. On Greek soil, for example, the personal interpretation of the resurrection could have been formulated in a different way: "Jesus has been freed from the prison of the body."

Together with this personal interpretation Marxsen formulates another of a functional nature, which for him should be placed first. As a New Testament basis he adduces 1 Corinthians 9:1, in which Paul speaks of having seen the Lord: his vision now has nothing to do with the reality of the person of Jesus but is to establish the basis of his faith. The purpose of the appearances, then, is to provide a basis for ministries, particularly that of preaching: "he commanded us to preach" (Acts 10:40ff.).

In a concise formula, which has become classic, Marxsen formulates the objective of preaching Jesus' resurrection in these words: "The cause of Jesus moves forward" *(Die Sache Jesu geht weiter)*. This states that, although Jesus is no longer present in history in visible form, his mission still carries on through the witnesses to the appearances. It also states that this mission of Jesus' is inseparable from his person and, therefore, that without the experience of having seen him, it would not have been possible to carry on his cause. Finally, it states that without this experience of having seen Jesus, everything would have come to an end. Nevertheless, he insists that this experience did not necessarily have to be expressed in terms of the resurrection of Jesus, which Marxsen regards as actually dangerous.

Marxsen has been criticized harshly and on several fronts. Objections have been raised above all to the contraposition he makes between event and *Interpretament* (as with Bultmann).[22] But we also need to appreciate the contribution his *Interpretament* has made to hermeneutics, even though Marxsen did not envisage it from this viewpoint but from the historical one of verifying what happened.

How he actually justifies it is debatable, but through this *Interpretament* Marxsen makes a radical statement on the nature of Christian life even after Jesus' resurrection. This life is a carrying on, and since Marxsen does not forget Jesus— "die Sache *Jesu*"—Christian life is the carrying on of Jesus. Seen like this, life for the disciples came to mean basically carrying on the cause of the historical Jesus. So the affirmation "Jesus is risen" is a justification of the disciples' mission itself, and the accounts of appearances are both required by and justify the mission: to carry on in history the activity and teaching of the historical Jesus.

If this is the case, if the resurrection is also the justification and requirement of mission—though not reduced to this—Marxsen sets us on a fruitful path for hermeneutics: availability for mission will be a prerequisite for understanding the resurrection of Jesus. Existence with its potential for salvation or condemnation must be taken seriously (Bultmann), and so must hope (as we shall see in Pannenberg and others), but we must also be open to a *praxis* (a reflection somewhat ignored by modern European theology but taken up in liberation theology).

In other words, we are not just beings of salvation or condemnation, nor just beings of hope, but also beings of praxis, to such an extent that if this were not the case we should not be able to understand the resurrection. In systematic terms the "resurrection" cannot be grasped only as a meaning concept but is also a praxic concept, as I said of the Kingdom of God.[23] By this appreciation of the *Interpretament* I am not saying that Marxsen understands mission and praxis as liberation theology does, but I appreciate the fact that he relates Jesus' resurrection essentially with mission.

Finally, Marxsen's denial that what happened to Jesus can be adequately expressed in terms of a single cultural expression, such as "resurrection of the dead," seems to me important for what it really states, not for what it seems to deny in reductionist terms. What happens after death is mysterious to such a degree that no one cultural expression can exhaust its reality and significance. In this sense Marxsen is right to criticize reduction of the expression of what happened to the terms of one cultural tradition—apocalyptic—and correct in reminding us that there are other cultural traditions for expressing what happens after death, such as immortality of the soul, even if the concept of resurrection is richer than others by including that of this life being full life, also bodily and societal and even cosmic, a dimension that is not required by other cultural traditions. Having said this, the basic criticism that can be made of Marxsen is that he does not seem to take into account what is central to apocalyptic tradition, that the resurrection of the dead expresses justice for the victims. I shall return to this as essential to my own reflections, but for the moment let me record that it has already been pointed out by Moltmann: "For Israel, hope in the resurrection was not an anthropological symbol, nor a soteriological one, nor did it refer to everlasting life or happiness, but it was a theological symbol to express faith in the triumph of God's justice at the end of history. . . . It is not a longing for life everlasting but 'thirst for justice.'"[24]

(iii) Wolfhart Pannenberg: Hope in the anticipated future. Pannenberg states that the resurrection of Jesus is the central event for *theology*,[25] since it is the source of revelation of the reality of God as power over the whole of existence,[26] and for *christology*, since from it the divinity of Christ is made manifest. The resurrection can bear such a wealth of revelation because it—even if only in anticipation, *proleptically*, in his terminology—makes present the end of history, which enables us to comprehend the whole of history, and so becomes, in Hegelian manner, the condition for the possibility of knowing the truth and the event that reveals God. Therefore, also, a theology based on the resurrection of Jesus is the true philosophy.

Besides this, Pannenberg insists that the resurrection is a historical event and has to be known as such through historical methods. One cannot, therefore, reduce its reality to the *meaning* of another reality distinct from itself, such as the saving value of the cross or the foundation of mission.[27] Pannenberg sees no special problem, in principle, in the resurrection being historical and criticizes the position of those who, in his view lightly, deny this historicity: "The fact that a related event brings out the analogy with what is otherwise habitually or repeatedly testified does not in itself constitute any reason for impugning its historicity."[28] (He is, however, also cautious. He knows that the subject is hotly debated, not only because of the difficulty in finding adequate historical methods but also "because it penetrates deep into the fundamental questions of understanding reality." In fact, he also relies on a sort of psychological argument: "One will decide to take this step [affirming the historicity of the resurrection and using it as the starting point for systematic christology] only on the intuition that it is no longer possible to provide a sustainable basis for christological statements along the traditional lines, that is, either starting with the idea of incarnation or that of the earthly Jesus' consciousness of power."[29] In the end he is obliged to admit that "my interest lies solely in that . . . this event, insofar as it is one, also has to be called historical.[30])

Furthermore, Jesus' resurrection has to be historical and verifiable, as theology cannot establish the reality of something solely on the basis of faith or revelation or scriptural inspiration, still less on that of a teaching authority. In this he is fully at one with the Enlightenment thinking according to which nothing can be known or should be accepted only on the basis of an argument from authority: "The theologian is in no way, for example, in the position of being able to say what happened in just those cases that remain obscure for historians."[31] But if Jesus' resurrection is to be viewed by theology as a historical event, this raises the question of a suitable method for establishing its reality, which, in turn, leads to the hermeneutical question.

History, for Pannenberg, is "history of tradition,"[32] and so "historical," in his terms, would seem to mean: (1) that it can be expressed in language; (2) that it appears in the context of a tradition; and (3) that it responds to a human metaphysical expectation. Following this course, the resurrection would be historical in that: (1) it has been expressed in the language of "resurrection from the dead"; (2) it is bound into the "apocalyptic" tradition; and (3) it responds to the "radical hope" found in human beings as possessors of the openness entrusted to all.

I do not propose to analyze this conception of what is historical, but I shall examine its consequences for hermeneutics. Above all, Jesus' resurrection cannot be understood without a view of history leading to an all-embracing and positive conclusion, because this is precisely what the phrase "resurrection from the dead" seeks to express, and this view of history is necessary for understanding what happened to Jesus as the anticipation *(prolepsis)* of this definitive end. If its reality is seen as only a fragment or as an isolated event—or in its wisdom variants of *carpe diem* or *vanitas vanitatum*—the resurrection of Jesus cannot be understood. Acceptance of a universal history that will come to a final fullness is, therefore, the condition for making it possible to understand the resurrection.

This view of reality derives from a tradition that developed on biblical ground (and so is contingent), but it has the potentiality to shed light on the whole of reality, the ultimate criterion of truth. Furthermore, this view of history requires a trusting openness toward its end—a radical hope, in other words. If we are not beings of hope, we can find no meaning in the phrase "resurrection from the dead." And this, Pannenberg states, is no longer contingent but belongs to the essential constitution of human beings and from a historical point of view—despite appearances to the contrary—is also a possibility today. (Recalling Bloch, he declares that no one dies with the thought of a total death.) In conclusion, to understand the resurrection of Jesus one needs a trusting surrender to the future, a radical hope that this will be a coming to fulfillment.

This transcendental correlation between *resurrection* and *hope* is a major insight of modern theology, shared by virtually all present-day theologians.[33] At work in it is the philosophy of hope elaborated by Ernst Bloch, which has been fruitful for the whole of theology in its reformulation of God as the "God of the future" and in its concept of history as "promise." Pannenberg is indebted to this intuition, using it to posit the future as God's mode of being[34] and hope in the future as a transcendental dimension of human beings.[35]

Pannenberg does not, however, specify the hope that is historically necessary today for understanding the resurrection. Moltmann, among others, was to criticize him for postulating only a generic hope, not the hope required by present-day history and not even that required by apocalyptic: a qualified hope, in the midst of and in the face of the negative aspect of history, a hope against injustice and death suffered unjustly.[36] As a consequence, Pannenberg fails to make his "God of the future"—an important and novel formulation—include, even if dialectically, other dimensions of the reality of God likewise rediscovered by theology: the crucified God, the God of victims.[37]

While Pannenberg's recovery of totality versus mere fragment and of hope versus mere facticity is important, liberation theology sees two major lacunas in his theology. The first is the *absence of praxis* on the way toward the fullness of history, to which I shall return later, here just citing the critique by A. González: "Despite the fact that Pannenberg has stressed the unity of event and interpretation, the continuity of history exists for him only on the level of interpretations (tradition), not on the level of praxis."[38] The second concerns the qualification of hope as *hope of the victims*, meaning his lack of partiality in the presence of victims. Even if only as a brief digression, I propose to examine this second deficiency, which permeates his theology and is reflected in his theological treatment of the life and destiny of Jesus.

For Pannenberg, the parameters for understanding the resurrection are adequately provided by two dimensions of Jesus' life: (1) his formally anticipatory (proleptic) character; and (2) seeing the end of his life in the context of the history of the traditions—the contradiction posed by his end: Jesus on the one hand claims God's authority for himself and on the other comes into conflict with the law, which in his day represented God. The resurrection is needed to confirm his claim and to overcome the ambiguity of his life: "To the extent that in Jesus' life the Jewish tradition came into conflict with itself, his appearance took on an ambiguity that could be resolved only if the God of Israel declared himself for him."[39]

There is, then, a relationship between resurrection and Jesus' life, but the cross is fundamentally absent from this relationship. It was soon pointed out that Pannenberg's explanation of the meaning of Christ's resurrection lacked the cross as a constituent feature, with the result that the cross became logically superfluous for understanding the resurrection, owing to his treatment of the cross of Jesus. The methodological principle of understanding an event on the basis of the history of traditions means that in Pannenberg the meaning of the cross is not unequivocal or clear in itself; that is, the cross needs the resurrection to have any meaning, but not the other way round.[40] He finds nothing in the traditions of the cross that sheds any light on the resurrection. And this lack of reflection on the cross of Jesus partly explains the lack of a critical dimension in his theology, which can be seen on various levels and certainly on that of hermeneutics.

In the first place, Pannenberg does not consider the cross in its primary *theologal* dimension as *cross*; rather, he gives the impression that the only meaningful thing about it is that Jesus should have died so that the Father could then show his power over the whole of reality. The "corpse" is more important than the "crucified," and the cross seems to be reduced to its aspect of making the resurrection possible. When the question of the meaning of the cross in itself is missing, two important dimensions of theology also vanish: one is the crucified God, with its correlation of the abandonment of Jesus on the cross; the other is the historical opposition between divinities, the rival gods who do battle against the God of Jesus, which raises the problem of idolatry.

In the second place, there is a lack of depth in his treatment of *sin* as the reality that brings death. If it is not seen in this way, Jesus' death has a casual character or at best has a certain inevitability only on the level of Jewish legal procedures but not on that of underlying reality. Jesus' death is no longer a reality that uncovers the true nature of sin. Pannenberg might say that, as the specific form of rejecting Jesus was putting him to death, the confirmation needed from God to resolve the ambiguity of his life would have to consist in bringing him back to life, but, by not going into the essence of sin as that which brings death, he cannot state that this rejection of Jesus *had to* consist in death and that God's action in raising him was a reaction to do justice to an innocent victim.

Finally, Pannenberg has criticized Karl Rahner for upholding the unity of cross and resurrection and for explaining the latter starting from the former, not the other way round.[41] I mention this critique because Rahner, by making understanding of the resurrection depend on understanding of the cross, supposes that the revelation of God and the demands this places on us come about through both cross and resurrection. In my paraphrase we have to respond to this God who is revealed in this way in both *obedience* and *hope,* both primary realities, without the first being deduced from a supposed absolute primacy of the second. In simple terms, obedience is what refers us to the negative side of history, to the cross, and what can also be interpreted as praxis against the crucifixions of history, while our being-of-hope refers us to the resurrection. Pannenberg accepts the second postulate and from there attempts to explain everything, but he does not know what to make of the first, with the result that hope becomes detached from the negative aspects we have to overcome and fight.

This is what is lacking in Pannenberg's theology of the cross: while accepting the negative side of history, he does not focus on the specific negativity of the crucified God. What follows from this, where hermeneutics is concerned, is that the hope of the resurrection becomes hope in a fulfilling future beyond death but not hope against the cross: this is our hope, but not the hope of victims. In my view this is the basic hermeneutical limitation in understanding the New Testament texts and definitely in understanding them from the viewpoint of the crucified of this world.

(b) European Catholic Theology

Catholic theologians, somewhat later than Protestant ones, have also concerned themselves with the question of hermeneutics. I propose to limit my considerations here to Karl Rahner, because of the intrinsic value of his treatment and because he tackles the subject—unlike the other theologians analyzed—from a substantially speculative standpoint.[42]

His basic affirmation is that the resurrection is the final resolution of something that has previously been destroyed by death. Furthermore, the resolution proclaimed in the New Testament is that of the totality of Jesus, of his person and his cause. If this person and cause in their earthly existence have already been saving, and if it is said of them that they are now definitively saving, then what follows is a conclusion that Rahner formulates brilliantly:

> If the resurrection of Jesus is the permanent prevailing of his person and of his cause, and if this person-cause does not mean the survival of a man and his history but the triumph of his claim to be the absolute mediator of salvation, then faith in his resurrection constitutes an intrinsic aspect of this resurrection and not an appreciation of an event that by its nature could exist exactly the same without being known. If the resurrection of Jesus is to be the eschatological victory of God's grace in the world, it is not possible to conceive it without an effective (though free) faith in it, a faith in which the very nature of the resurrection culminates.[43]

In effect, these words formulate a tautology, not a sterile tautology, however, but a fruitful one, since the words go to the root of the matter: an *eschatological*, and therefore definitive, manifestation of God in history that was not made apparent as such would be nonsensical. For hermeneutics this means—another tautology— that understanding of the resurrection requires *such a* faith in God. In simple terms, without prior acceptance that God can produce an eschatological event in history and that, if God does so, this event has to be recognized as such, there can be no understanding of the resurrection.

If one argues that this is precisely the point in question—to know whether God has produced such an eschatological event in history—the answer is that now we at least have texts that state this to be so, and that these texts confront us with the eventual possibility of such faith. Accepting them or not is one thing, but it is impossible *now* to deny the existence of such texts, which make these (possible) demands. What matters for hermeneutics is that these texts require a "new" modality of faith: openness to accept that God can act *eschatologically* in history and that this can be recognized—even if the ability to do so is also given by God. To sum up: the resurrection of Jesus shows the victorious manifestation of God, and if it is God who emerges victorious, this has also necessarily to be noted in a historical manner.

Rahner adds to this transcendental consideration the need for hope in one's own resurrection in order to be able to recognize what is triumphant in Jesus' resurrection, its "permanent prevailing." In this hope, thematic or a-thematic in form, we express the human longing for final resolution, for the ultimate triumph of life. And so, when we hear that Jesus' resurrection has taken place, we can understand it because it responds to our transcendental hope of absolute salvation—although it may well be that it is precisely this proclamation of Jesus' resurrection that enables us to thematize this self-understanding into categories.

Finally, Rahner points out that Jesus' resurrection is in itself an unrepeatable event, which means that we are forced to go back to the testimony of the original witnesses of the faith and have to take a stand in relation to this testimony, which in turn emphasizes the radical *otherness* in our understanding of the resurrection of Jesus. On the other hand, he states the possibility that we can still, in some way, experience *affinity* with the risen Christ. He says that we can, here and now, have

the audacity to place ourselves above death, with our gaze fixed on the risen Christ, who rises before us through the evangelical witness. And in this audacity (freely exercised) the risen Christ bears witness that he himself lives in the blessed and indissoluble correlation existing between transcendental hope in the resurrection and the actual categorical dimension of the resurrection itself.[44]

To sum up: Rahner states that grasping the resurrection is not only possible but *has* to be possible, that this grasp has to be to some degree real, since it would be a contradiction *in obliquo* to proclaim the resurrection of Jesus as the definitive victory of God now in history and for this victory not be known. For us to grasp this victory of God's, we need three things: (1) to be open to the possibility of this content of God's victory being communicated to us; (2) to expound a hope (since every human being in fact has it) in our own resurrection as our final resolution; and (3) to experience the repercussion of Jesus' resurrection as such in our own lives here and now.

To these reflections, which are most specifically his own, Rahner adds another, to which I have alluded but to which I return now for its implications for hermeneutics. I refer to the transcendental relationship he establishes between Jesus' death and his resurrection. Rahner states that according to the New Testament the resurrection is not what happens factually and chronologically after the cross but is rather what the cross of Jesus results in, by its very nature; that is, there is a mutual relationship of principle between cross that results in resurrection and resurrection of the crucified. This is not, then, a question of two juxtaposed realities but of two realities that refer to and explain each other.

I stress this point because, in virtue of the consequential development of both elements in this central affirmation, the now victorious life of Jesus would have been that of a crucified person, not simply that of a dead one. And, in parallel with this, the hope required would be not only a transcendental hope but a hope against the cross. It is true that without transcendental hope there can be no crucified hope, but it is also true that the two are not identical, as Pannenberg would have them. The first is required in any sort of desire to live on after death—and applies to the Christian sort, the Greek survival of the soul, the Eastern transmigration of souls, or any other. But to grasp the specific Christian afterlife we need hope "against the cross."

(c) Lessons from European Theology

Before moving on, let us reflect briefly on this survey of classic European theologians, to whom we owe the discovery of the need for hermeneutics, which has placed theology within a new paradigm.

1. The authors examined are all conscious of the fact that the texts dealing with the resurrection of Jesus cannot be read ingenuously, that we cannot approach them with the presupposition that we already know what "resurrection" means; in this way they belong to the generation of "masters of suspicion." I regard acceptance of this prior ignorance as not only *hermeneutically* necessary for avoiding any simplistic reading but also *theologically* and existentially fruitful, as without it—if we already knew well enough what resurrection was—the texts would confirm what we already know and so no longer be *revelation* of God.

Put positively, accepting the difficulty of the texts may well serve as a mediation of our recognition of our ignorance—even if not total or absolute—of what resurrection is, which means that we allow the resurrection event to be revelation, gift, and—therefore—salvation. In understanding of all that is mystery or shares in it we need to develop a knowledge also to be open to non-knowledge and, above all, to be on our guard against false knowledge, even if we have previously regarded it as good and true.

2. Nevertheless, some sort of knowledge of what resurrection might be clearly has to be possible, and if we are to understand it, the very texts of the New Testament require (logically) some sort of prior attitude. These requirements are judged in different ways—hence the diversity of the theologies examined—but can have significant formal coincidences among them, and in any case the attempt to interpret the texts can point to important considerations.

Of these, the following may be noted here: (a) that there should be an openness to grace, to allowing oneself to be given something by God, although authors vary in what they consider this something might be—salvation, the meaning of existence, faith. The central fact, however, is constant: we have to allow for the possibility of something being given to us. (b) There must also be some sort of ultimate hope, a conviction that in the final analysis history is neither absurd nor condemnation but salvation and that in the present there is already salvation, even if it is hidden. (c) There must be some affinity between the present life of the reader and what is said to have happened victoriously to Jesus, even though theologians express this affinity in very varied ways: the courage to place ourselves above death now, living as already saved beings, fidelity to the risen Christ in carrying on the cause of Jesus. The important thing, in any event, is that there should be some sort of continuity and not simply radical discontinuity—though the latter is obvious—between our actual life in the present and the unrepeatable event of Jesus' resurrection.

3. The variety of focuses depends on the theological conviction of each of these authors. Sometimes they present their conviction in open (excluding) debate with those of others. But history shows that basing everything on a single explanation, however complete it may appear, does not work, especially when dealing with mystery. So the phenomenon of diversity of explanations can perhaps teach us two things. One is that my own contribution, on liberation theology lines, however positive, will need to be complemented by others, now and in the future. The other is the feeling at least and perhaps the theoretical conviction that tackling the resurrection of Jesus—the mystery of the presence of the eschatological in history—is something that has to be done, though without facile agreements and eclecticism, by us all.

4. Finally, let me say that the hermeneutical requirements of the authors we have examined can help to overcome current limitations and faults, even if these do not relate directly to the resurrection. I believe, in effect, that although the question of how to understand the resurrection as an eschatological event seems a sophisticated matter, the subject actually has clear existential, human, and perennial equivalents: what our final view of existence and its meaning is, what we can hope for, what we must do.

So, even if this is simplifying matters somewhat, we can say that Bultmann's existential seriousness would be no bad thing amid the postmodern frivolities of our present world; nor would Marxsen's appeal to praxis in the face of the indifference currently inculcated; nor hope, even if only Pannenberg's version of it; nor Rahner's evocation of mystery against the present banalization of existence.

(d) Latin American Liberation Theology

Virtually all these developments in European theology took place before the emergence of the thinking proper to liberation theology. From them liberation theology learned the importance of hermeneutics above all, and it has incorporated some of their presuppositions. But it has also modified, radicalized, and broadened them, as the approach of Leonardo Boff demonstrates.

In his first work of christology Boff stresses that hope is needed in order to understand the resurrection, adds that this hope has to be such as to fulfill people at all levels of their being, and points out the numerous obstacles in the way of this being realized:

> We are essentially beings on the way, trying to fulfill ourselves at all levels, in body, mind, and spirit, in our biological, spiritual, and cultural lives. This aspiration is continually blocked by frustration, suffering, lack of love for and lack of unity with ourselves and others. The "hope" principle in us leads constantly to construct utopias.[45]

Boff further insists on the radical nature of hope by placing its correlation in utopia, in what has no place in history, and he points out its historical problems: "We all groan like St. Paul. . . . We all long like the writer of the Apocalypse for a situation in which there will be no more death, there will be no more weeping or cries or burdens because the old world will have passed away."[46]

On this level of reflection Boff is basically staying within the hermeneutics of hope, as developed by European theology, but in his later works he interprets hope more and more from the Latin American situation as one of injustice and suffering.[47] In *The Passion of Christ, Passion of the World*, published originally in 1977,[48] he still writes about *hope*, even if only in passing, but also of "a protest against the 'justice' and 'the law' that led to Christ being condemned."[49] He still talks of *expectation of salvation* but has discovered that "the Oppressed was the Liberator."[50] He still speaks of *utopia* but now rephrases it: "The resurrection of Jesus means the victory of life, of the right of the oppressed, of justice for the weak."[51] He still holds up *hope as a fundamental reality* but adds that we have to "live for truth and justice."[52]

So, from Latin America utopia has been modified, making it the object of the resurrection and of the hope necessary to reach it from the poor and the oppressed. This hope is no longer seen as a transcendental anthropological dimension of human beings but as something partial in its realization, and this is a major contribution to the hermeneutics of understanding the resurrection (one also made with great force by Moltmann in *The Crucified God*). Furthermore, even if only in passing, it is now stated that the continuity between the resurrection of Jesus and our present time lies not only in the *meaning* of our present life, formulated variously as the audacity to place ourselves above death or as salvation experienced as sinful and pardoned human beings, but in living now in such a way as to make this life "for truth and justice." Although Boff does not develop this thematically, he suggests here that *praxis*—and a particular praxis—is a presupposition for grasping Jesus' resurrection.

What Boff has sketched out—hope of justice for the weak and a life lived for justice, as hermeneutical principles, plus the undoubted popular-collective dimension of hope—is what I seek to develop in greater depth in the next chapter.

Chapter 3

The Hermeneutical Problem (2)

Hermeneutical Principles from the Victims

After that *tour d'horizon* I am now going to present my view of the hermeneutical problem. I start from the supposition that understanding Jesus' resurrection as an eschatological event is an analogous problem to that of knowing God through any divine action, with the added problem that, in this case, God's action is eschatological. This means that Jesus' resurrection has to be tackled from the most comprehensive viewpoint possible, since, although knowledge of God by definition has a purely intellectual dimension, this specific knowledge is attained through the whole of being human—what gives us both otherness and affinity with respect to God. Having said this—with Zubiri's realism—our access to God is a physical access.[1] I have put this elsewhere in less technical language: "Those who see God are those who go to God."

Approaching Jesus' resurrection from the most comprehensive viewpoint possible is already required, or at least insinuated, by the New Testament itself. It is true that, on the one hand, this asks readers to place their trust in those who have been witnesses to the appearances and so, in this way, to accept the reality of the resurrection. But, on the other hand, when the New Testament speaks of Jesus' resurrection, it relates it to all dimensions of the believer's situation. So it states that on the basis of Jesus' resurrection believers know who God is, who Jesus Christ is, how we have been justified and saved, what baptism means, what makes the new Christian liturgy possible, where the possibility of forgiving sins in the community comes from, and many other things.

Furthermore—and this is my main concern in this chapter on hermeneutics—the New Testament links Jesus' resurrection with those anthropological dimensions that, taken as a whole, express the totality of being human. Concentrating them for the moment, for motives of clarity, into Kant's famous three questions—What can I know? What must I do? What may I hope?[2]—produces the result that Jesus' resurrection is a reality in which an answer is given to all of them, and all gain an embodiment from the resurrection. So if we ask what we can know, the answer is that "the Lord has risen indeed" (Lk 24:34). If we ask what we are

35

allowed to hope, the answer is that "Christ has been raised from the dead, the first fruits of those who have died" (1 Cor 15:20). If we ask what we have to do, the answer is that "they went out and proclaimed the good news [of the risen Christ] everywhere" (Mk 16:20).[3]

The resurrection is, then, linked in the New Testament with fundamental human realities, and if this linkage is not seen in a purely arbitrary way, then these realities, duly actualized, will not only have light shed on them by Jesus' resurrection but will also, in turn, help us to understand it. So I want now to analyze the questions we all, explicitly or implicitly, ask ourselves, and the relationship they bear to Jesus' resurrection: *What knowledge, what praxis, and what hope* are needed today in order to understand what is being said when we hear that Jesus has been raised from the dead? The replies will above all take account of what the scriptural texts themselves require, but reread from the Latin American situation.

I add a fourth question to Kant's three: *What can we celebrate in history* (though this will be considered later, in chapter 5)? I do this because I believe that celebrating belongs to the totality of being human[4] and is not simply interchangeable with the dimensions of knowing, acting, and hoping, and because this question is implied by the very texts dealing with the resurrection. And I do it also because, however scandalous this may seem, without realizing what there is to celebrate in history it is impossible to understand the Latin American situation from which I interrogate the resurrection. But for now, let us see what hope, what actions, and what knowledge are logically necessary to an understanding of Jesus' resurrection event.

1.   The Hope of the Crucified: The Victory of Life over Death

Whether they formulate it in terms of "awakening from sleep," of "raising up what was put down," or of "life everlasting," the New Testament texts that speak of Jesus' resurrection express most clearly, from an anthropological point of view, the hope that triumphs over death. If human beings were not by nature "beings of hope" or were unable to fulfill this hope over the course of history with its ups and downs, the resurrection texts would in this respect be incomprehensible. It would be like trying to explain colors to a blind person.

Having said this—which may seem so obvious as to be unnecessary[5]—we need to ascertain what specific type of hope the texts mean, since they do not simply express a generic hope. I propose to dwell on this point at some length, since the hope that life can overcome death is what the texts themselves most directly and radically require if they are to be understood.

In this and the following sections I am going to proceed by analyzing first the requirements of the biblical texts in themselves and then, more systematically, the actualization of these requirements in the present.

(a)   The Hope of Life in Scripture[6]

When the disciples formulate the reality of the Jesus who has appeared to them, they make use of a language known in their day, deriving from the apocalyptic tradition of Israel, that of the resurrection of the dead. This is a metaphor drawn from everyday life: awakening from sleep. The metaphor states that a discontinuous change has taken place (there is no continuity between the sleeping state and the waking state) and expresses the radical superiority of the new state over the old. In this metaphor of awakening they formulate what has happened to someone who was dead/asleep. Jesus no longer sleeps but is awake; he is not dead but lives. The formula, then, states that death is not the absolute end of human existence, but, as this cannot be proved directly, it supposes, by correlation, the hope of some form of survival beyond death.

(i) Faith in a God with historical existence. Israel, despite being surrounded by peoples who believed in survival after death, did not initially develop a clear belief of life in the beyond. This shows, on the one hand, that it was not easily assimilated into the locally prevailing religious thinking, but above all that the development of its faith was based on *theo*logy rather than on a cultural anthropology influenced by the surrounding environment. In effect, the people of Israel, as they proceeded with their discovery of the nature of God, drew consequences for their understanding of themselves and their nation.

Israel knew God above all in relation to the real historical life of its people, and for this reason it was late in formulating the hope of a life beyond death. As Kessler observes, the ideas of "beyond the tomb" held by surrounding nations, especially Egypt, "were generally associated with a contempt for historical and earthly life,"[7] and this was something Israel, with its perception of this present earthly life as a gift of God, could not tolerate. So Israel thought of God in connection with life and the living—particularly with social relationships among the living—and its religion consisted precisely in bearing witness to this God. "The people had to concentrate all their attention and energy on this historical earthly mission."[8] So in the early stages the world of the dead, *sheol*, was not considered to be within Yahweh's sphere. For the believer the tragedy of ending in *sheol* was ceasing to be in communion with Yahweh.

This theologal concentration of earthly and historical life, in the name of its God, is what delayed the formulation of a hope in the afterlife:

> Israel knew the unsubstitutable nature of historical existence. It was destined to safeguard all dimensions of the exclusive rights of Yahweh, as God and Lord in this world, over earthly life in all its dimensions: that people had to learn through painful experiences what it meant to be called to serve this God with his universal rights. While this historical mission was insufficiently entrenched in the people's consciousness, the prospect of what lay beyond death brought the danger of evading their historical task. This is the deepest reason why Israel rejected the presupposition of a beyond, so obvious to the surrounding tribes, and did not project human dreams and vital aspirations beyond death.[9]

Such statements can only be called daring, since they venture into the unknowable will of God. But Kessler's assertion that death, as the end of existence, was not the greatest scandal to the Israelite faith is important, and it leads to these two conclusions. First, the affirmation of a beyond did not arise in Israel on the margin of and certainly not in opposition to historical life. The essence of its faith was always the affirmation of God as the God of historical life. Second, if Israel came to pose the problem of the beyond, it did so by broadening its idea of God and integrating into it the supremacy that the life of the people has for God. Undoubtedly, historical events had to happen for Israel to reformulate its faith in God. But these reformulations did not derive principally from self-centered anthropological longings but rather from its fidelity to a God of life and, as we shall see, to a God of justice. Fidelity to its faith in Yahweh is what led Israel gradually to affirm a life after death.

(ii) Communion with God beyond death. What was it that actually made Israel formulate its belief in the beyond? The reply can perhaps be summed up in two phrases: the lordship of Yahweh, and a reformulation of salvation.

The earlier and probably more theoretical development was a broadening of the notion of the *lordship of Yahweh.* From the prophets Israel was learning to understand this lordship as lordship operating in the beginning, which led to the formulation of a creator God at the absolute origin of time. But it also understood that this lordship extended into the future, and this gave rise to the eschatological hope that Yahweh would exercise his dominion over all peoples and over the whole of creation—and more, that Yahweh would be victorious against all the powers of earth and the cosmos. So the idea took shape that the future would be no obstacle to the sovereignty of Yahweh but would bring the definitive triumph.

The words of Isaiah 25:7—"He will swallow up death forever" (though they may well be an apocalyptic addition)—belong to this resulting eschatologization of Yahweh's lordship. From an exegetical point of view, it is not quite clear what the phrase means, since it could refer to those who will be alive in the time of salvation and will not succumb to death, or it could refer to a universal resurrection of a retroactive nature. But the important thing is that formulation of faith in the lordship of Yahweh now includes the overcoming of death.

The wisdom tradition adds a new element to this evolving faith. It tries to answer the question of why the just suffer and why, if they have lived faithful and essentially obedient to Yahweh, they have to break off communion with him in death. The traditional doctrine of retribution—that God, on earth, grants prosperity to the good and pours misfortune on the wicked—could not give an adequate answer to this question, since this is not what history taught. In any case, the question of why communion with Yahweh, with whom the just have lived in a relationship of total fidelity and trust, ends with death went on becoming more anguishing for believers.

The Book of Job is the greatest expression of this question, and the reply given there needs to be properly understood. It undoubtedly provides a new solution to the problem of retribution, but its most novel aspect is the formulation of a new faith: those who remain faithful to Yahweh *will not die forever*, will always remain faithful to him. This faith is expressed again in the Psalms: "God will ransom my soul from the power of Sheol, for he will receive me" (Ps 49:15). Communion with Yahweh lasts forever.

(iii) God's eschatological triumph over injustice. This belief that communion with God goes beyond death and, implicitly, that God's lordship extends over death also, was extended by a new and decisive element in the apocalyptic movement. This brings in the expression "resurrection of the dead" to describe what happened to Jesus. Briefly, this belief in the resurrection of the dead arose in response to a situation of extreme gravity for the just and faithful of Yahweh, but this crisis was produced by something very specific: the active *injustice* they were suffering at the hands of the worldly powers of the time.

In such a situation the problem is not why it goes ill with the just but why the powers of the world actively destroy those who are faithful to Yahweh—because they are faithful. The question is no longer the problem of divine retribution or that of communion with God, but the problem of injustice in history, the horror that history produces victims, and God's impotence or at least inaction in regard to the victimizers. This is the fundamental theologal scandal, that the power of injustice seems to be greater than that of Yahweh. Seen from the present, it seems that Israel for centuries was not worried by Yahweh not having power over death, but it *was* scandalized by God not having power over the injustice in history.

How to understand a just Yahweh in a history that produces victims was the agonizing question that arose in the apocalyptic movement, and the reply was that Yahweh will indeed bring justice. This is a message of comfort, of faith that history is in God's hands. Directly, then, the central message of apocalyptic, and its most important one in our own history, has nothing to do with the esoteric but responds to a human longing that in the end there will be justice, that the butcher will not triumph over the victim.

Two clarifications of this basic hope need to be made. The first is that the end of injustice coincides with the ending of this world as we know it, and therefore the triumph of justice is not described as renewal and transformation, however radical this is seen to be, but as the "end" of history, which differentiates apocalyptic from the prophetic movement and expresses a certain pessimism concerning the possibilities those believers saw in history: things can only change in a radically different history.

The second clarification, of which echoes are also to be found in the New Testament, concerns who will rise again. The first point to stress is that the final resurrection is never presented as the resurrection of a single individual but always as that of a collectivity. (The two great symbols of fulfillment that appear in both the Old and New Testaments—the Kingdom of God and the resurrection of the dead—are group, collective, universal realities. The idea of the purely personal fulfillment of an individual would have seemed absurd to them.) But once this is accepted, there is no uniform view on whether only the just and the victims of history will rise again, in which case the resurrection would be a salvific event in itself, or whether all the dead will rise, some to salvation and others to condemnation, in which case the resurrection would be salvifically neutral and prior to the judgment to salvation or condemnation, which would follow it.

This apocalyptic belief, relating resurrection and God's justice, developed gradually. The kernel of the idea is expressed in Isaiah 26:7–21, in the context of a grave crisis for Israel. The writer bitterly recognizes the failure of justice in this world and despairs of things changing:

> If favor is shown to the wicked,
>   they do not learn righteousness;
> in the land of uprightness they deal perversely
>   and do not see the majesty of the Lord. (v. 10)

The writer already knows what awaits the unjust and responds according to the traditional doctrine, which seems to set his mind at rest:

> Let the fire for your adversaries consume them. (v. 11)

And again, more radically:

> The dead do not live;
>   shades do not rise—
> because you have punished and destroyed them,
>   and wiped out all memory of them. (v. 14)

Justice is thereby safeguarded where the wicked are concerned, but the question still remains with regard to the victims. Yahweh then replies,

> Your dead shall live, their corpses shall rise.
>   O dwellers in the dust, awake and sing for joy!
>   (v. 19)

It is debatable whether this passage is dealing with resurrection from the dead in the literal sense or whether it refers only to the restoration of the people of Israel, though the two are not mutually exclusive. But the central point is that a radical hope in God arises in the midst of historical crises; the graver the crisis for the people, the more God's powerful salvation is hoped for. This text shows that faith in Yahweh is being deepened, without anything, even the greatest scandals in history, being able to put it to the test. The phase "resurrection of the dead" is then an expression of this powerful (and new) faith. In Kessler's words, "Faith in Yahweh generates the idea of actual resurrection of the sanctified just and audacious hope based on Yahweh himself."[10]

The unequivocal hope that there will be a resurrection of the dead appears years later in a specific context: the persecution undergone by many Israelites under Antiochus IV Epiphanes, who put many of them to a cruel death. This is the context of the final redaction of the Book of Daniel, in which (for the only time in the Old Testament) the actual resurrection of the dead, of the victims of persecution, is clearly stated: "Many of those who sleep in the dust of the earth [*sheol*] shall awake, some to everlasting life, and some to shame and everlasting contempt" (12:2).

This is undoubtedly a text of consolation and hope in a time of trial, but it is also a theologal text, and a novel and daring one: in the confrontation between a great (political) power and God, in the end God will win. While the prophets stress the existence of idols who are in conflict with Yahweh, here Yahweh's triumph is proclaimed. What this triumph will be like is not described uniformly. Daniel speaks of a world totally renewed and unlike the present one, after the universal tribulation; it breathes the pessimistic idea that this history cannot receive God, that a radically different world is needed for God to be able to show himself. Other texts—such as the beautiful passage in Isaiah 65:17–25—also speak of a radically different world but use the image of a renewed earth. In any case, the message of apocalyptic is hope in God's power to remake an unjust world and to work justice for its victims.

(iv) The hope expressed in Jesus' resurrection. Daniel 12:2 and Isaiah 65:17 have not become reality in history, which has continued without the dead being raised to life. But Israel's faith permanently adopted the hope of God's final victory over this world of injustice, which deals death and produces victims (though not all religious groups did. The Sadducees, for example, clung to the traditional doctrine of God's reward in this life and rejected the idea of resurrection on these grounds, which suited their purposes as they belonged and were related to the wealthy classes).

In Jesus' day expectation of God's eschatological action was shared by many, though Jesus himself hardly ever spoke of it in terms of *resurrection* but in the terminology of *Kingdom of God* and relied more on the prophetic tradition. In fact, it is only in Mark 12:18–27 (and parallels) that he tackles the subject of resurrection, in the debate with the Sadducees, and in chapter 13 in his apocalyptic discourse.[11]

The disciples, nevertheless, formulated their paschal experience in the terminology of resurrection. Further on, I shall analyze what they meant to say about Jesus by doing so, but first let us look at two types of text with important consequences for hermeneutics. One more generally taken into account is the need for hope in the universal resurrection and therefore in one's own. The other, normally ignored, is the need to make the hope of victims our hope.

As far as the first is concerned, although there were legends of the spiriting away of individuals, as in the cases of Elijah and Enoch, the raising of a single individual was a contradiction in terms in apocalyptic thinking. This means that by the mere fact of speaking in terms of resurrection, the disciples were associating Jesus' resurrection with a more general resurrection, the universal resurrection, in which they included their own. (An increasing number of people now think that what the disciples experienced and were given to understand in the post-resurrection appearances was the reality of the universal resurrection.) The first generation of Christians believed that Jesus' resurrection was the beginning of the universal resurrection (see 1 Thes 4:15, 17; 1 Cor 15:51): "The apostles did not proclaim the resurrection in itself or for itself, but as the precursor sign and first time of the general resurrection of the dead; and this, in turn, as the coming of the kingdom of God and of his pardon, the 'universal restoration' (Acts 3:21)."[12] It was only the second generation that became conscious of the temporal tension between Jesus' resurrection and the final parousia. In any case, Jesus' resurrection was expressed as that of the "firstborn within a large family" (Rom 8:29; 1 Cor 15:13; Col 1:18; Rv 1:5), which presupposes hope in a final resurrection, including one's own.

Where the second point is concerned, the significance of apocalyptic for the new Christian faith has to be sought in the former's *intention*, "expectation of God's justice,"[13] which means that the formula "resurrection of the dead" "was not an anthropological or soteriological symbol but something that helped faith in God's justice."[14] On the basis of this logic the first Christians preached Jesus' resurrection as God's reaction to human actions, as the justice God works for the one whom others unjustly put to death. This is how it appears in the earliest preaching, as narrated in stereotyped form in Acts: "You rejected the Holy and Righteous One . . . whom God raised from the dead" (3:14). In what happened to Jesus, apocalyptic hope in the triumph of justice is made real.

All this indicates that in preaching the resurrection of Jesus the first disciples were affirming that God's eschatological action in saving the righteous Jesus and doing justice to the victim Jesus has been realized and that this ushers in the end and fullness of time. The hope of the Book of Daniel, the hope in which the Maccabees died, is not an illusory but a well-founded hope. It is true that the butcher does not triumph over the victim; it is true that the idols do not triumph over the God of life.

(b) Rebuilding the Hope of Victims Now

We have seen that hope in one's own resurrection is postulated as a hermeneutical presupposition for understanding Jesus' resurrection. Modern theology, furthermore, has specified—in distinction from and sometimes in opposition to other symbols of hope, such as that deriving from Greek philosophy—that "its" symbol of hope has better credentials than others because the resurrection brings together the corporeal, social, and even cosmic dimensions of personal and historical reality.[15] With this, theology has recaptured basic aspects of the New Testament and has sought to put itself in tune with the demands of present-day anthropologies. With all this, however, it still has not touched on the essential point of what is implied in "the resurrection of the dead": justice for the victims. To do this, we have to go back to apocalyptic.

This expresses the most serious negative side of history: the victims. It also expresses a positive hope: that God can give them justice. In doing so it establishes a correlation between resurrection and victims. Hope applies directly to justice, not simply to survival; its primary subjects are the victims, not simply human beings; the scandal it has to overcome is death inflicted unjustly, not simply natural death as our destiny. The hope that has to be rebuilt now is not just any hope but *hope in the power of God over the injustice that produces victims*. "What is new and scandalous in the Christian message of Easter is not that one person has been raised before all the rest, but that it was precisely this condemned, hanged, and abandoned one."[16]

(i) The recipients of hope: The victims of history. If one takes the above seriously—and not just on the basis of a fundamentalist reading of the texts—Jesus' resurrection is hope, first of all, for those crucified in history. God raised a crucified man, and since then there is hope for the crucified. They can see the raised Jesus as the firstborn from among the dead, because they truly—and not just intentionally—see him as their elder brother. This gives them the courage to hope in their own resurrection, and they can now take heart to live in history, which supposes a "miracle" analogous to what happened in Jesus' resurrection. There is, then, a correlation between resurrection and the crucified analogous to the correlation between the Kingdom of God and the poor.

(ii) Universalization of the recipient by analogy. This does not mean that hope is de-universalized, but it does place conditions on it. In the first place, the setting of this hope is the world of the crucified, which is not an exceptional place but the most common of all human settings. We must not of course forget—as we religious people tend to do—that the cross of Jesus, before being *the* cross, is *a* cross and that there have been many more before and after it. Today there are vast masses who do not simply die but are put to death "at the hands of the pagans," men and women crucified, murdered, tortured, disappeared in the pursuit of justice. Many others die in the slow crucifixion produced by structural injustice. This is the setting for the universalization of hope, and from this place the resurrection becomes a symbol of hope to the extent that we participate, analogously, in the life and death of victims.[17]

Developing the analogy of the crucifixion is necessary but not easy. It could perhaps be said that when one's own death is not just the result of biological limitations or the wearing-down process involved in maintaining one's own life but rather the result of self-sacrifice out of love for others and to what is poor and the product of injustice in them, then there is an analogy between such a life and death and the life and death of Jesus. Then—and only then, from a Christian point of view—can one also share in the hope of the resurrection.

Outside this communion with the crucified Jesus, resurrection spells only the possibility of survival, and this survival—as the most classic teaching of the church spells out—is ambiguous: it can be either to salvation or to condemnation. For there to be hope of this survival being salvific one has to share in the cross of Jesus. This is the point from which resurrection hope can be universalized and become good news for all.

(iii) The scandal hope has to overcome. In Christian terms hope is against hope, as Paul says. Where resurrection hope is concerned, we are dealing with a crucified hope, not only because the expectation of survival after death brings its own darkness with it but because at the present time injustice brings death and one can see no end to its power. This is the great scandal.

If we take seriously the dualistic and antagonistic presentation of the action of human beings and the reaction of God in Jesus' fate—"you killed him, but God raised him"—we can then rephrase what constitutes the primary scandal of history and with what hope we should face up to it. A unilateral concentration on an action of God's that was only the bringing back of a *dead man* to life presupposes that this scandal is in the final analysis one's own death, meaning that what would make it possible to understand the resurrection would be the courage to hope in one's own survival. But if one hears that "you killed him," then the basic scandal is not directly death itself but the murder of the righteous and the possibility, a thousand times actualized, of putting them to death. (Even if only in passing, let me say that, in strict logic, the proclamation of the paschal kerygma should start with the prior question of whether we ourselves also share in putting the righteous to death. So Easter supposes—and as a central issue—openness to conversion.) The resurrection of Jesus, then, faces us with the problem of how to come to terms with our own death in the future, but in addition it reminds us that we also have to come to terms *now* with the unjust deaths of others in the present.

This is not to ignore the universal problem of death, nor is it to relegate the message of personal hope expressed in Jesus' resurrection to the background. But I do want to insist on the fact that there *now* exists an immense scandal, injustice that deals death, and that the way to tackle this scandal is—or can be, and in the midst of crucified peoples can most adequately be—the Christian way to tackle the scandal of one's own personal death also. In other words, the Christian courage to hope in one's own resurrection depends on the courage to hope for the overcoming of the historical scandal of injustice. In theologal language the question is whether God can do justice to the victims produced by human beings. As we have seen, Israel could live for centuries without personal death being a scandal to its faith, but it could not live with the scandal of faith in Yahweh and innocent victims existing at the same time. From then on, faith in God included the possibility of triumphing over injustice.

(iv) The hope needed at the present time. The foregoing means that hope must be not merely beyond death but against the death of victims, and this implies a formally *de-centered* hope, which fulfills the evangelical precept that forgetting oneself is the condition for rediscovering oneself in Christian terms; hope of one's own resurrection depends on hope of the resurrection of victims. Those for whom their own death is the basic scandal and hope of their own survival their greatest problem—however reasonable this may be—will have not a specifically Christian hope or one that stems from Jesus' resurrection but an egocentric hope.

What de-centers our hope is consciousness of the actual death of the crucified as that which is absolutely scandalous, a death that we cannot come to terms with and that cannot ultimately be relegated to the background of individual consciousness to make way for hope of one's own resurrection. This historical scandal should be the measure of what is scandalous about one's own death.

Having a hope for victims is the first demand Jesus' resurrection makes of us, but so is taking an active part in that hope. Being capable of making their hope ours, being ready to work for it, even if this makes us victims, is an irreplaceable hermeneutical principle. Outside this setting and this disposition, proclaiming that Jesus is risen can be interchangeable with the other symbols of hope in life beyond death that have proliferated and still proliferate in religions and philosophies—liberation from the prison of the body, integration into the absolute, transmigration of souls, and so forth.

None of this speaks of Christian resurrection, even though it has often been preached as such, but only of survival after death. There is a hope that can express—understandably—self-centeredness, that seeks "my" survival. But self-centeredness is never the *Christian* hermeneutical principle, and egoism still less so. Love, on the other hand, is. Those who love the victims, who feel total compassion for them, who are ready to give themselves to them and share their fate—such can see hope for themselves too in Jesus' resurrection.

These reflections can perhaps be seen as a contribution by liberation theology to the understanding of Christian hope.[18] Human transcendental hope is a necessary but insufficient condition for understanding Jesus' resurrection. The victims of this world have it, though they hardly ever speak of resurrection or invoke it. We have to slot ourselves into this hope, and by doing so we can rebuild—with different, though ultimately similar, mediations—the process followed by Israel's faith in a God of resurrection. As we progress in finding a God who is loving and on the side of the victims, so we can respond to this God with radical love for them, and this makes the question of the ultimate fate of these victims more acute. But we can also "hope" that the executioner will not triumph over them, and we can resign ourselves to a final and fulfilling hope.

One final thought: Such a hope is difficult; it requires us to make the hope of victims, and with it their situation, our own. But it is, nevertheless, true hope. It is like a gift the victims themselves make to us. It means that we have, in Ignacio Ellacuría's words, to "take the situation on ourselves," in this case the situation of the victims, but it is also true that "the situation takes us on itself" and that it offers us not only sin and the obligation to eradicate it but also grace and the courage to hope. The victims offer us their hope.

2. The Praxis of *Raising* the Crucified

This specific hope is the most essential hermeneutical requirement for understanding what happened to Jesus, which is why I have analyzed it at some length. But it is not the only one, and there are others that, even if they are not so clearly expressed in the texts, can be deduced from the way in which the post-resurrection appearances are formulated and from the disciples' reaction to them. One of these—decisive, in my view—is praxis. It is true that Jesus' resurrection is a transcendental response to hope, but not only are hope and praxis not opposed, they in some way require or can require each other. Hope arises from love, and where there is hope, love is produced.

The Kingdom of God is grasped in a concept of hope, but it is also a praxic concept, so that the Kingdom cannot be understood only as what is hoped for—having been promised—but also has to be viewed as what has to be built (the *verum quia faciendum*), something at whose service we have to be, so that without a readiness to build it, it cannot be grasped—which happens even more clearly in the praxis of struggling against the anti-Kingdom. Now this, even if in somewhat different and analogous terms, should be said of the concept of the resurrection.

Furthermore, the ultimate root of all hope is—in my view—always love. It is true that, conceptually, hope is correlative to promise, but in fact whether hope is generated or whether a promise is accepted depends essentially, I believe, on having seen, touched, and realized love; that is, it depends on the conviction that love is possible—so that without love there can be no hope. In other words, that the situation should by itself produce love is what makes it possible for it to produce promise and hope of itself. I say this on the basis of my experience in El Salvador; perhaps I could not argue it, but I have seen it in action. In theoretical terms one could say that "not every life is an occasion of hope, but that of Jesus is, as he took the cross and death on himself in love."[19]

(a) Openness to Praxis in the Appearance Accounts

For the disciples the essential thing was first and foremost, and programatically, to see themselves as *witnesses* (Acts 2:32) and not as mere *observers* or *spectators*. That is, they regard what they have been allowed to experience not simply as something to be registered in their minds, leaving them to decide whether to testify to it or not. The resurrection is rather something that demands being witnessed to and, therefore, something that in principle sets a mission on course. Anyone not open to mission could not understand what was being said about Jesus' resurrection. In this way, even if still in generic and stylized terms, I am saying that openness to witness—to a process of doing—is necessary for an understanding of the resurrection. So just as Rahner states that it would be a contradiction for the resurrection to happen as eschatological victory and not be recognized at all, so it would also be a contradiction for this eschatological victory to be known but not witnessed.

But furthermore, together with this subjective generic *openness* to doing (witnessing) on the part of the disciples, the appearance accounts contain a particular *charge* laid down by the risen Christ: the witnesses are entrusted with a mission. In general terms this is expressed as "being witnesses" (Acts 1:8; Lk 24:48), but it is also made specific. The risen Lord sends them out to preach, baptize, forgive sins, feed the faithful, and so on (Mt 28:19–20; Jn 20:23; 21:15, 17) and also, like the earthly Jesus, to heal and cast out demons (Mk 16:17–18). From the hermeneutical point of view, what is important in this observation is that, for the disciples, Jesus' resurrection and consciousness of mission seem to be inseparably bound together. Even if we should be clear which comes first, one is linked to the other.

This aspect should not be confused with, though it is related to, interpretation of the appearances as *legitimizing* the apostolate. From a historical point of view it was understandable for the disciples to make use of the appearances to this end also, so that, in order to be an apostle, one had to have been a witness to the risen

Christ (Acts 1:21ff.). The names of Peter and James would be mentioned explicitly to emphasize their position in the community (1 Cor 15:5, 8), and Paul would justify his apostolate, even without being one of the Twelve, on the grounds that the risen Lord appeared also to him (Gal 1:11–24; 1 Cor 9:1; 15:8–11).

In the present context, however, the important thing is not so much that the appearances are connected to particular *apostles* to legitimate them, but rather with *apostolate* as such to require it; in other words, what is decisive for hermeneutics is not *who can carry out mission* but rather *that mission must be carried out.* The fact that the resurrection was proclaimed as a mission is to be explained "not as additional or casual" but as "belonging evidently to the reality of the resurrection itself." It is a "constituent element of the very event of which that mission speaks."[20]

From this it follows that the apostolate—a praxis—is a hermeneutical principle for understanding the resurrection and that without it the resurrection cannot be understood as an eschatological event that essentially inspires praxis. This is why openness to mission on our part is essential, for without it Jesus' resurrection would remain dumb. This is what Moltmann expresses in various ways: "The paschal appearances of Jesus are, evidently, visions in which a call is made";[21] the appearances are not just a question of trying to understand earthly and human reality but of "offering the world something new";[22] the resurrection texts are not primarily texts relating a past but have to be understood "as a creative witness to revelation and to mission in the world."[23] Praxis, together with hope, is what establishes unity and meaning in history: "The nexus, which runs through the history of traditions, between the then and the now, is a nexus based on the history of promise and on the history of mission, since mission, in its Christian acceptance, means mission onward and outward. . . . Only in mission and promise, in duty and outlook, the work of hope, is 'the meaning of history' conceived in a historical way and a way that moves history on."[24]

(b) The Praxis Needed in the Present: Taking the Crucified People down from the Cross

Understanding today that Jesus has been raised by God entails the hope that we can be *raised*, but it follows from what has been said that we also have to be, in some way, *raisers*. Obviously this is said by way of analogy, but it is a necessary analogy, and if it makes us feel a little dizzy, perhaps Bergson's saying that God created us creators may help. The question this raises is what specific actions we have to be ready to carry out today.

I believe there are two sorts. The first consists in preaching the fact of Jesus' resurrection, and the second in serving the content of what we preach, a service of making real today what is expressed in hope of resurrection. In other words, it is a matter of *proclaiming the truth of a good news*—justice has been done to a victim—and making this truth *a reality*. This again is an analogy, obviously, since we cannot claim to be carrying out actions that reproduce the eschatological event of Jesus' resurrection, although we can—as Jesus did in his proclamation of the Kingdom—put *semeia* (signs) behind a particular *dynamis* (force).

In order to determine what specific course of action is needed today we have to consider the formal and material dimensions of Jesus' resurrection. *Formally*, the resurrection is a historically "impossible" action on the part of God, which means that adequate actions are those that show some degree of historical impossibility. They are not just any actions, doing some good thing, but those actions that express what appears historically impossible. In our time these could include the struggle against the idols of the world, overcoming a centuries-old resignation in people's consciousness, the churches forgetting themselves and turning toward the oppressed of this world, and so on. The fact that these things might come about provides a taste of historical impossibility, and precisely because they come about, even though always partially, we can affirm that the impossible has become possible.

Materially, the mission that expresses the content of hope is that justice be done to the victims of this world, as justice was done to the crucified Jesus, and so the course of action called for is to take the crucified people down from the cross. This is action on behalf of the victims, of those crucified in history, that tries in a small way—with of course no hubris—to do what God himself does: to take the victim Jesus down from the cross. As this course of action is on behalf of the crucified it is also automatically against the executioners and so a conflictive course, being conscious of the risks and accepting of them, on the side of the victims and open to becoming a victim oneself. Finally, being a course of action at the service of the resurrection of the *dead*, so of the resurrection of *many*, it should also be social, political, seeing to transform structures, *to raise them up*.

(If I may be allowed a brief digression, I should like to say that such reflections have been misunderstood as an expression of human hubris, of trying to do in history what God alone can do. Joseph Ratzinger wrote in this sense in 1984 in a private letter that was leaked and published in *30 Giorni*:

> In this context I should like also to mention the impressive, but ultimately shocking interpretation of the death and resurrection of Jesus made by J. Sobrino. . . . This lordship over history is exercised to the extent that God's gesture in raising Jesus is repeated in history, that is, through giving life to the crucified.[25]

I hope it is clear that I am not talking of repeating God's action, any more than I talked of bringing in the Kingdom of God in the previous volume of this work. What I do insist on is giving signs—analogously—of resurrection and the coming of the Kingdom. And this is also what Ignacio Ellacuría meant when he—for the first time, as far as I can establish—used the expression "taking the crucified people down from the cross"[26] as a formulation of the Christian mission.)

From a systematic perspective and in christological language we can conclude that the course of action needed today to grasp Jesus' resurrection is nothing other than carrying out Jesus' mission, with the *form* of the "impossibility" of the Kingdom becoming real and the *content* of "giving life to the poor." This action is also the place for verifying, in historical terms and partially, how reasonable it is to accept the truth of the resurrection. The partial verifications of this faith do not consist formally, as with Pannenberg, in that the faith makes a better (provisional) understanding of the whole of reality possible but in that it promotes a greater (provisional) transformation of oppressed reality.

From this standpoint Marxsen's intuition that "Jesus' cause moves forward" makes sense. Although the resurrection is by no means identical with what we do in following Jesus, it is also true that without being willing to perform the latter we shall not be able to understand the former. We do have to historicize the carrying-forward, since it is not any course of action that is carried out but that which reproduces Jesus' life, on the side of the victims and against the executioners. Then following Jesus introduces us into the hope of victims and becomes a course of action designed to put it into effect.

Putting oneself at the service of the resurrection means working continually, often against hope, in the service of eschatological ideals: justice, peace, solidarity, the life of the weak, community, dignity, celebration, and so on. And these partial "resurrections" can generate hope in the final resurrection, the conviction that God did indeed perform the impossible, gave life to one crucified and will give life to all the crucified.

These thoughts are analogous to those I expressed on the Kingdom of God. I said then that Jesus' liberating actions are only "signs" and "powers" of the Kingdom, not its fullness but pointers to it that generate hope in its possibility. In the same way it has to be said that partial "resurrections" in history are clearly not the final resurrection, but they generate hope in its being possible—and help us to understand it. What is specific to the reality-symbol of the resurrection is that the negative aspect our actions have to overcome is not just injustice and oppression but death and the cross.

Returning, in conclusion, to Rahner's words cited in the previous chapter, it has to be said that Jesus' resurrection is an event that *needs to* generate faith, since otherwise it cannot be understood as God's victorious action. But for the same reason, and more insistently, *it needs to* generate hope and action, since God would have achieved little—pardon the expression—if the triumph and love expressed in the raising of the Son did not generate hope and action in human beings. To put it the other way around—as mystagogy if not as pure logical deduction—we can say that hope and action are needed to grasp Jesus' resurrection, and not just any love and action but those that apply to the task of taking the crucified down from the cross.

3. The Mystery of Reality: History as Promise

The last question remaining to be answered is what we human beings can know. Where hermeneutics is concerned, this is the most difficult question, and the answer already contains some kind of hope, course of action, and celebration—or lack of them—as well as all kinds of metaphysical and epistemological prejudgments.

For the New Testament there is no doubt that Jesus' resurrection was something real that happened in history. "The Lord has risen indeed" (Lk 24:34); something real happened. This impression of reality is intentionally passed on, in some way, when verifiable events, such as Jesus' death and burial, are mentioned (1 Cor 15:3ff.) and when specific places, such as Galilee and Jerusalem (temporal data—the third day, forty days later—are more clearly symbolic), are instanced, which, even if not to be taken literally, do show concern to state that something *really* happened and that the New Testament *knows* this.

(a) Positivism, Existentialism, Universal History

According to nineteenth-century positivism, everything in history is related to everything else, there is a common homogeneity, and, as its anthropological counterpart, the subject of history is humankind, not God. So an eschatological event such as Jesus' resurrection, being in radical discontinuity—without analogy—with other historical phenomena and having God as its subject cannot be known as historical. The question then arises whether theology has any right to treat the resurrection as something real.

In the twentieth century, theology tried to respond to this challenge and move beyond "the fetishism" of positivism's historical events. Let us look first at two theologians who took opposed stances, Bultmann and Pannenberg. For Bultmann, on the one hand, Jesus' resurrection is not historical and can therefore only be the object of faith; furthermore, it *should not* be historically based, since this would make Christian faith impossible. For Pannenberg, on the other hand, the resurrection is historical—to which he adds, paradoxically, that positivism has an a-historical vision—and only thus can it be the object of theology.

Both ways of overcoming positivism, however, present serious problems for understanding the specific *reality* of the resurrection. Bultmann defines the essence of a historical event not in whether it can be described adequately "in itself" or in the causal context of events but from its significance. But he does not accept that the *future* can bring a qualitatively new significance: "Do not look around you at universal history; you should rather direct your search to your own history. The meaning of history lies always in every present, and you cannot observe it as a spectator, but only in your responsible decision."[27]

This attitude does not overcome positivism but is simply its obverse: "From this objectivization of history there is then born the abstract subjectivization of human nature."[28] And this subjectivization, however existential, also fails to make salvation possible in the unredeemed present, though Bultmann thinks it does. So Moltmann criticizes the lack of a future in his view of reality:

> Only with hope in the future of the world can believers bear the pain they feel at the wickedness of this world. The "amen" with which faith replies to the word does not yet mean the anthropological discovery of redeemed humankind, but the hope in that future in which God will one day make himself manifest.[29]

The foregoing shows that for Bultmann Jesus' resurrection has nothing to do with the meaning of universal history. But this is essential to it, as Pannenberg has shown. He goes beyond Bultmann in introducing the future into reality, but he does not take its *negative aspects* seriously. The negative side of history cannot be grasped simply by looking at universal history, since its negativity is precisely what makes an all-embracing understanding of history impossible. The negative side cannot be included in the whole as though it were one more element; rather, it is by overcoming the negative itself that history opens out, without our being able to decide in advance what the whole embraces. While pain, destitution, and injustice exist, history cannot be understood in its totality except by hoping against hope—even after Jesus' resurrection. Claiming to understand the totality while effectively ignoring the negativity is not possible in a Christian theology.

(Although the context is very different from that of the resurrection, I cannot resist citing A. González's critique of Pannenberg's view of history, as it shows how not taking the reality of the cross seriously leads to absurd conclusions:

> Five hundred years ago, the divinities of the American continent could not uphold their supposed explanation of reality since, in the same way as happened to the Sumerian god Enlil . . . they could not explain the changes brought about in the world of their adorers after the triumphant and destructive incursion of the first representatives of European Christian civilization. The missionary and universalist consciousness of Christianity was capable of explaining and even justifying such events, although at the same time it had to condemn all the excess that could not be reconciled with the very values of the Christian religion. The Dominican friar Bartolomé de Las Casas, without being an especially brilliant theologian, saw the inhabitants of that continent as "the scourged Christs of the Indies." That is, he thought that the face of the divinity was being shown in those heathens and not directly in the religious tradition of those who were scourging them. This thesis cannot be upheld without radically altering the conception of history held by Pannenberg.)[30]

(b) The Mystery of Promise

Jesus' resurrection points to the future, which means that reality itself appears as promise and points in anticipation to the future. This vision of reality derives from the biblical tradition, different from and opposed to the "eternal return" of Greek thought. It was developed in philosophy by Hegel and in theology, in pioneering though differing forms, by Pannenberg and Moltmann. What is common to both is that "every historical phenomenon carries, wrapped within itself, its own future, in which it is manifested as it is in itself, with its full significance. In definitive form, however, it will not become plain in its full significance, that is 'as it has been in reality,' until history itself has reached its end."[31]

For Pannenberg, what something is is decided only in its future, and so "truth is what will be made plain in the future."[32] On the other hand, "the future *seeks to* make itself present; it *tends* to its becoming a permanent present."[33] If reality is like this, then, Jesus' resurrection can proleptically anticipate this future, but, inversely, in order to grasp it one has to grasp reality in its anticipatory dimension.

Moltmann's approach, though related to Pannenberg's, is very different. For reality to be history supposes that the future is understood not only as the present unfinished, nor only as the possible "more" of the present, but as promise made present in history and *against* history.[34] This is how Moltmann describes promise:

> A promise is an offering that proclaims a reality that does not yet exist. . . . Promise links us to the future and gives us a meaning with which to grasp history. . . . The word of promise therefore always creates an intermediate space laden with tensions, a space situation between the handing over and the fulfillment of the promise. This provides us with a special ambit of freedom for obedience and disobedience, for hope and resignation.
>
> If the promise is taken to be God's promise, then it cannot be verified by human criteria. The fulfilling of the promise can contain something new, even within what is hoped for, and surpass in reality what was thought in human categories. . . . The not-yet of expectation exceeds any fulfillment that has already come about. So any reality of fulfillment that has already come about is transformed into confirmation, interpretation and liberation of a greater hope. . . . The reason for the constant added value of promise and for its permanent exceeding of history lies in the inexhaustible nature of the God of promise.[35]

Grasping reality as history means not only grasping what is temporal or unfinished in history but grasping the future on the basis of promise. Relating this to Jesus' resurrection means that, in order to understand the latter, it has to be seen also as promise, as God's definitive and eschatological promise: "Understood as event that makes the future accessible and opens up history, the resurrection of Christ is the foundation and the promise of eternal life in the midst of this history of death."[36]

Whether it is understood as prolepsis or promise, it still produces a degree of metaphysical vertigo to speak of the resurrection as that which is known in its essential relationship to the end of history. And this vertigo is increased if we affirm that the resurrection is the appearance of the eschatological in history and add to this that to know it as such is a gift and a grace given to us. The fact is that the resurrection points, in turn, to both *futurum* and *adventus*.[37] Insofar as it points to the *futurum*, it can be conceptualized from a philosophy, although this, in its turn, depends historically on traditions that speak of final resurrection. Insofar as it points to the *adventus*, it is related with coming, with grace, and with mystery. This has usually been described from the *becoming* of God in the incarnation, but it can and should also be described from the *coming* of God at the end of time. This mystery is what is implied in the understanding of Jesus' resurrection as promise.

It is debatable whether the resurrection, as a reality, is prolepsis or promise: I prefer to view it as promise. But we need to be clear that the problem goes deeper. It is a question of taking a view on the ultimate mystery of reality. If we ask what specific conditions this places on human intelligence, these, in my opinion, are two, which can be formulated as follows: openness to grace, and, so to speak, chastity of intelligence.

A promise, by definition, is what we cannot foresee for the future as pure extrapolation or as logical conclusion to a process; it is rather something that comes from outside, unexpected and undeserved. To grasp Jesus' resurrection as something real, then, we have to grasp reality as promise, and this hermeneutically presupposes openness to *grace*, allowing oneself to be given contents and even the capacity to know them. In Ellacuría's terms, in order to understand Jesus' resurrection we have to be ready to "take over reality," "be full of reality," and "shoulder reality," to which I would add that we have to "let ourselves be burdened with reality," which is why we can speak of theology as *intellectus gratiae*.[38]

On the other hand, we have to allow reality to be what it is, without deciding in advance what it ought to be. This attitude toward the mystery of reality is what I call *chastity of intelligence,* in order to stress that only an intelligence that does not want to seize everything, decide on everything, accept as possible only what it can know by extrapolating from what it already knows, can be shot through with grace.

In the final analysis, to know Jesus' resurrection we have to accept that reality is a mystery that is being shown to us gratuitously. In this sense the resurrection falls outside the scope of conventional historical proof. If, however, one confesses it as something real, then it is necessary to have the double attitude of faith in God's possibilities for intervening in history and an understanding of reality as that which bears within itself and points to an eschatological future. In this way it will be meaningful to state that by raising Jesus God has intervened, either anticipating the end of history (Pannenberg) or proclaiming God's definitive promise (Moltmann). In either case something has already happened in the present that points to the definitive future.

To end this chapter let me say that the reflections made in it have been made within the hermeneutical circle. Methodologically, I have examined the anthropological presuppositions for being able to know the event that is Jesus' resurrection, but it is very likely that I have done so in this way because we already have traditions concerning this resurrection that shape a particular anthropology and because I have reread those texts from the specific situation of the Third World, especially from that of its victims.

Within this circle—which does not just express an academic question—we move and progress in history. And it is this progress in history, not a pure philosophy, that in the end increases (or decreases) a person's conviction that the mystery of history was unveiled historically in what the disciples called Jesus' resurrection. In this sense the texts about the resurrection are for us, existentially, an invitation to view history *thus* and to progress and act in history according to this vision.

Chapter 4

The Historical Problem (1)

The Reality of Jesus' Resurrection

I began the analysis of Jesus' resurrection with the hermeneutical question in order to understand what we are dealing with when we speak of the resurrection. Having said this, however, we need to ask what happened: the historical problem. I have nothing specific to add to the exegetical debate about this,[1] and in this chapter I shall confine myself to a brief account of what the texts say. In the next chapter I shall examine an aspect that to me seems important: what a real experience of something ultimate, analogous to that of the witnesses to the appearances, might mean today.

I dwell on this because faith is a real experience of something real, and we need to know what reality there was at the outset of our faith. Faith needs witnesses, certainly, but it does not live *only* on acceptance of outside witnesses, as if it were a matter of forming an opinion about these witnesses. Faith forms opinions about reality and, in particular, about God. On the other hand, I believe that all Christians—and all human beings—consciously or unconsciously, can at some moment of their lives find themselves confronted with realities they can experience similarly, analogously of course, in the same way the first Christians did.

1. Accounts of the Easter Experience

In this section I shall set out briefly what others have expressed profoundly in order to draw some important conclusions from the accounts:[2] the experience of grace and of eschatological reality, the return to Jesus of Nazareth even in the appearance narratives, and interest in holy places.

(a) The Resurrection Event in Itself

The canonical writings of the New Testament say nothing about Jesus' resurrection in itself, which means that they did not give free rein to the imagination. Among the apocryphal writings only the Gospel of Peter, written toward the year 150, probably in Syria, narrates the resurrection:

But in the night in which the light of the Lord shone, while the soldiers were keeping guard by turns of two, a great voice sounded in heaven, and they saw the heavens open, and two men in great splendor came down from there and approached the tomb, and the tomb opened and the two young men went in. When those soldiers saw this, they woke the captain and the oldest among them, who were also on guard. And while they were telling them what they had seen, they saw three men coming out of the tomb and how two were supporting the third and a cross was following them; the heads of the two reached up to heaven, but that of the one whom they led by the hand reached beyond heaven. And they heard a voice that cried from heaven: "Have you preached to the dead?," and the reply came from the cross: "Yes." They debated among themselves and went to tell this to Pilate.[3]

This text may seem anachronistic, but for centuries Christian art has tried to depict Jesus' resurrection in itself, which puts faith on a false trail by conceptualizing the resurrection as a return to living under the conditions of our existence. The canonical gospels, for their part, never describe Jesus' resurrection; this is a matter of *fact*, but it is also a matter of *duty*, since in them the resurrection is conceived as an eschatological event and therefore cannot be represented. This makes the concept more difficult, since there is no image, but it also deflects wrong interpretations of what they do say and to what they do refer us: the appearances of the Risen Lord.

So, in order to know what happened to Jesus, we are of necessity referred to what happened to the disciples, who had certain experiences—today generalized as "the Easter experience"—without which it would not be possible to understand either the interpretation they made of Jesus of Nazareth or the origin of the church.

How to describe the reality of these experiences is an absolutely impossible task. One can perhaps say that "eschatological reality tangentially touched the historical existence of the disciples"[4] and that it did so in a precise way, in the form of an "encounter" with Jesus. The reality of this experience would then be at once historical and non-historical, and this ambivalence runs through the appearance narratives. In effect, they tell us where and when the appearances happened but absolutely nothing about the resurrection itself. It is said that the witnesses "saw" Jesus without changing their historical condition, but also that this capacity to see "was given them." They speak of the empty tomb—synoptically, for sure—but this fact is not adduced as historical proof of the resurrection. In systematic terms, "the disciples both live and do not live, at the same time, the final realities concerning Jesus. And this living at the same time in history and in eschatology—even if only tangentially and in spurts—is what the characteristics of the literary genre of these narratives witness."[5]

(b) The Appearances

The New Testament establishes Jesus' resurrection *because* he appeared to the disciples, a fact that was very early recalled in the pre-Pauline text of 1 Corinthians 15:3b–5: "that Christ died for our sins in accordance with the scriptures, and that he was buried, and that he was raised on the third day in accordance with the scriptures, and that he appeared to Cephas, then to the twelve."[6] This ancient text appears to be a confessional formula of Aramaic-Palestinian origin;[7] it takes up a very early formulation of Christian faith that (1) stresses the real death and burial of Jesus (though without any allusion to the empty tomb); (2) expresses the fact of the resurrection as God's action *(egegertai)*; and (3) adds the temporal precision of "on the third day," unusual in that it appears only in predictions of the passion, in the *logion* of the Temple in Acts 10:40, and is added perhaps to indicate that a prophecy was being fulfilled (cf. Jon 2:1; 2 Kgs 20:5; Hos 6:1ff.) or because of the popular conviction that the spirit left the body on the third day and then corruption set in. In any case, the origin of the formula is obscure, and it does not pretend to establish the actual moment of resurrection. "The third day" was also a generic expression for the time when God would act.[8] So, in summary, this most ancient formula states the content of the Easter experience to be: (1) the event of the appearance, which has become (aorist perfect *opthe*) Jesus by the power of God; (2) his manifest state (perfect durative *egegertai*) of resurrection and elevation toward a new unity with God, from which he—like the invisible Yahweh himself—can make himself present (appear) and prepare witnesses; and (3) this definitive beginning of the last times, of God's gratuitous and saving self-opening. The sending out of witnesses (the moment of legitimation) derives secondarily, but independently, from the appearance of the Risen Lord.[9]

What is said succinctly in this formula is developed in the appearance narratives. It is practically impossible to establish whether their details derive or not from historical recollections, but it is possible to give a minimal account of their structure. Taken as a whole, they offer the following scheme: (1) Jesus makes himself known to the disciples; (2) the disciples have to overcome a certain doubt or disbelief; (3) the Risen Lord charges them with mission. The central elements are that they insist on the encounter with Jesus as fundamental in their new life, that this encounter is real—in order to convince later believers who did not have this experience—and that by this experience they feel themselves urged (and also legitimized) to carry out a mission.

Together with this central message, there are many differences, so that the gospels here cease being "synoptic." With regard to the *place*, Mark 16, Matthew 28, and John 21 speak only of appearances in *Galilee*, and seem to exclude any earlier appearance in *Jerusalem*, while Luke 24 concentrates everything in Jerusalem, as does John 20. Which is the more likely historically is a matter for debate. Mark and Matthew may have placed them in Galilee because that was where the disciples fled, and perhaps also to show the shift to the Gentile world. Luke, for his part, concentrates all the Easter events in Jerusalem according to his theological-geographical scheme of describing Jesus' life as a great journey to Jerusalem, where he consummates his work. With regard to *time*—a reflection that has a more symbolical than historiographical intention—the Galilee traditions suppose that the appearances took place sometime after what is now called Easter Sunday, while in the Jerusalem tradition the appearances took place on Easter day itself. Another temporal difference appears in the ascension: in Luke 24:50ff. it occurs on Easter day; in Acts 1:6–11 it is placed forty days after.

With regard to the *content*, even given the basic scheme in common, the descriptions differ from one another. In all of them the disciples react to the appearance of Jesus, but they do so in different ways: in Luke with fear, since the disciples think they are seeing a ghost; in John, without any fear, but with joy; in Matthew with adoration. The motif of doubt appears in all, but to different degrees and with varying ways of overcoming it: in Luke Jesus shows his hands and feet and eats with them; in John 20 the recalcitrant Thomas has to touch his body; in Matthew, Jesus overcomes their doubt with words alone.

This diversity is possible and even inevitable owing to the type of experience the disciples are trying to relate. Differences in content are explicable by the diversity of their situations, long after the Easter event and in already established communities.[10] *Apologetically*, the disciples had to defend themselves against charges of having seen a ghost, and so they stress Jesus' bodily elements and actions, which was to lead gradually to a *massive materialism* alien to the original intention, which Matthew expresses best in presenting the Risen Lord as exalted.[11] Nevertheless, there is no free rein given to imagination. *Pastorally*, the gospels are addressed to communities far from the original experience and encourage them to believe in the witness of the apostles, as the case of Thomas paradigmatically demonstrates. If, finally, we ask what their purpose was in setting down these accounts of appearances, the answer is debated. To take two prominent opinions, Kessler sees the purpose in "the confirmation of the resurrection through the personal appearance of the Lord," while Wilckens regards it as trying to offer "proofs to legitimize those who held authority in the Church by virtue of the charge laid on them from heaven. Consequently, the mark of this tradition would be not preaching but ecclesiastical law."[12]

(c) The Empty Tomb

The account of the empty tomb appears in all the gospels, and is in fact the only account shared by John and the three synoptics (Mk 16:8; Mt 28:1–7; Lk 24:1–11, with Matthew and Luke depending on Mark). On the *literary* plane there is a fixed scheme: the women go the tomb, find it open (empty), an angel or young man tells them that Christ has risen and charges them to go and tell the disciples. John adds the appearance of Jesus himself to Mary Magdalen. This convergence of the accounts, based on Mark, suggests that, despite the divergences, the text is relatively early. The question of whether the tomb was *historically* empty or not has been given so many and varied answers that it is virtually impossible to reach any conclusion. Kessler has summarized the arguments for and against as follows.[13]

Those for are: (1) the women's testimony cannot be taken to be simply apologetic but has to be based on something real, since the testimony of women, in itself, had no value; (2) the temporal precision "on the third day" would make more sense if the tomb were empty; (3) the Jews, in polemics with Christians, did not deny the fact of the empty tomb but interpreted it in a different way (cf. Mt 28:13; Jn 20:15: the disciples had stolen the body, the gardener had taken it away); (4) the proclamation of the resurrection could never have succeeded if it had been possible to have shown Jesus' body in the tomb.

Those against—given in parallel to those for—are: (1) in a Hellenist context the testimony of the women could have been valid in itself; (2) the precision "on the third day" is theological, not historical; (3) the Jewish leaders could have had no interest in Jesus relatively soon after his death, since they would think that the Jesus issue had been finished on the cross; (4) it was not likely that anyone would have been able to open the tomb or have entrusted such an act to anyone, either Jesus' followers or his adversaries. In conclusion, it has to be said that "the question of historicity of the fact that Jesus' tomb was found open and empty is an open question. The truth of the biblical texts neither necessarily postulates the historical fact nor excludes it."[14]

Be that as it may, the New Testament never bases the resurrection of Jesus on the fact that the tomb was empty but on the encounter with the Risen Lord. This observation is factual, but it is also logical, since even if the tomb were empty, this says nothing about "where" Jesus would have been, and it can have nothing to say about his exalted reality. Furthermore, the accounts of the empty tomb are written not *in order to* prove the resurrection but *from* the already existing faith in the Risen Lord.

In the accounts, in effect, once the women have seen the open tomb, they do not draw the conclusion that Christ has risen; an angel has to announce it to them. Mark does not even say that the women saw the tomb empty, but that the young man first tells them that Jesus has been raised and then not to look for him in the tomb. And, curiously, Mark's account ends with the women fleeing in terror from the tomb, "and they said nothing to anyone, for they were afraid" (16:8). His account makes it impossible for them to have looked into the tomb. So the conclusion might be formulated in this way:

> In the beginning . . . the accounts did not pretend to relate that anyone saw the tomb empty and then believed in the Risen Lord; they show that faith in the resurrection was born not of finding the tomb empty but of the heavenly message; their objective is not properly biographical but theological. In the tomb, which symbolizes death, God, through his angel, proclaims to the community that he raised Jesus from among the dead.[15]

If one then inquires into the source of the early Christians' undoubted interest in the tomb and whether it was empty or not, evidenced in the four gospels, the reply may well be J. Delorme's: there is "a manifest interest, in the early community, in a tomb held to be that of Jesus, to which they went in a spirit of religious veneration, inspired by faith in Jesus' resurrection."[16] If this thesis is correct, then the tomb traditions serve neither apologetics nor theology but liturgical celebration. The Christians would have celebrated "Holy Week" and would have spent time by the tomb, which recalled and expressed Jesus' death and resurrection. This place would have served etiologically as a justification for celebration, even though they would have had no certainty (or concern) that Jesus was buried there—without excluding the possibility that he had been buried in a common grave.

2. The Reality of the Narratives and Their Meaning

I shall analyze the overall theological significance of the Easter event later. Here I want to concentrate on some of its elements, with regard to their reality and meaning.

(a) The Experience of Grace: "It Was Given Them" to See Jesus

In 1 Corinthians 15, and then in the gospels, Christ is said to have "appeared," expressed by the word *ofthe*. It is not easy to determine quite what this word means, but it could imply that Jesus "was presented and made visible" by God, or that "he presented himself and let himself be seen."[17] This gives rise to two types of reflection.

The first is concerned with the type of "knowledge" implied by *ofthe*. Linguistically, it does not appear to imply a simple vision corresponding to a christophany, though the description of the appearances implies more "seeing" (not necessarily with bodily eyes) than "hearing." Kessler, however, formulates a significant conclusion: "We can state with certainty that the appearances should not be considered in any way in the miraculous sense 'as prodigies that overwhelmed the disciples.'"[18] This means to say that the "vision" element with a particular content could well also be an *understanding* in depth, a *knowing* that they have met Jesus (living and exalted) and that in this they have understood the universal resurrection, the final victory of God.

The second reflection strikes me as more important. The word *ofthe* should not be translated merely as "was seen" but rather as something like "let himself be seen," with the implication that this was not an apparition accessible to everyone, but a specific action by God who "allows [them] to see" the risen Lord. Jesus' "allowing to see" and their "being made able to see" means that the appearances are, above all, expressions of gift and grace and that, therefore, the initiative comes from God.

For us today, whatever may have been the experience of those witnesses, the possibility of remaking this type of experience is gift and grace. And this brings us to the need for what Kessler called "radical modesty" and I call "chastity of the intelligence." In this way the encounter with the risen Lord, which points toward the future in its eschatological content, also points to what is inward: the initiative that comes from God.

In this sense it is obvious that the appearances present a serious difficulty to comprehension, but this problem does not begin with them, as though understanding God in his revelation and manifestation in the signs of the times were any easier. The possibility and difficulty begin with accepting that the initiative comes from outside, from God. What the appearances tell us is that the first disciples felt themselves to be blessed with this initiative from God and in a qualitatively different form from that in which others who came before them had been, since in Jesus' resurrection we meet the eschatological happening. Reflecting today on the possibility of reliving this experience, the first question we have to ask ourselves is, therefore, whether we accept the possibility of such an initiative. The root of the matter, as always, is still God.

(b) Eschatological Reality: The End Time

The central content of the appearances is Jesus "raised," but, precisely on account of this, by grasping his reality as "raised," the disciples are necessarily grasping the universal resurrection. They grasp "the event that reveals the final and definitive saving presence of God with which his saving presence at the end time becomes reality."[19] Understanding the risen Lord is, then, already salvific: history will be fulfilled, and this will happen soon, even before the narratives mention actual saving aspects (forgiveness, peace, joy, and so on).[20]

That the near approach of the final fullness was captured in the appearances is not directly demonstrable, but it is likely from the theological interpretation the disciples made of what happened to Jesus and from what took place soon after the appearances and was based on them.[21]

With regard to the theological interpretation, the mere fact of their choosing the language of resurrection points to the universal resurrection, and this is the formulation that survived, not that of exaltation or being caught up into heaven, both of which are secondary and appear at a later stage. Furthermore, in Matthew 27:51–53, it is said that when Jesus died many of the dead rose from their tombs, prefiguring, together with that of Jesus, the *universal* resurrection.

With regard to what then took place, we can say in summary form that (1) the disciples returned to Jerusalem, where the final eschatological events were to come about; (2) the first action of the community was to elect Matthias to make up the eschatological number of the Twelve (an event that was not repeated); (3) faith in the manifestation of the Spirit at Pentecost shows the firm conviction that the last times had already begun; (4) the sudden outbreak of baptisms is explicable only by the imminence of their eschatological expectation and that in the Lord's supper the "Come, Lord" is central; (5) the joy with which they break bread in houses and eat together is a prefiguring of the eschatological banquet; (6) the community understands itself to be that of the saints and chosen ones of the last times; and finally, (7) the community throws itself into preaching to the whole of Israel as though called to conversion before the imminent end.

These deeds are coherent with their theologal interpretation of Jesus' resurrection: God has raised him as "first fruits." And they are coherent with the oldest christology: Jesus is the one who has to come, who has to return soon as Son of Man in the universal judgment. It is, then, historically likely that the content of the appearances—what they were allowed to see, what was given them to understand—should have been as much the new reality of Jesus as the definitive action of God.

This also explains the crisis brought about by the delay of the parousia and the need to reorientate the essence of nascent Christianity. This delay meant that the "universal resurrection," the re-creation of reality by God, was pushed into the background, and that faith had to concentrate on the person and resurrection of

Jesus. And here perhaps lies the root of a most significant phenomenon that I shall examine later: the concentration by faith (and by christology) on the person of Jesus Christ and the gradual forgetting of the Kingdom of God.

(c) Returning to Jesus

The novelty of the appearances made recognition of Jesus difficult, and some of his words would have been unintelligible during his lifetime—the sending out on universal mission in Matthew 28:18–20, for example. In this way the appearances express both novelty and discontinuity. But the accounts also express continuity with Jesus. His attitude toward sinners, for example, does not change; in life he welcomes them and after the resurrection he sends the disciples out to forgive them. Neither does he vary in his relationship with his disciples: eating together, the fishing scenes, the primacy given to Peter . . . all refer back to Jesus of Nazareth.

There are two things, furthermore, that work programatically in the appearance narratives to show the element of continuity with Jesus. One is that the risen Lord is the crucified Jesus, an affirmation that should be taken not as a "dogmatic" thesis, as, let us say, Paul preached to the Corinthians, but as a primary reality: the risen Lord appeared to them with wounds. This is a radical way of identifying the risen Lord with Jesus and of overcoming any "magical" conception of the resurrection, as if it had left the actual reality of Jesus behind or in suspense. The other is that the appearances were experiences that took place, very probably, during the disciples' meals. In fact, the appearances often occur in the framework of a meal (cf. Lk 24:30ff.; Jn 21:21ff.; Acts 1:4, 10:41),[22] which makes one think about the relationship between experience of the resurrection and eucharistic celebration in the primitive community, so that the eucharist would be a Christian reinterpretation of the pasch, cross/resurrection. As a historical pointer, remember that the Christians celebrated the eucharist "on the first day of the week" (see 1 Cor 16:2; Acts 20:7), that is, the day on which they recalled the resurrection of the Lord.

One has to remember that meals were an essential thing in Jesus' life. The fact of the Last Supper, of meals with his friends, with women, with the poor and outcasts is undeniable. And the meaning of this indicates Jesus' central message: the shared table is a sign of the closeness of the Kingdom of God.[23] Jesus was not content to illustrate the nature of the Kingdom through "the apocalyptic metaphors of the wedding feast or the celestial banquet (cf. Mt 18:11; Lk 14:16–24); no, he anticipated them in his own meals to show precisely sinners (Mk 2:17) that God enters into community with them."[24] The plain fact, then, that experience of the risen Lord occurs in a meal expresses continuity with something essential in Jesus. The risen Lord is "the one of the shared table."

The appearances show a dialectical relationship between risen Lord and crucified Jesus, between pre-paschal meal and post-paschal meal (eucharist). The resurrection points to the future, as we have seen, but the disciples "recognized him by the marks of the nails and in the way he took bread."[25] The appearances are described, then, in such a way that the risen Lord is brought back to Jesus. This is also evident from the basic and decisive fact of who are witnesses to the resurrection—those who lived with Jesus and were attracted by him, by his message and his cause. It is a question of "this same Jesus" and of "these same disciples."[26] The continuity is clear and its consequence decisive: "The appearances of Jesus confirm existing faith. They are not a valid proof independently of it. . . . Such a formidable event did not have a single impartial witness";[27] "to have followed Jesus' own values constitutes an indispensable condition for being able to 'see' and 'recognize' him as risen."[28]

This can be seen also in the decisive role women play in the Easter events. Above all, the appearances to women are "such an important and unusual reminder that it has not been possible for it to be erased."[29] All the gospels tell that there was a group of women at the foot of the cross, and the synoptics specify that there were "many of them and that they had followed Jesus from Galilee" (Mk 15:40ff.; Mt 27:55; Lk 23:49). After Jesus' death it is the women who take charge of the burial of his body—these traditions being associated with that of Joseph of Arimathea.[30] They go to the tomb and are protagonists of the Easter events: they receive the announcement that Christ is risen and the instruction to tell this to the disciples (Mk 16:6ff.; Mt 28:5–7; Lk 24:5f., omitting the instruction), and Jesus appears to them before doing so to the disciples (to Mary Magdalen, Mt 28:9f.; together with the other Mary, Jn 20:11–18; longer ending of Mk 16:9f.).

So the women are undeniable protagonists and play a clearly superior part in the Easter narrative compared to the men disciples, though one has to be aware of how this is presented. In the first chapters of Mark, Jesus calls men disciples, without stressing the discipleship of women, but the men fail in their faith when Jesus foretells his passion. Then, in chapter 15, the women come to the fore: they "used to follow him and provide for him when he was in Galilee; and there were many other women who had come up with him to Jerusalem" (Mk 15:41). They are more faithful,[31] although in the end they are not said to have accepted the young man's announcement of Jesus' resurrection but to have fled in fright (16:8). This is so that neither the men disciples, nor even the women, but "Jesus alone is presented as the foundation of our faith": "The silence of the women allows Mark to show very clearly . . . that the cross of the risen Lord is the catalyst of all Christian thinking and that its shadow can hover over all following of Jesus."[32]

For our purpose the significant fact is that the women who were at the tomb, to whom the resurrection was announced and Jesus appeared, are those who had followed him from Galilee. Jesus has not only given new value to their existence in a patriarchal society but has called them to be disciples: "Jesus, with surprising freedom and without taking account of the ruling stereotypes in Jewish society of the time, included women in the circle of his disciples."[33] The names of five of them are preserved in the synoptics: Mary Magdalen; Chuza's wife, Joanna; Susanna; Mary, the mother of James the Younger; and Salome (Lk 8:1–3; Mk 15:40). These women led the itinerant and homeless life of the disciples and had given themselves to the cause of God's Kingdom. This made them just as much Jesus' followers as the men disciples, which is also stressed by the term used *(akolouthein)* to describe the disciples' following of Jesus.[34] Again, Easter is presented in relation to the life of Jesus, and those who experience him as risen are those, men and women, who followed him in life. "The Galilean women played a decisive role both in the extension of the Jesus movement to the Gentiles and in the continuation of this movement after Jesus' arrest and execution."[35]

The conclusion to be drawn from what has been said in this section strikes me as significant. In the Easter appearances there is an essential discontinuity: the dead Jesus appears as alive and the crucified Jesus as exalted. But continuity is also stressed. The resurrection has not transformed Jesus in such a way as to make his earthly life something merely provisional; rather, the resurrection gives definitive and lasting validity to that life. This means that Jesus will always be the way to Christ and that, correlatively, the following of Jesus then—and, by analogy, now—will be a necessary condition for having a direct experience of—or one analogous to that of—the appearances.

(d) Interest in Holy Places

We have seen that nothing can be said with certainty about the reality of the narratives concerning the tomb. Delorme's view seems to me both interesting and reasonable. I can only add to his exegetical argument that it is well understood after what happened in El Salvador, where the little hospital and the cathedral, the rose garden and the university chapel, the places where Archbishop Romero and the Jesuits were killed or are buried, have become holy places of pilgrimage. So has El Mozote, where hundreds of people were massacred and where a little monument has been raised, bearing the words: "They are not dead. They are with us, with you, and with the whole human race." The same is true of Las Aradas, where a cross has been erected to commemorate the peasants killed at the river Sumpul, on the frontier with Honduras, and of many other less widely known places. There is indeed a need to sacralize—make holy—martyrs, which happens by sacralizing the dates of their death, putting their lives and deeds into words, and by simple folk even attributing miracles to them. Sacralizing places belongs in this broader context.[36]

This sacralization sometimes coincides with history and geography: this is where they were killed or where they are buried. But the basic reason for sacralizing particular places and going on pilgrimage to them is not interest in just visiting the *ipsissimi loci* of martyrs (which are sometimes known, as in the case of Romero and the U.C.A. Jesuits, sometimes not, as with those of El Mozote and the Sumpul). Interest in visiting the places where they were killed or buried derives from the fact that they were beneficent and liberating in life and are perceived still to be so after death. The need to visit them comes from gratitude and the desire to ask for strength to go forward in history.

Sacred places have their own sacramentality and, given closeness in time, transform visitors *quasi ex opere operato*. So one can understand the disciples' concern to "locate" Jesus' tomb. Whether or not it was the place where they buried him, locating a particular tomb and going on pilgrimage to it were necessary in order to preserve a decisive memory, to display commitment and, above all, to show gratitude to Jesus.

3. History and Faith

What is historical in Jesus' resurrection? In conclusion, the following can be said. There are certain texts, those of the New Testament, that affirm that something happened to Jesus' disciples, something they attribute to their encounter with Jesus, whom they call the risen Lord; so much is historical.[37] Some of these texts embody traditions that are very ancient and close in time to the events narrated, and so can enjoy the presumption of historicity, while others are later and develop the earlier texts.

Also real is that a change was worked in the disciples, though experts differ on the magnitude of this change. In the *texts* it is clearly stated that there was a difference before and after Easter. This difference takes on various forms of literary expression: the places in which they were (from Galilee to Jerusalem); their behavior (from fear to bravery); their faith (from "We were waiting, but it is now the third day" to "The Lord is risen indeed"). The *narratives* are, then, composed in order to emphasize discontinuity: after they fled to Galilee, having betrayed, denied, and abandoned the master, "against all expectations, the phenomena of the appearances made them go back to Jerusalem."[38] The question at issue is whether in *actual fact* these changes were so radical.

Many authorities accept this change in the disciples, but others stress rather what there was of continuity. In a later chapter I shall set out the reasons for the latter approach.[39] For the present, Kessler can stand for many in showing the discontinuity:

> Shortly after the death of Jesus on the cross, the disciples who had disappeared, withdrawing to Galilee, suddenly and surprisingly presented themselves in Jerusalem. There, in the inhospitable and dangerous city of Zion and not in the safe Galilee, the disciples gathered to form the first community. This sudden and unexpected turn is related to the message that God had raised the crucified Jesus from the dead.[40]

In any case, it is certain that the Easter experience was what, gradually, led Jesus' disciples to radical changes. And it is also very important to remember that "only from this experience was there preaching and is there a New Testament. This was not written as a result of the impact made by Jesus' life nor of the impression produced by his death. All its pages—including those that purport to recall history—are only the products of the reaction provoked by the Easter experience."[41]

Where the sincerity and honesty of the witnesses are concerned, there seems to be no doubt. About the objective truth of what they state, whether anything truly external to them happened or whether they were victims of some sort of hallucination (psychological explanation), can be debated *ad infinitum*, though the texts give no grounds for a thesis of collective hallucination. The accounts of the empty tomb are not in any way put forward as proof of the resurrection. The *objective* conclusion, therefore, has to be the following: the disciples' faith in

Jesus' resurrection is historical and real; so is the fact that for them there was no doubt that this subjective faith had a corresponding reality that happened to Jesus himself. From a historical point of view, I do not think one can go further than this statement.

If we now ask ourselves today how we can today accept Jesus' resurrection *subjectively*, the answer is with *a reasonable faith*. We have to relate to the resurrection with *faith*, in the first place because we are among those "who have not seen and yet have come to believe" (Jn 20:29), even though this is not the primary aspect of faith, but more basically and in principle because the raising of Jesus is an eschatological act of God. In this sense the general affirmation that our relationship with God can only be in faith, and faith can be reposed only in God, is true of the resurrection. If accepting that the Exodus was an act of God, whatever the historical phenomena that may have occurred, is ultimately an act of faith, then accepting God's action in raising Jesus is as much so and more.

This faith is, however, also *reasonable*, and its reasonableness derives, in my view, from the conjunction of various things, from the "sum total of indicators" (Newman's well-known statement that many steel wires could have the same consistency as a rod). The *first* indicator is the existence of certain texts that confront us at least with the question of the presence of the eschatological in history and give a positive answer, while those who give this answer appear to be honest people. The *second* is the experience in our present-day history of some type of encounter with what we can call "something ultimate," as we shall see in the next chapter. The *third* is that believing acceptance of Jesus' resurrection generates (or can generate) greater personal humanization and more and better history, that it *founds history*. Of course—here as with faith in God—it depends upon each of us to tell ourselves what constitutes the reasonableness of this faith.

Given this way of understanding the reasonableness of faith, it follows that neither the resurrection nor the appearances of the risen Christ, still less the state in which the tomb was, can be used as quasi-mechanistic arguments to prove who God is and who Jesus is. In other words, Jesus' resurrection must not be used as "cheap grace"—the greatest danger of Christianity, according to Bonhoeffer—to save every human being from making the effort to find meaning in life and death, in transcendence and history; nor should it be used to justify any sort of fundamentalism. The resurrection is substantially an object of faith through being God's action and, furthermore, eschatological action.

For Christians, therefore, it has not provided a whole way, and certainly not a magical way, of carrying out the task every human being must perform: taking a view on what is presented to us as the ultimate reality. Inversely, conceiving a relationship between human beings and the eschatological in history can be present in secularized form in non-Christians, since all of us, I believe, are confronted with this question in one way or another, whatever the answer we give. For Christians, however, there is an invitation to this reasonable faith: the proclamation of the message that "God raised Jesus from the dead."

Chapter 5

The Historical Problem (2)

The Analogy of "Easter Experiences" throughout History

The previous chapter indicated that two *real* things concerning Jesus' resurrection have come down to us: some *texts* that seek to point to something objective that happened, and a subjective *faith*. I now move on to examine the possibility of experiences throughout history that, in one way or another, relate to the original Easter experience. I do this not to justify historicism—which allows no discontinuity in history, so that any understanding of the resurrection has to be on the basis of what happens in history—but to justify the risen Lord, in the sense that if his existence is really eschatological it may include some type of *breaking in* of the eschatological into our own history and mold our lives according to his eschatological life.

Such possible experiences will obviously not be identical to the original experience but analogous to it, so we need to define the relationship between the two. The essential difference between them is that the Easter experience, besides being the first, has fullness as its content, in the sense of anticipated fulfillment of the end of history, while experiences throughout history clearly depend on that first one for being understood as analogous Easter experiences; their content would make them experiences of finality, but without the distinction of referring to the finality of the end time. For this reason some would rather speak of experiences confirming the original Easter witness than of eschatological experiences throughout history.

Granted the difference between the two, I should here like to dwell on the similarity. Tentatively, I put forward actual experiences of finality that can serve, mystagogically, as an introduction to the original Easter experience. Reality is seen through reality, so besides taking account of the texts, to which we are always referred, we need to indicate actual experiences in order to understand Jesus' resurrection as something real.

1. On the Possibility of "Analogous Easter Experiences" in History

Let me first make two prefatory reflections, the first being an *a priori* one. On the one hand, it is clear that according to the accounts there is something unrepeatable in the experience the disciples had of the resurrection, even if this is no more than the fact of this being the *first* experience, to which any later ones—if they exist—have to refer back. In terms of systematic theology: "The experience of those who affirm that they have seen the risen Lord is now unrepeatable for us in its immediacy";[1] in terms of exegesis: "The appearances were not transmitted as an opening to ever new contacts with the risen Christ. On the contrary, they were presented as the unique act of accreditation of the first, basic, witnesses. After them, the first *contact* or *encounter* with the risen Christ will be that which takes place at *the end of time*."[2]

This would seem to exclude the possibility of any analogous experience in the present and would seem to refer only to the witness of the disciples. But on the other hand, since experience of the risen Lord is the founding experience of Christianity, it seems that it should be able to be remade and even *has* to be remade in some form throughout history. If only the first disciples had—and could have had—this founding experience, then the resurrection would be understood as the origin that unleashed faith, but once this had been unleashed, it would no longer *originate* anything. It would be a pure beginning, but not an originating origin. If Jesus' resurrection, however, is not just one event in history but the eschatological event, then we should not exclude its making itself evident in some way throughout history. The opposite would be less likely, since this would make it something forever extrinsic to us, and we could speak of "resurrectionism" in the same way as we do of "deism": in the beginning God showed Jesus as the risen Christ, but God then lost interest in him.

I would regard experience of resurrection instead as something handed down to us as an offer to be accepted—which is what the New Testament states—on the basis of the credibility of the disciples, but which can also be handed on to us as an invitation to remake it analogously. "In the end, the object of our faith is Christ raised in himself, not the experience of the first Christians,"[3] which means that our trusting acceptance, specific to any faith, does not end in the persons of the witnesses but in the reality of the risen Christ and in the God who raised him. In other words, the occasion of faith—which can be a testimony—is one thing; the act of faith, which always ends in the same divine reality, is another. This is a touchy proposition, but I believe it would be paradoxical if the most basic aspect of our faith were to remain totally alien to our own existence or be reduced to acceptance of a mere testimony.

My second reflection has to do with the fact that the Easter experience was limited to the companions of the historical Jesus (with the exception of Paul). On the one hand, this reinforces the unrepeatability of the original experience, parallel to the unrepeatability of following Jesus during his life. But if, on the other hand, the *continuation* of Jesus is held to be possible and even enjoined on later Christians—though in a way analogous to following him during his life—then it is plausible to argue that there can also be an analogous experience to the Easter experience. In any case, if such an experience can take place today, its place has to be the continuation of Jesus. (This observation has pastoral significance at the present time, with its proliferation of visions and charismatic movements, which might operate as successors of the Easter experience. Although they do not use such terms, these movements do claim that the eschatological is being made present to them in history, so it is worth examining what following of Jesus they contain and warning that without this they are very dubious.) I shall make my personal observations on this later, but I turn first to how others view the possibility of resurrection experiences in history.

(a) The Possibility as Seen in Modern Theology

Karl Rahner, writing from a systematic angle, affirms our essential dependence on the experience of the first believers in the resurrection, with the obvious implication that this was something unique and unrepeatable, so that not even mystical experiences can be equated with visions of the risen Christ. Nevertheless, Rahner himself adds that we hear the external message of the resurrection through the inner witness of experience of the Spirit, that in the audacity of placing ourselves above death—thanks to the apostolic witness—"the risen Christ witnesses to the fact that he himself lives. . . . Therefore we cannot say that it is impossible for us to approach the very experience testified. We experience Jesus' resurrection 'in the Spirit' because both he and his cause are presented to us as living and victorious realities."[4] So the experience of the first disciples cannot absolutely be separated from our own, and, this being the case, an experience analogous to theirs will also be possible in history.

As an exegete, U. Wilckens affirms that the purpose of the appearance narratives is not an invitation to have similar encounters throughout history, which will come to pass only in the parousia. Nevertheless, he adds that what is at the heart of early Christianity's discourse on Jesus' resurrection is "the creative omnipotence of God," to which the response is faith in the raised crucified Jesus, "consequently, *faith in God in its most sublime form*."[5] He does not clarify quite what this faith might be, but if this type of sublime faith were to be re-created in history—and I see no reason why this should not happen—this would be an objective re-creation of something analogous to what happened in the disciples' experience of the resurrection.

P. F. Carnley states that the Easter experiences are experiences of the Spirit of Christ and that therefore what happened in the appearances "can be experienced even now on principle: the continued presence of Christ as Spirit as a datum of faith in the present-day Church."[6]

E. Schillebeeckx states the matter clearly, from both the exegetic and the dogmatic standpoint. This is because, *exegetically*, he understands the appearances as conversion experiences: "Jesus once more offers them salvation; they experience this in their own conversion, which means that Jesus has to be living. In their experience of 'conversion to Jesus,' in the renewal of their own lives, they experience the grace of Jesus' forgiveness; here they experience that Jesus lives. Jesus is alive. A *dead man* cannot forgive."[7] (The historical presupposition behind this explanation is that the disciples—not just Peter—totally lost their faith during the passion and that it was from this point that they had to return to Jesus. An important dogmatic consequence would be that God can grant this forgiveness independently of Christ's resurrection. So the experience of the appearances would not be so unique and unrepeatable.) The appearances, then, are a form of expressing the original experience of forgiveness. And the *dogmatic* conclusion is, as I quoted in the Introduction, that "there is not so much difference between the way in which we can reach faith in the raised crucified Lord through the death of Jesus and the way in which Jesus' disciples came to the same faith."[8] Schillebeeckx does not reduce Jesus' resurrection to the conversion of the disciples; that is, he is not reducing what happened to Jesus to what happened to the disciples, nor is he denying God's initiative in this conversion. Faith in the resurrection is not human invention but gratuitous revelation. Granted this, however, he does not see the experience of the first Christians as something absolutely unique.

Commenting on this, H. Kessler says that Schillebeeckx sees "no 'essential' difference between the first disciples' mode of access to faith in the risen Jesus and our own; we too should be able to experience existential renewal in the light of the life of Jesus (through the apostolic witness, and this is the only difference), a renewal that would suppose certainty in faith that Jesus lives."[9] Kessler himself insists on the real priority of what happened to Jesus over personal experience, and to explain this he uses the interpersonal term "encounter": "The Other, who here is the raised crucified Jesus, approaches me and puts conditions for a possible knowledge of him in the encounter, at least for his part, in such a way that I, in turn, am transformed in the process of knowing."[10] Kessler prefers the term *encounter*—in the sense of an experience of illumination, a *disclosure*—to *conversion,* since the latter concentrates on and gives greater emphasis to the subject who is converted, while the former focuses on the one who works the conversion—God—and the result of God's action—Christ raised. With regard to the repeatability of the experience, Kessler distances himself from Schillebeeckx, but without completely rejecting him: "The original Easter experience, in effect, is analogous in other respects to the experience of later faith: the first witnesses, as we have seen, were not dispensed from believing (as they would have been, for example, in the face of irrefutable evidence, excluding any personal commitment) but were called to a faith that was a free response."[11]

He exemplifies this in the account of the disciples at Emmaus, in which he sees both similarities to and differences from the first appearances. The significant factor is that the faith of these disciples is not one based purely on the authority of the witnesses to the first appearances (the women and the disciples of Luke 24:22–24) but also on a personal and existential experience (breaking bread with Jesus: vv. 30–32). He draws this conclusion:

> Later disciples of Jesus can assent, through their own experience (albeit analogous-unequal) of the living and present Lord, to the testimony (rooted in the original and unique Easter experience) of the first apostles and confess: "The Lord has risen indeed" (Luke 24:34). The first apostolic witnesses, with their message—contrary to anything known or plausible—that the crucified Jesus was raised, invite us precisely to bring about our own experience of this. An experience that we ourselves can make . . . at the cost of committing our existence, of entry into the history of Jesus and into the practice of the living community. This invitation is permanent.[12]

Exp erience *(handwritten in top margin)*

(b) Analogous Easter Experiences throughout History

After that brief survey, what remains to be said? I have mentioned a few authors only, but perhaps enough to draw a double conclusion.

On the one hand, the New Testament presents the first appearances, self-manifestations of Jesus, above all to Peter, as unrepeatable, and in any case any other experiences of the risen Christ, supposed or real, throughout history are referred back to the original Easter experience.

On the other hand, however, these authors think—for speculative and theological, though not explicitly exegetical, reasons—that our present faith in the resurrection does not have to depend *only* on a testimony, but that it can and must in some way share in the experience of the first witnesses. We would otherwise— as I have already said—fall into a sort of *deism of the resurrection*, according to which the presence of the eschatological was made manifest in history at the beginning but not afterward.

This terminology—and that of the authors cited—may send shivers down our spine and produce metaphysical vertigo. But those who see the texts on Jesus' resurrection as a central element in the expression of their faith cannot keep silent on the matter. The authors cited, with a greater or lesser degree of caution, assent *theoretically* to the thesis of a certain repeatability of the Easter experience. "We enjoy certain possibilities of access and of understanding. The original Easter experience is, in effect, analogous in other aspects to the experience of later faith."[13] What I should like to add—with some daring—is a *phenomenological* analysis of such experiences. This seems to me decisive, in that what is salvific is *present-day* reality and experience. What molds us as human beings and as believers is not knowledge (even though true) *about* the resurrection and *about* the disciples' experiences but real experience *of* the resurrection (and of God).

(handwritten "4" in left margin)

(i) Experiences of finality in history.

Set to think what experiences can analogously re-create the experience of the resurrection, perhaps two courses can be suggested.

The first would be the experience of *visions*, which were certainly already important in early Christianity and have been put forward as possible throughout history.[14] Without prejudging the objective reality behind the subjective experience (and independently of the judgment of the ecclesiastical hierarchy on them), these visions are characterized by the appearance of some personal being—angels, saints, the Virgin Mary, Jesus Christ—with some message to be put into practice by the recipients.

As they are appearances of *persons* coming to meet us in history, these visions might be said to be analogous to the appearances of Jesus. This, however, does not strike me as an adequate argument. In the first place, these appearances (real or imagined) do not usually express the basic fact that God has done justice to a victim and that the eschatological has thereby broken into history. In the second place, the specific messages of those who appear do not usually express the basic message of the risen Christ but more peripheral things. In the third place, Paul makes a distinction between his own visions and his experience of the risen Christ.

Finally, these visions almost always have an esoteric (and sometimes a hysteric) component that chimes ill with the sobriety of the New Testament accounts. Circumstantial details tend to prevail over a deep experience of finality.

The other course, which to me seems more apposite, is *the experience of the irruption of something quasi-eschatological* into our situation. I bring this in because it is real and happens on a massive scale: its reality has come to meet us, "has appeared." (In El Salvador we can have no doubt about a reality that has appeared in its finality. These experiences are real and strike me as more credible than those of people who claim to have had visions or other esoteric experiences. Whatever interpretation one places on them, there can be no doubt that such experiences are real and, as real, at least give theology something to think about.) This seems to me the better mystagogy for showing us how to grasp the inrush of the eschatological, even if the christological dimension and final eschatology is not explicitly present in the experiences. Let me first put it phenomenologically.

Many people find that after years of being in a situation without seeing it, the reality of it is revealed to them. The reality unveils itself and shows itself for what it is: injustice that generates poverty, violence, lies, and death, but also a situation that generates hope, compassion, justice, and love. And it is also a fact that this experience of disclosure shows reality in its finality. Let me give two examples. A doctor who came from abroad to help the country wrote: "All the time I felt the pain of the daily life of the poor in the shanty towns and the rural areas. It was in the midst of this pain that I discovered something of what I was searching for, a God who was not only a greater but also a lesser God. Among you I found a good and just God, who walks with his people and who still suffers alongside those who suffer."[15] After living for some years among the poor and the victims, a North American sister, now dead, wrote these words: "My reflections are gloomy, sometimes even painful. Seeing the faces, listening to the stories, my heart cannot stop hurting. But I am not sad. . . . I find myself learning from these people what I had always hoped to be true: that love is stronger than death."[16]

Experiences (of "meeting," "learning") such as these happen; they are real, mediated not primarily by texts but by actual situations, and in them reality comes out to meet us. If we examine them more systematically, they show these characteristics:

1. In general, though there may be a pre-disposition to see things as they are, this does not usually happen; instead, reality, so to speak, takes the initiative and unveils itself. What it is in itself finally becomes clear, although it has been there—hidden or repressed—for a long time.

2. What is unveiled is reality "in final form." Through circumstantial historical realities some dimension of finality is unveiled.

3. This unveiling of reality is accepted with a triple gratitude. First, because what is unveiled sets us in the truth of the situation, the true principle and basis for building up what is human. Second, because much of what is unveiled is good and positive, better than what we have experienced before. Third, because the fact of reality being unveiled is perceived as a gift that does not correspond to previous "merits" or "expectations." Where it is least expected, in the poor of this world, reality as salvation has been made present.

Objective finality

4. This experience tends to mark life existentially. Its recipient is referred to a certain objective finality and is marked subjectively with a certain definitivity. What has been experienced brings a corresponding decision to live and work for something ultimate, such as justice, and to do so to the end—martyrdom—in darkness sometimes but with greater perception and conviction that this is the right course. The way forward has meaning and produces joy.

5. Normally, although the experience belongs to individuals, it is shared and generates community. We are grateful to the poor for being the vehicle of this unveiling and establish community with them, so that being-for-them and being-with-them becomes an element in the finality of one's own life. This gives rise to solidarity and community among those to whom reality has been unveiled in the poor and the victims of this world.

6. Finally, the type of life that arises from and responds to the reality unveiled usually shows the features of mission upheld against contrary signs: hope against hope, peace and calm against darkness, love against selfishness, and so on. In practical terms, this is a mission to establish justice and to help bring in the Kingdom of God, and it is being ready to give one's life for love—martyrdom—so that the poor may have life.

Experiences such as these are *real,* and they happen on a sufficient scale not to be seen as esoteric. As described above, they directly reveal their *anthropological* dimension, but it is not difficult to describe them from their transcendental correlative, their *theologal* dimension. Living in this way is a form of living adequately our creatureliness in accordance with the Creator. In this way we experience the inrush of what is true, good, and saving, of something final on the historical level, whatever religious understanding we may have of this. There is no need to express this as the inrush of the eschatological, but we do need to evaluate what there is of finality in this irruption.

Such experiences do, furthermore, show certain equivalencies with what is narrated of the appearances of the risen Christ. Formally, something final happens unexpectedly and without prior preparation: reality in some way "lets itself" be seen—the experience of grace implied by *ofthe.* The intensity of the experience means that it can be expressed as "the impossible becoming possible," analogous to life and justice triumphing over death and injustice. The community nature of the experience, which is to a degree contagious, though not mechanically so, recalls what sprang from the Easter experience; this probably happened at "meals," as we have seen, and certainly generated "community," so that what grew out of faith in Jesus' resurrection were not individual beliefs but communities, *ekklesia.*

(ii) The christological dimension of these experiences. What of the person of Jesus? I have said that the actual experiences described are not visions, which concentrate the experience on a person, but it is also true that the content of such experiences, what unveils them as something ultimate, points to a future, and offers salvation is a reality close to what Jesus was and did in life and certainly similar to what happened to him finally. The person, praxis, and destiny of Jesus

remain explicit reference points for these experiences. To say that "love is stronger than death" is an anthropological translation of the Christian experience of Easter: the cross leads to the resurrection. And in referring back to not only a greater but also a lesser God it theologally translates the christological reality that the risen Christ is the crucified Jesus.

We must then agree with Kessler that the resurrection concentrates God's eschatological action in history on the person of Jesus, and that in this sense present-day experiences are not identical with those narrated in the New Testament. But we must also stress that present-day experiences—though not linked to any "vision" of Jesus—can have a deeply christological structure; just as the resurrection proclaims that the life of Jesus of Nazareth was a true life and leads to true life and that resurrection shows the radical inversion of the condemned being the exalted, so these can appear in the experiences I have described.

We cannot expect appearances of the risen Christ like those narrated in the gospels to happen in history, but we can remake—or, more accurately, allow ourselves to be given the capacity for remaking—experiences of finality such as those described: that despite everything there is light and hope in the crucified people, that to react in mercy and love is the ultimate human beings can do, that giving one's own life so that others may live is living, and so on.

I am calling these experiences we bring about in history not "eschatological experiences" but "experiences of finality." None of these can fully reproduce the appearances narrated in the gospels. None of them can compel acceptance of the historical reality of Jesus' resurrection. But they can help us to understand—from their present-day *reality*—what the disciples affirm as a *real* thing: the crucified Jesus appeared to them raised. And, in my view, Christian faith lives when, throughout history, we not only accept a doctrinal testimony that, coming from outside, remains always something external to us, alien to us, but when we go on remaking this type of experience of finality.

Neither are we today witnesses of Jesus' original resurrection nor do the disciples' accounts, however credible for their honesty, confront us directly with the resurrection of Christ raised. But we can do two things. The first is to analyze the texts critically and honestly, as we did in the previous chapter, which can lead us to the conclusion that the disciples do in fact affirm the irruption of the eschatological into history. The other is for us today to have an experience analogous to that of the appearances, an experience of finality, with the noetic, praxic, and hope-giving elements mentioned in the previous chapter, plus the celebrational element, to which I shall turn next.

Historical analysis of the texts and analysis of experiences of finality are two different tasks, but I regard them as both necessary and complementary. It may very well happen that, even while reading the texts on the basis of such experiences, someone may not feel inclined to accept the resurrection of Jesus, for example. But it can also happen that these experiences can make the testimony of the disciples more believable, since something *analogous* is happening in our own history—the hermeneutical circle: *texts* that speak of irruption of the eschatological and *experiences* of finality.

2. Celebrating Historical Fullness: Living Now as Risen Beings

I have examined what type of experiences of finality we can have, analogous to those the disciples had in their encounters with the risen Christ. I should now like to look at what type of life in fullness we can have, under the conditions of history, that will, analogously, reflect the resurrection of Jesus. This reflection also has a hermeneutical significance: a reply to the question of what we can *celebrate* now in history—together with the questions of what we can know, what we are allowed to hope for, and what we have to do—is also needed in order to understand Jesus' resurrection. But its significance goes beyond hermeneutics: it concerns whether we can live now in finality in our own lives.

It has to be said *a priori* that, from a Christian point of view, this finality of life is nothing other than the following of Jesus, adapting this adequately to circumstances throughout history. But then we need to ask what the actual fact of Jesus' resurrection adds to this following, how it influences the aspect of "fulfillment," of "triumph," of "victory" in our own hope and in our actions on behalf of the crucified people. It is a matter of seeing what fullness there can be in our own lives now.

(a) The New Being in the New Testament

In the New Testament narratives it is clear that Jesus' resurrection generates reality and some type of historical fullness in the disciples. What there is of triumph in his resurrection overflows, as it were, into their lives. This comes out in the appearance narratives, which show the disciples experiencing not only hope and being sent on a mission but also peace, forgiveness, light, and joy, all of which is expressed as "victory" over uncertainty, darkness, fear. It could not be otherwise. Jesus has triumphed over his own fear, and they are therefore overflowing with joy.

This triumph, though, not only appears temporarily in the appearance narratives but remains present throughout the disciples' lives. In simple terms, as they are shown in the New Testament the disciples have worked a change in their lives, not only in that they have initially passed from fear to bravery, but also in that in the midst of the toils and trials that come upon them they act with freedom and joy.

This can be seen in the idealized descriptions in Acts. The apostles begin to preach without fear and with audacity, and they appear happy even in the midst of persecutions, "rejoic[ing] that they were considered worthy to suffer dishonor for the sake of the name" (Acts 5:41). It can also be seen in how the presence of the Spirit among them is recounted, more immediate and prodigious in Acts, more as a normal occurrence in Paul, but in both a presence that produces life and fullness. It can be seen too in Paul's own exultations and, programmatically, in the way the first Christians sum up both Jesus' person and his mission: good news, spreading the good news.

The disciples who have met with the risen Christ live a new life, with meaning and with joy. They do not appear to be "sad." They are afflicted but not forsaken, as Paul spells out (2 Cor 4:8ff.). In difficult moments they compare themselves to Jesus: "We are always being given up to death for Jesus' sake," but in the conviction that thereby "the life of Jesus may also be made visible in our bodies" (2 Cor 4:10).[17]

Finally, the disciples bear witness that they too already live in some form of fullness. It is not only that their expectation of the imminence of the parousia makes them live like new beings, but also that the content of triumph in the resurrection is not limited to Jesus alone but has overflowed from him and changed the quality of their lives. Even if only in passing, it is perhaps worth saying that herein lies, or should lie, the deepest root of what is new about the Christian liturgy. Its historical origin can be found on the sociological and religious levels in its continuity/discontinuity with the Jewish tradition. But its most original element consists in these first Christians "having something to celebrate," not just proclaiming truths or adopting ritual norms in the cultic sphere. They have to put their gratitude and their joy into words. They celebrate the Lord raised and exalted, and they express that his fullness has overflowed and reached them. This is what should make the Christian liturgy something definable in relation to other forms of worship, in theory and in practice.

(b) The Celebration of Fullness throughout History

If the above is true, today too we need to be open to the possibility of having some sort of experience of "fullness," "triumph," "victory" in history. Today too we need to see that the triumph in Jesus' resurrection has overflowed. If there were nothing of fullness and nothing to celebrate in history, it would be useless to go on repeating that Jesus' resurrection contains triumph and victory. So, without being in any way ingenuous and in the presence of the *mysterium iniquitatis*, we need to analyze what history contains by way of fullness.

In itself, the idea is traditional, though it has often been badly and dangerously understood. The Christians of Corinth, to take an example from earliest times, were so convinced that they were already living in fullness that they no longer hoped in their own final resurrection. They thought like this because they saw extraordinary signs everywhere—miracles, the gift of tongues, and the like—that seemed to triumph over everyday reality.

Paul's reaction against this unfortunate error is well known. The relevant point here is that to associate the fullness of the risen Christ with that of the believers is required by the very preaching of the risen Christ, but this does not in any way mean de-historicization, as the Corinthians claimed, but fuller incarnation in history. In graphic terms, their error consisted in thinking that the *less* they lived in the historical world, the *more* they lived in the world of the resurrection. (In 2 Timothy 2:18 the author criticizes those who claim "that the resurrection has already taken place," which leads them to believe that there is now no brake on their will, though in this way they are in fact doing the devil's will [cf. 2:26].)

This distortion of what it means to live now as risen beings has, from good and less good motives, been present in the history of the church. To take an example of current concern, the goodness and above all the superiority of the celibate religious life over other states of life has generally been justified on the grounds that it enables its participants to share already in the fullness of the resurrection *because* it removes them from the material conditions of existence and assimilates them to celestial ones.

But we do not live more in fullness through living less in the conditions of historical existence. This is not how the triumph in Jesus' resurrection is reflected; it is reflected in very different ways. Paul states it authoritatively in his debate with the Corinthians by stating the supremacy of love as the form the Christians' historical existence must take. This love is crucified like that of Jesus, on which Paul insists, but it is in this love that "living now like risen beings" will consist. To this love expressed in following Jesus we have to add the "triumph" element, in which two basic characteristics can be specified: it is life in freedom and in joy.

(i) Freedom as triumph over selfishness. Freedom reflects the triumph of the risen Christ not because it removes us from our material reality but because it places us in our historical situation in order to love, without anything in this situation being a barrier to loving. In Christian terms, the free are those who love and in the final analysis only love, with no other attitude to turn them away from loving. Paradoxically speaking, freedom is binding oneself to history in order to save it but—continuing the metaphor—in such a way that nothing in history binds and enslaves the ability to love.

There are loves and loves. Many—or at least some—can sincerely claim to have given their lives to the poor and victims and to love them sincerely, but it is usual for this love to coexist with bonds to other loves—party, revolutionary cadre, religious congregation, ecclesial institution—that nearly always mitigate, condition, or even distort the exercise of this first love for the poor (to say nothing of being *bound* by ambition for wealth and power). Of such people it can be said that, although there is real love, there is not total love because other ties—some quite understandable and legitimate in themselves—persist. But there are others, such as Archbishop Romero, who loved the poor and loved nothing more than them or as radically as them, with no ulterior motives, without other legitimate loves distracting him from this basic love, and without the risks incurred by this love dictating prudence to him. (I was always impressed by the freedom he had. Not only was he free to speak the truth to everyone, including himself, but nothing prevented him from doing good. He was not deterred by threats against his own person, or—which was more difficult—by threats to and destruction of the institutional platform of his church: bombs in the archdiocesan radio station and printing works, in Catholic schools, in the university, in clerical and lay residences, in seminaries. Not only this, but he had to accept the assassination of the major symbols of the church: priests, religious, catechists, delegates of the word, seminarians. But he did not give in, and this showed him to be a free man: nothing stood between him, as a person and as archbishop, and his love of the poor.)

Freedom is made present in this sort of love. Christian freedom is in the final analysis freedom to love. It is the freedom of Jesus himself as he claims: "No one takes [my life] from me, but I lay it down of my own accord" (Jn 10:18). It is the freedom of Paul: "For though I am free with respect to all, I have made myself a slave to all, so that I might win more of them" (1 Cor 9:19). This leads to his reminder that "the Lord is the Spirit, and where the Spirit of the Lord is, there is freedom" (2 Cor 3:17). This freedom has nothing to do with escape from history, and it does not even directly have to do with the right to one's own freedom—even though this right is legitimate and its exercise is becoming ever more necessary and pressing in the church. The freedom that expresses the freedom of the risen Christ consists in not being bound to history in what this has of enslavement (fear, paralyzing prudence); it consists in the greatest freedom of love to serve, without anything putting limits to or standing in the way of this love.

(ii) Joy as triumph over sadness. The other dimension of what is triumphant in the resurrection is joy, and joy is possible only when there is something to celebrate. Living with joy means being able to celebrate life, and the question is whether such celebration exists. Once again, this can appear highly paradoxical in situations of terrible suffering, like that of the crucified peoples, but it happens. Gustavo Gutiérrez recounts that at a workshop on popular spirituality in Lima the participants, poor and suffering, said: "The opposite of happiness . . . is sadness, not suffering."[18]

The fact that life can be celebrated is basic to understanding and living the resurrection of Jesus. This is of course not a matter of diversion, in its double meaning of entertainment and alienation. It is a matter of a radical honesty with reality, which enables us, despite everything, to recognize, together with others, what is good and positive, in small things and big things, which brings its own dynamic that is worthy of being celebrated. This honesty with the good in reality is what Jesus had when he rejoiced that the little ones had understood the mysteries of the Kingdom, when he celebrated life with outcasts, and when he invited his listeners to call God the Father of everyone.

This joy is also possible today. It is the joy of communities that, despite everything, come together to sing and recite poetry, to show that they are happy they are together, to celebrate the eucharist. To be honest with their own lives, they feel that they have to celebrate them. It is the joy of Archbishop Romero, besieged on all sides and by all powers, who was filled with joy when he visited the communities, and who exclaimed—seemingly rhetorically but most truly—that "with this people it costs nothing to be a good shepherd."[19] It cost him his life, but the people provided him with a joy no one could take away, and in this joy the triumph of the resurrection was made historically present to him. It is the joy expressed by these consciously paradoxical words of Karl Rahner: "I believe that being a Christian is the simplest task, the easiest and at the same time that light burden of which the gospel speaks. The more you take it up, the more it takes you up, and the longer you live, both the heavier and the lighter it becomes."[20]

I should like to end this chapter with some words by Ignacio Ellacuría, written shortly before his martyrdom, which, though they speak directly of hope, not joy, express what it means to live in fullness now:

> All this martyrs' blood spilt in El Salvador and throughout Latin America, far from inducing discouragement and despair, inspires a new spirit of struggle and new hope in our people. In this sense, if we are not a "new world" or a "new continent," we are definitely and verifiably—and not just for people from outside—a continent of hope, which is a highly interesting symptom of a future society compared to other continents where they have no hope and all they have is fear.[21]

This freedom and this joy express the fact that we can live now as new men and new women, risen in history. They make the following of Jesus not just the fulfillment of an ethical imperative, by asceticism or Kantianism, but the bearing of the mark of resurrection. This is graced following.

Jesus' resurrection is, in the final analysis, a Christian response to a permanent human question: the question of justice for victims, which is a question of sense or nonsense. To grasp it, we need hope, and we need a sense of mission, since "the resurrection *founds* history . . . opens an eschatological future."[22] But the resurrection can be not only "understood"—on this basis—but also in some way "lived" in believing following of the crucified Jesus.

We can live in history with resignation or desperation, but we can also live with hope in a promise. And this happens. Those who have radical hope for the victims of this world, who are not convinced that resignation is the last word or consoled by the claim that these victims have already served a positive purpose, can include in their experience a hope analogous to that with which Jesus' resurrection was first grasped and can direct their lives to taking the victims down from the cross. Furthermore, those who, in the midst of this history of crucifixion, celebrate what there is of fullness and have the freedom to give their own lives will, perhaps, not see history as nonsensical or as a repetition of itself but as the promise of a "more" that touches us and draws us despite ourselves. This experience can be formulated in various ways, but one of these has to be "walking with God in history," as Micah puts it, or as an encounter—in faith, in hope, and in love—with the God who raised Jesus.

Chapter 6

The Theological Problem (1)

The Revelation of God

I turn now to the theological problem: what is it that Jesus' resurrection reveals? As it is primarily an eschatological event, we must hope that it in some way reveals a totality, and in effect Jesus' resurrection reveals who God is, who Jesus is, and what we human beings are. Leaving this last element aside for the present (I have alluded to it in dealing with hope, praxis, freedom, and joy as realities related to the resurrection and will return to it under christological titles, which can also be read anthropologically), the resurrection led the first Christians to ask themselves who God was and who Jesus was, and they established a precise relationship between the two, so that action that reveals God is essentially relayed to and concentrated in what happened to Jesus; and, inversely, Jesus' reality is unfolded from what God did in him: "The resurrection and exaltation of Jesus, in effect, *contract and concentrate* God's eschatological action *in a single person*: Jesus crucified and raised. The ineffable mystery of God who contains all without being contained is shown to us visibly and perceptibly uniquely in the figure of a person: the man Jesus."[1]

Starting from this christological concentration of God's action, I should like to analyze in this chapter what Jesus' resurrection states about God. I do not propose to examine all that the Old and New Testaments say about God—creation, alliance, kingdom—but what derives from the fact of the resurrection, while keeping the immediate context of the cross. Specifically, I want to show that Jesus' resurrection (1) makes possible and requires a new theologal creed; (2) shows God's justice and partiality; (3) marks the triumph of the God of Jesus in the struggle among gods; (4) shows the dialectic within God himself—the greater God and the lesser God; (5) reveals God as God of the future; and (6) shows that God remains mysterious in everything.

1. "The God Who Raises the Dead": A New Historical Creed

"Faith in God is faith in the resurrection,"[2] and the first Christians formulated this faith in a succinct formula: "God raised Jesus from the dead," repeated (with slight variants) so often and so emphatically as to suggest that it is very ancient, the first form, in fact, in which the original experience is expressed.[3] The subject of the action is God, not Jesus rising through his own power, as later expressed in John 10:18. The resurrection is, then, an act carried out by God, through which God is revealed. And this way of grasping God's revelation is similar to that used in the Old Testament; recalling this will help us to understand God's mode of self-revelation in raising Jesus.

(a) The Structure of the Revelation of God in the Old Testament

First, in the Old Testament God is revealed not epiphanically but through histori-cal action.[4] This action provides the ground for a revelation of God to which a particular faith responds. And this action of God's is not any action but action that *liberates* victims. It forms the beginning of the *Credo* of Israel: "I am the Lord your God, who brought you out of the land of Egypt, out of the house of slavery" (Dt 5:6; cf. Ex 20:2; Dt 26:5–9).

In the second place, in the course of the Old Testament the historical actions through which God is revealed are progressively displaced toward the *future* (see 1 Kgs 20:13, 28; Ez 25:6, 8) until they reach this radical formulation: "For I am about to create new heavens and a new earth; the former things shall not be re-membered or come to mind. But be glad and rejoice forever in what I am creat-ing" (Is 65:17; cf. Rv 21:1).

Third, God is revealed progressively, universally, extending his lordship in time (from the creation to the final fulfillment) and in space (to all nations), while the *partiality* of his founding liberating activity remains constant, so that the ex-pression "in you the orphan finds compassion," which recurs in the psalms, can be called the true *confessio Dei* of Israel: "Yahweh's cause is quite simply the cause of the defenseless."[5]

Finally, God's revelation comes about *dialectically* and *confrontationally* in battle with other divinities. In the foundational event of the freeing from Egypt, this takes place against Pharaoh, as symbolized in the plagues. And the first com-mandment prohibits adoration of "rival" gods in principle, which raises the struggle to a theologal level: the struggle of the gods.[6]

(b) The New Testament

The New Testament shows an important parallelism with this structure of revela-tion. Here too revelation comes about through an action, and it begins with an action that is foundational and valid till the end of time—the resurrection of Jesus. This becomes the nucleus of the new creed.

Comparing it with God's revelatory actions in the Old Testament, Jesus' res-urrection appears as above all a *liberating* action. It is not just anyone who has been raised but a victim, and the reason for raising this victim is to do him justice, to free him from the oppression of violent and unjust death. Starting with this specific and *partial* action—God is the one "who raised Jesus our Lord from the dead" (Rom 4:24)—the formulation of the nature of God became universalized:

God is the one who "gives life to the dead and calls into existence the things that do not exist" (Rom 4:17). This action by its nature points to the *future*, to the final resurrection of the dead, so that in the end "God will be all in all" (1 Cor 15:28). Finally, it clarifies the *struggle of the gods*: "This man . . . you . . . killed. . . . But God raised him up" (Acts 2:23f.). God's life-giving action is reaction to the death-dealing action of the gods (through their agents).

The New Testament, then, follows the Old Testament way of proceeding in order to know God, with the essential difference that Jesus' resurrection is presented as a definitive and eschatological act: in history one can go no further than this. The New Testament also goes beyond the Old on another decisive point: God's action in the resurrection takes place after God's inaction on the cross. (The Old Testament has the mysterious figure of the Servant of Yahweh, of whom it is said that he will prosper. The Easter paradox of cross-resurrection is foretold, but not in the strictly theologal sphere.) In this way the same God is revealed in two distinct and even contrary ways, which establish a *dialectic* within God himself—the greater God and the lesser God, in my formulation—without either dimension suppressing the other. In this way the reason for the futurity of God is provided from within the very God. It is not just that in history we have the "already but not yet" but that the very God is affected by, and reacts differently to, what history holds of cross and hope of resurrection. Properly understood, "only in the end will God be God"; "God needs time" for history to overcome the ambiguity inherent in it so that God can show himself as pure positivity. I shall now examine in more detail what has been stated in very summary form.

2. A Just and Partial God, Liberator of Victims

The Christian God is revealed through action in history, and faith discovers God through relating him to this action. This being the case, it is of capital importance to determine why—according to the biblical texts—God decides to carry out such and such an action. This *why* will show the purpose of God's action and introduce us into the very reality of God.

(a) The Liberating Partiality of God in the Old Testament

Israel's most original creed relates God to freedom from Egypt, and it is vital to know why. Some think—and this is reflected in the first Vatican *Instruction on Liberation Theology*, in 1984—that the reason lies in God seeking to create a people with whom he can later make an alliance, so that this people will offer worship to him alone. This interpretation of the Exodus rejects any other that puts historical-political liberation at the forefront.

Juan Luis Segundo and Ignacio Ellacuría have both refuted this purely religious interpretation of the Exodus. For the former,

> The three oldest major sources—the Yahwist, the Elohist, and the Deuteronomic—are at one in showing Yahweh intervening on behalf of a people

that is already his, out of the compassion he feels in the face of the inhuman (call it political or not) situation this people is undergoing through its oppression and slavery in Egypt, and in order to give it a land of its own. . . . In the oldest traditions there is no trace of this supposed purpose of the exodus to "found the people of God."

For the latter,

Whatever the origin of these stories, their real basis is very precise: the cult (the covenant is a different question) does not give meaning to the liberation from Egypt, but rather the liberation gives its specific meaning to the cult, which celebrates and draws the explicit consequences of that historical experience, that historical praxis.[7]

I would add that the "religious" interpretation seems to attribute a certain self-centeredness to God, drawn from the human tendency to make ourselves the objective of all that we do, whereas God's logic is very different: "Since God loved us so much, we also ought to love one another" (1 Jn 4:11). In effect, the texts give a quite distinct reason. The Yahwist tradition has, "I have observed the misery of my people who are in Egypt; I have heard their cry on account of their taskmasters. Indeed I know their sufferings, and I have come down to deliver them from the Egyptians, and to bring them up out of that land to a good and broad land" (Ex 3:7f.). And the Elohist tradition: "The cry of the Israelites has now come to me; I have also seen how the Egyptians oppress them. So come, I will send you to Pharaoh to bring my people, the Israelites, out of Egypt" (3:9f.).

There are differences between the two narratives, but they have something basic in common. For the first time, God shows himself unequivocally as the God of Israel, and it is in this context that he reveals his name (vv. 13–15). The manifestation is intrinsically accompanied by an action, the liberation of the people, which in the Yahwist tradition is carried out directly by God, while in the Elohist it takes place—indirectly—through Moses. The basic point, however, is that this action by God is a reaction. It is not simply a question of God deciding to show himself or of using the oppression of a people as an *occasion* for his manifestation. This requires something previous, to which God reacts. And this previous something is the misery, cries, sufferings, and oppression of a people, with all of which God is related in a transcendental, not merely an occasional, manner.

Furthermore, by unifying the account of the Exodus and that of the "burning bush," the symbol of the Temple, the Yahwist narrative is effectively subordinating the Temple to the liberation. Written during the building of the Temple, this account emphasizes that it is not liberation that is for the cult—as if Yahweh's liberating commandment were at the service of a sacred place, the burning bush—but the opposite, the cult is for liberation.

God's self-revelation is, then, reaction to the suffering some human beings inflict on others—the suffering of victims. I have called this reaction "mercy," which should not be understood as a mere feeling and is historically determined by who the victim is. When the victim is a whole oppressed people, mercy necessarily becomes justice.[8] But what I am concerned to stress here is the basic affirmation needed to recognize the God who reveals himself: just as from a transcendental-absolute point of view we have to say that "in the beginning was the word" (Jn 1:1) through which creation came about (Gn 1:1ff.), so from a historical-saving point of view we have to say that "in the beginning was mercy for victims, liberation" (Ex 3).

Such a "beginning" has to be properly understood. It does not mean only that liberating mercy is at the start in time of God's manifestation, like the first step in a process in the course of which it may, later, be ignored or replaced. It means that it has to be understood as a *principle* that remains present and active throughout the process, providing it with its basic direction and content; that is, as an origin that *originates* important and lasting realities. This is in fact the case: God's reaction on behalf of victims—and against their executioners—remains a constant throughout the Old Testament (the prophets, wisdom literature, apocalyptic)[9] and in the life of Jesus (the reversal worked by the *Magnificat*, the beatitudes, and indictments)[10] and also in the final fulfillment that will bring about the destruction of "every ruler and every authority and power" (1 Cor 15:24f.). The liberating action in the Exodus is not just an occasion, but the permanent mediation of God's revelation.

(b) God's Liberating Partiality in the New Testament

I have dwelt at some length on the Exodus narrative because it gives an explicit *reason* for God's action, which helps in understanding the *reason* for his action in raising Jesus in the New Testament, which is generally less examined and—in my view—without drawing the due conclusions. Now the resurrection of Jesus, as the founding act of the New Testament, is also a *liberating* act: doing justice to a victim. (Just as with Jesus' miracles, the action through which God raises Jesus is not only beneficial but formally liberating, since the cross is not only an evil but the product of oppression. For this reason Jesus' resurrection enables us to call God a God of victims.) It is true that what happened to Jesus was soon universalized, so that cross and resurrection began to work as universal symbols of the destiny of every human being: the cross as the expression of human mortality and even of slavery unto death, and the resurrection as the response to the longing for immortality—so the raising power of God has been presented as the guarantee of that hope beyond death. All this is legitimate, but to rush into it is also dangerous; we need to go back to what is specific in God's action in order to grasp what it reveals of God and to identify what human being is raised, without taking it for granted.

In the discourses in Acts the human being who has been raised is identified as "the Holy One," "the Righteous One," and "the Author of life" (3:14f.). Peter sums up the life of the Lord: "He went about doing good and healing all who were oppressed by the devil" (10:38). The risen Lord, then, is Jesus of Nazareth, who proclaimed the Kingdom of God to the poor, denounced the powerful, was persecuted and sentenced, and throughout maintained a radical fidelity to the will of God and a radical trust in this same God, whom he called Father.

This description of the risen Lord is decisive for clarifying what the resurrection of Jesus reveals of God. God has raised the one who has lived in this way and who was crucified for doing so. God has raised an innocent one and done justice to a victim. Jesus' resurrection is then not only a symbol of God's omnipotence—as though God had decided arbitrarily and with no connection to the life and death of Jesus to show his omnipotence and thereby reveal himself as God—but is presented as the defense God makes of the life of the Righteous One and of victims.

What is specific about Jesus' resurrection is, therefore, not what God does with a dead body but what God does with a victim. The raising of Jesus is direct proof of the triumph of God's justice, not simply of his omnipotence, and it becomes good news for victims; for once, justice has triumphed over injustice. In the well-known words of Max Horkheimer, the longing of the totally other has been fulfilled, that "the executioner may not triumph over the victim."[11] God is the God who liberates victims.

This reflection leads me back to what I said in the first volume about the Kingdom of God. To establish the good news of the Kingdom, besides the notion Jesus had of it and besides what he did in its service, we have the "way of the addressee," the poor, so that Kingdom and poor cast light on each other. In the same way there is a transcendental correlation between the God who raises and the Jesus who is raised. Light is shed on what the reality of God is from the reality as victim of the one God raises. And this is none other than the victim Jesus of Nazareth.

3. A God against Idols

In the earliest Christian preaching, though in stereotyped form, Jesus' resurrection was expressed in a dialectic-antagonistic framework. This is how it appears in the six paradigmatic discourses in Acts: "This man . . . you crucified and killed. . . . But God raised him up, having freed him from death, because it was impossible for him to be held in its power" (2:23f.); "But you rejected the Holy and Righteous One and asked to have a murderer given to you, and you killed the Author of life, whom God raised from the dead" (3:14f.); "Jesus Christ of Nazareth, whom you crucified, whom God raised from the dead" (4:10); "The God of our ancestors raised up Jesus, whom you had killed by hanging him on a tree" (5:30); "They put him to death by hanging him on a tree, but God raised him on the third day" (10:39f.); "They asked Pilate to have him killed. . . . But God raised him from the dead" (13:28, 30).

(a) The Resurrection as God's Triumph over Idols

In all these texts, though the formulations vary slightly, God's action is presented as reaction to what human beings have done—which is in itself a very grave accusation and one that should not be glossed over in preaching. We should speak not only of the cross (and resurrection) but of crucifiers (and the God who raises).

The New Testament tends to play down the responsibility of the Jews for Jesus' death ("I know that you acted in ignorance," Acts 3:17), but this does not alter the relational dimension of God's action, so that what the resurrection *says of God* is going to be essentially related to what *others have done to Jesus*. So the resurrection reveals God if it is kept together with the human actions—putting the righteous one to death—that provoke this response. Therefore, while it is important to realize who the *addressees* (victims) are if we are to understand God's action as liberating, it is equally important to realize who the *agents* (executioners) are if we are to understand God's action as being part of a struggle.

This struggle is a way in which to express the antagonistic theologal structure of history, which contains the God of life and the idols of death, locked in struggle against one another. If on the cross God seems to be at the idols' mercy, in the resurrection God is seen to triumph over them. If the cross symbolizes the triumph of the idols over God, the resurrection symbolizes the triumph of God over the idols. If on the cross Jesus is the victim the idols generate by their nature, in the resurrection God gives life back to the victim, Jesus.

To put this in the form of a thesis: There is in history a mutually exclusive and antagonistic opposition both between the *mediations* of divinity (in Jesus' time, the Kingdom of God, on the one hand, and the *pax romana* and the circles that gathered around the Temple, on the other) and between the *mediators* (Jesus, on the one hand, and the high priest and Pilate, on the other), and this dialectic is introduced in the way God is revealed. According to this, God does not show himself in a history that is a *tabula rasa* with respect to his revelation, in which he could just as well reveal whatever he chose about himself, but God has to manifest himself actively against other divinities. So God shows himself through life, but by defending it from death; through justice, but against injustice; through setting people free, but doing so against slavery. . . . God's transcendence will be shown not only as beyond creaturehood but also as what is against creaturehood absolutized as an idol. In this context the resurrection shows, from God's triumph now, what the cross showed from his failure—that there is a struggle of the gods.

(b) Anti-idolatrous Praxis Corresponding to God

The resurrection demonstrates God's triumph, but *God being against idols*, in response to *the idols being against God*, is a situation that lasts throughout history. We need to draw the consequences from it.

Above all, we have to move beyond a sort of "resurrectionist" euphoria—not so much in fashion now as it was a few decades ago—by which God's real triumph in the resurrection would do away with the struggle of the gods throughout history. So we need to state that although Christianity is not formally a religion of suffering and sorrow—though it rightly has been accused of presenting itself as such—it is a religion of struggle and conflict, given the theologal structure of history, shot through as it is with the God of life and the idols of death. No attempt to transport ourselves to the triumph of the resurrection should make us ignore or minimize the historical-theologal conflict, whatever certain current siren songs or a theology of inevitability might suggest.

This also means that believing in the true God involves at the same time fighting against the idols. We have to believe in the God of the resurrection while being very conscious that the divinities of death exist and taking a combative stance against them. Fundamentally, this is no more than reinterpreting the first commandment—we must worship the true God—but at the same time not only not worship but act against other false gods. These are false not basically through being useless and inane, as their falsity is usually understood (sometimes in the Old Testament as well), but because they produce victims. This makes them *rivals* of God.

All this is relevant today. If we needed to defend the reality of God against modernity without denying humanity its autonomy, against postmodernity, we need to defend the struggle against idols in order to overcome the indifference—and even tolerance where it is fallacious—that sees history as a simple onward human march without powerful forces of opposition. Christians should not be able to see it like this, based, however, not on their view of the cross but on God's action in the resurrection.

4. A God-Mystery: The *Greater God* and the *Lesser God*

The resurrection, then, shows a God in conflict with other gods, but this needs to be seen within the totality of the Easter mystery. In this way a *dialectic* appears within God that cannot be synthesized throughout history, so that God's mystery is constantly reduplicated.

(a) God's Inaction and Action

The God who acts in the resurrection should not make us forget the inactive and silent God on the cross. In other words, although God's revelation has its own chronological process in relation to us, there is no reason to think that new manifestations of God totally annul earlier ones or even put them in the shade. (One might dare to say that in divine pedagogy God's manifestation on the cross comes before his manifestation in the resurrection, so that the latter may not be used to reduce the impact of the former.) Both biblically and dogmatically the cross-resurrection sequence makes up a unity, with one referring to the other. There is therefore no reason to suppose that the resurrection annuls what the cross reveals of God. Mark goes to great lengths to stress this.

This is clear christologically, since the risen Christ appears with the wounds of the crucified Jesus, and the gospels—though written in the knowledge of the triumphal outcome of resurrection—go back to Jesus and devote a disproportionately large space to the passion compared to their accounts of Jesus' life and even his appearances. But this has to be said theologally of God himself, and this needs to be stressed to avoid the danger of ignoring it, as though the God of the resurrection could annul the God of the cross. Not even after Jesus' resurrection does the New Testament eliminate—if one can use such a term—the "weakness" of God; it keeps it in all its poignancy, as can be seen above all in Mark and Paul. Nor does it elevate God's "power" in the resurrection to an absolutely definitive reality, since this power will be manifest absolutely only at the end, when "God will be all in all" (1 Cor 15:28).

In view of our present situation, after the bloodiest century in human history (Auschwitz, Hiroshima, the Gulags, Bosnia, Rwanda, and more), if, even after the resurrection, God is to be made manifest in history, it would seem that he is to be sought in history's crosses rather than in its resurrections. This is not masochism but being honest with reality. It will be possible to speak of the God of the resurrection—later—from these historical crosses. But if the crosses are disregarded, faith in this God degenerates into "cheap grace," which Bonhoeffer called the greatest danger of Christianity.

(b) Otherness and Affinity

This being the case, we then have to accept at once and serially both cross and resurrection as moments that reveal God—a dialectic that belongs to the very reality of God. Where this mystery of the specifically Christian God leads, and what mystagogy—if any—can be offered to guide us into it, is the most pressing problem, at least for believers—and, I should say, also an enigma that nonbelievers find difficult to eliminate completely from their lives. What should in no case be done is to eliminate one pole of the dialectic in order to keep the other, without trying to make them complementary in their revealing and saving reality.

The cross is a direct expression of the silence, the inaction, and the consequent powerlessness or at least inoperativeness of God. The manifestation of this inactivity and powerlessness does not formally have a liberative dimension, nor is it a reason for generating hope among the crucified, the victims. But if it is related to the powerful manifestation of God in the resurrection, then it can make God's liberating power *credible*.

The reason for this is that this specific impotence of God is the expression of his absolute closeness to victims and of his will to share their fate to the end. If God was on the cross of Jesus, if God shared in the horrors of history in this way, then God's closeness to us, begun at the incarnation and made present to us in Jesus' life, has been consummated. God's action in the resurrection is then not that of a *Deus ex machina* but one that expresses the intrinsic possibilities of God and makes the omnipotence apparent in the resurrection credible—something that is important, to say the least, to the crucified, who mistrust a power that comes *solely* from *above* without in some way having passed through the trial of *being here below*.

This mutual reference and complementarity of cross and resurrection as saving and liberating realities can be established from the biblical texts, such as Paul's "who was handed over to death for our trespasses and was raised for our justification" (Rom 4:25), but it has to be established first in experience, and in concept on the basis of this: the resurrection speaks of *otherness* with respect to victims, while the cross speaks of *affinity*.[12]

The resurrection says that God is radically other than human beings, that God has the ability to achieve what is completely impossible for them: absolute liberation and salvation. In the resurrection—the otherness of God—the *efficacy* of love has appeared. The cross, for its part, tells of God's affinity with victims; nothing in history has set limits to the closeness of God. Without this closeness God's power in the resurrection would remain not only as otherness but as *pure* otherness and therefore ambiguous and, for the crucified, historically threatening. But with this closeness, victims can really believe that God's power is good news. If I may say so, on the cross God passed the test of love. Once we have grasped the loving presence of God on the cross of Jesus, then God's presence in the resurrection ceases to be pure power without love, otherness without affinity, distance without closeness. And this makes God's power *credible*.

The fact that suffering affects God expresses, then, the overcoming of deism and of the *apatheia* of the gods, but from the point of view of the victims it expresses something more radical: the possibility of God not only saving suffering creatures but of saving them *in the human way*, by showing solidarity with them. It expresses the possibility of God being a God-with-us and a God-for-us, though, in order to be so, God himself has to define himself as a God-at-our-mercy.

What is actually good about this solidarity of God with victims is something not easy, by definition, for those who are not victims to determine and put into words, and in the final analysis it is a matter of a prime reality that cannot be deduced from the concept alone. But it can, I believe, be expressed in the following way: what is liberating and saving in a crucified God lies in victims being able to overcome radical solitude and orphanhood, to overcome absolute indignity.

The fact that God approaches and shares in the condition and fate of victims, and does so to save them, is seen as something good and as something that upholds their struggles, something that gives encouragement and hope, that is neither paralyzing nor alienating. The crucified God is finally experienced also as salvation because there is experience of communion with God. And this, like all communion, produces identity, dignity, and joy. This God—whatever his power—has credibility for victims because he has come close to them in their dimension as victims. And they feel joy at this.

How to relate and unify resurrection and cross is not a purely conceptual task. But it can perhaps be said that in the experience of victims the *raising-liberating* God expresses the efficacy of love and of salvation, and the *crucified-in-solidarity* God expresses credibility, grace, tenderness. The liberator God expresses otherness, the crucified God, affinity.

(c) Letting God Be God

Where the reality of God in himself is concerned, the cross-resurrection dialectic in God himself can perhaps be expressed by adding to the traditional words *Deus semper maior* (Augustine, rooted in John's "God greater than our heart") the equally metaphorical words *Deus semper minor*, used, though in a different context, by Rahner: "God is always greater (and, if you like, also for that very reason always smaller) than culture, science, the Church, the Pope, and everything institutional."[13]

In the conjunction of both things, otherness and affinity, being greater and being lesser, we can attempt to articulate the mystery of God and how this mystery, which can never be manipulated, and still less through the dialectic established, can also be good news.

It seems to me important to stress the reality of this lesser God, as theologians who take the suffering of victims seriously have done in different ways. From Bonhoeffer's "only a God who suffers can save us" to P. W. Gyves's "I discovered something of what I was searching for, a God who was not only a greater but also a lesser God," there is something in this God that draws victims. The fact is that any definition of God as power alone carries the danger of conceiving the essence of the divinity as pure power, or at least of defining divinity in terms of power—and victims have had a very bad experience of power.

I say this because Jesus' resurrection has often been used to present God *only* in terms of power—which is why we always need to bear the crucified God in mind. But we also need to move beyond the reductionism of the cross, which would have it that God reveals only his solidarity with the oppressed and not also the good news of liberation. This double danger can be overcome only if we take God's liberative action in the resurrection and his passive solidarity on the cross together. Maintaining this dialectic is what allows us, without trivializing it, to give God his new and definitive name: "God is love" (1 Jn 4:8, 16). People do not long for a love incapable of changing bad into good, but neither do they understand a love—as love—that does not come close to and act in solidarity with them.

5.   A God on the Way: The Futurity of God

In this chapter I have examined the *partiality* and the *crucifixion* of God, both insights of contemporary theology, the first from Latin America and the second from Europe. I should like to end by looking at the *futurity* of God, a concept that, though implicit in Paul's "in the end God will be all in all," has been rediscovered in our time under the influence of Bloch and his "principle of hope." This discovery converges with the theological evaluation of Jesus' resurrection so that, although this is understood as anticipation *(prolepsis)* or definite promise of the future, the revelation of God is seen as taking place definitively at the end of history.

I propose to examine the positions taken by various classic authors on the subject, from both a theoretical and existential context. The theoretical consists in approaching the futurity of God from the whole Easter mystery, cross and resurrection, not only from Jesus' resurrection as anticipation of the end of time. In other words, it is the dialectic within God himself—the *Deus maior* and *Deus minor*—that by its nature requires a future in which its ambivalence can be overcome, if pure positivity is to be found—at the end—in God. The existential context consists in understanding faith as a journey in history, but taking a specific way, hoping against hope, active and liberating, humble and clear-sighted at the same time. We have to move forward, then, not only because of the "not-yet" (the condition that makes the way possible) but because the "certainly not" exists and we have to build a future (the requirement to journey forward).

(a) The Future as God's Mode of Being

As a way into the subject, let us recall how European theology began to think of the futurity of God. Authors adopted three approaches, which can be called consequent futurity, pondered futurity, and critical futurity.

The chief exponent of the first, *consequent futurity,* is Pannenberg. He claims that theology has not yet thought of the future as God's mode of being, owing to the fact that, from Greek philosophy on, God has been seen in relation to the whole of reality, but seeing reality from its origin: there is a God who is "the origin of the world and of all that exists."[14] He calls this way of understanding God from the origin "mythic" and does so in a precise sense: mythic thought supposes that reality is already adequately constituted at the outset, so adopting this mode of thought has had serious consequences for Christian theology—its incapacity to think historically of Jesus' life and above all of his resurrection as an anticipatory moment and the revelation of God as the definitive end.[15]

For this reason and because Christian theology has depended on Greek modes of thought, Pannenberg concludes that "the future, as God's mode of being, has not yet been an object of reflection in theology,"[16] which for a biblical theology is not just one among many possible limitations but a serious lack, since the future is an essential element in the experience Israel had of God. The eschatologization of the reality of God culminates in Jesus, and this provides a possibility of developing a new dogmatic concept of God. From Jesus and his preaching of the future Kingdom we can think of "a God 'with *futurum* as constitution of being [*Seinsbeschaffenheit*],'"[17] and the classical attributes of the divinity—eternity, liberty, omnipotence, love—can be reinterpreted from the future. However, the ultimate truth of this conceptualization of God in the preaching of Jesus will depend on the act by God that unequivocally reveals the God of the future as creative power against death—the resurrection. The conclusion is this daring claim: "This implies, in a way, that God is still not,"[18] which is better understood when Pannenberg clarifies that "as power of the future, God is not any thing" and that God "is only in the mode in which the future exercises its power over the present."[19]

The concept that the future can be God's mode of being, or—if one prefers—viewing the transcendence-mystery of God not only from his *be-coming* in the incarnation, which is traditional and obligatory, but also from his *new-coming* in the future, has been accepted in modern theology, though with different emphases and with some criticism of Pannenberg, as we shall see next.

A second approach, which I call *pondered futurity,* is exemplified by Rahner and Schillebeeckx. Rahner, in his final period, redefines the mystery of God as the mystery of the absolute future,[20] and claims that "the content of Christian preaching consists in the open question of the absolute future and nothing more."[21] This futurity of God also operates as a criterion for verifying theology—what Rahner calls *reductio in mysterium*—and means, in the final analysis, that the mystery of God always remains a mystery.[22] However, unlike Pannenberg, Rahner does not concentrate everything in the future and in correlative hope. He claims that transcendence is also made present to us here and now in the form of a call to unconditional love of neighbor.[23]

Schillebeeckx also recognizes the primacy the future has acquired: "Instead of admitting the primacy of the past (and so of tradition) we now resolutely argue for the primacy of the future," and transcendence now acquires a special affinity with what in our temporality is called future.[24] But he asks if this unilateral conception of God, from the future, is not a new projection, which needs the past and the present to purify it: "Without this emphasis on present communion with God and on the past of Jesus, who is 'reminding' us of himself through the Spirit, it seems to me that the new 'concept of God' runs the risk of turning itself into a new mythology."[25]

Finally, there is a third approach, which might be called *critical futurity* since, while restating the importance of the future, it relativizes it as the absolute or, at least, the principal mediation of God's revelation. It does not simply complement the future with the present and the past but refers it to what there is still of the cross in present history.

Moltmann, on the one hand, sees God as "a God who has 'the future as a constituent characteristic.'"[26] This is the God of the promise who will be fulfilled in the future and is therefore the God of hope. "God acts in and within the present as future power," and this futurity of God is based on the resurrection of Jesus.[27] "All earlier statements about God taken from the history of Israel, from the law of the covenant, or from the existence of the world as such lose their force, being reduced to mere historical sayings, in comparison with this new eschatological self-definition of God as raiser of the dead."[28] On the other hand, however, Moltmann makes other claims that emphasize the present: "The question of God is posed on the ground of historical experience and in temporal concepts over and above that of his coming."[29] And above all, he stresses what I have examined: God is a crucified God and therefore is a trinitarian process that will culminate at the end of history.

Metz reaffirms that "what is human will always go on being a future" and that "Christian faith means trusting in the future as the future of the greater mystery of God."[30] But he qualifies and criticizes a one-sided concentration on the future, on the absolute eschatology "that presupposes a concept of an 'empty,' over-formal future that hardly has anything 'specifically Christian' in it any longer."[31] Therefore, according to Metz, the concept of God should not only be rethought from the future but also be reread from the *memory* of Christ, which includes not only the resurrection but also the cross. God becomes the totally other not *only* from his dimension of futurity but also from the dangerous nature of the memory of Jesus.[32]

Latin American theology also initially included the idea of God's futurity: the full manifestation of God is put back to the end of history, and hence God's futurity.[33] But from what I have already said, we can clarify this idea a little further. Seen from the totality of the Easter mystery—cross-resurrection—the reason why the manifestation of God is put back to the end of history is not only that history *cannot yet* reveal the totality, since only the end determines the process (as Pannenberg remarks in Hegelian manner), or since (to paraphrase Cullmann) in the resurrection God is *already* revealed but *not yet* in fullness, but that concentration on the futurity of God stems more radically from the cross of history remaining a massive reality even after Jesus' resurrection and from this cross being not only what rules in the short period before the parousia but also what remains as an essential element throughout history.

This means that in history cross and resurrection, word and silence, power and powerlessness, manifestation and hiding hold together and refer to one another, without any moment in God's one and only revelation having the capacity to annul another. For this reason, inherent in reality itself, and not only out of fidelity to a formal argumentation—only the end gives meaning to the process—God's self-revelation is made through a process and full revelation will come at the end, "when God will be all in all." The end is not only the ending of what is temporal as provisional; it is also a victory—"when all enemies have been vanquished"—over negative elements of history.

(b) Walking Humbly with God in History

The full revelation of God is not exhausted in the above reflections, obviously, but they may have helped to delve deeper into the mystery of God: the cross-resurrection of Jesus reaffirms his character of mystery and expresses in a completely new way what mystery is at stake. God shows himself as on the side of victims, and from there as universal God; he is revealed as active-liberator and passive-in-solidarity; and he is shown to be a God of the future, God on the way.

This is also essential for faith, since if faith is directed to this God—and not simply to any mystery—it will have to be configured by this partial, dialectical, and journeying reality. And so must faith in Jesus be. So, if the mystery of God requires journeying through history as its central element, we shall have to see not only how Jesus is the sacrament of the Father but also how he is the way to the Father and how faith in Jesus Christ takes on, in its existential reality, its *fides qua*, this double dimension of believing in Christ as the Son who makes the Father present (by bringing him down, so to speak) and who is the Way that leads (up) to the Father. (In passing, the virtually exclusive concentration on the human-divine tension in Jesus Christ has, in my opinion, put other, equally fruitful tensions in the shade—sacrament-way, as indicated above, or Messiah-crucified.) Then following Jesus will not be something added on to or required arbitrarily by an already formed faith but an element of the formation of this faith in the light of and directed to the mystery of God.

In concluding this section I should like to suggest that Christian identity can well be understood as the way of journeying in history responding and corresponding to this God. In this, I am not referring simply to the *homo viator* that all human beings are as beings-on-the-way. Still less am I encouraging a mere *stroll* through history, as a concession to the dominant relativization of the present day.

My purpose is rather to understand humanity from the God who is revealed in Jesus' pasch.

This means that responding and corresponding to the mystery of God has to take account, as a central element, of God's process and future. We have to respond and correspond here and now, but we have to understand the "now" also as having a basic orientation toward the future, as a stage in a process and on a journey. Therefore, whether we speak of the "walking humbly" of Micah or of the "following" Jesus demands, faith in God is a process that must, in my view, include the following elements: (1) hope in the resurrection, but in the presence of the crosses of history; (2) the humility to journey, without presuming to synthesize in history what can be synthesized only at the end, stressing that this is a particular humility required not only because of the littleness of creatures before their God but because of the very manifestation of God, dialectical, made up of silence and word, of action and inaction; (3) a journey in praxis—acting with justice, building the Kingdom—rather than just hope in expectation, since it is a question of God "being" all in all.

This specific journeying obviously requires that we "let God be God," with which God retains his mystery. But for many—as I have been able to illustrate from El Salvador—this course also produces joy and gives meaning to life, allows us to see that history and people give more of themselves, so that we can call this mystery *Abba*, Father. And while this happens, there will be human beings who—like Jesus—walk with God and journey toward the mystery of God. God converts them into a mystery of grace.

6. A God-Mystery: The Doxology

I began this chapter by recalling how the New Testament defines God on the basis of an eschatological action, final and insuperable in history, but I have insisted that this does not deprive the reality of God of his essential characteristic of *mystery*. In other words, the resurrection provides a novel reformulation of the mystery of the *fides quae*, while leaving us with and even augmenting the *fides qua*, the passage into mystery.

This is obvious, but I repeat it because the resurrection of Jesus could serve to smooth out what is mysterious in God, as if that had made everything clear. But this is not the case. Rahner said that mystery is not provisional in God but the reality of God insofar as he is incomprehensible and holy and that, therefore, even in the beatific vision God remains mystery.[34] He also said that, despite its numerous dogmas and innumerable moral and canonical prescriptions, Catholic theology really only says one thing: "that the mystery remains mystery for always."[35]

I should like now to examine how the resurrection not only does not reduce the mystery of God but rather increases it, and does so not only through its content, which is the eschatological reality, but also through the way intelligence works on this content.[36]

(a) Historical, Kerygmatic, and Doxological Statements

The reality of God cannot be experienced immediately, and in order to speak of it we have to mention those realities—actions, in the case of the biblical God— through which we think the reality of God is made manifest. "We speak, therefore, of God when we speak of another, but in such a way that this other appears from the point of view of his relationship with the reality of God."[37] Using language, then, we sometimes speak of historical realities in their relationship with God. But we sometimes speak of God directly.

Pannenberg call the language that, in intention, is direct language about God *doxological*. "Doxological assertions . . . tend to the eternal essence of God. They constitute a praise of the eternal on account of his works."[38] But access to these doxological formulations can be obtained only through *kerygmatic* formulations, which he describes thus: "Kerygmatic assertions express particular earthly happenings that are conceived of as events occurring by virtue of God. And in this sense of the 'works of God.'"[39]

The foundation of doxological statements does not lie in themselves, therefore, but in the realities that occasion this speech. Put in concrete terms, the passage of the Red Sea in the Old Testament is a *historical* reality (whatever the actual facts of the matter are), which, when referred to God, becomes a *kerygmatic* claim: "God freed his people from Egypt." Based on this claim as attributed to God through faith, we come to the *doxological* statement about God in himself: "God is liberating."

(b) Self-Surrender to the Mystery of God

On the same principle, the resurrection of Jesus can be described as an action that is *historical* in principle (with all the qualifications already made) in that it took place in history, as a *kerygmatic* statement in that this action is attributed to God in faith, and as a *doxological* statement in that it claims something about God in himself: God is one who raises; he is God of the victims; and so on. What concerns us here is that the step from historical to kerygmatic and then doxological statement involves not only a new formulation of the *fides quae* but also a new exercise of the *fides qua*. Pannenberg sees doxology as fundamentally adoration, in which what is characteristic of worship happens—"the surrender of the finite self to the absolute," in the Hegelian sense.[40] (Rahner, in his article on the concept of mystery, makes a somewhat convergent reflection. In the first place, he claims that human *ratio*, as a spirit of absolute transcendence, has to be conceived as the power that allows the mystery as such to be present. And in the second place, the actualization of this power comes about in an "unknowing" conscious of itself. Furthermore, and here is the similarity to "surrender," knowing reaches its full perfection only "when and insofar as the subject is more than knowing, that is: precisely free love." In the perichoresis of knowing and free love the spirit remains true to its essence and "reaches" the mystery.)

This idea is already present in negative theology, in that predicating certain attributes to God is done "in the knowledge that in God that is done in a different manner and one that is inaccessible to us."[41] But it is also present in scripture, since there any statement about God in himself is rooted in adoration. In scripture, unlike in scholasticism, "the word is rather sacrificed to God in adoration, and only contact between the one who prays and God, the experience of a new definite action by God, is capable of showing—always in a new and provisional way—what has been made of our words."[42] (For Pannenberg, unlike Hegel, the adoration expressed by doxology is not turned back to be subsumed in the concept but really means abandoning all representation: "Adoration has not been thought out sufficiently radically as long as the concept of the absolute and not the absolute itself has had the last word.")[43]

This brief analysis based on Pannenberg finds echoes in Catholic theology. Schillebeeckx also sees a transcognitive character in theological statements, since these purport "to articulate the content of a very particular act of trust in God," and he adds that theological statements are not only, nor can they be, logically true but that they should produce a doxology, since otherwise "we should . . . completely doubt their *theological* relevance."[44]

The conclusion from these reflections is that Jesus' resurrection is an action from which and from its attribution to him God is revealed in his reality-content, and because of this it is a statement of the kerygmatic kind, which can to an extent be controlled—hence the analysis of the preceding two chapters. But, through being a kerygmatic statement, it leads to a doxological statement of the reality-mystery before which all that is left is self-surrender, letting God be God. This surrender can be understood according to the cultic model or that of walking humbly, but the important thing is that God still remains a mystery.

Let me repeat what I said of God starting from Jesus of Nazareth. For Jesus, God is *Father*, but the Father is still *God*. Jesus rests in a God who is Father, but this Father *does not let him rest* because he is God. Similarly, starting from the resurrection, we can say that God is the *liberator of victims*, in whom we can trust, but this liberator is still God, to whom we must surrender.

Chapter 7

The Theological Problem (2)

The Revelation of Jesus

The resurrection of Jesus is narrated in such a way that it initiates a reflection on the nature of Jesus—not only on that of God. The resurrection does justice to the person of Jesus, confirms the truth of his life, and leads to the claim of his present fullness. In the simplest terms, all this will lead to the affirmation that Jesus *is* someone "very special," and this was to be (though obviously not in those words) the first expression of faith by his disciples and the first christological formulation. Gradually, as Christianity moved into the Greek world, the special nature of Jesus would be formulated in a specific way in the familiar terms of fullness of humanity and fullness of divinity. (If Christianity had stayed on Jewish soil, perhaps Jesus would have been confessed as the first eschatological prophet, without his nature being formulated in terms of humanity and divinity.)

This development also implied that relationship with Jesus had to be a relationship of faith, which supposes two things essential to any faith: (1) the *objective* reality of Jesus (what is believed) belongs to the sphere of the reality that, by its nature, requires faith to be approached: divinity, what ultimate reality may be; and (2) the *subjective* relationship of human beings (believers) with Jesus now includes surrender in availability and trust in his person. This faith will be expressed *theoretically* in orthodoxy and *practically* in orthopraxis, in such a way that the following of Jesus will come to be the basic element in Christian life.

Further on I shall examine how the objective reality of Jesus was considered as an object of faith, but I begin by looking into believers' faith in Jesus and his process.

1. The Origin of Faith in Jesus

Before analyzing the type of faith to which the resurrection gave rise, we need to ask whether Jesus himself, in his lifetime, gave rise to faith. The answer is important, since it helps us to know the type of faith the disciples came to have after

Easter and helps us to establish in what sense the overall cross-resurrection event (not just the resurrection) is essential to the final form of faith, that of the first Christians and our own.

(a) Theological Discussion on Pre-Easter Faith in Jesus

On the level of the text there is no denying that the New Testament tells of a change in the behavior of the disciples after the resurrection, although there is debate as to whether, historically, the change was as dramatic as the texts relate: from paralyzing fear, flight, and abandonment of faith to courage, strength, and faith. So we need to establish the continuity or discontinuity—and degree of each—of faith in Jesus before and after the Easter event. I propose to illustrate the discussion by reference to Schillebeeckx and Kessler.

Schillebeeckx polemically argues that there was a greater continuity than is usually accepted between before Easter and after Easter.[1] Although the disciples in fact abandoned and denied Jesus during the passion, this was more a failure in practice than a loss of faith. In support he cites Luke 22:31f.: "'Simon, Simon, listen! Satan has demanded to sift all of you like wheat, but I have prayed for you that your own faith may not fail; and you, when once you have turned back, strengthen your brothers.' And he said to him, 'Lord, I am ready to go with you to prison and to death.'" To this he adds the fact that Peter had already confessed Jesus, during his lifetime, to be an eschatological prophet and the Messiah (see Mk 8:29). So, while the disciples did deny and abandon Jesus, they did so out of cowardice, and it would not be right to speak of a (radical) loss of faith in Jesus.

This leads Schillebeeckx to argue also that the New Testament exaggerates in its presentation of the fear and disunity of the disciples during the passion. He believes this to be Mark's *theological* thesis, that "the disciples understood nothing of Jesus," but that this is not necessarily a *historical* argument, since even pre-Markan traditions seem to contradict this view. In any case, "for Luke there is no apostasy by the disciples: the passion and death of Jesus do not here establish a break in the faith of the disciples before and after Easter."[2]

This analysis backs up Schillebeeckx's thesis on the appearances: these are not the (only) cause of new faith in Jesus, and what happened after Easter would have been a "conversion" experience. (Here his view converges with J. L. Segundo: "The same transformation that worked in the disciples, despite its sudden and radical nature, if that can be taken at face value, can perfectly well be explained by their reaching a higher degree of faith in Jesus of Nazareth, dead on the cross.")[3] Peter, who had denied Jesus, was the first disciple to achieve conversion, according to Luke 22:32. Having earlier recognized Jesus as a messianic and eschatological prophet, he would have returned to following him and after his conversion taken the initiative in bringing the disciples together once more. Schillebeeckx, then, admits the new situation brought about by the resurrection, but as new experiences of faith after Jesus' death, experiences of his new presence. (Rudolf Pesch takes this argument further: the appearances are not the cause of faith in Jesus, which indirectly supposes that there must have been faith in him during his lifetime. So the genesis of faith in Jesus "lies, then in Jesus himself, in the faith he himself inspired." As proof, he adduces (1) Luke 22:31f., referring at least to Peter and perhaps to all the disciples; (2) Mark 8:27–30: proof of faith in Jesus as Messiah; (3) the disciples had resolved the debate over Jesus as Messiah before Easter; (4) Jesus had told them of the saving significance of his death and the possibility of overcoming his death before Easter.)[4]

Kessler, on the other hand, upholds the thesis of discontinuity.[5] The argument that the disciples kept their faith throughout runs counter to the general line of the New Testament testimonies. These all point to the cross as a break that marks a discontinuity, and nothing justifies holding that the debate on Jesus' messiahship had been definitively resolved before Easter. With regard to the historical sequence of events, shortly after Jesus' death, the disciples, who had fled into Galilee, soon and surprisingly reappeared in Jerusalem. There, and not in the safety of Galilee, they came together to form the first community.[6] Their going to Galilee expressed disillusionment with Jesus' mission, personal fear, and the end of what might have been "faith" in Jesus during his lifetime. The return to Jerusalem meant, by contrast, courage and enthusiasm for a new mission, following Jesus with all that entailed, and "faith" in him with astonishing creativity in its christological formulation. Furthermore, by the mere fact of returning to Jerusalem, they were expressing the rebirth of ultimate eschatological hope.

Besides this programmatic argumentation, Kessler objects that Schillebeeckx's exegetical base consists of a single text, Luke 22:31ff., and that this text comes from a tradition that cannot be used to support Schillebeeckx's claim, since the object of that tradition was to distinguish the honorific name of Cephas, not to prove that there was pre-Easter faith—a problem it does not tackle, since this tradition ignores Peter's denial. The Easter experience is not, then, fundamentally a conversion experience but something deeper.

(b) Faith in Jesus before Easter

Whether the cross was an absolute failure for faith (Kessler) or a relative one (Schillebeeckx) is important for discovering whether post-Easter faith depends wholly or only partly on Jesus' resurrection and to what extent, but it is also important for understanding the content of this faith and the origin of christology, which is what concerns us here.

On the one hand, there can be no doubt that in his lifetime Jesus had disciples who followed him honorably in hope and with dedication, that he provoked excitement and even enthusiasm, so that one can say that during his life Jesus seemed to them someone *special* to whose values they adhered—what Segundo rightly calls an anthropological faith in Jesus "radically united to his values."[7] On the other hand, there is no denying that the cross wiped out or at least weakened their faith. If this is so, post-Easter faith has some continuity with pre-Easter faith (the risen Christ is none other than Jesus of Nazareth), but the cross-resurrection questions and radicalizes this "first" faith while also adding new essential elements to it. Let us look at the first point, that of continuity.

(i) Formulations of faith during Jesus' life? To begin with *literary analysis*: in the synoptics there are only two texts in which the disciples make a *confession of*

faith in Jesus in the strict sense. In Matthew 16:16 Peter confesses him as "the Christ, the Son of the living God." In Matthew 13:33 the same Peter, after Jesus has walked on the waters, confesses, "Truly you are the Son of God." But these words do not seem to be historical, since in Mark the parallel to the first text does not mention the "Son of God" (besides showing a completely erroneous conception by Peter of what is really meant by being Christ [cf. Mt 16:22–23]) and Jesus himself forbids them to talk about it (the "messianic secret" of Mark 8:30). Mark's intention, then, would not be to show a faith in Jesus already in place before the resurrection but to provide grounds for a promise to Peter, whose faith as described corresponds not to the historical situation but to his later full faith. With regard to the second text, the parallel in Mark 6:49 makes no mention of this confession of faith but rather stresses the disciples' fear when they thought they had seen a ghost.[8]

Does this mean that the disciples saw nothing special in Jesus before Easter? Certainly not. The gospels attest to the fact that, even from what can be verified historically and without taking account of what they add to explain the disciples' faith after Easter, Jesus did and said things that must have drawn attention to his actual person, things that by their nature required them to decide about him.

In general terms it can be said that the disciples adhered to Jesus' cause and values and that they may even have regarded him as the Messiah they were waiting for. But if we want to analyze more rigorously if they had faith and what sort of faith, then we have to adopt some kind of *systematic viewpoint* on what we understand by faith. Here I define faith as trust and openness-availability to something that is held to be ultimate reality (*JL*, pp. 154–57). So I propose to list the gospel data as they present the ultimateness of Jesus, relating this to Jesus himself as the "ultimate." For methodological reasons I distinguish the relationship of ultimateness of Jesus to the *Kingdom* of God and to the *God* of the Kingdom.

(ii) The relationship of ultimateness of Jesus to the Kingdom of God. Where his relationship to the Kingdom of God is concerned, Jesus is presented in such a way that in his words and in his deeds he appears in a special relationship to it and its demands.

1. Jesus has the audacity to preach not only the coming of the Kingdom, but the *closeness* and the *certainty* of this coming—even if the beginning of the Kingdom is as small as a grain of mustard (see Mk 4:30ff.). Unlike the apocalyptics, then, Jesus does not proclaim salvation only for the future but claims that it is already arriving (see Mk 1:15), although in the end he was to change or qualify his vision in the apocalyptic discourse (Mk 13).[9] Furthermore, he dares to claim that the Kingdom has already come because he casts out devils (see Lk 11:20). These words and some of the signs he uses to express the presence of the Kingdom—meals with publicans and acceptance of sinners—are so scandalous that they had to lead to questions about who Jesus was, both by those who were for him and those against him.[10]

2. His scandalous freedom before the law, especially that governing the Sabbath (see Mk 2:31–33; 6; Jn 5:1–9; 9:1–16), before temple worship and its prescriptions, and before the traditions of the ancestors (see Mk 7:1–13f.),[11] coupled

with, on the other hand, his insistence on the *new* law of love (see Jn 13:34–35), on which he makes everything depend, in inner attitudes rather than outward keeping of the commandments—see the Sermon on the Mount—had to cause a great stir and, again, provoke questions about who this person could be.

3. His manner of speaking with authority, as people recognized (see Mk 1:27),[12] his counterpoint of "you have heard, but I say to you" (Mt 5:21f., 27f., 31f., 33f., 38f., 43f.),[13] his comparison with Moses (with the claim to interpret the law in a more authentic manner than he, as in Mark 10:4ff. with regard to marriage) make him out to be superior to all the major figures of the Old Testament and even to the Temple (see Mk 12:6).[14] The use he makes of the expression "amen, amen," "in truth, in truth I say to you . . . ," is also very particular.[15] As we know, in prophetic preaching this is used as a formula of legitimation—"Thus says the Lord"—and in prayer or in the discourses it is a desiderative formula to express "so be it." Jesus, on the other hand, does not use it to legitimate or to express a wish that things may be so. He rather begins with the formula "In truth, in truth I say to you" and does so to claim that "they are so."

4. Jesus also claims that eschatological salvation is decided by the attitude taken to him. In Mark 8:38, the oldest tradition, Jesus states that "those who are ashamed of me and of my words in this adulterous and sinful generation, of them the Son of Man will also be ashamed when he comes in the glory of his Father with the holy angels." In this passage Jesus does not identity himself with the Son of Man (as he does in Mark 10:32f., while Luke 12:8f. keeps the distinction), but he is bold enough to make salvation depend on how people react to him.[16]

5. Finally, Jesus demands radical following without giving any justification for this beyond the call itself. The phenomenon of following was not unusual in Jesus' time, since rabbis had disciples and envoys, and the Zealots—though they probably did not exist as an organized group until after Jesus (*JL*, p. 284 n.22)— were to demand total dedication to their cause, to the point of sacrificing one's life, so that the famous saying "take up your cross" may well have originated in such movements, since this was the fate of their adherents.[17] What is new with Jesus is that he demands following of the most radical kind, involving leaving everything unconditionally (see Lk 9:57–62) for the mere fact of having been called by Jesus and being united to the person of Jesus, not just to his cause, as illustrated at the outset of his mission. The logic of following is made to depend not only on the cause to which disciples are called—which would make follow-ing something logical in itself—but also on his person. Unlike the rabbis, Jesus does not organize following around the law, but around the Kingdom and his person. This is why it is he who "calls" disciples, not they who elect him—which implies a relationship that expresses some sort of faith.[18]

The conclusion is that Jesus is presented in such a way that he could really appear as someone "very special" in relation to what was the ultimate for him and for his audience: the Kingdom of God. In this way, the ultimate is seen to be intimately related to him. If methodologically in *JL* (pp. 67ff.) I began examining Jesus' mission and faith by setting him within the current of those who expressed hope of the Kingdom; if, that is, I looked at Jesus from the Kingdom, we now need to see that—according to the New Testament itself—the Kingdom also has to be seen from Jesus.

This is the objective reason that might give rise to a question about Jesus that could be called a "faith" question: the relationship of Jesus to what is ultimate about the Kingdom. Jesus himself provided the grounds for this, though without definitely saying what the Kingdom was or when it would come. But, as Rahner notes, "The pre-paschal Jesus is convinced that the new proximity of the Kingdom is begun *by means of* the proclamation he makes of this proximity."[19]

(iii) The relationship of ultimateness of Jesus to the Father. Touching on Jesus' *relationship with God,* the gospels bear witness to his total trust in the Father and his total availability to God. This is a relationship described in terms that differ from those used of other people's relationship to God. I examined this relationship in *JL* (pp. 135-59) and so merely recall the basics here.

1. Jesus does not address God only as Father but does so using the term *Abba,* which expresses an unheard-of closeness and intimacy, since it is the language of childhood. His contemporaries would have found it "inconceivable to address God with such a familiar term."[20] His use of *Abba* is, however, one of the most certain things about him historically, which means that his understanding of his relationship with God was really novel.

2. In the synoptics, when he addresses God, Jesus makes an important distinction. When he himself addresses God he calls him *Abba, my* Father, but at other times he speaks of "*your* Father." He makes, then, a distinction between "my Father" and "your Father" (Mk 11:25; Mt 5:48; Mt 6:32). The expression "*our* Father"—which would place Jesus together with others—appears only in Matthew 6:9 (the parallel in Luke 11:2 saying simply "Father"), when Jesus responds to the disciples' request to teach them how to pray with the "*Our* Father," although the *our* includes all the disciples but not him. The language shows his consciousness of a "special" relationship with God, which his audience grasped. This is obvious in John 10:30 and 38: "The Father and I are one . . . the Father is in me and I am in the Father," and also in Matthew's *logion*: "No one knows the Son except the Father, and no one knows the Father except the Son" (Mt 11:27; Lk 10:22). It is not clear whether these are authentic words of Jesus or not. Their authenticity has been denied from Strauss on, but now some exegetes (Jeremias, van Iersel) defend it.

Taking Jesus' special relationship with God and his special relationship with the Kingdom of God together, it is reasonable to suggest that the question of who Jesus is and the answer to this will include his being related in a very special way to ultimate reality and that, therefore, the disciples had to relate to him in a way different from how they related to other people. This would also, logically, explain the possibility that Jesus could have been suspected of blaspheming.

(c) A Systematic Reflection on Faith in Jesus before Easter

I am not competent to settle the exegetical questions implied in what has been stated above and in the debate between Schillebeeckx and Kessler, though I have to say that the latter's exegetical argumentation strikes me as more convincing. I should instead like to put forward some reflections of a systematic nature that may help us to understand better what post-Easter faith was compared to pre-Easter and so also to understand the development of christology. In the form of a thesis, the resurrection adds (can and has to add, if it is an eschatological event) something decisive to the faith held before Easter, to what we might call "first" faith. And it adds two things. The first, obviously, is *definiteness.* The other, and perhaps the more important, is having to *integrate the reality of the cross* into this new faith, this "second" faith. And having to integrate the cross means accepting that evil affects it ultimately, divinely. Let us examine this.

During his lifetime Jesus aroused expectations, hopes, and enthusiasm and could consequently provoke the question of who he was. His followers could see him as someone *very special* and could very well even have identified him as the awaited Messiah—whatever Jesus' own view on this. And if I may be allowed an *a priori* reflection, this possibility has to be stated, since if the disciples had before their eyes someone who *in reality* was a true object of faith, it would be a *contradictio in obliquo* for this not to have generated the question of who he was and not to generated any kind of faith. In other words, if God was in Jesus in a privileged form ("substantial," the dogma was to declare), it would be a contradiction for this not to be noticeable in any way. Or again, if the disciples had not been witnesses to something *special* in Jesus' relationship to God and the Kingdom, there would have been no reason for the resurrection to provoke faith in Christ or christology; it could, hypothetically, have been understood as a miraculous portent and nothing more. But the fact that it did provoke both faith in Christ and christology shows that *already* in Jesus' lifetime the disciples saw something special in him.

Even when this is the case, two questions remain to be answered. The first is what *believing in* Jesus could have meant during his lifetime, even when the disciples might have accepted him also as the Messiah. And the second is what role the cross—not just the resurrection—plays in later faith.

Believing in Jesus could have meant accepting his messiahship in some way, more or less completely *(fides quae)* and making his utopia, his values, and his manner of acting one's own *(fides qua)*. But that *such* a faith had a theologal dimension, that it included, that is, a relationship of ultimateness with Jesus, does not emerge clearly from his life. In simple terms, it was one thing for the disciples to have come to the conclusion that Jesus really was the Messiah, for example, and quite another for their relationship with Jesus to be one of ultimateness in principle.

If we go back to the distinction between God's *mediation* (the Kingdom) and *mediator* (Jesus), during Jesus' life, the disciples' faith would show in their accepting the values of the mediation and serving the Kingdom more than in accepting the ultimateness of the person of the mediator, which was subordinated to the ultimate that is God. The possible *faith* of the disciples would then be reflected in their total surrender to and trust in the Kingdom. This does not prevent one from speaking of faith before the resurrection, but it does qualify it. Even if they thought of Jesus as the Messiah, they would mean by this rather the closeness of the Kingdom than the unrepeatable and ultimate reality of Jesus' person.

We also need to ask ourselves if the cross was one more event in the life of that Jesus who—as a hypothesis—was believed to be the Messiah, or whether it was an event that—not only because it came at the end of Jesus' life but *because it was the cross*—determined the first faith. It is evident, if tautological, that before the cross, faith in Jesus, as *fides qua*, could not have the dimension of total surrender, since the totality of Jesus had not been manifested. Neither his possible messianism nor what the Kingdom of God is, as the content of *fides quae*, could include the cross, let alone the theologal dimension of that cross—the cross of the Son of God—although it could have been thought of as a necessary sacrifice for the advancement of the Kingdom. (In revolutionary movements there always comes the moment of determining what to do with the cross. Normally, people seek to find some continuity with the cause, so that the cross is understood as *necessary*—the price to be paid for liberation—and as *positive*—the mystique it generates [or can generate] in those who come after. But there is always still a problem in how really to recover those who have fallen.)

Nevertheless, for a theologal faith that would introduce Jesus into the mystery of God, the integration of the cross in that faith is not something optional, or obvious, since it means introducing it into the very God. In other words, it is possible to speak of the conversion experience of the disciples after Easter as "let us go back to Jesus' cause" (Schillebeeckx). But what happened after Easter was not simply a *recovery* of faith in Jesus, a faith that had been threatened to a greater or lesser degree by the cross, but *creation* of a new faith, of which Jesus was the central focus, but which now included the theologal scandal of the cross. This second faith rescues the first, but qualitatively it goes further.

The cross, then, is not just a subjective trial that the disciples have to *pass through* in order to recover the truth of Jesus; it is an objective—scandalous—fact, which has to be *integrated* into any earlier faith, even while it calls it into question. The scene of the disciples at Emmaus, for all its beauty, can also be read as a dangerous attempt to turn back to the past ("what was written in the scriptures") and not to begin to ponder the mystery of God in a new way—to see it, that is, also from the cross. (In the account itself, however, this danger is mitigated, since it is not said where and how the cross was foretold, but merely that this was God's plan. So the account refers the cross back to the mystery of God.)

All this means that it is possible to speak of *faith* in Jesus during his lifetime, but that before Easter the *theologal* aspect of this faith was not yet focused on him but on God and on a *messianic* God, one might say. Before the cross, faith in Jesus might have meant that what the disciples already hoped for was coming to pass in him (although they would have had to accept some modifications to their expectations). While Jesus was ushering in the awaited Kingdom of God, the disciples had some means of "controlling" who Jesus was and the truth about him; this meant that they could even accept him as the Messiah. So it was faith in what was already known in principle, not in what was revealed. But this faith lacked—by definition—openness to God's plan (his Kingdom) and God's envoy (Jesus) being different from what they had thought: *this faith lacked radical letting God be God.* In comparison with this, accepting Jesus' demands, though painful, was not all that radical, nor can it be used as an argument to show the depth of the disciples' faith, because for faith, the greatest test, the most radical and theologal, is that of letting God be God. This is why it does not seem to me correct to speak of the disciples having faith (with all that entails) before the cross-resurrection (and why Mark's stress on "not understanding" is a better pointer to the problem of faith than Luke's tendency to panegyric about the disciples, explicable because he is thinking more in terms of ecclesiology).

All the foregoing can be summed up as follows: the disciples' first faith during Jesus' lifetime *lacked being put to and passing the test*, which seems to me inherent in any biblical faith and not something believers can either experience or not. (In the New Testament John speaks of faith as a victory—see 1 John 5:4, with its parallel christological objective—that is, as what comes about after a struggle. But also in the Old Testament faith appears as what comes about from going through a trial, whether it is the faith of Abraham, of Jeremiah, of Job, or still others.) After the resurrection, when a specific faith in Christ had been generated, believers came to recognize that it was essential to their faith for them to recognize just what brought about the crisis—the fact that Jesus of Nazareth failed, suffered, and was sentenced. So the fact that after the resurrection the disciples turned back to the crucified Jesus and had the audacity to recount his life just as it was is also, among other things, their way of saying that this life had been the trial of their faith, that they had in some way failed when faced with it, but that now they are incorporating it as something special. Recognizing the risen Christ in the crucified Jesus was their way of expressing that their faith had emerged victorious from the crisis.

To finish this section, this may be the place for a systematic examination of the relationship Paul established between faith and Jesus' resurrection in these well-known words: "If Christ has not been raised . . . your faith is in vain" (1 Cor 15:14). Let me repeat that, even without any experience of resurrection, it would have been possible for the disciples to have some sort of faith in Jesus, since accepting that Jesus' life and work are the true life and the way to follow would already have supposed some kind of faith. As J. L. Segundo has written: "The resurrection was not an indispensable requirement for faith, or even for *religious* faith, in Jesus of Nazareth. There is a reason why the prologue to John's Gospel makes no mention of the resurrection: 'having seen his glory' is placed, for the evangelist, in pre-Easter episodes and culminates on the cross."[21] In other words, the disciples could have accepted in faith, even without the resurrection, that God was present in Jesus as he had been in other personages of the Old Testament. The question is not, then, whether the resurrection was absolutely necessary for the disciples to have any kind of faith in Jesus. The question is what the resurrection brings to faith and how it molds it in a way distinct from the faith that existed in the Old Testament and the faith in Jesus that might have existed before his death, whether the resurrection of Jesus happened as an eschatological event. And this is as relevant to the *fides quae* as it is to the *fides qua*.

With respect to the *fides quae*, if Jesus had died just like every other human being and if there had been no experience of resurrection, faith in Jesus would probably not have led to consideration of his unrepeatable relationship with God—which later led to the trinitarian formulation of the reality of God—or to consideration of how God was affected by the cross, the forces of evil. And with respect to the *fides qua* without experience of the resurrection, it is difficult to think that there would have been such conviction and self-surrender on the part of Christians—often to death itself—not only for Jesus' cause but for his person.

2. Faith in Jesus after Easter

Having examined faith before Easter, let us now turn to how the witnesses to the risen Christ began to express faith in Jesus and so to how the process of christology began. This came about in two different ways. One, that most discussed in christologies, is the *theoretical* way, the way of reflection on Jesus. Another, rarely mentioned though presupposed, is the *practical* way, how the first Christians confessed with their lives that the risen Christ made a radical and definitive "difference." This is the way of *orthopraxis*, and I propose to consider it first.

(a) The Practical Way

Faith in Jesus was expressed radically, above all, before Christians became clear theoretically about the reality of Jesus, during his life. The *ultimateness* of Jesus was confessed with the *ultimateness* of his life.

1. This appears in varying forms in the New Testament. According to Paul, we need to be of the same mind as Christ (cf. Phil 2:5); John gives pride of place to love for others, adding that Jesus has set us an example (Jn 13:15); the letter to the Hebrews exhorts us to remain steadfast by keeping our eyes fixed on him (12:2). What is at stake here is not so much the content as the seriousness: we have to be like this because Jesus was like this. There will be other motivations: reward, the coming parousia, the credibility it gives to the apostolate, and so on—and the example of Jesus is proposed also for courage during trials. The basic reason, however, the one on which all the others depend, is that "Jesus was like this." As Paul puts it, we have to live and die "in the Lord."

In the synoptics, the requirement to *configure one's own life* in accordance with that of Jesus emerges from the call to follow him. "Follow me" is Jesus' first and last word to Peter, as Bonhoeffer recalls.[22] This following soon became the central factor in the lives of the early communities. To gain a better notion of its importance, this is what it meant before the resurrection:

> Jesus never called the whole people to "follow him," but always and only select individuals, making them his disciples. . . . Following here means, in the first place, the unlimited communion in destiny that, following the Master, does not fear either privation or suffering. . . . The harshness of Jesus' demand of the person called by him can be explained only by his destiny of service to the Kingdom. This service had to be given in the same way as Jesus carried out his.[23]

While the "preacher" was not yet the "preached," "following" and "believing" were not identified with one another. After the resurrection, however, tradition

made the two come together: following and believing, being a disciple and belonging to the church, although the change is already insinuated in the different
strata of the synoptics and the addressees of the call become steadily more diverse. The key text, "If any want to become my followers, let them deny themselves and take up their cross and follow me," in Matthew 15:24–28 is addressed
to the disciples, while Mark 8:34 is addressed to "the crowd with his disciples,"
and in Luke 14:28–33 "none of you can become my disciple if you do not give up
all your possessions." As Schnackenburg has commented, "As these sentences
have been handed down, the boundaries between the demands made of the disciples and those made of the people in general have been confused."[24] What matters is the conclusion to be drawn: "Following and discipleship began to be the
absolute expression of Christian life in the post-paschal community, enduring in
the idea that all believers were placed at the same time in the service of the Christ
of God."[25] This explains the fact, without precedents in other religious movements, that the communities were openly missionary and they accepted any form
of suffering on account of this. The communities understood that their existence
was composed of following Jesus, going, so to speak, beyond what Jesus demanded.

2. Confessing Jesus through one's life is the most radical form of stating the
absolute character of Jesus. But this is radicalized even further through one's
death. Life is something given up only for what is held to be ultimate. Now the
New Testament testifies that in the life of the communities Christians had to be
ready to give up their lives for Jesus and that they effectively did so. There were
various reasons for persecution of the early church, but the basic one was its
fidelity to a certain type of life enjoined by Jesus and, sometimes, simply fidelity
to the *name* of Jesus.[26] However much it is idealized in the early chapters of Acts,
the courage of the first preachers shows their readiness for persecution and their
joy at being found worthy to "suffer dishonor for the sake of the name" (Acts
5:41). The martyrdom of Stephen and those who followed shows their readiness
to give their lives for Jesus. Confessing that there is only one Lord was, then, far
more than orthodoxy.

3. Together with this basic attitude, the New Testament describes practices
and attitudes that were required because Jesus required them (or, at least, because
this is what the first Christians thought). Such were the change from old forms of
worship (abandonment of sacrifices in the Temple), the regulation of marriage,
the possibility of celibacy, the extension of forgiveness to one's enemies, and the
like. These norms were upheld because they were what Jesus had said and done.

4. To this one should add that the first communities also "put the risen Christ
into action" (to paraphrase Gustavo Gutiérrez's "God must be contemplated and
put into action"). Experience of the risen Christ became not only possibility of
theoretical knowledge of who he was but also that of remaking his reality. This
experience, as already indicated, often took the form of a meal, and so meals in all
their dimensions—eucharistic suppers, communion in fellowship—and with their
consequences—possessing everything in common—became practices that in themselves already expressed faith in the risen Lord. (In the summaries made in Acts
of the life of the community—2:42–47; 4:32–35; 5:12–16—the central element

is the communion of life, which is expressed on all levels. Christians now have to be of one heart and mind, from which follows real sharing with the essential dimension that "no one should suffer want." And the meal with Jesus—the eucharist—provided the context for celebrating the coming of the Kingdom.)[27]

From these reflections we can draw the following conclusion: whatever the theoretical understanding of the first Christians, whether they called Jesus Son of Man or prophet, in actual life they were already bearing witness to the fact that for them Jesus was something unique, ultimate, and radical. This shows that there was faith in practice, which was accompanied by formulations of faith. The theoretical conceptualization of this primarily *practical* faith was later brought together above all in the title Lord: we have to live and die in the Lord, formed by him.

Let me say that this simple reflection is still decisive in Latin American faith (and christology). Many Christian men and women, independent of formulations, have said by their lives and deaths that they see something ultimate in Jesus. This is the equivalent *in practice* to what is confessed *by orthodoxy*, and the former is the origin and foundation of the latter, not the other way round. Practice, following, is what above all expresses that Jesus of Nazareth, crucified and raised, "makes a difference," that human beings "opt" for him when they have "caught" his enthusiasm and form themselves into a "people." They later put into words this experience that underlies theoretical christology, which they were to develop over the course of history, in accordance with the way God's revelation teaches us "to learn to learn."

(b) The Theoretical Way: The Origin of Christology

Alongside the practical way, the first Christians—of necessity—developed a theoretical way for expressing who this crucified and raised Jesus is, and what his relationship to the ultimate reality, God, is. So reflections arose, culminating in theoretical christology. This is the process of the *fides quae.*

I should like briefly to examine what the origin of this reflection was, what direction the first christology took, what interests prompted it, if and how it took up what was fundamental to Jesus and his proclamation of the Kingdom. The importance of this analysis consists in that, unlike what was to happen over the passage of time, we are here looking at something original and unrepeatable, "rooted in the contingent event of Jesus' actions, of his death and of his appearances once risen,"[28] as it was to be summed up in the early confession of faith in Romans 1:3ff. And this means two things. The first is that even after the resurrection, christology returned (and will always have to return) to Jesus; the second— the apologetic reflection, as it were—that the phenomenon of the appearance of Christianity as a whole cannot be explained only by analogy with other religious phenomena, since the crucified Jesus breaks all possible analogies.

(i) Early coming or exaltation? Between the years 40 and 50 the basic kernel of christology had already been completed: the one who was crucified was Son of God.[29] The question is how this conclusion was reached and what the starting point of the reflection was.

In order to establish what appears to be the original christology we have to take account of the earliest Judeo-Palestinian *texts* written in Aramaic, as they have come down in the first discourses in Acts (the exaltation) and certainly in the *maranatha*, as well as the *religious situation of the community*, which was living in intense eschatological expectation: "In the earliest period of the Aramaic-speaking Palestinian communities, the principal concern was focused on the future, within a high eschatological tension."[30] In short, the first reflection could have contained two elements: expectation of Christ's coming in the future and exaltation of him in the present, elements that are not mutually exclusive but which express different emphases.

One line of interpretation, looking to the present, claims that God has justified Jesus, that his life has been sanctioned as the true life. Jesus lives now in God and not only lives but has been exalted by God, which brings about a basic shift in reality. As in the *Magnificat*, the one who was humbled has been raised high. The eschatological time of salvation is now present, and the community is certain of this from the outpouring of the Spirit. According to this line, then, the earliest christology is that of *exaltation*.

Another line of interpretation, looking to the future, stresses that the community was at the highest point of its expectation of the parousia, for which it did not need an idea of exaltation or an intermediate time of Jesus glorified. Jesus has been taken up and will be constituted as Messiah in the sense of Son of Man in his imminent second coming. He will then exercise his true function of judging, which the Judeo-Christian community already attributed to him by calling him *Kyrios*. According to this line, the oldest christology is that of the Christ who is to come. The specific novelty of Christ would then consist in that in his second coming he will take on the functions of judge and congregator of the people of Israel.

"The one who is to come." Looking back on Jesus' life, it is quite probable that the first Christians should have thought—as later in fact happened—that Jesus was the just man, the prophet, the servant, as these figures appear in the Old Testament, and that they may well have designated the risen Christ as the just man raised up and the eschatological prophet.[31] Nevertheless, reflection on Jesus actually began in a different way. From very early on, texts appeared that related Jesus to the future. In Acts 3:20 there is the hope expressed that God "may send the Messiah appointed for you . . . who must remain in heaven until the time of universal restoration." And 1 Corinthians 16:22 exclaims, "Our Lord, come!"— *maranatha* (or "The Lord has come"—*maran atha*), an expression that was left in Aramaic in the liturgy and with which the New Testament also ends (Rv 22:20). This invocation is a daring theological creation, since it at one and the same time refers to Jesus as holding the Lordship and asks for his early saving coming as Lord. Both texts point christology toward the future, so that the risen Christ began to be identified with the one who is to come.

Expectation of a mediator figure who will appear at the end of time was present in the Old Testament in the figure of the Son of Man, and perhaps the first Christians were thinking of this when they spoke of Jesus as "the one who is to come." In any case, late Judaism could refer in these terms to a mediator who was to appear at the end of time. This mediator was thought of both as an individual and as a collective, but what is significant are the specific characteristics that describe him: he is the one who holds dominion over all the people of the Most High (Israel), with power over not only individuals but history itself (cf. Dn 7:26f.). This is why the term Son of Man could be used to formulate the future judgment and also the expectation of salvation.

In chapter 12 I shall examine in detail what is meant by Son of Man, but for the moment suffice it to say that the primitive community clung to eschatological hope and related the risen Christ to the one who is to come. Whether Jesus is seen as the one who is to come at the time of the universal restoration, or whether he is described in terms of the Son of Man who will come to judge and summon Israel together, the main fact is that the earliest christology related what was *special* about Jesus to what was to happen in the future, when the salvation of Israel is decided.

The exalted one. Understanding Jesus as "the one who is to come" was the means of expressing his special relationship with God, approached from the future. The experience of the resurrection, however, forced the disciples to reflect on his reality already in the present. This they expressed with the title Lord, *Kyrios*, although at the beginning they were content with the concepts of "exaltation," "enthronement," "being seated at the right hand of the Father."

To reach this theologization, the early Christians had two points of support. One was the indisputable fact of the inscription over the cross, which proclaimed Jesus king of the Jews, so Messiah. The other, more theological, was the text from Psalm 110 in which God tells the Messiah, "sit at my right hand." With this conceptualization they could express that Jesus had been singled out from all other human beings, and that this singling out consisted in his God raising him up and enthroning him, conferring dignity and power on him.

This appears in the first discourses in Acts, which take up an ancient tradition. Here it is said that God has exalted Jesus at his right hand and has poured out his Spirit (2:32ff.), which is backed up by the quote from Psalm 110:1. This places Jesus above David and makes him the true Messiah: "Therefore let the entire house of Israel know with certainty that God has made him both Lord and Messiah, this Jesus whom you crucified" (v. 36). The discourse in Acts 5:31 takes a step further and adds the soteriological dimension: "God exalted him at his right hand as Leader and Savior that he might give repentance to Israel and forgiveness of sins." Finally, in Acts 13:33, Psalm 2:7 is applied to Jesus: "You are my son; today I have begotten you." The psalm was understood messianically, and therefore applying it to Jesus was to name him as Messiah.

Though using different terminology, therefore, from very early times a christological line developed that claimed that, because he had been raised by God, Jesus has been exalted, shares in the dignity and power of God, and is, therefore, the true Messiah. His special relationship with God is also seen here in functional form. But it has to be stressed that in the texts of Acts it is not just anyone who has been exalted but the Jesus who went about doing good and died as a victim. Exaltation has to be understood also as confirmation of the true life, that of Jesus. And it should be understood as subversion of reality, as victory over the covering up of reality: the victim is proved right, not the executioner; God places himself—as in the *Magnificat*—on the side of the victim, not of the executioner.

(ii) Truth and salvation. Exegetes discuss whether both elements, exaltation and early coming, are or are not mutually exclusive. According to some, although the text of Acts 3:20 suggests that Jesus was caught up into heaven and will not show himself until his return—parousia without exaltation, as the ascension is described in Acts 1:11—it is highly probable that the idea of exaltation should also have appeared from the beginning as a consequence of the resurrection.[32] And with regard to the text of 1 Corinthians 16:22, in which the early *saving* coming of Jesus is prayed for, the Lord's supper, in which the expression was used, means that it has not only a sense of eschatological hope but also one of presence of and union with the Lord (Acts 2:46). Expectation of the parousia and exaltation would then be mutually related. According to others,[33] at the beginning there was only expectation of the parousia and not conviction of exaltation, although some communities—as would seem to have been the case in Corinth—not only accepted but focused on the Lord as the exalted one, without yet awaiting the parousia.

At the beginning there could already have been a variety of christologies, and from these beginnings the different schools emerged, some more "conceptual," based on the titles, as we shall see, others more "narrative," the gospels. From consideration of the future of Jesus as "the one who is to come," together with reflection on his present as "the one who has been exalted," there was a move to confess the reality of Jesus during his life and even before it, from everlasting. But perhaps we can already draw some major conclusions.

The resurrection led Christians to think deeply about three things. One was truth: Jesus' life had been the true life; being human consists in living like Jesus. The second was exaltation: this truth was not made clear in any form but through the inversion worked by the resurrection—the defamed one is the true one, the failure is victorious, the criminal is justified, the crucified Jesus is the risen Christ. Exaltation does not start from a clean slate: the one who was previously humbled to the extreme is exalted. And this exaltation does not appear as an *arbitrary* prize God bestows on Jesus but as the manifestation of the truth of Jesus' life. The third is hope. Jesus becomes the symbol of the possibility of salvation, both already in the present and in the future when he will come again at the end of time. His life and his destiny are not only his but overflow in the direction of others: there is salvation.

PART II

CHRISTOLOGICAL TITLES IN THE NEW TESTAMENT

A Rereading from Latin America

Chapter 8

The Titles and Their Problems

In the previous chapter we looked at the existential and theoretical origin of reflection on Jesus. This developed along differing lines, so that several christologies came to coexist. Before presenting these, I should like to begin with a brief analysis of the dynamism of faith in Jesus: that is, where the initial faith led and for what reasons. I will set this out in logical steps, conscious of the fact that chronologically the process was far more complex.

1. Dynamism in the Act of Christological Faith

In the first place, the disciples after the resurrection had a new faith that had passed the test of the crisis (the cross) and had seen itself confronted with confirmation by God (the resurrection). These events led, historically inevitably, to the question of who Jesus was. They had such potential that the christological response was bound to be *radical*, and so after Easter faith in Jesus was not only a *renewed* but a *new* faith. Not only was Jesus recognized, but cognizance of him reached its fullness—and an ever greater fullness (cf. Jn 16:13). Furthermore, because the cross and resurrection were events that took place in different and even contrary spheres of reality, holding them together could only be done dialectically (which happened very soon, as seen in Romans 4:25). The fact that a current of christological reflection existed was due, then, to the content of the object driving it and not only to the (Aristotelian) admiration that leads to knowledge.

In the second place, the most radical novelty of Jesus would consist in the undreamed-of relationship he had with God (although there is no linguistic or conceptual mention of *divinity*). This belonging of Jesus to God in no way supposed, at the beginning, any diminution of what later came to be called, technically, his humanity. "The fact that Jesus of Nazareth was a true man is for the New Testament something presupposed in all naturalness."[1] But it did suppose the peculiar and unrepeatable nature of this belonging. Various formulas were used to express this, and the one that became consecrated was "Son of God," to such an extent that "profession of the divine sonship of Jesus from then on became the distinguishing mark of Christianity."[2]

113

All this means that at the outset Jesus was not spoken of as *God*, nor was *divinity* a term applied to him; this happened only after a considerable interval of believing explication, almost certainly after the fall of Jerusalem.[3] It does mean that how to relate Jesus to God in the most adequate manner was a fundamental question, one to which the first Christians replied by relating to God first the events of his fate, as we have seen, and then those of his life, as we shall see later. They did not regard Jesus as an a-temporal and abstract revelation of God but saw him as related to God through real events. Jesus did not appear as an epiphany of the essence of God but related to God in important features of his own history. There was no apparent interest in establishing his divinity independent of his specific relationship with God. Put schematically and in logical steps that need to be fleshed out later, the process of understanding this relationship could be formulated in the following incremental words: God (Yahweh) no longer *acts* without Jesus; God can no longer *be thought of* without Jesus; God *is* not without Jesus; Jesus *belongs* to the reality of God.

In the third place, the purpose of this theoretical exercise is to relate Jesus to salvation—not only to God. In the New Testament there is nothing of detached curiosity to know who Jesus is; there is a committed concern, because it involved a matter of life and death—if and how Jesus saves. This means that from the beginning, as we have seen, Jesus was looked on as the one who will assemble his people in the future and the one who has power to forgive sins in the present. Jesus stands, then, in relation to salvation, and this salvific concern is what also guided reflection on the relationship of Jesus to God.

The concern to know who Jesus is—the question of christology—is not a concern to acquire new—categorized—facts concerning the nature of things but a concern to learn what God is showing and telling people in this Jesus of Nazareth and to learn whether what is shown is good for us. The answer the New Testament gives is positive, certainly, but it is important to relate the objective dimension of Christ as "manifestor" of God to the subjective dimension that this manifestation contains "salvation" for the human race. The fact is that the revelation of God to (religious) humankind is not a matter of adding new data to our knowledge of reality, data that we can react to freely, accept or reject, without anything basically changing in real life. What happens is that, in revealing himself God makes a difference to us: we pass (or can pass) on to a greater degree of humanization. Revelation and salvation are correlative, and so knowing what Jesus reveals of God is not merely a noetic concern but a salvific one. In simple terms, by revealing himself, God changes (or can change) our lives. This is the basic presupposition for understanding the first Christians' concern to *know who* this Jesus whom God raised was and what his relationship to God was. (But let me add that in the reimaging of salvation as brought by Jesus the "Kingdom of God" was relegated to the shadows—to which I shall return.)

In the fourth place, by this stage there was still no use of terms that were later, and still today, to become touchstones of whether or not there was true faith; formulated in abstract terminology, these terms were the *humanity* and *divinity* of Jesus. At the beginning of faith and of christology things were not formulated in this way, nor did orthodox faith depend on integrating these terms in its definitions.

What the New Testament was later to make explicit was that Jesus is intimately bound up with the reality and condition of human beings, so it reaffirms that he is truly *one with and for us*. It makes clear that he was intimately bound up with God, which meant that his reality had to be expressed in some way as a reality that is *of God* (cf. Jn 20:28).

Finally, let me say that in accepting the special relationship of Jesus to God and setting no limits on it, the seed of reflection on the radical novelty of *the very God* is germinated. By accepting that Jesus' historical existence belongs to God, trinitarian reflection is set in motion, with its three basic aspects: God, now the Father of Jesus, is still the ultimate mystery; Jesus, now the Son of God, is the historical expression of the Father; the Spirit, now the Spirit of God poured out in the resurrection, is the Spirit of Jesus, the power of God interiorized in believers and in the community to make following Jesus real.

The theologal novelty introduced by Jesus is, however, not only the trinitarian nature of God—which would be formulated only over time—but also that this "new" God presents a scandalous inversion of reality: the divine becomes real in the human and in what is humanly abased (cf. the words of Phil 2:6–8 and Heb 5:7f., perhaps the most hair-raising words from a christological viewpoint). Relating God to limited and suffering humanity came about early. And it was also temptation, in the sense that the process of reflection fluctuated between claim for and denial, or at least forgetting, of what was weak in Jesus.

2. Jesus' Relationship to God throughout His Life

After this logical reconstruction of the dynamism of faith, let us see how the relationship of Jesus to God was objectified and conceptualized. One way of doing this was to apply titles of dignity to Jesus, which I shall examine at length later. Another was to relate Jesus to God throughout his life, as the synoptics do and the Fourth Gospel does to an even greater degree.

What this relationship of Jesus to God in his life and his destiny consists in varies and so can be understood in more functional terms as sharing in some way in the lordship of God, or in more personal terms, as showing the sonship of Jesus in relation to a Father God. But besides establishing the fact of his relationship to God, the New Testament, especially in the synoptics, is concerned to show what occasioned manifestation of this relationship so as to establish *from when* Jesus exists in relation to God,[4] not out of pure curiosity but because this is necessary for understanding the content of this relationship.

The synoptics claim that this *when* has a history, so that the relationship of Jesus to God is not made clear all at once but through an ongoing process. Their main feature, however, is that as a whole they do not place limits to this process, so that the *from when* is continually extended: the relationship of Jesus to God comes to embrace the whole of Jesus' life, including his preexistence. (This process of christological reflection should not be read anachronistically from the adoptionism of the second century, according to which Jesus was not forever God but began to be so at a particular moment, on being adopted by the Father. The theological concern of the New Testament is different—to show the real relationship of Jesus to God forever and from all time.) The synoptics then return to rereading Jesus' life as a life *wholly* in relation to God, and they do so in such a way that this relationship is presented as one of growing intimacy, as union with God.

The decisive theological conclusion is that *the whole of* Jesus' life, not just one moment of it or another—which would be less basic and scandalous to faith—reveals God. In other words, not only is it a mystery—as generally accepted—that Christ should be in God *from all time*, but it is also a mystery that Christ should be in God—or that God should be with Jesus—*always*, including during his life and on the cross. The first, the preexistence, refers back to the mystery—the metaphysical mystery, let us say—of Christ, although the prologue to John understands it in terms of salvation. The second—the unity of Jesus with God in his life and on the cross—refers back to the historical mystery and is what makes the mystery of God a mystery that is at once scandalous and fortunate.

This process of reflection on the when and the what of Jesus' relationship to God developed through examining the *unity* of Jesus with God, as this was laid out especially in the gospels. At first this unity was viewed from Jesus' *destiny*, as we saw earlier. After the resurrection the relationship of Jesus to God was shown as the *exalted* at the right hand of the Father already in the present and as *the one who is to come* in God's judgment to bring the people of Israel together.

In the beginning, then, Jesus' unity with God was described in such a way that it comes about *after* the resurrection. But as reflection progressed, believers took it back into Jesus' *life*, which was a radical step for faith, since it was to make transcendence and history converge. Furthermore, this unity would be described as sonship. This can be appreciated in the following reconstruction, presented logically, whatever the chronology of the redaction of the texts.

The scene of the transfiguration (Mk 9:2–8; Mt 17:1–8; Lk 9:28–36) is told in such a way that the conclusion is "this is my beloved Son," with which the unity of Jesus with God is established before the resurrection (and, without doubt, in the context of the coming passion). Jesus' baptism (Mk 1:9–11; Mt 3:13–17; Lk 3:21–22) throws his sonship even farther back in time, since the scene is narrated in such a way that God says, "this is my Son, the Beloved, in whom I am well pleased." The scenes of Jesus' birth and virginal conception take this relationship back to the very beginning of Jesus' earthly life: "The child to be born will be holy. He will be called Son of God" (Lk 1:35) or "God with us" (Mt 1:23). In this way it was claimed that from the beginning—and so throughout the whole of his life—Jesus was in relation to God. Formulating this relationship in terms of "Son of God" suggested that it was a personal relationship.

Finally, the idea of preexistence (Jn 1:1) expresses that this relationship is transcendent, that it extends beyond time while touching history, and it relates Jesus to the personal reality of God in what can be called a metaphysical fashion. It is the beginning of reflection on the essential participation of Jesus in the reality of God, in divinity.

The conclusion is surprising (if not already known from dogma): God has *always* been in Jesus, and, the other way round, *all* of Jesus reveals God. It is also surprising in its scandalousness, since this "always" includes the obscurity and crisis of Jesus and above all the cross.

3. The Christological Titles in the New Testament

Another way of analyzing the diversity of christologies, and the one that I shall adopt from now on, is to look at the titles the various New Testament writings apply to Jesus. The difficulties of this way of proceeding are plain, since the titles can have different meanings in different times and places—as the history of forms of christology has shown—so that it is not easy to see exactly what they meant when they were applied to Christ. In this sense it is impossible to "systematize" the christology of the New Testament from titles, which does not remove their great importance, since they are concise answers to the basic and lasting question in christological faith—Who is Jesus?—which can be formulated existentially as "Who are you really, Jesus?,"[5] corresponding to the "And you, who do you say that I am?" of Mark 8:29 and parallels.

In the following sections I shall examine five titles: High Priest, Messiah, Lord, Son of God (with its concretion of servant and correlative of Son of Man), and Word. But first let us recall what titles of dignity are, what importance they have, and what dangers they hold.

(a) Riches and Dangers of the Titles

Certain terms are known as titles of dignity because they express something important and sometimes exclusive about a person (or a people) and therefore enhance the quality of those to whom they are applied. The christological titles operate thus, as *theoretical models* for expressing, and to an extent conceptualizing, from faith, the special reality of Jesus. This is their importance.

As to their origin, the majority derive from the theology of the Old Testament and others from surrounding religions. As to their content, some express more directly the relationship of Jesus to the Kingdom of God (such as Messiah, Son of Man, prophet), while others express his relationship with God (Son of God, Word). As to the aspect of Jesus' existence that they seek to enhance, some make clear the meaning of his earthly life (prophet, servant, high priest); some his significance in the future (Messiah, Son of Man, son of David); others his meaning throughout history (Lord, Savior); still others his transcendent reality (pre-existent, Word, Son of God, God).

The number of terms the New Testament applies to Jesus is high—more than thirty, according to Oscar Cullmann—and this simple fact invites reflection. On the positive side, the variety of titles granted to Jesus shows that the first Christians related him progressively to the whole of reality: to God, to the Kingdom, to humankind; to history and transcendence; to the present, the past, and the future; to hope and salvation. This means, on one hand, that there is no one title that, in itself and however exalted it may be, can adequately—and exhaustively—express the reality of Jesus, which is one way of saying that believers gradually came to see in him an ineffable mystery, one that could be named with no one name. It means that they came to see in Jesus a sort of excess of reality, which could only be approached from several angles. As Marcel Hengel has written, "The ancients did not approach mythical material differentiating it analytically, as we do, but thought accumulatively and in combination, according to a sense of 'plurality of ways of approach.' The more titles that were attributed to the risen Christ, the more possible it became to search for the unequalled singularity of his saving work."[6] In other words, the titles provided—upon closer study—a view of the totality of Jesus and so of the christology (or christologies) of the New Testament. This is what I hope to do in the second part of this book—to show the totality of Jesus according to the New Testament.

But the riches expressed in the variety of titles have a dangerous aspect. On the one hand, they make it possible to concentrate on a single title or on titles of a single type—the transcendent, such as Lord, Son of God, Word—while ignoring or downgrading the others, as history was soon to show. The use of the title "servant," for example, vanished quite quickly from the New Testament as a title, although the synoptics rescued its reality in their account of Jesus' passion. Another indication of this tendency is the difficulty the first generations had in recognizing that Jesus' death was not only death but *death on a cross*.[7] I am merely pointing to major dangers: the possibility of concentrating on one title to the detriment of others, or to rank them according to one's own interests, in which human hubris plays its part. In fact, relatively early and certainly in the Patristic Age, titles such as Lord, Son of God, Christ, and Word were preferred, while those of high priest (brother, faithful and merciful, victim of history) and servant (humiliated because loaded with the sin of the world, yet being light and bearing salvation) were forgotten. (We should also bear in mind that other important expressions the New Testament applied to Jesus were not taken up in later christologies, perhaps because they were not titles in the strict sense: the "brother" of the letter to the Hebrews, the "good news" of Paul and the synoptics, the "slain lamb" of Revelation.) As I have repeated several times, it was to the credit of the gospels, of the synoptics above all, to have recovered essential aspects of Jesus such as his weakness and his cross. And we should remember that, before the synoptics, Paul always saw Jesus as the crucified one (1 Cor 1:23) and the servant (Phil 2:7f.).

(b) Correct and Incorrect Use of the Titles

The titles are explanatory theoretical models, and believers necessarily had to make use of them. But we have to understand clearly how they should be applied to Jesus, a question of supreme importance, since how their application is understood governs whether the titles can be useful christologically or will be dangerous and even harmful. To overcome this danger we need to distinguish the different stages in the process of applying titles to Jesus.

The *first stage,* both logically and chronologically, is that of applying to Jesus titles of dignity whose meaning is already known, at least in principle; for example, to show Jesus' importance, he is said to be *the Lord.* In a Jewish world in which God was called Lord, or in a Greco-Roman world in which certain persons were designated as *kyrioi*, this was a significant way of expressing the meaning of Jesus: Jesus is not just another man, since he is *Lord*; neither is he just one lord among many, but *the* Lord. The same is true of the other titles.

The logic of this manner of proceeding is clear, but we need to be aware of what is happening. Epistemologically, one proceeds from knowledge of the known universal-generic to the unknown particular-specific, from the importance of the title—known, logically, before the advent of Jesus—to its application to Jesus. The title, then, is what shows the importance of Jesus. This manner of proceeding is positive and, in any case, inevitable. It is the way of showing both Jews and Gentiles the unique importance of Jesus. But it also carries the serious danger of understanding the specific content of a title independently of the reality of Jesus (and, in extreme cases, even contrary to the reality of Jesus). This makes a second stage necessary, the more specific and Christian one, that of relating Jesus to the titles, which proceeds in the opposite direction.

In this *second stage,* epistemologically we move from the particular-specific to the universal-generic—that is, from Jesus to the titles. If in the first stage the reality of Jesus is understood on the basis of titles that antedate him, now the titles are understood on the basis of Jesus' reality. It is this reality of Jesus that will explain the content of the titles, not the other way around. What the titles really mean, in the sense now of *christological* titles, can only be known by starting from Jesus. So, properly speaking, the New Testament does not say "Jesus is Lord" but "Being Lord is Jesus," and so forth.[8]

This is more than a play on words, and on it depends correct understanding of Jesus and of faith in him, both the *fides quae*—how orthodox we are in confessing Jesus—and the *fides qua*—how willing we are to accept Jesus and to change our "natural" understanding of the titles. This is why I have insisted that Jesus is the best safeguard of Christ and that following Jesus is the best safeguard of Christian identity. Furthermore, if we did not proceed in this way—from Jesus to the titles—Jesus would, strictly speaking, not reveal anything new; rather, we would see in him—with surprise and gratitude, perhaps—a confirmation of what we *already* knew. In other words, if we know what being Lord means, we do not need Jesus to tell us what it is. What we will be doing is appreciating that Jesus fulfills the conditions of being Lord, so that this title can appropriately be applied to him.

But the New Testament does not proceed in this way. It says that before Jesus we did not know fully what it was to be Lord, although we had a previous notion of it. And it tells us, furthermore, that not only was our previous notion not adequate but that it could be—and historically it is, as often as not—erroneous and even contrary to how it is verified in Jesus, because it expresses exactly the opposite of what the title means as seen in Jesus. It can, then, hide our own ignorance, but also and above all our sinfulness in filling the content of the title with our own interests. Paradoxical though it may seem, there is also an intrinsic danger in applying the titles of dignity to Jesus. It is dangerous to have decided before Jesus that we already know in what true lordship consists. What it means to be Lord can only appear—without dangers—in Jesus: being Lord is serving, which is what

John and the synoptics (especially the anti-triumphalist Gospel of Mark) systematically and scandalously claim.

To give another classic example, let us recall how the letter to the Hebrews applies the title "high priest" to Jesus. The letter uses the terminology and conceptualization of "high priest" to show the unique saving importance of Jesus. But it makes clear that with only the previous understanding of the concept of high priest derived from the Jewish religion, not only will we not know Jesus but that we do not know him, that, furthermore, we distort him, because what Jesus has done is precisely to abolish the nature of the old high priest. What being a high priest is can only be known from Jesus, and those who claim to know the reality of this high priest before Jesus and apart from him not only do not know him but radically misrepresent him.[9]

When the New Testament applies titles to Jesus it operates in two (logically) different ways. The first, needed to show *that* there is faith in Jesus, consists in claiming that Jesus is someone very special, exceptionally related to God and carrying out God's will for people. This is what those who heard the message should have understood when it was preached to them that Jesus was the prophet, the Lord, even when they were—later—told that he was God. The second, needed to show *what* faith in Jesus was held, consists in saying that being Lord, being prophet, being high priest, being Son . . . was what Jesus was. Even being God was what appeared in Jesus. We always have to come back, then, to Jesus of Nazareth.

According to this, the growing acceptance of a title applied to Jesus presupposes two things. At a first stage, it presupposes openness to *faith*, if one likes, but real understanding of the title presupposes a disposition to *conversion*, to the acceptance that we do not know what it is to be Lord, or even what it is to be God, before Jesus. This is what the audience should have grasped when Mark says that "lord is the one who serves," when Paul insists that "the Messiah is the one who was crucified," and when the letter to Hebrews says that "the true high priest is the one who offers himself as victim." From this point of view, closing off the possibility that Jesus reverses the content of the titles is the expression, on the christological level, of the sinfulness of human beings.

Studied in this double direction, from the titles to Jesus and from Jesus to the titles, the titles can present Jesus as revelation and in this sense are an important way of developing christology. Then, but only then and for this reason, the titles become, on the one hand, necessary conceptualizations of faith; on the other, we can then move beyond an ideologized (in the pejorative sense) reading of them, setting them to serve our own interests; finally, we can then make them fit instruments of christology. This is the later and mature *third stage* of applying titles to Jesus, in which we have overcome the temptation of ourselves controlling the content of the title and now can indeed and in truth say what was said from the beginning, that Jesus is Lord, prophet, Son of God, God. A present-day example can illustrate this. In El Salvador we often use the title Monsignor, on its own, when referring to Monsignor Romero. But if any should think that they know Romero and the quality of his life through calling him Monsignor, they will have understood nothing and will be in grave danger of distorting the title on the basis of what they already know is meant by "being Monsignor." The truth of Romero is what gives real dignity to the title Monsignor and not the other way around.

4. Christological Titles at the Present Time

These methodological observations on what the christological titles in the New Testament are, what purpose they serve, and how they should be understood seem to me important for faith and for christology at the present time.

(a) The Need for Christological Titles throughout History

From the beginnings of faith no one title was sufficient to describe the reality of Jesus, so titles appeared in various places and proliferated over the years according to the needs produced by history and cultures. This is a permanent lesson of the New Testament. *[Many titles]*

The fact that only the titles that appear in the New Testament are said to be inspired does not mean that it is not legitimate to apply titles to Jesus throughout history. And so, even if the formulations mentioned below are not understood in the same way as the so-called titles of dignity in the New Testament, and whether they are called titles or not, it is legitimate for Teilhard de Chardin, in an evolutionary context, to call Christ "the omega point of evolution"; for Karl Rahner, in an anthropological-existential context, to call him "the absolute bearer of salvation"; for Bonhoeffer, in a context of secularism and nostalgia for humanity, to call him "the man for others." And in Latin America, in a context of oppression, it is perfectly legitimate to call him "the liberator." *[→ No]*

But besides being legitimate, this way of proceeding is necessary. What is happening when we today apply titles or concepts of dignity such as those mentioned above to Christ? Simply, we are saying what we see in him and thanking him in a meaningful expression for what we believe to be the best of what is human and divine, what gives most hope, best stimulates the practice of charity, and makes us live in thankfulness; what we have to put into words in order to be honest with our faith in Christ and with our vision of reality. This is what in fact has happened in Latin America through calling him liberator, and this is what happens whether we call him defender of the poor, revolutionary for truth and justice, or the cosmic Christ. The creation of new titles or terms of dignity is necessary to such an extent that if today or throughout history the creativity and initiatives for "naming" Christ creatively did not exist, we should have to doubt that we understood Christ adequately and even that we understood the reason that led the New Testament to apply titles of dignity to him. *[mention of Sophia or Christa]*

Having said this, we need to remember that at the present time as well we have to be careful not to fall into the same trap: we must not find ourselves making Jesus—through the titles we apply to him—an invention in our own image and likeness and one serving our own interests. To take the example closest to home for me, what we mean by calling Jesus liberator cannot be determined absolutely beforehand from before Jesus. It is certain that, historically, liberation has had forms and historical mediations that go and have to go beyond Jesus, and it is true that the Spirit always leads us, in a way, beyond Jesus. But it is also true that in the actuality of Jesus there is something of *norma normans*, and so in calling him liberator *today* we have to bring essential elements of the *yesterday* of Jesus into this concept; for example, that the fellowship of the Kingdom is liberating, but so is sonship with respect to God; that we liberate from the sin of the world by attacking it from outside, but also by shouldering it from inside; that we have to liberate others, but that we also have to allow ourselves to be liberated, to be graced. At the present time we have to learn how to learn, as J. L. Segundo perceptively repeats, but learning *today* must also be done from the *yesterday* of Jesus.

(b) The Contribution of the New Testament Titles to the Essence of All Christology

For my analysis I have chosen certain titles that, taken as a whole, express, or at least introduce into, the fullness of Jesus what came to be called his humanity and his divinity, his person and his saving function. What I want to stress is that these titles bring us into the reality of Jesus in a precise manner. So the *humanity* of the high priest will be not just any humanity but that which is exercised as fellowship and solidarity. The *salvation* brought by the Messiah will essentially include giving an answer to the popular hopes of the poor, the weak, the victims. The *lordship* of Jesus is saving, but it also leaves us with the task of making him Lord of history. The *sonship* of Jesus is definitely that of the weak, that of the servant, that which incarnates him and makes him brother of the crucified people. The *sacramentality* of the Word proclaims that the human can make God accessible and that, from now on, there is no need to add anything to humanity to reveal God, though it must be defined.

In this way I am trying also to prepare a precise understanding of christological dogma. I am trying to retrieve dogma not only from the viewpoint of the *vere homo*—Jesus is truly a human being—but also from that of the *homo verus*—in Jesus true humanity has appeared in its guise of fellowship, solidarity, mercy. The same can be said of his divinity: not only from the *vere Deus*—Jesus is truly God—but also from the *Deus verus*—in Jesus the true God is made present, the God of the victims, the one at the mercy of human beings.

Keeping the deep truth of Chalcedon is not just a matter of accepting—and placing alongside one another—a perfect humanity with body, mind, and will and a perfect divinity, but of accepting the reality and actual expression of all of this in and from Jesus. In this way too, while analyzing the titles applied to Christ, I am sketching major areas of Christian anthropology: how to exercise our humanity in a mediating, saving, son-like manner, open to transcendence, and how to make it the sacrament of God.

(c) The Need Today to Retrieve the Essentials of the New Testament Titles

To end this introduction to the New Testament titles, I should like to advert to the anomalous situation of the christological titles at the present time. In my view, our true faith in Christ does not seem to be greatly nourished by calling him Lord, Christ, Word, to say nothing of Lamb of God, high priest, servant. I sincerely do not believe that our faith, even the faith of the best of us, would change much if we dropped these titles, and in principle there would be nothing wrong in doing so, since the object of faith, as we know, is not our words about Christ—the terms in which we formulate his reality—but his person. It is surrender in trust and openness to the mystery of God; put in christological terms, it is following Jesus to the end.

This does not make it less shocking that the titles those first believers applied to Jesus to say in whom and in what they believed should today mean very little or almost nothing. For example, the title "christ" has become a proper name—Christ—and hardly suggests to anyone the decisive importance of its original content: the Messiah who gives a hope to the masses. This shows the need to get back to the central contents of the titles and see if they have any meaning today. This does not, of course, obviate the need for investigating the origin of these titles, their significance in the story of Jesus and the rest of the New Testament, and so on, but it does mean that they need to be related to our situation today, assuming that by them something important is being said.

With respect to the first task, historical and exegetical investigation, I have nothing very new to offer, though I shall point out what seems to me more important than is generally admitted by the experts. My more specific contribution will be in reflection on the present-day practical importance of the titles, seen specifically from the victims of the Third World, since, although they were formulated in different and distant cultures, the realities expressed in them—salvation, liberation, hope, the presence of God in history—have a perennial significance, but one that needs to be brought up to date. In other words, I want to see what the fact that the New Testament applies these titles to Jesus can say to believers today and, the other way around, what present-day reality says about being able to and having to restore their value to them.

Chapter 9

High Priest

The Mediator—
Human "without Additions" but "with Definitions"

earthly work

High priest is a title that, together with those of prophet and servant, is appropriate for referring to Jesus' earthly work and for expressing its significance theologically. From a historical point of view, *prophet* refers to Jesus' denunciations and his upholding of victims. *Servant* refers to his own persecution and cross. *High priest* refers to his function of mediator and so of savior. I concentrate here on the last title—and on the reality that lies behind it—since I have dealt with Jesus as prophet and servant in the previous volume (pp. 160–79), not from the point of view of the titles but from Jesus' life and works: his historic denunciation of idols and his fate on the cross.

central concern of human kind - Salvation

I begin this examination of the titles with that of high priest because it is the vehicle for expressing, in the concepts and formulations of the time, the central concern of humankind and certainly of the Christians of the New Testament: the possibility of salvation. By calling Christ high priest, believers are intrinsically relating Christ and salvation and doing so in a specific manner: he is the *mediator* of salvation. This is decisive since, for the mentality of the time, a mediator was essential for salvation, and this is the reason for the basic importance of the title. But furthermore, through reasoning how and why Christ is the mediator of salvation, we reflect on the essence of his person; that is, we do christology, with, in this case, insistence on his *humanity.*

This is the sense in which I propose to analyze the title of high priest applied to Jesus, but—as with the other titles—I shall do so on the basis of the questions and problems thrown up by our present situation. In this way, present-day reality will guide the questions that, systematically, I ask of the titles. And, vice versa, I expect analysis of the titles to help our understanding of present-day reality. In this way I hope to avoid turning the titles into museum pieces—as so often happens—with no meaning except for specialists.

In the case of the high priest, the title refers to salvation and, specifically, to the priestly mediation that makes this possible. So this chapter has three main sections: the first deals with the deepest dimension of the priestly character, its *theologal* dimension; the second examines the historical form this character took in Jesus, its *christological* dimension; the third looks at the consequences for christology: in Christ what is mediating, priestly, and saving is what is human "without additions" but "with definitions."

1. The "Theologal Revolution" of the Priestly: God Accedes to Being Human

Let us begin with the theologal, not with the christological, so as to determine as theoretically profoundly as possible what the problem of salvation and its solution are about. Even if beginning with the theologal has something artificial about it, since the actuality of God in the New Testament presupposes God's manifestation in Jesus, it still seems to me the right place to start because it provides a deeper insight into the concept of priesthood.

(a) Distancing from and Access to Divinity

Salvation is a complex concept, since it depends on the multiple oppressions and wants from which human beings need to be saved. Here, however, I understand *salvation* as an all-embracing concept. In anthropological language *saving* means overcoming the dehumanization of the human. In religious imagery it means overcoming the distance between God and human beings, a distance deepened ethically by sin but brought about more profoundly by the radical difference between divine and human nature. In positive terms, *salvation* means achieving humanization and deification.

Staying with religious imagery, the commonest solution religions find to the problem of salvation is a ritual one. Human beings have to approach God but are radically incapable of doing so, even if they act ethically, because they dwell in a merely human world, alien to the divine: "In order to approach God, the decisive factor is to enter into a different world, the world of the sacred, the radically distinct and separated from the profane, the sphere of the divine and supernatural. Well now, we have access to this sphere and this world through rites and ceremonies, which separate us from the profane and make our access to the sacred possible."[1]

The priest is a decisive factor in this means of access to the divine, since he is the human embodiment of the sacred, separate from the profane, and therefore able to mediate between both spheres. The theater in which this mediation takes place is worship, and within that its focus is sacrifice, above all expiatory sacrifice. Although it is expressed with differing shades of meaning in different religions, at least in those that surrounded the biblical world, what is central to the priestly office is enabling human beings to be purified ritually from their sins and have access to God. Priestly means and is mediatory in this precise sense.

This gives rise to the basic question: do the Old and the New Testaments share this same view of salvation? On the one hand, they uphold the anthropological basis: human beings are beings in need of salvation. On the other hand, however, their solutions differ. The Old Testament provides a cultic solution to the problem, common to all religions, though in tension with another non-cultic type of solution, found in the various covenants God makes with his people. The New Testament, for its part, changes the perspective radically and proposes a different, non-cultic solution. It is important to know why, and the reason is theologal: in Jesus a very different God from that of other religions and, to a large degree, different from that of the Old Testament is made manifest. Therefore, what is or is not mediating-priestly has to be understood primarily from the newness of this God.

(b) Revolution in the Reality of God

At the risk of over-elaboration, let us examine the characteristics of this "new" God, since they are what will lead to this change in the significance of the priestly. I should like, therefore, to expound what I call revolution in the reality of God, which takes account of the whole of the New Testament. One needs to bear this in mind, since any discussion of mediation normally and rightly adduces the letter to the Hebrews, in which the *mediator* is radically different from that of other religions. So the newness of the mediator is discussed, but not usually the newness of *God*, which is more primal and undoubtedly more decisive for understanding the nature of priesthood.

1. In the New Testament the transcendent God is no longer a separate and distant God but is the God who *has come to* human beings. The manner of his coming is not only a condition for making his manifestation possible but the content of his own reality: God makes himself known in his coming to human beings and makes it known that (an essential part of) his reality consists precisely in his coming to us. This coming, then, belongs to God essentially. It is not one among other possible contents of God's reality but the central content, as the incarnation expresses: God is no longer without this coming to us, God is "God-with-us" (Mt 1:2–3). The transcendent God, without ceasing to be that, is the God who has come to us in Jesus.

2. This coming of God is good for human beings and is *the supreme good*. However trivial it may seem, this is essential for understanding how Jesus (and all of us) can be mediator and priest. God comes to us because God is good and comes as what is good for us. This is what Paul is seeking to express when he claims that it is good news for the (saving) justice of God to have been revealed in the gospels (Rom 1:16–17). God's approach is not, therefore, in order to judge better but in order to save, and so his coming is in itself salvific: it is a sign of primal goodwill. In other words, by coming close to us, God has forever broken the symmetry of being possibly salvation and possibly condemnation (in Rahner's expressive phrase). This is why Jesus presents God's coming as supremely good for us: God's coming in a "Kingdom" and his coming as "Father" are both expressions of a good God, a God who forgives sins, heals the heart, humanizes, and fulfills.

3. The formal characteristics of this coming are the following: God's approach is *free and gratuitous* (see 1 Jn 4:10), one that does not depend on, nor can it be

forced by, the will of human beings, nor do we have to strive for it; it is an *active* event (Lk 15:20) that comes out to meet us and is not content with just "being there"; it is also a *permanent* event, not just a sporadic one (in Christ); and it is an *irrevocable* event, not dependent on human response (Rom 5:8). Furthermore, as it took place in Jesus, this event is *partial to the weak* of this world, the poor, the despised, those excluded in various ways, those regarded as sinners, all those for whom living is a heavy burden (recall the essential partiality of the Kingdom of God and the resurrection, examined above). This partiality, as a fact, cannot be argued further: it simply is, as both the Old Testament and the New Testament show. This "being thus" belongs to the content of the mystery of God, and accepting this "being thus" of God is central to the act of faith. But, although it is a mystery that cannot be deduced, this partiality shows how apposite it is for God's love to show itself as mercy and tenderness through being addressed to little ones, and to show itself as justice through being addressed to those who are little because they are oppressed. This does not exclude the universality of God's salvation—seen in historical terms, it reinforces it—but it does mean this must be understood from partiality and not vice versa.

4. The sphere of God's coming is the *life and history* of human beings in all their needs: for forgiveness and healing, for bread and hope, for truth and justice, as Jesus' life and actions demonstrate. God does not come *separate* from this life and history but in them; he does not grant salvation by *separating* us from this life and history but by healing us, empowering us, and communicating himself to us in them.

5. The saving coming of God is *opposed to the world of sin.* This means not only that some will not accept it, or that others will not be grateful for it, but that the world of sin will rebel against it. The reason this is so is the *mysterium iniquitatis*. But God himself has already in his coming taken on the fact that the world of sin will act against him, culminating in the cross of Jesus. The cross shows that there is opposition to the death to the coming of God, but it also shows that the coming of God is unconditional, that God not only wants to offer salvation but wants to offer himself for the sake of this salvation, which is a scandal to the Jews and folly to the Gentiles (1 Cor 1:23).

6. The God who comes goes on being the *holy and transcendent* God. But his holiness is not distancing from the historical world but the greatest possible incarnation, so that we can come to be "perfect . . . as [our] heavenly Father is perfect" (Mt 5:48). His transcendence does not consist only in being beyond history—in order to revitalize it—but in an active drawing of history into himself so that hope may always be maintained and history may give more of itself (cf. Rv 21:1; 1 Cor 15:28).

(c) Revolution in the Priestly Reality

All the above concerning the "new" God is vital for understanding the "new" priestly reality. The solution to the problem of human access to God changes radically because *God* is like this. It is not we who accede or have to accede to God in search of salvation but God who "comes down" to offer it to us. Our encounter with God includes an active response, but this is no Promethean effort, and it takes place in a double dimension.

First, we should *respond* to God in gratitude, in faith, and in hope, the central content of which is precisely acceptance of the fact that God has come gratuitously as salvation. Second, we should *correspond* to the reality of the God who has come to us by making ourselves good news and salvation for others, by being ourselves expression of the coming of God to humankind, according to the programmatic phrase in Johannine theology: "Not that we loved God but that he loved us . . . we also ought to love one another" (1 Jn 4:9–11). Our encounter with God has, then, the structure of otherness and affinity, of response and correspondence to the God who has come. And in the fulfillment of both things lies salvation.

So the mediating and priestly character of world religions and the Old Testament has changed *because* its basic presupposition—our understanding of the nature of God—has changed, and with this the old priesthood has automatically been abolished, even if this is not mentioned in the letter to the Hebrews. To sum up, there is nothing created that serves as efficient cause of the saving coming of God, nor is it necessary that there should be. To claim that there is—as the so-called just did at the time of Jesus—is blasphemy in the strict sense, because it is going against the deepest aspect of God himself and of God's will. The old priesthood is, therefore, superfluous, and worse, it is a threat against the reality of God.

(d) Brief Definition of the Theologal Priestly Reality

In light of the above, it may be asked whether there is still any particular sense in talking of priesthood and mediation. The reply to this has been given by God himself, and so cannot be worked out *a priori*. God himself, by coming to us in saving guise, has reserved to himself a historical expression of this coming (which is Jesus and which, in principle and by analogy, all of us could be), and had to reserve this to himself in order to be able to accede to us in our history and historicity. This historical expression of God's coming is still necessary and possible. It is necessary because God has self-determined to go on coming to us, and so goes on needing historical expressions of this coming. It is possible because it is possible throughout history for us to carry Jesus forward and carry out his life.

This enables us to make the following definition of priestly mediation. Directly, this mediation is the historical expression of God's coming to us. All actions that express this will be priestly actions. All those persons and/or groups who carry out these actions will be priests. By derivation, everything that helps us to respond and correspond to the God who comes to us will be priestly and mediating. Saying "by derivation" is not to undervalue this dimension of mediation, since our responding and corresponding to God is precisely the setting of salvation. It is said to uphold what I have called the "theologal revolution": God's coming to us takes logical precedence over our seeking God. This is a theoretical statement but one with profound practical and pastoral consequences. In priestly mediation, in effect, we should use various means and argue in various ways to enable us to enjoy salvation, but without losing sight of or relativizing the supreme argument that it is God's goodness—and its historical embodiment—that is ultimately what moves us to accept the God who comes.

2. The "Christological Revolution": The True Priest? Jesus

If we move from the God who comes to the mediator, in the New Testament this is Jesus. In the imagery I have just been using, Jesus is—both at once—the expression of God's access to us and the way for us to accede to God. This double movement is clearly expressed in the gospels. Jesus is, above all, the historical expression of the good God coming to human beings, since, before they do anything, "the Kingdom of God is at hand," and they can address God with confidence, calling him "Father." This *previous* goodness of the God who comes will be Jesus' supreme argument for his call to conversion, as we can see in the parables. Jesus is then also the expression of how creatures can have access to God, in trust and faith, in mercy and self-giving, in prayer and love. Using John's more technical language, we can make the following synthesis: Jesus is, in the first place, the *Word* of the Father, come to us on his own initiative, not out of the will of the flesh (Jn 1:13)—descending access; in the second place, Jesus is the *Way* to the Father (14:6)—ascending access. Jesus is, then, mediator through being the sacrament of God with respect to us and through being the way for us with respect to God. (According to this, the efficacy of the mediator, which historically has been understood more on the lines of efficient cause [Christ's action succeeds in bringing together two separate realities: God and humankind], can be understood along the lines of symbolic cause [God's descent to us in Jesus] and of exemplary cause [our ascent to God in Jesus].)

This is the theologal revolution in terms of the mediator. But there is also another revolution in the nature of this mediator: the mediator is a human being, and because he is, he can exercise mediation in both directions: from God to human beings and from us to God. This strictly human nature of the mediator, without additions, is the second revolution of the priestly, the *christological* revolution. Jesus' humanity as mediator is present in the whole of the New Testament, especially in the gospels, but the letter to the Hebrews expounds it in detail. Its central claim is that the high priest is the Christ, who is Jesus of Nazareth, which is an authentic revolution in theory and practice and one that has, in my view, still not been adopted in all its implications.[2]

It is true that the letter makes Jesus high priest through his being the Son exalted at the right hand of the Father, who can intercede for us because he has penetrated into the sanctuary. But in analyzing the nature of this mediator in historical and specific terms, the letter expresses what I have called the second revolution: to put it somewhat provocatively, to be the mediator requires no "additions" to human nature but does require "definitions." In this way, analysis of the title high priest takes us, not only descriptively, in the manner of the gospels, but also theoretically and technically, into the realm of what was later to be called the humanity of Christ.

(a) The First Stage: The Importance of the Title High Priest

As I have said, in the New Testament the titles serve at a first stage to express the importance of Jesus. So let us look, though briefly, at the origin and meaning of the title *high priest*.

A theology of the high priest was developed in Judaism; his importance lies in his being related to an eschatological figure, which was made possible by interpretation of Psalm 110:4 and of the mysterious figure of Melchizedek in Genesis 14:18ff. The psalm is a psalm of kingship and assigns to the king the functions of the high priest in the context of his enthronement. With regard to the figure of Melchizedek, at the time of Jesus one line of thought attributed eschatological traits to him, and through being made superior to Abraham he was given an unequalled importance. In this way the title high priest came to express an eschatological figure, and so to designate a personage as high priest was equivalent to calling him the prophet of the end time. The title was, then, suitable for bringing out a person's importance. We are here at the first stage of the application of the title: Jesus is someone very special, and to express this he was proclaimed the high priest.

Jesus himself, however, did not see himself in terms of the concept of priest, even of ideal high priest. (Sociologically, Jesus was a layman of the tribe of Judah, which, in the present climate of institutional understanding of priesthood, can be repeated only with impotence and even irony. But this fact, though interesting, is not decisive, since the letter to the Hebrews argues for his high priesthood not from the fact that he did not belong to the tribe of Levi but from the actual exercise of his humanity.) He gives rather the opposite impression, as confirmed by his attacks on the Temple and his probable struggles against the priestly caste, not to mention the fact that, historically, the high priests were those mainly responsible for his death. But the letter to the Hebrews proclaims Jesus as high priest, and we need to ask why, since his life and activities do not suggest the application of this title to him so much as of others, such as eschatological prophet, Messiah, son of David, and so on.

The reason for this application is not clear. It could reside in the need to show that in Christ, God's plan as manifested in the writings of the Old Testament, in which the priesthood is evident (Vanhoye), was being fulfilled. Or it could be that for the eschatological community—as the Qumran community thought— ideal sanctity was typified in the conduct and purity of the high priest (Jeremias). There was a need, then, for the community to proclaim Jesus as the true and effective priest, but—unlike what happened with the application of other titles— there was only one factor in Jesus' life that related him to priesthood: his sacrifice. The task for the letter to the Hebrews was, then, to reinterpret priesthood and sacrifice in such a way that Christ would appear as the true priest.

In its presentation of Christ the letter does not leave aside Jesus' transcendent dimension; on the contrary, it proclaims him Lord and Son of God, goes so far as to say that he is "the reflection of God's glory and the exact imprint of God's very being" (1:3), and the quote from Psalm 45:7–8, which appears in 1:8–9, could be taken to refer to what was later called his divinity. But in having to argue the case for the priesthood and sacrifice of Christ as true priesthood and sacrifice it presents them with great originality and dialectically—affirming and denying—finds itself forced to stress what will later abstractly be called the humanity of Christ.

(b) The Second Stage: The Polemic Definition of Priesthood from Jesus

The exposition made by the letter to the Hebrews is not merely positive and peaceable but proceeds dialectically, and it does so because it has to answer the questions of a community in crisis and overcome its questionings. In proceeding in this manner it will be applying the title of high priest to Jesus at the second stage I discussed earlier: whatever previous idea of priesthood the community held, like it or not, being priest and mediator is being what Jesus is.

The community to which the letter is addressed is one suffering tribulations and discouragement. Its members are tired of the sufferings they have to endure as Christians (10:32ff.; 12:3ff.) and dispirited by the non-arrival of the parousia (3:14; 6:12; 10:36ff.). In this situation the religion of the Old Testament offered a powerful and attractive influence, above all on worship, as did certain forms of angel worship. So the writer has to encourage them, but he also has to unmask their false hopes, and in doing so he states what salvation means and what the characteristics of the true mediator are.

(i) The polemic against the efficacy of worship of angels. The first polemic is concerned with the worship of angels. The letter presupposes the existence of a surrounding religious culture based on the worship of angels, an echo of which can perhaps be heard in the letter to the Colossians: "Do not let anyone disqualify you, insisting on self-abasement and the worship of angels" (Col 2:18). This worship must have been expressed in ritual "matters of food and drink" and "observing festivals, new moons, or sabbaths" (Col 2:16). It was, then, a ritual and cosmic form of worship, a-historical, attractive in being a seductive mixture of false mysticism and religious formalism.[3] Further, the logic behind this cult is attractive to natural reason: the angels are "closer" to God and can therefore "better" guarantee a liturgy that gives access to God.

It is against this background that what the letter polemically states (Heb 1:5–14) should be understood: Christ is closer to God, is seated at the right hand of God (1:3), and is therefore superior to and more excellent than the angels (1:4). But—and this is where the surprise comes—he is so not because his existence is more cosmic and less historical, more "angelic" than that of the angels, so to speak, but precisely because it is *less* angelic and more human, because he has lived more submerged in history. So from the start the letter stresses the earthliness of Christ, and it constantly returns to the historical process of Jesus' life. It claims that Christ is at the right hand of God and is superior to the angels, but it recalls that this is the result of a process: "When he had . . . he sat down . . . having become." And so that no doubt should remain about Jesus' earthly nature, it not only stresses the process by which he approached God but also states, audaciously, that he was originally "made lower than the angels" (2:9).

From the outset, then, the letter's thesis is polemical: we have to change our understanding of what access to God means on two important points. The first is that closeness to what is human, not distance from it, grants access to God. And the second is that nature, even if it is "angelic," does not have the potentialities of history. (This "angelic christology" is anachronistic only in appearance, since there is still an innate tendency to think we are closer to God the farther we are from the reality of human history, as shown by the proliferation of spiritualist movements, apparitions, and the like [however understandable such movements may be], and also by an understanding of the liturgy as the presence of authority surrounded by an "angelic" solemnity. The conclusion is still the same: "The better mediator will be the one who is closer to God and more distanced from human beings." And I have to say that the ecclesiastical authorities do not usually warn of these grave dangers as seriously as they do when someone insists on the humanity of the mediator.) This is why there is more perfection and possibility of mediation in Christ. He began "further" from God than the angels, since he started "closer" to human beings and like them in all things, "yet without sin" (Heb 4:15). Distinct from and in opposition to the angels, Christ guides humankind not from above with celestial instructions but from below. He himself follows the path toward God, and it is he who follows it for the first time and to the end: he is "the pioneer of . . . salvation" (2:10). Equally, neither does the glorification of Christ at the end appear as an automatic concession to his quality of Son after his death—independently of what his life was like—but through it.

(ii) The polemic against the efficacy of Old Testament worship. The second and better known polemic touches on Old Testament worship. The letter states that the priests of the old covenant could not carry out what they promised—to mediate between God and humankind—so their worship was ineffective. Above all, it states that with the coming of the true priest worship has been abolished. The most important aspect for christology is the point-by-point comparison of the old priests with Christ, since in this way the letter progressively clarifies—by denying and affirming—the nature of the true priest.

In the Old Testament the priest, because he is consecrated to God, has to remain aloof from the profane sphere; furthermore, his separation signifies superiority over the people, all of which is expressed in the rite of consecration and in numerous ritual prescriptions. Christ, on the other hand, to become the high priest, makes himself like others in everything; he is put to the test (2:18; 4:15), he suffers abuse (11:26) and even death (2:9). The Old Testament priest is severe, so the sons of Levi are praised by Moses for killing those who had gone over to idolatry (Ex 32:29), and when Moses blesses Levi he praises him for having abandoned his parents and having ignored his children (Dt 33:8–11). Christ, on the other hand, is merciful (Heb 2:17; 4:15). The Old Testament priests are weak (7:28), mortal, and therefore bearers of a perishable sacrifice (7:23), sinners themselves and incapable of entering into the intimacy of God (9:8ff.). Christ, on the other hand, is "holy, blameless, undefiled, separated from sinners" (7:26).

The conclusion is that under the first covenant the sacrifice offered by the priests is ineffective (9:9), the sanctuary is "a sketch and shadow" (8:5), and the cultic regulations are "for the body" (9:10). In short, the letter criticizes the "system of separations" that characterizes the Old Testament priesthood: "The ancient cult, marked by irremediable outwardness, did not renew people deeply, nor could it place them in an authentic relationship with God."[4] Christ, by contrast, offers himself; the rites are his own life and death; the sanctuary is the real course of history. Christ does not go into the sanctuary with the blood of goats and calves (9:12, 25) but with his own blood (9:12). In this way the exteriority of the old priesthood, which mediated between God and humankind, is broken, and the "reality principle" is introduced: it is real and historical existence that makes access to God possible (or impossible). Jesus' offering is pleasing to and accepted by God, not through an arbitrary decision on God's part but on account of the actual content of Jesus' life. Because his life is without sin, because it is filled with the Spirit (9:14), because it expresses the will of God (10:5ff.), Jesus' life is truly mediatory and conveys access to God.

The letter, then, sets out the difference between the two types of mediator and the superiority of the priesthood of Christ over that of the old covenant, to the point where this is abolished. To demonstrate this, it argues *a priori*, recalling that under the first covenant the priesthood was based on God's call to Aaron, of the tribe of Levi, from which the priests came, while Christ is constituted priest according to the order of Melchizedek, with the essence of the argument lying in the fact that the figure of Melchizedek is presented as superior to that of Abraham (7:6ff.). Here then—aside from the esoteric aspect of the argument—is an etiological reasoning: Christ is superior to the ancient priesthood through his origin. But the reasoning in the letter is mostly *a posteriori*—from the fruits both priesthoods have produced.

(iii) The salvation the high priest brings. This true priest *does* convey salvation. Apart from the language and the theoretical model employed by the letter to explain what salvation is and how it is produced (see *JL*, pp. 262–64), the claim is clear and repeated and rings out triumphantly: Christ "became the source of eternal salvation" (5:9); brought "many children to glory" (2:10); caused us to be "sanctified" (10:10); gave us "confidence to enter the sanctuary" (10:19). More concretely, in religious-soteriological language, it says that Christ offered a single sacrifice for sins (1:3; 10:11–14); that he purified "our conscience from dead works to worship the living God" (9:14); that he left "our hearts sprinkled clean from an evil conscience" (10:22). There is no doubt, then, that the writer of the letter to the Hebrews sees Christ as the mediator of salvation. Our concern here is with the nature of this mediator, but first let me make three short digressionary observations.

The first is that the letter seems to reduce priestly action to Jesus' death. As is known, however, it is general practice, certainly in Paul and Mark, to make Jesus' death into a compendium of his life, the unfolding of the incarnation. This means that Jesus' sacrifice, according to the letter, can, and in my view should, be read as the consequence and expression of his mercy and faithfulness.

The second is that the letter seems to reduce salvation to the religious dimension, specifically to the forgiveness of sins, ignoring the breadth of the plural, historical, and transcendent salvation that appears in the gospels. This, however, is not the case. It is clear that forgiveness of sins is central in the whole of the New Testament, but it is not seen as an expression of salvation on its own but in relation to other forms of salvation. For Paul, justification goes well beyond simple forgiveness: it is the enabling of a new life. In the synoptics, forgiveness (or, more accurately, welcoming of sinners) appears together with Jesus' healings, both in the context of the coming of the Kingdom. Relating the Jesus of the letter to the Hebrews to that of the synoptics, we can conclude: "Jesus is the mercy of God in person, coming to this world, approaching us concretely, physically, touching us in our temporality and in our flesh, so that we give ourselves trustingly and unconditionally to this action of God's and change it into what God is, mercy. Pardoned, we are in our turn capable of mercy."[5]

Furthermore, we should bear in mind that the letter presents the work of Christ as the new and definitive covenant, superior to that made on Sinai (8:5) and foretold in Jeremiah 31:31–34, the text quoted in Hebrews 8:8–12 and 10:16ff. This covenant, though it can be accompanied with rites of worship, is salvation as forgiveness of sins, but it is more than this, as Jeremiah's text shows. What the salvation conveyed by this new covenant is can be gleaned from what the letter says of the new form of life of those graced by the covenant. In the passage following the mention of the new covenant (10:17), a summary of the new Christian existence is proposed as "full assurance of faith," "confession of our hope without wavering," and "love and good deeds" (10:17–25; cf. chaps. 3, 4, and 11 on faith; 12 and 13 on hope; 12:14—13:21 on charity). From the whole of the response made possible by the new covenant, we can grasp what the salvation conveyed comprises: living in faith, hope, and love.

The third digressionary point is that although by using the traditional priestly imagery the letter presents mediation as serving human access to God, it in fact also presents it as serving God's access to us, as we have seen earlier. This appears in Jesus being shown as God's initiative, and our concentration on him as salvation. It might be said that we have to "go with him to God," but this Jesus has been given to us, and "with him God has come to us." "Looking to Jesus" (Heb 2:2) shows us a way, undoubtedly, but it is also an invitation to see God and experience God's power. Not for nothing is Jesus the "exact imprint of God's very being" (1:3).

3.   True Humanity: Mercy, Faithfulness, Self-giving, Solidarity

In establishing what effective priesthood consists in, the letter to the Hebrews reflects on who this Christ the true priest is. This has consequences for the theology of priesthood and of ministries (needless to say it is vital to establish what true priesthood is and what relationship it bears to the ministerial [derived] priesthood), but for the time being I am concentrating on its consequences for christology. Here the specific contribution of the letter is that christology, in biblical terms, has to return to Jesus of Nazareth; in dogmatic terms, it has to stress the real humanity of Christ; in actual and existential terms, it has to make Christ's solidarity with the weak an essential element in humanity.

(a) Humanity "without Additions"

The letter gives exalted titles to the high priest—Lord, Christ, Son of God—but it stresses his human reality and so repeatedly uses the name of Jesus, above all in the context of weakness, suffering, and death, to describe Christ's earthly mediating existence.[6] This is not just stating the obvious, nor is the purpose in mentioning Jesus' name simply to identify who this high priest is. The concern is to bring out his concrete, historical, earthly existence. And the first thing it says of this Jesus is that he is really human and shares in the human condition, who "in every respect has been tested *as we are*, yet without sin" (4:15). Yet more: who "*had to become* like his brothers and sisters in every respect" (2:17).

This Jesus needs no categorical addition to his humanity to be able to be a mediator, such as belonging to a particular tribe—that of Levi—or receiving, as ministerial priests do, a special faculty. His not needing any "additions" to his humanity is the deepest meaning of the admonition the letter gives: "For it is evident that our Lord was descended from Judah, and in connection with that tribe Moses said nothing about priests" (7:14).

Christ does not, then, derive his possibility of being mediator from anything *added* to humanity; it belongs to him by his practice of being human. It does not come to him from a superhuman dignity (as religions generally understand priesthood), or from an added sociological category. In this sense, insisting today that Jesus was "lay" not only has a polemical value in the present ecclesial situation; it is another way of insisting on the basic fact: "layman" or "priestly minister," so to speak, Jesus is God's mediator through being human and not through any other *added*, let alone *separating*, category.

(b) Human with Particulars: Mercy, Faithfulness, Self-giving

While Jesus' humanity needs no "additions" to be mediating, it does need "particulars." Some of these are *natural* and inevitable, while others are *historical*, the fruit of freedom, and so capable of mediating God.

In Jesus his humanity took shape, naturally and inevitably, in one gender and one race: he was male and Jewish. But this does not mean that these particulars are essential to his capacity of being mediator. As we have seen, being mediator is being human (correctly specified). In Jesus' case this humanity is made present *in and through* his maleness and Jewishness, but could, strictly speaking, have been made present through femaleness and non-Jewishness. Formally, Jesus can be mediator through being human, not through being male or Jewish, although in his case humanity took male and Jewish form.

These natural, necessary, and inevitable particulars are not the ones that make Jesus' humanity mediating; this depends on another set of particulars, those that are free and historical. The letter already claims this, indirectly and polemically, by comparing how differently the priests of the old order and Christ exercise their humanity. Christ lives in proximity to others, not apart from them; he deals mercifully with them, not sternly; he is innocent and close to God, not sinful and distant from God; he offers his own life, not that of animals. There are, then, different and even contradictory forms of carrying out being human, and the true priest does so in a particular way.

So the letter describes various important aspects of Jesus' humanity, but it also takes on the task of setting out, programmatically and in thesis form, what is specific and special to that humanity: in his lifetime Jesus was merciful to the weak and faithful to God (cf. 2:17; 4:15). Both things are historical embodiments of Jesus' humanity.

1. Concerning *mercy*, suffice it to say that the letter stresses Jesus' compassion when faced with the weaknesses of human beings: "For we do not have a high priest who is unable to sympathize with our weaknesses" (4:15). And the reason for this is given: Jesus shares in and so knows the weakness of humanity. This way of regarding mercy is not so obvious in the synoptics, but it is possible to find convergence between them and the letter. In the gospels, too, it is mercy that moves Jesus to act, as he himself acknowledges programmatically (Mt 9:13; 12:7) and as the synoptics show on many occasions: He has compassion on the crowd (Mt 14:14); he is moved with pity for a leper (Mk 1:41), for two blind men (Mt 20:34), for those who have nothing to eat (Mk 8:2; Mt 15:32), for the widow of Naim whose son has just died (Lk 7:13). And in at least four accounts Jesus heals after the plea "Have mercy on me" (Mt 20:29–34; 15:22; 17:15; Lk 17:13). (Mercy is also the basic property Jesus uses to describe God as well as the complete human being.)

2. Concerning *faithfulness* to God, the letter shows Jesus in his creatureliness and the weakness contained in this, a condition for making theologal faithfulness possible. So it is said of Jesus—centrally and consciously—that he is like all others except in sin (4:15). (The idea of Jesus' sinlessness is implicit in 2 Corinthians 5:21; 1 Peter 1:19; 2:22; 3:18, and elsewhere. "The sinlessness of Jesus was being claimed before the letter to the Hebrews, but the writer of this was concerned with it in a special way on account of the priestly nature of his christology. . . . The Letter . . . besides mentioning the absence of sin, first presupposes the possibility of sinning. So the possibility of Jesus being tempted plays a more important role here than in the synoptics.")[7] He had to "become like his brothers and sisters in every respect" (2:17), including being tempted; he was "tested, as we are, yet without sin" (4:15). And this true and genuine humanity of Jesus is also expressed on the theologal level: Jesus places himself before God in humility, with "prayers and supplications, with cries and tears, to the one who was able to save him from death" (5:7, referring to Jesus in the Garden), and in darkness, since, "although he was a Son"—which makes what follows scandalous—"he learned obedience" (5:8).

His creaturely faithfulness is also characterized by process, by having to journey in history. The letter several times says that Jesus "came to perfection," but it does not spare him having to *come to be* human. Christ is Son from his origin and will be so forever, as his priesthood is forever, but this "ever" has a history and in this Jesus' faithfulness has been shown. Faithfulness to God means letting God be God, and this is what appears in Jesus. Tersely and with a clarity unequalled elsewhere in the New Testament, the letter says that Jesus was related to the mystery of God in faith. Jesus is the one who has first and most fully lived faith

(12:2). The letter, then, states Jesus' creaturely faithfulness, which the synoptics show descriptively.[8]

3. Besides these two particulars of Jesus' existence, which the letter deals with systematically, there is an essential third one; Jesus' *self-giving*. In the letter's imagery mediation is carried out fully by the mediator offering sacrifice. From this point of view what the letter does is to discount sacrifice as something "added on" and to require it as "historic actualization" of humanity. So the rituals of worship are described as "regulations for the body" (9:10) and so ineffective and incapable of achieving access to God. And then, with no more reasoning than the self-evident, it states: "It is impossible for the blood of bulls and goats to take away sins" (10:4).

We have already seen that the offering Christ makes is inseparable from his very existence: the "rites" are his own life and death; he enters the sanctuary not with blood of goats (9:12, 25) but with his own blood (9:12). Here the structure of exteriority characteristic of the ancient priesthood, its "add-ons," has been broken and the structure of reality and historical embodiments imposed: Jesus' life is an expression of the will of God (19:5ff.), and Jesus' self-giving is filled with the Spirit (9:14). Reading this self-giving from the point of view of the synoptics, we can say that it is the consequence and culmination of his faithfulness to God and his mercy toward people. This self-giving is what enables him to be mediator and is, therefore, a historical embodiment of his humanity. Faithfulness, mercy, and self-giving are then embodiments of (not additions to) what is truly human. (It might be worth noting here that in specifying these embodiments the letter is not falling into any sort of Anselmianism—even a backward sort—but is, above all, stating how Jesus was in actuality. The mediator *is* like this, the letter states; it then elevates this into a thesis: the mediator *must be* like this.)

(c) Humanity as Solidarity

To round off this chapter, let me say that one more essential element of Jesus' humanity has to be added to all the foregoing: his solidarity with others—understanding *solidarity* here in its broader sense of loving co-responsibility among the members of the human family.[9] The letter tells of this descriptively by recalling his participation in human weaknesses and limitations. And it states it programmatically in the beautiful expression, "Jesus is not ashamed to call them brothers and sisters" (2:11).

The phrase "brothers and sisters," which has unfortunately not generated a christological tradition on a par with the title Son (and others), is fundamental. With it, Jesus' humanity is stated to be realized in terms of solidarity, so that all true humanity has to be in solidarity. Jesus is, finally, the mediator and the Christ, not only through being a human being but through being a brother. The first is necessary but not sufficient: the necessary and sufficient condition is to be human in the mode of brother- and sisterhood. This does not eliminate the otherness of Jesus with respect to human beings, but it defines it from affinity: Jesus is like us as "brother," but he is different from us as "elder brother," as shown in two important statements.

With regard to faith, Jesus in his life is presented as a believer like ourselves, our brother in relation to God, since he was not spared having to pass through faith. But he is also presented as an elder brother because he lived faith as its "pioneer and perfecter" (12:2). He is the model, the one on whom we have to keep our eyes fixed in order to live out our own faith. Christ is the definitive witness who, like all the witnesses cited in chapter 11 of the letter, gives assurance in faith. Where the final fulfillment is concerned, Jesus has already gone into the sanctuary, but he has done so as "forerunner on our behalf," so that we too may enter (6:20). He is the first to make the journey, the firstborn. That is the way he has left us, and so salvation comes upon us not only in the manner of efficient cause—Christ interceding for us—but in that of exemplary cause: Jesus has left us the way he himself has trodden. This otherness as "elder brother" should not, however, make us forget the more basic affinity of his being, essentially, "brother."

(d) Two Consequences for Christology

The letter stresses the humanity of Christ, but it also defines it. The fact is that one can have a truly human nature because it includes body, soul, will (today we should add freedom, selfhood, self-possession, and more), all realities proper to this nature, but this in itself still says nothing about the actual exercise of human nature, which can be very diverse.

The first definition the letter makes is in not being content to state what would be the equivalent of *vere homo*—that Jesus is *truly* a human being because he shares in human *nature,* where the *vere* adverbially qualifies the fact of possessing this nature—but in presenting Christ as *homo verus*, the *true* human being, through the actual practice of humanity, where *verus* is an adjective qualifying the actuality of Christ's humanity. In this sense the letter is saying that in Jesus what it is to be truly human has been revealed, and let me say that this in itself is already saving, since it takes us out of our endless doubt and anguish over what we are and helps us to overcome the temptation to cover up our true nature and to define ourselves in Promethean terms.

It is also saving in another, related way. In effect, the letter establishes Jesus' constitutive relatedness to God: he is the Son (the first title given to him, in 1:1). But, as we have just seen, it also establishes his constitutive relatedness to us: he is our brother. And this is essential to christology: just as the synoptics insist on the constitutive relatedness of Jesus to the Father (and with the Kingdom), the letter mentions both the "vertical" constitutive relatedness—Son—and the "horizontal"—brother. It thus recovers, though in different terms, the basic intuition of setting out Jesus' relationship to the Kingdom of God.

I shall return to this, but it seems important to pick it out from the start: there is no christology with only a (vertical) constitutive relatedness to God; it has to contain, at the same time, a (horizontal) constitutive relatedness to us. Jesus is not only *vere homo*; he is also *homo verus*—and not only this but *frater verus*.

Chapter 10

Messiah

Keeping Alive the Hope of the Poor

I began with an examination of the title high priest because it expresses the fact that, as mediator, Christ brings salvation. I take messiah next because messianism is essential to an understanding of Jesus and because it is still needed in the Third World, since it embodies a dimension of salvation and expresses the hope of the poor for liberation. For some years now, however, with the paradigm of postmodernity and others, messianism has been ignored, if not ridiculed, and this makes it necessary to return to it. In this chapter I want to look at the need to take the reality that lies behind this title messiah seriously once more and to do so in a precise context, which—provocatively—I formulate as follows: throughout history Jesus has been "de-messianized," and so the Messiah needs to be "re-messianized," a process already started to some extent in the New Testament, as we shall see.

To explain this paradox, let me say for a start that *the anointed*, *messiah* in Hebrew, *christos* in Greek, is the specific title used to designate Jesus in the New Testament, so that his proper name, Jesus, and the title applied to him, Christ, have come to be put together as Jesus Christ. The importance of designating Jesus as *Messiah* can also be seen in the fact that it appears in all the writings of the New Testament, from the traditions that express the beginnings of faith and christology (Acts 2:36: "God has made him both Lord and Messiah") to the deepest theological reflections of Paul, Hebrews, and John. The title, moreover, passed from Jesus to those who believed in him, so that "the disciples were . . . called Christians" (Acts 11:26), first in Antioch. Then, it would seem that two important things happened in the New Testament period. The first is that the title messiah underwent a major change when it was applied to Jesus, and the second is that, by becoming a proper name and being used routinely, it ended by becoming an abstract noun, a designating rather than a signifying term.

This is what I now want to examine. I start with a brief analysis of the significance of the title and the vicissitudes through which it has passed, and then go on to see how the central content of the title messiah can be made relevant today.

1. The Core of Messianism: The Hope of the Poor

(a) The Hope of the People in the Old Testament

The hope of peoples and of the poor runs through the history of humankind. Israel formulated this hope as the Kingdom of God but also linked it to the appearance of a saving figure. In the imagery we are used to, it hoped for *mediation*, a changed world, and it hoped for a *mediator*, a savior. Messiah and messianisms, therefore, have nothing esoteric about them but are expressions of peoples' hope.

It is not easy to determine exactly what this savior meant for Israel, but what seems clear essentially is that the messiah would be a public figure, sent by God to save God's people as a people. And because he was related to the people, he could be described in terms of royalty and, more generally, in political terms. So at the start "the anointed" was applied to the king of Israel (1 Sm 9:19; 24:7, in times of the historical monarchy) and especially to the king as God's representative (2 Sm 7:12ff.), to whom an eternal reign is promised. As history gave the lie to this promise, the messiah was gradually changed into an eschatological figure, that is, into an object of hope for the future. In the exile, and when there was no longer a throne of David, the idea seems to have been forged of the appearance of a king who would set Israel free (Ps 89:4f.), restore the kingdom, triumph over the Gentiles, and internally promote the true religion:

> I will take the people of Israel from the nations among which they have gone, and will gather them from every quarter, and bring them to their own land. I will make them one nation in the land, on the mountains of Israel; and one king shall be king over them all. . . . They shall never again defile themselves with their idols and their detestable things, or with any of their transgressions. . . . My servant David shall be king over them. (Ez 37:21–24)

The hope of bringing the whole people together again appears also in Isaiah 11:1–6, but now stressing the inner transformation of society: a just king will appear who will finally impart justice, defend the weak, and bring about reconciliation and peace.

(b) Expectation of the Messiah at the Time of Jesus

At the time of Jesus there were various expectations concerning the figure of the messiah: whether victory over enemies would be brought about by God himself or by the messiah through prodigious deeds; whether the messiah would be priest or king; whether he would be a "warrior king" (as in, for example, Wis 17 and 18) or a just and peaceable king (Zec 9:9f.). But there is an important common thread running through all this. In the first place, the hoped-for messiah would be descended from David; he would, therefore, be a historical figure, not a mythical, cosmic, heavenly one. In the second place, he would carry out his mission on earth and install a historical reign—a more accurate description than "political reign." Finally, this messiah would be a public figure (so could be thought of as a political figure in this sense), but the decisive thing was that he would respond to the hopes of the people and would act to transform the situation of Israel.

As far as Jesus himself is concerned, it is a fact that he appeared in the midst of messianic expectations and that he caused a great stir in his time, so it is quite likely that the people would have asked if he was "the one who is to come" (Mt 11:3; cf. Dt 18:15, 18). The placard on the cross saying "King of the Jews," which is clearly historical, shows that the people either thought that Jesus saw himself as such or hoped that he was. It is clear that Jesus aroused some sort of hope in the people, and the word best suited to describe this at the time was *messiah*.

On the other hand, Jesus provided no firm grounds for claiming that he understood himself to be the Messiah in the sense of the awaited king or, more generally, political figure, and he certainly did not in the sense understood by the Zealots, who could have existed in Jesus' time as an incipient movement, though they did not become an organized group until later. In any case, Jesus shows no sign of typical Zealot activity (with the possible exception of the expulsion of the traders from the Temple), nor does he act on a wider scale like a descendant of David—and John 6:15 shows him fleeing when the people wanted to make him king. However, neither is it completely clear from the gospel narratives that Jesus definitely denied being the Messiah; or, said with greater caution and propriety, in the interpretation made by the synoptics it does not appear that Jesus absolutely denied responding to (some of) the messianic hopes of the people. (At the judgment before the high priest [Mk 14:62; Mt 26:64; Lk 22:67] Jesus does not give a clear answer to the high priest's question about his messianism but seems rather to evade it, as if he were trying to focus the discussion on another aspect, that of Son of Man. Something similar happens in the scene before Pilate [Mt 27:11; Mk 15:2; Lk 23:3], with the same evasive "You say so" to the question of whether he is a king, to which John adds a conversation in which Jesus takes the initiative: "Do you ask this on your own, or did others tell you about me?," ending with, "My kingdom is not from this world" [Jn 18:33–37]. And when Peter confesses him as the Christ [Mk 8:29], Jesus' reply shows that Peter has not only understood nothing but has completely distorted Jesus' real nature. In these key passages of the gospels Jesus is presented in such a way that he neither confirms nor denies that he is the Messiah.)

We can also ask whether Jesus saw himself as "son of David," which would be an equivalent way of knowing himself to be the Messiah. For a start, though, it would not be possible to establish historically that Jesus was actually descended from the family of David, since the genealogies in Matthew and Luke are more theological than historical in purpose and were formulated at a very late stage, even if the text "descended from David according to the flesh" (Rom 1:3) is an early tradition, showing that the communities were convinced that he was so descended. Jesus himself only once (Mk 12:35–37; Mt 22:41–46; Lk 20:41–44) mentions the relationship of the messiah to David, quoting Psalm 110:1. In this exegetically problematic passage Jesus could be meaning to say—beyond whether he saw himself as the Messiah or not—that the messiahship of the messiah did not stem from a fleshly reality—being a descendant of David—since the messiah is greater than David. On his own messiahship, Jesus left his audience, once more, in the dark.

The conclusion has to be that we cannot know for certain whether Jesus saw himself as the Messiah or not. One interpretation claims that he did, so that the "messianic secret" would be a creation of Jesus himself in order to avoid the misunderstanding of a "political" messianism rather than his own more "spiritual" one. Another denies it, making the messianic secret the work of the community. What is most relevant here, however, is that the gospels as a whole show that, on the one hand, Jesus did not understand himself as a Messiah-king but that, on the other, the people did relate him in some way to the hopes they had long placed in a messiah.

(c) The Development of the Title in the New Testament

Despite the ambiguity stemming from Jesus himself, all layers of the New Testament call Jesus Messiah, Christ, and make this a central title and a proper name. So the Gospel of Mark, despite its anti-triumphant tone, at least raises the question of Jesus' messiahship. The Gospel of Matthew is less scrupulous and makes this messiahship a central feature, presenting Jesus as son of David in its two preliminary chapters. The title appears nine times in the course of this gospel, with the aim of showing that in Jesus the promises of the Old Testament have been fulfilled. The Gospel of Luke also calls Jesus son of David in the infancy narratives in order to show that these promises have been fulfilled in him. All the other New Testament writings speak of Jesus as the Christ with complete acceptance.

How did the first Christians come to this conclusion when it is not clear that Jesus understood himself as the Messiah, even if his life was largely told in terms of the reality designated by this title? The answer to this question concerns us not in order to understand the exact sequence of events but to know if there was a major shift in the New Testament period in understanding messianism, when and why it came about, and what the first Christians actually meant when they applied the title messiah to Jesus.

If we accept Hahn's thesis, the Easter experience would not have led immediately to a confession of Jesus as Messiah.[1] The title would not have been applied to him from the beginning but with the deepening of reflection on the Son of Man who will come in the parousia. At a second stage, the Messiah would have been related to the "exalted one" after the resurrection and with the "Lord" in the present, and the title would have helped to explain the sort of "power" the risen Christ then had. The decisive step—both novel and scandalous—would have been taken at a third stage, when the title was related to the passion—and in effect Jesus is called "king of the Jews" by Pilate and the soldiers (Mk 15:1–20). This, which would have been a historical event for the first Christians, would have led them to rethink what being Messiah meant, thereby effecting a spectacular change in their understanding of the savior and of the salvation brought by him: the Messiah brings salvation—the original conception—but in an unsuspected way, through the cross and his death. The content of salvation is now understood not so much in terms of the Kingdom of God as in terms of redemption from sins. Finally, at a later stage, the title messiah was used to describe and interpret Jesus' work on earth, especially his working of miracles, which would not have been present in the Jewish concept of the messiah. It would appear to have been the Hellenist community that brought about this change: through understanding his earthly activity as a new Moses or as the eschatological prophet, they applied the title messiah also to describe his life.

Exactly how this process came about cannot be judged exegetically, but the conclusion seems important, at least from a systematic angle: with the title messiah the whole reality of Jesus, past, present, and future, could be described. So the title became simply coextensive with "Jesus" and so could be converted into his own proper name. In this way the title became definitively assured, but at the price—in my view—of losing definition and in particular of becoming detached from the Kingdom of God.

In mentioning "Jesus Christ" (Jesus Messiah) we are speaking of a "person" who can be designated by a name, but gradually the original content of messiah as savior and restorer of the people became lost. And, curiously, the title messiah became a proper name where Jewish thought was disappearing. The one who changed it into a definitive title was Paul, who excluded the Jewish connotation of earthly and political king from it and introduced the new Christian meaning of salvation into it. However, not to be too simplistic about this, we should remember that in Romans 1:16–17 and 3:21–26 Paul related salvation to the revelation of the *justice* of God and, furthermore, that the Old Testament background of *justice* does not permit a merely spiritual reading of salvation. The Christians of Jewish origin, for their part, kept the title for obvious reasons, since for the Jews *messiah* was the key term for designating the one they were waiting for, even though this forced them into the arduous theological and apologetic task of showing that a messiah like Jesus, crucified and raised, so unlike the one hoped for by the Jews, was already foretold in the scriptures.

2. "De-Messianization" and "Re-Messianization" of the Messiah Today

I now move from the New Testament to the present in order to reread the title messiah, evaluate the changes effected in the New Testament, and offer a solution to the paradox mentioned. I should also like to reflect on the other paradox, of which the New Testament is much more conscious: the proclamation of a *crucified* messiah. But let us first look at the present situation with regard to messiahs and messianisms.

The First World or, if one prefers, the globalized world with its postmodernity, does not seem receptive to messiahs or messianisms. It no longer has a place for the utopias of the poor and shows an obvious lack of leaders who want to support them. If one adds to this the fact that history has also shown the real dangers attendant on messianisms (populism, paternalism, dictatorship, ingenuousness, fanaticism, aggression),[2] the conclusion is that there is little point in talking about messianisms, and that to do so can be tolerated as at best a sin of young nations.

J.-B. Metz is speaking for many when he says, "There is a new outlook, a new mentality in Europe; a new spectre is stalking Europe: a variant on what is discussed in intellectual circles as postmodernity. There is an everyday postmodernity of hearts that banishes the poverty and misery of the so-called Third World to an incomparably greater distance."[3]

The conclusion is that, just as years ago secularization questioned the content of the title Son of God in order to diminish divinity, postmodernity is now—objectively—questioning the title messiah in order to diminish popular utopias and hopes. Nevertheless, the poor of this world, who make up the great bulk of its population, need utopias, which can be as simple as life and dignity being possible, but which are utopias for them in the strict sense, since life is precisely *what cannot be taken for granted* and what there *is still no place for* in this world. This same Third World goes on hoping for the appearance of leaders with hearts of flesh, not of stone, who will provide them with hope and ways to life.

For this basic reason—the need the crucified peoples have for utopias, messianic hopes, or whatever, and the inaction, lack of interest, or contempt shown toward this need by the ruling system—I propose to reflect on messiahs and messianisms as seen today, since "messianism has always been and will be the best shock tactic for tackling the problems of the present, opening oneself to a future filled with hope."[4] (Those who warn, even when they do so in good faith and with a certain measure of reason, that postmodernity is good for tempering exalted messianisms, can be answered by reminding them that messianism is good for awakening sleeping and soporific free-market democracies.)

(a) Theological Caution: "De-Messianization"

The recent eclipse of messianism has historical roots, but it also has theological ones, since in some sense it begins straight after Jesus' resurrection (although—decades later—it was recovered in the synoptic view of Jesus and his proclamation of the Kingdom). One can put forward the thesis that two things have happened to messianism over the course of history: one is that priority has been given to the mediator over mediation, to Christ over the Kingdom of God; the other, related to the first, is that the mediator has come to be understood more on the lines of *Son of God* (which relates him to the *person* of God) than on those of *Messiah* (which relates him to the *will* of God, the *Kingdom* of God). I shall discuss the reasons for this later, but the decisive one was most probably that the parousia did not come about as expected.

(i) A mediator without mediation: toward a Messiah with no kingdom. After the resurrection, *Christ*, meaning *the Messiah*, became a proper name for Jesus, but the title gradually lost definition and specificity, and a process began that I have—perhaps provocatively—called the *de-messianization of the Messiah.* This process was able to come into being through the plurivalence and ambiguity of the concept of messiah, as we have seen. On the one hand, it is clear that by calling Jesus Messiah Christians were claiming that a longstanding hope of Israel, the appearance of a savior, had been fulfilled in his resurrection; on the other hand,

however, it is not so clear what model of savior could or should be used for understanding Jesus.

In other words, after the resurrection Jesus was understood as *savior*, and was therefore called *Messiah*, but the concept of the salvation he brought underwent a change: what was central in the Old Testament, that salvation would be the historical salvation of an oppressed people, no longer seems to be a central element in messianism. Christ gradually ceased to be presented in the semblance of the Messiah who, particularly after the exile, appears in correlation with the hope of the poor, as the just king who will finally impart justice, defend the weak, and bring about peace and reconciliation. So let us look first, tentatively and cautiously (so as to avoid simplifications and anachronisms), at the direction the process took so that we can situate it later in a theological and historical context.

First, the hope of *historical* salvation, brought about in history, was replaced by that of transcendent salvation, which will take place in the parousia, as the universal resurrection. This does not mean that the New Testament no longer gives importance to earthly realities—that it does is shown by its ethical demands, the call to charity, care of the weak, and so on—but that these things now seem more like ethical requirements *following from* an already formed faith than like reconstructing the central reality brought by Jesus, which is in correlation with his messianism and is the central element in the formation of faith. Salvation is furthermore concentrated on salvation from sins (plus freedom from the law and from death) and little by little becomes salvation in the *singular*, with the tendency to downplay *plural* salvations, of body and soul, as they appear in the Old Testament and in the gospels.

A second point is that the correlative of messianic hopes is no longer the *people* with their own hopes but the individual and the community with theirs. Again, this does not mean that the New Testament discards the notion of collectivity, of the people, since what springs from faith in the resurrection of Christ is precisely a community, and the nascent *ekklesia* expresses its own identity in terms that all imply collectivity: people, body, temple. But on the other hand it is also true that—for understandable historical reasons—the actual hopes of the peoples as historical peoples, what today we would call their cultural, social, and political aspirations—as basically human as individual or community aspirations—tend to disappear. These are such hopes as for slavery to cease and freedom to come, for wars to end and peace to supervene, for repression to stop and justice to reign; all in all, for death to cease and life to remain. So the "messianic" hopes destined to be fulfilled by the Messiah would tend to disappear.

And finally, specifically, there is less importance attached in understanding of the Messiah to what in the prophetic books of the Old Testament and in the synoptics is the direct recipient of hope: the *poor* among the people, the historically impoverished and excluded. Once again, the New Testament has not lost the idea of the partiality of God and of God's Christ, since in principle the social inclusion of Gentiles, women, and slaves means, in historical terms, showing partiality. But neither can it be said that Christ will be preached to those waiting for the "just king" of Isaiah, for the Messiah who will bring justice to orphans and widows and will therefore be partial.

These are the cautions. Let us now look briefly at the context that historically situates—and so qualifies—what has been said, remembering furthermore that every text of the New Testament was *canonized* in the *overall* context of the Bible. The early Christians went on reading the Old Testament—in which the people's hopes appear clearly—and refer to it as *the* scripture, which suggests that the process of "de-messianization" was not as straightforward as the above summary might suggest.

On the other hand, concentration on the mediator is already implicit in the experience of the resurrection, which concentrates God's eschatological action on a singular person, Jesus crucified and raised (although it refers to a *collective* universal future). Historically, expectation of the imminent parousia, the welcome de-nationalization of the understanding of the people of God, and above all the historical littleness of the communities and their insignificance for changing society, all combine to make it most improbable that they could have considered the problems and hopes of the poor en masse—structurally, we should say today—in order to give a historical answer to them.

All this needs to be properly understood. I am not underrating the novelty claimed in the New Testament: that Christ brings salvation and forgiveness of sins, and that his Spirit can re-create "new men and women." But I do want to insist on the change effected in understanding of the word *messiah,* brought about precisely when it was applied to Jesus as a proper name. This brings us to a central problem in the New Testament, one that goes beyond the well-known step from the Jesus who preaches to the Christ who is preached, although it is also expressed in this step. This, in my view, is the matter of a change in understanding of God's plan: the *kernel* of the kerygma is no longer directly the coming of the Kingdom but the appearance of Christ. Although mediator and mediated are still related, the "good news" of God is now concentrated on the appearance of Christ and not so much on the coming of the Kingdom, is focused more on the mediator—the one sent by God—than on the mediation, the actuality of a world transformed according to the will of God. The step was undoubtedly taken little by little. At the start, expectation of "the one who was to come," the Son of Man, was convergent with and could be equivalent to expectation of the coming of the Kingdom. But the two things gradually drifted away from one another.

(ii) Priority of the Son over the Messiah. In addition to the above and following on from it, the mediator came to be understood more in his relationship to the *person of God* (which was better expressed in the titles Lord, Word, and Son) than in his relationship to the *Kingdom of God*, which is the relationship implied in the title "messiah" in the Old Testament tradition. In present-day terms, the innermost reality of Jesus is seen more and more as *sonship*, sacrament of the Father, historical presence of God in this world, and this—really good news, obviously—is the greatest thing that can happen in history. In this way, although it is applied to him as a proper name, the title Christ (Messiah)—with all that it entails of relationship to the salvation of the poor and to the Kingdom of God—

will not be the most distinctive one given to him. The most distinctive designation will be that of *Son of God.*[5]

This, put here in abstract terms, has had consequences—some of which strike me as serious—for faith and theology, since in just this point of messianism a virtually absolute break between the Old and New Testaments would seem to have taken place, a break that could, moreover, be taken as an advance in revelation of God and, above all, an outdating—not to say abolition—of the Old Testament and its popular hopes. Put systematically, the danger consists in ignoring the fact—or its no longer being so present as in the Old Testament and the synoptics—that the good news also applies to mediation: a world, God's creation, after God's own heart, in which the appearance of the mediator and his reality as sacrament of "the person" of the Father can relegate to second place how important it is for God for his will to be done for this world—for this world to be changed according to his will.

Let me repeat here what I said in the first volume, and pardon the irony. Sometimes one has the sensation, after centuries of history, that some Christians see the Father in heaven absolutely happy because the mediator, the Son, has appeared on earth. This mediator (and some communities) has turned out well for him, so it is no longer so important for creation to have turned out well for him. Irony apart, though, there is very little logic in this, since it is precisely the sending of the Son that expresses God's definitive commitment *to his creation* (see Rom 8:18–25), which does not eliminate but heightens the problem of how his creation is faring. They may be anthropomorphic, but it would do no harm to reread the words of Genesis in order to reflect on what God might—still today—feel on seeing his creation: "The LORD saw that the wickedness of humankind was great in the earth. . . . And the LORD was sorry that he had made humankind on the earth, and it grieved him to his heart" (6:5–6). This indignation of God's is what we need to recover and maintain in order to reassess the importance that the mediation, *God's* creation, has for God.

(b) The Theological Urgency: "Re-Messianization"

It could be objected that this is how things happened and so how we have to accept them. There are two things to be said about this. First, more theologically, the change cannot ignore or exclude but must include what Jesus' true messianism was, something the synoptics make clear, particularly by going back firmly to Jesus and making his relationship with the poor central, which, theoretically, will become more actual through the nonappearance of the parousia and with Christians facing up to the acute problem of salvation in history. Second, the Third World is still crying out for mediation. This is why I talk of the need to *re-messianize* Christ, the need for *a Messiah with a kingdom for the poor*. It is clear that the New Testament, overall, rejects the Messiah as political and warrior king, but it would be a serious distortion to make Christ into the Messiah of a purely spiritual kingdom without incarnation, into a universal Messiah with no partiality for the poor, without effective mercy for their sufferings, without demanding that justice be done to their oppressors.

(i) A liberating Christ. This brings us to the messianism of Christ at the present time, and to speak of this we have to start by overcoming two prejudices that will never entirely go away—as shown by the way the church is now turning in on itself after the boldness of Medellín.

The first is that, although Jesus did not seek to be a political Messiah, still less a king, shaping the *polis*—in the direction of the Kingdom of God—was still central for him and he would use his power to do so, even if this power was not political or military power but the power of truth (proclaiming the utopia of the Kingdom, denouncing the anti-Kingdom), the power of love (with its correlatives of mercy and justice), and the power of witness (his faithfulness to the cross). So what is dangerous about denying the political aspect of the Messiah Jesus is not recalling his rejection of being a warrior and nationalist king and of a theocratic kingdom, but rather stripping the notion of Messiah of the oppressions and hopes of the poor and the victims, on one hand, and the need to use a power on the other. This power, being the power of truth and love, is no less *powerful*, and so also conflictive, as the recent history of Latin America shows. The danger lies in making the essential saving relationship between messiah and masses disappear.

The second prejudice lies in the reductionism of tackling the problem purely from an analysis of the title messiah. We should not say, "Jesus is the Messiah" but, "Messiah is Jesus." If we approach the synoptics from this standpoint, we find a Jesus who, independent of titles, resembles the "just and partial" king of Isaiah, who seeks to install law and justice, who shows mercy to the weak and denounces the oppressors, who takes note of the hopes of the people, and especially of the poor, as shown in two key texts in which Jesus proclaims the good news to the poor: Matthew 11:2–6 and Luke 4:16–20. And this should not be excluded after the resurrection, since it opens up new horizons of understanding (the Messiah as savior and forgiver of sins) but does not invalidate Jesus' life, being rather its most solemn confirmation, even though the chronology of the writings of the New Testament shows that it took some time to *go back* to the story of Jesus.

Which title is used to name this Jesus is secondary; the main point is that this Jesus expresses the core of the messianic hopes of the poor in the Old Testament, even though he brings about profound changes in their theocratic, nationalistic, exclusivist, military, and other similar conceptions. This is what the synoptics show, and this is why they present Jesus in essential relationship to the Kingdom of God, since "the messianic hope was focused initially not on an actual and particular figure but on the coming of the Kingdom of God."[6]

Today too, as in the time of the synoptics, it is urgent to reclaim the central element of the title messiah to avoid falling into the paradoxical situation where Messiah—Christ—is the term most widely used to refer to Jesus yet without suggesting anything of biblical messianism or bringing anything to the hope of the poor. This is precisely what liberation theology has tried to do by applying the title *liberator* to Christ. The faith of Latin American Christians and the christology of liberation have given meaning back to the title of messiah. That of liberator aims to reclaim the central element of the earliest meaning of the title: in history someone will appear who will bring salvation to the poor and the oppressed; a just king will appear who will free the mass of the people from their slavery. This is how Jesus is seen by many in the Third World. This does not imply a return to the Old Testament, purely and simply, let alone viewing the liberator as a nationalist, theocratic, warrior king. It means reclaiming and upholding the essential: keeping the oppression and hopes of the poor before one's eyes and giving them an answer.

The historical situation of Latin America makes this reclamation of Jesus' messianism possible and actually requires it. With or without the title of liberator, it is clear that Jesus has to be viewed in this light, since otherwise he would not do justice to the true situation of Latin America or to the true nature of a Christ who is Jesus of Nazareth. This, indeed, is what Puebla sanctioned when it recognized that "many segments of the People of God" are searching "for the ever new face of Christ, who is the answer to their legitimate yearning for integral liberation" (no. 173). This does not mean reducing the totality of Christ to what is expressed in the title liberator or, more precisely, a reductionist interpretation against which Puebla warns: turning Christ into "a politician, a leader, a revolutionary, or a simple prophet" (no. 178). But it does make possible and require a christology that develops overall from the liberating messianism of Jesus.

We need to avoid pitfalls, such as making the title liberator into a magic formula to resolve all problems, or of reducing Christ to being the answer only to social hopes, ignoring those other personal and inner dimensions of the human spirit, including those of the poor, or of fanaticizing the poor and deceiving them in the name of a liberation that would work virtually *ex opere operato*. But the intuition remains valid: Christ, by definition, is Messiah, and this messianism today can and—very largely—must be described as liberation. It is sad to have to recall that Christ is liberator, but through this tautology, Christ Liberator, we can perhaps regain the need and urgency of the messianic utopia.

(ii) A crucified Messiah: the "messianic mystery." In order to regain the messianism of Christ, we need to return to Jesus of Nazareth. But then we come up against an unexpected element: Jesus is a "crucified" Messiah. And this also has to be incorporated into present-day understanding of the Messiah.

In the first place, it has to be viewed positively, since a crucified Messiah destroys the human tendency to see messianism in a magical light: "The magic man will come in whose hands all responsibilities will be discharged and from whom we shall receive all solutions and lands flowing with milk and honey."[7] A crucified Messiah crucifies—and so cures—messianic conceptions tending to the mechanical, magical, and egoistic. This is what the temptation stories express (Mt 4:1–11; Lk 4:1–13).

In the second place, it has to be seen as something scandalous: a crucified Messiah confronts us brutally with the *mysterium iniquitatis*. The best messiahs throughout history, people like Archbishop Romero, are persecuted and done away with in three years. Why is this world, God's creation, capable of killing its best, those who bring it salvation? And the most generous revolutions—with grave faults and errors but also with great measures of generosity and popular hope— are attacked implacably and unmercifully until their disappearance is achieved.

Why does this world not give them a chance? Why does it flatten them—and use those who are not better but very often worse than the original revolutionaries to do so? "Only ten years later, nothing is left but the question, 'Where is that God who seemed to pass through the history of Nicaragua?'"[8]

These are the hard facts of history that cannot be passed over, and this brings me to a final consideration. Scripture scholars call the warnings Jesus gives to his audience in the synoptics not to divulge his marvelous works the "messianic secret." (Xavier Alegre observes astutely that not only does Jesus impose the messianic secret during his life so as to avoid misunderstandings, so to speak [Mk 1:25; 1:34; 1:44; 5:43; 7:36; 8:26], but that the evangelist carries it on even after the resurrection. And he adds that it is not by chance that Mark's original gospel ends abruptly at 16:8—verses 9–20 being a second-century addition—without scenes of appearances but with the angelic command to go to Galilee, the place where Jesus was active and where his death was first plotted on account of his actions. This—not Jerusalem—is the place to meet the risen Christ. All this means that the "incomprehension of his followers"—a historical reality corresponding to the messianic secret—continues even after the resurrection.)[9] Whether the gospel accounts in which Jesus asks for the secret to be kept are a device by which the community explained why Jesus did not openly proclaim himself to be the Messiah, when the community was claiming that he was (Wrede), or whether the prohibition stemmed from Jesus himself, not to reject the title for himself absolutely but in order to prevent misunderstandings (Cullmann), the important thing is that these accounts warn against any messianic triumphalism.

A still more basic aspect to be stressed, it seems to me, is the brute fact that the Messiah finished on a cross for being *consistently* Messiah—that is, for proclaiming hope to the poor and denouncing his oppressors. From this point of view we now have to speak not of a messianic secret, real or hypothetical, but of the *messianic mystery*: the true Messiah, defender of the hope of the poor, finishes on a cross.

At the present, as in the past, messiahs and messianisms do not magically resolve the problems of history. And not only that. Those who offer the best of messianic hopes and practice—whether an Archbishop Romero or the protagonists of a revolution—have to listen to the sentence, "He deserves to die." Messianism and crucifixion are linked, then, in the New Testament and in history, and this is why it is important to bear in mind both that the Messiah was crucified and that the one who was crucified is the Messiah.

In a thought-provoking text Christian Duquoc upholds a "historical nonmessianism as the basis of the sense of a messianism founded on Easter," and points out that "the messianic ideology has been contaminated by the same logic as oppression: it tries to conquer power instead of changing it, making it different": hence the "need" for messianism to be "crucified." But he also stresses that it would be misinterpreting the messianism of Christ to make it something purely spiritual and mystical. With all the reservations he expresses, he recalls the basic aspect, which I have also tried to establish:

Jewish messianism is at root the certainty that the God of the alliance is the God of those deprived of hope; he takes up the cause of those stripped of all power. Jesus does not in any way reject this movement; on the contrary, he radicalizes it by expressing in practice that a power, even a religious one, that is indifferent to despair, oppression and even distortion, is a perverse power.

The new messianism "does not provide too many indications where means are concerned," but for the purpose of this chapter what is important is that "God ceases to be a support for destructive powers and becomes the God of the 'poor.' . . . God is still clad in the trappings of a king, of a political leader, though not now to impose a new imperialism but to impose justice."[10]

To conclude: the real context in which we can examine messianism adequately is not the content of hope—people's earthly hopes or transcendent saving hope—but the nature of power: whether oppressive power is used or renounced. Christ, the Messiah, is the one who is crucified, without power; but this crucified one is still Messiah, Christ, someone who takes up the hopes of the poor, of the masses, who channels their energies and sets them to producing.

This re-messianization of the Messiah requires a re-messianization of the church and of theology, and the task is necessary, utopic, and also urgent: "Only utopically and with hope can one believe and have the strength to endeavor, with all the poor and oppressed of the world, to turn history back, subvert it, and launch it in another direction."[11]

Chapter 11

Lord

The Lordship of Christ, Hope, and Theodicy

The first Christians soon expressed what the nature of Christ was in the *present* through the generic notion of *exaltation*, as we have seen, but throughout the New Testament they expressed it more radically by conferring on him the title of Lord *(kyrios)*, which expresses exaltation with power, his sovereignty in the present.

The content of this title is extremely dense, since it brings together meanings deriving from Judaism, Hellenism, and—possibly—Eastern religions, and, above all, because it gradually became the means of expressing very diverse aspects of the nature of Christ. So the title Lord expresses his current presence in the community and in the cosmos, the intimate relationship of believers to Christ, and the intimate relationship of Christ to God, above all on the *functional* level of the exercise of his lordship. In short, as Cullmann says, the application of the title Lord to him does not exclude the possibility of applying any other title to him, with the exception of Father.[1] To this one needs to add that as time passed the title acquired a polemical and existential significance, since in proclaiming Christ *kyrios*, believers had to renounce other divinities, and this became their life, as Revelation attests.

As we have already done, we can ask ourselves how much of all this is present when we Christians of today confess Christ as Lord: it may not be much, and it may be that "the Lord" has become, like other titles, basically a *designating* but not *signifying* title. In order to reclaim the relevance of the title I shall make a rereading of it from the exercise of lordship by Jesus of Nazareth and in the context of major problems of today. Specifically, I propose to examine (1) the possibilities the title offers as a *formula of faith* and some of its dangers; (2) *service* as the most specific aspect of Christian lordship; (3) *hope* that the lordship of Christ can mold persons, communities, and history; (4) the question of *theodicy* and Christian responsibility for "making Christ Lord in history"; and (5) the need to unmask and combat other *kyrioi*, the *idols* of today. First, though, some words on the origin and meaning of the title, to help us to understand what "Lord" says and

152

what it does not say when Paul incorporates the title into his christology and makes it central to it.

1. The Origin and Meaning of *Kyrios*

In the Old Testament there are various terms used to express the reality of lordship. In Hebrew, *baal* means owner, possessor, despot, and in the religious context it always refers to the divinity. *Adon* means the lord who has sovereignty over persons, and *adonai* means "my Lord," an expression that was not used in everyday conversation but was the form in which God was mentioned to avoid pronouncing the name of Yahweh. Aramaic has another term, *mar*, used by the disciples, but not in the Old Testament, as a title applied to the divinity. In Hellenism, the word designating the one who holds lordship is *kyrios*, a title that gradually acquired religious meaning through Eastern religions and the cult of the emperor, so that the *kyrios* came to have unconditional power, in effect divinity, assigned to him. The Septuagint translated the Hebrew *adonai* into Greek as *kyrios*, and at the time of the first Christian communities it already had a religious meaning. So when Christians applied this title to Jesus, they related him in some form to the divinity, making him a sharer in God's sovereignty.

Looking at its usage in the New Testament, Jesus is called "Lord" in the gospels several times, but they do not yet make any reference to his relationship to God, although the expression should not be regarded as one of mere courtesy in daily discourse.[2] What the disciples meant by calling him lord during his lifetime can be gathered from the passages in which they call him both lord and master.[3] When they call him master (*rabbi* in Hebrew, *didaskalos* in Greek), the use is spontaneous and unreflecting and has no further christological significance. But when they use the expression *the* master (*o didaskalos*, in the nominative), then something specific is being claimed for Jesus—his authority and, above all, some type of special bond between his person and those who follow him. Recognizing him as master would then express a specific relationship, personal and binding, which is what would also be meant by calling him lord. This is why the expression lord appears often in the gospels in the context of the disciples' following, and it denotes two things: one is Jesus' sovereign authority in calling people to follow him; the other—a logical supposition—is Jesus' capacity to mold the characters and lives of his followers in a specific way. So lordship is not a pure and arbitrary authoritarianism, to which people have to respond in servility, but a capacity for summoning and molding, to which the response is availability.

If we now ask where, when, and why the New Testament communities applied the title lord to the risen Christ, the answers are quite varied.[4] It is worth analyzing them, if only summarily, because this title is, more than any other, the product of (possibly) very diverse traditions, and knowing them leads to a better understanding of the variety and riches of its meaning when the title is used by Paul. It is also worth it because the origin of the title lends itself to discussion about whether Christianity changed radically by regarding Jesus no longer as Son of Man and prophet (in the Jewish tradition) but as the one who is present, with power, in worship (in the tradition of Eastern religions). So let me, in the form of a brief excursus, set out first the various statements on the subject that might be called classical and then provide a synthesis of the different meanings of the title once it has been taken up by Paul.

At the beginning of the twentieth century, controversy was unleashed with the suggestion that the title came from pagan cultures. In 1913 Bossuet wrote that the religious title *kyrios* was Eastern in origin, used in mystic circles in the veneration of their divinities.[5] Christians, no longer expecting the second coming, were concentrating on worship; that is where they felt the presence of Jesus, and in order to express this they made use of this religious title. His conclusion is that worship took the place of eschatological expectation and Christianity broke away from its roots in Judaism and the Jesus movement to re-root itself in pagan religious ideas. Lohmeyer upheld a similar thesis.[6] At the time of Jesus there was a widespread longing for a savior, earthly or heavenly, to appear. Among the Romans this was expressed by applying the titles lord and Son of God to the emperor. What the Christians would have done through their contact with the Hellenic world in Antioch was to transform Jewish faith in a messiah Jesus into faith in a Jesus who was Son of God and Lord. So, for both these authors, the title *kyrios* would derive from pagan religious cultures and would mold Christianity to take on elements of these cultures.

Cullmann ventured a different and contrary opinion: the origin of the title should be sought in the worship of the dawning Christian community of Palestine. He deploys an *a priori* argument in support of this thesis: The very existence of the community presupposes that Christ, as exalted, is already present in it: "How is it that after the death of Christ a particular community was able to come into being? If Jesus' followers really placed all their hopes in the future . . . one cannot see clearly what could have been the source of the impulse that gave birth to a community in which enthusiasm ruled and whose life was dominated, wholly and entirely, by manifestations of the Spirit."[7] But he also argues *a posteriori*: as a matter of fact, the very ancient expression *maranatha* appears in the earliest communities (1 Cor 16:22), used in Aramaic within a Greek text. The *mar* component of *maranatha* has a meaning very close to that of *Kyrios Iesous*, something like "lord of heaven" or "heavenly sovereign." The expression can be understood either as a confession of faith—"Our Lord comes"—or as a petition—"Lord, come!" According to Cullmann, the second meaning is the more accurate, since Paul translates confessions of faith into Greek but not prayers, and Revelation 22:20 also uses the expression in the imperative as a prayer, and not in the indicative as a confession of faith. Cullmann himself, however, associates both possible meanings of the formula with the eucharistic context in which it is used. On the one hand, there is no doubting the eschatological hope expressed in the "Come, Lord!," which would describe Jesus in much the same way as calling him Son of Man sought to express. But on the other hand, Jesus would be experienced as present in the community in the breaking of bread, and his coming would have taken place in some form (1 Cor 11:23–29). So the community was unifying its longing for the future coming of Jesus with his actual presence; it was not only waiting for the parousia but living it in the eucharist. It is most probable, therefore, that the

Palestine communities were already invoking Jesus as Lord, though Cullmann admits that it was in the Hellenist communities that the content of the title was deepened and radicalized. (Kramer took the view that with the title *kyrios* the community was confessing—in its worship—the presence of the Lord in the community and in the cosmos, but that he was not being related to either the past or the future, which would invalidate Cullmann's thesis that the title originated in the early Aramaic-speaking community.)[8]

According to Hahn, the title had a secular origin and was used during Jesus' lifetime, as we have seen.[9] After Easter the earliest tradition introduced a double meaning into it: the unlimited power of Jesus and the total submission of the community. On the other hand, in the liturgical gatherings "our Lord" was invoked, but in expectation of the parousia. Only later was this idea combined with that of messianic exaltation and enthronement in the present, based on Psalm 110 but also motivated by the delay in the parousia. In this environment the Greek translation of the Septuagint played a major part: the title *kyrios* that appears in it was applied increasingly to Jesus, without this necessarily leading to ideas of his divinity. Only in Hellenist Christianity of pagan origin did the idea of the divine essence of the exalted *kyrios* finally take root. The hymn in Philippians 2:6–11 would stand at the threshold of this development.

Finally, Schweizer represents an intermediate position.[10] The Palestinian communities had two basic convictions: the first was the expectation that Jesus was to come as judge of the last days; the other was that he appears to his disciples as the master, determines their lives, and requires obedience, and this too is a source of hope. The step to *kyrios* was taken because the prophets called the judge who was to come *marana*, which explains why in the liturgy Jesus was called *judge, mar,* and *lord*. The Lord of the end of time has become the Lord present now and the *kyrios* of the eucharistic community. And just as there were worship communities that invoked their *kyrioi* (Osiris, Atis) to free them from evils, this also helped Christians to see Jesus as Lord of the world.

After this brief survey we can now pull together and organize the different elements expressed in the title as they are used by Paul. *Kyrios* expresses, first and foremost, *the living reality of the Lord who is at work in the community*. So the community expresses its faith by confessing him as *kyrios* (Phil 2:11; 1 Cor 12:3; Rom 10:9); its liturgy is the celebration of the table or supper of the Lord (1 Cor 10:16–22; 1 Cor 11:20), who guarantees the unity of the community; proclaiming the gospel is carrying out the Lord's work (1 Cor 9:1; 15:58). In the second place, the *kyrios molds and regulates the daily life of the community*: divorce and remarriage (1 Cor 7:10f.), the place of virgins (1 Cor 7:25). Third, *Christians have an ongoing personal relationship* with the *kyrios*, whom they address in prayer, as Paul states of himself (2 Cor 12:8). Fourth, the *kyrios molds the history of salvation*: he will appear in the parousia to judge and finally unite himself with the community (1 Thes 4:15–17; 3:13; 1 Cor 1:8; 16:22). And already now, until the parousia, he exercises a reign over the living and the dead (Rom 14:9) and over the cosmos (1 Cor 15:24f.). Finally, Paul constantly uses the expression "in the Lord" to *shape the whole of Christian life, both personal and in community.*

Whatever the origin and evolution of the title may be, then, it became an essential part of the New Testament. Overall, it was Paul who worked out the lordship of Christ theologically, although he would have found *kyrios* already applied to Christ in the Hellenist communities. Among the great variety of meanings, its central one is that of *active presence* in the community, in worship, in history. And this being so, we should inquire not only into the origin of the term but also into the *historical* situations and experiences that led to the conviction of this presence of Christ. Briefly, these could be of two types: first, the gifts or charisms experienced in liturgical assemblies; then, the experience of solidarity among believers, above all at the shared table. In other words, experience of creativity and of life, in liturgy and daily living, is what historically manifests the actual presence of Jesus. The conclusion is that, in place of being viewed primarily as Son of Man or Messiah, Jesus began to be seen also as a being in the line of divinity present in the community. This marks a decisive step in faith and in christological reflection, one that goes beyond the experience the disciples had with Jesus.

2. Reflections on the Lordship of Christ

If we now ask how much of the foregoing is present today in the minds of those who invoke Christ as Lord, what they understand by invoking him in this way, what importance this has for their faith and their following of him, the answer is not at all clear. Perhaps the charismatic and Pentecostal movements understand what they are saying (leaving aside whether what they understand by "the Lord" corresponds to the reality of Jesus), but others will probably have only the concept of a vague lordship of Christ over history, which they will normally not bother to investigate, or they will simply use the title Lord as one more way of naming Christ. And so we say, "The Lord says . . . " or, "We ask you, Lord . . . " without knowing exactly whether we are addressing Christ or God the Father.

I do not want to exaggerate, but it seems to me that a vitally important title—and with it a decisive New Testament christology—has been relegated to the history of christological *concepts* and no longer has any real relevance to the present-day *reality* of faith, theology, and Christian life, with a corresponding loss to all three. The solution to this problem does not lie in changing our current language, but it does require us to introduce the implication of calling Christ "Lord" and not something else into our understanding of faith and into Christian practice. The following reflections are designed to help this.

(a) Christian Understanding of "the Lord Jesus" as a Formula of Faith

The title *kyrios* was used from a very early date as an inclusive expression of the nature and content of the new faith, which shows that it is not just one more title but of decisive importance. In fact, the title appears in two *homologies*, community acclamations in the liturgy, which express its gratitude and submission to

Christ. These homologies are *Kyrios Iesous* (1 Cor 12:3) and *Kyrios Iesous Christos* (Phil 2:11). A third text, Romans 10:9, can be considered a definition of faith, a sort of condensation of what we might call primitive dogma, because it states a saving event. Let us examine these three texts, with a brief reflection on each of them.

(i) Orthodoxy and orthopraxis. Romans 10:9 says, "If you confess with your lips that Jesus is Lord . . . you will be saved." This must be a very early formulation of faith, pre-Pauline, found in a still more condensed and primitive form in the phrase "call[ing] on the name of the Lord" (Rom 10:13; 1 Cor 1:2). In the Old Testament this invocation is addressed to God himself (cf. Jl 3:5, which Paul is quoting in Rom 10:13), which means that the New Testament is making a bold claim that will mark the development of christology: the salvation that comes from God— and definitely only from God—now also comes from calling on Jesus. So he is no longer considered only as *mediator* of salvation but is invoked as *grantor* of salvation. In functional terms, this expresses his nature as being part of the divinity.

This is what is basic and novel about the definition: it expresses faith in Jesus. Being a definition, it refers to orthodoxy, that is, to how to formulate faith correctly. But, looking from the life of Jesus and from the present, we need to put some reservation on a "pure" definition of faith. Jesus' life is known to demonstrate the priority accorded to orthopraxis over orthodoxy (see *JL*, pp. 189–92), even when confession of faith includes proclamation of the Lord. Jesus deliberately states, "Not everyone who says to me, 'Lord, Lord,' will enter the kingdom of heaven, but only the one who does the will of my Father in heaven" (Mt 7:21), and in Luke 6:46 he asks, "Why do you call me 'Lord, Lord,' and do not do what I tell you?"

These texts perhaps express the conjoining of the titles master and lord during Jesus' lifetime, with the implication that calling Jesus lord without behaving like Jesus-the-master is seriously inconsistent. Matthew 10:24, "A disciple is not above the teacher, nor a slave above the master" (said after speaking about persecution) follows the same line, expressing the common destiny in persecution between the Lord and those who follow him. In Matthew 8:21, to the request, "Lord, let me first go and bury my father," Jesus replies, "Follow me and let the dead bury their own dead," which shows just how radical following him has to be.[11] The synoptics, then, warn against the danger of separating orthodoxy and orthopraxis and of the uselessness of the former without the latter.

This danger, nevertheless, becomes more real after the resurrection. What now has to be done in order to be saved could be focused and concentrated on invoking Jesus correctly. It is not that confession of faith excludes orthopraxis, but there is a danger of which one has to be careful, as Juan Luis Segundo has perceptively seen: "The question 'What must I do to be saved?' is not answered with, for example, Matthew 25:31ff., but by mentioning joining the community, whose constitutive element is nothing other than faith in Jesus Christ: 'Believe in the Lord Jesus and you will be saved, you and your household' (Acts 16:31; cf. 2:37, 41, 46)."[12]

(ii) The possibility of cursing Jesus. In 1 Corinthians 12:3 the following assertion is made: "No one speaking by the Spirit of God ever says 'Let Jesus be cursed!' and no one can say 'Jesus is Lord!' except by the Holy Spirit."

The second part of this versicle is a homology, and makes plain the importance of the Spirit, since it and only it enables us to confess Jesus as Lord, which means to say that this confession expresses what is deepest in Christian faith. But, on the other hand, the first part expresses the possibility, not only of not knowing Jesus, but of cursing him, which is really surprising in a community that calls itself Christian. What historical context led Paul to make this incredible statement is not clear. Perhaps, as Cullmann says, the justification Christians gave for having cursed Jesus would be that the Spirit had brought them to do so—in accordance with Matthew 10:17–20: "Do not worry about how you are to speak or what you are to say; for what you are to say will be given to you at that time."[13]

In the community in Corinth the problem was not, then, confessing a *kyrios*, the risen Christ, but confessing the *kyrios* who Jesus is. Hence Paul's reaction: without the Spirit we cannot confess Christ as Lord, but if we are moved by the Spirit—as the Corinthians prided themselves on being—then we have to go back to Jesus, to confess *him* as the Lord. (Forgetting or even rejecting Jesus, in theory but above all in practice, has been a perennial temptation and danger throughout history. It is not merely that we Christians do things contrary to Jesus but that we do not see our true value in acting as Jesus really would—in poverty, humility, denunciation, and a host of other things—seeking instead to find pseudo-justifications for our actions in the Lordship of the risen Christ, in the power, exaltation, finality, solemnity, triumph, and victory of the risen Christ. And we do all this in the name of the Spirit—or of church customs and laws.)

(iii) The scandal of Christ Jesus: a crucified kyrios. The letter to the Philippians (2:11) declares that "every tongue should confess that Jesus Christ is Lord." "Lord" is a new name given to Christ, and it is "the name that is above all names." The *Iesous Kyrios Christos* then becomes a definition of faith. This provokes two observations.

The first is not very important for analysis of the title lord, but is, indirectly, for that of messiah. This is that the homology is not formulated just as "Lord Jesus" but as "Lord Jesus-Christ." This implies that Jesus Christ is becoming one name, and implies that Christ, the term that originally translated the title messiah, is losing its strength and has become a second name for indicating Jesus (as Lohmeyer has shown), which can be imagined only in a pagan-Christian, Greek-speaking community and not in the Jewish community in Palestine. As I have already said, this shows the beginning of the de-messianization of the messiah.

The second observation is more important. It concerns the reason the hymn in Philippians gives for calling Jesus "Lord," since the christological confession appears only at the end. This reason lies in the *kenosis* and abasement of Christ. In the logic of the New Testament there is no attempt to exalt suffering but only to establish that what happens in this abasement—specifically, Christ emptying himself of the divine condition to take on the condition of a servant and of an ordinary person—is pleasing to God. (For the concept of "what is pleasing to God," see *JL*, pp. 227–30.)

In this way the same sort of novelty appears that we found in examining the titles high priest (himself the victim) and messiah (crucified). Just as not anyone can be mediator, but only the one who is faithful and merciful to the end, so not anyone is lord, but only the one who has emptied himself, the crucified Jesus. The gospels put this in simpler terms: not anyone is lord, but the one who lowers himself.

In sum, then, the definition "Jesus is the Lord" expresses something new and unheard-of: the putting of Jesus, in some sense, on the same level as Yahweh. The fact that calling on the Lord Jesus, without further ado, should be seen as sufficient for salvation—on the level of orthodox confession—presents him as "beyond" a simple mediator. This is the direction the New Testament takes in designating what will later, in more precise language, be called the *divinity* of Christ. This is the first stage of applying the title—saying "Jesus is the Lord."

This development, however, is not simple, nor is the orthodox definition sufficient in itself, since it can be perverted, as in the case of the Corinthians, and it has to go in tandem with practice. Above all, it is not evident and cannot be trivialized, not only because predicating the lordship of Christ of any human being is not evident, but for the reason adduced for predicating it of Christ: his *kenosis* and abasement, which brings us back to the eternal scandal that the divinity of Christ is shot through with crucifixion. This is what is at stake in the second stage of applying the title—saying "Lord is Jesus."

(b) Lordship as Humble and Non-Triumphalist Service

Before moving on to the positive and specific content of the title (which I do in the next section), let us pause for an obvious but always necessary reflection. Christ, the Lord, is of course not a despotic *baal*, but the actual exercise of his lordship is not simply like that of a *kyrios* with power either. In the gospels, which tell of Jesus' life, but also in texts that speak of Christ after his resurrection, there is absolutely no apotheosis of power or of lordship; what appears is a power that might be described as "strength-to-serve," as energy to give life, with no traces of a power that triumphs magically over history.

(i) Power and service in Jesus of Nazareth. The gospels make very clear what being lord means. Jesus is not in any way an anarchist, but on the other hand he changes the significance of lordship to make it fit his vision of the Kingdom: "Whoever wishes to be first among you must be your slave" (Mt 20:27; Mk 10:44), a text whose importance makes Luke place it immediately after the Last Supper (22:27). And to make the novelty of what he is proposing clear to the disciples, Jesus tells them: "You know that among the Gentiles those whom they recognize as their rulers lord it over them, and their great ones are tyrants over them. But it is not to be so among you" (Mk 10:42–44; Mt 20:25–27; Lk 22:24–27). He himself provides an example of how overturned the notion of lordship is by washing his disciples' feet (Jn 13:1–15)—made more extraordinary if one remembers that rabbis, masters of the law, let themselves be waited on by their disciples.

This is very well known. Jesus of Nazareth worked a radical change in the notion of power. But it might be argued that after Jesus' resurrection, being now exalted, the Lord above all and over everything, the power of Christ could be reworked in the direction of dominion and subjection (basically like a *baal*, as has happened throughout history). In fact, this has always been the temptation of a church of Christendom in any of its forms, as has been expressed in the one-sided majesty of much of Christian art and above all in the theoretical and practical understanding of impositional, if not downright despotic, church authority. The christological presupposition for this has been an understanding of Christ as all-powerful Lord. And so what could never be done by invoking Jesus of Nazareth—poor, persecuted, serving—seems to have become possible and even right, seen as giving glory to God, in calling on Christ as Lord. This is why we always have to go back to the historical Jesus, the safeguard for the truth of the complete Christ. And in this sense it is well to remember Bartolomé de Las Casas's somewhat simplistic but deep theological comment: "The church has no more power than Christ had as a man."[14]

Even when it is starting with the risen Lord, however, the New Testament does not make him arbitrarily or manipulatively all-powerful, let alone despotic. As we shall see next, the risen *kyrios* inspires and molds; he does not impose or distort. His power is not expressed in manipulating history from above but in inspiring and giving life. And this, without doubt, would be the prime verification of whether historical and ecclesial lordships are being exercised in a Christian manner, even *after* the resurrection.

(ii) Service out of humility. There is more: The New Testament not only does not describe the lordship of Christ as authoritarian or despotic; it—even with a positively shaping force—describes it in terms not of triumphalism but of humility. In its "policy statements" it says that the powers of this world—and human hearts of stone—are subject to him in principle but not annihilated. This will happen only at the end time. The opacity, negativity, and badness in history have not been eliminated by the lordship of Christ.

This has to be stressed, because believers often seem to smooth out the passion in history—when they do not ignore it or, worse, produce it—and console themselves with the statement that, "In any case, Christ has already conquered the world," which produces a type of alienation no less dangerous for being subtle. This is why we need to recall that the New Testament presents the lordship of Christ as humility in history, as a process that has its final referent in the Kingdom of God, which will arrive *after* all the powers of this world have been overcome (1 Cor 14:24ff.). And Christ himself, the Lord, is first the one brought to nothing, the one who has passed through humiliation and *kenosis*.

(c) The Lord as Fashioning Principle of Life and History: Hope

What I have just recalled is important for preventing the lordship of Christ from being understood on the lines of worldly lordships and powers and for understanding it adequately and salvationally. But having said that, we need to analyze positively what Christ being Lord means.

In the New Testament *lordship* means, formally speaking, the presence of Christ in this world, in such a manner that believers are subject to him, but in such a way that they are fashioned in a particular manner and in this find salvation. The lordship of Christ does not operate as magic, but it does generate hope; it is possible to live humanly in history, and liberation from the powers of evil is possible. Put as a thesis, this is the brilliant theologization Paul and his school make of a title that was even earlier applied to Christ. Let us now look at the personal, community, and cosmic aspects of the lordship of Christ.

(i) The lordship of Christ that fashions believers. Paul uses the expression "in the Lord" often and in a variety of contexts to show how believers ought to behave in different situations. He uses it in generic form in his greetings in his letters, but he also uses it in a particular sense in relation to different aspects of the Christian life. So, for example, he states that ministers should "have charge . . . in the Lord" (1 Thes 5:12); he tells the Philippians to "rejoice," to "stand firm," to "be of the same mind" in the Lord (Phil 3:1; 4:1–4); he teaches the Corinthians how to live in the various states of life: the "slave" as a "free person belonging to the Lord" (1 Cor 7:22), the widow "free to marry anyone she wishes, only in the Lord" (7:39), "woman . . . not independent of man or man of woman" in the Lord (11:11); speaking of himself, he states that the Corinthians are his work, "the seal of [his] apostleship," in the Lord (9:1f.). Beyond particular instances, he lays down the basic thesis that in all ways life is to be lived "in the Lord." So the whole of Christian life is covered by the injunction "serve the Lord" (Rom 12:11), developed as "always excelling in the work of the Lord" (1 Cor 15:58). The whole of Christian life is life in the Lord: "If we live, we live to the Lord, and if we die, we die to the Lord; so then, whether we live or whether we die, we are the Lord's" (Rom 14:8).

According to this thesis the lordship of Christ over believers is not an arbitrary sovereignty, still less a despotic power imposing subjection and servility. Lordship rather means Christ's capacity for fashioning the life of believers and, correlatively, expresses an invitation/request. "Submitting oneself to the Lord" is allowing oneself to be conformed to the life of Christ. The proclamation of this possibility is good news and its achievement is salvation. What lordship adds specifically is that this new form of being "is possible" precisely because Christ is Lord, because he "has power" to fashion us in his likeness, an idea that Paul formulates in various ways.

Sometimes he explicitly relates Christ the Lord to the Spirit (2 Cor 3:17; 1 Cor 6:17), and this Spirit of Christ is the one who brings about the union of believers with Christ. In other terms, without using the lord terminology, Paul categorically states that the purpose of God's work is that we should be "conformed to the image of his Son" (Rom 8:29). And in personal and existential language he applies it to himself in the well known "it is no longer I who live, but Christ who lives in me" (Gal 2:20).[15]

The lordship of Christ in relation to believers, then, means personal relationship with Christ, which is at once binding and empowering. The former means that, through being the Lord and so *other* with respect to ourselves, Christ is the ultimate model, beyond which there is no appeal, for how we should act in all situations in our lives and in the whole of our life and death. But this model also has an actual content, which is what we have to reproduce in our lives, which points to *affinity* and supposes going back to the actuality of Jesus, since it is the life of Jesus that has to be reproduced.

So, to sum up, accepting the lordship of Christ involves formulating a demand but above all formulating a hope: believers have to be conformed to Christ, but this is, above all, *possible*. And this possibility is guaranteed by the "power" of the Lord.

(ii) The lordship of Christ over the church community. In several texts Paul places the Lord in relation to the community, above all to the liturgy, in which Christ is made present. He exhorts the Corinthians all to be "in agreement" "by the name of our Lord Jesus Christ" (1 Cor 1:10); the rite of excommunication is to be carried out "in the name of the Lord Jesus" (5:4ff.); they are confirmed in their faith in victory over death "through our Lord Jesus Christ" (15:57); he encourages them to stand fast in faith because "in the Lord your labor is not in vain" (15:58). And because he is their Lord, the community can address Christ in prayer (2 Cor 12:8; 1 Thes 3:12ff.) and God through him (Rom 1:8; 7:25; 2 Cor 1:20; Col 3:17). ("Praying" to Christ and worshiping him presuppose his exalted status, his presence now in the community, and addressing him as a reality belonging to the sphere of the divinity. We are here far from the Son of Man and the intercessor high priest, even if in some way the mediating function of Christ is still kept in praying to God through him.)

In various circumstances, in order to encourage and inspire the community, Paul reminds them of the Lord. The lordship of Christ is not imposition but request/invitation to act in such a way as to build up the community. Its manner of acting is not authoritarian but inspiring and empowering. Not only individual believers but the whole community can and should be conformed to Christ.

(iii) The lordship of Christ over the cosmos. Relatively soon, belief in the lordship of Christ over the whole of reality became a central tenet of faith itself. This was expressed in the succinct formula "Lord of both the dead and the living" (Rom 14:9).

As to its *geographical extent*, this lordship of Christ is universal and extends over the whole world. Christ is the head of creation: "all things have been created through him and for him . . . and in him all things hold together" (Col 1:16f.), including "thrones or dominions or rulers or powers" (1:16). This, then, is a lordship broader than that exercised over the church, and it has a different sense: in the church believers become conscious of the lordship of Christ, while in the world this lordship can remain unknown—an "anonymous lordship," to paraphrase Rahner.

As to its *temporal extent*, the lordship of Christ belongs to a definite period of history. According to the theology of Luke and Paul, it begins with the resurrection-ascension and will end with the parousia, "when he hands over the kingdom to God the Father" (1 Cor 15:24). This is the time of the lordship of Christ, and it is also the time of the church—although to avoid the perennial temptation to return to a Christendom model of church I must stress that this coincidence applies to *time* but not to *power*. It is Christ who exercises lordship in history, not the institutional church.

I shall examine the consequences of this lordship of Christ over the whole of existence for believers and the community in the next section, in the context of theodicy, since such a lordship is in no way evident. But let me now sum up the essential consequence of what has been said: for individuals, community, and history *hope is possible*, precisely because Christ is Lord, because he has power. But this has to be complemented with two reflections. First, that the lordship of Christ of necessity leads to the question of theodicy and to that of the responsibility of believers (and all human beings) to make him Lord of history. Second, that the lordship of Christ is exclusive and antagonistic in relation to other lords, and so proclaiming Christ as Lord is, essentially, conflictive. This is what I want to look at in the two following sections.

(d) The Lordship of Christ and the Question of Theodicy

(i) The questioning of theodicy. History, even under the lordship of Christ, continues to display a radical ambiguity. There is a world of grace, but there is also a world of sin, and verifiably of abundant, cruel, and lasting sin. There is the great and lasting paradox that sin has power and that the Lord of history does nothing to eradicate it. Even more, in Paul's daring words, we are "completing what is lacking in Christ's afflictions" (Col 1:24).

This leads us to the deepest problem of history (I write at a time of conflict in the former Yugoslavia, of ecological disaster in the Great Lakes, of the impoverishment of the continents of Africa and Latin America), and christology has to take this problem seriously, without making it banal or supplying merely philosophical answers. In other words, I do not see how one can say "Christ is the lord of history" in the world we live in without being overawed by the scale of the problem this statement implies.

When around the time of the Second Vatican Council the biblical vision of a God of history was rediscovered (I am thinking of works such as Daniélou's *The Mystery of History*), theology heaved a great sigh of relief, since this superseded the concept of a God of nature, but I am not sure it realized what was happening. (And perhaps something similar may be happening now. There are major advances in the theology of the cosmic Christ, with obvious contributions to solving problems such as the diversity of religions and the universality of Christ. But the problem of theodicy remains, perhaps even more acutely: that of the coexistence between a now clearly cosmic Christ and poverty and injustice on a now clearly cosmic scale.) The theologal, philosophical, even aesthetic gain was evident, but what about any real progress? Salvadoran peasants who have endured number-less horrors ask: "How many times we tell ourselves that God acts in our history. . . . But, father, if he acts, when is this going to end? And so many years of war and so many thousands of deaths? What's the matter with God?"[16] Ignacio Ellacuría wrote: "God the Father had and/or acquired many poor children. . . . This is a massive fact that cannot be passed over by anyone—theologian, pastor, or prophet—trying to talk about God."[17] And a voice from the First World states: "In a world in which human reason and freedom have produced the realities of this twentieth century, speaking of continuity between the human and the divine can only mean that the ultimate mystery of existence—God—is not a Friend of the human race but more likely an Enemy: God creates with the sole aim of de-stroying."[18] Wherever one looks, the question of theodicy becomes more glaring and wounding simply through confessing the lordship of Christ. So let me now see if I can find a way of shedding some light on the problem.

(ii) The Lord has a body in history. Using imagery distinct from that of lordship, but close to the concept in reality, Paul has related Christ to humankind in a creative and novel way—and one that, if its consequences are fully drawn, is scandalous. He states that Christ is head of a body, the local community (1 Cor and Rom), of the whole church, and even of the whole of humankind (Eph and Col). The novelty of this theologization consists in making Christ be present not only *in* the community, *in* the church, and *in* the world, inspiring them and fash-ioning them, but also *through* them, which includes, in some way, being at their mercy. Community, church, and world are not only *settings* of Christ's presence but also *sacraments* of his being and instruments of his actions. They are not a descriptive *ubi* but a substantive *quid*.

In the first letter to the Corinthians the problem Paul has to resolve is that of threatened unity, and to resolve it he states that there are varieties of gifts but the same Lord (12:4). But in developing the idea, he compares these gifts to a single body (12:12), adding cryptically "so it is with Christ," to conclude, "Now you are the body of Christ" (12:27). In Romans 12:5 he states that "we, who are many, are one body in Christ." Here he is still not saying clearly that Christ is the head of the community and that this is his body, but by using the metaphor of the body he is indirectly relating Christ to the *whole* community and doing so—which is my main concern here—in such an intimate way that he compares the relationship to bodily union. So he asks, "Do you not know that your bodies are members of Christ?" (1 Cor 6:15). And speaking of the eucharistic celebration he reminds them that "we all partake of the same bread" (10:17), referring to the body of Christ (10:16). The community is, then—even if this is not stated pre-cisely here—the body of Christ, not just the actual place in which Christ is made present.

This appears more clearly in the letters to the Ephesians and to the Colossians. In these letters Christ is described as "head" of the church, which is his body (Col 1:18; Eph 1:22; 4:15; 5:23). The basic idea behind the comparison is that the building up of the body starts from the head (Eph 4:12, 16; Col 2:19). Christ is the savior of the body of the church (Eph 5:23), nourishes it and cares for it (5:29) and gives out the various gifts in it (4:11). The conclusion is that there exists an intimate relationship between Christ and the community of believers.

(iii) The responsibility for making Christ present in history. The New Testament dwells on the downward movement from the head to the body, but we can look into the upward movement from the body to the head. Being body of Christ is a mark of glory for the church, but if it is taken seriously, it also expresses its greatest responsibility: to make Christ present in history. To quote Ellacuría once more: "The historical corporeality of the church implies that the being and actions of Jesus Christ 'are embodied' in it to enable it to carry out an 'embodiment' of Jesus Christ in the actual events of history."[19] So the presence of Christ in history depends, in a way, on what his church is. In affirming the lordship of Christ, the church is stating two things. One, directly, is the transcendent possibility of Christ, as Lord, influencing history. The second is that, in believing that Christ himself accepts, so to speak, being mediated by the church, it confesses its responsibility for making him present in history. The Lord is still—partly—at the mercy of the church. (This is not a subtle form of making the problem of theodicy disappear: "Faced with the scandal of the evil in the world, [taking the responsibility away from God and] assigning it to human freedom."[20] I shall come back to this in chapter 16, on Nicaea, in connection with the relationship between suffering and God.) This, I believe, is what is at stake when in ecclesiology it is said that the church is the sacrament, the body of Christ. In one of his brilliant phrases in the letter to the Colossians, Paul states that he rejoices in the sufferings he is undergoing for their sake and then adds, without any apparent logical or necessary connection, "In my flesh I am completing what is lacking in Christ's afflictions, for the sake of his body, that is, the church" (1:24). The now exalted Christ, the Lord, needs to go on suffering throughout history for the sake of his church. And he does this through a historical entity, the person of Paul. Christ, then, has decided to make himself present in history, but in order to do so he needs the church to reproduce the work of Jesus in history. He "needs" us in order to be Lord.

The fact of Christ having a body in history cannot be deduced from examining the concepts underlying the title lord, since he—as Lord—could have remained distant from believers and all human beings. But he did not do so. It is part of God's plan that the Lord, the one who is usually so far from and above his "subjects," should be so close to them that they form his body. This in no way denies that the Spirit of Christ is greater than his body, which is no more than reaffirming the basic tenet of faith: the initiative always comes from above, as gift and grace. But it does imply that it is the church that has to set about producing this Spirit and that it can reveal or conceal the Spirit. In other words, the actual practice of the lordship of Christ depends, to a large extent, on us. It is our task, in history, to express this lordship and make it credible to the rest of humankind. (I have already seen that this idea is not pleasing to Cardinal Ratzinger, who sees it as Promethean, an expression of hubris, as though we were trying to make God's action ours. So I repeat: the initiative comes from above, but an important element in it is that Christ incorporates us into his lordship of history.)

(iv) The lordship of Christ and the building of the Kingdom. The New Testament nowhere spells out precisely what this cosmic lordship of Christ is. It states that the powers of this world are subject to it, but that they are not yet annihilated, which will happen in due course, "after he has destroyed every ruler and every authority and power" (1 Cor 15:24), so that only at the end, once death has been overcome, will Christ hand over the Kingdom to the Father and God be all in all (15:24–28).

According to this, between resurrection and parousia it falls to the church, as body of Christ, to make him present in a history in which powers contrary to the Lord exist. In working terms the "state," the "emperor," and "wealth" are not the final powers in history, since they are subject to Christ, which generates the hope of being able to triumph over them. But, on the other hand, without being naive, as these powers are not yet destroyed, to put it mildly, this will happen only at the end. With this hope and this realism Christians should work on the world, but the question of what they should be doing remains. In this context the International Theological Commission has made this notable statement: "In perfect consonance with this principality of Christ is that principality which is usually carried on in history and in human society, above all through signs of justice, which appear necessary for preaching the Kingdom."[21]

This text places the lordship of Christ in the final context of the Kingdom of God, relates it to the present historical situation, and actualizes it, above all, in signs of justice. According to the logic of the text, if—impossibly—nothing showed signs of transforming the historical situation, it would make no sense to go on confessing Christ as Lord. Turning this around, we can say that if, in the name of faith in a Christ who is Lord, believers shape the world in a way different and contrary to its present direction, opposing and struggling against other lordships, then the transcendent assertion that Christ is Lord can be verified in historical terms. The task remains largely in the hands of believers (and of all human beings). And this is also a way of facing up to the question of theodicy from praxis: making the Lord be Lord. (In a different context, *Gaudium et Spes*, no. 19, expresses the same idea when it states that one of the reasons for atheism is that we Christians have concealed rather than revealed the face of God. An important part of God is in our hands.)

(e) The Struggle against the Lords of This World

The New Testament confesses Christ as not only Lord but as the *only* Lord: "There are many gods and many lords—yet for us there is one God . . . and one Lord, Jesus Christ" (1 Cor. 8:5–6). This means that the title is the content not only of a homology, a confession of public faith, but of an excluding confession, which— by its very nature—had to lead sooner or later to confrontation with those who accepted the existence of other lords. The confession *Kyrios Iesous* was to become a polemic confession and, for Christians, a conflictive and dangerous one.

This proclamation of the uniqueness and exclusivity of the lordship of Christ is similar to proclamation of the uniqueness and exclusivity of God, which is in itself polemical. (In view of the present debate over the uniqueness [or lack of it] of Christ, it may be useful to make the following observation. The New Testament, in comparing other lordships with that of Christ, does not speak simply of lordships *different* from that of Jesus, but of *opposed* and *excluding* lordships. From this point of view it is important methodologically, when examining the diversity of religion and lordships, to analyze first their opposition to or convergence with that of Jesus. Remember Jesus' saying, "Whoever is not against us is for us" [Mk 9:40].) The first commandment orders recognition of a single God (Dt 6:4), but in the presence of and in contrast to other gods who are *rivals*. From this it follows that faith in God has to be not only monotheistic and monolatric but also essentially anti-idolatrous.

(i) Conflictivity of the Kyrios. Seen from its conflictivity, the title *kyrios* can be considered first and foremost as a replica of the *kyrioi* of the religions (as Bousset and Lohmeyer originally suggested), although these were usually more tolerant than belligerent in the Greco-Roman world, which suggests that the conflictivity of the *Kyrios Iesous* derived not from a specifically religious context but from the political one of the Roman Empire. The text of 1 Corinthians 12:3—"No one speaking by the Spirit of God ever says 'Let Jesus be cursed!' and no one can say 'Jesus is Lord' except by the Holy Spirit"—should be understood in a climate of persecution in which Christians were being forced to curse Christ and proclaim Caesar as *kyrios*. It is questionable whether this was already happening when Paul wrote to the Corinthians, although Acts 17:7 might be adduced as a historical argument: the Jews tell the magistrates of Thessalonika that Christians "are all acting contrary to the decrees of the emperor, saying that there is another king named Jesus." Regardless of when confessing Christ as lord began to be politically polemical, it did happen: Pliny wrote to Trajan that under interrogation Christians had to confess "Kyrios Caesar," offer him victims, and curse Christ. There is an early account of this in the martyrdom of Polycarp (c. 155) and suggestions of it already in the New Testament.[22]

In Revelation, written at a time of overt persecution, the theologal conflict is historicized. The "beast" and the other kings "will wage war on the Lamb," but he will conquer them. In this context he is declared to be "Lord of lords and King of kings" (Rv 17:14). The title lord then expresses—and its content enables it to do so more radically than those we have already examined—not only the "new" faith of believers but also its necessarily dialectical dimension: the Lord had to be confessed in the midst of and against other lords, and the early Christians risked their lives for this. To this, however, we have to add what is most basic and up to now has had to remain implicit only: what is conflictive is not the title, publicly proclaiming Jesus as *kyrios,* but acting socially and ethically in accordance with Jesus of Nazareth—who was also to be confessed as *kyrios.* This is shown by the very fact that even before their public—and provocative—use of the *kyrios,* Christians suffered persecution in their own families and within their own Jewish people. It was only later that attacks and persecutions came from the Roman political authorities.

The danger and permanent threat posed by the new faith was ultimately not in proclaiming a Jesus who is Lord but in proclaiming a Lord who is Jesus and in acting in accordance with this faith: this is what had already happened in Jesus' own death. The Jews could accuse him of wanting to be king, but what they were really trying to do was to show Pilate that the subversive impulses of his preaching were "politically dangerous."[23] Jesus and his enemies present two different systems, each claiming an opposing direction of human life; both were practical systems, and so their contradictions applied on the level of everyday life. This was also the most threatening aspect of the new faith after the resurrection (whether the title *kyrios* was used to confess Jesus or not): "The Christian faith introduced a critical seed with regard to the world, which always carried the probability of conflict and confrontation. . . . A coherent Christian attitude will always keep a certain critical capacity for its social surroundings and should not he afraid of having to take on conflict."[24] (This applies to the first letter of Peter, more anxious to find some agreement with the state than Revelation. But despite this, the message is that there can be no Christian faith without risk of persecution, owing to the objectivity of Jesus' message. The New Testament actually shows Christians opposing the political authorities to differing degrees: less virulently and seeking accommodation in 1 Peter, very virulently and uncompromisingly in Revelation.)

(ii) The conflict at the present time. In our times the polemical character of confessing Christ as Lord is still applicable. Today too there are *kyrioi* persons—but mainly structures, political, economic, military—that tyrannize and oppress. This is not a matter of *odium fidei* according to orthodoxy but of *odium iustitiae* according to orthopraxis. It is not a case of reneging on Christ in support of Caesar but of actively (and sometimes defenselessly, as with massacres) opposing Caesar's purpose. This means that the persecutors can be as baptized as the persecuted.

Since they are structures rather than persons, the lords of this world can increasingly pass unobserved, since they seem to belong to the order of *nature* (leisure culture, free market, globalization) and not to the order of *history,* which we human beings make. They do not yet seem to demand—as the idols unmasked some years back did—an explicit cult and orthopraxis; simply being in today's world is enough, and acceptance of these *kyrioi* will follow naturally. Because of this, it would be naive to go on confessing the Lord without unmasking, denouncing, and fighting these false lords.

This is happening. In Latin America many believers have proclaimed the lordship of Christ through their deeds, and as a result they have been brought before Caesar, have been threatened, defamed, imprisoned, tortured, and murdered. They have also proclaimed the *only* lordship of Christ, not in a fundamentalist way but in the real way, through truth and justice and the measures that seem most appropriate. This is literally subversive, and this is why today can produce accounts of martyrdom as moving as those of Polycarp or Stephen. The concept of *theology of story* did not originate in Latin America, but stories are told here, and they give a very good idea, theologically, of what it means to proclaim Christ Lord. This is what Fr. Rutilio Grande said in his homily preached in Apopa on February 13, 1977, one month before his martyrdom:

It is dangerous to be a Christian in our country! It is dangerous to be truly Catholic! In practice it is illegal to be a genuine Christian where we live, in our country. Because inevitably the world that surrounds us is radically founded on an established disorder, in the face of which the mere proclamation of the gospel is subversive. . . . I very much fear, dear brethren and friends, that very soon the Bible and the gospel will not be allowed to pass our frontiers. We will get them pulped and nothing more, because all their pages are subversive.[25]

The confession "Jesus is the Lord" is a conflictive confession, but it is above all one filled with hope. The title *kyrios* expresses that Jesus, through being that, has *power* to shape the reality of believers, of the church, and of the world, despite so many powers being against him. This power is that of salvation, not of subjection. He exercises it through the Spirit, not in ways that stifle humanity, responsibility, and liberty. Invoking Christ as Lord ultimately means having and holding on to that hope.

The Spirit was at work in the New Testament period and is also at work today in the church and in the world. While it produces fruits of truth, commitment, and witness—and because it does—we can go on affirming that Christ is Lord and has power. And, turning this around, if, hypothetically, Christ today no longer had the power to shape the lives of believers, there would be no sense in proclaiming him Lord. This is one way of expressing the basis of faith: that there will always be people conformed to Christ, that God's initiative will always, in some way, emerge victorious.

This is happening at the present time in many places. In Latin America, for certain, there are believers who have lived without submitting to the powers of this world, for whom neither life, nor death, nor things present, nor those to come, have been able to separate them from the love of Christ (Rom 8:39). They are those of whom we can say with Paul, "The world or life or death or the present or the future—all belong to you" (1 Cor 3:22). By living like this, freed from subjection to other lords, they express the truth that Christ is Lord. They make him Lord in history.

Christ's being Lord at the present time is not, then, a title that applies to him alone; it also implies the exercise *in actu* of this lordship through the activity of his body in history, believers and all human beings. The confession "Christ is the Lord" is therefore also a working confession: it expresses commitment to make him Lord.

Chapter 12

Son of God/Son of Man/Servant of Yahweh

*The Man Who Came from God
and the God Who Came in Man*

Examination of this title leads us into something we have not yet explored, the *personal* relationship of Jesus to God. As priest, Jesus expresses the humanity he mediates between God and human beings; as messiah, he is the anointed of God who sums up hope of salvation; as Lord, he acts with power—in God's fashion, be it said—to mold believers and the community. Now, in calling him Son of God, the New Testament gradually moves to present Christ in his personal relationship with God, and it does so in such a way that faith in the divine sonship of Jesus becomes what distinguished Christians: Jesus is the Son of God. He is not merely an earthly messiah but "belongs to God." Strictly speaking, this title does not mention divinity in the sense in which this was to come to be understood in the councils, but it expresses a unique relationship of Jesus to God, and this was to lead to his nature being no longer adequately described only by affirming his true humanity.

This is the most important aspect for *christology*, but to understand the title comprehensively and in its Christian originality we also need to bear in mind, as a sort of counterpoint, the tradition of the Son of Man and the tradition of the beloved Son as suffering servant. While literal divine sonship was a scandal to the Jews with their monotheism, sonship in the manner of a servant was equally scandalous to the Greeks. They could accept the "communicability" of divinity and so the existence of "sons of gods" on the basis of communication of power and sharing in it. But the abasement and *kenosis* of divinity was folly, as Paul was to tell the Corinthians.

The importance of the title is also *theologal*. The metaphorical language of "son" necessitates reference to a "father," as John's theology was to make magnificently clear. Put in plain language, the man Jesus bears a "family likeness" to God and so makes God present. Put in the dogmatic language of *communicatio idiomatum*, what is said of Jesus must be said of God himself. Ultimately, what was said is that in Jesus God has appeared in human form, as the liturgy of Christmas so finely puts it: "The love of God has appeared." It is true that from the Son our view of God is changed, but above all, from him we know God "a little better." "In Jesus is the very God who comes with all his fullness of love for us."[1]

Finally, the title has *anthropological* importance: we are all daughters and sons of God. If believers were called Christians in Antioch, God's plan is that we should be "conformed to the likeness of his Son" (Rom 8:29). (Tradition was to say that we are by grace what Jesus was by nature. Rahner boldly claimed that "the *unio hypostatica* is distinguished from our 'grace' not by what is affirmed in it, but both cases [including that of Jesus] are grace.")[2] Unlike the other titles, then, this one expresses not only *who Jesus is for us*—his salvational dimension—but also *what we can be through him*—the exemplary dimension: we can be children of God, and our salvation is fulfilled in becoming so. "See what love the Father has given us, that we should be called children of God" (1 Jn 3:1).

To finish this introductory section, let me say that these reflections are still central to faith, but they are also a challenge. Psychology and feminist theology today both examine the limitation of the father metaphor in its correlation to the son metaphor. And from the point of view of victims we have to analyze the metaphor of sons and daughters in its correlation to father. This is the background from which we need to approach the various traditions concerning the Son.

1. The Traditions of Jesus as Son of God[3]

The idea of a divine sonship is not exclusive to Israel but has more universal roots. In the religions of the ancient East it was reckoned that kings were engendered by gods—in Egypt the pharaoh was the son of the god Ra—and the same was thought of the Roman emperor in New Testament times. In the Hellenic world not only kings but anyone out of the ordinary—miracle-workers, for example—could be considered as children of God, divine beings *(zeios aner)*, since they had divine powers. Hellenism also knew sons of gods who died and rose again, as in the Gnostic myth of the redeemer and his mission to the world.

In view of these outward similarities it has been suggested that the origin of the Christian title Son lay in surrounding pagan thought, and for Harnack this also represented the beginning of the (spurious) Hellenization of Christian dogma. Nevertheless, this conflicts with the central fact of the New Testament, and this needs to be said at the outset: Jesus was crucified, and "[anyone] crucified was for educated men of antiquity no more than an example of criminality, shame, and ugliness."[4] So paganism, at the start, had no point of contact with what was central to christology, and if the latter had been based on the former, pagan theologies would inevitably have had to produce Docetist Christian christologies, since the humanity and death of Jesus could have been accepted only as mere "appearance." Furthermore, paganism accepted the (divine) sonship of human beings on the basis of the power they possessed, and there was no place for the (preferential) sonship of "widows and orphans." Nevertheless, the Hellenic world contributed the important idea of the "communicability" of divinity, which was to become decisive in future christology, when a more "metaphysical" understanding of Jesus' divinity was worked out.

Judaism, for its part, owing to its radical monotheism and the absolute transcendence of God, neither understood nor could understand the expression *son of God* as a product of the communicability of divinity. The idea that God could "beget" or communicate his own reality to human beings was totally alien to the Old Testament. The phrase in Psalm 2:7, "You are my son; today I have begotten you," so much quoted later in the New Testament, did not have—and could not have had—a literal meaning but referred to the enthronement of a king. The title, then, means something completely different from what it means in other religions. It means that a person or people is chosen by God for a special mission, which on the one hand is a sign of the divine benevolence but on the other exacts obedience from the chosen—which, essentially, expresses some type of personal relationship, though not as radically as the Greek idea of communicability of divinity. In the Old Testament, either the whole people, chosen for a special mission and required to be obedient (Ex 4:22; Hos 11:1; Is 30:1; Jer 3:22; Is 63:16), or an individual, such as the king representing the people (2 Sm 7:14; Ps 2:7; 89:27), could be called "son of God." (As I insist on "partiality" for understanding sonship, it is worth noting the "democratization" implied by calling not just an individual but a whole people "son of God.")

The consequence for christology is that the application of the title to Jesus should not necessarily be traced back to paganism, since "the title 'son of God' is not at all alien to the Jews of Palestine,"[5] nor are the ideas of preexistence, creative mediation, and mission associated with it,[6] though the New Testament goes further and transforms the understanding of sonship. But neither is the meaning of the title in Judaism sufficient to account for its application to Jesus. There was something in Jesus himself that cannot be derived from any other tradition.

So the New Testament contains two distinct formulas to express Jesus' sonship, deriving from independent traditions. One calls Jesus "Son of God," and the other calls him "Son." The first, overall, expresses a *functional-personal* relationship between Jesus and God, and the second expresses an *essential-personal* relationship with God. To these traditions a variant of the first should be added, that of the "beloved Son," which relates Jesus to the suffering servant of Yahweh, and I would add—as a biblical and systematic counterpoint—another, that of "Son of Man."

(a) The Tradition of the Son of God: The Man Who Came from God

In the New Testament the title Son of God is applied to Jesus early and appears in all its strata. (According to Hahn, the same process as with all the other titles could have applied. At an early stage, the first communities in Palestine used the title Son of God for Christ, when they connected it with Jesus' final work at the end of time, adding that God has adopted and enthroned Jesus for this heavenly task. Later, in Judeo-Hellenist Christianity, the title was applied retrospectively to the historical Jesus, since in the diaspora Judaism had already made use of the expression "divine person" [*zeios aner*] to denote one who had received the Spirit and special powers. The most radical step would have been taken in Hellenist Christianity. In this context the gift of the Spirit was seen not as empowerment for a mission or for working wonders but as penetration by the Spirit in the personal reality of Jesus. This would be the origin of the later understanding of Jesus as a divine being. From the point of view of history of religions, the very idea of coming to express Jesus' reality in terms of divinity would have been made possible by the Hellenist context.)[7]

Let us start with the use Paul makes of the title, in order to evaluate its importance and content. On the one hand, he does not use it as consistently as he does "Lord"—only fifteen times as opposed to 184—and he strangely uses it more in Romans and Galatians, so in polemical letters against the *Jews*, than when writing to the *Corinthians* (a mere three times), even though these were immersed in a Hellenist environment, which shows that proclaiming Jesus Son of God is not an indication of the beginning of a spurious process of Hellenization. Although the use Paul makes of the title is quantitatively little, qualitatively it appears in important contexts, covering practically the whole of Jesus' nature and work, which is an indirect way of saying that God (the Father) is present in the whole of these.

(1) The Son of God is mentioned in relation to the central fact of the *sending, handing over*, and *death* of Jesus on the cross. The Father sends the Son (Gal 4:4), does not spare the Son (Rom 8:32), the "Son of God . . . loved me and gave himself for me" (Gal 2:20). (2) The title also appears related with the *exaltation* of Jesus. Romans 1:4, an ancient pre-Pauline formula, confesses that in the resurrection Jesus has been declared Son of God with power according to the spirit. (3) In later texts the Son appears as *mediator* of creation (1 Cor 8:6), which suggests preexistence, and as the *image* of the Father (Col 1:13ff.). (4) Salvation is conceptualized from the Son: the handing over of the Son brings about our *reconciliation* with God (Rom 5:10). We can be conformed to the Son (Rom 8:29) and can call God *Abba*, Father (Rom 8:14; Gal 4:6). (5) Finally, in the context of the history of salvation, the Son will return at the end of time (1 Thes 1:10) with the specific purpose of subjecting himself to the Father so that God may be all in all (1 Cor 15:28).

The title is used, then, at important stages of the life and destiny of Jesus, related most particularly to God, and so it makes it possible to know better who Jesus is and who God is. To attain this knowledge, one important route is comparing this pre-Pauline title with the more specifically Pauline one of Lord. This comparison reveals that the title Lord expresses the relationship between the exalted risen Christ and the community, and the title Son of God expresses the relationship of the risen Christ to God the Father. The title Lord would then be used as an invocation in worship and in personal life, while the title Son of God was used to proclaim the *ultimate reality of Christ in himself in relation to God*, in other words, "particular culminating theological statements."[8] In the view of the synoptics it would express the constitutive relatedness of Jesus to God—simultaneous with his constitutive relatedness with the Kingdom of God.

When Paul uses the title Son of God he is saying that Jesus is not only messiah ("Son of God, according to the flesh"), crucified and confirmed by God in the resurrection, but more than this. He is "identical to a heavenly being, before all ages, mediator between God and God's creatures, that is: mediator at the same time of God's saving revelation."[9] In this way, the title Son of God expresses not a pure speculation about the (metaphysical) nature of Jesus originating in Hellenism but a salvational concern. The title expresses good news: "In Jesus God himself has come to us," and simultaneously asserts a truth: "the risen Christ is totally related to God."[10]

If we ask what historically established the application of the title Son of God to Jesus and gave it the meaning we have discussed—beyond Hellenism and the Old Testament—two distinct reasons can be adduced. The first and more radical is the interpretation of the experience of resurrection not only as confirmation of Jesus as *messiah* (of earthly character) but of someone who "belongs to God."[11] Very early on, in fact, at the time of Saul's conversion (around the year 36 or 37), the title had become central to the new faith. Paul spent several days "with the disciples in Damascus, and immediately he began to proclaim Jesus in the synagogues, saying 'He is the Son of God'" (Acts 9:19f.). The second and more historical grounding reason is the memory of the relationship of Jesus of Nazareth to God the Father during his lifetime. Toward the end of the New Testament the synoptics were taking the title for granted, and so what Matthew and Luke do in their infancy narratives is, so to speak, "argue" the case for Jesus' sonship on the basis of his divine provenance and origin. Their stories of the conception and birth of Jesus suppose that Jesus is the Son of God. Matthew is concerned to show that Jesus was really descended from David, but in the last link of the chain he changes the repeated formula "N was the father of N." He says that Jacob was the father of Joseph but then adds, "the husband of Mary, of whom Jesus was born" (1:16), which establishes that Jesus was born of Mary, not from a human father but from the Holy Spirit (1:18), which states his divine origin. Luke begins his genealogy only with Joseph, whose son Jesus "was believed" to be. His true paternity comes from on high, so the child "will be called Son of God" (1:35).

Mark, anti-triumphalist, appeals as ever to sobriety, defending the title from any danger of becoming a manipulatable myth. He presents Jesus as a "hidden" Son of God, in the same way as he speaks of his messianism. At the start of his public life it is the demons who call him Son of God (3:11), and Jesus tells his disciples not to say it. Only at the end of his gospel, when Jesus has died on the cross, does the evangelist formulate a clear confession of faith: "Truly this man was God's Son!" (15:39), but he places it in the mouth of a pagan, the Roman centurion. What is basic to all the synoptics, however, is showing what it was in Jesus that made such an impact that they connected him in such a special way with God. This was his openness and his availability to God, his prayer entrusted to his *Abba*, and his obedience to God. As I said in the first volume (*JL*, pp. 135–39), Jesus trusted in a God who is a Father in whom he can rest while at the same time being available to a Father who is God and will not let him rest.

In conclusion, Jesus "had a unique way of placing himself before God,"[12] and this led Christians, on the one hand, to state that "Jesus came from God" and to proclaim him as Son of God, going beyond what the title previously offered its theologians. And on the other hand, it led to the conviction that "God came in the man Jesus," that God had appeared in this world in the guise of goodness and absolute mystery.

(b) First Counterpoint: The Tradition of the Son of Man

The synoptics apply the title Son of God to Jesus, and yet Jesus himself never mentions it, while he does speak repeatedly of the Son of Man: it appears sixty-nine times in the synoptics, always in Jesus' mouth, and thirteen in the Gospel of John. Discussion on the origin and significance of this title is unending—whether it is an honorific title or not, whether Jesus used it of himself or of another or it was applied to the first community—but for our purposes here the relevant fact is that is regularly serves as a counterpoint to the title Son of God (and so safeguards this from future mythical and Docetist interpretations).[13] Beyond what the linguistic parallelism suggests, it is worth noting that from very early on Jesus' nature was formulated as a dual whole: "descended from David according to the flesh . . . Son of God . . . according to the Spirit" (Rom 1:3). And although this expression should not be understood in the sense of future patristic and conciliar reflections, maintaining the intrinsic tension of this duality was to be the specific character of the dynamism of christology—an opportunity and a problem still with us today.

With regard to its meaning, in the Old Testament "Son of Man" can express dignity—as late Judaism used the term of a mediator who would appear at the end of time, first mentioned in Daniel 7:13: "As I watched in the night visions, I saw one like a human being coming with the clouds of heaven. And he came to the Ancient One and was presented before him. To him was given dominion and glory and kingship, that all peoples, nations, and languages should serve him. His dominion is an everlasting dominion that shall not pass away, and his kingship is one that shall never be destroyed"—or can simply mean "human," perhaps with the suggestion of littleness in relation to God. It can be used of an individual, or collectively. So in the Book of Daniel it is the "holy ones of the Most High" who will receive the kingdom in 7:18, but later it is understood individually (see the Ethiopian Book of Enoch and 4 Esdras). In the New Testament the expression is used of Jesus and came to describe his historical nature and destiny. In this way the totality of Jesus, described more transcendentally under the title Son of God, is now described more historically. Let us look briefly at how the totality of Jesus is revealed by the title Son of Man.

The oldest meaning relates the Son of Man with "the one who is to come," which establishes a relationship between the eschatological nature of the Kingdom preached by Jesus and the eschatological aspect of the person of Jesus—as perceived after the resurrection—described in operative and salvific terms: "And I tell you, everyone who acknowledges me before others, the Son of Man also will acknowledge before the angels of God" (Lk 12:8f.), a text that shows the Son of Man's role at the last judgment. (This text does not identify Jesus with the Son of Man but makes an explicit distinction between them, which suggests that it is historical, or at least that Luke's version is the original and that Mark, in 10:32–33, was the one who made the identification of Jesus with the Son of Man.)[14]

Although the transition has been made from the Jesus who preaches to the Christ who is preached, a fundamental characteristic of Jesus has been maintained: his expectation of the end.

To this understanding of the Son of Man as the one who is to come, the clearest from tradition, two others were added (though it is debated whether this is a question of a title or of a mere designation). One is that the Son of Man is earthly ("the Son of Man has nowhere to lay his head" [Mt 8:20; Lk 9:28]) and active ("the Son of Man has power to forgive sins" [Mk 2:10]; "the Son of Man is lord of the sabbath" [Mk 2:28]). This development, according to Hahn, became possible only once the equality of persons between the Son of Man and Jesus had been affirmed and was necessary once Jesus was understood as God's plenipotentiary here and now on earth. The other and more specifically Christian added meaning is that of the Son of Man as a figure who suffers and rises again, as in the three announcements of the passion in the synoptics: "Then he began to teach them that the Son of Man must undergo great suffering, and be rejected by the elders, the chief priests, and the scribes, and be killed, and after three days rise again" (Mk 8:31; see Mk 9:9–10, 31–32; 10:32–34). This development belongs to the last stage of tradition and is paradoxical in itself, since it unites the dignity of the judge who is to come with suffering, passion, and death.

The title (or expression), which keeps the ambivalence of designating both historicity and transcendence, expresses the totality of Jesus' humanity. At the start it points to the future so that the appearance of his humanity will be found there, but later it pulls this appearance back to the present of Jesus' life and historical destiny. To do so, it unites in one expression such disparate elements as power and failure, bringing salvation and himself experiencing condemnation. Overall, "Son of Man" enables the whole "story of Jesus" to be told. Playing on the ambivalence mentioned, we might say that this story is the story *of a man* and that, at the same time, the whole of it *is full of dignity*. This *story of the man* is what acts as a counterpoint to the *story of the Son of God*.

I propose to end this section with a structured (I hope not too artificially) reflection showing what there is of *man* and what there is of *dignity* in the Son of Man.

(1) If the term *human being* is used as an honorific title, this is saying that dignity does not accrue to Jesus or any other human being from anything added to their human nature but from a deepening of what is human. (2) The functions of judging and convening the people of Israel, which are specific to the Son of Man, are not entrusted by God arbitrarily to any human being but to the one who is the true human being. This is the one who can judge not arbitrarily and from without but from what is truly human. (3) If the one who is able to save does so not because he has a power that has been given to him from outside but because he is truly human, then the notion of power loses its arbitrary and oppressive aspects. This is because the appearance of what is truly human is always salvific and, conversely, what is salvific makes what is truly human appear. (4) Through being truly human, the Son of Man is subject to the passion and the cross and, conversely, the resurrection is to confirm him as the true human being, as the one who has lived the true life. I have already said that the Son of Man can be what he

is (judge, convener) through being human, but I would here add that he is now able ultimately to be so through being a victim. And in this sense it is good to recall that in the Old Testament the Son of Man can be either an individual or a whole people. (John Paul II, on his visit to Canada in September 1985, said that on the day of judgment the nations of the South would judge those of the North: "The poor nations—and by that we have to understand various classes of poverty, not just lack of food but also deprivation of liberty and other human rights—will judge those who take these goods from them.")[15] Mocked humanity is that which can judge what is human, and it is also—surprisingly—what in history is open to a "benevolent" judgment.[16]

This is the first counterpoint to the Son of God. Beyond the antithetic/complementary parallelism the language suggests, beyond whether there were points of contact in the development of both titles (or expressions) or not, what matters is that throughout the whole of the New Testament, and certainly in the synoptics, the counterpoint is kept up: Jesus is personally related to God, he is on God's side, comes from God; yet Jesus shares in what is human, he is on man's side, comes from the earth. The lesson to draw is that there is not yet any hint that one aspect is to the detriment of the other. Being Son of God happens in Jesus in the manner of the Son of Man. God's goodness needs the goodness of a person and, conversely, the goodness of a person needs the goodness of God. As Leonardo Boff says, "only God can be so human."

(c) Second Counterpoint: The Tradition of the Beloved Son, the Pais Theou

The New Testament contains a tradition of the beloved Son that relates Christ, the Son of God, with the servant of Yahweh. This is a more radical counterpoint than the previous one, and it derives not from juxtaposing traditions but from delving deeper into one of them, that of the Son of God.

(i) The son and the servant. In several New Testament passages in which Jesus is spoken of as Son of God there are allusions to Old Testament texts that mention the "beloved Son," in whom God is "well pleased," an expression taken up in, for example, the scene of Jesus' baptism (cf. Mt 3:17 and Is 42:1). (An equivalent expression is "chosen one," which John uses in his account of the baptism [1:29]; he is related to the "lamb" who takes away the sin of the world, who is the equivalent of the suffering servant.)

In the New Testament the word *Son* (from the "beloved Son" texts) is translated by the Greek word *uios*, but in the Septuagint this term is translated by *pais Theou*, which literally means "child (of God)." The replacement of *uios* with *pais* is understandable, since both "son" and "child" imply a relationship to a *father*, the first directly, the second indirectly. But what concerns us here is that the Old Testament also applies the word *pais* to the *servant of Yahweh*. There is, then, a linguistic relationship between the terms beloved *son* and *servant*, but the relationship is not only linguistic; it applies to content too.

The New Testament, in effect, frequently refers to the songs of the servant to explain the totality of Jesus' nature: his calling, mission, and destiny. The synoptics make clear allusions to Isaiah 42:1 (the servant chosen to impart justice); in Matthew alone this servant is alluded to in the baptism scene (3:17), in an account of numerous healings (12:18–21), at the transfiguration (17:5), and in the parable of the murderous vineyard tenants (21:37ff.). In all these texts the reality of the servant *(pais)* is translated into language of Son *(uios)*. In John the figure of the suffering servant is very much present, although expressed in a different register: the Son of Man has to be lifted up (on the cross [3:14]); the good shepherd is the one who gives his life for his sheep (10:11); the term *lamb* embraces several aspects of the suffering servant: he goes to the slaughter like a lamb (cf. Is 53:7). John 19:36—"None of his bones shall be broken"—is an allusion to the paschal lamb also offered as expiation of sins (Ex 12). What matters is the conclusion: the beloved Son of God, united to God and obedient to God, is the one who takes on the figure of the servant. He is the acceptable Son of God because he is the servant, understanding the servant in his overall reality: the one who carries out his *mission* on earth and who is ready to suffer the *fate* of the cross.

The *reality* of Isaiah's servant is, then, important for understanding Jesus as Son of God. But in addition to this, the first chapters of Acts produce an explicit christology based on the title *servant (pais)*. In chapters 3 and 4 there are four allusions to Isaiah in which Jesus is spoken of as the servant, and in the last three of these the word is used as a technical term, as a *title*. In his second address to the Jews, Peter tells them that God "has glorified his servant Jesus" (3:13) and that, "When God raised up his servant, he sent him first to you" (3:26). In the prayer of the community in Jerusalem, after Peter and John have been freed by the Sanhedrin, they recognize that the authorities have "gathered together against your holy servant Jesus" (4:27), and they ask God to stretch out his hand to heal so that "signs and wonders [will be] performed through the name of your holy servant Jesus" (4:30). (At least in the texts of Acts 3, the *servant* means not only the chosen one of the first three songs of Isaiah, but also the suffering servant of Isaiah 52—53. In Acts 8:32ff., Philip also explains Jesus to the eunuch on the basis of Isaiah 53:7–8.)

These texts express a very ancient christology:[17] Jesus is the servant of Yahweh, and the figure of the servant is sufficient to explain who Jesus is—a christology whose origin could lie in Peter's personal experience, since the four quotations from Acts 3—4 are addresses by Peter or prayers of the community together with Peter. Furthermore, in the first letter of Peter, regardless of whether the letter is by Peter or not, there is a presentation of Jesus' sufferings (1 Pt 2:22ff.) based on quotations from Isaiah (53:5, 6, 9, 12).

This christology based on the title servant soon disappeared from the New Testament, but in the synoptics the reality underlying the title resurfaced, and this reappeared in post-apostolic texts in the context of the liturgy (1 Clement, the *Didache*). In the *Shepherd of Hermas* a tension that runs through primitive christology is insinuated: either Jesus is only servant (making it difficult for him to be son) or he is only son (making it difficult for him to be servant). This dilemma shows how difficult it was for the early church to unite sonship and suffering as a servant, a problem as acute as how to unite divinity and humanity—the

Greek version of the problem. However, the unity of both elements was upheld from the beginning.

Why the title servant soon disappeared from use as a title may be due to various reasons: concern with expressing the glorious and powerful aspects of Christ, for which other titles were more useful—the specific emphasis of the title Son of God is deliberately exalting—or an unconscious tendency to downplay the suffering and humiliated dimension of the one who was confessed as exalted and Lord. In any case, there is a need—certainly in the Third World—to reclaim the Son-servant relationship, since it would be sad that in a crucified world the *title* of Christ that best suits it, that of *servant*, should be unused and mean nothing.

The New Testament itself expresses from the beginning and then restates as a central element the *reality* that lies behind the title. The gospels do so in narrative language and taking up the complete reality of the servant: his choosing/mission and his fate. Let us now look at these texts, since they express what I have called the counterpoint: the Son of God is a suffering Son.

(ii) Christ and doulos. The idea of the Son-servant appears in different guises according to the different contexts within the New Testament. Let us examine this in two major texts.

We have already seen that the Letter to the Hebrews emphasizes that Jesus was like us in everything except sin, which proclaims not his true humanity in the abstract but his sharing in human weakness, both on the historical level, emphasizing that he is brother like us ("for we do not have a high priest who is unable to sympathize with our weaknesses" [4:15]), and on the theologal level. (In much the same way, in John's prologue the *logos* becomes flesh [*sarx*], with the connotation of the weakness of the flesh.) The letter insists on the "divine" nature of Jesus and makes this central from the start—the "heir" is the exalted *Kyrios* (1:2). Nevertheless, it also stresses that his relationship to the Father is from the weakness of a creature: "In the days of his flesh Jesus offered up prayers and supplications, with loud cries and tears, to the one who was able to save him from death, and he was heard because of his reverent submission. Although he was a Son, he learned obedience through what he suffered" (5:7ff.). Christ "endured the cross, disregarding its shame" (12:2). In short, "the *doxa* of the Son of God does not admit of separation from the shame of the cross."[18]

It is, though, important to know what the paradox serves. The first text (Heb 5:7ff.) ends, "and having been made perfect, he became the source of eternal salvation for all who obey him"; the second, "so that you may not grow weary or lose heart" (12:3). In both cases soteriology is stressed, in transcendent form in the first and existential in the second. (There are other texts in which this paradox is expressed. In 2 Corinthians 8:9, a text much quoted in Latin America and a key text for Medellín [*Poverty of the Church*, 7], Paul uses a common metaphor to explain the contrast and the salvation Jesus brings: "For you know the generous act of our Lord Jesus Christ, that though he was rich, yet for your sakes he became poor, so that by his poverty you might become rich." The language is clearly metaphorical, but the metaphor is used to make three important statements. The first is the fact that he discarded his divine condition. The second is the salvific intent: "so that . . . you might become rich." And the third is the means: the "generous act"—love, in the final analysis. The riches-poverty metaphor is most useful in Latin America—and elsewhere—for expressing *kenosis*. It is only one possible expression of humiliation, just as money, Mammon, the example Jesus uses, is only one aspect of idols [Mt 6:24; Lk 16:13; cf. Lk 16:9]. But in any case these examples show that scripture finds the riches-poverty area good for exemplifying important realities. Paul uses other antitheses elsewhere: justice-sin, messiah-curse, to show the structure of christology.)[19]

The longest and most considered text in the New Testament for showing the Son in the guise of the servant is the hymn in Philippians 2:6–11, even though it does not use the terms *Son* or, strictly speaking, *servant*.[20] The hymn, which antedates Paul, describes the change from divine condition to that of a slave and requires consideration here. The first stanza speaks of Jesus, not of the intra-trinitarian *logos*, and the incarnation is presupposed without being explained, which it is only in John's prologue, although it is also implicitly present in Galatians 4:4 and Romans 8:3.

In the hymn the subject is Jesus, confessed now as messiah, not the intra-trinitarian *logos*. This Jesus is "in the form of God" *(en morphe Theou)*, a formula that needs no philosophical understanding. It does not mean simply the divine essence but the manifestation of the divine dimension of human beings with its splendor and its effects. Christ could have had the theoretical temptation to act "divinely," but he did not do so. This is what was to be told in narrative form in the temptations: Jesus' messianism strips itself of its possible "extraordinary" condition and abases itself. (By comparison with us, Jesus is not "in the image of God" but "the image of God." In this type of theorizing the background is Adam, who sought to be like God, while Jesus does not seek it, since he is. But he does not cling selfishly to this image.)

This is what is implied by the word *harpagmos* (which is difficult to translate, related to concepts such as "rapine" and "booty"): Jesus not only does not seek to "exploit" what is not his for his own ends (as happened with the angels and demons and even Adam himself [see Gn 3:5] but does not make use of what is his, "equality with God" [*to einai isa Theo*]). Furthermore, he takes on another form and condition, that of a slave *(morphen doulon labon)*. This is where *kenosis* lies: not in the incarnation but in stripping himself of the divine dimension of being human (a dimension that belongs to every human being by nature) and taking on the form of what is weakest in human nature. (Although it might appear oversimplified, this meaning of *kenosis* can be gleaned from the texts in which Paul speaks of his free *renunciation* of being supported by the community [see 1 Cor 9; 12; 15; 18].) So the "humbling himself" is described in terms similar to that of his becoming flesh, *sarx* (Jn 1:14) or to that of his being sent in "sinful flesh" (Rom 8:3).

So the hymn is a radical affirmation of Jesus' human form through an abasement that changes him into a *doulos*, a slave. It also stresses his decision to *take the form of* a slave, with which *kenosis* is presented not only as what happens to him, out of need or through fate or even from faithfulness to his mission, but as what he freely and consciously chooses, which increases the novelty and scandal. And finally it states that this *kenosis* is the hallmark of Jesus' life and of his progress toward the end, to death, to what Paul adds to the original hymn: "even death on a cross." This is the Son–humbled slave. He obviously bears a close resemblance to the Son–servant (which is why I brought the analysis of *kenosis* into this chapter) but with significant differences.

The first, as González Faus has noted,[21] is that in the hymn *kenosis* as such is fruitful for Jesus himself: it gives him a name that is above every name, but it says nothing directly about his saving relevance with regard to us, which does appear clearly in the servant: his suffering is expiation for our sins. This lack of the soteriological aspect, however, is not complete, since, even if only indirectly, we can view as salvific for us the fact that the cosmic powers ("every knee should bend, in heaven and on earth and under the earth"), which are in mythological language the roots of human slavery, have been defeated. With *kenosis* and exaltation, "not only is Christ glorified, but he opens the way to glory for us. . . . The surrender of human existence to death has been superseded by this 'Savior.'"[22]

The second difference may appear subtle, but it is important in situations such as that of the Third World. *Kenosis* expresses the fact that Jesus took on "human form" in its weakness and burdening. The servant, nevertheless, expresses the form of "victim." In *kenosis* Jesus strips himself, whereas the servant is stripped. The two things do not have to be absolutely distinguished, but they are not the same. *Victim* is a historical-dialectical concept that indicates being actively humiliated by others. Therefore, the servant not only shares in the human condition of suffering but bears our sins (historical sins, in the Latin American interpretation),[23] which destroy him and leave him looking no longer human, let alone divine.

In any case, both the *doulos* and the *pais* bring salvation. Technically, this is expressed in both cases by Jesus accepting affinity with the human condition and, more radically, with victims. If *closeness* is already a salvific reality, *humiliation* is more so for victims. Humbling oneself is coming to be in communion with "those below," a theoretical model for understanding salvation that differs from and is more radical than that of Greek theology.

This is the second counterpoint, and it is more radical in concept than that of Son of Man. The Son who makes God present is the humiliated one and the one who puts himself at the mercy of human beings. He is himself a victim because he comes to a real world, that of the anti-Kingdom. And the God who approaches in this Son is also the God who becomes present in a real world and puts himself at its mercy.

2. The Tradition of the Son

The christology of the Son of God has been elaborated with the greatest profundity in the Gospel of John, though formulated and conceptualized differently from the synoptics. Christ is "the Son," and his correlative is no longer simply "God" but "the Father." An intimate and exclusive relationship exists between the two.

The Son is the focus of this gospel, no longer in hidden fashion as in Mark but now openly and publicly. Let us look at this first in its more "dogmatic-formal" formulation and then in its more "concrete-existential" one.

(a) The Dogmatic-Formal Perspective

In the Gospel of John the Son comes from God, and he is the only one who comes from God: he is the only-begotten, the *monogenes* (1:14, 18). This is an absolute statement, one that stands up on its own with no supporting argument—in the same way as do Matthew's and Luke's statements that the Spirit and not a man was the origin of Jesus' conception—and is upheld despite the fact that his parents are known (7:27) and that he comes from Nazareth (1:45; 7:41). The gospel, then, feels no need to argue the case for the unique relationship of Jesus to the Father owing to his origin, nor does it feel the need to state, even if paradoxically, the "double" origin of Jesus, "descended from David according to the flesh and . . . declared to be Son of God with power according to the spirit," as in Romans 1:3. The central affirmation is absolute: Jesus is the Son because of his *provenance* from God—which would be decisive in patristic christology.

The gospel stresses the essential *unity* between the Son and the Father: "The Father and I are one" (10:30); "the Father is in me and I am in the Father" (10:38), a unity expressed as mutual knowledge (10:15) and unity of will (5:30; 4:34). Its external expression is working together (5:17, 19, 20): the Father works with the Son, not just through the Son (8:16). And the reason for this unity is that "the Father loves the Son and shows him all that he himself is doing" (5:20). This unity is also expressed *soteriologically*, since the Son shares in the life of the Father in order to pass it on to us: "So just as the Father has life in himself, so he has granted the Son also to have life in himself" (5:26). Finally, from the perspective of *salvation history*, the Father sends the Son (8:42) and the Son returns to the Father (16:28). The Son's time is the same as that of the Father (9:4).

In various ways, then, and on different levels of Jesus' being, he shows himself in unity with the Father. The "Jews" understood what was being said here and were scandalized (10:32, 36). According to the gospel, they attacked and persecuted Jesus because he based such an extreme claim on his own witness (5:30f.; 8:13f.). In an affirmation of principles, Jesus refers himself to the Father alone so that the Father will be the one who bears witness to him: only the Father can make Jesus known, which is to stress the ultimateness of Jesus, beyond which it is impossible to go. But Jesus also defends himself in two ways. One is the *way of honesty.* He challenges people to take an attitude to what he does: "If I am not doing the works of my Father, then do not believe me. But if I do them, even if you do not believe me, believe the works" (10:37f.). The other is the *way of works*: "Anyone who resolves to do the will of God will know whether the teaching is from God or whether I am speaking on my own" (7:17).

Finally, John's gospel stresses that this unity is differentiated, since the Father is "greater" than the Son: "the Father is greater than I" (14:28). In working terms, John stresses the essential dependence of the Son on the Father: "My food is to do the will of the one who sent me and to complete his work" (4:34); "I always do what is pleasing to him" (8:29); "I do as the Father has commanded me, so that the world may know that I love the Father" (14:31).

So the relationship of the Son to the Father is presented in dialectical terms: John shows both the *unity* between Father and Son and their *differentiation* in terms of the Son's obedience to the Father. By the first he claims that Christ belongs essentially to God, his divine reality. By the second he claims that this participation in God's reality is not by way of "fatherhood" but by way of "sonship," which will both make possible and force reflection on the trinitarian being of God. To sum up, let me quote Kasper: "The Son is the person who submits himself unreservedly in obedience to God. Thus he is wholly and entirely transparent for God; his obedience is the form in which God is substantially present."[24]

(b) The Existential-Actual Perspective

The above texts provide a synthesis of the personal relationship of Jesus to the Father. In christological terms they state that Jesus' being belongs essentially, not only functionally, to God. But these texts make us dizzy, so to speak, and, however impressive, can be relegated to a theoretical christology, one that gives no actual content to the unity of Jesus with the Father and certainly none to the nature of the Father himself. So let us look briefly at what might be meant by Jesus being "wholly and entirely transparent for God."

It will help us to understand this if we recall that the whole of John's gospel can be seen as a plea for this unique transparency; the gospel has been written "so that you may come to believe that Jesus is the Messiah, the Son of God" (20:30f.; cf. 21:24f.),[25] or, in Old Testament language, "the glory," "the divine transparency," "the fullness of love and loyalty." The problem is how to prove this assertion, and John's solution consists in presenting Jesus' works as "signs" that express the works and the reality of God.

John presents his gospel as a plea because many people do not accept Jesus' works as true "signs" but misinterpret them radically. This is what the Jewish leaders do; they are also fearful that Jesus' works and signs might lead to ruin (11:47f.), as are the crowds (cf. 6:26). The underlying reason for this attitude is a deformed and false idea of God in terms of power, which Jesus renounces: "Unless you see signs and wonders you will not believe" (4:48; cf. 7:3f.).

Having established the context of the plea, let us look at the "proofs" the gospel adduces in support of Jesus. In John 5 and 9—10 Jesus produces two signs that should bring acceptance of his "transparency" with respect to God. Both cases involve healing a person in need—a blind man and a paralyzed one—who functions as an example of a wider collectivity of people in need: in the porticoes of the pool called Beth-zatha there lay "many invalids—blind, lame and paralyzed" (Jn 5:3). Jesus cures the paralyzed man (5:8–9) and gives sight back to the blind one (9:1–7). These deeds are the "signs" that should produce acceptance of Jesus and of his showing forth of God, but this does not happen because the implications of such acceptance are very profound—his intimate relationship with God, his belonging to the reality of God. To quote Barreto once more: "This is the sign before which ways fork and opinions divide: a man, the man Jesus, who does good, heals paralytics and blind people, remedies very human needs as an expression of the way God is present to and relates to us, acting through him and showing himself as Father."[26]

God, for Jesus, is a God who goes on working, who shows a loving care for his creatures, especially those in need. This love and care are above the law (the paralytic is healed on the Sabbath [5:10]) and so the chiefs of the "Jews" could not see a "sign" here, even if the reality of God was expressed in these deeds. For people to see this, they needed to be in sympathy with God, which ultimately means loving like God and even being willing to give their lives for such love. This produces a hermeneutical circle that cannot be analyzed further, involving knowing God, being in active sympathy with God, and knowing the transparency of Jesus with respect to the Father: "The deeds Jesus performs . . . express the Father's love. But they can be understood only if we love people with the love God has for us. . . . Those who do not have the Father's love and compassion cannot generate activity like his. This is what Jesus reproaches the Jews with: they will never understand what he is doing because they do not have this love."[27]

It should be stressed that John's gospel deals principally with what Jesus *does*, not only with transmitting a message, and that this is the ground for understanding his unity with the Father: "The unity between him and the Father is perceived in the convergence of their actions. The work to which Jesus appeals is not simply a work like that of the Father: it is the Father's. . . . The condition of Son is made clear in the works (10:34f.; cf. 5:19–23). Jesus is not merely the bearer of a message from the Father but is the expression of the Father himself, in that the Father is present in him and acts in him."[28] What I have called "the transparency of Jesus with respect to the Father," his personal unity with God, consists, then, in making God's love present, a love that is in no way sophisticated but is as human and compassionate as that expressed in making a paralyzed man walk and a blind man see.

Without dwelling further on it here, let me finish this section by saying that in the Johannine tradition of the Son the counterpoint is also present, and to a radical degree. The "glory" or "transparency" reaches its culmination in the "hour" or event of death (cf. 12:23, 27f.; 13:31; 17:1). God's love consists in giving life, and for this it is necessary to give one's own life.

3. Reconsideration of Father and of Sons and Daughters

I have dwelt longer than elsewhere on the biblical analysis of this title because it expresses something central to Christian faith: Jesus' unique relationship with the ultimate, his "family feeling" with God. Jesus is—also—from God, and God appears in him in human guise as good and as mystery, as presence and hiddenness. Hence the importance I have given to the counterpoints, to prevent the title Son of God from becoming banal and coming to mean simply that Jesus shares in an abstract divinity already known in advance of him.

The title expresses good news above all. For some time, people have been questioning whether the term *father* and, correlatively, those of *sons* and *daughters*, are adequate to describe human existence in a religious sense.

(a) Critique of the Concept of Father

Father is a term heavily weighted with meanings. It necessarily expresses origin and provenance; it can also express power and authority, with their corresponding subjection and infantilism, on the one hand, and protection and love, with their corresponding gratitude and love, on the other.

In general, father symbolism is used to explain the basic structure of being, in which it operates negatively. As the founding act of religion and society, Freud posits not trust in the father but rebellion against him to free ourselves from tyranny: the children end by killing him, showing that *father* is absolutely not an adequate term for expressing the positive side of a reality in which we can trust.[29] For others, biblical religion stems from the faith of Abraham, who had to face up to whether or not to kill his son (which has made possible sacrificialism in theology and unparalleled oppression in Western society).[30] For others still, Christianity consists precisely in elevating human beings to divinity (Erich Fromm), a positive elevation because it symbolizes human victory over the "father," the law, and oppression; alternatively, the essence of Christianity would lie in seeking to elevate Jesus to the Father's level, but as reparation for having murdered him (Herbert Marcuse).[31]

More recently, the exclusivist use of the term *father* has been questioned by feminist theology. As I see it, there are two basic issues. One is the reductionism and, above all, the impoverishment resulting from naming God only by the metaphor Father, without simultaneously complementing this with that of Mother. The other is the standpoint from which God is approached: this is effectively patriarchal and so subjecting of women; it has founded and justified oppressions of women in history and seriously distorted the image of God. The following quote from Elizabeth Johnson can stand for many:

> Feminist theological analysis makes clear that exclusive, literal, patriarchal speech about God has a twofold negative effect. It fails both human beings and divine mystery. In stereotyping and then banning female reality as suitable metaphor for God, such speech justifies the dominance of men while denigrating the human dignity of women. Simultaneously this discourse so reduces divine mystery to a single, reified metaphor of the ruling man that the symbol itself loses its religious significance and ability to point to ultimate truth.[32]

Such criticism is valid, and I think we have to uphold two elements in order to deal with it. One is going back to the Son who *is Jesus* and the Father who *is Abba*. The authoritarian, infantilizing, patriarchal, and sacrificialist conceptualization that can be present in *Father* can also and should be theoretically attacked from the tradition of the Old Testament and from the experience of Jesus: "Too often this predominant symbol has been interpreted in association with unlovely traits associated with ruling men in a male-oriented society: aggressiveness, competitiveness, desire for absolute power and control, and demand for obedience. This certainly is not the Abba to whom Jesus prayed."[33] The other is to introduce feminine characteristics—also present in scripture—on as deep a level as masculine ones: maternal tenderness (Isaiah), a spouse's love (Ezekiel), defending and being tender with the weak ("You are the father of orphans and widows"): "It is also possible to see God the Father displaying feminine, so-called maternal features that temper 'his' overwhelmingness. . . . Thus gentleness and compassion, unconditional love, reverence and care for the weak, sensitivity, and desire not to dominate but to be an intimate companion and friend are predicated of the Father God and make 'him' more attractive" (Johnson). Ivone Gebara is more radical in her critique: "If it is no longer possible to speak of a personal God with autonomous existence, of a being divine in himself, separate from everything that exists, then neither can we speak of his will or his plan. . . . Nor is there any sense in the traditional catechesis about Jesus as Son of God the Father . . . within an outdated cosmic and anthropological scheme."[34]

In essence, critique of what is dangerous in the father concept can only be creative praxis in relation to God. Christological faith sets no limits to this praxis, since the relationship it establishes is between humankind (although this is in male form in Jesus) and God. What it does state is that in Jesus true sonship has appeared, which relates to the goodness and the hiddenness of the ultimate (whether this is called father or something else). It seems to me that these two things—the ultimate goodness of reality, against all appearances, and the defenselessness of this reality in the face of evil—sum up the reality of the "Father" according to the New Testament—and this is what has to be upheld in Christian faith, whatever language is used.

(b) Critique of the Concept of Sons and Daughters of God

In the Third World the most specific critique is addressed not so much to Father language (though it might well be in view of the nature of many fatherhoods) as to its correlative of Son, at least objectively. Without using words in their debased sense, it is scandalous to call "sons and daughters of God" those who seem to live—though in a different sense from what Bonhoeffer meant—*etsi Deus non daretur* (as though there were no God). Put plainly, they seem to live "abandoned by God's hand," "made a Christ," destroyed and disfigured, as though there were no creator God (call this Father, Mother, It, All, or Nothing), and as though they were not his-her-its creatures. Therefore, to avoid falling into the routine language trap and even if it is not usual in a work of christology, let us make a brief digression on the situation of the "sons and daughters of God" at the present time.

(i) Brief digression on God's creation. The human *species* is not in danger of extinction; its growth is rather seen as part of the problem. But people have now

begun to use a new language to express the practical *nonexistence* of millions of human beings—the excluded, those who do not count, the surplus. Human beings are of no concern, a lack pointed out some years ago, at least in Latin America:

> The essence of the population of the Third World today, unlike what happened up to a hundred years ago, is that it is, from the point of view of the First World and its economic needs, a surplus population. The First World still needs the Third World for its materials, its space, its nature, if only as a dump for its poisonous waste, and its raw materials are still needed. . . . What is no longer needed is the greater part of the population of the Third World.[35]

The human *family*, the sons and daughters of God in relation to one another, presents a cruel and macabre spectacle, that of Dives and Lazarus, growing ever farther apart from and more antagonistic to one another. To give just a few facts, expanding a little on what I said in the Introduction: According to the United Nations, the gap between rich and poor nations is growing: in 1990, average income in the developed nations was sixty times that in developing ones; the wealthiest groups earned 180 times what the poorer did. I have already said that, in 1997, 358 persons, whose assets exceeded a billion dollars, had a combined annual income greater than 45 percent of the world's population. By 1998 these assets were held by only 225 individuals. The facts, then, are terrifying. While we can now envisage the possibility of eradicating poverty within a foreseeable future, the international will to cooperate is in decline.

It has to be recognized that the *solutions* put forward have been bad, and in 1998 the World Bank and the International Monetary Fund accepted the fact that their financial policies had been erroneous. The promised funds do not extend to all, and so the cruel decision has to be taken as to which nations will live and which will die. And, as Ellacuría used to say, a bad solution is worse than no solution at all.

The planned cultural *dehumanization* to encourage consumerism, the trivialization of life, the individualization and real isolation of persons and peoples—despite globalization—leads people to ignore, lose interest in, and despise others. And if modernity was characterized by expectation of salvation—the coming of the kingdom of freedom, the classless society, or whatever—postmodernity is limiting, if not canceling, expectation itself. The conclusion is that the world economic structure imposes resignation, by necessity, and discouragement for those who had hope. For the present world economic system to succeed, there has to be "the geoculture of despair and the theology of inevitability."[36]

Finally, the whole situation is subject to a coverup, sometimes crude, but usually subtle. The U.N. charter proclaimed that "all human beings have been created equal," but in order to have rights and dignity it is better to have been born in New York or Bonn than in El Salvador or Chad; it is more important to have been born a "citizen" of a particular nation than merely to have been born. The universality of human dignity has always been an illusion and a deception. What prevents it is partiality, but in the opposite direction from the will of God: the universal rule has been partiality toward the powerful minorities.

(ii) The mystery of the beloved Son. This is the reality that challenges the routine assertion that we are all sons and daughters of God. God has come to have a world that bears little resemblance to what he wills: sons and daughters who do not reflect the life and dignity of God. And the scandal does not go away by drawing a distinction between natural and supernatural, as though it were possible to be sons and daughters of God on this second level despite what happens on the first level, because God made "them in our image, according to our likeness" (Gn 1:26). Nor does it go away by saying that the poor and the victims can be rich in virtues, which is often true. The conclusion is that, if we believe in a God Father, Mother, of life, the mere repetition that we are sons and daughters of God cannot fail to sound sarcastic.

We are once again faced, then, with the problem of theodicy, which in my view is more radical than the problems just enumerated, as the situation of women and oppressed cultures and races indicates. Obviously it is not enough to change or add concepts and terms. Whether God is called *Abba*, Father, Mother, All, or a name taken from other religions in place of that from the biblical-Western tradition, the dark side of reality remains, as does, above all, the situation of the victims; none of the above names tempers *this* problem. (The idea of simply not naming God in any form does not help either. This can be a help in expressing the experience of God as something mysterious and holistic and in overcoming reductionisms, as Ivone Gebara seems to suggest in the illuminating article cited above, but in my view it does not remove the situation that gives rise to theodicy.) To move forward—if, indeed, there is a way forward in these matters—three courses occur to me.

The first is *the way of honesty*. In the church of Latin America this has been said for many years now, and it would be a bad mistake to think that "the time has passed" (as some people frivolously suggest). It was said in pastoral language at Medellín, and Puebla reasserted it vigorously: "We brand the situation of inhuman poverty in which millions of Latin Americans live as the most devastating and humiliating kind of scourge" (no. 29). The faces of the "sons and daughters of God" are children struck down by poverty, frustrated young people, indigenous people in subhuman situations, exploited peasants, ill-paid workers, marginalized and overcrowded urban dwellers, disregarded old people (nos. 32–39). And Santo Domingo in 1992—so trite in many of its texts—amplifies these "faces" (which could perhaps without oversimplifying be related to the "form" of the hymn in the letter to the Philippians or the "aspect" of the fourth song of the servant in Isaiah) as a sign that the human family is not progressing but moving backward. I quote at length because of the way the text fits our situation:

> Faces disfigured by hunger, the result of inflation, overseas debt and social injustices; faces disillusioned by politicians who promise but do not deliver; faces humiliated on account of their own culture, which is not respected and is even despised; faces terrorized by daily indiscriminate violence; the anguished faces of abandoned youngsters who wander our streets and sleep under our bridges; the suffering faces of humiliated and ignored

women; the tired faces of emigrants, who find no worthy welcome; faces made old by time and work of those who lack the minimum needed to survive worthily. (no. 178)

These hundreds and thousands of millions of human beings are today the "blind, lame, and paralyzed" who crowded the pool of Beth-zatha with its five porticoes (Jn 5:2f.). And this situation—even if it may seem out of place in a work of christology—has to be made a central concern in order to "save theology from its cynicism."[37] In speaking of a Father God and of his sons and daughters, let us at least hold on to and not cover up the truth of the situation.

The second course is *the way of praxis*. We are faced with a situation similar to that deriving from the title Lord. If we are in any way responsible for or collaborate in, by action or omission, the generation of poor and victims, it would be better if we keep silent on the subject of a Father/Mother God and on creatures who are his/her sons and daughters. It is our task, as I said when examining the lordship of Jesus, to make the fatherhood and motherhood of God in history real.

The third is *the way of boldness in faith*. The mystery of the servant still applies today. Today too the beloved Son is the one chosen to "maintain justice and do what is right" and to be a light to the nations, as the first three songs in Isaiah proclaim. And the beloved Son is also faithful to the point of being destroyed for the sake of completing this mission on earth, as the last song indicates. And it is in this Son and not in any other—as Isaiah's beautiful and deep words proclaim—that God is well pleased.

To finish, let me repeat what I said of martyrdom in the first volume (*JL*, pp. 264–71). There is an analogy of the beloved Son. In our world there are those who carry out a mission and are destroyed by it, ending up like the suffering servant, weak and powerless; there are many martyrs who today express this total identification with the servant. There are others, however, who express only the servant's final destiny, without a prior praxis to bring it about: they are simply poor (often women, children, and weak old people), and they die as victims. So now when we ask who is the beloved Son in today's world, we have to take both groups into account. Here I concentrate on the second, the vast majorities, the millions and even billions of human beings who are still forgotten, to all practical intents and purposes, by virtually all the powers of this world—and often by theology. This is where the partiality of God's fatherhood comes in, and, correlatively, the partiality of sonship. "Father of orphans and protector of widows is God" (Ps 68:5), as it says in the Old Testament. Puebla spoke of the poor in this same biblical tradition: "Made in the image and likeness of God to be his children, this image is dimmed and even defiled. That is why God takes on their defense and loves them" (no. 1142).

The presence of God in the suffering servant is a mystery in the New Testament and remains one throughout history. It is also a mystery that God's "family look" is seen in the mocking of humanity. The tragedy is that we can fail to see and even distort who the servant is today. I end this chapter with two quotations.

Michael Novak, theologian of capitalism, claims that the current expression of the suffering servant is the business corporation:

For many years one of my favorite scripture texts has been Isaiah 53:2–3: "For he grew up before him like a young plant, and like a root out of dry ground; he had no form or majesty that we should look at him, nothing in his appearance that we should desire him. He was despised and rejected by others; a man of suffering and acquainted with infirmity; and as one from whom others hide their faces he was despised, and we held him of no account." I should like to apply these words to the modern business corporation, an excessively despised incarnation of the presence of God in this world.[38]

Gustavo Gutiérrez cites these words by César Vallejo: "The lottery-ticket seller who cries, 'I've got the winner!' has some element of God."[39] It is in such poor people that the face of God appears, in mocked humanity. That we should be able to see something of God in them is not something that can be planned; it just happens. Some seem to express only their lack of human form, their failure to value their divine condition, which comes to them with creation. (Without being ironic, I have written elsewhere that many millions do not need to make the meditation on "the two flags" in St. Ignatius's *Spiritual Exercises* [no. 146f.] to be chosen to live in poverty and to have been placed with the Son. This is one way— even if a shocking one—of entering into the analogy of the beloved Son.) These poor people, like the beloved Son, make God present, a silent and hidden God, but still God.

Chapter 13

Word

Truth and Good News

preexistence

I have left analysis of the title *logos,* Word, to last. It continues the line of thought according to which "God has appeared in Jesus." But this is deepened, and so the *logos* brings the unity of God with Jesus "from everlasting" (preexistence) and the coming into being of God himself (incarnation) and shows Jesus—in everything he does and says, and in all that he is—as revealing of the Father.

In the history of christology the title *logos* is of great importance because it "bridges the gap" between Judaic and Hellenic culture. It was also decisive for preaching Christ as a mission to the Hellenic world, just as the title messiah was for preaching him in the Judaic world. Hence the New Testament title *logos* can be analyzed as the scriptural basis of *future* patristic and conciliar christology.

I am going to examine it in its capacity to shed light on the presence of the transcendent in history, which I shall do by means of a reflective meditation on the prologue to John's gospel. I shall also examine its capacity to illuminate major aspects of revelation: the dialectic between past and present in revelation of God; revelation as communication of God who is, first and foremost and formally, good news and not only truth; and revelation as victory over lies and not only as overcoming of ignorance. But first let me make a short presentation of the origin and meaning of the title.

1. Origin and Meaning of *Logos*

The word appears only in John's writings and in its most specific sense in the prologue to his gospel. As for its origin, it is certain today that there are numerous reflections on the *logos* in both Hellenism and Judaism.[1]

(a) Hellenism

In Hellenism the *logos* is a basic reality. It is used to affirm and uphold the idea that beyond empirical reality there exists a reason, a meaning. At the origins of

Greek thought, the *logos* was viewed as the law of the universe that governs all things, and Plato made it one of the ideas. There was, however, no speculation about whether the *logos* could become a substantial reality in itself, a basic problem that was later to worry Christian theology. In Philo the *logos* already appears as a sort of intermediary essence between God and humankind, related to the Wisdom, already personified, of which the Old Testament speaks. In Gnosticism the *logos* is a mythic essence, also mediatory, which is personified as creating, revealing, and saving. There is even talk of incarnation, though not in the sense given to it in John's prologue but in a mythical-Docetist sense. In the surrounding religions there was also mention of a revealing and saving *logos* (Hermes, Theot), and in these the process of personifying the *logos* was speeded up for the sake of popular religious feeling.

Whatever the form in which the *logos* was conceived and personified, the basic aspect for theology lies in the conviction that existence is shot through with reason and meaning. This means that existence is not only the object of salvation or condemnation but is also an object of meaning, possessing intrinsic transparency and light. This is what is related to God from the believing viewpoint and what will also mean that theology both can and should be "rational."

(b) Judaism

Judaism also contained deep reflection on the Word, deriving from two distinct traditions. One bears on the creative word of God *(debar Yahweh)* and the other on "wisdom." In the first chapters of Genesis the way in which creation comes about is described sometimes in craft terms (God works the dust of the ground [2:7]), but structurally creation comes about through the word: "and God said," and all things were created (1:3; cf. Ps 33:6) and were all good.

This creator word acquires a separate identity: "God sent out his word" (Ps 107:20). In Isaiah 55:10f., the efficacy of the word of God is stressed and is virtually personified. But it is in the Judaism of the diaspora that the movement to hypostasize and personify the word begins. "The source of wisdom is God's word in the highest heaven" (Ecc. 1:5), and the "word" is first spoken of on its own, without the qualification that it is "the word *of God.*"

The other Old Testament tradition on the word focuses on wisdom, which is personified as anterior to all creation: "Before the ages, in the beginning, he created me" (Sir 24:9); "The Lord created me at the beginning of his work" (Prov 8:22); "I came forth from the mouth of the Most High, and covered the earth" (Sir 24:3). This wisdom is present in history and "[takes] root in an honored people" (Sir 24:12). It is identified with the law (see 24:23). (There are rabbinical texts that identify wisdom with the Torah, which is then hypostasized as "daughter of God.")[2]

In the development of these speculations, wisdom and word become interchangeable. A certain notion of personification begins to appear, when the word is considered as a reality in itself, and of preexistence with respect to the whole of creation, which, as I have said, will be important for the *future* of a christology of the *logos*, since the word is the person of Jesus Christ. But before analyzing the application of the word to Christ, let us look at two historical-existential characteristics of the word in the Old Testament.

The first is that the word is the necessary vehicle for the challenge God poses, this dimension of challenge being what makes God present for us. "The God of the Bible cannot be grasped as neutral; he ceases to be God the moment that intimation ceases."[3] This is why God has no image but only a voice. So God said to Moses, "Then the Lord spoke to you out of the fire. You heard the sound of words but saw no form; there was only a voice" (Dt 4:12). Accepting the relationship with God is, then, being open to being challenged by God's word, and the contrary, neutralizing this challenge, is ceasing to relate to God.

The second is that human beings can not only *neglect* the word but *reject* it. And this rejection expresses not only a generic human sinfulness but the specific sinfulness of creatures before a God who speaks to them and warns them, who argues with them and even implores them, recalling the good things he has done for his people. Rejecting the word of God is another form of the *mysterium iniquitatis*, expressed here in the explicit relationship between human beings and God himself. It may seem obvious, but it needs restating: through having a voice, God is also accepting the possibility of being not only unknown but actively ignored and rejected, as the prophets of the Old Testament powerfully denounced.

(c) The New Testament

In the New Testament *word* as a term to designate Christ in an absolute sense appears only in the prologue to John's gospel (1:1).[4] It is not applied to Jesus in his life, nor is it likely that it would have been, since calling Jesus *logos* implies an already developed christology and supposes a certain sense of his incarnation and preexistence. Its *Sitz im Leben* is not liturgy or preaching or catechesis or parenesis but explicit theological reflection in a world already religiously and philosophically somewhat removed, in both time and space, from the origin of Jesus, and one in which reasons have to be given for faith. Let us now see how the gospels relate Jesus to the reality of the word.

The four gospels and above all the source Q give many of Jesus' words, but in John's gospel—even leaving the prologue out of account—the word of Jesus has a special meaning. "Word" is what is heard phonetically with one's ears (2:22; 19:8), but it is above all what one has to hear with faith and hope: "Very truly, I tell you, whoever keeps my word will never see death" (8:51; cf. 8:31; 5:24).

The word of Jesus is not related to God only because Jesus turns to God for his justification; it *is* the word of God: "I have given them your word" (17:14); "your word is truth" (17:17). Jesus appears not as someone who *brings* the word, the truth, and the life but as the one who *is* the word, the truth, and the life. Finally, this relationship between Jesus and word in the gospel is so intimate that *word* is the term reserved for describing Jesus' work. So in 1:23, when John the Baptist appears preaching, the evangelist consciously refers to his preaching not with the term *word* but with *voice*: "I am the voice crying in the wilderness," which makes a clear distinction between Jesus and the Baptist. What the gospel is seeking to do with all this is to enable the reader to progress from understanding of the word *spoken* by Jesus to that of the Word that *is* Jesus, a word made flesh. So the word preached by Jesus is truth (17:17), and Jesus himself is the truth (14:6). It is true that the use of *word* in the singular occurs in other important places in the New Testament: there is the word of the cross (1 Cor 1:18) and the word of reconciliation (2 Cor 5:19), but in the Johannine writings this absolutization reaches its height: the word is Jesus.

2. John's Prologue: A Reflective Meditation

This word made flesh is what John presents in the prologue. In a dense summary he sets out the reality of the *logos* according to a temporal scheme full of different concepts: his preexistence; his mediating role in creation; his revelatory function, so radically superior to any other previous revelation; his incarnation; his rejection of some and welcome for others; his saving function. In one sense it can be said that the prologue sets out "the history of the word," the paradigm of what, in Christian terms, transcendence in history means, the reality of a (divine) *logos* that becomes history, humanizes and saves it, and also remains at its mercy.

(a) Preexistence and Divinity

The origin of the Word lies "in the beginning," an allusion to Genesis 1:1, but with one important difference: in Genesis what is in the beginning is God, who—by means of the word—creates everything. In John's prologue the Word *already is* in the beginning. It does not appear as something created, or, as in Greek thought (which would re-appear with Arius), as the first and most eminent of creatures. With this manner of presenting the Word, from a temporal perspective—"in the beginning"—the prologue equates the nature of the Word with the nature of God: the *logos* is "with God."

    This equivalence is made plain, although in dialectical form, in the formulations that follow. "The Word was God" (1:1c): it is not, therefore, a creature or emanation of God, but neither is it simply identified with God, with what in the New Testament is *o theos* (Father God), as is made clear in the continuation. The translation of 1:1b is extremely difficult: NRSV and JB both have, "and the Word was with God"; NEB, "The Word dwelt with God." Neither these nor any other definition expresses an identification of the Word with the *theos*, the Father God.

(b) Mediator of Creation

The first function of the Word is to be the mediator of creation: "All things came into being through him, and without him not one thing came into being" (1:3; cf. 1:10), which means that the whole of creation is "shot through" with this Word, that our world and our history bear traces of the Word, an idea already found in Paul (1 Cor 8:6; Col 1:16) and in Hebrews (1:2). Perhaps the *semina verbi*—Justin's brilliantly apologetic formula—are insufficient to reproduce what is said in 1:3. Deepening the intuition, we can say that "the universal teaching of God is inserted in human hearts from the creation, since the Word-wisdom of God, by which everything was made [1:3], contained life, and this life was the light of all people [1:4f.]."[5]

This mediating Word is then specified in anthropological and existential terms: "What has come into being in him was life, and the life was the light of all people" (1:4); "The true light, which enlightens everyone, was coming into the world" (1:9). What is asserted, then, is neither a purely objective/natural creation nor mediation but a "human" creation, which in itself is light and life. And if these texts are related to the words in the gospel, "I am the way, the truth, and the life" (14:6) and to Jesus' whole person, then what the hymn affirms is not simply the goodness of creation as coming from God, as in Genesis 1, but a qualified goodness. Life, truth, love—all the best we human beings desire—are already in bud at the beginning, "modeled" on Jesus.

According to the hymn, people can meet Jesus. To bring this about, Jesus needs to be presented only moderately well, so to speak, since there is an affinity between people and the life the creator Word infuses in us. According to John, people feel impelled toward Jesus by an irresistible force, since this Jesus is in the bowels of their being (cf. 6:44; 12:32).

As this Word is the mediator of creation, creatures learn the manner of "creating," that is to say, the Father's way of working. This is an important idea. On the one hand, it has the grandiosity expressed by Bergson's statement that God created us creators. On the other, there is nothing esoteric or mysterious about it: rather, as we saw in the previous chapter, God's working is doing good to the needy, curing a paralytic: "My Father is still working, and I also am working" (5:17), as Jesus says when he has healed him. God's working is not esoteric but expresses the deepest aspect of being human. This is why Barreto says, "It is face to face with life or with its absence, death, sickness, human degradation, that it becomes clear whether people have learned from the Father or not."[6]

Here the text interposes a reflection of a historical nature and makes a statement of principle. Although what exists at the start is only life and light (as in Genesis what is created by God is only the good), history shows that there is also darkness. Light (and life) is in conflict with darkness (and death). In the face of this historical experience the hymn emphasizes the triumph, in principle, of the former over the latter: "The light shines in the darkness, and the darkness did not overcome it" (1:5).

(c) The History of the Word: Becoming Flesh in History

The hymn continues and works a radical shift: it moves on to narrating the "history" of the Word, the culminating moment of its approach to people. This is what, according to Cullmann,[7] is specific to John's prologue and differentiates it from earlier Judeo-Hellenic reflection on the word: its account of the person of Jesus gives it a radical and new direction. The external formulation might be the same as that of a hymn to wisdom, but the fact that the Word became flesh, history, is something totally new.

In history, the Word had a precursor, John the Baptist. He was not the light, but he had two important functions: he was a witness testifying to the light and, pedagogically, prepared the way so that all might believe in the light (1:6–8, 15).

The basic statement, the one that forms the central part of the prologue, is that the Word came to us, truly and irrevocably: "The Word became flesh and lived among us" (1:14). The central mystery of the Christian faith, the Emmanuel, "God with us," of Matthew 1:23, "the goodness and loving-kindness of God our Savior" (Ti 3:4), is here fundamentally affirmed. The Word, that which can be equated with God, has become what is not God: it has become *sarx*. This means that it has become not simply the humanity of Jesus—the truly human nature of which dogma was to speak—but his historical reality, to which weakness, especially as made evident on the cross, *sarx* in the sense of the weak side of human nature, is essential. In historical language it is said that the Word "pitched its tent"—like nomads in the desert—among us, in order to journey through history like us and with us.

That Jesus is truly human is stressed by various New Testament writings, most impressively by the letter to the Hebrews, as we have seen. What is special to John's prologue is the resounding affirmation of God's *becoming*, that what is truly human—no more, no less—is God, and that this God, in order to come to be with us, has become not-God. And so we can state that "we have seen his glory" (1:14c). The invisible, inaccessible mystery of God has become accessible in what is not-God. This glory is—once more—nothing esoteric; it is not an abstract divine condition. Glory is faithful love, love situated in history and in the midst of a conflict that reaches to death. "Glory" is in opposition not to what is human but to what there is of darkness, opacity, hatred in human nature.

The text continues with the history of the Word and tells of people's reaction to this definitive approach. The first thing it says is surprising and disconcerting: "He was in the world . . . and the world did not know him. He came to what was his own, and his own people did not accept him" (1:10f.). The incarnation is here historicized in a terrifying but nonetheless real way: the Word did not become flesh in any world but in the real world, the world of sin in Johannine theology, the anti-Kingdom in the terminology of the synoptics. Not even "his own" accepted him. The incarnation is something real; the Word takes flesh in a history of darkness that does not know the light and acts against the light. The rejection of the Word is stronger here than in the Old Testament, since now God is rejected in person. And this rejection also expresses the conflict of Jesus' life and the reason for the need to remain faithful to the end, of which the letter to the Hebrews also speaks, thematically.

John's gospel tries to explain this rejection—a vital task. Those who reject Jesus, he says, do not know God (5:38–42), which "relates to their lack of the love they get from him, a lack in turn related to their searching for their own glory."[8] There is a tautology here, a sort of circle that ultimately concerns human affinity (or lack of it) with God. Those who do not hear the Father cannot come to knowledge of Jesus. In simple terms, those who are not in tune with God's values ("it is right to heal a person in need, even on the Sabbath") are not in tune with

God.[9] (This what J. L. Segundo calls "anthropological faith," which from a logical point of view must come before understanding of revelation.)

(d) Salvation

"But to all who received him, who believed in his name, he gave power to become children of God" (1:12). This is the objective of the coming of the Word: to save. This is a reality understood in various ways in the New Testament and here formulated as follows: salvation is what happened and appeared in Jesus (*charis kai aletheia*, "grace and truth," which taken as a whole means fullness). But it is also important to note the order of the two terms: grace, love, life have logical priority over truth and light.[10] I shall return to this further on, but we can now formulate the basic thesis: salvation does not consist primarily in a knowing but in a being (being loved and being loving). Salvation and the element that has priority—"from his fullness we have all received, grace upon grace" (1:16) (or, perhaps better, "above all a love that responds to his love")—are clarified below.[11] This expresses salvation in terms of love, of being loved and of loving, so the prologue is saying that to live in love is to live saved.

This is what is then stressed in the gospel. Jesus' new commandment, by which his disciples will be known—how to share in his fullness, in the language of the prologue—is to love one another (Jn 13:34f.). The norm, motivation, and empowerment for this love is "as I have loved you" (13:34). In the first letter of John the idea is similar, although here related to God himself and so, being theologal, more radical. God is love; God has loved us first; we should love one another (1 Jn 4:7–11), "and those who abide in love abide in God, and God abides in them" (4:16). In love we share in the fullness of Jesus and of God. There is no better formula for saying that salvation exists.

(e) Revelation

The prologue ends by presenting Jesus as the one who makes the Father known. It does so positively but also polemically: "No one has ever seen God. It is God the only Son, who is close to the Father's heart, who has made him known" (1:18). The Word is revelation and can be revelation because he has seen the mystery of the Father, which is hidden from everyone else. "Those who have seen me have seen the Father" (1 Jn 14:9). Jesus is the one who shows the Father.

This is the supreme revelation. The objective reason for it has now been given: Jesus has seen God. No one can speak of God as Jesus does. And the—polemical—consequence has to follow: revelation in the past, the scriptures, sacred to the Jews, have been superseded forever. If in John's gospel Jesus' word is compared to scripture itself (2:22; 5:45f.), in the prologue it is shown to be above it: "The law indeed was given through Moses; grace and truth came through Jesus Christ" (1:17). (Note that this is not a question of "abolishing" scripture, as is the case with the worship of the Old Testament in the letter to the Hebrews, but of going beyond it. What John's Jesus does denounce is "the perversion of institutions implied by the surreptitious introduction into them of a God who is the principle of murder and lies . . . and who converts what should be an instrument of life into one of death.")[12] All biblical personages before Jesus pronounced words, but he has spoken *the* definitive word, because he himself is *the* Word of God.[13] The letter to the Hebrews says the same thing in its first lines: "Long ago God spoke to our ancestors in many and various ways by the prophets, but in these last days he has spoken to us by a Son." Jesus' life is, then, the word of God, and God's word is nothing other than the life of Jesus.

(f) God's Initiative: Grace

To finish this section, let me say that God's approach to us happens through God's initiative and only God's: "born, not of blood or of the will of the flesh or of the will of man, but of God" (1:13). Here there is an objective parallel with what Matthew and Luke present as virginal conception, not in language that connotes a biological portent, however, but in theological language and so more radical: the initiative proceeds from God and only from God; God's definitive approach to us is gift and grace. Nothing has forced or can force or needs to force this approach.

This is another way of expressing the basic message of the whole New Testament: God has loved us first; his love is not a reaction to the good we might be or do, but God is original benevolence. In Paul, God sends his Son "while we were still sinners" (Rom 5:8). In Luke, God runs and puts his arms around the prodigal son (cf. 14:20). In 1 John 4:10f., "In this is love, not that we loved God but that he loved us." Gratuitousness is there from the start.

John's prologue shows Jesus as the Word and the Word as God: "the Word was God" (1:1). Other passages of the New Testament also state that Christ shares in the reality of God: "He is the reflection of God's glory and the exact imprint of God's very being" (Heb 1:3); "For in him the whole fullness of deity dwells bodily" (Col 2:9). In other texts he is related linguistically to God: "our great God and Savior, Jesus Christ" (Ti 2:13); "through the righteousness of our God and Savior Jesus Christ" (2 Pt 1:1); "the Messiah . . . God blessed for ever" (Rom 9:5);[14] "But of the Son he says, 'Your throne, O God, is forever and ever . . . therefore God, your God, has anointed you'" (Heb 1:8f., citing Ps 45:7f.). Finally, there are two texts, both in the Johannine writings, which call Jesus "God." The gospel ends—in its first ending—with Thomas's confession, "My Lord and my God!" (20:28), and the first letter of John also ends with a confession: "He is the true God and eternal life" (5:20).

The New Testament, then, relates Jesus intimately with God along the lines of what would later be called his divinity. But two clarifications need to be made. The texts that speak most clearly of Jesus' divinity are late; they work as an arrival point, from the historical flesh of Jesus. And the concern they demonstrate is not speculative—about what the essential reality of Christ might be—but salvific, and this is the reason for analyzing his relationship with God, the ultimate source of salvation.

This brings to an end our analysis of the application of titles to Christ in the New Testament. In synthesis, we might say that any title that expresses what is good and true, just, hope-bearing, and liberating, any title that expresses what is best in humanity and in divinity, is applied to Jesus. The only thing the New Testament does not call Jesus is Father.

3. Jesus, God's Presence in Our History

The *logos* of John's theology has been a key concept in christology from its origins. In the Fathers it was to be basic as a bridging concept between Judaism and Hellenism. In modern theology Rahner made the *Word* a symbolic reality *par excellence*, a systematic concept for understanding the incarnation. I shall discuss both these elements in Part 3. Here I concentrate on the Word as revelation of God in history. Let us see how John's *logos* sheds light on current problems in the field of revelation.

(a) The Basic Statement: We Can Know God

The resemblance between the beginning of the letter to the Hebrews and the prologue to John is well known: both present Christ as the revealer by antonomasia. But while the letter focuses on the superiority of Christ over other mediators of revelation, the prologue turns him, as it were, toward us, placing its emphasis on what the Word is for us and on what we can and should do with it.

Above all, the Word expresses the possibility of knowing God and the way of coming to know him. It is the answer to the eternal human question: Who is God? God is what is manifest in the Christ who Jesus is. And God is this in a very precise way: God is not merely what Jesus' words or actions point to but is what Jesus *is*. And, conversely, Jesus is not merely one who talks wisely *about* God—even though he does so with more wisdom than anyone else—or even only one who carries out the will of God—even if he does so more radically than anyone else—but *is* the flesh of God in our history. God takes flesh, and he takes the flesh of Jesus, and, conversely, the whole of Jesus shows God. (This is not to deny the presence of God in other human realities; it rather justifies this, since it expresses the fact that God needs no more than *sarx*, without further additions, in order to become present in history.) So to make God present, Jesus represents a movement that is not exclusive of other people but inclusive of them. What Christian faith says is that God becomes present in humanity, that God certainly became present in Jesus, and that God is not going to become more present in anyone other than in Jesus. (I shall come back to this in Part 3.)

This means that God himself has provided the means of annulling his radical otherness in relation to us and of doing so without ceasing to be God and therefore mystery. In words that everyone can understand, when Jesus welcomes poor people and sinners, God welcomes them; when Jesus castigates oppressors, God castigates them; when Jesus rejoices in eating with publicans and prostitutes, God rejoices; when Jesus suffers on the cross, God suffers on the cross. . . . When we ask ourselves intellectually and existentially who God is, the answer is to look at Jesus:

> What God is becomes visible in a man. Now according to John, what God is is shown in what God does in and through a man. Jesus does not articulate language about God solely through his speeches but, principally, through his deeds. And not just any deeds: the sign above all others is the laying down of his life as an expression of his love (13:1; 15:13).[15]

Jesus is, then, by definition, the mediator for knowing God and the way to go to God. And there is an important pastoral conclusion to be drawn from this dogmatic thesis: wherever there is interest in Jesus, whenever Jesus draws and inspires people—even if they do not confess him entirely—something good and humanizing exists. The life of Jesus is the best mystagogy toward his own mystery and is—whether one knows it or not—being on the way to God. What one has to be careful about is that this Jesus is Jesus of Nazareth, not any other.

(b) The Dialectic of Revelation: Past and Present

Jesus is the definitive presence of God in history, and yet there is a disconcerting phrase in John's gospel: "It is to your advantage that I go away" (16:7). The reason Jesus gives is that it is only once he is absent that the Paraclete can come, and when he comes "he will guide you into all the truth" (16:13). The paradox is remarkable: the Word *of God* has become present in this world, and yet it has to be *completed* and it is good that it should be. (In another surprising passage, which can be taken as a parallel, Jesus tells his disciples that "the one who believes in me will also do the works that I do and, in fact, will do greater works than these" [Jn 14:12].) And this also points to the solution to a problem in Christian life and in theology, since both have to live in time.[16]

The revelation of God communicates truth and makes God present but—owing to its temporality—as process. It is a *pedagogy* to enable us to come to recognize truth throughout history. In support of this thesis Juan Luis Segundo cites the constitution *Dei Verbum*, which, referring to the Old Testament, states that revelation, even through imperfect and transitory matters, shows "the true divine pedagogy" (no. 15). Revelation, as pedagogy, is the process the very God sets in train, through which God *teaches us to learn*. Segundo illustrates this with the magnificent text from St. Augustine's commentary on the Gospel of St. John: "The Lord himself, in that he deigned to be our way, did not seek to hold us back but to pass on."[17] (Continuing the pedagogy metaphor, there comes a moment when good teaching withdraws, though remaining present in another form.)

The revealer, the Word, does not bind us to himself. Rather, he refers and encourages us to go to our own incarnation in history, to go on searching for and receiving light and life in it. The very word of truth is what requires us to seek ever more truth, to "discern" the truth. The revealer is the one who requires us to be always open and alert to (possible) new revelation. At the same time, nothing of this annuls the fact that the Word, who is Jesus, is the primary criterion for "discerning" the revelation of God today. (This dialectic of "yesterday and to-day" is present in the very makeup of John's gospel. The "today" is the novel work of the Spirit, the Paraclete, and the same Spirit brings Jesus back to mind. In the gospel the earthly life of Jesus and the life of the community are fused into a single narrative.)[18] Jesus is the greatest historical expression of the reality of God, and the structure of all discernment is made plain in his own life.[19] The Word binds us to the basic structure of Jesus' life for us to know God and releases us for us to discover and re-create the basic structure of that life in every historical circumstance. In Pauline terminology, the Word is not letter but Spirit. But this Spirit refers us back time and again to what Jesus "wrote" with his life so that we can "write" the life that belongs to us.

This dialectic between past and present in revelation is what, dogmatically and pastorally, is at stake for theology in reading the "signs of the times."[20] As we know, the constitution *Gaudium et Spes* speaks of the "signs of the times" as events and tendencies that characterize an age (no. 4)—signs of the times in a *historical-pastoral* sense. But this is not the deepest meaning of the expression, even though theology seems to use only this sense. In effect, the same constitution refers to "authentic signs of God's presence and purpose" (no. 11)—signs of the times in a sense we can call *historical-theologal*. If one takes this seriously, it means that God is still manifesting himself today. But at the Second Vatican Council itself there were already serious difficulties in the way of understanding and accepting this.

The need to examine the signs of the times as what characterizes an age was obvious to a Council that sought to question itself on the relevance of the mission of a church that had to accommodate itself to a new world. But there was great debate on what was said on the historical-theologal signs (in no. 11). In his commentary on this paragraph of *Gaudium et Spes* Joseph Ratzinger stated that, from the "Zurich text" onward, signs of the times were to be interpreted as "the voice of God," which was not accepted in its full radical implication, for exegetical, christological, and ecumenical reasons—Protestant observers might see it as a weakening of the *solus Christus* and *sola scriptura.*[21] But although the formulation was modified, the intention of the final text is still to complement the past with the present, recalling the actual presence of Christ and the Spirit in history. (Seeking God and Christ in the present—and their relation with the past—is a problem that takes on major dimensions in the life of the church. In terms of *dogma*, it means thinking seriously about the Spirit of God and its "real" existence, which can be seen at work throughout history. In terms of *spirituality*, it means asking oneself about the possibility of discerning, individually and in common, the will *of God* today. In terms of *exegesis*, it means not petrifying texts or making them into letters without spirit: this applies both to scriptural texts and, above all, to those of the councils. In terms of *history*, it means not sanctioning as universal and permanent what was decided for a particular circumstance: this applies to intra-church decisions above all. In terms of *common Christian sense*, we might say that a God and a Christ who have no "today," who do not speak, who do not show themselves, would be a sorry God and a sorry Christ.)

The revelation of God implies, then, both *memory* and *imagination*. The memory of the *sarx* of Jesus remains essential, since in it God is made present, even though, as history demonstrates, we can use every sort of subterfuge to forget, domesticate, and manipulate Jesus of Nazareth, especially the fact that he died a criminal's death on a cross. (There should be no need to recall that Latin American theology has given great weight to the historical Jesus—the past—and has declared him *norma normans*. There is no danger, then, of forgetting the past; this, however, does not remove the need to ask after God and his Christ in the *present situation*, not just in *texts from the past*. In the present—postmodern, globalizing, free-market—it seems almost in bad taste to mention conflicts and crosses and to make Jesus' conflicts and cross central, despite the fact that both conflict and cross, for the sake of upholding the weak and denouncing the powerful, are the best-documented historical facts in the gospels. The dangerous memory is indeed *dangerous*, and the most radical way of neutralizing its danger is removing the *memory*. A subtle mechanism is at work here, similar to "forgiving and forgetting" after crimes have been committed, which is why we have to remember both the victims and the executioners.)[22] *Imagination* of Jesus is as essential as his memory, though difficult. Conjecturing "what Jesus of Nazareth would say and do today" presents the difficulty of any extrapolation but also adds the virtual impossibility of integrating a historical and theologal fault of major significance into present-day thinking: the Kingdom of God that Jesus preached as imminent did not come; neither did the parousia the first Christians also believed to be imminent. We must not trivialize these differences but "learn to learn." This is what Johannine christology encourages us to do.

(c) The Dialectic between Truth and Good News

The Word, being revealing, communicates truth, but at the same time it is *good news*. The ancients used to say that *verum et bonum convertuntur*, but we have to ask ourselves which of the two, according to Christian faith, has priority, if such a priority exists. If we effectively move beyond a notion of God's revelation as communication (arbitrary, though usually called "free") of pronouncements (however true); if we seriously accept that God's self-revelation is the mystery of God "happening" in history; and if we accept that this happening of God as reality is the highest good and that this highest good is not only the pronouncement but what is really communicated, then the term *revelation* recovers what is original to it, and so John's prologue can again be read as what it is: the appearance of a reality that is good news and not just information about Jesus and God, however true and splendid.

To say it in theoretical terms first: Rahner (here following the renewal initiated by Karl Barth) defined revelation as not so much "self-revealing" as primarily "God's self-giving," although in the case of Jesus' cross he no longer speaks of "self-giving" *(Selbstmitteilung)* but of "self-saying" *(Selbstaussage)*.[23] Zubiri, for his part, states, with philosophical precision, that God's revelation has the whole person as its correlative, not only intelligence.[24] And González, commenting on Zubiri, formulates the matter thus:

Revelation, in its aspect of communication, is not primarily the handing-over of a *logos* but something both more modest and more radical, which is the physical gift of God to us. . . . Ultimately, Christ did not found Christianity by transmitting a message, a cosmovision, a rule, and values but, more radically, by making Christians. Through his deeds he molded the "I" of those who surrounded him. . . . Our "I" is nothing other than our being, and what Jesus' works would bring us was to be this deiformation according to the being of Christ. . . . In any case, the decisive aspect of deiformation, with all its individual, social, and historical aspects, is a personal dynamism set in motion by Christ.[25]

In these reflections the distinction is not formally between truth and good news but between *logos* and reality, between the handing-over of the word and that of the reality of the very God, and the important point is the priority given to the second over the first. But if this is the case, if we presuppose that by definition God's self-giving is "a good thing," revelation is then—logically—good news before being truth.

Let us now go back to John's theology. The prologues to both the gospel and the first letter are shot through with the feeling of good news. They do not merely state a truth—which turns out to be good news—but directly share a good news, which is firmly held to be true. Considered as (a truth that is) good news, the prologue to the gospel states that in this world of darkness light has appeared, that in this world of death light has appeared, and that in this world of provisionalities—including Moses and John the Baptist—the definitive has appeared. Seen from our standpoint, it is saying that in this world we can be sons and daughters of God, totally as gift and grace. We can be "human."

Furthermore, though, the prologue specifies what the good news consists of, what the good that has come to us with the Word is. In verse 17—difficult to translate, not so much for the actual words *charis kai aletheia* as for their true meaning—its content is made plain. Literally, both terms can be translated as "grace and truth," both being symbol words that in themselves express something absolutely good. Most modern English versions stay with "grace and truth," but other translations attempt to specify and detail the content of these two symbol words on the basis of their equivalents in the Old Testament: "love and faithfulness," "love and loyalty," "compassion and goodness," "faithful mercy," "merciful love and faithfulness," are other suggestions.[26] What all these translations purport to transmit is the content for us of the good news that the Word has become flesh. So the fullness we have received is the *hesed*, the compassion of God. It is, then, a *grace*, with the specific connotation of God's partiality and tenderness toward the poor of this world. And it is *fidelity*, God's trustworthiness, that of a solid rock *(emeth)*.

Whichever the most correct translation may be, the important thing is the very fact of making concrete what "grace and truth" means from the Old Testament understanding of God and, above all, from Jesus of Nazareth: the good news is that God loves us (grace), such as we are, human, weak, and little, and that this love of God's includes, as of its essence, God's compassion and mercy toward us.

It is a conscious, condescending love. What is also good news is the irrevocability of this love, God's faithfulness to himself and in regard to us (truth).

It would perhaps be an unjustifiable degree of extrapolation to see the poor of this world as the immediate addressees of John's prologue, since the Word is "the light of all people." But I do believe that the "faithful mercy," attributed to the God of the Old Testament and then to the Father of Jesus Christ in the synoptics, is good news for them. In any case, I think that in order to understand the prologue as good news one has to understand humanity not just in its factual sense but specifically in the sense of *sarx*, its weakness, what is in need of human mercy. This applies to all people, but certainly to those who are weak and oppressed for historical reasons.

Let me say too that revelation as self-giving of God, that is, as communication of God's reality, not just of a *logos*, also appears, if stylized, in John's theology: those who persevere in faith in Jesus as Son of God and who persevere in love remain in God and God in them (cf. 1 Jn 4:15f.). This "remaining" supposes an interaction of realities, not just a conceptualization of truth.

The conclusion to be drawn from this section is that God's revelation is not only "truth" but is at the same time and with logical priority "good news." This does not mean, of course, that the two have to be separated. Truth in itself, through the fact of coming into being, already has a liberating potential and is good news: "The truth will make you free," Jesus says (Jn 8:32). In a world of lies and deceit, the desire for truth is already a good thing in itself, even before concrete truths are spoken. So, for instance, Archbishop Romero was good news, very largely, for his desire for truth and commitment to speaking truth against lies. He generated hope that "truth is possible," which is good news.

Having said this, however, it is not the same to understand God's revelation as basically noetic, though with liberating possibilities, as to see it as a basically *euaggelic* phenomenon, a bringer of good news and hope. The consequences of this are important: it means that theology has to be based on truth and that it is its task to establish that the good news is *true*. (The 1990 document from the Congregation for the Doctrine of the Faith, *The Ecclesial Function of the Theologian*, was headed with the words, "The truth will make you free," while Mark headed his gospel, "The good news of Jesus Christ, the Son of God" [1:1]. The two are of course not opposed, but neither are they exactly the same.) Above all, however, theology has to communicate that God's truth is *good news*, something that tends to be overlooked by theologies concerned with establishing "truth" in a world that questions it.[27] And the same, in my view, applies to documents issued by the magisterium: even though they are dogmatic and should be convincing, they should contain at least traces of good news. Pastorally, this means that the church's evangelization has to start from and make "good news" central (however obvious this may be) and rethink the conditions (witness, credibility, objectivity) needed to make evangelization a communication of this good news.

This can be seen clearly in two examples from our own time. What the pontificate of John XXIII communicated—certainly doctrinal: it convoked a council— was above all good news. At the time of writing, the impression is the opposite: many truths are put forward (some of them very well formulated), but joy and hope seem absent, while suspicion and even fear grow in the church: "John Paul II continually exhorts the Catholic faithful to root out fear. Strange paradox: the Instruction on the vocation of theologians just produced by the Congregation for the Doctrine of the Faith is riddled with fear."[28] As Ignacio Ellacuría wrote, playing on the words *mater et magistra*, "The 'maternality' of the church should take priority—without canceling it—over its 'magistrality.'" Maternality is what molds (helps to christify, deify) people and is correlative to good news.[29] Let me finish this section on revelation, truth, and good news with these words by J. L. Segundo: God reveals something to us when he "makes a difference,"[30] and with these from St. Augustine, whom he quotes, "If you do not make me better than I was, why do you speak to me?"[31]

(d) Revelation as Triumph of Truth over Lies

John's gospel makes use of antonyms (light–darkness, angel of light–angel of darkness, and so on), a technique that may derive from Qumran and could point to the beginnings of gnosis, and this applies also to the theme of revelation. This of necessity posits the knowledge-ignorance duality, so that revelation always implies some sort of overcoming ignorance. But, in John, revelation also appears in the context of a deeper and more central antonym, that of truth–lie, brought out in the conversations between Jesus and the Jews. Let us look briefly at this.

(i) The devil is a murderer and a liar. In the discussion on Jesus and Abraham (Jn 8:31–59) Jesus asks "the Jews" this key question: "Why do you not understand what I say? It is because you cannot accept my word" (8:43). In other words, Jesus is asking himself why they do not see God's revelation in him. And the answer is that people in fact have two distinct and even mutually exclusive vital forces—an idea parallel to that of the forces of the Kingdom and the anti-Kingdom, of God and idols. These two forces each spring from a different "father." For Jesus, the father is his Father God, who orders him to heal even on the Sabbath (Jn 5:19–30), and Jesus acts in accordance with his wishes. For "the Jews," the father is the devil, whose wickedness is described in terms of him being a murderer and a liar, the latter concept being repeated no less than five times in one verse: "He . . . does not stand in the truth, because there is no truth in him. When he lies, he speaks according to his own nature, for he is a liar and the father of lies" (8:44). Jesus here makes clear that the difficulty in accepting God's revelation—accepting the truth—lies not in the ignorance of "the Jews" but in their lying. "If you were blind, you would not have sin. But now that you say, 'We see,' your sin remains" (9:40). They are possessed by a force that not only is ignorant of but also rejects Jesus and his word.

This should be enough to show that revelation does not take place on a *tabula rasa* but in a world that tends to lie and cover up. Our problem is, then, not just to move from ignorance to knowledge, but more basically, to go from lies to the truth. (Paul sketches a similar idea in Romans 1:18—3:20: original sin is oppressing the truth with injustice [1:18], comparable to the binomial lie–murder. The results of this lie and injustice are crushing: God's anger appears [1:18]; creatures lose their sacramental quality of making God present [1:19f.]; people's hearts are darkened [1:21]; and all the evils of history come about—God giving people up to them (1:24–32]. The situation is such that only the Son can put it right. "But now . . ." [3:21] things have changed radically.)

Besides being a liar, the devil is a murderer and is so "from the beginning" (Jn 8:44; cf. Rv 12:17), logically before being a liar. "Cain, who was from the evil one, murdered his brother" (1 Jn 3:12), so the allies of the devil are also murderers (see Rv 13:7, 15–17). This can carry on down through history: "All who hate a brother or sister are murderers" (1 Jn 3:15). We can debate which evil—murder or lying—comes first in closing us off from revelation. (In a short article I have inquired into the order in which God's commandments are broken. There are undoubtedly various impulses in human nature that unleash sinful processes, but it is perhaps not far from the truth to say that what annihilates other people— plunder, death—comes first and only after committing such sins do we lie about them. In thesis form: scandal–death–always seeks to hide–lies.)[32] The main thing to realize is that opposition to the truth produces an active sin (1 Jn 2:9–11) and that if God's revelation is to emerge victorious, it has to triumph over this sin. In effect, truth has to triumph over evil, which is expressed in murder and in lies. This evil can become truly scandalous, a sort of sin against the Holy Spirit (Mk 3:29–30): "The dramatic denunciation running through [John's] gospel is that the concept of God can be perverted to the point of exchanging it for a principle of death and lies (in this order: death then lies!)."[33]

Finally, another shape opposition to revelation takes is "the world." At the Last Supper, Jesus speaks in revelatory terms: "I have made your name known" (7:16), but he adds, "to those whom you gave me from the world," the place of murder and lies. The world not only *does not know*; it *hates*. Jesus tells his disciples that the world hates them (1 Jn 3:13; Jn 17:14), and he accuses "the Jews" of seeking to kill him (Jn 8:37). The world actively works against the truth.

The conclusion is that the revelation of God's truth must triumph over lies, over the evil one, and over the world. And this means that not only must God's truth be made plain but also that sin must be unmasked and, in this sense, also "revealed." The criterion for doing this is clear: "The children of the devil are revealed in this way: all who do not do what is right are not from God, nor are those who do not love their brothers and sisters" (1 Jn 3:10).

(ii) Who will free us from this world of lies? What I have said about the need to triumph over lies and not only to overcome ignorance remains absolutely essential in today's world. This world cannot prevent information on the reality of poverty and oppression being made available, but it is not interested in having these things known as central realities that should mold the collective consciousness and conscience. Rather the opposite is happening: in a thousand ways things that clamor to be heard (the death of the Great Lakes) are forgotten; what is obvious (that globalization is not resolving poverty but maintaining it and even increasing the gap between rich and poor) is passed off as ambiguous and ambivalent; and hysteria takes over ("We have reached the end of history").

Therefore the problem I am indicating now is not just that of the murdering evil one but that of the lying one, who today takes the form of the "covering-up one." A gigantic coverup, besides which Watergate looks insignificant, today hangs over the whole world. In other words, if Kant woke us up from the dream of dogma, we have still not awakened from our other deeper and more dehumanizing dream—nightmare, rather—of cruel inhumanity. Faced with this, what is to be done? How can we know reality and know God? How can we let God be revealed to us and reality be shown to us?

Above all, we have to be honest with reality, allow things to be what they are, without manipulating the truth of what they are, even though we must undoubtedly do all in our power to change them. And this respecting things in their reality—our will to objectivity and truth—can also be a mediation for the theologal attitude of letting God be God. We also have to return to prophecy, not only as denunciation of actuality but also as example and unmasking of the reasons for the coverup. Antonio Montesinos, in Advent 1511, preached his famous sermon to the Spanish slave owners of Hispaniola. He denounced them for torturing, ill treating, and killing, and in no uncertain terms: "You are all in mortal sin; you live in it and you die in it." But perhaps the most interesting aspect is his strictures on what they "knew" and "did not know": "These—are they not people? Have they not rational souls? Are you not obliged to love them as yourselves? Do you not understand this? Do you not know this? How can you be so sunk in depths of such lethargic sleep?" In the present-day world we can, once more, experience being faced with the sin against the Holy Spirit, and we can ask ourselves now what we can do to remedy it. Let us then return to John's theology, which sets out ways toward the truth.

In the first place, John states that no one has ever seen God (Jn 1:18a; 1 Jn 4:12a), but he puts forward two ways to knowing God. According to the prologue, the only Son—the Word—knows God, he who is "close to his Father's heart" (1:18b). But in the first letter we know God because God lives in us if "we love one another" (1 Jn 4:12b). "The place given in the gospel to revelation by means of the Son is taken in the letter by experience of God in the exercise of mutual love. This, as 1 John understands it (3:16–18; cf. 1:3–6), is the only way of experiencing God and the way of making God present and manifest."[34] This love, therefore, is not only a commandment, an ethical requirement, but is also a principle of knowledge: without this love we cannot know God or his Christ. (There is a parallel here, though it may seem a distant one, with the conception of following Jesus as epistemology—that is, as the principle of knowing Christ. I shall return to this later, but see also what I wrote in *JL,* pp. 62–63.)

The second way is more scandalous. In John's gospel knowing God—the correlative to revelation—is identified with knowing the one God sent "in the act of laying down his life."[35] "And I, when I am lifted up from the earth, will draw all people to myself" (12:32); "they will look on the one they have pierced" (19:37). For Paul too the cross is the ultimate revelation: "But we proclaim Christ crucified . . . Christ the power of God and the wisdom of God" (1 Cor 23f.). Both John and Paul interpret Jesus' cross as an expression of the Father's love (Jn 3:16; 1 Jn

4:9f.; Rom 5:8) and so can present it as revelation. But it can also be viewed from another angle. Active opposition to God's revelation, the lie of the world, is so great and so powerful that only a very special event can reverse the force of this lie and open us to honesty with reality. In the New Testament this powerful event is the crucifixion of Christ. The aberration is so vast that it can be overcome by God only through the upheaval brought about by the Son's cross. This still applies today. The crucified people (Ellacuría), the pierced people (Romero), have the power to unmask lies and coverups, and they also have the strength to try to overturn history. The world of the poor and the victims is what opens our eyes to the true reality, what triumphs over lies as well as just overcoming ignorance. And then we are better able to understand the revelation of God.

Chapter 14

Jesus as *Eu-Aggelion*

The communities of the New Testament *theorized* the reality of Jesus of Nazareth in order to express the idea that in him there is salvation, and this is what all the titles examined so far say. Nevertheless, the New Testament also uses the expression *eu-aggelion*, good news, to describe the person, work, and fate of Jesus. So let us end this part by examining Jesus as good news.

1. Jesus, *Eu-Aggelion*, and Orthopathy

The New Testament interprets *what happened* to Christ as what brings about our salvation. Paul, for example, states that Christ was "handed over to death for our trespasses and was raised for our justification" (Rom 4:25), which in a second phase of development was to be expounded in accordance with various theoretical manners of understanding: "Christ has redeemed us with his blood"; "He is the expiation for our sins"; "He has set us free from the law"; "He intercedes for all time."

This theorizing by believers, though basic, is derived later than the historical event of Jesus; we cannot, therefore, say that Christ is savior without having experienced (or understood in some form, even if only through tradition) just *what* Jesus of Nazareth *is*. (If this sounds like pre-paschal reductionism, it can be read in another way. The presence of God in our history—revelation, self-communication—should "make a difference," as I said in the preceding chapter, since it would otherwise be an empty promise. What happens in Christianity is that the way God makes a difference is through what Jesus was and did and what happened to him. All this could and should be theologized, but no theory of it can be put in its place.) The Jesus event is what at the beginning "made the difference" and what could, later, be theorized, after his Easter fate. But this movement cannot be reversed; we cannot go back from theorization to the experience of the reality of Jesus.

What I now want to examine is the "good news" dimension of Jesus of Nazareth. Let me say at once that if this dimension is introduced into Christ, it means that in our relationship to him we have to add what, for lack of a better word, we might call *orthopathy* to *orthodoxy* and *orthopraxis*. By *orthopathy* I mean the correct way of letting ourselves be affected by the reality of Christ.

(a) Three Meanings of Eu-Aggelion

According to the New Testament, and bearing in mind what has just been said, *eu-aggelion* can mean three things: (1) what Jesus proclaims and initiates, the *Kingdom of God*, is gospel, to which we respond substantially in orthopraxis; (2) Jesus' *pasch*, his death and resurrection (from which there is no reason to exclude his life), is gospel, to which we respond substantially in orthodoxy; and (3) *Jesus' manner of being* in his service to the Kingdom of God, and in his relationship to the Father, is gospel, to which we respond substantially in *orthopathy*.

Of these three meanings the New Testament spells out (linguistically) the first two: what Jesus proclaims—the Kingdom of God—is good news; and *Jesus himself* in his saving destiny of cross and resurrection is good news. The first is brought out more clearly in the synoptics and the second in Paul, with both meanings being brought together best in Mark: the good news is what Jesus brings and what is proclaimed of Jesus as crucified and risen. As any piece of good (or bad) news is essentially aimed at a particular audience, this has to be specified. With the first meaning, the audience is the poor of the world, in the line of Isaiah taken up by Luke, while with the second meaning, the paschal kerygma, the audience is universalized. Everyone is the audience—Jews and pagans, men and women, free persons and slaves—although within the universality there is a partiality—for pagans, women, and slaves.[1]

I do not propose to dwell on this aspect, which is well known, but I do want to examine the third meaning of *eu-aggelion*, which, though based on the New Testament, is not adequately brought out by the other two alone: Jesus' *manner of being* in relation to the Kingdom of God and the *Abba*, which, strictly speaking, goes beyond his message, his activity, and his praxis. This manner of being seems to me, in the strict sense, good news that cannot properly be reduced to the two previous meanings. (Schillebeeckx, for example, asks, "What is decisive in the New Testament and so in Jesus' manifestation: his message, his activity and praxis, his faithfulness to death, or his resurrection?" He sees these, rightly, as false dilemmas, since the good news is the sum total of the Jesus event. His list of elements, however, even if it should not be taken in a technical sense as trying to cover the whole of Jesus' reality, lacks the element I am examining.)[2]

Jesus was in fact confessed as mediator of the Kingdom of God, but this does not yet say *how* he was a mediator, what spirit he brought to carrying out his mission, if and how he won the love and trust of the weak, what credibility he had for them. . . . In other words, proclaiming and serving the Kingdom of God can be done in various ways: from above, with power, distanced and even authoritarian, fighting the sin of the world, certainly, but only from outside; or from below, incarnate in the weak and sharing in their fate, shouldering the burden of sin in order to eradicate it. It is, then, possible to be the mediator of the Kingdom in various ways, and what I am seeking to stress is that Jesus was so in such a way that he was already good news through his *manner of being such*. (The same can be said of his manner of relating to God in trust and readiness. But this, by its very nature, is less easily observed, and so I concentrate on the impact made by his manner of being in relation to the Kingdom.)

This third meaning of *eu-aggelion* is well expressed in some summing-up statements in the New Testament that, strictly speaking, do not refer either to the Kingdom of God or to the paschal mystery but to that Jesus who, by his manner of being, brings joy and is, therefore, good news. Jesus "went about doing good and healing all who were oppressed by the devil" (Acts 10:38); "Jesus is not ashamed to call them brothers and sisters" (Heb 2:11); "For the grace of God has appeared" (Ti 2:11). This could also be argued *a priori* from the final definition of God given in the New Testament: God is love, and for us love has a *how,* without which it is not love, even if it is something advantageous and liberating. This *how* that makes it possible for God to be known as love is Jesus' manner of being, and, to put it the other way around, the manner of Jesus' being is in itself good news.

(b) Jesus' Manner of Being as Eu-Aggelion

We can now ask what specifically it was that made Jesus good news in the sense described, what aroused interest among the poor people who "came to him from every quarter" (Mk 1:45), the rural population of Galilee, despised by all the religious movements.

What made such an impression was undoubtedly Jesus' *message* of hope, his *liberating* deeds—miracles, casting out demons, welcoming outcasts—and his work of denouncing and unmasking the powerful; that is to say, his service to the Kingdom of God was what attracted their attention. But his *manner of being* and making the Kingdom also made a great impact.

In Jesus they saw someone who spoke with authority, convinced of what he said, not like those who spoke as unreasonable fanatics or salaried officials. In their tribulations they flocked to him, and in asking him to solve their problems they always seemed to find the decisive plea, "Lord, have mercy on us." Children were not frightened of him, and women also followed him. People came to him, and at the end of his life he found his greatest protection in these people. One woman could not contain her enthusiasm and expressed it with the greatest vivacity: "Blessed be the womb that bore you!" In Jesus, the poor found someone who loved them and defended them, who sought to save them simply because they were in need. His followers, the disciples, men and women close to him, were impressed by his genuineness, truth, firmness, and, above all, his goodness. Such a thing, then as now, is not common, makes an impact on the collective consciousness, and is good news. To paraphrase the much-quoted text of Micah 6:8, we might say of Jesus that he was *good at being* a mediator because he *did justice,* and that he was a *good* mediator because he *loved with kindness.*

The gospel narratives, then, produce a clear echo of the positive impact Jesus made through his actual manner of being, and this impact is, in my view, the most decisive factor in being able to speak of Jesus as good news: "Jesus' words, through the intensity of the relationship they established with all outcasts, gave them the desire and the strength to break the chains of fate that bound their freedom."[3] The kerygma is focused on Jesus' destiny as good news, but here "good news" is already an *interpretation*—a positive one—of this destiny. So it has a derived character: the cross was interpreted salvifically—for which support was sought, more or less successfully, in the theologies of the Old Testament—and so the reality of the risen Christ had to be interpreted salvifically, which was ultimately a faith experience, even though, once this was made, Jesus' resurrection could be grasped as the start of the universal resurrection and so as possible salvation for all.

Jesus' life and manner of being, though, are good news in a more direct way: his actuality is what causes joy. We have to guard against "horizontalizing" the good news and ranking Jesus against others who have also been good news (as people used to be warned against Renan and his famous *Vie de Jésus*). But, on the other hand, we also have to remember that faith is not just acceptance of an *interpretation*, nor is the act of faith in its deepest sense acceptance of a witness; ultimately it is confrontation with and acceptance of, in trust and availability, a historical reality that leads beyond itself, and which can indeed then be interpreted transcendentally and be an object of faith. The good news of Jesus in the New Testament is not only a belief—that the pasch brings salvation—but also an experience of salvation—that Jesus' mercy, honesty, loyalty, and fidelity are good things for the human race. (If we claim that experience of Jesus' resurrection would be enough to proclaim him as good news, we have to remember that while the resurrection indeed expresses something positive, it is not the resurrection "of anyone" but that of Jesus. The eschatological positivism of the resurrection presupposes the historical goodness of Jesus. And from here we can, perhaps, find an intrinsic logic to what it takes to be an apostle: to have been with Jesus in his life and to have experienced his resurrection. Both things, not just the second, are what allows one to preach the *eu-aggelion*.)

(c) The New Adam as Theorization of the Historical Eu-Aggelion

This meaning of "good news" is in some way theorized in the New Testament by calling Jesus "Son of Man" and, above all, "the new Adam." In the ancient thinking common to the religions and to Greek philosophy, there existed the idea of an *ideal man*, or more precisely of *the ideal of man*, which responded to the desire for what we human beings really are to be made truly manifest and for this manifestation to have saving efficacy. By calling Jesus "Son of Man" Christians would have been confessing, perhaps unconsciously, that in him had appeared, finally, the good news of what is truly human. This could be seen more clearly if he was called the second Adam. In the surrounding religions the appearance of the true man was pushed back to the beginnings, and so the *first man* was the true man. In Jewish theological thinking this was impossible, because at the beginning stood not the true man but sinful man, Adam, which is why Jesus could not be called simply "Adam" in the New Testament but had to be "the second Adam." (The Ethiopian Book of Enoch resolved the problem by shifting original sin from Adam back to the fall of the angels.)

Paul is the one who develops the theology of the second Adam in the tension between discontinuity and continuity. In Romans 5:12–20 he stresses the contrast between Adam and Jesus, whereas in 1 Corinthians 15:35–53 (dealing with the question of how the dead are raised and what kind of body they have) he empha-sizes both the discontinuity and the continuity between the two. There are two forms of *body*, he says—the animal body and the spiritual body (v. 44). The first, typified in Adam, is living soul, earthly; the second, Jesus, is spirit that gives life, heavenly. And because this "new" exists, we can be raised.

Paul, then, speaks of Jesus in discontinuity from Adam but also in continuity with him. The discontinuity is obvious, and this is why Jesus is not simply given the title of Adam. He is, however, called the second Adam, which seeks to indi-cate a continuity, the significance of which is important for us: what has appeared in Jesus is the truth—hidden, frustrated, so often disfigured, but always looked and longed for—of the first Adam, the human person.

The conclusion is that Christianity was to say from its infancy, and to go on explaining later, that, in effect, Jesus of Nazareth has made the ideal man mani-fest. The early communities understood this as his appearance in the future as Son of Man, eschatological judge, and summoner, while Pauline theology was to see it as set against what had been in the beginning, *Adam*. In the context of good news, what concerns us here is that Jesus is, finally, the tangible appearance in history of what is truly human.

(d) Jesus as Good News in Contemporary Christologies

In conclusion to this section, let us see if and how the person of Jesus as *eu-aggelion* and the corresponding *orthopathy* feature (or not) in academic christologies. In my view they have generally not featured but have been rel-egated to the realm of piety, or perhaps both have been subsumed into the *saving* dimension of Christ. But, as we have seen, in both theory and reality *eu-aggelion* and salvation, though intimately related, are not quite the same thing. Salvation is good news, of course, but it need not include the savior's *manner of being*, and in this sense it does not exhaust the concept of *eu-aggelion*. I should say that christologies fail to analyze this difference adequately and, faced with the criti-cism that they are purely speculative, stress that their presentation of Christ—like that of the New Testament and the Fathers—is motivated by soteriological con-cern.

This is true of contemporary christologies, but I do not believe it to be suffi-cient. Without the *essential* characteristic of good news, in the sense explained above, the identity of Christ is cut short (despite any amount of orthodoxy sur-rounding it) and his relevance is much diminished, if not excluded. Some theolo-gians have indeed seen what is at stake in a christology that fails to communicate good news and so have given an account of the good news found in Jesus. This is also the most basic way of relating christology and spirituality. Let us look at three examples.

Latin American christology has certainly insisted on the fact that the good news is the mediation, the Kingdom of God, but it has also stressed the impact made by the person of the mediator. As Leonardo Boff writes:

> In contact with Jesus, everyone is brought up against him- or herself and with what is best in them: each person is brought back to his or her origins.[4] For me, the most important thing said about Jesus in the New Testament is not so much that he is God, Son of God, messiah, as that he went about doing good, healing some and consoling others. How I should like that to be said of everyone, including me![5]

Karl Rahner, writing in more speculative vein, asked how omniscience and love, omnipotence and goodness, beauty and wisdom, could come together in history— in other words, how the mystery of God could show itself as truly human and in human fashion, not only *understandable* by human beings but also *good* for them. The answer is Jesus:

> Oh infinite God, you commanded the sea of your infinity not to drown the poor little redoubt that encloses the little plot of my life, but your infinity even allows for its protected extension. Only the dew of gentleness should drop from your sea on to my tiny field. You came to me in human words, because you, infinite One, are the God of Our Lord Jesus Christ. He spoke to us in human words, and there is now no reason for the word of love to mean anything I might fear, because when he says that he—and you in him—loves us, then this word comes from a human heart. And in a human heart, such a word has only one meaning, only one beneficent meaning.[6]

Ignacio Ellacuría was impressed by how Jesus combined justice and compassion for the people. One of his pupils recalled:

> In a theology lecture Fr. Ellacuría was analyzing Jesus' life, and suddenly reasoning departed and his heart took over. And he said: "The fact is that Jesus had the justice to go to the depths and at the same time he had the eyes and the bowels of mercy to understand human beings." Ellacu was silent for a while and then finished saying of Jesus: "He was a great man."[7]

In these texts the accent that makes the person of Jesus good news varies: he takes us to what is most authentically and originally human, according to Boff; he brings together what is hard to bring together, for Ellacuría; he expresses love and only love, in Rahner's words. The important thing, however, is the conclusion to be drawn: to put the reality of Jesus into words, it is not enough to call him God and man, or even savior and liberator. We have to mention his manner of being, his closeness, honesty, tenderness toward the weak. This—with which his human, divine, and saving being is shot through—is what produces courage, inspiration, and joy. This is what makes him good news.

2. The Need for *Eu-Aggelion* in Today's World

The examination of Jesus as good news obeys a christological requirement intrinsic to the New Testament, but it leads to a more general contemporary question: whether anything of the *eu-aggelion* can be found in the world situation today. This is the basic problem for believers and indeed for all people.

Let me mention briefly that, with regard to the situation of the churches, Schillebeeckx in 1974 pointed to two main reasons why the churches are emptying. One is that "we are losing the capacity for presenting the gospel to the people of today with a creative fidelity, together with its critical aspects, as good news"[8] (to which I would add that theology in a secularized world has concentrated on demonstrating the *truth* of faith in the face of Enlightenment questioning—hence ☆ the efforts of the best theology to make this truth reasonable—but not so much its *good news* dimension, perhaps because the latter has a dimension of gift and grace that is alien to the former). The other is the atmosphere of fear, disillusion, and mistrust in case the gospel should triumph over the limitations and sins of the institution. With regard to the social situation, we live in a world in which the news is not generally good, and in which goodness is not news. What is worse, while expectation of salvation—the coming of the kingdom of freedom, of the classless society, or whatever—was, in principle, constituent of modernity, postmodernity or free market or globalization is limiting, if not canceling, expectation itself. The greatest hurdle facing evangelization is the lack of conviction that good news is possible. So I end this chapter by turning to Jesus as good news in the present world situation.

(a) The Impact of Jesus Today

What is it about Jesus that makes an impact today, that makes him good news? The answer matters, since in a world in the throes of secularization on one hand and disillusion on the other it is not enough merely to repeat the doctrinal content of faith in Christ: he has to be presented in his humanizing capacity. Based on the gospel accounts and on the experience of the poor and victims, we might propose the following analysis.

Jesus' mercy makes an impact, as does the primacy he accords to it. There is *mercy* nothing before or behind this, and it is the basis for his definition of the truth of God and of human beings. Jesus' honesty with reality makes an impact, with his will to truth, his judgment on the situation of the oppressed majorities and the oppressing minorities, his being a voice for the voiceless and a voice raised against those who have too much voice. Jesus' reaction to this situation makes an impact, being a defender of the weak and a denouncer and unmasker of the oppressors. Jesus' faithfulness in upholding honor and justice to the end in the face of internal crises and external prosecutions makes an impact. Jesus' freedom in blessing and in cursing, in going to the synagogue on the Sabbath and violating it, his freedom, in short, in not allowing anything to stand in the way of doing good, makes an impact.

So does his desire to put an end to the misfortunes of the poor and to see his followers happy—hence the beatitudes. So do his welcoming of sinners and outcasts, his sitting at table and celebrating with them, and his joy at God's revelation in them. So do his signs—only modest signs of the Kingdom—and his utopian outlook embracing the whole of society, the world, and history. Finally, his trust in a good and close God, whom he calls Father, and his openness to a Father who is still God, a mystery that cannot be manipulated, make an impact.

Seeing each of these aspects—honesty and truth, mercy and faithfulness, freedom, joy and celebration, attention to small needs and breadth of outlook, trust in the Father and openness to God—made reality in one person is always a breath of fresh air. Seeing people like this is good news. But what also makes an impact, and perhaps a greater one than the foregoing, is that aspects difficult to reconcile appear combined in one and the same person. In Jesus there is mercy *(misereor super turbas)* and prophetic denunciation ("Woe to you, you rich!"), strictness ("Whoever would come with me, let him take up his cross and follow me") and gentleness ("Your faith has saved you"), trust in God (*"Abba,* Father") and solitude before God ("My God, why have you abandoned me?").

And so one could go on. The important thing is that—however appropriate the above description—the gospels present a Jesus who embodies everything most human and who incorporates every human quality at one and the same time, and this still draws people to him today. Using the terminology previously employed, we might say that Jesus is not only *good at* mediating the Kingdom, effective in his theory and practice, but a *good* mediator, welcoming, compassionate, trustworthy for the poor and afflicted, the recipients of the Kingdom.

(b) Keeping Jesus as Good News: Present-day Witnesses

Rahner said, in bold and beautiful words, that a human person is "a deficient way of being Christ." If this is true, then we should "make up today what is missing in the passion of Christ," but we should also, and logically first, be good news to the world. (This is the deepest sense in which witness is essential to evangelization, as *Evangelii Nuntiandi* says: "The Good News should be proclaimed, in the first place, through witness" [no. 21].) And this is what happens.

In our world people such as Archbishop Romero are good news, *eu-aggelion,* and in him its three meanings converge: (1) his service to bringing in the *Kingdom of God* (his preaching, the hope and utopia he radiated); (2) his *paschal* fate, the ultimate solidarity and love his death expressed, and his hope of rising again in the Salvadoran people, whose liberation will come to be a reality; (3) his *manner of being,* close to the poor and the victims, and a prophet to the oppressors; his craving for solutions to the conflict; his compassion and goodness; his firmness and honesty. All this made him human and attractive. His closeness and solidarity, his honor, tenderness, and courage brought joy. The poor were glad to have not only a good *archbishop* who carried out his duties well, but a *good* archbishop, close to them and merciful. His *manner of being,* apart from the results of his actions, was already good news. And it is from this fact, not apart from it, that his paschal fate, his death and "resurrection in the Salvadoran people," can be understood as *eu-aggelion*. (He also demonstrated the transcendental relationship between [good or bad] news and its addressees. Like Jesus, Romero was good news to the poor, but the oppressors found him the worst sort of news.)

In places where there is persecution, many others have been witnesses to the end. This massive fact, taken as a whole, is also, though scandalous and hard to understand for those who are alien to it, good news. Jesus' death and the deaths of modern martyrs are good news, even if in a different sense from that of soteriological interpretation. (Luke, in particular, describes Jesus' death as that of a martyr. This is clear from the fact that in Acts he describes Stephen's death in similar terms [7:55–60], so that in presenting Stephen as the proto-martyr, he proclaims Jesus as the martyr by definition. But besides this, he explains why: Jesus is murdered because he upheld a cause, that of the poor. Most to the point here, Jesus dies upholding particular values: he heals the high priest's servant, wounded by one of his disciples [22:51], forgives his enemies [23:34], trusts in the Father [23:46]. This reason for his death and this manner of dying make Jesus good news.) Martin Luther King Jr. is good news in his willing acceptance of death for defending the cause of his oppressed people. Alfred Delp and Dietrich Bonhoeffer are good news, killed for defending humanity against Nazism, strong and generous in their time in prison and at their trials. Ignacio Ellacuría is good news, returning from Spain to El Salvador knowing the danger he was in, staying at his residence despite being targeted, and then killed. Ita, Maura, Jean, and Dorothy are good news, assassinated simply for their faithful accompaniment of the poor.

It is paradoxical but true: martyrdom, the ultimate witness to the absoluteness of love, truth, and justice and to the manner of living love in freedom, without hatred, with hope, contains much that is good news. Martyrdom, however, normally appears only in situations of persecution, beginning in New Testament times. The Book of Revelation, written at a time of persecution, confesses Jesus as "Lord of lords" but above all as the martyr. Jesus is "the lamb that was slain" and the "faithful witness" (Rv 1:5).

In a world such as ours, full of lies and cruelty, martyrs tell us that truth and love, firmness and faithfulness, and love to the end are possible. And that is good news.

(c) The Good News of the Shared Table

The fact that Jesus both proclaimed and was himself good news also explains why Christianity took root and spread. From a historical and psychosocial angle, two things can be stated. The first is that "Jesus gave religious expression to the actual situation of the vast majority of the Jewish people in first-century Palestine"[9] and offered them a *hope*: the end to misfortune is at hand, the Kingdom of God is coming near (Mk 1:14). The second is that Jesus conferred personal *dignity* on the masses of the people of his time. He freed them from overwhelming oppressions, particularly religious oppression, which weighed like an intolerable burden on the shoulders of the poor—hence the importance of his words, "My yoke is easy, and my burden is light" (Mt 11:30). He gave them back self-esteem, with which they overcame the powerlessness they felt and the contempt to which they were subjected: "Your faith has made you well"; "Your faith has saved you"

(Mk 5:34; Lk 7:50). He concentrated entirely on the obvious, central fact, covered up through most of history, including by religious mechanisms, that love is the most important, most human, and most divine thing there is (Mt 22:34–40; Mk 12:28–31; Lk 10:25–28), the love that John calls "new" (Jn 13:34) even though it must also be the oldest.

This manner of living with hope and dignity that Jesus unleashed is what made such an impact in the Palestine of his time and in the Greco-Roman world. In summary form, it is good news that "we all have something important to contribute" (charisms), that "we are all sons and daughters of God," and that "everything is summed up and burned up in love."

The new faith, then, had the capacity to restore personal dignity to the outcasts of history. This capacity was also expressed and sacramentalized socially in the shared table. The good news Christianity introduced historically, and which the good news of the person of Jesus expresses socially, is that those who for centuries had been separated—the poor, pagans, slaves, women, those whom the Jews despised and the Roman Empire marginalized—could sit around a single table: "This universal opening and its capacity for cultural and social integration is one of the reasons that explain the rapid spread of Christianity."[10] What Christianity introduced into the situation of the time was, then, two convergent elements: the good news of the person of Jesus, and the good news of the shared table. Both become intelligible when one is referred to the other.

How Jesus has been proclaimed and how the table has been shared have varied over the centuries. Eusebius of Caesarea, a historian who compares the Kingdom of God to a banquet, describes the banquet held to mark the closure of the Council of Nicaea, ending by saying that the scene seemed to symbolize the Kingdom of Christ, looking more like a dream than a reality. Leaving aside the exactness of Eusebius's description and his theology, this banquet was not in fact a shared table—rather the contrary—and did not express the Kingdom announced by Jesus, whose divinity—ironically—had just been proclaimed. Centuries later, Fr. Rutilio Grande, a month before his death, brought together the good news of Jesus and the good news of the shared table:

> The material world is for everyone without frontiers. So it is a common table with long cloths, like this Eucharist. Each with his or her own stool. And the table, the cloth, and the utensils should reach everyone. Christ had good reason to signify the Kingdom by a supper. He spoke a lot about a banquet, a supper. He celebrated it on the eve of his total commitment. And he said this was the great memorial of redemption. A table shared in fellowship, at which all have their setting and their place.[11]

Throughout history it is the shared table that has continued to "make the difference" to the outcasts of this world. It is what makes it possible to hope for salvation and to present Jesus as *eu-aggelion*. It is the social expression of the personal good news that is Jesus. And as in the case of his lordship, Jesus also leaves the means for him to go on being good news in our hands—the building of the shared table.

PART III

CONCILIAR CHRISTOLOGY

Chapter 15

Introduction: Concentration on the Mediator, Jesus Christ, to the Detriment of the Mediation, the Kingdom of God

In this third part I am going to examine the second basic phase of christology, the christological statements of the early councils. I propose to introduce them in chronological order and within the traditional framework—the divinity and humanity of Jesus Christ and the specific relationship between the two. As our concern here falls into the area of systematic theology, I am going to examine the conciliar texts with brief references to the Patristic Age on one hand and from the problems of present-day existence on the other.[1] Let me also say at the outset that while these texts are useful theologically, besides being normative, they are also limited and even dangerous, as is widely recognized today. Above all, they are texts that launched christology on an original and ambivalent course, one already begun in the New Testament and which I propose to take stock of in this introductory chapter and the excursus that follows it.

1. The View of the Victims

The conciliar texts are particularly useful when analyzed in their formal elements: the specific, radical, and original relationship between transcendence and history, the absoluteness of what is human, the unexpectedness of God, reality as mediator of salvation.[2] Their usefulness also depends on viewing them in their historical context from a proper viewpoint. Let me say at the outset that the viewpoint here is that of the victims of this world, a concept that needs a brief explanation, since it is not usually dealt with in the patristic and conciliar context. One thing that emerges from an examination of this *viewpoint* is that modern *culture and thought patterns*, which differ from those of Greek thought in their concepts of history and freedom (which makes understanding the content of dogmatic formulations difficult) and in their concept of truth (which makes the means of analysis difficult), have to be taken into account, thereby placing demands on hermeneutics.

But also, and more importantly, the viewpoint has to take basic account of *the actual situation of our world*, which tends to be forgotten. Now *objectively* the situation of our world (including that surrounding us moderns or postmoderns) is massively a situation of victims, and, *subjectively*, there are millions of human beings with a more or less explicit awareness of this fact, depending on the degree to which they have internalized the reality of oppression and the need for liberation. In order to understand the conciliar texts, therefore, we have to overcome the difference in culture between then and now, bearing in mind that "now" is not merely Western modernity and postmodernity but also the varied cultures of Asia, Africa, and Latin America (which gives christology adequate historical identity), but we have to do this from the objective *situation* as it actually is (which gives its relevance historical identity).

I am not affirming this need to adopt the view of the victims out of habit or upholding it out of formal adherence to liberation theology; I am doing so because I believe that this viewpoint is a necessity for any form of thinking in a world that is one of victims, and it is certainly so for a Christian form of thinking. "Christ set his chair of redemption among the poor."[3] This does not mean that modernity's viewpoint is not also necessary (particularly where modernity, even if diffusely, postmodernly, impregnates culture); nor does it mean that the view of the victims is a panacea for understanding and interpreting dogma. And adopting this viewpoint cannot, of course, mean forcing texts and reading into them what is not there. All this said, however, I remain convinced that the victims are a setting for reading and understanding dogmatic texts as well as biblical ones.

It has to be said *a priori* that any statement about Jesus Christ, if it is true, will have something to say about his crucified people and that, conversely, any statement about the latter will shed light on him. This is, evidently, a conviction belonging to a specific christological faith and so ultimately not arguable, which does not make it irrational, since such a conviction is produced by the correlation, already analyzed, between the Kingdom and the poor, resurrection and victims, plus the daily experience that rediscovers this correlation afresh every day. It also has to be stated *a priori* that "in some way the setting is the source (of revelation) in that it makes the latter produce one result or another."[4] (What is said here about the setting for understanding revelation will be applied analogously to the setting for understanding the conciliar texts.) This happens clearly when scriptural texts are analyzed, since in them the essential relationship between God's revelation and victims exists, and so the view of the victims sheds light *directly* on biblical texts. The same does not happen with conciliar texts, which make no mention of the poor or victims, so the viewpoint of the victims can shed light only more *indirectly* on these texts. It still does so in a real sense, however, referring them to the history of revelation and offering heuristic suspicions on what they say and what they conceal, above all on why they say some things and conceal others and what this saying and concealing mean. Let us look at this point by point.

In the first place, the view of the victims helps to *detect* major lacunas in the conciliar statements, such as the absence of the Kingdom of God and the God of the Kingdom and of their correlatives of anti-Kingdom and idols, on the theological level, and of the absence of Jesus of Nazareth and of his constitutive relationality with respect to this Kingdom, on the strictly christological level. It also helps to detect the reductionism of salvation, on the soteriological level, and the absence of the poor as its primary addressees, all of which tend to be overlooked from views other than that of the victims.

In the second place, it facilitates *due recognition* of the radical nature of important *contents* objectively indicated by dogmas: the relationship of God to suffering; the humanity of Christ as *sarx* and the incarnation as humbling; adequate understanding of the *communicatio idiomatum*: the limited human is predicated of God, but the unlimited divine is not predicated of Jesus.

In the third place, it helps to *relativize problems* previously regarded as serious, such as the—spurious—hellenization of dogma, and to suspect the existence of more serious and decisive ones. One of these is the influence of power—ecclesial and imperial—in christological reflection and the transformation of faith into the political religion of the empire. In other words, it helps to find inculturation, with its advantages and problems, and to record what is essentially counter-cultural in Jesus. Another is the unilateral direction the christological endeavor took: deepening the relationship between Jesus and the *person* of God (Yahweh in the Old Testament, the Father in the New Testament) at the cost, as I have said, of virtually completely forgetting the relationship of Jesus to the *Kingdom* of God. This forgetting, in my view, is what initially made it possible to equate "Christendom" and "faith in Christ," something that would have been impossible if that Christ had been conceptualized in relation to the Kingdom with the same theoretical depth as that with which he was conceptualized in relation to the Father. In simple terms, the post-Constantinian church—which would still have been sinful in any shape—would not have been able to justify on principle the aberrations it committed had it had a christology of the Jesus of the Kingdom, but with its christology without Jesus and without the Kingdom they were "justifiable."

Finally, the viewpoint of the victims enables us to restate and provide a better answer to the question—relevant today for several reasons—of Christian universalism, a subject I bring up here since it has traditionally been taken for granted that adequate universalization of Jesus Christ began (in practice and also in principle) with the possibilities offered by Greek thought (greater than those provided by the Jewish mentality). But the viewpoint of the victims challenges the idea that a *concept* (not just that of the Greek world) is the only or best way of expressing the universality of Christ, and it also provides a partial, though massive, historical reality, that of poverty, in relation to which such a universalization can develop.

I shall come back to this last point, but I should like to say something here to establish the christological importance of the view of the victims, and I do so in the words of Aloysius Pieris, a Christian, an Asian, and a theologian, who has acutely faced the problem of Christian universalism. In his "Universality of Christianity?" he establishes two principles, fundamental for what they deny and reject as well as for what they affirm and put forward, for understanding the reality of Jesus and his universality. This is what he states: "(1) Jesus is the contradiction between Mammon (money) and Yahweh; (2) Jesus embodies the defensive alliance between the oppressed and Yahweh."[5] From this he produces the conclusion that concerns us here:

> The universality of Christianity is based on these two principles. But returning to these basic elements is equivalent to burdening ourselves once more with the cross, the cross we have abandoned for centuries. . . . We find ourselves, then, faced with a christology that is not designed to answer philosophical questions about persons and natures. . . . Rather, the affirmation of faith that Jesus embodies the defensive pact between Yahweh and the oppressed continues a *christology that can be translated into a praxis in Asia, and in fact in any other part of the world. This praxis alone changes Christianity into a universal religion.*[6]

(Pieris takes it as obvious that no Asian today would understand a single word of the language of Chalcedon—which applies to virtually everyone else as well. But the important thing here is that he does not suggest translating the *concepts* of Chalcedon into other Buddhist of Hindu concepts but presents the work of Jesus of Nazareth in relation to God and the poor. In this, in this Jesus acting like this, he finds a universalizing potential and principle.) This quotation may sound radical, but the task—though this is probably not something that would concern the writer—applies equally well to dogmatic christology: the universality of Christ is possible on two conditions. The first is that Christ should be able to appear in historical and actual, and therefore partial, terms and not solely in conceptual, and therefore universal, terms, even though these seem to aid his universalization. In the situation our world is in, the partiality that will allow religious universality to come about is the conflict between wealth/idols and poverty/oppressed. The second condition is that this Christ can be put into practice. A Christ translated as radical rejection of wealth/idols and radical closeness to and defense of the poor/oppressed can be understood theologally from God and as the will of God, and he can be understood "in Asia, and in fact in any other part of the world."

On the basis of *this* partial/praxic understanding of universality the dogmatic statements of the councils can be understood and interpreted, at least in their latent intention, and their true metaphysical and soteriological universality can be expounded. But, let us recall, what makes possible *this* universal interpretation of Christ, which corresponds to Jesus of Nazareth and to the situation of our world, is the view of the victims.

This view is what will guide my analysis of the divinity and humanity of Christ. But before this, let us in this chapter and following excursus look at the problems, limitations, and possibilities offered by the Patristic Age. Taken as a whole, the thought of this period is ambivalent for christology—which will require a certain amount of "on the one hand . . . on the other" on my part. Specifically, in this chapter I want to examine (1) the novelty of the period in comparison with the New Testament; (2) the constant element of salvific concern; and (3) the loss of the Kingdom of God. In the excursus I want to examine the Patristic Age from the problems posed by the inculturation of Christianity and also by the counter-culture it brings with it. So I shall say a little about (1) the Hellenization of christological thought (which is studied and evaluated in a number of ways); and (2) the process of transforming the Christian faith into a political religion (which is generally passed over in christology).

2. Novelty in Comparison with the New Testament: The Loss of the "Reality Principle"

The process of christological reflection continued after the New Testament and without the discontinuity suggested by the very expression "New Testament," used to indicate something complete and closed off in itself. Major changes were, however, gradually brought about, and I deal with their most basic aspects here. The whole process was obviously much more complex than this, but it is important to understand the overall process and its basic causes, since these still impinge on us.

(a) From the Story of Jesus to His Transcendent Reality

Still fresh in the New Testament is the memory of Jesus of Nazareth, or at least contact with those who knew him in his earthly life and were witnesses to his resurrection; even after christologies such as that of Paul, the synoptics returned to Jesus. This fact, that the New Testament not only *presents* the story of Jesus but *goes back* and *has to go back* to it, however much it theologizes it (which it certainly does, but "historically," not just liturgically or doctrinally), is still an impressive one. Schweizer, referring to Mark's gospel, says that the most notable thing about it is that it should have been written.[7] And for Käsemann,[8] giving his famous 1953 lecture, the central question is why the early church went back to Jesus of Nazareth and his cross when it had already enthusiastically proclaimed his resurrection and exaltation.

In formal terms, the central presupposition of the christologies of the New Testament is what we might call the *reality principle*. This means that the attributes, however egregious they may be (lord, exalted, word . . .), remain attributes, while the real and historical subject is still Jesus of Nazareth. Faith (and, indirectly, theology) is referred back to "what we have heard, what we have seen with our eyes, what we have looked at and touched with our hands" (1 Jn 1:1), although this, obviously, was to become analogous with the passage of time. Now the Fathers of the church were increasingly to have only texts concerning Jesus, which—existentially obviously—need not exclude either faith or christology but does mean that the latter can wander off on conceptual paths without the contrast provided by the actual reality of Jesus or his memory as a central plank. (It may seem obvious, but those who knew Archbishop Romero or at least people who were in touch with him found this of great value in reflecting on him. This is particularly notable now that the process for his canonization has begun, and there is a danger of canonizing a "selected" Romero—priestly, churchy, pious,

[handwritten marginal note: Reality Principle]

but not conflictive, Salvadoran, or prophetic. The "watered-down" Romero that some would like to put forward is unthinkable and intolerable for those who knew him.)

The New Testament builds its reflection on this reality of the historical Jesus and his resurrection. The Patristic Age, on the other hand, became progressively removed not only from the historical Jesus (a tendency already present in the New Testament, although overcome in various ways within its texts, explicitly in the synoptics but also in other layers—certainly in the letter to the Hebrews, 1 Peter, 1 John, and, its way, in Pauline theology; see *JL,* pp. 55–60) but also from the resurrection as a historical-eschatological event pointing to the end time, and it was increasingly to understand the reality of Christ from his historical origin (birth) and his transcendent origin (preexistence).

The process of reflection developed over time. The earliest preaching about Christ contained what was most historical about Jesus—his public life, "beginning in Galilee after the baptism that John announced" (Acts 10:37)—and, when seeking a successor to Judas, they had to choose "one of the men who have accompanied us during all the time that the Lord Jesus went in and out among us, beginning with the baptism of John until the day when he was taken up from us" (Acts 1:21f.). Later, gradually, Jesus' public life—his story—declined in importance and disappeared, to the extent that everything was reduced to the final event, that he "suffered under Pontius Pilate." On the other hand, a theme that had not featured in the narrative of Acts was introduced: "begotten and born of a Virgin." And this—Jesus' origin—which began as a late addition, ended by being the most determinant element in christology.

So, from then on, the Christian faith would be concentrated on the incarnation, "on the moment when the Son of God came down to earth,"[9] which presupposes his preexistence, his transcendent origin. It is true that in some way theology never abandoned the earthly element of his story, as Gnosticism did, but "it built its own space beyond the 'life of Jesus.'"[10] Christology's concentration on the incarnation did not necessarily mean—as it might be interpreted today—ignoring Jesus' life and fate. This is because, thanks to their concept of nature, the theologians of the first centuries could see in the incarnation—as in a sketch—all that happened historically throughout the course of his life. The church Fathers' Christianity is by no means Gnosticism; they rather fought determinedly against this. Their theology is always, in some fashion, memory; it always has, in some form, a real referent: the Christ event. But neither can it be denied that their manner of referring to the real Jesus has changed from that of the New Testament, of the synoptics above all (and from that of our own time). Moingt pertinently concludes:

> Recollection has been reorganized and amplified through being handed on: now it remembers, in the first place, the birth of Christ and contemplates in this the coming of the Son of God in flesh. To the point where the theology of Christ is going to be built up, for the most part, as discourse about his birth, thereby distancing itself, in its form, from the gospel narrativity, becoming a theology that owes more to speculative intelligence than to memory.[11]

To sum up this process schematically, we might perhaps say the following:

1. In the first three centuries a series of shifts was forged with respect to the New Testament seen as a whole: from a christology based on the future (parousia, universal resurrection) to one based on the origins (birth, preexistence); from a means of determining Jesus' identity based on his historical person and praxis (the one who went about doing good, was crucified, and raised by God) to another based on his divine provenance (begotten by God); from a functional vision of Christ as savior and universal power to another vision concentrating on the ontological makeup of his nature and on his divinity; from a plurality of titles applied to Jesus to a concentration on the titles Son of God, Lord, and *Logos*.

2. The New Testament was used, clearly, but more and more as *proof* of a theological thesis (done as much by Arius as by Athanasius) than as an original revelation that had to be "let be." It was not that the New Testament was simply replaced by reasoned reflection, but the latter increasingly imposed norms for reading the former. "They [the gospels] were no longer asked to tell the story of God with men in his Christ; they are interrogated and interpreted with the intention of penetrating the secrets they hide, the mysteries of the nature of Christ, which people try to discern beneath the appearances of history."[12]

3. Neither Nicaea nor Constantinople (the later council more concerned with history) mention actual events in Jesus' life but encapsulate the whole of his existence in the incarnation, passion, resurrection, and ascension. His story then disappears. A century after Nicaea, Chalcedon makes a statement that is still surprising. If Nicaea had to say that Christ is "true" God in order to combat Arius (and to show that the divinity of Christ is something that is clear in the gospels), Chalcedon had to add that Christ is "true" man, which is indeed clear from the gospels. This shows the great change in viewpoint that had taken place.

4. The Patristic Age did not work out a christology of the life of Jesus, and a long time was to pass before this was done. St. Thomas Aquinas was to tackle "the mysteries of the life of Christ" in twenty-five questions in the third part of the *Summa Theologiae*. It is true that the humanity of Christ is not treated as history here, but at least the intention of "going back to Jesus" is apparent. Suárez was to do the same. (Ignacio Ellacuría wrote: "What was formerly—and much less today—dealt with under 'the mysteries of the life of Jesus' as something peripheral and ascetic should regain its full meaning, on condition, clearly, that an exegetical-historical reading is made of what Jesus' life really was.")[13]

5. On the level of theological method, what was to happen was that doxological and not historical statements were taken as the starting point. The New Testament begins with the history of Jesus and—doxologically—incipiently points to his preexistence, lordship, divinity. . . . At the councils, what is the end point of faith was taken as established, as a basis for discussion: "The language of faith has not varied, but its *predication* has been turned around, with the attribute becoming the subject. It was said that Jesus Christ is Son of God and Lord; now it is said that *the* Son of God is Jesus, since he became man and showed himself as Jesus Christ."[14] In conclusion, "The outlook of the faith has shifted: Christ used to be referred back to the beginning of history; now we see the Son descending

from his heavenly eternity, and when he is considered in his historical condition, the height from which he has come down is never forgotten."[15]

Comparing this christological process with that of the New Testament, two things stand out. The first is that the New Testament takes account of the *whole* of Jesus' public life, which it recalls, from his baptism to the cross. And the second is that this memory is handed down in the form of *narratives*—gospels. The theological reflection—speculative, we might say—of Paul and John also deals with this handing on of memory, but both are conscious that the ultimate referent of their reflection is a real Jesus. In the Patristic Age all was to be concentrated, gradually, on the incarnation—believed as a real event but viewed as so transcendent that it came to overshadow the rest of Jesus' real life. The reality principle was here undergoing a devaluation.

It might be said that this process is inevitable and that we find ourselves in the same situation or worse, but this is not the case. Of course we cannot return to the actuality of Jesus, but we can take the reality principle seriously and decide on ways of allowing ourselves to be guided by it. Present-day christology, at least in Latin America, is conscious of this and tries to base itself on it. It does so by reevaluating the *reality* of Jesus of Nazareth, recalling it and understanding it as *history*. And it does so also by seeking his *actual presence*—said not purely metaphorically—in his body in history, above all in the martyrs and in the poor. This is not pure piety but theory: the crosses of history are a mediation of the cross of Jesus. And, importantly, through being real, they lead to its reality.

Faith takes an attitude to reality, and the theoretical-christological texts that help faith are those that help to recapture the reality of Jesus. "Looking to Jesus" (Heb 12:2) is more than a pious evocation; it is the call to the reality principle, from which the whole reality of Jesus can also be unfurled conceptually. Ultimately, Jesus as a *reality* is understood and accessed from *realities*.

(b) Christology and Works

Together with this basic innovation in theoretical approach, others develop as reflection distances itself from the New Testament. I am going to deal with two of them briefly next: the relationship between christology and works, and that between christology and community. These subjects have not been covered as much as the preceding one, so I shall approach them tentatively, putting forward some thoughts and doubts, however provisional. We have already seen that in the New Testament *faith* in Christ includes both theoretical and practical elements, in such a way that very soon, within twenty or thirty years, on the one hand, Jesus was proclaimed Son of God, while on the other, "following and discipleship began to be the absolute expression of *Christian existence* in the post-Easter community."[16] This double, theoretical-practical, dimension of faith is also present in some way in the *christologies* of the New Testament, although we should not expect its theologians to express modern epistemologies relating theory and practice.

These christologies display the invitation/demand to remake Jesus' life as a requirement stemming from Jesus himself or from the theologians of the New Testament: following in the synoptics, being of the same mind as Christ in Paul, doing Jesus' deeds in John. . . . What matters is that Jesus is not presented only as an object of faith, or even only as the source of hope for salvation, but as a person whose reality has to be reproduced, in some way, in one's own life. Strictly speaking, there is no reason to interpret the practical response to this invitation/demand as an epistemological characteristic proper to christo-*logy*, but neither can we merely juxtapose the theoretical and practical sides of christology. And so, Paul's *life* can be viewed as the practical expression of his theoretical christology. (For J. O. Tuñi, "Pauline christology would be a real enigma without Jesus of Nazareth." Tuñi also sees Pauline theology as an exegesis of the historical and existential aspects of Paul's own life.)[17]

Works, then, were required from the outset and, in some way, not only by faith, which is evident, but also by theoretical christology, which in turn they made possible. But these works were also facilitated by the actual historical situation: the first Christians formed small millenarian movements composed of communities with eschatological expectations, with the enthusiasm of all beginnings, as evidenced by the tradition that virtually all the apostles died as martyrs. (Regardless of whether it is true or not, this legend is worth pondering. Just as the church has insisted on the symbolic and eschatological value of "the twelve" who were at the start, so we should also insist on the symbolic and witness value of "the twelve martyrs." On them, and on their *end* as martyrs and witnesses, the church is founded.) And this non-theoretical element, which can be called existential or practical, was also central in the first few centuries, and vitally so, owing to the situation of persecution. Some of the great christologues, such as Ignatius of Antioch and Justin, died as martyrs and related, as we shall see, the reality of martyrdom to christology. As time went on, however, it became clear that the massive growth in numbers of Christians would not, by its nature, allow such radical experience and fate, and the situation became worse in the fourth century, when the Christian faith became the "religion" of the empire, first tolerated and then official.

What I want to stress here is the outcome of this. For whatever reasons, following, *doing*, became divorced from *theoretical* christology. The Christian life, as ascesis or spirituality, was of course encouraged, but christology—as an exercise of the intelligence—was gradually changed into a conceptual exercise, separated from the practical life of embodied faith and basing itself only on visualized faith. (In Ellacuría's terms, we might say that the christology of that period began the understanding of the christological endeavor as "taking account of Christ," but did not, as christo-*logy*, include "taking on Christ" and "taking Christ over.") This is where we have to look for one of the reasons for the one-sided intellectualizing tendency of christology. (If I might appeal to current experience as a counterweight, one of the reasons why Latin American christology is so specific is the demands the actual situation imposes on following Jesus, and this orthopraxis *as such* is, perhaps, the most powerful impetus to the *theoretical* working out of some elements essential to christology, including the understanding of Jesus/Kingdom of God/poor and of the paschal mystery of death/resurrection. In this sense, actions are what to a large extent guide the theoretical course of christology and what force it to overcome a one-sided intellectualism.) Historians of dogma do not deal with this subject, but I regard this uncoupling from works as one cause of the de-historicization of christology. The "details" of living the faith failed to reflect the "grandiosity" of theoretical philosophizing on the incarnation, and yet those details are precisely what, ultimately, revalue the "mysteries" of the life of Jesus and so of his history. In any case, even before the current epistemologies of praxis, the reflection in Mark's gospel, that in order to have God's thoughts we have to follow Jesus, should have had enough resonance.

(c) Christology and Community

There are theologians in the New Testament: there could even, following the Jewish tradition, very soon have been what we now call schools of theology: "In a Jewish context a Christian community without at least some scholarly and theological activity is unthinkable."[18] What there are above all, however, are communities. For christology to come into being, the personality of theologians such as Paul and Mark was important, but so were the different aspects of the community. In the synoptics above all, christological reflection combines memories of Jesus with the actual situation of the communities. Christologies would not have been simply teaching put out to the community to be accepted but, in some way, products of the community. If Mark's Jesus is anti-triumphalist, Luke's the defender of the poor, Matthew's both upholder and overcomer of the Law, this is because ecclesial triumphalism, the coexistence of rich and poor, and the Law were serious problems for the communities. If the Christ of 1 Corinthians is a scandalous Christ, crucified, this is because the enthusiasm of the charismatics made them want to know nothing of Jesus of Nazareth (1 Cor 12:3). This is well known, but I recall it here in order to examine what relationship existed between christology and community in the Patristic Age and whether it had changed from that in the New Testament. The suspicion has to be that christology was distancing itself from the original reality of the communities.

This needs some explanation, since it is usually said of the Patristic Age, as a positive comparison with what was to come later, that its christology was *popular,* and the main reason generally given for this is that most of the theologians of the time were bishops and therefore pastors, which meant that their theology was imbued with a homiletic, catechetical, and parenetic flavor. It takes up the problems and concerns of the bishop's flock, and in this sense there is no divorce between theology and the people such as was to come later. *Popular* here means extending beyond the purely "academic" sphere into that "of the people."

But if this is true, it is not clear what and how the people contributed to *theoretical* christology, in what depth and on what level of reality the faith of the communities was related to the reality of Jesus. It is the case that there were serious disputes among the people over the preaching of the *theotokos* (Mary as God-bearer) led by Proclus and Nestorius, that monks and soldiers invaded the conciliar chamber, that Arians and anti-Arians fought each other, and that there would later be exiles, persecutions, and even executions in the name of a christology. Theology reached the people, but one can still ask in what sense it was "popular." And there is no clear answer. As an illustration of this, let me recall what Juan Luis Segundo says about God's revelation: "Revelation . . . supposes . . . the formation of a people that transmits a wisdom from generation to generation. Through the ever-imperfect doings of the community, this 'people' becomes tradition."[19] Here revelation is related to the formation of a people, and in a similar vein I should like to see in what sense christology is an element in the formation of a people, which would make it "popular." This can come about in two ways.

Popular can mean a christology that is a component of the popular culture (such as "Christ the King" in areas of Christendom, or "Jesus saves" among Pentecostal movements), or a symbol of historical, geographical, or ethnic identification (such as, in their day, an Arian or Nicene Christ), all of which can lead to debates and polemics. But on a deeper level, *popular* can mean a christology that gives voice to the life, hopes, praxis, and mission of the community. *Popular* here means that which generates a people and a community at the deepest levels of their being.

These diverse meanings of *popular* can be illustrated by the phenomenon—ecclesial and social—generated around liberation theology. On the one hand, it is certain that this theology has penetrated into the cultural environment: it is talked about and debated, even by those who know little or nothing about it. But it is more deeply popular in that it expresses the *real being* of a community; liberation theology or, more accurately, its central nucleus as understood by the people (and by its opponents, when they are lucid) is what gives identity to communities, what makes them grow, work, struggle, and even produce life, what becomes the theoretical *referent* of their Christian way of life and being. This theology is what the communities themselves help to generate, and it is what accompanies them on their way.

In which of these two senses is patristic christology popular? It is impossible to be precise at this distance in time, but I should say that it is more in the first sense than in the second. Allowing for all cultural and other differences and even taking account of the pastoral dimension of those bishop-theologians, its method in theoretical reflection gradually came to resemble that of the Greek philosophers more than that of the writers of the synoptic gospels or, if I may be permitted the anachronism, that of the "committed theologian" or "organic intellectual" in contact with the bases of the people of God. The bishop-theologian would have been conscious of accepting one christological formula or another, would have been orthodox or heretical in varying degree, would have been present—even noisily—in synods and councils (even if he was unlikely to have known all the finer points of what was at stake in affirming or denying the *theotokos* formula), but he would—in my view—increasingly have become a mere recipient of christology. Unlike the New Testament communities, in which discussion in the communities was existential (what to do about the poor and the rich in Jesus' way, for example), by the Patristic Age it could only be circumstantial-ideological. It is true that councils, to be valid, had to be "received" by the people of God (and viewed from today there was a remarkable amount of discussion as to whether

Nicaea, and still more Chalcedon, had been received by the local churches or not, a discussion that went on for a very long time). But this still does not tell us whether this *receptio* was "popular" in the second sense given to the term here.

After that digression, let us return to the comparison with the New Testament. In this the contents of christology affect the community on a basic existential, practical, and social level. The image of Jesus that the texts—particularly the synoptics—put together (and theorize over) not only hands on teaching, answering the question, What can I know?, but also hands on hope, the need for commitment, and celebration, thereby answering the other questions: What can I hope for?; What should I do?; What am I allowed, gratefully, to celebrate? Christ is in relationship with the communities, and christology is "popular" by reason of *primary* concerns of believers *as human beings*. And this—not just the theoretical doctrinal aspect—is what generates the identity of communities and peoples. This is what the community lives on and with which it makes its history.

In the Patristic Age there was a gradual loss, in my opinion, of the relationship between Christ and community at this primary level. Being Arian or anti-Arian and, later, Catholic or Protestant (but not being for or against liberation theology) would depend more on geographical circumstances than on the faith, hope, and commitment of a particular community in its actual life.

The conclusion has to be that in the Patristic Age there was a gradual loss of the popular-communitarian dimension by comparison with New Testament times, and this supposes a loss also of the historicity of christology and of the reality principle: the historical actuality of Jesus became increasingly irrelevant for christology, among other reasons because the actual reality of the communities ceased to be a heuristic and hermeneutical principle of christology. Let me say that this process has been reversed, many centuries later, in Latin America: "We . . . have cause for joy [in seeing a] search for the ever new face of Christ, who is the answer to their legitimate longing for integral liberation" (Puebla, no. 173).

3. The Constant: Concern for Salvation

Let us turn now from some major differences between this period and that of the New Testament to what remained constant: concern for salvation. The christology of the church Fathers and the early councils is not a purely speculative undertaking but, like the New Testament, is at the service of concern for salvation. The two things were to be separated completely only later, in the Middle Ages, with Anselm's *Cur Deus homo*, but in the Patristic Age there was an intrinsic relationship between christology and soteriology; "Soteriology comes to be and will go on being the hermeneutical principle of christology."[20] Whatever may have been the limitations of the soteriology of the period, it has bequeathed us this formal element: christology was worked out in terms of soteriology. (This, which is generally accepted with some enthusiasm, is criticized by Pannenberg: one cannot make christology depend on soteriology, since modernity requires that the truth of things be based on what they are and not on something foreign to them, whether authority or concern for salvation.)

(a) Concern for Salvation as a Formal Dimension of Christology

The Patristic Age shares a basic tenet of both Old and New Testaments, and furthermore, through having to answer its adversaries, deepens it. Against Marcionism and Gnosticism it affirms that there is no difference between the creator God and the saving God, that creation is good and the result of love, not the imperfect action of a demiurge. Creation, furthermore, has been brought about through the Word, and this same Word is the mediator of salvation. Jesus Christ is, then, mediator of creation and mediator of salvation. Salvation will, therefore, consist in the remodeling of fallen creation. (If this is taken seriously, it means that not even in salvation are there "additions" to the reality created by God [in its concrete actuality and not as hypothetical *natura pura*]. What saves or condemns is reality, and so salvation is love [received and given] with no additions and damnation is egoism [produced and undergone] with no additions. "*God* has silently lived *our* very life," says José Ignacio González Faus in a fine expression of "without additions.")[21] The keystone in this remodeling is Jesus Christ "sent into the world to 'redo the work' that he had carried out at the start. The Son saves all that needs to be saved. . . . He saves all that he takes on of human nature and nothing more than he takes on. . . . In the Son made man salvation is already brought about just as it should be brought about at the end of time and in eternity, through the union of human beings with God."[22] Here we have the budding direction to be taken by the development of christology, and we need to appreciate above all the centrality of this fact: patristic christology expresses the conviction that there is salvation and that this is fundamentally *sharing* in the life of God, *theopoiesis*, divinization, with the christological variant of *anakephalaiosis*, recapitulation.

I am going to illustrate this soteriological *pathos,* concentrating on certain texts of Irenaeus. He conceives the content of salvation as communion with God: "The glory of God is a living person, and human life is the vision of God" (*Adv. haer.* 4, 20, 7). (This was classically paraphrased by Archbishop Romero as "The glory of God is the poor person who lives," which is certainly a notable example of rereading the Patristic Age from the viewpoint of victims.)[23] The grace of the Spirit that God gives to us "will make us like him and fulfill the Father's will, by making us in his image and likeness" (5, 8, 1).

This also makes clear that the one who saves is God, that the mediator of salvation is Jesus Christ, and that this mediation is effected basically through the incarnation (which in some way, "as in outline," also includes the passion and the resurrection). Christology is thus seen to be at the service of salvation, and the latter will set conditions (still without Anselm's distinctions) on the former: "The Word of God, of his boundless love, became what we are that he might make us what he himself is" (5, 1, 1). (The means of salvation described is not entirely extrinsic to us; in history we pass through a process of salvation, which consists of the realization of our own dynamism, implanted by God, a dynamism that is sometimes beautifully described as the Spirit becoming "accustomed to dwell among the human race and to 'rest on' men and to dwell in God's creatures" [3, 17, 1].)[24] The incarnation comes about in order that "he himself might unite through himself us to God" (3, 4, 2). This "becoming flesh" certainly has a biblical basis, but the absoluteness of Ireneaus's conviction stems from the incarnation being necessary for salvation, "*salus autem quoniam caro*" (3, 10, 3), which predicts what was to become the classic double principle of soteriological christology: "If God does not give us salvation, we do not possess it with certainty. . . . If it is not we who are united with God we do not partake of immortality" (3, 18, 1). "We should not be able to have a part in incorruptibility and immortality except on condition of being united to incorruptibility and immortality. But how could we be united to incorruptibility and immortality, had not incorruptibility and immortality previously become what we are, in order that what was corruptible should be absorbed by incorruptibility and what was mortal by immortality?" (3, 19, 1).

This understanding of the beginnings was later split into two classic statements. In the Arian controversy Athanasius defended the divinity of Christ *a priori*—this being the main point—in order to assure salvation: "For us men it would be as useless for the Word not to have been the true Son of God by nature, as it would for the flesh he took on not to have been real."[25] And to confess the fullness of human nature that Christ had to express, also *a priori*, there is the well-known statement by Gregory Nazianzen: "What has not been taken up has not been healed. What is united to God, that is what saves."[26]

These texts summarize the salvific logic of the Patristic Age, which Irenaeus also expresses in the concept of "recapitulation." In general terms, Christ "was incarnate and made Man; and then he summed up in himself the long line of the human race, procuring for us a comprehensive salvation, that we might recover in Christ Jesus what in Adam we had lost, namely, the state of being in the image and likeness of God" (3, 17, 1).[27] And arguing in greater detail, he claims that Christ "passed through all the ages of life" (3, 18, 1). This is about not divinization but recapitulation, though the logic is the same: the reality of Christ has to be of a particular nature in order to be saving. This is not Anselmianism but (speculative) reflection on scriptural texts, guided by concern for salvation. (In the context of recapitulation, Irenaeus asks whether redemption had to come about through the spilling of blood—and in lands of persecution and martyrdom it is more than mere curiosity to know why—saying: "If the blood of the just had not been spilt, in no way would the Lord have had to shed blood. That blood has had a voice from the beginning, God told Cain after he had murdered his brother. [All this] showed the recapitulation of the blood of all the just and prophets spilt since the beginning, which would have to come about in his person" [5, 14, 1, 7ff.]. Here, clearly and very early, is a departure from and overcoming of the sacrificialism that has been traditional in the soteriology of the church.)

(b) The Limits of This Soteriology

Patristic christology has a grandiose vision of Christ, and yet it makes no impact in Latin America (or in other parts of the world), even if one concentrates on its essential soteriological dimension. Why not? The reason, I believe, lies in the fact that, besides being distant and difficult to understand, this christology is incapable of providing an answer to today's questions, since the notion of salvation that guides it is foreign to the line begun (or begun anew) in *Gaudium et Spes* and culminating in Medellín. It would be anachronistic to seek a present-day understanding of salvation in that period, but it would also be sheer voluntarism to claim that it provides a universal soteriology inspiring for all ages.

I should like to stress that the difficulty does not lie, basically, in the obvious cultural distance hermeneutics has to bridge, since we are also at a distance from the world of the Old Testament prophets and from that of the synoptics, and yet we can find sufficient coincidence with both *in our actual situation*. In this context it is important to recall that the Patristic Age has proved fruitful for ecclesiology, so that the ecclesiological revolution brought about by Vatican II derives very largely from it. But the reason for this is not the validity of patristic thinking on the subject *in itself*; it is that there is a coincidence of *real* and not only of *conceptual* problems: in this case, the desire of the church to be the organ of salvation, the sacrament of Christ, the people of God, the community that makes unequals equal. This coincidence—in which, furthermore, the Patristic Age still holds critical lessons for the present—is what has not come about in christology.

There are other difficulties besides this basic one. In the first place, salvation was to be increasingly linked to the spilling of Christ's blood in the passion, so that Christ was still confessed to be fully human, despite the theoretical problems this involves. The underlying purpose was to make possible his suffering, which is what can save. In other words, the sacrificial notion—not that of Irenaeus—of the mediator of salvation was upheld. In the second place—and this brings us closer to the heart of the Patristic Age—there remains the serious problem of how human beings can *share* in the nature of the mediator beyond some vague expression like "sacramental sharing in the perfect and complete Man." Moingt says it all in a passage that deserves quoting in full:

> In Irenaeus, the theology of the incarnation finds its place within a fine theology of history, whose horizon opens on to the coming of the Kingdom of God, as in the time of the apostles. The same was to happen with Tertullian. But the view of salvation was not to remain fixed for long on this eschatological horizon of an end of history converted into the Kingdom of God. It then began to shift from earth to heaven, to detach itself from history, to concentrate on the transformation of human nature, become incorruptible and divinized, and to show itself satisfied from here below with divinity procured by grace and the sacraments in conformity with the aspirations of Greek piety and with the promises of its "mysteries." This view of salvation was to reinforce the tendency of theology of the incarnation to detach itself from history and re-form at the timeless instant of union of the Word with humankind.[28]

Seen from the view of the victims, the conclusion is that we need to reshape the patristic concept of salvation on three major points.

The first is to make *divinization* and *humanization* complement each other or converge, making the latter historical in line with historical utopias (in parallel with the positiveness of divinity) and presenting it, dialectically, in opposition to the all-pervading de-humanization (in parallel with the victimization produced by the idols, on which patristic christology, naturally, had nothing to say). It is not that divinization is not of decisive importance—Ignacio Ellacuría was given to citing Augustine's "To be human one has to be more than human"—but that on its own it is not enough, since—again as Ellacuría used to say—there is no salvation history without salvation in history.[29]

The second is to introduce into the concept of salvation in the singular Jesus' concept of plural salvation, of body and soul, of person and society, transcendent and historical—the words are the not very expressive ones of the magisterium, but they mean integral liberation in the sense used at Medellín and Puebla. This means, ultimately, recovering the Kingdom of God, with which I shall deal in the next section.

The third is to posit the personal appropriation of salvation in a form different from that used by the Fathers, so that sharing in the divinity of and becoming conformed to Christ become truly historical, as they have to be in following Jesus, and not merely intentional or sacramental.

The soteriology of the church Fathers is a good expression of the radical translation of Greek thought into the singular, making salvation transcendental and absolute. Following this absolutizing *pathos*, salvation could well be formulated today as "meaning" in progressive theology, as "liberation" in liberation theology. But there still remains the task of historicizing this absolutizing salvation, making it accord with the evils we suffer and with the longings God implants in human hearts. In this, the Patristic Age offers no help.

4. Christological Neglect of the Kingdom of God

In this period the process already begun in various ways in the New Testament period was to reach its culmination: the Kingdom of God makes no appearance in christological formulations. This is a definite fact, and on it and its implications I offer the following thoughts.

With regard to a *theo*-logy, which now means a specifically Christian one, the Kingdom should be essential for understanding the nature of God. As Juan Luis Segundo writes: "Jesus, fully human at the same time as perfect God, thereby makes us understand what this concept of divinity actually in fact entails. And the answer is that God has to be understood following the key provided by Jesus' life, which is none other than the historical project of the *Kingdom of God*, with the specific contents he gave it."[30] But the Patristic Age did not follow this logic. Its deepening christology provides the *formal* element of Segundo's statement (Jesus expresses the divine nature), but it is incapable of adopting the *material* element that comes down from the synoptics (Jesus stands in an essential relationship to the Kingdom). So, even though it was absolutely central for Jesus (also a divine being), the transcendental relationship between God and Kingdom was lost, with the latter saying (virtually) nothing about God. God's mediation (the Kingdom) was to disappear from the theologal scene (although some of its elements would not necessarily vanish from the ethical/moral scene), leaving only the mediator (the Son). (It would seem as though—in the end—God was interested only in "the Son," who—if I may be allowed the expression—"turned out well," but not interested, or not "so much," in the creation. In this scenario everything would be perfect in the world of the liturgy, in, with, and through the Son, but the same perfection was not to be expected of the real world, as though this were not *God's* world.) Both the grandeur and the perils of the concentration-reduction can be found in Origen's phrase: Christ is the *autobasileia tou Theou*, the Kingdom of God in person. (Another aspect that contributed to the theologal devaluation of the Kingdom was relating God to *creation*, something obvious in Hellenic thought, and not to the *exodus*, something obvious in biblical thought on account of its historical character, God showing partiality to the victims.)

Where *ecclesio*-logy is concerned, this neglect of the Kingdom also had serious consequences. The reality of the Kingdom, including its finality, was transferred to the church, a transference that had something inevitable about it and could even have a certain legitimacy as long as the church worked for and became a sign of the Kingdom, but something that was also very dangerous. As we shall see in the following excursus, the church came to regard itself as the ultimate, not merely without duly stressing its differentiation from the Kingdom of God, but taking its place with a hubris inconceivable as coming from Jesus of Nazareth, conceiving itself *in principle* (whatever might have been its actual activities, holy or sinful) on the basis of power. It could even come to be anti-Kingdom and to lack a reality—the Kingdom—that could judge it.

Where *soterio*-logy is concerned, the conclusion is obvious and I have already examined it: the plural needs from which humankind has to be saved are not considered, nor are the various areas of actual existence in which it has to be saved. But this also has consequences for *christo*-logy. I have already said that in the Patristic Age, as in the New Testament period, christology depends on soteriology, which is true, but it is a more universal truth than is generally recognized. Damnation and salvation are culturally and historically conditioned concepts, so that the history of the different christologies (biblical, Hellenic, Antiochean, Latin, medieval, Reformation, and modern European, Latin American, African, and Asian), which cannot be reduced to uniformity of content, do share a common concern for salvation: "In a particular culture and in a specific age, all (christological) confession brings the most basic questions of meaning and hope into relationship with the life, teaching, death, and person of Jesus, the wandering Jewish preacher."[31]

If we apply this assertion to the start of christologies, in the Jewish world, misfortune and damnation, even if with varying shades, were seen in terms of corruption of history and of personal fault; this is why salvation had to be thought of as redemption of the sinner and also essentially redemption of history on God's part, that is, as the Kingdom of God. In Hellenism the view of the world was completely different, cosmocentric, and salvation was understood as "elimination of uncertainty through knowledge *(gnosis)*, of mortality through immortality, and of imprisonment in matter through intellectual liberation. In short, salvation meant overcoming finitude, removing the barriers of existence through 'deification.'"[32]

The consequences for christology are clear. If salvation is conceived in biblical terms as the Kingdom of God, then Jesus will be regarded as following in the line of the prophets, as messiah. If salvation is viewed Hellenistically, in terms of liberation from finitude, then Jesus will be seen in terms of mediator between the finite and the infinite, which produces a basic need for (and gives an internal logic to) the christology of the two natures.

Viewing this change (from biblical to Hellenist) from the viewpoint of the victims of today, there is more need of a soteriology—as ground, though not as culmination—on biblical-Jewish lines, which could and should be completed by that of the Patristic Age, than of the other way around. As Aloysius Pieris says—and here I finish where I began—a Jesus who puts God and poor together against the idols and oppressors is today a "more universal" Christ. The "anti-Kingdom" goes on expressing the basic sin of the world, and the "Kingdom of God" goes on expressing a more universal hope. Neglecting it is a serious matter. And this serious danger, without anachronisms, should be taken into account when reading patristic texts.

Excursus

Christianity in the Greco-Roman World

In this excursus I want to look at two basic events that took place in Christianity as it spread through the Greco-Roman world, which constitute a change from the New Testament. One is the shift in the "theoretical manner of thinking," which had a direct influence on christological reflection, and the other is the change in the "religious self-understanding of Christianity as a whole," which had an indirect influence. At the end of this excursus I shall look briefly at these changes from the viewpoint of the inculturation of the Christian faith and also of its counter-cultural potential.

1. The Shift in the "Theoretical Manner of Thinking"

In the Patristic Age Christianity immersed itself into a culture that was both highly developed and foreign to the biblical tradition. In this culture it not only proclaimed Christ but justified this proclamation, was open to dialogue with the Greco-Roman world, partly defined it, and was partly defined by it. This process could have not come about, but it did, and it developed in matters essential, not peripheral, to the faith: God, Jesus Christ, the Spirit, salvation. All this was done with an astonishing pathos of daring, creativity, and willingness to venture into the unknown, which in itself was already an expression of faith *in actu*. But it also had its price and its dangers.

(a) A Thought-provoking Paradox

At the first stage of post–New Testament christology (although the process began earlier) the biblical conceptualization of Christ began to coexist alongside the Greek, and from the time of the Apologists of the second century the bridge between the two was provided by the concept of the *logos*, which brought two differing theoretical languages together. As J. Moingt says, "The title of *logos* given to Christ was the outcome of this mutual recognition of Christian thought and Jewish thought."[1] (Moingt also claims that the Christian Apologists of the second century used the term spontaneously in the sense given it by the philosophical

239

thought of the period: "The term *logos* has the same meanings and functions in the discourse of the theologians as in that of the Stoic philosophers.")[2] The most decisive event for the development of christology, however, was the meeting between Christianity and the Greek concept of divinity, to the point where, without this meeting, faith in Jesus would probably have been formulated in different terms, such as that of "eschatological prophet," for example. The fact is that the gospel accounts and the preaching of the apostles, as a whole, did not "aim to make the divinity of Christ recognized in the way in which Christian discourse tried to do in the first half of the second century."[3] This does not mean that the impulse to confess the ultimateness (divinity) of Christ is not present in the New Testament, but the way in which it was conceptualized would not have been historically possible except in the Greek cultural environment.

The point at issue here, however, is that proclaiming Christ's divinity—which up to Nicaea was understood fairly fluidly—led to a fruitful paradox, both because paradoxes are always thought-provoking and require concepts to be fully examined, and because, as they are never fully resolved, they help to keep the "mystery" of things, which is essential in analyzing the nature of Jesus Christ. The essence of the paradox here is that, while the Greek concept of divinity allowed for it to be handed on, which helped with claiming divinity for Christ, this still had to be explained to both Greeks and Jews, who—logically—were disconcerted, though for different reasons. The Jews were scandalized at this denial of the absolute singularity of God, and Trypho, as Justin relates, asked: "Answer me first on this point: How are you going to prove that another God exists besides the creator of the universe?"[4] The Greeks, as Celsus challenged the Christians around the year 178, argued as follows: "Either God really changes in himself, as they say, into a mortal body . . . or he has not changed but makes those who see him believe he has really changed. But in this case he is deceitful and a liar."[5]

This would mean that the paradox entailed by the new faith can be formulated like this: If one holds to the immutability of God (in accordance with the *apatheia* of the gods), this necessarily produces a Docetist understanding of Christ. If one holds to the true humanity of Christ, this leads to one of two things: either denying his divinity, which is intolerable for Christian faith, or affirming the mutability of God, which is intolerable for the Greek mentality. The conclusion is that one has to choose between the true humanity of Christ without God and Christ with God but without flesh.

Christianity did not choose either, and thus showed, in my view, what formed its major greatness at the time, that is, a "no contest" approach that it has kept to often throughout history—not choosing between grace and freedom, or between faith and good works, to take the most current example, though it has often emphasized the superiority of one over the other and even pitted one against the other. From a theoretical standpoint this avoidance of a contest that would have mutilated the reality, as they saw it, forced Christians to deepen their thinking in unexpected and creative ways, but it also forced them to adopt a philosophical (or quasi-philosophical) approach to the nature of Christ, his humanity and divinity, and the relationship between the two, which brought a whole new dimension to their thinking about Christ.

So the positive outcomes of this process were: (1) upholding *in actu* the mystery of Jesus Christ by the mere fact of upholding the paradox, and (2) having to give a reasoned account of what they confessed, and so being forced to examine the concept more deeply. I shall look at these more closely in the following chapters, but this new theoretical way of thinking also had ambiguous and dangerous results, which I shall examine now.

(b) The Priority Given to Speculation

Upholding the paradox pushed thinking into a more speculative course, to the detriment of more historical and narrative forms. This speculative disposition became evident in the analysis of the nature of Christ, and so—though done in order to be able to proclaim him God and savior without contradictions—the answer to the question *who* Christ is was replaced by another: *what* Christ is—if and how he has a body, if he has a soul or if its place is taken by the *logos*, if he has one will or two, if he is in all ways like us. . . . And then it had to be asked how these elements could be squared with the fact that his nature is also divine. In the ironic but well chosen words of Paul van Buren, "The problem can already be seen in the works of Justin Martyr, in which the author insists on the fact that Jesus was a man, with a body, mind, and spirit, and yet without any historical relationship to the rest of humankind. . . . He was someone like us, but he was not one of us."[6]

The result of this new way of proceeding was that christology became speculative in a very precise sense; this brought a high price to pay: the process of conceptualization advanced on the back of the formal dynamism of thought, without allowing itself to be guided mainly by what I have called the reality principle. Christological thinking had not yet reached the point of elevating the reality of Jesus Christ to a theological concept,[7] but the need to produce theological reasoning and to argue in a specific direction was to derive fundamentally from the demands of a way of thinking that was increasingly hypostasized in itself. The statements about Christ would not show that Christ *is such* because this is how "we have seen and touched him," but because this is how he has to be thought of and *so how he has to be* in reality. In this sense, the most important thing that happened in the Greek world was not just that conciliar christological statements were made, which centuries later would be called dogmatic, but that a *doctrine* about the ontological constitution of Christ began to arise, and with this the very idea of what would later be understood as dogma became possible: a teaching put forward with authority to be believed. (Our current notion of dogma was established in the nineteenth-century church; this is why I speak of the "possibility" of the appearance of dogma. In the early Fathers of the church the term *dogma* means rather the commandments and moral recommendations of Christ, as in the *Didache*, the first letter of Clement, and Ignatius of Antioch, and although the Apologists gave it a more intellectual tone, it still did not have its present meaning: at that period dogmas were the basic doctrines of the faith of Christ's apostles. Furthermore, dogma was not distinguished from faith in action but was rather the expression of that faith. "Liturgy was dogma in prayer, while theology was doxology.")[8]

(c) The Use of the Category of "Nature"

The basic concept Greek philosophy employed to explain reality was that of *na-ture*. (The term *physis*, "nature," was used in the councils together with other close or related concepts. Although its meaning is not quite the same from one council to another, the following explanation by González Faus sheds light on the relationship between nature and other explanatory concepts: "*Ousía* is simply the [abstract] essence of a thing. *Physis* describes this essence insofar as it is the principle of action and, therefore, with a certain connotation of its actual being. *Hypostasis* clearly indicates this essence insofar as it is *an* actual reality and, therefore, insofar as it subsists in a subject. *Prosopon*, more vaguely, looks at the essence insofar as it appears as a reality.")[9] By comparison with biblical and modern understandings, this concept had severe limitations, which were to mortgage christology for centuries. Let us look at two of them.

The first is the removal of Christ from history. *Nature*, in effect, led one to know what a thing is, its components, characteristics, and limitations. But when that *thing* is a person with freedom, unless we know how this freedom was exercised, we do not know much about that *thing*. Without history we do not know much about people, and this is a basic problem for christology. It might be said that the nature of Christ—double, what is more, divine and human—is his principle of action, but without the story of what these actions were we know practically nothing about Christ, either in his human nature or in his being as savior. (Speaking of divine *nature* is nonsense on two levels. On the first, the *divine* reality is unrepeatable and so its nature cannot be abstracted as is done with other, repeatable realities. In the biblical tradition *God* is a proper noun, not a common noun. So, on the second level, applying the same formal concept of *nature* to a divine reality and to a human one can only lead to misunderstandings. Rahner's attempt, for example, to understand Christ's humanity as signifier [sacrament] and his divinity as reality signified, is something different; it breaks the symmetry implied in *two natures*.)

The concept of nature introduces what is permanent, fixed, immutable, universal into thought while ignoring or undervaluing what is historical, changing, contingent, practical, partial. And it is just this second category that is the *essential*, the non-negotiable one, I should say, in the biblical and specifically the gospel understanding of God's revelation and of salvation. When the "nature" category is used on its own, Christ's story and freedom, specificity and partiality are lost. And they are just what have to be kept. As Ellacuría wrote:

> It is in personal stories and in the history of peoples that God has been truly present. . . . That history far more than nature is the proper place for God's revelation and communication is a statement of incalculable importance for theology and for Christian praxis: it is in history far more than in nature that we are going to make the living God present.[10]

In other words, a universalism based on the eternal nature of things will not allow us to make the actuality of Jesus' life and death central—nor the reasons for his death. It loses his constituent relationship with the Kingdom of God and God's partiality for the poor. The option for the poor, as an essential reality identifying both God and Jesus, is alien to Greek thought, not only because it is "for the poor" but also because it is an "option." What is actual and underivable disappears from reflection. (In graphic terms, referring to the start of this process, already visible in the New Testament, Juan Luis Segundo states: "This same love that emerges victorious in the Fourth Gospel has to pay it its tribute. It becomes divine to the extent that it disembodies Jesus from a conflictive history in which he is specifically on the side of the poor. . . . The conflict the Fourth Gospel recognizes is that between Jesus and what we might call the "mechanism" of the world. And this is no longer dealing with the real world that makes people poor and marginalizes them.")[11]

Another serious limitation, related to the previous one, is the diminished revelatory capacity attached to the nature concept. Making use of this concept means trying to understand Christ and his novel aspect on the basis of something that, in principle, is already known or at least knowable. That is, it logically presupposes that we already know, from before Jesus, what divinity is and what humanity is, so that we can say that in Christ both realities are to be found. (In this context, the renewal of the theology of revelation is significant, in its variants as far apart as those of Barth and Bultmann, Rahner, or Pannenberg, as is the emphasis they place on the fact that revelation is *given* to us, not [just] *confirmed*. Analyzing Pannenberg's theology, J. Mártinez Gordo stresses that "God can be known only through God himself, through his mediation in the historical actuation of Jesus.")[12] From this point of view, dogma was to add only *one new* element—the *way* in which both natures were *combined* in the one person of Christ, even though *this* specific element was to be very important, as we shall see, and on this point dogma did in fact express revelation.

(d) The Relationship between Dogmatic Formulations and the New Testament

There is no denying that the Patristic Age introduced a new discourse in relation to the New Testament: "By now a discourse of orthodoxy and of authority has been created, since neither scripture nor tradition are any longer sufficient for expressing the faith."[13] What does this novelty mean in relation to the christologies of the New Testament?

To answer this question, we need, on the one hand, to recall that, in the understanding of the church the christologies of the New Testament are normative and in a certain sense insuperable, while the conciliar christologies do not possess this same degree of definiteness. (So, for example, in 1984 Pope John Paul II and the Monophysite patriarch of Antioch signed a document of union between their churches, without the pope imposing the formulations of the Council of Chalcedon. It recognizes that the differences in terminology and interpretation between the concepts used to define the reality of Jesus are not substantial. "In words and life we confess the true teaching on Christ Our Lord, despite the differences in interpretation of this teaching that arose at the time of the Council of Chalcedon.")[14] On the other hand, however, we need to examine the possibility of moving forward in christological formulation and conceptualization, and we need to ask ourselves what such progress means. So, in dealing with a *theological proof*, "Theological problems cannot [in the Patristic Age] be resolved exclusively by means of arguments based on scripture but have to be translated to the plane of philosophical concepts,"[15] which is what the Patristic Age did, in this marking an advance on the New Testament. But, in dealing with the *deep understanding of the faith*, the answer is not so simple.

Starting from faith itself, we have to say that, on the one hand, we can know *no more* than is contained in revelation, since this is the ultimate source of all knowledge. But can we know *the same things in a better way*? Our answer has to be guarded. In a culture such as the Greek, we may gain in conceptual clarity by speaking of Christ in terms of *nature,* but we may lose in historical actuality by comparison with the New Testament. If we want to understand the meaning of the salvation God grants us, is it better to start from the theory of divinization or from the father's embrace in Jesus' parable of the prodigal son? On the existential level, the answer seems clear to me, but it is also important to find some sort of theoretical answer, which, in my opinion, can point in two complementary directions.

One is the distinction Karl Rahner makes between logical and ontic explanation: "Logical explanation—in general terms—explains by distinguishing, but in order to explain one set of things it does not express another."[16] That is, it does not delve into the content of knowledge. Ontic explanation, on the other hand, explains by starting from another set of things, by giving the cause, for example.[17] In these terms, conciliar dogmatic christologies would be logical explanations, which cannot add to the content of New Testament statements.

The other, already touched on, consists in considering dogmatic statements as doxological, as coming at the (provisional) end of a process of understanding that begins with the New Testament. (*End* here does not have the sense Rahner rejects, as though Chalcedon put an "end" to reflection and christology could not progress beyond its dogmatic formulations. Rahner sees these as a departure point, not an arrival point.[18] My view is that *end* means that the statement is no longer amenable to reason, so the only course is "surrender" to mystery.) At this end, understanding surrenders because it no longer controls its content; this is particularly true of the basic statement of Chalcedon. But this surrender has to remain related to the process of understanding that began with the New Testament, which continues and always has to return to what was at the beginning, the Christ of the New Testament and, first and foremost, Jesus of Nazareth.

In any case, both considerations lead to the same conclusion: patristic and conciliar christologies cannot be understood without going back to the New Testament, and the latter is the essential route to understanding the former. It is still also true, however, that explanations—even if they are only logical ones, in Rahner's terms—are necessary if we are to be able in some way to formulate and understand the reality of Christ at a particular period.

The conclusion is the need for a reading that operates in two directions: from the Patristic Age to the New Testament, and from the New Testament to the Patristic Age. We shall have to speak of hypostatic union, but we also have to go back to biblical language: "The goodness of God has appeared." Only by keeping both languages can we—especially at this distance in time—make sense of conciliar christology. This double reading will also help us today to learn how to think of and express Christ in relation to our own time and to the past, which for us includes the New Testament statements and the conciliar definitions. Then we can well call Christ "the omega point of evolution," "the man for others," and "the liberator."

(e) Concept and Narrative

Besides the formal reason for going back to the New Testament (that it contains God's foremost revelation, as we have just seen), there are other major ones, among them the neglect of story in patristic christology. In this, "theology had made innumerable speculative advances, but it had distanced itself from the 'stories' of salvation."[19] And these are precisely what the New Testament provides, particularly in the synoptics. The burden of the need for narrative to precede concept and even of its priority in initial confrontation with reality has been well expressed by Leonardo Boff: "Abstract analysis of who God is and who man is will not lead us to understand who Jesus God-Man is. It was through living with Jesus, seeing him, imitating him, and deciphering him that his disciples came to know both the God and the man."[20]

If this was true for those who shared their lives with Jesus, today we need to find some sort of equivalent reality that will help us approximate to this experience and enable us to conceptualize it. This is what story achieves and what makes it necessary for theology to be (also) narrative, as J.-B. Metz has claimed. Concept and narrative are not opposed to each other, but they are not the same, and both—not only concept, as was supposed for centuries—are needed in theology. On this continent Gustavo Gutiérrez has recently reminded us of the same thing: "It is not that logical argument and systematic thought have no place in theology; what matters is that they should always refresh themselves with a faith that does not reveal its whole meaning except in lively and life-giving story."[21]

Furthermore, when discourse turns on something belonging in the past, story is clearly irreplaceable and becomes *memory*: "Remember, O Israel"; "Do this in memory of me." This memory is the most appropriate way of understanding the past, since story brings in the listener, telling of an experience and by its own nature and dynamic trying to convert this into the listener's own. Story invites, stirs, encourages, but does not force.[22]

Finally, as Metz also stresses, the Christian story is *dangerous* memory, recalling the life and death of one who was crucified. If what is "dangerous" about this memory is "told," then it is not just something to be understood conceptually (the why and wherefore of the cross) but an invitation and a challenge to adopt a particular attitude to it. In this perhaps lies the reason why the story of the cross is told in liturgy and in spirituality but not in theology, not even in that of the councils, in which the *truth* on which all else was to be based was supposedly established.

In the passage by Aloysius Pieris quoted earlier, he expresses the same suspicion, beginning the sentence in which he tackles the theoretical subject of the universality of Christ with an eloquent "but": "*But* returning to these basic elements is equivalent to burdening ourselves once more with the cross, the cross we have abandoned for centuries."[23] This shows the correlation between neglect of the story and abandonment of the cross.

To return to the Patristic Age: in its christological formulations concept is not added to story but comes to replace it. This is what has produced the need *at the present time* to reread patristic theology taking account of what there is of story and dangerous memory in the New Testament. Otherwise, it would be very difficult to avoid the sensation *today* that doing christology is (merely) philosophizing about the makeup of a unique and unrepeatable being, named Jesus Christ, but one lacking in personal, historical, ongoing, encouraging, and challenging attributes. This can be avoided only through story. This can also be seen from the view of the victims, and from there I will finish this section with a few short observations.

The first and most basic one is that story is *especially* necessary and irreplaceable in a situation where victims suffer acutely and hope against hope: "There are sufferings in the face of which theological discussion must fall silent. Only narrative is possible. Narrative alone *rescues* for future history the sense of freedom surrendered bound up in these stories of suffering, apparently conquered, suppressed or revoked by death."[24] So it is not by chance that Latin American countries have produced, at the same time, theoretical christologies and witness accounts, while elsewhere story is accepted as a possibility and even as a necessity for theology *in theory*, but in the event stories fail to find a place in christology (certainly not current stories, and sometimes not even those from the gospels), in which basically concepts (alone) are proffered.[25] But a theology that does not include story in some way, except for tolerating it in pastoral theology or spirituality, is defending itself most effectively from the reality that surfaces, challenges, and inspires in story. And this is what I see happening—though not deliberately—in the christology of the Patristic Age.

The second is that the memory expressed in the Christian story is the *memoria passionis* but also *celebratory and hopeful* memory: it has to recall a meal, the last one Jesus celebrated, and a hope, that there is a future for victims. This is what—surprisingly for Western theologies—the witness accounts from the world of the poor and victims show—and perhaps these theologies cannot hear them because of where they come from. But if theology fails to listen to them, it deprives itself of an experience of grace, of the fact that it has been offered something good in these stories.

The third is that the story is told and spread also so that it can be translated into action, as an invitation and a challenge. This is certainly what the gospels do, not just passing on information in story form but recounting a life, an attitude, a work to be reproduced, carried forward.

The fourth is that story should not be understood as just a fragment but as having a universal potential. The idea of "concrete universal" is valid for story too. It needs to be interrogated for a concrete structure, and so one that cannot be deduced but can, as structure, somehow be made capable of being universal.

My final observation—and the one most pertinent here—is that stories from the past shed light on those of the present but are also, in turn, illuminated by these. The first and foremost story, in effect, is always real life. The narrative of Jesus' life sheds light on our lives, but it is also true that ours shed light on his. The base communities express this simply by seeing present-day lives that resemble Jesus' and telling their story. As Gutiérrez rightly says: "Calling to mind, for example, the life and death of a man of our time such as Archbishop Romero is telling, faithfully and creatively, the life and death of Jesus in the Latin American present."[26]

This is the change that is taking place at the present time in the way theoretical christology is being done. But at another time there was another change, affecting theory but mainly works, that had a great influence on the way faith was lived and, indirectly, on christology: the Christian faith became the new religion of the Roman Empire.

2.   The Change to "Seeing Itself as a Religion"

Another major change took place in contact with the Greco-Roman world—the process through which Christianity turned itself into the official religion of the empire. On the surface this change took place independently of explicit christology, but I consider that it was made possible by the disappearance and distortion of the very concept of the Kingdom of God. In this sense it was related to a particular vision of Christ. This does not mean that concern for salvation, or for ethical and social aspects, disappeared.[27] Far from it: there are splendid texts connecting christological orthodoxy with the poor that are truly concerned with the Kingdom. Ignatius of Antioch wrote to the Smyrneans: "Note how all these heterodoxies on the subject of the coming of the grace of Jesus Christ to us are contrary to the spirit of God himself: they have no concern for love, none for the widow, the orphan, the afflicted, the prisoner, the hungry, the thirsty."[28] Here orthodoxy is linked to compassion and justice for the poor. But in general the Kingdom of God ceases to be decisive and is no longer present in the overall way Christianity sees itself. The worst aspect is that, in both theory and practice, the Kingdom was replaced by the church, acting as the final authority on earth and making use of a power strictly contrary to that of the Kingdom—without, that I can see, christology exercising any restraint on it.

To show the development of this process, I am not going to examine texts but more generally—and I believe more effectively—look at the way in which Christianity gradually became the political religion of the empire. Putting the conclusion first, what was to happen was that the church, instead of seeing itself as distinct from the Kingdom, with the mission of being its servant and sacrament, and instead of judging the empire from the standpoint of the Kingdom of God, began to see itself as the equivalent of the Kingdom and came to concern itself principally with its (advantageous) relationship with the empire. It tried and managed to make itself into a political religion in the Greco-Roman world.[29]

(a) Christianity and State at the Outset of the Church

Mutual collaboration between religion and state appears in the oldest religions—including that of Israel—and the relationship between the two is based on a double reality. On the one hand, power, expressed in the state, exerts a fascination and, among ancient peoples, also possesses a sacral and numinous character. This is why one of the classic ways of understanding divinity has always been through manifestations of state power. On the other hand, the state needs an ideological element that will integrate society, and in antiquity this was explicitly its religion. This is what lies behind political theology (as opposed to the natural and mythic theology of the Greco-Roman world) developed by the Stoics, which influenced the first generations of Christians. As Moltmann has written:

> According to ancient political teaching, state and gods always go together: there cannot be an atheist state any more than there can be a stateless god. *Polis* and *civitas*, *nomos* and *dike* are essentially religious concepts. In accordance with ancient social teaching, the primary obligation of the state was to accept the country's gods and to venerate them properly. Thus the well-being and peace of the country was assured, and its citizens came together thanks to the bond of a common religion.[30]

When Christianity began to spread through the empire, it came up against political religions that served to integrate and consolidate a people, to make myths about its origins, and to glorify its history. This gave rise to the searching question of what Christians—who were deliberately moving into all areas of the empire—could specifically offer to fulfill these roles, which would inevitably devolve on them with the passage of time. Above all, they had the example of Jesus' approach and attitude to political power. Jesus found nothing numinous in this, but rather looked for such a quality in what was little and weak: state power was no sort of divine manifestation for him. Yet this example set by him did not always guide the actions of the church, which at times acted in a totally contrary manner.

In the early stages of Christian expansion there was no serious conflict with the state, and it would be anachronistic to have expected any. Even in the passion narratives in the gospels and in Acts, Caesar's representatives are treated with a certain respect. Submission to authority is enjoined (Rom 13:1; 1 Pt 2:13), as is payment of taxes (Rom 13:6) and praying for kings and for all those constituted as authorities (1 Tm 2:1f.). What is being described here, apparently, is a peaceful coexistence between the new faith and the state. The state does not appear to be a problem for faith—not that it is judged positively from the standpoint of the Kingdom of God, but simply that it has not yet posed a problem.

Toward the end of the first century the situation changed. The state, far from posing an attractive temptation, was harshly rebuked, though, once again, not directly for being anti-Kingdom, but on account of the persecution Christians were undergoing under Domitian. This is what the book of the Apocalypse recounts.[31] The Roman state is described as a "beast" (chap. 13), probably personified in the emperor Domitian (v. 18), and faith in Jesus is opposed to this power (14:12). Understandably, "for the church of the martyr . . . the state was predominantly a manifestation of 'this world' in the pejorative sense,"[32] but it is important to recognize that, however understandably this came about, it was also an enemy on account of the animosity it was showing to the budding church.

Whatever illusions the first Christians may have had about presenting themselves to the empire as the true religion, this temptation was overcome by the force of the actual situation, in which "the expectation that Christianity would penetrate to the ends of the earth had worked out quite the reverse."[33] Instead, persecution was showing the lordship of Christ in its true dimensions. Jesus is "the lamb standing as if it had been slaughtered" (Rv 5:6) and on this account "worthy to receive power and wealth and wisdom and might" (5:12). In the Apocalypse the temptation to become integrated into the state as its political religion is conquered by the very situation of persecution.

(b) Toward a Political Religion of the Empire

In the following generations the situation became ambiguous, and in the end Christians were to succumb little by little to the temptation to turn themselves into a political religion, useful to the Roman Empire. While it was true that during the persecutions many Christians opposed the state with all their might, it was also understandable that they should seek to come to an arrangement with the empire and to make this arrangement as beneficial as possible.

In this context a Christianity understood fundamentally as *faith* in Jesus, in a raised Christ who had been *crucified*, placed Christianity at a disadvantage in comparison with the official religions. According to Stockmeier, this situation "undoubtedly reinforced the tendency to propagate Christianity as a 'religion' and, in the same way as other cults, to stress the positive role it could play for the empire."[34] It is understandable that, in time of persecution, Christians should have sought an alliance with the state, but it is surprising how quickly (according to Stockmeier) they fell into the pattern of a political religion. "The many voices of the overall church show an understanding, with reservations certainly, but in the final analysis tending toward the model of relationship between religion and state."[35]

The basic method of integration into the state was the church putting itself forward as the best religion for the empire. This process culminated, to all intents and purposes, with Constantine, but it had begun earlier. To give some examples: Mellitus of Sardis (d. 172) describes church-state relationships enthusiastically, reminding the emperor Marcus Aurelius that Christian philosophy has brought his empire fortune and blessings, power and greatness, and he promises him prosperity for himself and for his descendants as long as he protects the Christian religion. Origen (d. 254) went so far as to promise military success if all the subjects of the empire became Christians, since Christian prayer—he claims—possesses even more power than that of Moses for overcoming foes: Christianity is therefore the most effective religion politically. The convert Lactantius (d. 320) viewed the Christian religion as the leaven of an ordered society. Eusebius of

Caesarea (d. 339) saw the Edict of Constantinople as the fulfillment of the promises of the Old Testament: the church has brought together all the religious aspirations of humankind. And these wishes were granted: Christianity gained an
ever greater moral function in society, thanks to its stabilizing influence.

(c) The Church in a Position of Power

These voices are not the only ones that have come down from antiquity, but they
do indicate the direction Christianity was moving in at the time. In 311 the emperor Galerian promulgated the edict of toleration, based on the supposition that
Christianity was a political religion, and when Constantine incorporated it—tolerating it alongside others—as the state religion, he was complying with a wish
expressed by several generations. What is called the conversion of Constantine
was not a conversion to the Christian faith but a change of religion. Constantine
was concerned with divinity, understood according to the Gnostic thought-cur-
rents of his time: religion had to serve him to consolidate his empire, and so the
church should take on functions similar to those of the pagan cults. The Edict of
Milan (313) makes clear that, while the validity of other cults was recognized, it
was the task of the Christian cult to assure the health of the empire. Furthermore,
however, Constantine saw his emperorship as a religious mission: the emperor
was seen as "God's lieutenant."[36] The outcome was:

> Constantine carried through the recognition of Christianity and its integra-
> tion into the religious-spiritual structure of the Roman empire obviously in
> line with his own convictions, which, despite his personal experiences, cor-
> responded broadly to the Roman tradition. He granted Christianity equality
> of rights precisely as a religion, even if one with a special character, and he
> gradually subordinated it to the state.[37]

Constantine sought to be bishop over all and claimed to possess the final authority over conciliar decisions. He, a converted layman, not even baptized—and
not bishop of Rome—was the one who convoked the Council of Nicaea (emperors were to convoke the first five ecumenical councils) to resolve the divisions
between Arians and Athanasians, and it was he who put the ecclesiastical resolu-
tions of the council into effect and he who was later to exile Athanasius, even
though the council had decided for him. But the most significant aspect is that "he
prepared the Council of Nicaea in such a way that the bishops who gathered there
from all parts of the empire returned totally cognizant of their new function in the
service of the state, of which they were now officials."[38]

In the year 380, with the Edict of Theodosius, Christianity moved from being
a permitted religion to being the official state religion. In the edict the Christian
religion is spoken of as that which is based on the Father, the Son, and the Holy
Spirit—that is, it is referred back to the content of the Christian faith, but its
functions are still those of any religion. This meant that it was laid down as manda-
tory by the state, and those who did not observe its practices were to be punished
not only with divine wrath but also with "the punishment of our will, which we
have received by divine command."[39] In this way the transformation—structurally

speaking—of Christianity into a political religion was completed, a development for which Christianity itself had long been preparing, with unfortunate consequences. "By an extraordinary but almost fatal reversal of the situation, Christianity, which just before was still a proscribed religion, had begun to become a state religion."[40]

The paradox of this process was that Christians were gradually to come to accept the sacred nature of the emperor, in the name of which they were previously prosecuted. Everything that surrounded the emperor became divine: his palace was a sacred place, and to refuse him veneration was a sacrilege, which, according to Athanasius, could rightly be punished with the death penalty.

The church became the official religion of the Roman Empire not because Constantine declared it as such but because it had been building up its power in various areas until all other (pagan) forms of worship were prohibited. The great irony is that, in Segundo's words, "Christianity became official to the extent that the persecution formerly directed against it was now directed against paganism, wiping it off the map. This was political power 'imposing the truth' by force," and, "when one accepts the use of political power to 'facilitate' acceptance of this truth and suppression of error, there is a high price to pay."[41] Aguirre makes a similar observation: "A church that was marginalized and persecuted very quickly, once it became the guarantor of the ruling ideology, marginalized and persecuted in its turn."[42]

3. Inculturation, Culture, and Counter-Culture

To end this excursus, I propose a reflection on inculturation, a question for the present time, adding a shorter one on the counter-cultural dimension of faith, not usually brought into the discussion.

(a) Inculturation: Hellenization and Politicization

For centuries these two developments, Hellenization and politicization, were accepted without discussion, though this is no longer the case. On the theoretical level inculturation has been discussed in the context of the Hellenization of dogma. Some see this as meaning a loss of the biblical aspect, and therefore as harmful. Others—as we shall see in the following chapters—see the way the Greek mentality was adopted as an actual de-Hellenization (the rejection of and victory over Gnosticism, for example) and a positive trans-Hellenization, progressing beyond Greek thought in metaphysics and anthropology, and so judge it to be beneficial.

From the aspect of inculturation, this "change in the theoretical way of thinking" has to be seen as the most successful case of *desire for inculturation*, even with all its gains and limitations, and the Third World should be able to appeal to it today, in the name of what was done at that time. The paradox is that that inculturation, the "most successful," has been precisely one of the things that has stood in the way of subsequent inculturations and placed obstacles in the way of dialogue with both cultures and religions and with philosophies. The burden of this paradoxical fact has been the ecclesiastical conviction, little discussed until recently, of the superiority of Greek culture over any other and its potential for universal adoption, greater than that of any other. (The fact that this type of christology produced dogma obligatory for all time, a universal and often exclusive christology, contributed to this paradoxical "universal inculturation.") In any case this "universalization of a specific inculturation" is also responsible for a good part of present difficulties with the Patristic Age and of indifference to it. (It also gives rise to the suspicion that the church's present drive for inculturation expresses not only fidelity to the "inculturable" nature of the Christian faith but also the need to make reparation for the injustices committed against other cultures.)

Be that as it may, there is the second phenomenon of the early centuries: the accommodation and, in that sense, inculturation of Christianity into the religio-political structures of the Greco-Roman world to the point where it became the political religion of the state, which—whatever the exact chronology—had directly harmful consequences for the church and indirectly harmful ones for christology. (Both Hellenization and politicization were tendencies that gradually made themselves felt, so it would be wrong to date the beginning of Hellenization in christological thinking to the middle of the second century—since it could already have been present in some ways in the New Testament writings—or the church's relationship with power to Constantine and the year 313. We must not be simplistic, but at the same time there is no escaping the conclusion: philosophy [directly] and political power [indirectly] both made themselves felt in christology.) Just as "Hellenization" of the theoretical mode of thinking marked the way of doing christology for centuries (only much later was modern philosophy accepted for conceptualizing the faith and only recently were biblical and narrative theology added to speculative theology), so the religious politicization of faith marked the way the church saw itself in the Middle Ages, in the coming of Spaniards and Portuguese to America, and in any form of Christendom.

It is very likely that this was practically inevitable from a historical point of view, since it fell to the church to fill the social and cultural gaps left by the collapse of the Roman Empire, but the results were serious. (Moingt also thinks that "by sealing in itself the alliance between Judaism and Hellenism, Christianity provided itself with the means to impress itself quickly on the Roman Empire.")[43] If I have insisted on this second (and more harmful) form of inculturation, it is so as not to reduce the debate on the Patristic Age to the Hellenization of dogma and to tackle it also as the Greco-Romanization of the church, which was also, indirectly, to have consequences for christology.

(b) Culture and Counter-Culture

There is a great demand for inculturation today, and rightly so. This is due to the fact that the absolutization of one cultural, theoretical, and practical form of Christianity, the European (Greco-Roman-Latin-Germanic), prevented other inculturations, which has been a theologically mistaken and humanly unjust way of proceeding. It has shown contempt for other cultures and has served to oppress them, violating cultural and religious rights, as we say today.

This is the background to the call for inculturation today, particularly among colonized peoples. They are showing the following: first, a desire to counter-attack, putting forward what is positive in their religions and cultures, countering the contempt they have suffered from; second, their need for a reparation of the religious oppression to which they have been subjected. Faced with this call, it is important that we should recall the capacity the Patristic Age showed for concili-ating and taking on the "other" in Christian faith. It would be an absurdity and a real contradiction today to praise (and far more to impose) Greek and Byzantine liturgies, which are already inculturations of a predominantly Jewish tradition, and to ignore (still more to ban) inculturations in other cultures—above all those of the poor.

The Patristic Age, however, can teach us another lesson: the church also has to be conscious of the counter-cultural dimension of the faith, which comes out very clearly from what the church has done and what it has not done. Struggling against the limitations of Greek thought was counter-cultural and brought beneficial re-sults. Not struggling against a political and imperial religion meant ceasing to be counter-cultural and brought harmful results, as we have just seen. So, once we accept the need for inculturation, we also have to ask ourselves how counter-cultural the Christian faith has been.

Let us begin by asking if there is something *transcultural* in Christian faith—what is, so to speak, "the most Christian of Christian," a question akin to that of the canon within the canon. The importance of deciding what might be transcultural consists, on the one hand, in that it is just this that should be inculturated (and can be, since it finds some type of correspondence in all cultures, all of which are God's creation). But, on the other hand, this transcultural element should also act in some *counter-cultural* way in all cultures (beginning with the biblical one), since all cultures are also inclined to sinfulness.

What is transcultural in Christianity? (Or in any religion, since the question is not exclusive to Christianity, which should help in interfaith dialogue.) It is diffi-cult, and strictly speaking impossible, to *formulate* it adequately, since any for-mulation, including the biblical one, is already cultural. We are dealing with some-thing ultimate in believing human beings, to which they respond, above all, with their life, their work, their hope, and their faith. But if we must try to put it into words, we might say that what is transcultural about the Christian faith (as this is seen in the view of the victims) is God and the Kingdom proclaimed and initiated by Jesus; it is belief in and the utopia of justice; it is the work of following Jesus and the experience of the grace of the love of God, "who has loved us first," poured into our hearts.

This can be said of various cultural embodiments. And this is also what should act counter-culturally, "this" being clearly understood as applying to what is cen-tral and transcultural in Christianity (and analogously to what is central and transcultural in other religions) and not to unjust impositions by a conquering church. The counter-cultural was very much present in Jesus' attitude to his own

Jewish religion and culture. It was also present in the New Testament period and in the Patristic Age, in both theoretical and practical forms. But soon Christianity inculturated itself in what was harmful and sinful in the Greco-Roman world and ceased to be counter-cultural.

(c) Neglect of the Kingdom and the Counter-Cultural

I have mentioned neglect of the Kingdom of God several times already, but here I want to relate it to inculturation and what is counter-cultural. This neglect led to Christianity ceasing to be counter-cultural when it needed to be and adapting itself to a worldly and sinful religiopolitical way of being. And the church was able, inhumanly, in the name of the faith, to wipe out heretics and pagans, and to turn itself into the church of Christendom.

From the viewpoint of the victims, this neglect and distortion of the Kingdom and its replacement by a church in power has perhaps, over the centuries, been more decisive in shaping Christianity than the (good or bad) Hellenization of dogma, at least in the following sense: the positive side of "Hellenization" can go on being fruitful, while its limitations and dangers can be overcome, as present-day christologies show. But the "worldly politicization of Christ," the fact that the church passes itself off—no longer crudely, but still subtly—as the ultimate, as the Kingdom of God, is a much more difficult sin to eradicate and a far more perennial temptation.

(d) Theology and Power

Finally, let me say that on the theological level it remains surprising—and shocking—that an age that developed an impressive theology of the divine—the Trinity—did not work out a theology of this God "outward," a theology of the world as God wishes it to be. It may be said that it did this in dealing with the incarnation, but here the "outward" does not embrace God's world, God's creation, with the same pathos. It is surprising—and shocking—that an age that developed an impressive christology and soteriology should ignore the Kingdom of God. And it is also a major limitation that in that age the divinity and humanity of Christ should have been protected from the danger of *being denied* but not from the greater danger of their *opposites:* idols and inhumanity.

The ultimate reason for producing this excursus is to recall this fact and to try to prevent it from happening over and over again in history. That the church is limited and sinful is obvious and inevitable. For it to commit aberrations is distressing and scandalous. But that its christology, however sublime it may be, should not at least be able to raise the alarm that the church is distorting its identity and its mission would be shocking and, when all is said and done, unacceptable.

This is not said anachronistically in order to minimize the achievements of patristic christology, which I shall consider in the following chapters. Neither am I saying that this christology distanced itself completely from Jesus and the Kingdom of God, since it upholds them indirectly and implicitly, by insisting on the humanity of Christ, for example. But I do want to say it as an important reminder: the errors and sins of the church are bad enough, but it would be worse if there were no shriek of protest at their being committed. Then, one would think, there would be no solution. And for some shriek of protest to emerge when we do not do what we should do, we have to get back to the ultimate, central "inculturable and counter-cultural": Jesus and the Kingdom of God. This, at least, is what is clear in the view of the victims.

One final observation: in the conversion of Christianity into a political religion, the christological undertaking was influenced, to a greater or lesser degree, by political power. "A church that carries out a particular political function will relate dogma to it. I am not saying that it will deform or betray it. But it would be unthinkable for it to play with fire without getting singed."[44] It is not possible to think in the same way from the sphere of power as from the sphere of oppression. (This becomes more obvious when considering Christendom and shows clearly in those who hold power in the church. The aberrations and errors committed throughout history by the hierarchy and the magisterium, above all by popes, are due, I consider, to the distortion of the Kingdom of God and the resulting way the church saw itself as a power. As González Faus has suggested: "The temporal power of the popes . . . will emerge in the course of this study as a highly influential and very harmful factor in the exercise of the ordinary magisterium.")[45] It is more difficult for christology to meet and focus on the Jesus of the Kingdom, who denounces and unmasks the idols of this world, when it is close to them— not to say even one of them—than when it is on the side of the victims. This is not to say that the situation totally determines the exercise of intelligence, but it does influence it greatly, at least in deciding the importance of subjects to be examined, in generating fruitful suspicions, and in advancing new courses. (It was not chance that made the intellectual thrust of Vatican II so different from that of the councils of the Middle Ages, Trent, and Vatican I. At these, in effect, the church was thinking from and for power, even if with good intentions. At Vatican II, though, what was at stake was whether the church should be in power or not. By deciding, in principle, that it should not, it thought of the faith from a different aspect. On this, Pedro Casaldáliga observed, with his usual good sense and daring, that the most important "council" was Medellín, because at that the bishops began to think from the situation of the poor.) Nor is it to say that worldly ecclesiastical power can directly determine the contents of christology, but indirectly and unconsciously it can move it in a wrong direction.

So, having warned of the dangers, I should like to end this excursus on the positive note of the Patristic Age's impetus to inculturation. This is how Moingt ends his article "Christology in the Early Church":

Then it was the Greeks who were knocking at our doors: now it is the refugees, the poor with no hope, the disappointment of the old holy lands. The Gnostic apocalypses have become reality and covered our horizons with clouds. We need constantly to be converted to the other, precisely to the other who suffers. Unbound from myth, the truth of yesterday, that same truth, has to become reality in history today.

Chapter 16

A God Who Can Suffer

The Pathos of Audacity and Honesty

Having set the scene for the thought of the age, let us now move on to examine conciliar christology. I propose to follow it in chronological order, starting with analysis of the divinity of Christ, moving on to his humanity, and then to the relationship between the two.

The reason for starting with an analysis of the *divinity* of Christ proclaimed at Nicaea is not just chronological—the fact that it happened first—but also methodological and existential, since from the outset this presents us with the basic question: in Jesus Christ the ultimate reality has been shown, to which human beings can relate only in faith. "Nothing created can be an object of faith," Karl Rahner said. Turning the statement around, if something is not created, it can only be an object of faith. This has the result that the relationship of human beings to Jesus Christ will have to show the existential—and not only conceptual—depth of *fides qua*, of unconditional trust and active openness.

This is further deepened when we recall that the definition of the divinity of Jesus, as it was established in the patristic theology of the fourth century onward, is not found in the New Testament (even though there are statements such as that of Philippians 2:10 that "at the name of Jesus every knee should bend," as has to be done before Yahweh [cf. Is 45:22–24]), and when the Patristic Age sought to proclaim it unequivocally, this proved problematical in view of the actual events of Jesus' life and death. Therefore, if Jesus' divinity is accepted, an unsuspected novelty is introduced into divinity, which will lead to the need to ask, in speaking of God as in christology, "God? That is (the one who becomes absolutely present in) Jesus (the man from Nazareth)."

The problem is not going to be, then, only if and how a human being can be God—which smacks of mythology—but if and how *this* limited and crucified human being can be God—which threatens to scandalize reason. The first is a question that, since the Enlightenment, has to be answered. The second remains an insoluble problem. Jesus Christ is God *despite* the cross, and this "despite" will be "a cause of scandal" but also the "cornerstone" of Christianity. It will certainly be fundamental for the victims.

In this chapter I am going to look first at Nicaea's statements on the divinity of Christ, with a minimum of patristic context. I shall then reflect on the consequences that follow for an understanding of God from the fact of Jesus Christ belonging to the divinity. I shall end with a reflection on the significance the fact that suffering affects divinity has for the victims.

To finish this introduction, let me say that I have subtitled the chapter "the pathos of audacity and honesty" because the council Fathers upheld the divinity of Jesus Christ even without knowing where affirming the divinity of a crucified man was leading them. This is what I have called honesty with reality, even though here it is a case of honesty with a *believed* reality.

1. Early Reflections on the Divinity of Christ and Their Problems

The New Testament, as we have seen, contains expressions that contain the seed of what will produce confession of the divinity of Christ in the strict sense, which supposes that reflection on the divine reality of Jesus has not a deductive character, as if believers already knew what divinity was and verified it in Jesus, but a doxological one. The definition of Jesus' being as divinity is produced by the understanding of faith: "Jesus is identified as 'Son of God' not by virtue of a preestablished principle, as though we already instinctively possessed the measure of the divine, but on the basis of his word (his promise of the Kingdom of God), of his deeds (the signs that anticipate this Kingdom), of his approach (creative freedom), of his resurrection (his victory over death)."[1]"The concrete, historical interpretation of the Son of God predicate means that Jesus' divine sonship is understood not as supra-historical essence but as reality that becomes effective in and through the history and fate of Jesus."[2] What germinated in the New Testament took root in the Greek world. Let us look briefly at how the process developed.

In the Hellenic world the *logos* of John's prologue acquired great missionary importance for preaching Christ, just as *messiah* had done in the Jewish world. John's text was used for attempting to convince the pagans that "Jesus Christ alone has been begotten as the unique Son of God, being already his Word, his First-begotten, and his Power. By the will of God he became man. . . ."[3] Strictly speaking, this *logos* is not yet said to be God (consubstantial with the Father), but something is claimed for him that will have great importance for reaching this conclusion: his *preexistence.* This does not signify something purely temporal but relates him to the creation and links the *logos* with action specific to the divinity. The *logos* was present at the creation with the divine attributes of Power, Wisdom, Spirit. Christ, then, existed before being born; he was not a human being like others but closer to divinity. On the other hand, the *logos* was not totally assimilated to God, and his divinity is functional, so to speak, rather than metaphysical. This shows two things. The first is that there was an early general acceptance of the *quasi-divine* nature of the *logos*, though not in the form of simple assimilation; the second is that the *divinity* of Christ was seen at these early stages in a fluid manner, which gave rise to the crisis that erupted with Arius. Let us recall the antecedents for this.

In the third century adoptionism reappeared in Rome, not as in the Judeo-Christianity of the Ebionites but in the context of trinitarian theology: the strict monotheist concept could not accept Jesus as the natural Son of God. According to the refutation made by Hippolytus, the adoptionist position claimed that Jesus came to be Son of God, either when the Spirit descended on him at his baptism—the position held by Theodore of Byzantium, its best-known defender—or later in the resurrection. The logical burden is that there can be only one God. (It is interesting to recall the biblical reason adduced to establish the *when* of Jesus' adoption: Jesus performed miracles only after his baptism, at which the power to do so was given him by the Spirit. This means that divinity was understood, specifically, as having to do with power.)

On the other hand and following a contrary trend, attempts to explain the relationship between the human and the divine in Christ developed into a christology of the *logos-sarx*, according to which the *logos* could take the place of Jesus' soul, thereby denying or undervaluing the physical existence of his soul. This model for understanding the unity between human and divine exalts the latter and devalues the former. This, paradoxically, is what led Arius to deny the divinity of Christ.

The polemic was unleashed when Alexander, bishop of Alexandria, maintained that the Son is *co-eternal* with the Father and *is begotten* by the Father, which was apparently new usage. (Moingt agrees that these are new arguments, "at least insofar as they claim the authority of faith."[4] They do not seem to be, however, as these statements are, at least implicitly, found in John's prologue, in New Testament use of Psalm 2:7—"today I have begotten you"—and in the first attempts by the Apologists to explain the divinity of Jesus Christ, such as, among others, Justin: "The Word who is with him being begotten before creatures" [2 *Apologia* 5]; "In the beginning . . . God begat a certain rational power of himself . . . the Word and Wisdom, these being this God begotten of the Father" [*Dialogue* 61]. Tatian tries to explain the begetting of the Word "by sharing, not by division . . . the begotten Word in the beginning in turn begat our creation for us" [*Discourse against the Greeks*, chap. 5].) Arius would not have had a problem with the idea of something new being introduced into Christianity, but its content did not accord with his Hellenic idea of the immutable God. Against this position he employed speculative arguments; there cannot be two immutable principles; an act of begetting cannot be attributed to God. He also used biblical arguments, which were to prove more decisive, turning on the difference between the incarnate Word and the Father as he appears in the New Testament.

The Arians gathered all the passages in which the nature of Christ is shown as creaturely, limited, humbled, especially those that showed his sufferings, and in this way reached the nub of the problem: the Word, as principle of limited activities and subject to suffering, could not be divine. Therefore a strictly divine Word could not be present in the limited and suffering Jesus of Nazareth, as he is presented in the gospels.

We are here faced with a basic question for faith and for christology: either Christ was God and could not suffer, or he suffered and so could not be God. The fundamental achievement of Nicaea, in my view, was to have faced up to this dilemma, not simply saying yes or no to the divinity of Christ but saying yes in consciousness of this difficulty. Though lacking the grandiosity of Chalcedon, here is the essence of the confession of the mystery of God and of God as specific mystery.

Arius did not say that Christ "is not God" but that he "cannot be God," even if he is the most exalted of creatures. The first is what the council had to face up to (Christ is God), while the second is a task for theology (how he can be God, being at the same time a limited and suffering human being). Behind the debate lies what I have called the *fluidity* of the confession of the *divinity* of Christ. Even if this were accepted, formulas such as those of Bishop Alexander extend the concept of this divinity and pose the question of how *divine* the divinity of Christ is.

Athanasius of Alexandria, with Eustathius of Antioch the great adversary of Arius, gathered all the latter's theses in his three books of "Against the Arians." He grants that they would be right if the reality responsible for the personality of Christ—taking the place of his soul—were solely the Word. But this is not the case. Athanasius supported the *logos-sarx* christology, and his solution consists in assigning the sufferings the Arians mentioned to Christ's *sarx* or in simply denying these sufferings. He enumerates the deeds and sufferings of Jesus that appear in the gospels and distributes them between *logos* and *sarx.* So, for example, the agony in the garden would be a welling up of his fearful flesh, and weeping is a property of the body. Throughout Jesus' life all these limitations can be explained without their being attributed to the *logos*. And in his death this was separated from his *sarx*, so that henceforth it was still not affected. So, all in all, the Word was not subject to limitation, or suffering, or weakness of the flesh.

The problem for Athanasius—and his quest for a solution—was like that for the Arians: how the Word can share both a fleshly and a divine form of existence. Athanasius claimed that the Word did not lose this divine form, and this is the only Arian thesis he refuted. He did not, therefore, face up to Arian denial of Christ's soul; he only attacked its consequences. In doing so he left the question in the air, and he failed to tackle the key question: whether a divine being could suffer.

2. Nicaea and Its Significance

To resolve the Arian problem, the emperor Constantine, in 325, summoned the First Ecumenical Council of Nicaea, and at it the true divinity of Christ was affirmed against Arius. I have mentioned this point in the preceding Excursus, but it needs to be made again here, since it first surfaced at Nicaea. At this stage

the church came out from the shadows, took stock of its power, of its universality; Christianity emerged victorious from three centuries of struggle against paganism, became a state religion. A historical event of such magnitude was bound to make itself felt in the document produced by this council: in its form—it speaks in the name of and with the authority of the universal church, it imposes its definitions and decisions on all the churches, and confers a sacred character on them by hurling anathemas against those who oppose them—and likewise in its content—it confers the supreme honors of divinity on the founder of Christianity.[5]

The dogmatic statement was made in a "symbol of faith," in a creed, that is. It is formulated in language drawn from tradition, with its roots in the New Testament, but it introduces clarifications and new elements ("new words," they were called at the time) that were not previously in the tradition. And it includes, for the first time, even if only in the term *homoousios*, conceptual terminology of a philosophical bent. This is what the symbol says:

> We believe in only one God, the Father almighty, creator of all things, of those visible and those invisible, and in one Lord Jesus Christ, the Son of God, born as only-begotten of the Father, that is, from the being of the Father, God from God, light from light, true God from true God, begotten and not made, one in being with the Father *(homoousion to Patri)*, through whom all things came to be, those in heaven and those on earth, who for us men and for our salvation came down, became flesh, and became man *(enanthropesanta)*, suffered and rose on the third day, ascended to heaven, and will come to judge the living and the dead. And (we believe) in the Holy Spirit. (DS 125)

Let us briefly examine this formula.

(a) A Formulation of Belief Already Held

The first thing to note is that this formula takes the shape of a liturgical profession of faith, which is why it begins, "We believe." The bishops came disposed to confess the traditional faith of their churches, which meant that the formula was not going to proclaim a *new* reality concerning Christ that was not already believed—even though the council, on account of Arius, was to be forced to clarify and refine the meaning of what was already believed, which is doing theology, not proclaiming faith.

The formula refers back, then, to belief in the divinity of Christ, which in tradition was based on the twin New Testament pillars of John's gospel: creation and provenance, which coincide in formulating the reality of Christ from his origin. Jesus is not a creature, since "all things came into being through him" (Jn 1:3); and Jesus is truly Son of God, in the literal sense, since he is begotten as the Father's only Son (1:14, 18). In this way, the divinity of Christ is viewed from his origin, not from the life and death of Jesus.

(b) Conceptual Precisions and a New Element

Nicaea adds some precisions and one new element to this basic truth of faith. The most important precision is the adjective *true*—"*true* God from *true* God"—insisting on the fact that the divinity of Christ should not be understood in any way other than that the Son is really God. In doing so, Nicaea put an end to the state of *fluidity* in understanding the divinity of Christ.

In the New Testament and in tradition, God—the divinity—is a definite reality, the Father. However, a new focus was needed to tackle the divinity of Jesus Christ: he is divine not by *being* God (the Father) but by *being in a specific relationship* with God (the Father). And in order to express this specific relationship adequately, Nicaea introduced a conceptual novelty in relation to tradition: *homoousios*, consubstantial with the Father. The Arians accepted that Christ is like *(homoiousios)* the Father, but not that he is of the same nature. Hence the need to express such a major conceptual difference with precision.

This relationship between Father and Son came to be expressed, as to *provenance*, in the Son being *begotten*, not created (nor produced by any other means: emanation, leading out . . .). And as to *content*, the Son is *consubstantial*, of the same substance as the Father, which means that he is "properly and absolutely all that God is by substance, possesses all the properties of the divinity without difference of kind or degree."[6] The council did not intend to become involved in philosophical-theological discussion and speculation by introducing this new conceptual element, but in fact it ventured along this path, with all its attendant dangers and possibilities: "We should grant the council the merit of having sought to raise the unity of Father and Son to the plane of being, whereas earlier tradition had left it on the plane of economy."[7]

(c) The Absoluteness of Reality: The Divine and the Non-Divine

Even if it did not intend to, but certainly on an important point, Nicaea went beyond Greek metaphysics and worked a real de-Hellenizing. According to Greek thought there exists a series of intermediate beings (demiurges, demons, angels, aeons, and so on) between the divine and the human, the uncreated and the created, so that Christ could be the most exalted of these intermediate beings without being truly God or truly human. It was in this context that the council made its radical statement: Christ is not an intermediate being but is of the divine being. "The Son is by nature divine and is on the same plane of being as the Father, so that anyone who encounters him, encounters the Father himself."[8]

By approaching the divinity of Christ in this way, Nicaea also brought about a rejection of the Greek understanding of being: being is either divine or non-divine, and there is no halfway house. (Even if only in passing, it is worth mentioning that this view of being underlying Nicaea serves to increase understanding, metaphysical and theological, of the notion of *hierarchy*. It is possible to maintain that created beings can reflect uncreated being to a greater or lesser extent, but in relation to this they are all radically equal, non-divine, before being distinct from one another. What is created neither needs to nor is able to take on the uncreated in order to carry out a function or special ministry.) In doing so, Nicaea produced a (philosophical) statement of the absoluteness of earthly being—whether this is understood as nature, as at the time, or as history, as now. (The letter to the Hebrews made the same claim in rejecting an "angelic," that is, intermediate, christology and basing salvation on the "earthly" existence of Jesus.) And although it does not actually tackle it, Nicaea approached the root problem of whether and how non-divine being can receive, show forth, and reveal divine being.

This is better understood by recalling that in the symbol of Nicaea the subject of all that is predicated is formulated as "the Lord Jesus Christ" and not as "the Word," with which divinity is predicated of something that is—in some way, although precisely how is still not specified—also non-divine. The council did not examine what this non-divine is with the same clarity as it applied to the divinity of Christ and said only that Jesus Christ "became flesh, and became man." That is, it did not tackle Arianism's other thesis, the denial of Christ's soul. This was probably due to the presence of the question of *logos-sarx* christology, taken up by Athanasius, among others, probably without realizing the problems it led to. It was not until the Council of Constantinople that the humanity of Christ was proclaimed, and not until Ephesus and Chalcedon that it was spelled out fully.

(d) The Content of the Divinity of Christ

We also need to inquire into what the divine element is, since the Bible speaks not just of *divinity* but of *Yahweh* in the Old Testament and of the *Father* in the New Testament. To say that Jesus Christ is of one being with the Father does not mean that he shares in one *ousia*, divinity, with a universal and repeatable entity (as human being or nature has). That is an abstraction to which nothing concrete in reality corresponds, and so there cannot be a singular application of this supposedly universal being—although the New Testament, even if only in two places, mentions *divinitas*: *theiótes*, referring to God in Romans 1:20, and *theotés*, referring to Jesus, "in whom the fullness of deity dwells bodily," in Colossians 2:9.

What does it mean, then, to say that Christ is of one being with, consubstantial with, the Father? In the credal formula it means that "he possesses the fullness of *domination* (*dominus*: Lord) over the world and history by which divinity is defined, and exercises it in union with God in the field of the work of creation and the work of salvation."[9] This shows the outcome of the struggle against Gnosticism, that is, the rejection of a god outside history and with no history of its own. In this context the God of the Old Testament would (alone) be a creator God, lord and savior of history. The radical addition made by the New Testament is that now this same God has history by virtue of the Word present in it. And, conversely, being consubstantial with the Father is sharing not just in the *divinity* but also in the *lordship* of the Father. Speaking of the divinity of the Son, something new for a human being, involves, since Nicaea, speaking also of the historicity of the Father, something new for a divine being.

(e) Concern for Salvation

Finally, the Nicene formula carries on the earlier concern for salvation. The formula itself picks up the basic fact that the incarnation is "for our salvation." And in the theological debate this concern appears explicitly after the "of one being with the Father." Athanasius expresses it in the judgment already quoted: "For us it would be as useless for the Word not to be the true Son of God by nature as it would be were it not true flesh that he became."[10] The clarifications and the new element are, then, for the sake of soteriology. The true *divinity* of Christ is necessary for what he *became* to be able to be *saved*, and his true *humanity* is necessary for what God wanted to save to *become*.

3. The Theologal Novelty

Nicaea introduced technical language and categories in order to define christological faith so that "there could be no escape-route" for Arianism. In doing this so comprehensively, however, it set dogma on the track of essentialism, on the one hand, and on that of a radical conceptualizing of God whose consequences would emerge only over time, on the other. As B. Sesboüé has said, "Nicaea's 'of one being,' which for a long time seemed too much, was in fact too little."[11] Affirming the divinity of Jesus Christ in effect produced a radical change in the conception of divinity. In other words, one cannot say that *Jesus* Christ is of one being with the Father and leave the notion of the Father (God, "the holder" of divinity) untouched. (First, one has to ask whether "God" stops being a name exclusive to the Father and comes to express a divinity shared with the Son. According to Moingt, this is what happened in the formulations of Bishop Alexander: with the eternal begetting of the Son, "the Father is stripped of his personal statute of only God. . . . Divinity ceases to be identified with the individual whose exclusive prerogative it constitutes, the creator God, Father of an incarnate Word; it is now seen as a common good."[12] The Cappadocians also seem to suggest this, though Gregory of Nyssa felt obliged to write a treatise contradicting it, titled *Quod non sunt tres dii.*)

The two postulates—and the intrinsic tension between them—that were to guide all subsequent development also made their appearance at Nicaea. One is the *christo*-logical postulate of "having transferred the principle of Christ's existence to God, at the same time transforming his historical existence into eternal existence."[13] The other is the theological postulate that Nicaea "has reordered the concept of one God to make room in it for another, for a Son."[14] Nicaea was, above all, a theologal council, since "it made room for Jesus in God." This was the council's great theologal revolution, even if its final definition stayed on a certain level of abstraction, which was later to be resolved with the *communicatio idiomatum.*

This theologal novelty prompts two reflections, moving beyond what was debated at the council, though in some way implicated in this. The first is on the definition of God's being. The second is on the fact that God is affected by suffering and its significance.

(a) Partiality in God

Nicaea declared the Son "of one being" on account of what Jesus *is* (only-begotten Son of the Father), but not on account of what Jesus *does*. The actions of Jesus of Nazareth (who is now declared of divine nature) are not taken into account in order to "redefine" God. And this means that Nicaea was not to move beyond a view of the divinity (of the Father) of an essentialist and non-historical type, which both the Old Testament and the New Testament do. This lack of historicity was not overcome even by introducing Jesus into the sphere of the divine.

One important consequence of this was that, even with Jesus "inside" the divinity, universalization *versus* partiality persisted. On the one hand, as we saw in the previous chapter, revelation of God (and hence "definition" of God) comes about through historical actions, definite of necessity but also partial, the fruit of God's unassailable freedom. "The God who comes down to set his people free," "the God who comes to us in a kingdom for the poor," "the God who raises the victim Jesus" is a definite God but also a partial and even dialectical God, on the side of some and against others. But, *later*, God was to become—with no distinctions—a God of all.

This great change took place during the Patristic Age; Nicaea was not responsible for it, although this council, precisely because it introduced Jesus into the divinity, could have returned to the specific biblical notion of divinity and of how God is revealed—but it passed over the opportunity. The result was that, in place of a God who acts concretely and historically, a God who acts universally and transcendentally, the creator, survived; in place of a God who exercises lordship over historical processes, a God who is universal lord survived; in place of a God who saves the oppressed, the poor, and the marginalized, we were left with a God who saves anyone and everyone. Put simply, in place of a God who is "father of orphans and widows" in the Old Testament and *Abba*, whom little ones can call on, and "God of the kingdom," who brings hope to the oppressed in the New Testament, a universal, creator, lord, and saving God is maintained. Yahweh, the Father of Jesus, is God, but without any sure way of knowing what the life, work, and fate of his Son Jesus reveal about him.

The dangerous aspect of this precipitate universalization could be avoided by taking it fully but keeping in it—dialectically, maybe—the material and partial aspect that produced it: the inclusion of Jesus of Nazareth in the divine being. But when this did not happen, it could be seen as "Hellenizing" in the negative sense: an understanding of God led by universal considerations rather than by material ones (those belonging to Jesus) and from which the partiality that distinguished the God of Jesus has vanished. This, rather than the use of Greek concepts (Nicaea's "new terms"), would be the danger of Hellenizing.

Against this it might be argued that by speaking of a creator God, lord, and savior, history is already being introduced—in some fashion—into the concept of God: in fact the Fathers spoke of the *economy* of God, of God's material disposition in view of salvation. This is true, but only in a manner without origin or shape, as is proved by the fact that recovery of history and partiality in God is something recent in ecclesial conciliar theology. Vatican I (1870) still spoke of God along the lines of divine *nature*. He is a living and true God, creator and Lord of heaven and earth, but, in addition to the abstract and a-historical tone of this language, his attributes are universal: all-powerful, eternal, unmeasurable . . . (DS 3001). In this context it is a perhaps insufficiently valued achievement of Vatican

II to have expressed the reality of God in terms of history, to have *narrated his nature*, even if only in outline form. (This is done above all in the constitution *Dei Verbum*, nos. 2–4. The text presents only the basic outline of the history of God and does not lay any stress on God's partiality—for which we would have to wait till Medellín. The main fact is that it is done: it is no longer enough to speak of the nature and attributes of the divinity; God's history also has to be told.)

Despite what has been said above, the fundamental fact about Nicaea is that it did "make room for Jesus in God." In this way the seed of making God material and partial was sown, even if from a different viewpoint from that of the Old and New Testaments—no longer from God's actions, historical, material, and partial, but from his essential relationship with an actual person. Nicaea said that Jesus was God, thereby opening up an unknown path. Later, following the *communicatio idiomatum*, it would be said that the materiality, historicity, and partiality of Jesus had to be predicated of God. According to Nicaea, God is still a God without history, but he now has one material aspect: the being of Jesus. This statement would be difficult to uphold, as later debates seeking to "eliminate" the materiality of Jesus from the divine being were to show. On this account, the great merit of Nicaea was to have "made room for Jesus in God."

(b) God and Suffering

The reason why Arius did not accept the divinity of Christ was basically the suffering of Jesus, the incarnate Word. Whatever may have been the explicit understanding of the bishops and theologians at Nicaea, the logic of their thinking led them to have to take a stand on the relationship between God and suffering. In the faith of the church God had always been considered in relation to human beings and as on their side. But now he appears as one of them, and the consequences of this have to be drawn: God suffers like them and has himself decided to place himself at their mercy. This is what was at stake—implicitly but actually—at Nicaea. And this is what can be seen more clearly when the reading is made from the viewpoint of the victims.

Going back to Arius, let us recall that for him Christ not only *was not* God, but he *could not be* God owing to his limitations and sufferings. The council, despite this, proclaimed the divinity of Jesus Christ and so had, in some way, to relate God and suffering. This is the basic fact, and it was to say something specific about the Christian faith. Moltmann's well-known statement may need some modification, but I agree with him that without a crucified God there is no *Christian* theology. As González Faus has written:

> By placing the terms God and suffering together, the Council of Nicaea places us in front of the two most decisive questions that have arisen in human history and life. And by answering in the affirmative, that there is a link between both, it exposes the very nerve of Christian faith, in all it has of unexpected and unhoped-for irruption, which does not fit easily into human capacities for explaining nor in human desires and is rather judgment on and condemnation of these.[15]

As far as I know, commentators on Nicaea do not usually address this aspect.

The council, then, upheld, implicitly but effectively, the novelty—at once scandalous and blessed, through being saving—proclaimed in Paul and Mark of the relationship between God and suffering. Out of fidelity to the texts of the New Testament and without knowing exactly where they led, the council Fathers accepted the *divinity* of a *suffering* Christ. I have called this the pathos of audacity and honesty. This is what should be emphasized, but we also need to reflect on the reasons for it and its consequences.

Nicaea had reasons, above all biblical ones, for making God and suffering converge. Seen from today and from the viewpoint of the victims, and in line with the council's soteriological concern, we might perhaps formulate the following technical reason for relating them: without *affinity* there is no salvation. And this affinity has to reach down to the deepest levels in human beings, to where the expectation of salvation is most necessary and, at the same time, seems most difficult to achieve—in suffering.

This affinity can be expressed in various ways. Greek theology coined the axiom, "What has not been taken on has not been redeemed," and Latin theology, "Without the spilling of blood there is no salvation." (What is decisive is not the particular philosophical model in which this saving affinity is expressed. Showing *how* taking on what is human and sacrifice bring about salvation is a problem for theological reasoning, but what matters is to stress the fact itself: without some form of drawing together, of affinity between the divine and the suffering human, there can be no salvation. On models of salvation, see *JL*, chap. 8[2], "Why Jesus Died.") In Hegelian form Moltmann says, "Only when every calamity, abandonment by God, absolute death, the infinite curse of condemnation, and sinking into nothingness are in God, is communion with this God salvation."[16] And these are Bonhoeffer's words: "God, nailed to the cross, allows them to throw him out of the world. God is impotent and weak in the world, and only in this way is God with us and helping us. . . . Only the suffering God can help us."[17]

This view of faith sees the divinity being affected by suffering, and this was the view underlying Nicaea, even though Greek thought gave it no theoretical support but quite the contrary. It also implies that this fact can be salvific. That reason is scandalized by this is evident, and at first sight it is distressing to think that mystery, excess of light, can also become enigma, excess of darkness—which I considered in the meditation on the crucified God in the first volume (pp. 233–53).

This God-suffering relationship, however, has not only to be upheld, I believe, by formal fidelity to the texts of the New Testament, as in saying, "That is the way it is," but also can be (and in my opinion must be) taken up in theology as a condition for making expression of the ultimate reality of God possible, both in its *content*—God is *love*—and in its *form*—God is *mystery*.

Where God's reality is concerned, there is no avoiding the question of how God's love is possible without it being affected, to some degree, by the situation of human beings. The Greeks arrived at the idea that God is what is perfect and also what is good for human beings (Plato), but they conceived his perfection as a lack of need, since satisfying need implies change. Therefore, God cannot love human beings, and still less can he love them by sharing in their history, since this would imply sharing in their suffering. The "thought that thinks itself" (Aristotle's God) is the perfect example of God's changelessness and *apatheia*. God moves and draws the whole of existence as final cause, but he does not love human beings, nor can they love him. "In friendship with God, there is no place for mutual love, or even for love. Because it would be absurd for someone to think he loves Zeus."[18] As often happens, this view of God has its anthropological counterpart: the perfection of human beings cannot consist in friendship but in intellectual contemplation, since in the former we depend on others whereas in the latter we depend on no one—we do not allow ourselves to be affected by anyone—and so become like the gods.[19]

> He who is self-sufficient needs neither services from others nor the enjoyment of their affection, nor their company, but is very well able to live on his own. This becomes very clear if we observe what happens with God: it is obvious that God, who has no need of anything, will not need friends either, or anything that might affect him in such a way that it controls him.[20]

I see this as the most basic question at stake at Nicaea: not just whether Jesus Christ, a being who is also human, is God, but what being God is. This takes us well beyond Greek thought but also beyond that of the Old Testament; implicitly, it conceptualizes the basic intuition of the New Testament concerning the death of the Son of God on a cross and the wisdom of God in Jesus' cross. And all these scandalous assertions, which produce metaphysical vertigo, are made, in the final analysis, in order to be able to say that God loves human beings and loves them in a human way.

Nicaea did not reflect on how the suffering humanity and the divinity of Jesus Christ are related, a task that was left to the future, but it did make a declaration of principle, in the knowledge that thereby the Christian faith was left wide open to Arius's reproach, "You believe in a God who suffers." But in this way it also went beyond Greek thought from another viewpoint: God's being contains an essential core of mystery, which cannot, therefore, be controlled by reason. And once God is allowed to be not controllable by, but rather controller of, reason, God appears as God. In simple terms, in the Christian understanding God has not only attributes (being creator, father, savior . . .) but also the form of being mystery. And an effective—perhaps the most effective—way of showing God's ineffability and uncontainability is having transcendence and suffering coexist in God—his greater being and his lesser being, *Deus semper maior* and *Deus semper minor*, as I said in an earlier chapter.

This is what by virtue of its own content—and not just through a possible religious approach prior and alien to it—requires us to "let God be God." This God, in whom transcendence and suffering coexist, is not a confirmation of our idea of God, nor is it a controllable modification of this idea; it is pure revelation. This is where what is most original and most worth keeping in Nicaea lies, and the reason for it is to make human salvation possible, according to Athanasius's desires; for God to be able to love us in such a way—by sharing in our suffering condition—that we human beings can grasp that love. The debate, beginning with Harnack, on the (negative) *Hellenizing* of dogma and the (positive) task of *de-Hellenizing* it, saw this task being carried out by going back to the christology of the Fathers and the New Testament, thereby avoiding introducing the theoretical categories of Greek thought. The suggestion is sound, but one can go beyond it and say that the deepest de-Hellenizing consists not in "abandoning something"—in this case Greek conceptual categories—but in "adding something"—a God who suffers. (Kasper is correct, though my interpretation goes further: "Arianism was an illegitimate hellenizing, which dissolved Christianity into cosmology and ethics. As against this, Nicaea represented a de-Hellenizing: for dogma, Christ is not a world-principle but a salvation-principle" [p. 178].)

4. Which Christ Do Victims Believe in: Arian or Nicene?

(a) Preamble on Theodicy

The world's suffering, in all its manifestations, abounds and superabounds. Our world is a vitiated creation, contrary to the will of God, which is obvious to all except those who "by their wickedness suppress the truth" (Rom 1:18). And this affects God. These days the problem is best seen in the universalization of poverty. As Ellacuría wrote: "The problem of the poor is God's problem. . . . The poor are the failure of God the Father. . . . The impotence of God in history is something that has to be accepted in Christian confession of God's omnipotence."[21] González Faus has noted that "according to one Christian tradition, a very genuine but carefully ignored one, the most telling argument against the existence of God is the existence of the poor."[22] (They are not just poor, but pauperized, as senior officials of the United Nations have made clear: we are moving from "the unjust to the inhuman" [J. G. Speth, 1996]; the world will to help with development has diminished [W. Franco, 1997].) Beyond the fact of poverty lie the victims of cruel and aberrant violence, the shame of humankind. From Europe the Christian J.-B. Metz and the Jew Elie Wiesel press us to keep alive the *memoria passionis* of the victims of Auschwitz.[23] In more recent years we have had the victims of El Mozote, Haiti, East Timor, Rwanda, Bosnia, Kosovo. . . .)

   In this situation we have to speak not only of God's suffering but of human suffering before God. The question of theodicy—always a problem for religious people—arises: how to reconcile God and suffering, how God can exist if suffering exists, above all the widespread and cruel suffering inflicted on the innocent, for which there appears to be no justification. The problem is obviously still with us, even though people have tried a thousand ways of reconciling God with the existence of evil and come up with a thousand different answers. One answer, which always sounds offensive, is: Why put the blame on God, when it is human beings who produce suffering? Another offers the majesty of religion: Who are you to call God to account? Another points to real experience, even though it smacks of cruelty if taken seriously and is hardly convincing: God produces good from evil. Yet another appeals to the lesser evil: God cannot abolish human freedom, even if this produces evils, since to do so would be a greater evil.

Something in human nature, nevertheless, prevents us from accepting answers like this that try to explain the inexplicable so that God will emerge unscathed from the trial. (In his prologue to *Hoping against Hope*, Reyes Mate writes: "Nor can God shelter from this event [the Holocaust]. The Christian theologian [Metz] rejects the common recourse of traditional theodicy: blaming the scandal of evil in the world on human freedom. But the suffering of creatures is, first and foremost, a question that has to be addressed to God, if it is true that God is good and all-powerful.") And so some, the logico-rationalists, come to the conclusion, even though it resolves nothing either, that God does not exist or, ironically, that not existing is his only excuse in the face of suffering. Others, loving humankind and tormented believers at one and the same time, protest, and so Ivan Karamazov says that while innocent children suffer he does not want to know about God and his heaven, even if the scandal spreads to there.

In our day the problem has been posed again with one of its postulates modified: God is not completely all-powerful, since he too is subject to suffering. This would seem to abolish or at least reduce the scandal of theodicy—not of suffering—though not on the lines of cheap grace. As Bonhoeffer says, the same God suffers, and it is just because of this that this God can save us. Nevertheless, this theology of the crucified God has not silenced the question of God and suffering.

J.-B. Metz is perhaps most responsible for keeping the question alive at the present time, and he insists that suffering has to bring theology down to earth.[24] With respect to Bonhoeffer, Moltmann, and Dorothee Sölle, he is critical of the theology of the "suffering God" and of the attitudes it has led to: the "aestheticism" and even a sort of "euphoria" at the God who suffers with us. He demythologizes a suffering that, in essence, is turned into merely "a victorious and comradely suffering-with," underestimating its negativity. And he also demythologizes a suffering that would be simply a "symptom and expression of love," since suffering can also lead to nothingness.[25] He writes of God: "When we speak of a suffering God today, this is often the same as a critical rejection of the creator, almighty God. We no longer dare to speak of God's omnipotence in view of the atrocious state of his creation. If he were omnipotent, would it be possible to see him as anything other than an apathetic and cruel idol?"[26]

How, then, should we approach the problem of God in view of suffering? What is the proper attitude to theodicy, if such a thing is possible? (Note that I am not speaking of an "answer," since theodicy is a mystery, or an enigma, but one in the face of which, as with any mystery, one has to take some attitude.) In my view, such an attitude could or should include the following elements. The first is *indignation* on account of human suffering, leaving something unrecoverable to be kept in this indignation (which can be against what human beings do or against what God fails to do). (Some years ago I wrote on the subject of theodicy: "The basic scandal does not consist in the existence of destitution despite the existence of God, but simply in the existence of destitution. Theodicy is not a problem constructed theoretically by introducing God into the scheme of overall understanding

of reality, but a problem that is there independently of this theoretical construction. So the basic question is how to justify humankind.")[27] The second element is
the utopic ingredient of *hope*, that God—with or without the power to overcome
suffering—will have the power to support human beings in their hope (Metz and
Wiesel's "despite everything") and in their actions (Ellacuría's "turning back history"). The final ingredient is the *honesty* to "take stock of a horrible reality" in
order to "take charge of it and take it on oneself." In simple terms this means
deciding to *work* for justice and mercy, to *walk* humbly in history with God,
through the darkness, protesting, but *always*. (Metz analyzes "sensitivities to
theodicy" in language, in experience of God, and in praxis, and insists that these
are the three basic levels on which the problem of theodicy has to be maintained,
not ignored or set aside.)[28]

   Next I want to look into God and his relationship with suffering, to see if this
is good or bad, but all from the viewpoint of the victims themselves, from the
"authority of those who suffer,"[29] even with no guarantee of being able to represent their view adequately. (I have already said in the Introduction, but would
like to repeat here in the context of the victims' suffering, that I sometimes think—
consciously exaggerating—that *Christian* theology is, ultimately, an impossible
task. Allowing for all necessary qualifications, it seems to me that the poor and
the victims, in general, cannot do theology, as this is understood conventionally,
and that those who can are not poor and almost never victims. One can go on
discussing theoretically whether or not the poor can do theology: Segundo says
they cannot, while Gutiérrez and Boff claim they can. Ellacuría held that the poor
provided *light* rather than theological *content;* he saw light as more important
than working out content. José-María Castillo has firmly upheld the theology of
the base communities.[30] I seek to draw attention to the fact that it is not so easy to
be sure than one can express the view of the poor.) So I am going to change
method and register of language and set out in personal and narrative form—
narrative theology being irreplaceable when one comes to such subjects—if and
how suffering affects the poor's faith in God (theodicy) and if and how the fact
that God can also share in suffering (the divinity of Nicaea) affects their hope of
liberation. In simple and deliberately provocative terms we can ask which Christ
the poor prefer, that of Arius or that of Nicaea.[31]

(b) The God Victims Believe in: A Historical Overview

From my experience in El Salvador it seems clear to me that victims—at least at
the present time, though things can always change in the future—believe and
hope in a powerful and saving God. Some of them have made this clear in terms
of the liberation process: they believe in the biblical God, who freed his people
from Egypt and who comes close in the Kingdom announced by Jesus, a Kingdom that will be the end of all misfortunes. How widespread this "new faith" in
God is compared to the traditional Christian resignation of the poor is something
that would need to be researched, but for our purpose it is enough that this experience of God should be real to some extent and should be deeply felt. The questions
that then arise are whether these victims—those who have had their consciousness

raised—are open to the notion of a God who suffers, what such a God means to them, and whether accepting this God is a liberating experience or exposes them to the danger of sliding back into religious alienation.

In summary form it can be said that (1) among these victims God still has absolute primacy as something ultimate and powerful; (2) in the midst of oppression they have discovered the liberating dimension of this God; (3) they sometimes have doubts—which can extend to the level of protest, as in theodicy—about this God; and (4) ultimately, they also find the crucified God a source of liberation. Let us hear it in their own words, though with a prior caution: Western readers should be aware that the poor are not given to formulating protests against God as might be done in the West—or might have been done before postmodernity—but spring to God's defense when he is attacked. So, for example, when a European journalist, an agnostic, asked a peasant from Chalatenango—respectfully—how he could believe in God when he, his family, and his village had suffered so many atrocities, the peasant replied, quite naturally and with equal respect: "You don't understand. God gave us our head to think with, our heart to love with, and our hands to work with. It is we who do the evil, not God."

A logical reconstruction of the faith of victims will show that what comes first for them is their unshakable faith in God. As a whole, victims do not doubt God but thank and defend God, even at times when the protest of theodicy ought to arise. A European priest who went through the war in Morazán, a zone badly affected by repression and fighting, asked how this was possible when the people had gone through so much—bombings, disappearances, murders, massacres. . . . And yet they could say, "Yesterday we were bombed and we were saved by God. . . . God acts, father. . . . God is with us, father, because if God had not been here, it would have been even worse."[32] That is how they express their faith in a saving and powerful God.

Sometimes, however, things are not like that, and a reaction sets in. Understandably, the priest in question, whose origin and education had exposed him to the Enlightenment, reflected in these words on the massacre at El Mozote:

> More than a thousand peasants murdered. I am not exaggerating. I saw many of the mutilated bodies decomposing. Days later there was still an intolerable stench. The houses destroyed, all the people in them dead. . . . In that little town that for me was joy, there were women and children, those children we never see playing in the woods. . . . El Mozote, such a cheerful settlement, with so much life. . . . When I looked at the heaps of the dead, the destruction, I couldn't bear it. How is it possible that just here, where I have come so many times to say that God is a God who is close to us and loves us, who is not indifferent to suffering—that just here such an appalling massacre has taken place?[33]

Not only the priests but the peasants also asked the same question (and it bears repeating): "How many times we tell ourselves that God acts in our history. . . . But, father, if he acts, when is this going to end? And so many years of war and so many thousands of deaths? What's the matter with God?"[34]

Finally, sometimes a difficult synthesis results, in the outcome rather than in the concept, naturally. This God whom they believe to be liberating because he is the God of life can mysteriously, secretly bring hope when he himself appears subject to suffering, when he shows himself as a crucified God. The peasants do not think of things in these terms, but in my opinion their language and concepts express them with greater weight than do our theories. It would not occur to them to use phrases like "a crucified God," but they rejoice in having a God who comes close to them through his suffering. They clearly understand that if the cross expresses closeness, then there is also "something good" in the cross.

It is very important to insist on this. The good they find in the cross is not due in these cases to the fact that this is how salvation is proclaimed in the kerygma, or to the possibility of the cross leading to resurrection, which, in general, they accept as Christians and hope for in their work and struggles, but is due to something more fundamental. This is that the cross, in itself, already speaks of closeness to their own situation. And as they, besides being poor and oppressed, are those who are distanced and marginalized, anything that means closeness already brings something of salvation with it. Without realizing it, they share some of Paul's intuition that in the cross there is, also, good news. They share this intuition because they have existentially related cross and love. In their language this would be associated more with a crucified Christ than with a suffering God. But what they are proclaiming, in either case, is that "theologal closeness" is good.

(c) The Salvation of a Crucified God: A Historical Overview

If we return to the question of which Christ concerns victims, the one who worked miracles or the one on the cross, Arius's or Nicaea's, or which God, that of the Exodus or that of the suffering servant, the reply is a complex one, and in order to make it comprehensible I am going to use the categories of *otherness* and *affinity* as saving categories. The poor do not use these terms, but on the basis of historical analogies—how they see salvation in non-poor people approaching them—it should be possible to glean something of what they think of a Christ-God who suffers.

It is a repeated historical experience in El Salvador that many non-poor have moved close to the victims—from Archbishop Romero and Ignacio Ellacuría to many other priests, religious sisters, and professional people. Sociologically, these people express *otherness* with regard to the poor, and it is just in this otherness that the victims see the possibility of salvation. They come to see that otherness with regard to themselves—economic, political, professional, ecclesiastical—need not be oppressive but can be empowerment, capacity to serve, and so capacity to save. So if one asked the poor if they would prefer an Archbishop Romero without otherness, living like them in penury, unprotected and incapable of defending them, they would answer no. In graphic terms, there are already four million poor in El Salvador, and they have no interest in adding even one more to their number. They are more interested in otherness being able to be power, service, and so salvation. Schematically, they hope that power will be service.

This, however, is not the whole truth. It is also a fact that when the people who come close to them share to some extent in their fate (kidnapping, defamation, persecution, lack of protection, murder), that is, when together with otherness they show some sort of affinity, the poor of this world feel that something good has happened to them. In other words, affinity toward them is also saving and even liberating, even if the salvation it produces is distinct from the salvation that otherness as power can bring. So when the non-poor with prestige and power have shared in the sufferings of the poor even to the extent of martyrdom, the poor have experienced—in the midst of tears and protests—something salvific.

Archbishop Romero expressed this joy resulting from affinity in these much-quoted, paradoxical words: "I am glad, my brothers and sisters, that our church is being persecuted, precisely because of its preferential option for the poor and because it is trying to become flesh in the interests of the poor. . . . It would be sad if in a country where people are being murdered so horrendously we did not count priests too among the victims. They are the witnesses to a church incarnate in the problems of the people."[35] Romero saw something so saving in the cross, not just as the way to *resurrection* but as *already* the expression of *incarnation* and incarnation following on to the end; that is, he saw the cross as affinity—the greatest possible affinity—with victims. This appears to be just what the victims of this world understand as salvific: the closeness of those who are deprived of power. And this is why, if we try to answer the question of which God the victims prefer, that of the Exodus or that of the cross, or which Christ, that of Arius or that of Nicaea, the reply is dialectical.

It is clear that the victims are waiting for a new exodus and for the God who has the power to bring it about. But even if it is not obvious, in fact it is also true that the victims find something good in a God who is subject to suffering. They experience, then, the integral liberation that comes from God dialectically, in two different and complementary ways—one made possible by God's otherness, the other by God's affinity. Logically, the first comes before the second, but the second can also be real and can be unified with the first. And this means that the salvation they experience in a crucified God is no longer just the comfort they have always found in the crucifixion but a comfort united to desire and work for liberation in history. In terms of theodicy, God, transcendent and close, powerful and crucified, moves them to hope and to action. God does not change his suffering, but God can change them to eradicate their suffering.

All this may not be obvious, but it is factual. At the end of the day, it is something that can only be experienced, not extrapolated from prior concepts, and that is why I have chosen the route of historical narrative and not merely that of conceptual analysis. In strict logic it might well be that the victims would reason in the following terms: if there is to be liberation, God cannot be crucified, and if even God is crucified, that means there is no possibility of liberation. In this case the cross in God and liberation coming from God would be mutually exclusive. In other words, if we can ask what suffering enables God to do, we also need to ask what it prevents God from doing: if even God suffers, what will deliver us from suffering? But it could also happen that victims would think that a God absolutely distinct and removed from them, particularly in the deepest part of their being, their suffering, "could not be trusted either."

What has been said in this simple language can perhaps help us to understand what—at least implicitly and unconsciously—was at stake at Nicaea. Historians tell us that the council insisted on proclaiming the divinity of Christ, although he shared in suffering, because otherwise there is no salvation. This argument is, at bottom, *a priori*. The Greeks thought that salvation required affinity, and so they insisted that divinity should partake of nature, which of necessity includes limitation and suffering. The contribution of the reflection I have made is *a posteriori*: affinity produces some sort of salvation in history. The fact that Jesus Christ also suffers—more so if he is God—brings salvation. It is good for mystery to come close to the point of affinity with victims.

All this needs to be understood properly. It is not a matter of lapsing into "dolorism" or of not recognizing that salvation comes from the totality of the mystery of Jesus Christ—incarnation, proclamation, and initiation of the Kingdom, denunciation of the anti-Kingdom, cross, and resurrection. What is at stake is recognizing that the cross "stage," even logically separated from the resurrection, can be perceived as salvific because it expresses affinity with the victims of this world.

I said at the beginning of this chapter that Nicaea, by dealing with the being of Jesus Christ as divinity, is putting faith before us. This means that what has been said in the last two sections may be accepted or not; the outcome of one or the other, though, will, in my view, be not an analysis of texts but one's own life experience and life's journey. What Nicaea ultimately offers us is a definite pathos for the journey: the audacity to confront paradoxes and conceptual scandals and the honesty to introduce suffering too into a God of life and hope, without knowing where this will lead us.

Chapter 17

A Human Christ

The Pathos of Reality

The New Testament takes the humanity of Jesus as an evident fact. "The New Testament takes for granted the fact that Jesus Christ was a real human being" (Kasper, p. 197). It was only when Christianity took root in the Hellenic world of Gnosticism that questions began to be raised about his true humanity, which "soon became a problem of life and death for the church, [which] became involved in what was perhaps the most serious crisis it had ever had to sustain" (Kasper, p. 198). Modern theology certainly has in principle overcome the temptation to deny his true humanity, and so progressive, political, and liberation theology all insist on "going back to Jesus." Nevertheless, this return to Jesus—to his true humanity—is a perennial task and should never be taken for granted. I am going to mention three current reasons for this, to be kept in mind as help to fruitful reading of the patristic and conciliar debate over the true humanity of Jesus.

First, it is true that in our time the official church encourages us to investigate this humanity: the International Theological Commission recognized that "making clear in a more apt fashion the participation of Christ's humanity and of the mysteries of his life" is a present-day requirement.[1] It usually, however, insists more on the danger of reducing Christ to the merely human—and, more specifically, to his prophetic and political aspects—than on the danger of devaluing his humanity, as has happened in many movements within the church.[2] The temptation to "dehumanize" Christ is understandable, since a divinity "made human" produces joy but also causes terror. On the theoretical level, the *communicatio idiomatum*, if taken seriously, is at once *fascinans et tremens*. The fact is that one cannot predicate the properties of divinity from the humanity of Christ (we cannot say that the humanity of Christ is infinite, omnipotent, eternal, and so on) in the same way as we should the properties of his humanity from God (the Son of God was born, suffered, died . . .). In other words, we have to "humanize" divinity, but we cannot "divinize" humanity—which ought to make us rethink, in theory as well as in practice, which is the more dangerous reductionism for Christian faith. This, as one can easily understand, is disconcerting for the proponents of "cheap grace." Furthermore, there is always practical fear: Jesus' "follow me" brings serious requirements, and his mere presence is upsetting. In Dostoyevsky's legend, the Grand Inquisitor, a high official of the church, asks Christ to go away and not come back. One concludes that upholding Christ's humanity is always a problem.

The second reason is the felt need for his humanity to appear. The Enlightenment proclaimed the autonomy of humanity, and with that came the suspicion that the divinity of Christ absorbed and "de-humanized" his humanity. Theology has always insisted, against this accusation, on demythification. Rahner, for example, repeatedly said that Christ is really human, not a God "cloaked" or "disguised" in humanity. But this demythification—especially when imbued with a Promethean component—does not produce a genuine humanization ("Build a God or rebuild mankind," said Rostand), which is why we have to go back to the humanity of Christ, though not only or even principally now to demythify it, but so that what is truly human can appear in this world.

There is still a widespread call for this true humanity to appear today. We are not awaiting—as in former times—the appearance of an eschatological figure, the ideal man, the new Adam, but the longing remains. And the answer is not simply to confess the true humanity of Christ but to be able to put forward the *ecce homo*, to be able to say, "This is being human."

The third reason is ecclesiological. Besides the danger of christological Docetism there is the (perhaps even greater) danger of ecclesial Docetism, if not necessarily in theoretical form, nonetheless actual and existential: this is the *unreality* of the being and mission of the church. This comes about when the church (with all its virtues and faults) gives the impression of having built itself a world different—and distant—from the real one, in which it can act well or badly but in which it does not share what is obvious in the real world, its "joys and hopes . . . griefs and anxieties." (These opening words of *Gaudium et Spes* can be seen here as above all a denial of and move beyond ecclesial Docetism.) This unreality can permeate not only the life of the church but Christian life in general. In this context the classical discussions on the humanity of Christ can help us to grasp the need to uphold the "reality principle," to view Christianity as, above all, a real thing in a real world.

Going back to the "humanity" of Christ is, then, neither a trivial nor a superfluous task. What this humanity was in effect—the history of Jesus' life, work, and fate—was the subject of the first volume of this work. I want to go back to it more formally here in the shape of an examination of the early councils, analyzing the debates and doubts produced, the difficulties that arose, and the reasons for upholding his humanity in the presence of the divinity that seemed to absorb it. As I see it, we can learn three things from this process: (1) the conviction that Christ is truly human and the intuition that only this Christ can bring salvation; (2) the *pathos* with which his humanity was defended; and (3) the *will to uphold it*, even when it had ceased to be obvious by virtue of the definition of his divinity. This teaches us to learn the decision to uphold the "reality principle" at the present time.

1. The Intuition of the Age

When Christianity was introduced into the Hellenic world, it had to face up to Gnosticism, which questioned the humanity of Christ in theory and practice. This danger provoked—with some waverings—a firm conviction that in my view is the most important inheritance the age has bequeathed to us: humanity is real, and not even divine reality can deprive it of its reality. In graphic form, just as human beings have to "let God be God," so God "lets humans be human." This, furthermore, is necessary for salvation to be possible. In more precise terms, humanity is the condition of possibility of salvation, and this is the reason why Christ had to be "*truly* human"—to which I would add that the appearance of the true human is already salvation in itself, offered and initiated: Christ is the "*true human being.*"

This intuition carries a pathos, shown in the struggles of the Apologists against the Gnostics. Down to our own time the words of Ignatius of Antioch defending the flesh of Christ so that his own martyrdom would make sense, or those of Tertullian, begging us "not to be ashamed of the flesh that saves us," still have the power to move us. From this viewpoint the most important thing the councils were later to do would be to express the intuition in terms of the pathos mentioned: whatever is meant by being human, *that* is Christ. In other words, in Christ everything is real that can be called human (against Gnostics and Docetists). And in Christ (the man) nothing is real over and above what is human, which would be explained later by defining that his human nature is not mixed or confused with his divine nature but is real, without "borrowing" anything from the divine. Humanity "without additions" is what will reveal God and what will make salvation possible. This is the importance of the "*vere* homo," an affirmation made *a priori* in order for Christ to be salvation.

The affirmation of "homo *verus*" has a different logic: we know what is truly human because *that* has appeared in Jesus, in his constitutive relationship with God and with history, his mission, his actions, and his fate. This is what formally makes him the revelation of humanity (and of God) and what makes him savior in the manner of exemplary cause. If the "*vere* homo" expresses the condition of possibility for Christ to take on our existence, the "homo *verus*" expresses the actual form humanity takes and so makes it the offer of salvation, or salvation initiated. In yet other words, the *humanity* of Christ is necessary for the former, according to the theoretical thinking of the age. The *story* of Jesus expresses the latter, and following him is its fulfillment.

By translating *nature* as "story," however, I am also indicating something important that is missing from the Patristic Age. The debates of the period revolved around a yes or a no: whether Christ had or had not human nature with all its components (body, spirit, soul, will). But what was not debated was the actual "exercise" of humanity, human nature in action, so to speak, the story of Jesus; neither was whether this exercise was correct or not debated (though obviously the former was taken for granted). This is a serious limitation, since what is truly human has to be understood in the actual form it takes and, furthermore, in dialectic form: what is truly human comes about *over against* a spurious exercise of what is human. The opposite of the truly human is not *absence* of humanity (or of some of its components) but *presence* of inhumanity (through a spurious exercise of humanity). Therefore, the humanity of Christ, insofar as it is true, has to be presented also as *victory* over what is inhuman.

Following these lines, I propose to examine the humanity of Christ from two viewpoints, even though these cannot be clearly separated. The first is that of the Patristic Age and the councils: Christ is "*vere* homo." The second is more that of the New Testament and the present time: Christ is the "homo *verus*."

2. "*Vere* Homo": Pathos for Humanity

(a) Denial of the Flesh of Christ

In New Testament times there were already signs of a widespread Docetism, more popular than theoretical. In the first letter of John the writer feels the need to address these cutting words to his community: "Every spirit that confesses that Jesus Christ has come in the flesh is from God, and every spirit that does not confess Jesus is not from God" (1 Jn 4:2; cf. 5:5; Jn 19:34). In his second letter he states with complete clarity: "Many deceivers have gone out into the world, those who do not confess that Jesus Christ has come in the flesh" (v. 7). The threat to the faith is so grave that the author calls these deceivers "antichrist" (ibid.; 1 Jn 4:3).

Together with this generalized Docetism, other more theoretical ones made their appearance. Central to all of them was the idea that the human existence of Christ—the history of Jesus, his birth, public life, death, and resurrection—is appearance *(to dokein)*, while some teachers, such as Simon Magus and Basilides, concentrated on denying that Christ could suffer in any way. Trying to seek a solution that would, on the one hand, satisfy reason (which always comes down against a suffering God) and, on the other, the Christian faith (which is bound to confess a Christ who can suffer through being human), they say, for example, while it is true that at his baptism the Jesus-capable-of-suffering was united with the Christ-incapable-of-suffering, this unification disappeared in the passion.

Marcion poses the problem in more theoretical terms. The incarnation was simple appearance because "if Christ had been born and had, in truth, taken on humanity, then he would have ceased to be God, losing what he was through taking on what he was not."[3] His disciple Apelles insisted that the flesh adopted by Christ is not flesh like ours but a heavenly body, proceeding from the astral world and coming down to ours through the celestial spheres.

In a Gnostic environment Docetism was practically inevitable from the soteriological perspective also, as a classic example will show. The Gnostic Valentinus claimed that salvation was a drama unfolding in both the upper world, where the divinity lives, and the earthly world, where human beings live, which are linked by an intermediate world. Salvation consists in freeing the divine spark there is in humanity, and so Christ came down to the human world and became united with Jesus, although this Jesus was not the one described in the gospels but an intermediary essence. What this Jesus carried out on earth did not count toward salvation in the final analysis but was only a sign of what happened in an intermediate world where salvation was indeed decided. This consists in what there is of divinity in the earthly world returning to the upper world. The earthly as such, fallen humanity, made up of body and soul, remains without salvation.

(b) The Pathos: The Struggle against Docetism and Gnosticism

This threat to the humanity of Christ operated on two levels, basically corresponding to two periods. In the first, the *basic conviction and pathos* appeared: Christ was human, like us, and without this there is no salvation (this is the work of the great Apologists, true defenders of the flesh of Christ). In the second, the *conceptual argumentation* for the humanity of Christ made its appearance. This does not mean that pathos and concept belong to clearly distinct periods, but I am treating them separately because pathos, rather than concept, represents the earlier conviction, so that concept derives from pathos. I note this because it may be that today we are living in a somewhat similar situation. Faced with some of the ways in which churchmen and ordinary Christians act, a cry goes up: "Without Jesus of Nazareth there is no solution," for the faith, for the church, for theology; this conviction is what later becomes conceptualized in theoretical analyses. But the conviction in itself, we need to note, has its own being and is not purely a doctrinal conclusion. This conviction is what generated the pathos in support of Jesus of Nazareth. Let us now look at some important examples of this pathos in the Patristic Age.

Ignatius of Antioch lays stress on the flesh of Christ and formulates this in a series of vigorous antitheses: "One is the bodily as well as the spiritual doctor, born and not born, walking in the flesh and yet God, proceeding both from Mary and from God, first capable of suffering, then incapable of suffering, Jesus Christ Our Lord" (Eph 7:2). In this manner he delves deep into the antinomy of humanity and divinity, but more to the point here and without even mentioning it, he rejects Docetism in the very point it sees as its strength: "despite being divine," we might say, Christ "is truly human." In the confrontation with Docetism he brings out the importance of Christ's humanity for salvation: "to vilify the incarnation implies vilifying salvation" (*Smyrn.* 1:1–2).

Faced with the imminence of martyrdom, his own as well as that of others, he states that by rejecting martyrdom one rejects salvation: "If we are not ready to die for him, to imitate his passion, we shall not have life in us" (*Mag.* 5.2). And with existential profundity he draws the christological conclusion that interests us here: "If, as some say, [Christ] suffered only in appearance . . . why am I in chains? Why am I longing to fight the wild beasts? I shall be dying in vain, and I am bearing false witness against the Lord" (*Trall.* 10). There is, therefore, a relationship between martyrdom and salvation, and the theoretical basis for this is communion in the (martyrial) flesh of both Jesus and the martyrs. With this same logic he accuses the Docetists of—at one and the same time—denying the bodily life of Christ and being incapable of following him to martyrdom, with which they deprive themselves of salvation (*Trall.* 10).

Ignatius finds another way of affirming the truth of Christ's flesh. The heretics do not show solidarity with those who are being persecuted; in the text cited above, "they do not care who is imprisoned." In this way "they cut themselves off from the eucharist, not confessing that it is flesh of Our Lord Jesus Christ, the same flesh that suffered for our sins" (*Smyrn.* 6:2; 7:1). Irenaeus of Lyons, attacking Marcion's dualism, insists on the unity of God's plan, which covers everything from the creation to the consummation. The decisive moment for saving history is in the "recapitulation" of everything, and what matters most is that the central point of God's plan lies in the *incarnation* of Christ (*Adv. haer.* 3:16:6). The incarnation is in itself the mystery of God's "becoming," but the point here is what God becomes; "The Word of God became what we are to convert us into what he is" (5:1:1). Against Gnosticism he affirms the absolute necessity of the flesh: "If it is not the human that is united to God, we do not share in immortality" (3:18:1). In summary form, *salus autem quoniam caro* (3:10:3). Besides, the flesh of Christ is not only the condition for salvation to be possible but is also what can express the (human) means of carrying this out. Irenaeus says: "Not a messenger, nor an angel, but the Lord himself gave them life, because he loves them and has pity on them. He himself has redeemed them" (*Epid.* 88). And when he asks himself why Christ shed his blood he gives, among others, the very human reason that it was to persuade human beings of the generosity of their Lord (cf. *Adv. haer.* 5:1:18ff.). Salvation is here spoken of as what human beings hope for, but he also speaks of a savior who is credible through his generosity and love. Christ "has humanity" and furthermore "is human."

Tertullian prefigures practically all the classic problems of christology: the two natures, their coexistence and differentiation, and the unity of Christ: "We see him God and man without doubt according to both substances" (*Adv. Prax.*, 27). Where the humanity of Christ is concerned, he insists that this is a complete humanity soul and flesh, in the language of his time. Against those who maintain a "spiritualized" flesh or an "unfleshed" spirit, he states that "in Christ we find soul and flesh, put in the simplest and starkest terms: that is, soul soul and flesh flesh" (*De carne*, 13).

He attacks Marcion's Docetism passionately—"The proclamation of the flesh of the Lord will provide the measure of our resurrection" (*De carne,* 1)—and shows why Marcion finds it so hard to accept flesh in Christ. The fact that Christ can have flesh is not in itself "impossible or dangerous," and so Marcion can only deny the flesh on the grounds that it is "unworthy" on account of its origin in human birth. Tertullian then counter-attacks in these well-known words:

> But how were you born? If you hate man who comes into the world in this way, how will you be able to love anyone? You don't even love yourself. In any case, Christ did love man thus formed in a womb, covered in dirt, brought to light through shameful parts and fed in a ridiculous manner. He came into the world through him, preached through him, and through him lowered himself in humility to death, even to death on a cross. He had to love

him, since he redeemed him at this cost. And in loving him, he loved his birth and his flesh, since nothing can be loved with the exception of what makes it be what it is. . . . If being born and flesh make man redeemed by God what he is, how can you claim that Christ must be ashamed of what he redeemed or that all this that he would not have redeemed if he did not love it is unworthy of him? (*De carne*, 1:4)

The birth of Christ excites Marcion's contempt, but it is an essential condition of salvation. Tertullian argues:

No angel ever came down to be crucified. . . . There you have the reason why the angels do not take flesh through birth. . . . Christ, in order to save man, had to come from the very place [a woman's womb] into which man had put himself bringing condemnation upon himself. . . . Tell us that a crucified God is wisdom or free us also from this folly. (*De carne*, 6, 5)

The conclusion is this:

Spare us the one and only hope of the whole globe; for you are destroying the indispensable shame of the faith. All that is unworthy of God is for my benefit. I am saved if I am not ashamed of my Lord. . . . But how was all this to come about in him in truth if he himself was not something real, if he himself did not have a being that could be crucified and be buried and die? It is impossible to call Christ man if he does not have flesh. (*De carne*, 6, 5)

And then the soteriological argument appears again: "No soul can obtain salvation . . . except when it is flesh. Flesh is to this extent the touchstone of salvation" (*De resu.* 8). *Caro cardo salutis* is another fine expression of this basic intuition: "God lived with men as man that man might be taught to live the divine life: God lived on man's level, that man might be able to live on God's" (*Adv. Marc.*, 2:27).

In these vigorous texts Tertullian makes our salvation depend on the true incarnation. This is what I have called the pathos for the flesh of Christ, which is the most appropriate expression of the faith, with its novelty and scandal value: a divinity who is not ashamed of humanity but takes it on. (This scandal reappears periodically throughout history. Nestorius [fifth century] thought it *unworthy* of the divinity of the Word to attribute to him the properties of the flesh united to him: birth, passion, death. Cyril of Alexandria reproached him for "blushing at the humiliations of the incarnate Word.")[4] Humanity seems to be unworthy of divinity, and yet it is central to faith. Humanity is not only worthy of divinity but is necessary for God to save, and so Tertullian's famous *credo quia absurdum* should be understood not as a sign of irrationality but as a—surprised and grateful—acceptance of a divinity truly made flesh.

(c) The Conceptual Debate

This pathos of faith did away with Docetism, but Jesus' humanity remains an existential embarrassment, and so there has been a tendency to suppress it, all of which can be justified theoretically. This is most likely to happen through confessing his divinity. The debate on the humanity of Christ lasted for three or four centuries and can appear tedious to those unversed in the subject, so the brief summary below can hardly do it justice.[5] Nevertheless, I trust it will be found useful, since it shows, on the one hand, how deep-rooted the tendency to mutilate the humanity of Christ is, and on the other, the strength of the believing instinct to uphold it.

The importance of the debate can be appreciated better when we realize that it deals not simply with the "flesh," although this can express the totality of humanity, but also with the "soul" and "will" of Christ, signifying the deepest dimensions of his being. In other words, the debate can be expressed in this way: Granted that Christ shared in the corporeity of humanity, was this at the deepest levels of his being, at the level of knowing, willing, deciding . . . ?

(i) The soul of Christ. In the third century the theologians of Alexandria laid greater stress on the divinity of Christ than on his humanity. So Clement tended to spiritualize flesh and attributed the Greek *apatheia* to the body and soul of Christ. Origen understood the incarnation from above: humanity is divinized and seems to have no proper integrity of its own. In Antioch the tendency was the opposite. Paul of Samosata cast doubt on the divinization of Christ and stressed his humanity, particularly the existence of his soul, so as not to make Christ's human activity depend on a divine principle.

The ecclesial reaction came at the Synod of Antioch in the year 268. The presbyter Malcion, charged with rebutting the teaching of Bishop Paul, upheld the doctrine of *logos-sarx* in order to emphasize the divinity of Christ: Christ did not have a human soul, but its function was carried out by the divine *logos*. The synod condemned Paul, but by doing so on the strength of Malcion's thesis devalued the humanity of Christ once again—and this at an ecclesial synod. At Nicaea both Arius and Athanasius upheld the christology of the *logos-sarx*, and the council itself did not take a stand, contenting itself with the statement that Jesus Christ "became flesh and man" (DS 125). But once the polemic had been unleashed, the Arian debate and thesis quickly resurfaced.

Apollinarius, bishop of Laodicea and a close friend of Athanasius—for which he was excommunicated by an Arian bishop—defended and emphasized the unity: Christ is one nature, *mia physis*, synthesis of absolutely divine *logos* and *sarx*, the latter understood as without a spiritual soul. The reason given for this was speculative: if his humanity had had a body and a soul, this would then be a complete nature and Christ would then be a conjoining of two natures—which is impossible. Christ is one nature: his whole vital impulse derived from the divine *logos* and there is no need to state that his body was one true nature. To guarantee the unity of Christ, Apollinarius damaged his humanity.

Reaction against Apollinarianism came first at the synod of Alexandria in 362, convoked by Athanasius. The "Paulinists" (after Paulinus, bishop of Antioch) stressed the question of the soul of Christ, probably invoking the soteriological argument: What has not been taken on has not been made whole. The Apollinarists did not deny that the savior possessed a body with spiritual activity, but they did insist that the principle of this spiritual activity was the Word. The synod did not solve the problem, and the polemic continued in Antioch between the presbyter Vitalis, an Apollinarist, and Epiphanius, who upheld the totality of humanity in Christ: "I say that he is a perfect man who possesses all that is in man and all that man is . . . and has not failed to take on any part of man,"[6] insisting on the soteriological argument.

Vitalis traveled to Rome to seek support from Pope St. Damasus, but he, as soon as Vitalis had left Rome, wrote three letters to Paulinus in which he sought to uphold the total humanity of Christ. As opposed to the christology of *logos-sarx* he proposed that of *logos-anthropos* and so reaffirmed the unity of Christ, denying that two sons existed, one human and the other divine. In support of the overall humanity of Christ he invoked the soteriological argument. In this situation a new council was needed—despite the opposition of Athanasius—to clarify what Nicaea had left in the air.

In 381 fifty Fathers gathered in Constantinople. The Acts of this council have been lost, but its ideas were preserved in later writings. The council worked out a symbol of faith similar to that of Nicaea, without adding any theological definition that might have shed light on the truth of the humanity of Christ, but with a first canon anathematizing the Apollinarists as heretics. The following year a new synod met in Constantinople, with virtually the same participants. According to Theodoret, the synod reaffirmed that "the Word of God is totally perfect and from all time, but in the last days for our salvation he became a perfect man" (*Church History,* 5:9). Fifty years later, in 431, the Council of Ephesus was to declare of the humanity of Christ: "[Christ] is perfect man . . . flesh animated by a rational soul" (DS 250). Twenty years after that, in 451, Chalcedon was to proclaim that he is "perfect in his humanity . . . truly man with a rational soul and a body . . . of one being with us as to humanity, like us in all things but sin" (DS 301).

(ii) Christ's human will. Chalcedon did not put an end to the debate, and the problem resurfaced in dealing with Christ's will. Let us look briefly at this debate—which is also interesting for the way in which bishops, popes, and emperors challenged one another, one of the outcomes of the process described in the Excursus above.

Sergius, patriarch of Constantinople, accepted the two natures but only one divine-human operation; in later language, only one will (hence the term Monotheletism). Sophronius of Jerusalem and Maximus the Confessor regarded this as a betrayal of Chalcedon. In 638 the emperor Heraclius published a decree forbidding talk of "one or two wills" and professing "a single will of Our Lord." For his part, Pope Honorius had declared in 634 that only one will existed in Christ (DS 487) in order to stress Christ's obedience and under the assumption that human will, at least in its actual historical manifestation, is opposed to God and that therefore one cannot speak of human will in Jesus. Honorius was also able to appreciate that, from a pastoral point of view, the language of one or two wills mattered little, "a matter for grammarians," he called it, in which popes should not become involved.

With matters standing thus, Maximus the Confessor continued to affirm that denying the human will is denying the human nature of Christ. (Piet Smulders describes what was at stake in these words: "If the human freedom of Jesus is no more than the passive instrument of his divine will and is deprived of any autonomy, the man-God ceases to take on precisely that reality which in man constitutes the site of rebellion against and obedience to God.")[7] He persuaded Pope Martin I to convoke the Lateran Synod in 649; this proclaimed "the two wills of the same one Christ, our God, the divine and the human" (DS 510). The tensions persisted, and the emperor Constantine IV proposed a new council to be held in 681. The new pope, Agatho, accepted the convocation, condemned the Monothelites and also Pope Honorius for his support of Sergius; later, however, in approving the council, he did not condemn him for heresy but merely accused him of negligence. On the subject of christology the Third Council of Constantinople reaffirmed what had been said at Chalcedon, but it did so in more telling language in speaking of the human will of Christ. This is real, though always subject to the divine will (DS 556). Smulders sums this up in these words:

> As human he acts with authentic human freedom. With his free decision to be the form and expression of the Son among us he affirms and realizes his divine obedience and his divine love for humankind. As human he voluntarily "follows" the Word, which speaks to him in such a way that it is himself. It is precisely in this perfectly human obedience to the Word of God and his faithfulness to Humankind that Christ is the Word and the saving revelation of the Father.[8]

Using the language of human *will*, more telling than that of mere *nature*, reaffirms the full humanity of Christ and clarifies—by removing it from any mythological understanding—"the essential participation of the human freedom of Christ in the work of salvation."[9]

So ended the *conciliar* debate on the humanity of Christ. The conclusion was that Christ was a true human being, what we today understand as a person. This means that the term *nature* as it appears in the council documents should now be replaced by *person* if they are not to say something different from and even contradictory to what they set out to say. As Christian Duquoc has written: "In Chalcedon's definition, self-awareness, freedom, moral dignity derive from the concept of *nature*."[10]

In this way, faced with the will and the freedom of Christ, patristic and conciliar theology had to go back to a person with will and freedom—had to go back in some form, that is, to Jesus of Nazareth. The great merit of the Third Council of Constantinople was perhaps, "to have gone back to concentrate on the actual historical life of the son of God."[11] And in this way too, even in a highly conceptual form, the pathos with which the process began was maintained: Christ is really human; were he not, he would be no use to the human race.

3. Lessons for the Present Time

I have devoted some space to the debate on the humanity of Christ because it provides lessons that are still important today. However much the paradigms change, the question of what is human, the temptation to ignore or to distort it, and the longing for what is truly human to appear do not go away.

(a) Countering Recurrent Docetism

A *first* lesson to be learned from the debate is that *what was obvious ceased to be so* and that, even when synods and councils reaffirmed it, denial or less than full acceptance of the humanity of Christ resurfaced periodically. In 451 Chalcedon had to define that Christ was *truly* man and *of one being* with us, in symmetry with what Nicaea had said about his divinity a century earlier. And over two centuries later, in 681, the Third Council of Constantinople had to define his truly human will. What cannot be seen (his divinity) was defined first and upheld with greater ease than what can be seen (his humanity). This makes one think.

At the time there were various reasons for this: the cultural environment of Gnosticism; the theoretical difficulty of accepting a complete human nature once the "of one being with the Father" had been defined; the existential repugnance at accepting a divinity affected by limitation, indignity, and suffering. Nowadays things are different, but people live without Jesus and effectively reject him, and we can speak of a new Docetism, the existence of an esoteric Christ in various guises.

Many people are seeking an esoteric Christ who will give meaning to millions of miserable lives—which is perfectly understandable. Others seek Christ—or his religious equivalents—in order to overcome the tedium induced by a civilization of wealth—which is less understandable. Furthermore, a human and committed Christ like Jesus is *avoided* and even *rejected* on account of the threat he poses to an established faith and church. There is still an (unconfessed) fear that a human Jesus, the one from Nazareth, will appear in the world and the church. "Don't come back," as the Grand Inquisitor pleaded with him!

When one takes this context into account, it can be useful and challenging to recall the conciliar debates. In this sense the first concern has to be to uphold the humanity of Christ. Despite the theoretical *impasses* to which simultaneous confession of the human and the divine in Christ led, the councils produced ever clearer statements on his humanity and refused to break the tension by denying either his transcendence or his immanence. By doing so, even though the councils give the impression of knowing too much, they actually show that they know rather little. In other words, the excess of knowledge carries the essential element of renouncing a definitive knowledge (*chastity* of understanding), which is a guarantee that they are dealing with ultimate mystery. Furthermore, the knowledge they built up about the humanity of Christ unfolded in an atmosphere that encouraged devaluation of it: it was a *victory*. What mattered was being true to the essential: Jesus Christ, divine, is perfectly human.

It is also positive that the councils presented the true humanity of Christ "without frills" (either human or superhuman), as I commented when discussing the title high priest. The councils do not mention any addition to the humanity of Christ but rather reject the great temptation of the period: to use divinity as the great "add-on." On the contrary, his divinity coexists with his humanity, but without mixture or confusion, as Chalcedon formulated in all clarity. It does not come to the aid of humanity; this relies only on itself, with all its possibilities and limitations. The councils stress that Christ has *everything* human (body, soul, will), but *only* what is common to all human beings. (It is perhaps worth recalling that the councils did not actualize Christ's humanity in either his maleness—with its supposed superiority over femaleness—or his Jewishness. Such qualifications are not determining for making Christ a human being—united to God and saving.) That Jesus would have had, for example, besides the knowledge he acquired, an *additional* vision of God and infused knowledge, were problems medieval theology would grapple with, but they were not very important in the Patristic Age, and certainly not for the Antiochenes, great defenders of the humanity of Christ and at the same time prepared calmly to admit their possible lack of knowledge. (The Alexandrian tradition, more focused on the divinization of Christ, along with Augustine, was different, propounding the idea of an understanding of Christ free of any ignorance.)

(b) The Need: To Recover the Dialectic and Specification of Christ's Humanity

I have made the point that, where Christ's humanity is concerned, we need to go beyond the councils, formally as well as materially, since it is not enough to assert that Christ is truly human, which they indeed do. We need to add that in him is shown what is truly human—which they do not do. From this angle, and from its consequences in the present, the councils reveal two serious deficiencies: lack of dialectic, and lack of specification of what is human. The synoptics and the letter to the Hebrews show Christ as human in a specific form and against inhumanity, but this is not expressed by the councils.

(i) Lack of dialectic about humanity. The dialectical perspective for proclaiming the humanity of Christ is still needed today. When recovery of the humanity of Christ began, there was an insistence on *demythification*, on the assumption that a Christ without true humanity finally becomes a myth, but also on the—precipitate—assumption that everything human is already humanizing. Nevertheless, it is clear that a simple return to Christ's humanity has not resolved the problem. It is possible to be "factually" human, with no mythic tinge and no hint of divinity, and yet be "inhuman" through hubris in the face of mystery and unconcern and oppression in relation to others. This is the world we live in, the world of genocide in Rwanda and the destruction of the Amazon rainforest.

The opposite of humanity is, then, not merely absence or lack of humanity, but inhumanity. And this we have to fight against. So a demythification that leaves room for Jesus' humanity is not enough: his humanity has to be proclaimed as triumphing over inhumanity. The synoptics present this graphically in the scenes of the temptations: Jesus is not a cosmic or celestial messiah (which takes care of the basic demythification) but a human messiah. But this still does not tell us what the problem in the temptations is: it is whether to be a serving or an imposing messiah, whether to be a messiah in human or inhuman mode. So the actual *way* in which Jesus exercises his messiahship should be seen as *victory* over an inhuman messiahship.

(ii) Lack of specification of humanity. Lack of specificity is another serious limitation of the councils. According to the New Testament, true humanity consists of *faithfulness* to God, letting God be God; *mercy* toward other people; and *surrender* of self. It also involves *fellowship and solidarity*, which is why Christ is presented in the New Testament as not only *human* but as a *brother* (Heb 2:11). Finally, it also means upholding these specifications, journeying to the end and in preparedness to surrender one's very life.

All this, so clear in the New Testament, has not always been so throughout history. Confession of the true humanity (and divinity) of Christ has been articulated as though the existence of the church depended on it. But the fact that this humanity takes the form of fellowship and that it provides the—christological—basis for the human family and for solidarity among people has not had repercussions in either the dogma or the life of the church. For centuries, the church has not been able to see "brothers and sisters" but only "others"; worse still, it has seen "rivals" or even "enemies" in very many of the inhabitants of the planet. Vatican II stated that "by his incarnation, the Son of God has united himself with everyone" (*Gaudium et Spes*, no. 22). But it is essential to understand this humanity in terms of fellowship. Progressive and liberal theologies have upheld the humanity of Jesus to save him from myth. But his fellowship and solidarity have not been upheld with the same zeal, producing the risk of falling into self-centeredness and even selfishness.

(c) The Challenge to Be Real

To end this chapter on the humanity of Christ, let me say that this can well work as a sort of "reality principle" within christology and lead us to consider the "reality" dimension of our lives, individually, as Christians, and within the church. Perhaps I may be allowed a personal reflection on the matter. In my view, those of us who live as a minority on the planet—those who are able to take life for granted—have the basic problem of becoming *real*. We can ask ourselves if we are human, if we are Christians, if we are on the way of perfection, if—as we asked earlier—we are authentic. But, as I see it, in our world such language still does not express a more fundamental and primary problem: if we are *real*, it is in a world in which the vast majorities, unlike ourselves, cannot take life for granted. So the first thing we have to do is ask ourselves seriously what this matter of "being real" in the world means; then we have to ask whether, in relation to this meaning, we are living as exceptions and footnotes, so to speak, in social Docetism and metaphysical appearance.

Personally, I have always been impressed by Ellacuría the philosopher's apprehension of reality as, above all, inhuman poverty, the cruel and unjust deaths of most people—to the point where he dared to challenge Heidegger: "Perhaps, instead of asking why there is something and not nothing [Heidegger's well-known question in *Was ist Metaphysik?*], he should have asked himself why there is 'non-'—non-being, non-reality, non-truth and so on—instead of 'entity.'"[12] And Ellacuría the theologian insisted, as I have said many times, that "among so many signs as always appear, some challenging and others barely perceptible, there is in every age one that is the main one, in the light of which all the others should be discerned and interpreted. This sign is always the people crucified in history."[13]

Ellacuría's words express reality on the basis of its flagrant denial. They should not be read masochistically, but they need to be read so that, among other things, they can help us to understand what we mean by "being real." Being real at the present time means, above all, being actively involved in the most solid reality, that of unjust poverty and indignity, allowing oneself to be affected by it and responding adequately to it. In negative terms, if Bosnia, Kosovo, Rwanda, and Congo do not affect us deeply, do not move our hearts and minds, then we are not living in reality in any shape or form, and not only are we not ethical or Christian or authentic or saints but we are not real; we are unreal. We shall have become exceptions or footnotes; we shall have fabricated an alternative reality (which may be historical, cultural, or religious) in which to live.

If this reality of the sin of the world, with its corresponding desires and hopes, with the goodness and the joy of the victims, does not shape our whole being, our knowledge, our hope, our work, and our celebration, we are not real. In more existential terms, if we have not at some point felt shame at living on an unjust and cruel planet, one that we have made with our own hands, and in a human *family* that is no such thing but more like a *species*, now divided into two subspecies, those who live and those who die, then we are not real—and worse still if we despise the great majority of our brothers and sisters who are poor, marginalized, and victims. In positive terms, when our joy consists in—truly—celebrating the triumphs, little or great, of the poor, then we are real.

The problem of being unreal or real should be expressed on various levels, including the ethical one, without doubt, but it goes deeper. In Kantian terms, it consists in being wrapped in a sleep we now call that of unreality, the root of many evils. "How are you sunk in such lethargic sleep?," Antonio Montesinos flung at the Spaniards on Hispaniola five centuries ago. In order to be real we have to begin to awaken from this sleep; this is the founding grace of a new life.

A word is needed from this perspective on ecclesial Docetism and how to overcome it, even if it seems that the church has no such problem. It is often said, for example, that we must love the real church, but *real* here means simply "as it is." The problem of the limitations and sins stemming from the church's institutionalizing are often ideologized by appealing to "incarnation." My comment is simply that there is no doubt that the church is as it is and that it exists in this world. But this does not make it real in the sense explored above; within its "reality" in the sense of "being as it is," it can still be Docetist. And as darkness gives way to light, let us look at this from the positive example of what a real church is.

Many things can be said about Archbishop Romero, including that he built up an evangelizing church. I should rather say that, above all, he built up a "real" church. This Salvadoran church, together with impressive achievements, had its limitations, errors, and faults, but no one could doubt that it was Salvadoran and real. As Romero said in a homily preached September 15, 1979, "I rejoice, brothers and sisters, that the church should be persecuted, precisely on account of its preferential option for the poor and for trying to take flesh in the interest of the poor." Or, even more forcefully on June 24 of that year, "It would be sad if, in a country where assassinations are taking place on such a horrific scale, priests too were not found among the victims. They are the testimony of a church incarnate in the problems of the people." In case it might be thought that the reality I am asking for in the church is masochism, for Romero the church was real also because it was the place for expressing grace, faith, commitment, and the hopes and values of the people of El Salvador. This is what moved him to say: "With this people it is not hard to be a good shepherd" (November 18, 1979). These are not words only for piety or even only for commitment; they are also for clarity, for finding criteria by which to evaluate whether the church is real or not. Archbishop Romero's church certainly was. Conversely, a church that is not poor in a time of poverty, that is not persecuted when people are being murdered, that is not committed at times of commitment or does not inspire commitment in a time of indifference, that has no hope in times of hope or does not encourage hope in times of discouragement, that does not celebrate when the poor celebrate or try to console them in times of sorrow—this is not a real church. It might say, subtly or brutally, that this is not what it is mainly for. It might say, more sophisticatedly, that its first concern is to proclaim the word of God. But the result is the same: distancing itself from reality, and so unreality. This has been the ecclesiological translation, throughout history, of the old christological Docetism. Hence the need and urgency to recall that, over many centuries, Christian faith has depended on proclaiming the humanity of Christ—and this is what the church has struggled for.

Perhaps these reflections may help to bring back a sense of the importance of the "*vere* homo" of christology, of the fact that God did truly take on a *human nature*. And, conversely, the conciliar declarations may perhaps help us to take reality seriously and to fight against unreality.

John's text, "And the Word became flesh and lived among us" (1:14), expresses not an abstract "becoming" by God but, if one can use such words, a "will to reality" on God's part, a will to become real in the flesh of not just anyone but of the poor and the victims. (This understanding of *sarx* as the weakness of the flesh is the one that probably became current in the first two centuries, as in Tertullian, for example. Later, the terminology of *human nature* was more widely used.) This will to be *sarx* operates as the "reality principle." But, let us recall, this "will to reality" (the taking on of a human nature, as it was expressed at the time) was from the first the most debated principle in the church. It was easier to accept the divinity of Christ than it was to accept his humanity. And, right down to the present, the major problem is still *Docetism* in christology and *unreality* in the church.

Perhaps these reflections may also help us to progress beyond the "*vere* homo" and to see in Jesus Christ the "homo *verus*." In today's world we have lost the innocence of humanity depending simply on the possibilities of human nature: hence the need and desire for a Christ who will not only have a "human nature" but will also be human in a "human" way. This has to be upheld in times of crisis and in periods of ordinariness. Francis of Assisi sought to be *repetitor Christi*.[14] Ignatius of Loyola sought "inner knowledge of the Lord so that I may love and follow him more."[15] At the dawn of liberation theology, José Miranda went back to "the humanity" of Christ with a specific purpose: "Christ died so that we should know that not everything is permitted, but not any Christ but the one whom reason cannot bring back, the historical Jesus."[16] Puebla established and praised the "legitimate longing for a liberator Christ" (no. 173). And so one can go on, to the petition Marxists used to address to Christians a few years ago: "Give us back Jesus." All this shows the importance of going back to Jesus of Nazareth, to the "homo *verus*."

Beyond christology, the humanity of Jesus is what Christianity can offer today so that humanity may have a future. Nietzsche proclaimed the death of God, but as Metz points out, with that he also proclaimed the death of humankind,[17] which might perhaps be seen today in the trivialization of existence and, above all, in callous indifference to the victims. From a believing point of view, this is a powerful argument for returning to the humanity of Jesus. And in symmetry with Nietzsche's prophetic cry, we might perhaps see the "resurrection" of humanity as the mystagogy leading to the "resurrection" of God.

Chapter 18

God in History

The Pathos of the Whole

1. The (Provisional) Culmination of a Process

Divinity and humanity are dimensions predicated of the being of Jesus Christ, but such predication still does not, strictly speaking, tell us who he is; even more, when both dimensions are upheld, this seems to become an impossible task. Despite this, discussion of Jesus Christ did not come to an end after the first two councils, and it is still impressive to see how theologians and council Fathers progressed farther and farther down a cul-de-sac without ceasing in their efforts to shed light on the mystery of Jesus Christ, driven by a sort of primal "honesty with reality." In my view, the greatness of Chalcedon consists in maintaining this honest *subjective* approach while keeping its *objective* correlative: the primacy given to the unity of the whole, even when this whole has to unite, without confusing, such distinct realities as transcendence and history. So Chalcedon was to affirm that Jesus Christ is one divine being—a comprehensible statement in principle—and not two, that he subsists in two forms of being, in two natures, human and divine, the relationship between the two of which it described with the well-known adverbs *inconfuse* (without confusion), *immutabiliter* (without change), *indivise* (without division), *inseparabiliter* (without separation).

Chalcedon was respectful of the reality and therefore did not attempt to make the *how* of the relationship between the two natures comprehensible. Furthermore, the four adverbs are defined in the negative, which means that the conciliar definition states what does *not* happen in the union of the natures but not what positively does. In doing so, it abandons any positive explanation of the mystery of Jesus Christ, but it does provide positive pointers to it. (From an epistemological point of view, christology can only show that "it is not contradictory for one 'actual human nature' to exist in personal fashion on a divine ontological level."[1] Beyond this classic statement, theology can, positively, clarify the specific epistemology needed for understanding the mystery of Jesus Christ and offer a mystagogy for doing so.)

Recalling Rahner's definition of God as "holy mystery," we can say that the definition helps us to progress in the *holy* dimension of the mystery: the irrevocable *approach* of God to human beings—*achoristos*, with no way back—in which mystery functions as "excess of luminosity." And it helps us to progress in what this "holy" has of *mystery*, not attempting to explain the *why* of this irrevocable approach—mystery functioning for us as "excess of darkness." By upholding the paradoxical unity of the being of Jesus Christ and not attempting to explain the *how* of the relationship between the divine and the human, Chalcedon affirms what in the subtitle to this chapter I have called "the pathos of the whole," without doing violence to this reality but respecting it as it is and in the hope that, at bottom, this reality is indeed one (good, true, saving) and not split apart into pieces.

In this chapter I am going to examine the Council of Chalcedon as the culmination of conciliar christological reflection, although in fact the question was not cut short and the debates continued for two centuries. First, I present a very brief history of the discussions that led to Chalcedon, so as to see what was at stake; then I provide a critical analysis and positive reinterpretation of the definition. In the following chapter I attempt a doxological rereading of the definition with the specific epistemology required, followed by a formal rereading in order to see what light Chalcedon sheds on reality: transcendence in history and the sacramental character of reality. The epilogue then examines the revolution in the concept of God that comes about through the *communicatio idiomatum*.

It hardly needs saying that Chalcedon is difficult to understand today, which means that it is usually simply ignored by normal believers and relegated to study by experts. Nevertheless, I am one of those who consider its definition to be important, not only for the purposes of the magisterium but for those of theology, since it can clarify the mystery of Jesus Christ and of God as well as the structure of reality. For its importance to emerge, however, the definition has to be considered from two viewpoints: *epistemologically*, as a *doxological* and not merely conceptual statement, and *metaphysically*, from its *formal* structure rather than from its actual contents.

Saying that the definition is a *doxological formulation* means that it makes a transcendent statement about the basis of historical situations, without these forcing the statement (even though they suggest it), that the definition can therefore be understood only by following the historical course that led to its promulgation and, in the end, by not attempting to control it. This involves surrendering our human nature, *sacrificium intellectus*—chastity of intelligence, we might say—all of which I believe to be good for human beings. In other words, the definition is an expression of faith, but it is so not only as a proposal made by a council so that it should be believed but, intrinsically, because its content can be grasped only through (surrender in) faith.

What I should like to make clear, in order to understand what was at stake in the Chalcedonian definition, is that there is no need to deceive oneself into thinking that it suffers *essentially* by comparison with New Testament ones, as if these were not equally doxological and did not share the same difficulty. When the New Testament says that in Christ "the grace of God has appeared, bringing salvation to all" (Ti 2:11), it is using more telling language, closer to everyday speech and so more accessible, and it is conveying the important message that Jesus is good news. When Acts says that God "raised [him] up" (2:32), or John's prologue that "the Word became flesh" (1:14), they are also using language that—as language—is more accessible than dogmatic language (though not as clear as the first example above) and that also picks up important traces of Jesus' being: his relationship with the Father, his coming to be, and so on. But none of this gives the New Testament definitions an *essential* epistemological advantage over dogmatic ones; they are equally not comprehensible in themselves but only through a course of learning and a surrender in faith. There is a difference between both types of definition, but this does not amount to a qualitative leap in the ease or difficulty of understanding what they are stating: a specific coexistence between transcendence and history. The conclusion to be drawn from this is that just as the New Testament definitions have to be taken doxologically and then express something important, the same is true of the dogmatic definitions, which can then, I believe, also tell us something important.

The definition also becomes telling and meaningful if it is read *from its formal structure*. This means that the whole is made up of various elements and that the important statement the definition makes is *what* reality is expressed through the *specific relationship* among these. To make the definition telling we need to analyze how its various elements, difficult to unify, are related: the final reality is made up and unified as such by maintaining and respecting its elements, however "un-unifiable" they may seem.

This process reaches its culmination in the being of Jesus Christ, but we can exchange realities and experiences that make it likely, with all appropriate analogies. The question then becomes whether there are "reverberations of Chalcedon" down through history. To answer this—mystagogically—I am going to take two experiences, one drawn from the personal sphere and one from the social. In doing so I remark that, methodologically, it seems important to compare the definition of Chalcedon not only with *texts* but also with *situations* that went before and came after it.

The type of personal experience to which I refer is well known as a tendency in religions: the human longing to be united to what is the Ultimate, the Divine. The biblical tradition also provides evidence of this longing through the metaphors it uses for the union between divinity and humanity: the union between husband and wife, the vine and the grapes, the body and the head. José Ignacio González Faus expresses it succinctly on the theoretical level: "The intuition of non-duality without identity is virtually a common heritage of humankind as the best expression of the relationship between God and the non-divine."[2]

The second type of experience lies in the social sphere, and to illustrate it I should like to bring in a conviction—a surprising one perhaps—that grew on me during the conflict in El Salvador. It concerns the work of the popular movements for liberation. To find some point of comparison with Chalcedon, let me say that the work of liberation can function here as the basic unity, with two different elements usually operating within it: religious faith (transcendent) and the struggle for justice (historical). The temptation that resulted was either for one dimension to merge with the other so as to absorb and weaken it or for both to go their separate ways without each drawing strength from the other. The lesson to be drawn is that both one thing (the mixture or cutting out that makes the identity proper to each dimension disappear) and the other (the division or separation that leaves one unrelated to the other) were harmful to the cause of liberation. In simple terms, it is good for liberation (the one reality) that the two dimensions (faith and justice) should exist. It is good that either should respect the identity of the other without absorbing it, should "let it be" in the reality of its own identity (just as it is good to "let God be God" and "let humans be human"), without forcing one dimension into the other and without them being separated. And it is bad that one should absorb the other, that politics should manipulate the people's piety so as to make it serve its purpose completely, or the other way around (violating "without mixture or confusion"); it is also bad that piety should detach itself from praxis, or the other way around (violating "without division or separation").

When this happens, both dimensions come out the losers, as does the overall reality. (The same loss has come about in very different historical situations, such as when the faith has tried to absorb history—in theocracies or Christendom—or, for believers, when secularism has tried to absorb religion.) When the irreducibility of both is maintained, on the one hand, together with their mutual reference, on the other, then both—faith and justice, transcendence and history—come out the winners: their single reality is more productive when its dimensions of transcendence and history are both respected and when the correct relationship between them is maintained, without reducing one to the other. (Both Romero, pastorally, and Ellacuría, theologically and politically, insisted on this, and this was perhaps one of the greatest contributions both made to the course of events in El Salvador, if not the fundamental one.)[3]

So much for the description of an experience and a conviction: Would it be too far-fetched to say that, from a formal point of view, the debates over Chalcedon and those over the work of liberation have something in common? However far this analogy can be taken, I believe all theologians (if not all the faithful) need to find some historical experience that will act as an analogy for them in helping them to interpret Chalcedon. In any case, the essence of Chalcedon consists in the pathos of maintaining the unified and differentiated whole that, existentially, shows itself in the hope that there can be unity—or, more precisely, union—with respect for acceptance of differences and in the trust that this respectful acceptance can unify further and better.

To end this rather long introduction, let me say a word about what the view of the victims can contribute. Basically, perhaps, just one thing: it can open our eyes to the relationship between God and what is small. In the first place, this means God taking on, and respecting, humanity not only as distinct from himself but as small, weak, limited, and mortal: "The union of God with humankind, as it came about in Jesus Christ, is historically a union between a God emptied of his primary version and the world of the poor."[4] In the second place, it means that the humanity God took on, in its littleness, reveals God, even if sometimes as the *Deus absconditus*.

2. A Short History

Let us begin with a brief account of what happened prior to Chalcedon. This summary will be superfluous for experts and perhaps too condensed for non-experts. Nevertheless, it seems to me important to give at least a minimal account of the *process* and *debate* through which the definition of the reality of Jesus Christ was produced. The first helps us to read the definition as a *doxological* formula, that is, as a statement that has to sum up the course followed (the process). The second helps us to read it in its *formal* aspect, that is, from what was at stake—the proper relationship between the human and the divine (the debate). In any case, I think it is important for us to feel (if that is an appropriate term) that, given the direction taken by christological thinking in the Greco-Roman world, Chalcedon "hit the mark," that it not only formulated the vision of those who won the debate but also expressed a truth that opened the way to "more."

(a) The Debate before Chalcedon

Once the true divinity and humanity of Christ had been accepted, the obvious problem was that of the relationship between the two: whether and how they made up a single whole. Broadly speaking, by the fourth century two schools of thought had come into being, those of Alexandria and Antioch. The former emphasized the divinity and thereby apparently facilitated understanding of unity, but with the tendency to do so to the detriment of the humanity; the second emphasized the humanity, which made it difficult to understand its unity with the divinity. From the viewpoint of soteriology, in the former the theoretical model for understanding salvation would be divinization, the work of God; in the latter, through the stress laid on the full humanity of Christ, salvation came to be understood as the reparation of humankind (in the West as expiation of sin), the outcome of the work of Jesus. This was the context that produced the great christological dispute during the fifth century, which started with a series of sermons on the Virgin Mary. The polemic was unleashed by an apparently minor event. The community of Bishop Nestorius (d. *c.* 451) of Constantinople was divided over calling Mary the Mother of God *(theotokos)*. The priest Proclus upheld this in his sermons, while Nestorius's chaplain Anastasius contradicted him: "If anyone calls Mary Mother of God, let him be anathema." Nestorius became a third party to the debate with the thesis that "Mary did not bear the divinity in her womb . . . but a man made the instrument of divinity, and the Holy Spirit did not make the God-Word from the Virgin . . . but made her a temple for him" (*Sermo* 8).

This denial of the title *theotokos* was consistent with Nestorius's christology. He accepted both the complete divinity and humanity of Jesus Christ, but the unity between them did not reach the deepest level of his being; it was rather of a moral nature, like that of "the captain of a ship." In more sophisticated language, he claimed that the unity was brought about by God assuming humanity, for which process he used the term *prosopon*, meaning the mask used by actors to represent a character in the theater. Ultimately, Nestorius was trying to safeguard the *true* humanity of Christ against vestiges of Arianism (the superman) and Apollinarianism (the non-man), and could not find a way of sharing this with his divinity. So he made Christ's final being a third thing, in which divinity and humanity were both present.

The opposing christology was represented by Cyril of Alexandria, whose primary concern was to safeguard the unity in Christ, although to do so he risked putting his true humanity at risk (basically following in the line of Athanasius and *logos-sarx* christology). Cyril upheld the famous definition *mya physis sesarkomene* (one nature—of the divine Word—made flesh) derived from the Apollinarians, who disseminated it as though coming from Athanasius, which produced Cyril's tenacity in upholding it. After endless debates and disturbances— Nestorius's sermons being sent to Cyril and to Pope Celestine, two harsh letters sent from Cyril to Nestorius (and corresponding replies), delegates sent by both parties to Rome, and Nestorius being condemned by the Synod of Rome in 430— the emperor Theodosius convened a general council to be held at Ephesus in 431.[5]

From a dogmatic point of view, the council approved only Cyril's second letter to Nestorius (February 430; *Creeds*, pp. 296–98), which dealt with the whole problem of the unity of the two natures. Its essence can be summed up in the following five points (see DS 250): (1) Christ is a true unity (Cyril's insistence) and not a moral or apparent unity (as Nestorius seemed to imply through his use of the term *prosopon*); (2) this unity does not suppose that the Word ceased to be fully divine in becoming flesh but that he went on being so; (3) this unity requires the "joining" of two natures that are distinct, and the means by which they are joined is *hypostasis* (a difficult term to translate, but not the same as *physis*); (4) concerning the humanity of Christ, this is made up of body and soul and so is a complete and true human nature; (5) thanks to this unity, one can say that Mary was the Mother of God, and in general whatever is predicated of the man Jesus can be predicated of God (a statement present in embryo in Ignatius of Antioch and culminating in the *communicatio idiomatum*).

Ephesus did not succeed in bringing peace to the opposing factions, and in 433 a "symbol of union" was drawn up, probably composed by Bishop Theodoret of Cyrrhus, through which the Antiochenes sought to eliminate all vestiges of Apollinarianism in Cyril, while recognizing his strong insistence on unity. This definition also failed to bring peace. Cyril gave the impression of backtracking and expressed mistrust of the Antiochenes. A sympathizer of his, Eutyches, archimandrate of the Cyrillian monks of Constantinople, rejected the definition and accused its defenders of Nestorianism. "Our Lord—it says—is (the product) of two natures, but after their union I confess that he is of only one nature" is the formula he repeated. So once again the divine nature takes over the human nature. In ever more sophisticated language, the basic problem, the true humanity of Christ, keeps reappearing.

In 448 Flavinius, patriarch of Constantinople, convoked a synod, put forward a compromise definition, and condemned Eutyches. The following year, in support of Eutyches, the emperor convoked a further council at Ephesus, presided over and manipulated by Dioscorus, bishop of Alexandria, who was a supporter of Eutyches. He refused to allow Pope Leo I's "Tome to Flavian" (bishop of Constantinople) to be read out, rehabilitated Eutyches, and deposed Flavian; the council broke up in violence. From a theological point of view it represented a complete triumph for the Monophysite Alexandrian line taken by Eutyches. On hearing what had happened, Pope Leo exclaimed, "*In illo Ephesino non iudicio sed latrocinio*" ("That synod of Ephesus was not a judgment but a robbery"), from which it has generally been known as the "Robber Synod."

With the death of the eastern emperor Theodosius II and the accession of Marcian in 450, the tide turned against Eutyches. The emperor convoked a new ecumenical council, due to be held at Nicaea, but because he could not be there in person, he transferred it to the city of Chalcedon, from where he would be able to follow it more closely. Pope Leo I, opposed to a new council for fear of the disturbances it might cause, tried to have it held in the West but without success. He then tried to prevent it from tackling doctrinal issues and to confine it to disciplinary ones, so that the Nestorian line might be reinstated in the reaction against Eutyches, but he failed in this too. In effect, the council was controlled by imperial officers for its duration, from October 8 to November 1, 451. Some six hundred eastern bishops took part, together with the papal legates and two bishops from Africa. The debates took place in a rarified atmosphere and led to the condemnation of Dioscorus, the isolating of his supporters, and the condemnation of the "Robber Synod" of 449, on the one hand, and the recognition of the orthodoxy of Flavian (who had died on his way into exile in 449) and that of various other theologians who had been condemned with him, on the other. In the midst of these upheavals the most important of all conciliar dogmatic definitions on Christ was made.[6]

(b) Chalcedon's Definition

It is worth recalling that the council Fathers were not minded to produce a new definition; it was the emperor who required it in order to do away with divisions, and this produced two new developments in comparison with previous councils. The first was that the council did not produce a new symbol of faith, a narrative pastoral *credo*; the second that it composed a theoretical-technical text. What began at Nicaea with the term *homoousios* reached its conclusion at Chalcedon. The council Fathers themselves were aware of the pastoral difficulties this would cause and so recognized that this language was not suitable for catechesis or needed for affirming true faith in Jesus Christ, being designed only for the refutation of heresy. This is what they said:

> Wherefore, following the holy Fathers [of Nicaea], we all with one voice confess our Lord Jesus Christ one and the same Son, the same perfect in Godhead, the same perfect in manhood, truly God and truly man, the same consisting of a reasonable soul and a body, of one substance with the Father as touching the Godhead, the same of one substance with us as touching the manhood, like us in all things apart from sin [Heb 4:15]; begotten of the

Father before the ages as touching the Godhead, the same in the last days, for us and for our salvation, born from the Virgin Mary, the *Theotokos*, as touching the manhood.

We confess one and the same Christ, Son, Lord, Only-begotten, to be acknowledged in two natures, without confusion, without change, without division, without separation; the distinction of natures being in no way abolished because of the union, but rather the characteristic property of each nature being preserved, and concurring into one Person and one substance [*hypostasis*], not as if Christ were parted or divided into two persons, but one and the same Son and only-begotten God, Word, Lord, Jesus Christ. (DS 301, 302; *Creeds*, pp. 352–53)

Properly speaking, this definition proclaimed nothing fundamentally new in relation to earlier councils: the true divinity, the true humanity, and the true union of Christ. Nevertheless, because it had to take a stand in relation to the debates then raging, it brought out essential truths. These are summarized below.

(i) The divine-human relationship. I begin with the second paragraph of the definition—which, in a way, is intended to be explanatory—as it is the one that supports the statement—not explanation—of what is put forward in the first paragraph as doxological statement. Its basic novelty lies in the words "in two natures," which does a fundamental service to the true humanity. Before then, the usual expression was "*from* two natures," which left mainly in the shadows what happened to the humanity once the union between divine and human had taken place in Christ. The expression "in two natures" stresses that the human nature goes on being true, even after having been taken on by the Word.

The definition insists that the relationship between the two natures does not erase their difference: the divine goes on being divine and the human goes on being human; it also stresses the specific relationship between them: "without confusion, without change, without division, without separation," all negative (Greek *a-;* Latin *in-*) adverbs, denoting that they are not trying to explain "how" the union functions but to safeguard it from false interpretations. The relationship between divine and human comes about without confusion and without change, which is stated to counter the latent danger of Apollinarianism, the divine element swallowing up the human, and against Eutychianism, which makes it disappear. Furthermore, the relationship is without division, stated against the Nestorian danger of dividing transcendence from history, and without separation, against the danger of making the relationship reversible. In simple terms, God has taken the decision to "tie himself" to humanity, "respecting it." And, the other way around, humanity—and the weak side of humanity at that—is declared capable of being the bearer of God, without ceasing to be human and weak. Humanity keeps its own identity without the need to borrow anything from another reality, not even the divinity. And this is forever, irreversibly.

In this way, using the relationship between transcendence and history, even if in an abstruse formulation, the council proclaimed what constituted the mystery of Christ. Christ is the unrepeatable and supreme expression of reality through the specific relationship between divinity and humanity found only in him. What needs to be emphasized is that not even the Chalcedonian definition "claims to explain, ultimately 'how' God and man coexist in Christ, and this is the very reason for the mystery, which cannot be understood through any positive definition,"[7] and in this way it maintains the mystery of the being of Christ—and, by derivation, the mystery of all human life. So the definition expresses mystery as *fact*.

Besides this, however, it also introduces a basic *content* into mystery. Put as simply as possible: "there is not the one without the other, always respecting the fact that the other is other." The definition is, then, the expression of a metaphysical respect for existence; each ambit of existence has its proper identity, which has to be respected. God—even at the moment of becoming human—does not manipulate humanity to his advantage but lets it be as it is, including its limitation: this formed the crux of christological debates over centuries. Equally, humankind—even at the moment of being taken on by God—cannot manipulate God to its advantage.

God in Jesus goes on being God, which is why not even Jesus' story deprives him of the element of mystery, with its characteristics of unpredictability and unmalleability. Our response to Jesus Christ has to be faith, but not faith that is just received belief; it has to be faith that enables us to correspond to the divinity expressed in him. And humanity in Jesus goes on being human, not only with its proper limitations but with its proper possibilities, which enable him to humanize and save, but not by going beyond or against them as though he could exercise a super-power or super-science.

All this is said to be "forever": the relationship between divinity and humanity is *inseparabiliter, achoristos,* "with no turning back." The fact that existence is like that in Jesus Christ is, then, no "experiment" on God's part, waiting for results so as then to take a definitive decision; it already is God's irrevocable decision. God, forever, has come to humanity and has also placed himself at the mercy of humanity. Humanity is, forever, what can be and has been taken on by God, however small and weak it may be. Furthermore, in the way God became human in the event, humanity was what was weak and small, *sarx.* This is good news both through what it says and through the seriousness with which it is said: "forever." And the result is that from that moment on there will be no other way for humanity to go to God, and also that anything truly human will always be a way to God. (This is another definition of humanity "without additions"—though "with actualizations"—spoken of above.)

(ii) The unity of Jesus Christ. In order to safeguard his humanity, Nestorius tended to divide Christ, whereas Cyril emphasized his unity—though leaving some suspicions about what happened to his humanity. Chalcedon resolved the question by stating that in Christ there is a *prosopon,* a *hypostasis,* translated as "person," which subsists in two natures. The positive statement being made is that Christ is a unity and is not divided into two parts. But the language and imagery employed, seen from today, can only lead to confusion and even to error. To overcome this problem, I am not going to try to find new concepts equivalent to those of

Chalcedon that might make the definition comprehensible. (Theology made many attempts at this some decades ago, speaking, for example, of "the working of the created act through the uncreated act" to relate nature and person. The attempt can be compared to that of finding more telling and meaningful terms to express the real presence of Christ in the eucharist, such as transignification or transfinalization, to replace the discredited transubstantiation.) I propose merely to attempt to paraphrase the definition in order to bring out its deeper meaning and its saving significance.

For a start, Chalcedon does not say what it means by *hypostasis* (subsistence). And where the language of *nature* is concerned, to speak of a divine "nature" is a contradiction *in obliquo*, since the God who becomes present in Jesus Christ is not, as we have seen, repeatable, and so cannot be abstracted or adequately described by the concept of *nature*. Where the "human" nature of Jesus Christ is concerned, the problem is of another kind: one can speak, without offending logic, of *nature*, but this then excludes his history, and this, as we shall see, is the source of practically all the limitations of Chalcedon. With regard to the plural "natures," it is clear that here the concept of nature cannot serve as a genus to which two species can belong, one divine and the other human. The unity resulting from these two "natures" cannot, therefore, be a sum of the two or a sort of "supernature." (We shall see later that the concept of *sacrament* can serve to express this unity better.)

What the definition is positively seeking to express is that what makes these two realities subsist in one is divine, but a further clarification is needed. This divine principle does not cancel out the totality of what we today call "person." The definition states that this ultimate principle is *prosopon* or *hypostasis*, which led to the union of the two natures being called the "hypostatic union." But we must remember that for Chalcedon the term *person* is ontological, not anthropological, and so, as we saw in the previous chapter, it is perfectly possible (as the definition logically takes for granted) for Christ's human nature to possess qualities we should today call personal, such as freedom, self-awareness, moral dignity. What Chalcedon is then stating is that what is ultimate and uncommunicable in the actual being of Christ is in the Son, not in his human nature. "This actual nature, by the mere fact that it does not determine any mode of being of its own, exists in another totality: its mode of being is that of the Son, its manner of being and of 'owning itself' is the same as that of the Word of God."[8] Chalcedon is affirming that the humanity of Jesus Christ subsists in the Son, has its existence in the gift of God to humankind. By this it means, simply and deeply, that what is "ultimate" in Christ is divine.

Using a more biblical and dynamic terminology we could perhaps say the same thing in other words by stating that the overall reality called Christ is God's "initiative" and that this initiative is what makes him *be*, what calls his human nature into being, what "personalizes" him. As for content, in the language of the gospels Jesus Christ is "God with us," "the goodness of God appeared among us," "the word of God who has pitched his tent among us." As for coming to be this, at the *start* of everything there is God. Jesus Christ does not come from "blood or the will of the flesh" but "of God" (Jn 1:13). What is at the start is always God's initiative, God's love (cf. 1 Jn 4:10). This initiative is what makes humanity *be* in taking it on or what takes on humanity, making it be. What Chalcedon does is to root God's initiative in Christ and proclaim that this God *is* now really in humanity and that humanity is *from* God. From the salvational viewpoint this radically upholds the fact that the initiative for salvation comes from God and that salvation, in the final analysis, consists in the fulfillment of what every human being is inchoately: in deiformation.

This ultimateness Chalcedon gives to the basic unity—despite being dual—of Jesus Christ is a radical overcoming of all Manicheism, Marcionism, and dualism. The ultimate is not dispersion but recapitulation, not disencounter but encounter. The ultimate is the utopia of the last time, when "God [will] be all in all" (1 Cor 15:28), anticipated in Jesus Christ. One final observation, already suggested: unity is not achieved at the expense of identity; it does not "de-nature" the "natures," and so we can say that this unity is enriching, because it unites what is diverse, and that it has a dynamic potential through the dialectic established within diversity.

3. Limitations: Criticism and Reinterpretation

It is a commonplace of contemporary theology to criticize the definition of Chalcedon. To take just one example, B. Sesböué makes the following observations, reading the definition with modern eyes;

> (1) Chalcedon employs an inadequate conceptual language. (2) Its dualist scheme introduces a fictitious oneness into the term "nature." (3) And it calls the unity of Christ into question. (4) Chalcedon is concerned with a christology from above. (5) It proposes a Christ deprived of human personality. (6) It ignores the historical dimension. (7) The aftermath of Chalcedon has shown that the council failed to resolve the christological problem.[9]

The basic limitation of the definition, the root of all its others, is its concept of nature, which excludes history from its understanding of reality and historicity from its understanding of being human. For purely pedagogical reasons I am going to group the criticisms into three: lack of the concrete, lack of historicity, and lack of relationality. As for the content, these limitations affect major theological areas: revelation, salvation, christology, theology, and so on. I shall try to reinterpret them going beyond the Chalcedonian definitions, and in doing so I take account—without forcing it—of the view of the victims.

(a) Lack of the Concrete

(i) The non-revelatory universal. The definition uses the universal terms *divinity* and *humanity,* thereby giving the impression that it knows—at least in principle— what was divine and what was human before Jesus appeared. In this way, strictly speaking, the definition is not serving original revelation.

Universal concepts prevent the content of the definition from being seen as an expression of *revelation*. And as, furthermore, these concepts are abstract, reason is left with the choice of filling them with actual contents, which can be done in three ways. Reason (that believes) can specify the contents *from a Christian standpoint*, allowing itself to be guided by (the story of) Jesus. But it can also do so *inadequately*, even with good intentions, reading this story selectively and eliminating from it what does not fit with its previously held universal concept of human and divine nature. And it can do so *sinfully*, deciding on its own account what is human and what is divine, even against the evidence provided by Jesus—a possibility that cannot be ruled out, since human reason is also concupiscent, is subject to hubris and is inclined to suppress the truth.

I am speaking in general terms and of possibilities, but history shows that such possibilities become actualities as often as not. In other words, the universality of the definition has not put a brake (either in speculation or in pastoral practice) on many aberrations in the presentation of Jesus Christ. The conclusion is that the Chalcedonian definition can be read as a true statement but not as a vehicle of revelation, as a questioning of our image of God and of humanity, or as good news that God is like this and humanity is like this.

Christian revelation, however, has a distinct and even contrary logic, and this is expressed most radically in christology. We know who God is and what being human is from Christ and not the other way around. God is not any divinity but the Father of Jesus, and being human is not simply possessing a reasonable animal essence—however "complete," "perfect," and "true" this may be—but being like Jesus. Otherwise christology empties revelation of its questioning and evangelical character, deprives reason of the grace of "letting itself be given truth," and can even collaborate in the hubris that usually accompanies such knowledge. As with the application of titles to Jesus, there is an application of concepts to Christ that can hide rather than reveal.

(ii) Revelation: the relationship expressed in the four negative adverbs. Despite this limitation, the definition does contain a decisive element in the service of revelation of God by stating *how* the two (supposedly known) realities, divine and human, are related to one another—a relationship that not only is not known beforehand but, even after being declared, remains beyond the control of reason. For the union to be hypostatic and in the form expressed by the four negative adverbs is a mystery in the strict sense. *Epistemologically*, its understanding is "given to us"; *existentially*, for God to be like this "makes a difference." God appears as redoubled mystery in *taking on* non-divine being together with his own divine being—and in the manner of the four negatives. At the risk of tautology, Chalcedon shows that the christological mystery is a possibility in God. In God there exists the possibility of creating something that, while different from God, belongs to God, and that God should create this in order to be able to express himself to himself.[10] This God is a "new" God, and so there is revelation here. This is a *mystery* God, "incomprehensible," who does not cease to be a mystery even when revealed. And this God is *holy* mystery, good news, "good that God should be so," who relates to humanity in this way, without diminishing

humanity but respecting it. And it is also good news that this union should be forever, irrevocable. The correlation of this active possibility in God to relate to humanity in this way is the possibility in human beings of being taken on by God, which makes them "pure reference to God" and sharers in the mystery, "indefinability brought to itself."[11] This is also good news.

Putting divinity and humanity into this specific relationship—not merely accepting their coexistence and juxtaposition—was the *formal* revelatory achievement of Chalcedon. The council gave direct expression to what the reality of Jesus Christ is but also to the mutual reference between God and humanity, so that—after God's free self-determination to be "like this"—this reference becomes essential to any definition of what being divine and being human means. God actualizes his mystery christologically. God is the possibility, made reality, of taking on humanity. Being human is the possibility, made reality, of being taken on by God.

(iii) Further limitation: lack of specificity in the relationship. A formal reading of the definition—as opposed to a simple translation of its concepts into more modern ones—can still be fruitful. But the limitations remain, even within this formal reading. In speculative terms we have to ask what this divinity that has the capacity for taking on non-divinity is, what this humanity that has the capacity for being taken on by non-humanity is.

In the definition—and here I come back to the lack of history—the divinity that takes on humanity is not presented as the God of the Exodus, of the prophets, of the beatitudes, of the Kingdom, of the cross, of the resurrection. Nor does the humanity taken on appear as being weak and victim on the one hand, or compassionate, altruistic, and committed on the other. The hypostatic union may be the highest expression of the relationship between God and humankind, between transcendence and history, in symbolic and dramatic terms, but it does not show—as actually happened—an actual God present in an actual Jesus or this actual Jesus making this actual God present.

This still leaves the question of why this hypostatic union took place between *this* God and *this* human being rather than between a powerful God and an important personage. It is a good thing to ask ourselves this question, not because it has an answer but because it refers us back to the "original surprise," fortunate or scandalous depending on one's point of view, of God's manifestation and self-communication. Without actualizing God and humanity, christology can present the hypostatic union as a "drama" and an "aesthetic," but it will not have—even if this seems a comparatively modest requirement—a "history" of God's compassion and mercy toward the victims of this world.

This is why we have to come back not only to the grandiose-conceptual but also to the actual-real. And this is where the essential relationship between a God of the victims and victims who rely on God does indeed appear. The "Father of orphans and protector of widows . . . God" (Ps 68:5), the God of the Kingdom for the poor, becomes reality: God is a God poured out to weakness, and weakness has been taken up into God.

To finish this section, let me say that starting from this point makes the assertion of God's presence in the world of the poor (on which Latin American liberation theology has insisted so much) more understandable: "Just as you did it to . . . the least of these who are members of my family, you did it to me" (Mt 25:40; cf. Medellín, *Peace*, no. 14); "With particular tenderness he chose to identify himself with those who are poorest and weakest" (Puebla, no. 196); "The sign of the times is always the crucified people" (Ellacuría).

The view of the victims does not, naturally, create the grandiose idea of the hypostatic union, but it does—modestly—point to the way to make it actual and to safeguard its specifically Christian content. Is there in God a self-determination to express himself in what is weak and little, in the poor and the victims, in service and solidarity? And, conversely, do poverty and solidarity contain a likeness of nature to divinity? These are the Christian questions.

(b) Lack of History

Conceptualizing Jesus' being in terms of "nature" diffuses his actual being,[12] can serve even to deny or distort it, and leads theology into dangerous paths. (Wiederkehr's words can stand for many: "There is no denying that there is a danger . . . in the powerful tendency to abstract formalization. As the abstractness of terminology increased, so the actual content of the human subject 'Jesus of Nazareth' and the theological profiles of the 'God and Father of Jesus Christ' were diluted.") I therefore propose to examine the definition in three of its expressions, turning to the history of Jesus to move beyond it.

(i) Perfection and imperfection. Docetism, Apollinarianism, and Monophysitism all have the devaluation of the humanity of Jesus Christ in common. The question is why this tendency is so recurrent, why by the year 451 Chalcedon still had to state that Jesus Christ *is* consubstantial with us, *is* truly human. Even in the seventh century it was difficult to allow Christ a human will insofar as that will expressed true humanity.

The burden of this resistance to accepting the humanity of Jesus Christ, even though it is clear from the New Testament, is that it is not congruent with divinity to unite itself to humanity *because* humanity is imperfect, changes, comes to be, is subject to temptation, crisis, suffering, death. . . . These aspects, undeniably attributed to Jesus in the New Testament, are seen as negation and limitation *because* humanity is understood in the conceptual terms of *nature*: hence the logical tendency to Docetism.

Looked at from *history*, however, and from the corresponding *historicity*, such limitations need not necessarily mean negation but can even be seen as positive aspects of humanity. So the New Testament does not fight shy of mentioning Jesus' crises and temptations, and the synoptics give them a lengthy treatment, so that—from the viewpoint of this section—the most important thing about the account of the temptations is the fact that it was written at all. Nor does it fight shy of saying the Son does not know "the day" of the coming of the Kingdom and is mistaken in proclaiming it close at hand. The New Testament writers state all this quite naturally, even after confessing their faith in Jesus Christ, because what is limitation from the point of view of humanity as nature is positive from the point of view of humanity as history. As Karl Rahner said summarily: "For us in history, and therefore for Jesus too, this 'erring' is preferable to knowing every-thing in advance."[13]

When reality is viewed historically, sin alone is denial of humanity, which is why the letter to the Hebrews insists on the double fact of Jesus' likeness to us in all things except his radical difference in sin. Weaknesses, not knowing, groans and tears—even faith—do not indicate imperfection, because they belong to Jesus' *history*. Furthermore, in his case they are vehicles for achieving perfection.

The councils had the courage to accept the incarnation—a basic and revela-tory *formal* element—and so they had to say that God became the "other," be-came a limited and suffering human being. But the temptation to reject this al-ways remained beneath the surface when they expressed this becoming and being the "other" in terms of nature. This temptation was strong for good reasons: the union of God with limited and imperfect humanity will sooner or later lead to "contaminating" God's perfection, and so the *communicatio idiomatum* sanctioned it. In this way the problem of change and suffering—as perfection or imperfec-tion—was introduced into the very God. *Nature without history*, one has to con-clude, always leads to the grave danger of denying the flesh of Christ and the truth of God.

(ii) The cross as sacrifice or as self-giving. The decisive point of this argument is the cross, which is also decisive because of its significance for soteriology. The cross, as "nature," spells only shedding of blood, a "sacrifice" that—of its na-ture—would bring unknown benefits and effectuate the mediation between hu-mankind and God. How dangerous this is can be seen from the remains of Anselmianism and sacrificialism still current today. The cross as *history* is some-thing else. It is not the simple shedding of blood but the product of historical causes; it expresses a manner of being and of living and a way of relating to human beings: love. Our understanding of soteriology will depend on—and be very different—whether we see the cross as nature or as history.

The cross as history is the history that led to the cross, and this is well known: Jesus defended the weak against those who were oppressing them, came into conflict with these, remained true to his cause, and was killed because he was a nuisance. The cross came about, therefore, for defending the weak, and this makes it an expression of love. We can then say that the cross brings salvation, that the cross is *eu-aggelion*, good news. Love saves, and in the end love, in its various expressions, is the only thing that saves.

Without Jesus' history, the cross spells shedding of blood, death, and nothing more. Soteriology then turns into magic or the arbitrary cruelty of a god. With Jesus' history, the cross spells love, and a soteriology without magic or arbitrary cruelty becomes possible. Besides, this crucified man has lived humanly, with love, and so the cross is the radical expression of Jesus' self-giving *throughout his life*. Also, and above all, this life of Jesus' can in itself be offered as salvation; in it, the true life is shown. Reproducing it in history is living in truth as already

saved. The inviting exemplariness of Jesus ("their eyes fixed on Jesus") is effica-
cious historical soteriology.

In passing—and to clarify the difference between cross as nature and cross as
history—the problem remains with us today, if in a different form. To take an
important example, in the process for the beatification of Archbishop Romero,
there are debates about what title he should be given (though it seems that it will
be martyr), and this is the start of a problem that could—hypothetically—become
a danger. If he is beatified as a martyr (and not as bishop and martyr), what counts
essentially from the canonical point of view is his death itself, which would mean
that his past life and the historical reasons that led to his death—with the exceptions of the hatred of the faith and now, perhaps, the hatred of justice—will not be
essential, or at best will be secondary. The danger is that, in effect, a Romero
without history could be beatified, or that his history could be not absolutely
essential. This is what would signify understanding martyrdom as nature, not as
history. The process of his greatest official exaltation could be the means of distorting his figure: Romero the Salvadoran, in the flesh, who defended the poor
against their oppressors, who denounced and unmasked these, who remained faithful—in obscurity and in joy—to the will of God, and all this to the end. This is
martyrdom as history. I have already said that the danger is hypothetical, but let
me add that I hope they do not beatify Romero the martyr *secundum naturam*,
with which they could be beatifying a watered-down bishop, but *secundum
historiam*.

Let us return to Jesus. The lack of history is evident not only in Chalcedon's
understanding of the cross but also in theoretical soteriology in general. Traditionally, what is saving in Christ is something that can be described in universal
terms, even if these are as distinguished as divinization, ransom, expiation, redemption. The actual historical manifestation of Jesus, what was shown to be
loved by God in Jesus' life and his "exemplarity," more modest historical models, do not seem to be sufficient. And yet Jesus saves by showing us that there is
a foreseeing love, God's irrevocable initiative, by showing us the way to live in
response and correspondence to this love, and by offering us the strength to follow this route. This saving model of "exemplariness" also includes—most essentially—the "cross."

Something analogous could be said of the resurrection, remembering what
was said in the first part of this book. Resurrection, as *nature*, means simply
coming back to existence, and for the living it means simply expectation of life
beyond death. Resurrection, as *history*, is something different. It is doing justice
to a victim; it is the hope that the butcher will not triumph over the victims and
that we may be able to share in this hope.

Cross and resurrection *as nature* ultimately tend to show a cruel God, on the
one hand, and a *deus ex machina* on the other. *As history*, cross and resurrection
reveal a God who is love. Nature without history will always present the danger
of falling into sacrificialist cruelty with the cross or magic with the resurrection.

(iii) "Being" and "becoming." Adoptionism is not a current theoretical problem,
but it might be useful to adduce it as proof in examining the problems of the

concept of nature. When some christologies, for example, say that Jesus "is becoming Son of God," they normally provoke the accusation of adoptionism, as if
"becoming Son of God" were something that happened all at once and functioned
as the other side of the coin of "God becoming man." (Even here, one needs to
consider the possibility of understanding the incarnation as an evolution, so that
Jesus would be the high point of God's approach to humankind, but a point prepared and expressed in successive previous approaches. If this sounds surprising,
remember Irenaeus's words on the "Spirit's slow habituation to flesh.") Nevertheless, the language of "becoming," of "coming to be," though it too has its
dangers, is apt for bringing out certain aspects of christology that are not strongly
expressed simply by talking of "being," in the language of nature, that is.

The first thing to remember is that Jesus has a history and that he will always
go on revealing what he is through that. Precisely because his being Son of God is
a full reality, it needs a full history, with all its incidents and developments so that
it can reproduce and introduce us into the fullness of his being Son. In other
words, the revelation of the full sonship of Jesus cannot be made all at once. A
proof of this, as we have seen, is the New Testament's efforts to think of the
original "moment" of this sonship as belonging to various historical moments:
preexistence, conception, birth, baptism, transfiguration, resurrection, exaltation,
parousia . . . before concluding that Jesus had been Son of God forever and through
all these moments.

The dynamic and process character of this cannot be explained by the concept
of nature, since this would suppose that the divine sonship either exists or does
not. Neither, though, can it be explained by any one incident in Jesus' life, any
one aspect of his behavior, or his fate alone; it can be explained only by the whole
of his history, which means that only through the historical process of Jesus can
the fullness of his sonship be revealed. The *a priori* reason for this is simple: not
even Jesus of Nazareth can make "the whole of divinity" present at a stroke; he
can do so only through a process. Let me add that this has implications for our
own filiation process, which Paul calls "becoming" sons and daughters in the
Son.

The second thing to remember is that the process character of Jesus extends to
the utmost depth of his theologal relationship with the Father, which the concept
of nature is, once again, radically incapable of describing. This is not an *a priori*
statement but an observation drawn from the New Testament. In the form of a
historicized account, the gospels demonstrate Jesus' closeness and obedience and
faithfulness to the Father; in a more reflective vein, the Letter to the Hebrews
shows the process of his becoming Son. (John's theology puts forward a more
majestic image of the Son, without totally excluding Jesus' progress in history.)
Jesus has to be made perfect (Heb 2:10), so the writer makes the most daring
statement that Jesus is the "pioneer and perfecter of our faith" (12:2). The letter
not only shows the process character of Jesus' humanity but introduces this into
the historical relationship of Jesus to the Father.

The terminology of "becoming Son of God" can undoubtedly lead to misunderstandings, but I think it would be worse to abandon historical language to
describe Jesus, including his relationship to the Father. This language cannot state

that the divinity is coming to be—as though humanity could, Prometheus-like, steal the fire of the gods little by little—but can stress the appearance of this divine sonship in the history and through the history of Jesus. What Jesus "is"— Son of God—unfurls and is captured in a doxological statement, but this is precisely why historical statements are needed.

> The scriptural eschatological-historical understanding of reality does not involve any supra-historical concept of essence; being is here understood, not as an essence, but as actuality, that is as being active. The statement, "being is coming to be," is of course not the same as asserting that being consists in becoming. It is in history that what a thing *is*, is proved and realized. In this sense Jesus' resurrection is the confirmation, revelation, putting into force, realization and completion of what Jesus before Easter claimed to be and *was*. His history and fate are the history (not the coming to be) of his being, its ripening and self-interpretation. (Kasper, p. 165)

These clarifications may be useful for overcoming any sort of spurious adoptionist concepts, but they do not eliminate but rather stress the fact that Jesus' sonship is shown to us through his history and that only from the final fullness of that history can he come to be known as Son of God: "Thus it also becomes clear that the full meaning of Jesus' pre-Easter claim and manifestation, his dignity as Son of God, dawned on the disciples only at the end and after the completion of his way: that is, after Easter" (ibid.). What needs to be emphasized in this correct statement is that the precise revelatory moment of the end depends on Jesus' way, which is not precise but truly historical. At Easter—which, in its turn, is the prolepsis of the end—Jesus comes to show himself as what he "is." But this "is" contains a history, without which Jesus would not have achieved his being Son of God, once through God's plan the Son had become flesh.

Nature without history will always be a danger, since it leads to talk of the Son's *being*—which indeed tells us very little—but not of the Son's *history*— which is what will show us the way.

(c) Lack of relationality

A final limitation of the nature concept is that it weakens and gradually devalues *relationship*, which is a serious limitation for christology, since Jesus is shown during his lifetime in essential relationship both to his Father and to the Kingdom of God. Relationality is, then, constitutive of Jesus, even if its specific significance varies according to whether the Father or the Kingdom (self-giving or service) is its specific referent. (The conciliar definitions confess Jesus Christ as "Son," terminology that speaks of *relationship* with the Father, but here the question is that of the intra-trinitarian relationship in which the historical relationship of Jesus of Nazareth with the God he called Father would be subsumed but not made clear or actualized.)

The basic way to overcome this limitation is to go back to the history of Jesus. But we can also look for theoretical support in a concept equivalent to that of nature but capable of describing Jesus and including relationship as central. This equivalent concept might be that of *person* (dogmatically legitimate to use, as we have seen), though this might be taken in a de-Hellenized sense, since, left to its own inertia, Greek thought tended to understand *person* as mere subsistence. Here I propose to understand it from *self-giving* (in Hegelian terms) and from the *dynamism of selfhood* (in Zubiri's).

(i) Relationality with the Father: sonship as self-giving. Dogma affirms the relationality of Christ with the Father by proclaiming his divine *sonship*, but we need to examine what sort of relationship is meant. As we have seen, dogma proclaims that the Son is begotten of the Father and is consubstantial with him, which can be affirmed in accordance with the Greek idea of the communicability of divinity. Sonship then means relationship with the Father in the sense of *provenance* from him. Its biblical basis is in the statements in John's prologue, and its aim is to express the idea of being "consubstantial" with the Father. In this case, the concept of nature can be used to express the reality of provenance, but this concept, in itself, does not serve to express what there is of historical and personal relationship between Jesus and the Father. For this, the concept of person is needed, as it developed during the debates on the Trinity—in two directions, one focused on the subject's spiritual self-possession, and the other on self-giving. The second is the one that helps to understand Jesus' relationship to his Father. (Augustine defined the persons of the Trinity as relationships, Richard of St. Victor as *ex-sistentia*, which was deepened by Scotus and systematized by Hegel: abstract personality is recovered in giving oneself to the other.)[14]

Being a person is being able to enter into a relationship with another, which is fulfilled in *self-giving*, so that Jesus is constituted as person precisely in this self-giving to this "other" who is God. In this self-giving Jesus rescues and actualizes his generic personality. The way he keeps it up to the end, absolutely radically, demonstrates his special and essential relationship to God. What makes this radical self-giving possible and requires it—and demonstrates it—is Jesus' history down to his end on the cross, and nothing of this can be grasped in the term *nature*. As Pannenberg says: "Jesus' self-giving to God had the character of self-abandonment not in his giving himself to his mission, which he embraced clear-sightedly and accepted wholeheartedly, but only in his self-giving to God in the midst of the darkness of the fate of the cross, which must above all have represented the failure of his mission."[15]

This relationship of Jesus to God *in the way of historical self-giving*—not only in the way of provenance—can also be described in the term *sonship*. (However obvious it may seem, it needs to be pointed out that a relationship of self-giving to another can take various forms: friendship and motherhood for one; servility, slavery, and the like for another.) The biblical basis of this sonship is clearly brought out in the synoptics: Jesus' closeness to the Father, to the point of calling him *Abba,* and his availability and fidelity to him, letting him be God. Its theological usefulness consists in the fact that this relationship of closeness and availability can be understood as a kerygmatic statement, which cannot be said of the statements on his provenance in John's prologue, on the basis of which we can make the doxological affirmation of the *divine* sonship of Christ (see chapter 6 above for kerygmatic and doxological statements).

This also means that the identity of Jesus with the eternal Son is established not directly but only indirectly, on the basis of the historical, observable sonship of the man Jesus with respect to a God-Father. As Pannenberg says: "The unity of the man Jesus with the Son of God can be inferred only by taking a *detour. . . .* Only Jesus' personal communion with the Father proves that he is one and the same thing as the Son of this Father."[16] Identifying the historical sonship of Jesus with the eternal sonship of the Son is a doxology beyond the mind's control. (A systematic understanding has been sought through an analogy between sonship and creatureliness: "The creaturely relationship between humankind and God as the basis and origin of our being human is absorbed into the intra-divine relationship between the Son and the Father as the basis and origin of his being divine.")[17] The divine sonship of Christ can then come to be expressed through the following stages: (1) establishing Jesus' historical relationship with the Father as self-giving; (2) understanding this self-giving as an expression of sonship, as Jesus' unity with and differentiation from the Father; (3) identifying this sonship of Jesus with that of the eternal Son.

Going back to Chalcedon, the definition affirms a specific *coexistence* of humanity and divinity in Jesus Christ, but it does not express Jesus' primal personal relationship of self-giving: *closeness* to a God whom he calls Father and *availability* to a Father who goes on being God. This is a serious lack, since "it is precisely in his incomparable relationship with God, when he knows himself to be empowered by God, when he lives, works, and prays from the Father and for the Father, that the New Testament reveals the dignity of Christ and his unity with God." (The *theologal* consequence is also serious: that Christ's divinity "could not do other than appear increasingly closed in on itself.")[18] This is why we need to rethink Jesus' sonship starting from his historical relationship with a Father God.

One final consideration: when his sonship is understood on the basis of *provenance* (Christ is the begotten one), then more stress is placed on consubstantiality, and Jesus' sharing in divinity comes to the fore. So, for example, Christ shares in the "lordship" of God—and this quality can then be sought in his life, in miracles, casting out demons, absolving sins, and so on, thereby starting on the slippery slope of viewing divinity essentially as power. But if Jesus' sonship is seen principally in terms of *self-giving*, then there is more stress laid on his relationship with the Father, and in this relationship Jesus appears as the *pais Theou* (who precisely on account of this is constituted Son of God). In this way the novelty— and the scandal—of the divinity of the Father is also preserved. The Father not only begets divinity, so to speak, but also begets a Son who is also a servant, and in him is well pleased. The Father becomes related not only to humanity but to humanity in the form of servant. And let me say that this observation on divinity is no less important in situations of crucified peoples.

(ii) Relationality with the Kingdom: Jesus' work. The Kingdom of God, which is absolutely central for Jesus, does not feature in any form in the Chalcedonian

definition: Jesus Christ does not appear in relation to the Kingdom. And this relationship has to be rescued, for only from the Kingdom can we overcome the reductionism of salvation (in the definition "for us and for our salvation" still appears, but nothing more). We rescue the God who has poor sons and daughters. We also rescue, if only by implication, the negative dimension of reality, the anti-Kingdom. Finally, we rescue what is essential for the victims: that they are the privileged addressees of the Kingdom and so the creatures privileged by God. The problem is, then, how to rescue the relationship of Christ to the Kingdom of God from the definition in some way and without falling into artificiality.

The Father to whom Jesus relates is, also and essentially for Jesus, a God of the Kingdom. God decided to be not God alone, but God related to what is not God. And this plan of God's is fulfilled not only in the incarnation but also in the real advent of the utopia of a Kingdom (of God) in which human beings can be people (of God). (This is central to liberation theology. "Just what Jesus came to proclaim and bring about, the Kingdom of God, that is, is what should become the unifying force in the whole of Christian theology.")[19] The conclusion is that a Jesus related to this God will also be related, in an *essential* and not merely an accidental manner, with this God's will and particular plan for his creation.

In order to rescue the relationship of Jesus to the Kingdom of God, the fundamental thing is to go back to the synoptics. But, as we have just done in examining his relationship with the *person* of God, it may perhaps help if we replace the concept of *nature* in the definition with that of *person*—understood here in Zubiri's terms: "This personification, being person, I say, consists precisely in being one's own. If I may be permitted the ugly word *ownness* (to make myself understood quickly), I shall say that the problem we have to face up to is just that of the dynamic and evolving transition from selfness to ownness. This is the dynamic of ownness." A. González explains it like this: "Persons are not something prior to their activity; personal reality is a dynamic reality in and for itself: it is the dynamic of ownness." From this it follows that "the person of Christ cannot be thought of as a subject coming before his actions. . . . Being a person and knowing oneself to be a person are things that come about precisely through human actions to the extent that these bring reality itself into being."[20]

From this point of view, not only is Jesus' work not alien to the core of his personhood; it is what constitutes it. And since the sphere of his activity and work is the Kingdom of God (and against the anti-Kingdom), the work that is most formally directed to the building of the Kingdom and the destruction of the anti-Kingdom will be the most constitutive of his person. Building the Kingdom belongs, then, essentially to the person of Jesus, which is another way of affirming the essential relationship of Jesus to the Kingdom of God and to the God of the Kingdom, as the synoptics do. (I have viewed this work as what is most historical about the historical Jesus, which is also the way that can lead to confessing him as the Christ and can serve as the basis of christology; see *JL,* pp. 67–70.)

It is, then, possible to rescue the relationship of Christ with the Kingdom of God from the definition, by understanding nature as person. The fact of the matter is that while the (metaphorical) terminology of *Son* exists to express Christ's relationship with a *Father* God, there is no word in the *conciliar* tradition to express his relationship with a God *of the Kingdom*. (The definition speaks of "our Lord Jesus *Christ*, but here Christ, messiah, does not yet denote relationship to the Kingdom as God's utopia corresponding to the hope of the poor.) Even if the language is not very adequate, might it not be possible to think of the relationship as between the *anointer* (God) and the *anointed* (Christ), united in one same will to build the Kingdom? In this case, Christ would share essentially in the transcendent liberating work of *God*. His work and love on earth would be the historical version of God's transcendent activity and love.

These ideas have been developed in some form in Latin American theology: action also places human beings in relation to God. Liberation theology, in effect, stresses that God exists and God's utopia exists, that God's person exists and God's will exists; therefore, "God has to be contemplated and put into action."[21] We have to *respond* to God (maintaining his otherness) and to *correspond* by doing his will and so remaking his reality (maintaining affinity). This second way of relating to God, corresponding to God, comes about historically through making God's Kingdom, through molding creation as God would wish it.

This emerges clearly from the Jesus of the synoptics, who, furthermore, warns of two grave practical dangers, with theoretical repercussions, in speaking of the relationship between human beings and God. Jesus tells us it is not enough to "say Lord, Lord," but that we have to *do* the will of his Father, with the resulting hermeneutical implication: without a "doing" there is no proper understanding of or relationship with the "Lord," with the divinity. He also says that there are two lords, God and Mammon, between whom we must choose, serving one and hating the other, which introduces a specifically anti-idol practice into hermeneutics. This is what Jesus did, acting positively for the Kingdom and against the idols of the anti-Kingdom, and this, more than nature, is what makes him a person.

The Chalcedonian definition, then, is lacking in actuality, history, and relationality. What I have set out here is an attempt to overcome these lacks theoretically. But the positive aspect should not be overlooked: Chalcedon provides the content of *what* it is that has to be historicized—divinity and humanity—and of *how* this should be done—respecting the four negative adverbs, which state what is not to be done. This may seem like a small contribution from one point of view, but from another it is an important aid to a correct view of the whole—the conjunction of humanity and divinity, within the imagery available at the time—and how their different elements are to be related.

Chapter 19

Formal and Doxological Readings of Chalcedon

Following Jesus as an Epistemological Principle

The preceding chapters have studied the conciliar definitions, examined their concepts, criticized their limitations, and put forward reinterpretations. I have tried to make the definitions easier to understand, or at least not to put unnecessary obstacles in the way of their comprehension. In this final chapter I want to propose two ways of reading the christological definitions that will also help to this end. The first is a formal reading, rereading the definitions not only for the actual statements they make about Jesus Christ but for what they have to say about reality and its structure. I have in fact done this in earlier chapters when analyzing reality as suffering that affects God himself (the basic problem at Nicaea); reality as absolute, despite the dead ends into which this absolutism (in maintaining the humanity of Christ) can lead; reality as differentiated, so that, depending on how its elements are related, the same reality can offer possibilities or dangers (the relationship between the natures, in Chalcedonian terms). What I propose to do now is to reread Chalcedon's definition as a *holistic definition*, in order to help to understand the radical unity of reality, its humanity and its divinity.

The second is a doxological reading of the definition, that is, as a definition that expresses an ultimate reality and requires a *specific epistemology*. In my view, whatever terminology and philosophy are applied, the basic epistemological problem consists in how human reason ought to operate in order to be able to *make*, meaningfully, statements about the unrepeatable being of Jesus Christ in himself: Jesus Christ is a divine being. And let us remember that, in principle, this problem has no easier solution even if we abandon this phraseology and express the reality of Jesus Christ differently—such as in biblical language (Jesus Christ is "the Lord," "the Son," "the Word") or in current theological terms (Jesus Christ is "the absolute Bringer of Salvation," "the integral Liberator")— since the reason for the difficulty lies not in the abstruseness of the language or the inadequacy or obsoleteness of its concepts but in the fact that Jesus Christ is confessed as a *divine* being ("truly," as Nicaea said). The conciliar terms, just like the biblical and the current ones, are then limit statements, and this means that their understanding has to come through a specific epistemology. (To this one has to add that the christological definitions express a "qualified" divinity, as it were. The person of Jesus Christ is divine, but this divinity is confessed in a specific way, since it subsists in two natures. The mystery of the divinity becomes re-doubled mystery. It is the mystery of a God who, furthermore, "makes room" for humanity, which goes beyond the "simple" mystery of God. And, by derivation, it is the mystery of humanity being "radically open" to God.)

1. A Holistic Definition

My concern with this formal reading is not purely theoretical or philosophical-speculative; it is prompted rather by an intuition that has a long tradition behind it: a unified whole—not simply the sum total of all that is real—has *meaning* and, above all through religions, offers human beings meaning. Coming to be and to belong to *that* whole is, in some way, *salvation*, above all because, without ceasing to be human, we are taken up into the divinity.

Let us begin by recalling well-known matters. Whether under the Greek concept of nature, in which *kosmos* means order, a form of expressing meaning—not absurdity, as in the formless *tohu bohu*—and so integration into it is some form of salvation, or under the concept of history, especially in its Hegelian version of "history of the absolute" (in which negativity and even "the speculative Good Friday" can be integrated, so that there can be both reconciliation and salvation), an important strand in *philosophical* tradition has always conceived reality as a unified whole. This becomes clearer in world *religions*, whose ideal is to overcome the infinite distance separating divinity and non-divinity and bring about their intimate union, an ideal extending to mystical dimensions. (In the Old Testament this intimacy in the relationship between God and Israel is expressed in terms of that between husband and wife, though without going so far as to include sexual union.) *Anthropologically*, it is clear that unity in diversity offers salvation, which is expressed clearly in various forms of interhuman relationships: justice, friendship, fellowship, love—especially that which binds men to women. (Besides the significant fact that the Song of Songs, an expression of erotic *unity*, was integrated into the canon, St. Bernard used the image of a kiss on the lips to explain the unity of divinity and humanity in Jesus Christ. In him both parts are active and passive. It is a unique kiss: "God's kiss of the world is the *logos*, and humanity's kiss of God is the human nature of Jesus.")[1] *Sociologically*, I have already commented on (in examining "ecclesial Docetism") the salvation that produces "real beings," sharers in the human family such as it is, with no need to feel ashamed of being on a planet without really belonging to it, in the manner of exceptions or footnotes. (See chapter 9 above on "high priest" and the need for the church to be, above all, "real," that is, to share in the "reality" of our world, especially in its suffering aspect.)

The conclusion has to be that uniting, not separating, is what brings salvation. In order to *be* (persons above all), we have to *be* within a whole. Putting this intuition into Christian terminology from its contrary, the ancients used to say, "ubi peccatum, ibi multitudo" ("where there is sin, there is separation"), to which they added, "sub specie contrarii, ubi gratia, ibi unitas" ("where there is grace, there is unity"). Turning this around, we can say, "Where there is unity, there is grace, there is salvation."

Now in this context the first thing the christological definitions say is that this unity, first and foremost, is possible because it is real, and is so precisely in what would seem to be most impossible—in the unity between divinity and humanity. Jesus Christ, in effect, is *one* being: he is not separation. He is an all-embracing being who integrates all that there is, divinity and humanity. He is not a fragment of reality; he is reality *for always*, not something provisional.

This is said in abstract terms and needs bringing down to earth, but if this is the case, Chalcedon is not just one way of formulating the reality of Christ; it also put into words the possibility of radical and all-embracing unity, in which it expresses good news. Its desire, at the least, is that separation will not have the last word, that reality will be more than a mere fragment without wholeness, mere becoming without direction, mere wandering without a goal. Even if its language is abstruse, the definition presents us with the possibility of a unified and definitive whole, integrated so as to include salvation—the importance of which is clear in today's world with its fragmentation and consequent trivialization of existence.

(a) The Biblical-Christian Tradition

Before looking at the Chalcedonian definition from this aspect, it is worth recalling briefly the holistic logic of the unity of existence in the biblical-Christian tradition: the unity between what is divine and what is not divine, in constant tension. In scripture God is the creator, infinitely distant from his creatures, whom they cannot call to account: "Where were you," he asks Job, "when I laid the foundations of the earth?" (Jb 38:2). In a different context, in a singularly beautiful passage God also affirms his distance from creatures: "for I am God and no mortal . . . and I will not come in wrath" (Hos 11:9). (The whole verse stresses not the "metaphysical" distance between creator and creature so much as the essential difference in the way each behaves: "I will not execute my fierce anger; I will not again destroy Ephraim; for I am God and no mortal, the Holy One in your midst, and I will not come in wrath." Numbers 23:19 is another verse that expresses this same difference in kind in God's actions: "God is not a human being, that he should lie, or a mortal, that he should change his mind. Has he promised, and will he not do it? Has he spoken, and will he not fulfill it?") For all this distance, however, this same God always appears in relation to human beings and in such a way that the relationship between them constitutes the whole of reality. (This holistic vision differs from other more naturist ones found in other religions and cultures, in which nature comes directly into the overall scheme. In the biblical tradition nature would be integrated into the whole through human beings, because it is at their service. Throughout history, this has been understood in an instrumentalist sense—manipulative and so criticized today—through which nature loses its own identity and becomes subject to, in the sense of oppressed by, human beings. But it can also be understood in a humanized and sacramental sense, as St. Francis of Assisi did, for example.) From the start, then, the identity of the creator God has been defined by his radical distance from creation, but again from the start the same God has introduced a—metaphysical, perhaps—closeness to his creation: "In the image of God he created them" (Gn 1:27). And when history properly so-called begins, God decides, so to speak, not to be God "alone," a God-in-himself, and establishes a relationship with humankind, sacramentalized in Israel. And so, however much the Old Testament traditions on God vary, they have this much in common: God is a God-*of*, a God-*for*, a God-*with*, and never a God-*in-himself*. He becomes a God of and for the people, and himself expresses the mutuality: "I will be their God, and they shall be my people" (Jer 31:33). This decision by God not to be God "alone" but God "in relationship" is the burden of biblical holism.

Jesus' message also can and should be understood holistically, since it places God in essential relationship with what is not God: the overall scheme is described by Jesus as the Kingdom of God. In this, what we today call transcendence and history are intrinsically related to each other, convergent in a whole—a fact that very soon attracted the attention of liberation theology when it made the Kingdom of God its central tenet and insisted seriously on its holistic potential (see *JL*, pp. 105–34).

According to this, and in technical language, from the Kingdom of God the overall scheme can be defined generically as "transcendence in history," and the Kingdom of God facilitates this understanding, since its "Kingdom" is history and "of God" transcendence. "What this conception of faith from the Kingdom of God does is place God in indissoluble conjunction with history" and overcomes "the dualism of kingdom (earthly) and God (heavenly)."[2]

Finally, in the New Testament tradition the end of history is described in clearly holistic terms, when the Son hands the Kingdom to the Father and then "God will be all in all" (1 Cor 15:28). (As Christ is also present at the start—John 1:1—there is a holistic christological beginning.) Or, according to the utopia of Johannine theology, "that they may all be one. As you, Father, are in me and I am in you, may they also be in us" (Jn 17:21). (Oscar Cullmann drew attention to the fact that the holistic vision developed in Israel alongside the principle of deputation throughout the history of salvation. In this manner the dynamism of the original wholeness was narrowed down through deputation to emerge once more in a now definitive wholeness. So the scheme of salvation history would then be creation-Israel-Jesus Christ-church-final fullness.) This holistic vision of the biblical tradition lasted. Marcion was rejected and condemned because he separated creation from salvation, the Old Testament from the New, the creator God from the saving God: he "de-totalized" existence. The overcoming of Marcionism or of any type of Manicheism was the means of sustaining the original holistic vision. In a positive vein, Christian holism was deeply and finely expressed in Irenaeus's idea of the recapitulation of all things in Christ. The burden of this way of thinking is that unity—which includes divinity and humanity—is good, welcoming, saving. What saves is wholeness, not fragmentation; unity, not separation; reconciliation, not antagonism.

(b) Chalcedon as a Holistic Definition

The Chalcedonian definition effectively falls within holistic tradition, to a profound degree. The debates between Nestorius and Cyril revolved around the unity of Christ—remember Cyril's *mia physis*. And despite the difficulty posed by accepting *two* such absolutely distinct natures, the unity was upheld: *"unum* nobis Christum et Filium effecerunt"* (DS 250), according to Ephesus; *"unum eundemque* confiteri Filium dominum nostrum Iesum Christum"* (DS 301), according to Chalcedon.

In this definition what unifies is divinity, *hypostasis*, which, in religious language, is the guarantee that true unity can exist and that this is salvation. The definition also presupposes that that unity has come into being through the incarnation and that its purpose is salvation: "for us and for our salvation he was made man *(enanthropesanta)*" (DS 125); "for us and for our salvation, born from the Virgin Mary . . . as touching the manhood *(kata ten anthropoteta)*" (DS 301).

(i) Karl Rahner's speculative explanation. After that brief reminder of what I said earlier, let us now make a short excursus into Rahner's thesis on the unity of divinity and humanity in Jesus Christ, a true and deep expression of holistic reality. Its originality lies in two things: the first, in understanding humanity with essential reference to divinity; the second, in understanding the relationship between both elements according to a sacramental theoretical model, so that Jesus is the sacrament of God and humanity is the sacrament of divinity. I shall develop the first point later. On the second, I should say that, speculatively, Rahner is trying to explain how the *sarx* of John 1:14 is the real symbol of the Word and is so to such an extent—he adds—that "if I had to write a theology of symbolic reality, christology, as the doctrine of the incarnation of the Word, would, clearly, have to form the pivotal chapter,"[3] and its development would revolve around this unique phrase: "Whoever has seen me has seen the Father" (Jn 14:9).

(ii) Three earlier theses. Understanding of the unity of divinity and humanity in Jesus Christ involves acceptance of the following three dogmatic theses:

1. The first thesis is: "God can become other." The fundamental dogma of Christianity affirms this primary possibility in God, a statement that enunciates a finality beyond the reach of thought, but which is basic: "The absolute, or rather the Absolute, possesses, in the pure freedom of its infinite absence of relationship, which it always maintains, the possibility of becoming the other."[4] If this is so, if God himself can—freely—become other, then his actions *ad extra*, creation and incarnation, cannot be understood as two magnitudes existing in parallel with each other; they are rather "two moments and phases in the real world of a process that is one, even if internally differentiated, of God's exteriorization and alienation within what is distinct from him."[5] And the priority of his actions *ad extra* resides in the incarnation, so that this is the condition for making creation

possible. ("Power-becoming-history is his primary freedom. . . . His being able to be creator, the faculty for constituting the merely other into himself without giving himself, of making it arise out of its very nothingness, is only the derived, limited, and secondary possibility that, in the end, is based on the said primary possibility, although it could also function without this.")[6] Human nature is possible because Jesus is possible (and actual). According to this, we can understand ourselves in any hypothesis only on the basis of a possible incarnation of God, so that if that had not taken place, we should always be inquiring into our essence. "In order radically to understand what we are we have to understand that we exist because God wanted to become human."[7]

2. The second thesis establishes the condition for God to "utter himself" *ad extra* (in what is not God) without ceasing to be the absolute mystery: God can utter himself *ad extra* and go on being God because he can utter himself to himself *ad intra*. "God's immanent uttering himself in his eternal fullness is the condition for uttering himself coming out from himself, and the latter is the continuation of the former."[8] If within the Trinity there were no possibility of God expressing himself that was not a threat to the being of the Father—to his going on being unoriginated, that is—then God would not be able to utter himself *ad extra* and at the same time remain God, the one who eternally withdraws himself through being without origin. God, in communicating himself, would give himself totally; this would be without the duplicity of self-giving and withdrawing. This affirms the possibility that God's coming to be *ad extra* being an expression of himself depends on God being able to express himself internally and going on being the unoriginated God.[9] There can be a human reality that is a sacrament of God if expressing himself within himself is an attribute of God.

3. The third thesis is that "only the Word can become incarnate." Scripture definitely asserts that it was the Word that became incarnate and gives no grounds for thinking that it could have been another person of the Trinity that did so (as did tradition before Augustine). Beyond this assertion, however, in order to understand the thesis and its transcendence, according to Rahner, we must have a particular (transcendental/circular) understanding of what being human means on the basis of the incarnation. This is that if being human could be understood independently of the incarnation, then the Word would have no radical affinity with what "being human" means; then, however, being human would have no affinity with the Word, and the incarnation would have been one among many possibilities for the Word: it would not be clear why God had chosen humankind in order to express himself. If, though, human beings are essentially the *expression* of God, then it becomes more understandable that it should be the Word, the intra-trinitarian *expression*, who became human. Within the Trinity, it is the function of the Word to be expression, and he therefore has a certain affinity for expressing himself outward in what—humankind—is the expression of God.[10]

To sum up these theses: God can become other than God, and the overall reality that results from this is by definition a reality in which its two elements are radically united. The whole resulting from God becoming other is holistic and as deeply so as possible.

(c) Jesus, Real Symbol of the Word

This overall reality cannot, obviously, be understood as mere coexistence or juxtaposition of two things. Seeking an adequate theoretical expression for it, Rahner uses the sacramentality of the real: the human, Jesus, is the real symbol of the Word—by which false or inadequate interpretations are left behind. The basic error would consist in viewing human nature as the previous element, given and known before the incarnation, since in this case human nature would be seen as a uniform, which would indicate God but not be his real symbol; it would be an arbitrary sign, put on from outside, which really *does not* manifest God, even if by God's positive decree this human nature referred back to God. Neither can nature be seen as an instrument manipulated by God from the outside but without telling us who God is.[11] It is not strange—Rahner added, writing forty years ago—that when such suppositions are implicitly or explicitly present in a christology Christ is revealing the Father through his *teaching* or through his *powerful* actions but not through what he is.

Refusing to understand the unity of the divine and the human in Jesus Christ as subsequent, that is, as the union of two realities that—even if only logically—could exist independently of one another is still more grave. The Word did not take on a human nature already constituted logically; he took on human nature in creating it and created it in taking it on; he took it on in alienating himself. The humanity of Christ is, then, that created reality which becomes the Word when the Word alienates itself, goes outward from itself. And this human nature remains the symbol of the Word for always, including in the beatific vision. "The eternal significance of the humanity of Jesus for our relationship with God" does no more than affirm that since the incarnation the human Jesus is the real symbol of God and that therefore—not being provisional and transitory but a real symbol—he is the mediator for all eternity.[12]

(d) Jesus Christ and the Unification of Human Beings

I have spoken of a holistic christological definition, but this "totality" directly involves only one person. So if the totality is to be salvation for all, a universal potential must exist in Jesus, capable of taking all up, deifying them, and thereby offering them salvation. Continuing with Rahner's reflection, this is possible through the mutual conditioning of christology and anthropology. Being human—despite what we know about it empirically—is indefinable, "indefinability come to itself," "pure reference to God," which reaches its fullness in Jesus. Seen the other way around, finite humanity is a secondary manner of being Christ. "Mankind arises when God seeks to be not-God."[13]

There is, then, continuity between Christ and being human, which means that the latter can be taken up by the former. Or, more accurately, the difference is not absolutely radical, and it should be sought not in the difference between grace and hypostatic union, since both are God's mysteries *ad extra*, but in the overcoming of all ambiguities in Christ. "The *unio hypostatica* is distinguished from our grace not by what is affirmed in it, which on both sides (in Jesus too) is grace, but because Jesus is the affirmation for us while we are not also affirmation but receivers of God's affirmation in our regard."[14] Ultimately, Rahner is stating that humanity—with the necessary qualifications—can come to be in fundamental union with God. Chalcedon is then a fundamentally holistic definition.

We can perhaps reach a similar conclusion through an anthropology of biblical stamp. Although modern Western anthropology, with its emphasis on individuals in their inalienable responsibility and constitutive freedom, does not make the corporative anthropological idea of co-humanity easy to grasp (it seems to belong rather to the basically societal anthropologies of primitive peoples), this does represent an important tradition in the church. The Second Vatican Council—in the context of the atheism it seeks to repudiate in order to offer a true humanization—presents the person of Christ as the New Man and points to the possibility of incorporating all human beings into him, "For by His incarnation the Son of God has united Himself in some fashion with every man" (*Gaudium et Spes*, no. 22). This statement is theoretically understandable in the light of the idea of "corporative personality" in biblical thought, strongly defended in his day by Oscar Cullmann.

We have in fact already seen that the New Testament uses terms that understand individual human beings within the greater reality of the human family. So the risen Christ is presented not just in himself but as the "firstborn" of the resurrection (cf. Rom 8:29; 1 Cor 15:13; Col 1:18; Acts 3:15; Rv 1:5), that is, in essential relationship with other human beings (so that the experience of appearances of Jesus could well be interpreted as a sort of vision of the universal resurrection). We have also seen that, although in a more stylized form, the letter to the Hebrews presents Jesus as "the pioneer and perfecter of our faith" (12:2), that is, as the "first" among a cloud of witnesses (who can be thought of as being summed up in him), one who invites others to join with him. Several christological titles show the ambiguity or ambivalence of being able to refer either to an individual or to a collectivity: Son of God, Son of Man, suffering servant. (In a remarkable passage in his sermon of October 20, 1979, Archbishop Romero said, "In Christ we find the model of the liberator, a man who identifies with the people to the point where interpreters of the Bible do not know whether the Servant of Yahweh proclaimed by Isaiah is the suffering people or Christ come to redeem us.")[15] Finally, the same letter to the Hebrews tells us that "the one who sanctifies and those who are sanctified all have one Father. For this reason Jesus is not ashamed to call them brothers and sisters" (2:11).

The New Testament also relates and brings together all believers and, ultimately, the whole human race in Christ from other points of view as well. Paul's is indicated by his theology of the body of Christ. In the first letter to the Corinthians and the letter to the Romans, in which he speaks of the unity of the community, he stresses the unity of all believers, and he adds that the risen Christ is made present in the eucharist: "Because there is one bread, we who are many are one body, for we all partake of the one bread" (1 Cor 10:17).

Paul also speaks of "all of us com[ing] to . . . maturity, to the measure of the full stature of Christ" (Eph 4:13), a passage that is not simply referring to individual

Christians reaching a state of "perfection" but of perfect humanity in a collective sense, meaning Christ himself, who has created "in himself one new humanity in place of the two" (2:15). (Christ is thus the prototype of the new humanity re-created by God [see 2 Cor 5:17] in the person of the risen Christ as the "last Adam" [1 Cor 15:45], after having given death in him on the cross to the lineage of the first Adam, corrupted by sin [see Rom 5:12f.; 8:3; 1 Cor 15:21]. Created "in true righteousness and holiness [Eph 4:24], he is also "one only" because in him all divisions among people disappear [see Col 3:10f.; Gal 3:27f.], as the *Jerusalem Bible* comments on Ephesians 2:15.)

The corporate deputizing appears in the central passage of Romans 5:15–19: "Therefore just as one man's trespass led to condemnation for all, so one man's act of righteousness leads to justification and life for all. For just as by the one man's disobedience the many were made sinners, so by the one man's obedience the many will be made righteous" (vv. 18–19). The unity of existence at its deep-est levels is central to Christianity. Its basis is faith in a God who unites himself forever to a human bring, Jesus of Nazareth, and through him to all of us. Estab-lishing this holistic unity and its saving quality seems to me to be the lasting significance of both Chalcedon and of the New Testament.

2. A Doxological Definition

Let us now examine the Chalcedonian definition as a doxological definition, that is, as a definition that speaks of Jesus Christ as God-in-himself.

(a) A Specific Epistemology

I said in chapter 6 that statements about God in himself are possible only through a *process* of understanding. Here I apply analysis of doxological definitions to the conciliar texts. The understanding process begins (1) by establishing histori-cal actions, which (2) are, in faith, referred to God as God's actions, so that (3) those actions allow us to make statements about God in himself.

From the epistemological point of view, in this process reason *controls* the first step and, in some way, even though faith is active in it, makes up the second. But grasping the reality of God in himself is possible only in the *surrender of reason* to the mystery of God (with its analogy of the adoration that happens in worship). If one takes the Exodus as an example, (1) a liberation from Egypt happens (or is narrated as happening in history); (2) the event is attributed to God, so that God, on the basis of his liberation action, comes to be known as "the God who liberated Israel from Egypt"; and (3) the reality of God in himself, essen-tially, one might say, is confessed, so that we can state, "God *is* liberating."

This process of understanding God can help, even if only analogously, in un-derstanding how reason operates in coming to make christological definitions. They too say of Jesus Christ that he is God (what is ultimate in him is *being* a divine person), and this reality has to be formulated in a limit statement that re-quires a process of understanding and a final surrender.

The process begins with *the human reality of Jesus*, which in principle is historically verifiable. That his being is truly human was demonstrated in the previous volume. Here I want to add only that Jesus' story could—and should—be read "Chalcedonically," in such a way that his humanity does not cease to be that (unchanging), is not absorbed by the divinity (unconfused) or separated from the divinity (undivided), and all this lasts to the end (unseparated). Summarily, we can say that, in his life, Jesus refers to God without God "de-humanizing" him, and so to the end, despite crisis, agony, and death. (What happens to the divinity in Jesus' life is not verifiable but can only be inferred and believed. But, once accepted in a later faith, we could and should say that in Jesus of Nazareth God comes close to humanity, without this humanity "de-divinizing" God, although it does actualize God to a scandalous extent.)

This human reality, now approached through faith, is *placed in relationship with God*. This is what New Testament and patristic christological reflection do in various ways, as we have seen in earlier chapters, through titles and theological interpretations of his life. The outcome is to establish a special relationship between Jesus and God.

The process *ends with confessing the divinity of Jesus Christ* in himself, which, incipiently in the New Testament and explicitly after Nicaea, comes about through surrendering reason to mystery. (In the case of the divinity of Jesus Christ the need for the surrender of reason can also be seen from another viewpoint if we examine how the link "is" functions in the dogmatic conciliar definitions. When we speak of the divinity in general and say, "God *is* liberating," the "is" can be understood, to some degree, from the analogy of being—even if in the analogy too the final step requires mental surrender, since something is being predicated of God by way of affirmation, negation, and eminence. But in christology not even this analogy of being helps toward a solution, since the "is" of the definition operates in a way completely beyond the control of reason. The verb "is" does not work in the same way here as it does in other forms of words. The statement "God *is* man" "cannot identify the reality expressed in the subject of the phrase—God—with that alluded to in the predicate—being human, being born, and so on—in the same way as it does in our usual statements.")[16]

For epistemology, what matters is the conclusion: understanding the reality of Jesus-Christ-in-himself can be achieved only through a doxological statement. In this precise sense the conciliar definitions are arrival points that sum up and sustain the beginning of the process and its development. They are significant as marking (though always provisionally) the end of a process of understanding that begins in the New Testament and, within that, in the texts that deal with the actual life and fate of Jesus, to which were added—later—the theological interpretations the New Testament and the Fathers of the church made of these. And they end in the surrender of reason to mystery.

This epistemology includes, then, two essential elements: the *way* of understanding, which begins with some reality of a historical nature, and the *surrender* of reason at the end of the process. These two elements—way and surrender—are what I want to look at now, not only in their theoretical cognitive dimension but also in their working historical reality. I want to examine the way to doxology as following of Jesus and the surrender of reason as the surrender of the whole person.

(b) The Following of Jesus: The Working Way to Doxology

To give meaning to the conciliar statements, with logical and chronological priority accorded to Chalcedon, we need to travel a *conceptual way*: who Jesus of Nazareth was, how the New Testament rationalized him (the theologies of Paul, John, Hebrews, the synoptics, and so on), and the later church tradition (the theologies of the Apologists and the Fathers).[18] Without traveling this *conceptual* way, the definitions will always remain unintelligible. To this, however, I want to add a *working* way, meaning nothing other than the following of Jesus: remaking the structure of his life, work, and fate in history. In this way following Jesus will be not just an anthropological, ethical, and salvific reality but one functioning also as an epistemological category. It would, I believe, be ingenuous to think that traveling the *theoretical* way could suffice to understand the christological definitions, as if concepts could be understood only on the basis of other concepts. At times, before being theoretical, this way was historical.

(i) Following as a source of understanding. In order to know Jesus Christ we have to follow a way in which we can come to be (or not be) in affinity with his reality. What brings us together with him is the following *(way)* of Jesus *(affinity)*.

Following means journeying with, being and doing—in today's terms—what Jesus was and did. On this journey we acquire consciousness of *otherness* with respect to him, since, in comparison with us, Jesus appears as the "elder" brother, as the radical initiative that comes from God and has to render accounts to none other than God. But the point I want to make now is that following also implies *affinity*, greater or lesser, naturally, with Jesus.

The following of Jesus consists, in the first place, in remaking his life and praxis, and this remaking can bring about "an inner knowledge" (as the mystics say) that is not simply based on texts concerning Jesus, which always remains to a certain extent extraneous to our reality. What Jesus' relationship to God is can be known—or glimpsed—through us remaking his trust in the Father and his openness to God. What proclaiming and bringing in the Kingdom mean can be known—or glimpsed—through us remaking his compassion for the poor, his acceptance of outcasts. What his denunciation of the anti-Kingdom is can be known—or glimpsed—through us remaking denunciation of sinful structures. What living with spirit, with freedom, with grace means can be known—or glimpsed—through us remaking the spirit of the beatitudes. Jesus' *being thus* can be known in depth through us *being thus*.

Second, this *being thus* is what shows itself open to transcendence in history and hence to theologal transcendence. An effective way, at least phenomenologically, of grasping transcendence in history is that of maintaining in our own lives the tensions that arose in Jesus' life and work. This means upholding the practice of justice, with the conflictivity this implies, while at the same time seeking reconciliation; sustaining effective practice while working in the spirit of the beatitudes; maintaining the struggle against poverty while seeking one's own impoverishment; keeping alive an imperishable hope in the coming of the Kingdom while doing so against all hope, out of honesty with reality; carrying out work designed to bring in the structures of the Kingdom and to create the new humanity at the same time. All these mean combining things that are difficult to combine, but in this way history is made to bear more fruit than it was pregnant with, to give more of itself. We can experience this *more* in the following of Jesus. If you like, we can experience a sort of "echo" of God's transcendence.

The conclusion is that the theoretical way of understanding has to be supplemented with—and as a major component—the historical way—following—since only in that can we build an affinity between ourselves and the reality of Jesus, which is what makes inner knowledge of Christ possible. Confessing—afterward—Jesus Christ as the ultimate provides the surrender, the leap of faith; before this, it is of the greatest importance to determine as precisely as possible where this leap is to take place. Outside the following of Jesus, in my view, we have no sure means of knowing what we are talking about when we confess Jesus Christ. (We have already seen the dogmatic reason for this. Jesus' existence does not remain absolutely alien to ours, so knowledge of him can originate—in the most radical manner possible—with us remaking the hypostatic union—analogously, of course. The fact that we can *be* like Jesus is what will in the final analysis make it possible for us to *know* Jesus. In New Testament terms, God's plan is that we should come to *be* sons and daughters in the Son.)

(ii) The surrender of reason. The process of understanding ends with surrender, which supposes active willingness not to control the mystery of Christ, not—in a way—to know: what I have called chastity of intelligence. This surrender has been described in tradition as *obsequium rationabile*. It is *obsequium* because following is subject to the obscurities and the ups-and-downs of history. The same course of following can, therefore, be verification or temptation for one's own faith, depending on whether it leads to more life or seems to end in absurdity. As a result, even following could be a place from where not to make the leap of faith, since it could be that, following Jesus, we could reach the conclusion that this way does not lead to the ultimate but is illusory.

The leap of faith can, however, also be *reasonable*, but this statement needs some criterion on which to base it. Traditionally, the "reasonableness" of faith has been able to be ascribed to indications of Christ's particular being (self-understanding, miracles, and so forth) or to his resurrection, understood as an unrepeatable miracle. But from the viewpoint of following, the basic criterion is based, as I have said, on what following itself produces: we experience existence giving more of itself and doing so by offering, freedom, dignity. In any case, in following we have the subjective experience that "it could not be any other way." And the objective correlation of this experience is that this "more" should happen to the benefit of those who have been most deprived of life, of freedom, of justice, and of dignity.

Such formulations can of course be debated and improved upon: what I want to stress is that the criterion of the reasonableness of faith is related to the Jesus who is followed (whether it is possible for the Kingdom to be extended and the anti-Kingdom diminished), and not only to the (unverifiable) Christ who is confessed in faith (his universal lordship). Now if the following of Jesus (a historical reality) can provide this experience of the "more," then it can make sense to confess that in Jesus true life has appeared and God has become present in him. The leap of faith and limit-statement about Christ can still be made (or no longer made); if it is, then this act of faith also becomes victory, as in Johannine theology.

In theological tradition the element of surrender has been formulated most radically as *sacrificium intellectus* or, in more biblical language, as the surrender of the whole person to God—taken up once more by Vatican II, as in *Dei Verbum* (no. 6). This happens in the noetic way of understanding, which ends in adoration, but it is most apparent in the historical way of following. In this, noetic surrender goes with surrender of the person: following Jesus to the end means readiness to give out of one's own life and even one's actual life. *Sacrificium intellectus* is then integrated into *sacrificium vitae*.

In Latin America this has been more than words. The following of Jesus to the end affirms faith in Jesus, and far more so if this end is martyrdom, since life is something one surrenders reasonably only for something this is truly held to be ultimate. (I do not believe that it is possible to lay down one's life for something penultimate, something purely *ideological*—a doctrine of whatever stamp—as, lamentably, the martyrs of Latin America have sometimes been accused of doing.) Rahner sees it as quite possible that "the moral personality of Jesus, summed up in his word and his life, should actually produce such a strong impression on individuals as to make them give themselves unconditionally in life and death to this Jesus."[18] In these words Rahner is seeking to demonstrate the possibility of an "orthodox Jesuanism" in places where the language of orthodoxy damages rather than helps faith in Jesus Christ. But beyond this pastoral intention, this "unconditional giving" is surrender, the leap of faith, at least implicit faith in Jesus.

Understanding Jesus Christ requires surrender, but, conversely, where such surrender exists he is being proclaimed as ultimate divine reality. *Fides quae* (in who Jesus Christ is) depends chronologically and logically on *fides qua* (the very act of believing in Jesus Christ). There is, then, a correlation between the act and the object of faith. The object of faith will *a priori* require a particular act, but in turn the quality of the act will say something essential about the content of its object. Now if there is an *act* of faith in Jesus that places absolute trust in him and makes oneself absolutely available to him, then one is implicitly but really affirming something absolute about the content because there has been true surrender, a leap of faith.[19]

Establishing this transcendental correlation between the act and the object of faith, between *fides qua* and *fides quae*, can remain on the level of purely conceptual tautology and so, to the extent that it does so, sterile. But it can be fruitful if the basic content of *fides qua* is brought in—surrender in life and death to Jesus, the *following* of Jesus *to the end*. If no limits are set to following, we are making a journey that leads (or can lead) to doxological confession of the divinity of Jesus Christ.

(iii) Putting the christological experience into words. The journey and the surrender together make up the christological experience, which is a sort of categorial reverberation of the ultimate experience of faith. From this point of view, the definitions do indeed put experiences into words. Experience is the source of understanding; it is "prior in some way to 'metaphysical' christology."[20] And without this experience language will remain pure phoneme.

The experience precedes the putting into words, but the latter in turn follows the former by necessity. Reality always seeks to express itself; it fights to "make itself heard." Christological verbal expressions have been varied throughout the course of history. They can be densely conceptual, such as the conciliar definitions; they can be both linguistically and conceptually simple, such as, "he went about doing good . . . for God was with him" (Acts 10:38); or they can be sophisticated, such as the following by Karl Rahner:

> God has promised me himself in Jesus totally and irrevocably, and this promise can now not be refused or revised despite the infinite possibilities at God's command: he has set the world and its history a goal, a goal that is himself, and this position is not only something eternally present in God's thought; it is something already installed by God within the world and history: it is Jesus, crucified and raised.[21]

From Latin America the experience can be put into words with the simplicity of Puebla: there is a search for "the ever new face of Christ, who is the answer to their legitimate yearning for integral liberation" (no. 173). Or it can be said that Jesus Christ has irrevocably brought "the good news of the definitive mediator of the Kingdom of God for the poor."

Any form of words, though necessary, should be self-critical. Christological language, seen from faith, must in its turn allow God to take it up and destroy it in order to express himself.[22] It should even be conscious of its possible sinful use, which would happen, for example, if its definitions (biblical, dogmatic, modern) were read in such a way as to detract from Jesus of Nazareth turned to the poor (the most perennial problem) or from humanity in its feminine or non-Western forms or in such a way as effectively to exclude the Kingdom, the power of the anti-Kingdom, and the like; or again in such a way as to disguise the fact that Christ is God's initiative.

What can ultimately overcome the limitations of any form of verbal expression is christological experience—following and surrender—because it offers a real referent: the life and fate of Jesus. Only in this way shall we have any hold against the "metaphysical vertigo"[23] produced by the conciliar definitions. In its turn, christological experience should be collated with biblical and dogmatic definitions so as to draw both questioning and encouragement from them. As always, we are faced with a hermeneutical circle. But the circle is broken by what originated it: the experience that the following of and surrender to Jesus produces in believers.

Finally, let me say that something being good news engenders a specific need for putting it into words: the good news produces joy and gratitude, and gratitude cannot remain dumb forever. When christological forms of words stem from gratitude, then they are recovering *in actu* the dimension of good news possessed by Jesus Christ. And conversely, if this were not the case, if there were no gratitude, the definitions would be trying to express the reality of Jesus Christ to clarify it for limited or dangerous ideologies but leaving out its being good news—a more serious problem, probably, than that of orthodoxy.

(c) Following and Spirit in Knowledge of Christ

I have insisted that in order to gain understanding of Jesus Christ we need a *journey*, that of following, and *surrender* of the whole person, which presupposes some type of affinity on the journey. In Johannine theology the one who shows the truth of Jesus and who leads us into all truth is the Spirit. The question, then, is to see how following and Spirit converge in coming to know Jesus Christ. My thesis can be formulated thus: the following of Jesus is the *channel* we have to follow (the christological dimension), and the Spirit is the *strength* given to follow it in today's conditions (the pneumatological dimension).

Following and Spirit do not coexist in juxtaposition; they cannot, naturally, generate different, let alone contrary dynamics. They are rather convergent realities that respond to distinct spheres of existence. Following is the structure of life, the *channel* marked out by Jesus along which to journey, and the Spirit is the *strength* that enables us to carry on following this channel in a real and relevant manner throughout history. So rather than "carrying on," we should speak of "carrying out," and so the whole of Christian life can be described as "carrying out Jesus with spirit." The "carrying" refers to the channel of the authentic life mapped out by Jesus' life; the "out" refers to the perennial need for bringing up to date and openness to the novelty of the future; the "with spirit" refers to the strength needed to undertake this journey in the actual situation.

The Spirit did not invent, so to speak, the structure of following down through history, since that structure was already established in Jesus. In Ellacuría's construction, the basis of this structure can be described as "taking stock" of reality (being actively involved in reality: the *incarnation*); "taking charge" of reality (proclaiming the Kingdom and combating the anti-Kingdom: the public life, *mission*); "shouldering" reality (the burden of reality, conflicts, persecution: the *cross*); "being taken up" by reality (utopia-producing grace: the *resurrection*).

This is what we have to re-create in following Jesus, and this is what Jesus has bequeathed to us. "Convincing ourselves of this," in the face of temptation to ignore it or distort it, and re-creating the structure of Jesus' life according to actual needs, not mechanically, is the work of the Spirit, which has always led us back to Jesus of Nazareth and revealed the truth of Christ to us throughout history. Following should not suffocate the Spirit; it requires it, rather, so that they refer mutually to one another. (Notable followers of Jesus have—at the same time—been open to the Spirit. Francis of Assisi sought only to be *repetitor Christi* and to carry out the gospel "without gloss," yet he introduced a whole new wave into social and church history. Dietrich Bonhoeffer, a notable theologian of following, brought unsuspected novelties: "living *etsi Deus non daretur*," calling Jesus "the man for others," and in his personal life taking part in a plot against Hitler [which cost him his life: the unexpected and—among theologians—rare novelty of martyrdom]. Oscar Romero led a revolution in the church [greater than those normally originated by people who devote themselves exclusively to cultivating the Spirit], but one wholly based on re-creating Jesus' life: incarnation in the existence of the poor, mission in the service of the Kingdom and against the anti-Kingdom, taking up his cross, and so on.)

Today, with the proliferation of movements relying on the Spirit (more as an expression of the marvelous and esoteric than as the reality that inspires following of Jesus), in which—with all due respect—the Spirit sometimes seems to be invoked as a *deus ex machina* rather than as the Spirit of the God of Jesus Christ, it is incumbent on us to stick to the thesis: the Spirit gives us strength to follow, but the following—and not esoteric conceptions—is the proper setting for the Spirit. The way that leads to knowledge of Jesus Christ is "following with spirit" but not the action of the Spirit cut off from following.

This is my basic thesis, and I should like to illustrate it now from the life of Jesus of Nazareth. Once the basic structure of this life has been established, we need to examine whether and how the Spirit becomes present in it, so that following Jesus will—for us—be carrying out in history not just a life "deprived of spirit" but one "full of spirit." In other words, the Spirit is made present not only in the *subjectivity* of those who follow Jesus but also in the *object* of their following. If we go back to Jesus' life, then, we find, on the one hand, that he said little about the Spirit and nothing about its personality, but, on the other, that he is described by the evangelists as possessed by the Spirit of God: at his baptism, in the temptations, at the start of his public life in the synagogue at Nazareth, and so on. The synoptic tradition even reifies this Spirit to some degree by regarding it as a "power" *(exousia, dynamis)*: "power had gone forth from him" (Mk 5:30; Lk 8:46).

More than this reifying (and personalizing) interpretation of this power that went forth from Jesus, however, the synoptics show what I see as more primary and basic: Jesus' life is shot through with a special power; it is a life "inspired by the Spirit of God," which means that following Jesus at this point of history will be following someone who, in his lifetime, was filled with the Spirit, and so following this "Jesus with spirit" will include his followers' readiness to let themselves be affected by whatever "spirit" might be for them. (Although the distinction is not always clear, I am using "Spirit" and "Spirit of God" [capital S] to refer to the Holy Spirit, the third person of the Trinity, and "spirit" [lower case] to refer to the Spirit's actual manifestations in history.)

The fact that Jesus lived, worked, and died "with spirit" is undeniable. There is no way his life can be seen as something mechanical: he is shown as coming up against the real world of his time in a particular, novel, and unflagging manner. These particular "ways" of coming up against the real world are the "spirit" with which he lived in the various spheres of life, which can—later, from faith—be interpreted as manifestations of the Spirit of God. Let us now look, systematically, at these manifestations of the Spirit in Jesus: the Spirit of *newness*, the Spirit of *truth and life*, the Spirit of *ecstasy* toward the Father.

(i) The Spirit of newness. Jesus positions himself as a creature before God. In the scene of the temptations, composed so as to tell us that Jesus discerned God's will concerning the central purpose of his life, Jesus is debating with the devil only in appearance; his true interlocutor is God. He tries to discern what (new) good there is to do and how he should do it: Jesus' life is imbued with the spirit of *discernment*. To serve what he discerns, Jesus employed his freedom: the Law, the Temple, religious traditions were all relativized, denounced, or abolished as the occasion demanded. Most important, he exercised this freedom not to defend some liberal idea but to defend love, justice, and mercy: Jesus' life is imbued with the spirit of *freedom*. Between the beginning and the end of his life an un-foreseen newness comes in: God, the Kingdom, discipleship, and healings were very different matters in the early days in Galilee and in the final days in Jerusalem. Jesus is open to newness: he trusts in a God-Father who is close to him but who is still the immovable God-mystery. Jesus died and moved toward the final future in openness to this newness: Jesus' life is imbued with the spirit of *newness* and openness to the *future*.

(ii) The Spirit of truth and life. The Spirit not only becomes evident in *attitudes* but provides contents—"Lord and giver of life, who has spoken through the prophets." For Jesus, his own life meant giving life, defending those whose life has been taken from them; he himself lived through providing life for the poor: Jesus' life is imbued with the spirit of *life*. Jesus "spoke with authority," convinced of what he was saying, not like irrational fanatics or paid officials. He was not naive about truth, not did he assume that it abounded in this world—not so much on account of general ignorance as because of lies and the generalized structural deceit. This produced his debates concerning truth, beginning with the truth of God, his unmasking of what sought to pass as God and was not God, his denunciations of idols as active rivals of God, who are not inert but who act against God: Jesus' life is imbued with the spirit of *truth*. Jesus' actions are governed by the "new commandment," of which he "gives an example." Mercy—which defines the full human being (the good Samaritan) and the heavenly Father ("moved with pity, he went out to meet his son")—is also what defines Jesus himself, who acts after the plea, "Have mercy on me": Jesus' life is imbued with the spirit of *love and mercy*.

(iii) The Spirit of ecstasy. The word *ecstasy* is a dangerous one: it can indicate the esoteric and the a-historical. But there is perhaps no other with which to describe this specific action of the Spirit of God, who has the power to work the miracle of setting us free and taking us out of ourselves. Paul states that it is the Spirit who makes us call God *Abba*, Father, the term Jesus uses consistently and naturally, with the sole exception of his cry from the cross, "My God, my God, why have

you abandoned me?" Jesus' life is imbued with the spirit of prayer; his is a graced life. His mission shows no hubris or Promethean attitude; his acceptance of God's initiative shows in everything he does. The Kingdom has to be served, but it still grows even when human beings are not on the watch for it. The Kingdom has to be made, but we still have to pray, "Thy kingdom come": Jesus' life is imbued with the spirit of *gratuitousness*. This is where Jesus' true *ecstasy* appears, his basic other-centeredness, his going out from himself: I say this because the ecstatic is usually the realm attributed—often most inappropriately—to the Spirit. No conventionally ecstatic or even mystical or trance states are recorded of Jesus, but we are told that he "went out of himself." In completely unextravagant but deeply historical words, Jesus goes out from his own self—that self that so often resounded in triumph: "You have heard . . . but I tell you"—and hands it over to the Father: "Not my will but yours be done."

Whatever one may think of this analysis, the conclusion has to be that Jesus' life is imbued with spirit, independently of what he may have said about the Spirit. For Jesus, in effect, as for any human being, "being spiritual" is determined not by speaking *about* the Spirit but in being and speaking *in* the Spirit and *with* spirit: "a power went forth from him." And when this happens, God's power can be present "even to move mountains"—not, though, as falling back on esoteric powers but as the ultimate choice to do good.

What does all this mean for coming to know Jesus? It means that following the historical Jesus today does not (mechanically) reproduce a life lived mechanically by Jesus but reproduces and brings alive (with spirit) a life that was lived with spirit. Following is, then, the setting where manifestations of the Spirit come about and the place for "getting in tune" with the Spirit of God. And, as a result, it is the place for recognizing—doxologically—that it is the Spirit of God who teaches us who Jesus is, which is the power of God "to do even greater things."

The New Testament, Chalcedon, and the later theologies have the audacity to define the ultimate reality of Jesus Christ. What I have tried to say in this chapter is that understanding them, whatever their worldviews and forms of words, requires us to follow both a theoretical and a historical route. Along this route we experience whether Jesus of Nazareth is drawing us into history in a more adequate way, enabling us to play our part in it in a more human way, to stand outside ourselves in order to be for others, to walk in hope toward an absolute, unknown, mysterious, and utopic future, to walk with God and toward God.

The route on which we can make this experience is, in the final analysis, the following of Jesus, always set in history "with spirit" and always actualized by "the Spirit of God." This is what following Jesus as an epistemological principle means.

Epilogue

Memory and Journey

I had originally planned to end with an epilogue on Christian identity, which, following what I had said in the first volume about Jesus of Nazareth and in this one about Jesus Christ, would express what it means to be a Christian today. But the idea was pretentious, since the New Testament already shows not one but several forms of Christian identity. It would also have been a far-reaching task, and I have settled for a more modest title and scope for this epilogue, concentrating on two aspects of this identity. Throughout the two volumes I have tried to show that, from Jesus Christ, Christian faith has good news as its central content: Jesus proclaims and brings in the good news of the Kingdom of God; he himself—through his fate, his actions, his whole being—is good news; his resurrection brings hope to victims and, through them, to all. I have dealt with the dogmatic definitions, too, in such a way as to bring out not only their truth but their dimension of good news: it is good that existence is a whole and that its divine and human dimensions converge without mixture or division. I have also stressed the dialectic opposite to good news: the anti-Kingdom, the idols and their agencies, existence stymied or distorted. . . . With this, Christian identity acquires realism and is required to make resistance to adverse forces and shouldering the burden of reality part of its essence. Finally, I have also insisted on the following of Jesus and on its basic structure—which has to be remade with spirit and in the Spirit—and on the fact that this following is the way to God.

Both volumes are made up of these elements and the christology underlying them. This christology, it seems to me, is in the end a sort of parable about Jesus Christ, which, like all parables, forces its readers/hearers to adopt a stance and make a decision. In his parables Jesus was effectively saying to his listeners: "Do you think the father was right to celebrate the return of the son who had left his home, or is the elder brother right to protest this attitude? Which one do you identify with?" In much the same way, faced with one christological text or another, readers have to make up their minds: "Is it true that Jesus, his God, the Kingdom, are true referents of humanity; are they both good news and a challenge to struggle against the idols and their agents and works? Or is this all pure illusion and would it be more sensible to disengage, to domesticate the spur of human existence in either epicureanism or stoicism, to look away?" It is in the theoretical, but above all historical response to these questions that, in my view, we build up—or destroy—Christian identity.

I am not going to repeat what has already been said in these pages to throw light on the answer, but I should like to end by putting forward two reflections that may help to set us or keep us in the Christian way of being and journeying in history in a particular manner. The two reflections are on *memory* and *journey*, and I have chosen these from among other possible elements because both are logically required by christology and because both seem to me necessary at the present time.

1. Memory: Things to Remember

In this epilogue I am not going to introduce here subjects I have not already tackled in some form. What this epilogue adds lies in the viewpoint: memory. I say it like this because of the permanent—and certainly actual—danger of forgetting. Let us, then, look at what we have to remember today out of faithfulness to Jesus.

(a) The Undeducible Originality of Jesus' God

I have spoken of the undeducible originality of the Christian God. I should now like to demonstrate it in another—and perhaps surprising—way, building on the dogmatic reflection of the last few chapters. I start with this quotation from Juan Luis Segundo, which may not appear at all clear, as he himself admits:

> I was saying . . . that the primitive nature of some of the instruments employed [at the council]—such as the notion of "nature"—has made many people think that Chalcedon has been left irredeemably behind. I believe, nonetheless, that quite the opposite is happening, or should happen. The depth of that conciliar definition has perhaps not been fully grasped yet. And if it has not been then what happened afterwards should not be seen as the "results" of Chalcedon but, strictly speaking, as the results of forgetting it, with the christological distortions that were to be feared.[1]

The writer is referring to God in these provocative words. He is saying that Chalcedon can teach us something important about God but that this important something is usually left out of account. What is perhaps still more shocking is that he deduces the important thing about God he wants to mention from a particular interpretation of the *communicatio idiomatum*, preceding the above quotation.[2]

As a brief reminder of the process, Nicaea started the journey of confessing the personal unity of Jesus Christ, which was debated explicitly at Ephesus, prompted by the *theotokos* controversy—whether Mary was or was not Mother of God. By answering in the affirmative, Ephesus laid down a basic principle: what is stated of the two natures has to be predicated of the ultimate divine subject. So if

Jesus was born of Mary, if he suffered and died, this cannot be denied of the Word. The reason for this is that what is predicated of a single subject cannot be separated.

This is what led to the formulation of the *communicatio idiomatum*, but Chalcedon introduced something new: the two natures in which the *logos* subsists are not mixed, from which Segundo draws this conclusion: "If they are not mixed, each and every one of the things we can perceive directly in the story of Jesus will be properly and fully human. His divinity will be beyond our perception: we can only infer it."[3] This means that we can predicate what we see in Jesus of God. But what can we predicate of Jesus basing ourselves on an inference of what God is? What happens in reality is that the *communicatio* works only in one direction. We can say of God that he had a mother, that he suffered and died, but we cannot say of Jesus that he was unmoved, all-powerful, immortal, omniscient. . . .

Segundo's conclusion is that,

> As we picture it today, the question of whether Jesus was God . . . would have consisted in knowing whether the less familiar term—Jesus—fitted or not into the universally familiar category of what [a] God was. But however the question may have been put and answered in the early centuries of the church, by the time of Ephesus and Chalcedon it can clearly be seen that the question has been put the other way: how far did Jesus clarify or correct what was understood by God?[4]

This leads to my first reflection on Christian identity: we must not start by presupposing that we already know who God is, nor must we think that at a particular point in the faith process God ceases to be "mystery," a dazzling "excess of light." Acceptance of our "unknowing," which always needs Jesus Christ, is an essential element in our knowledge of God. We saw this, in another context, in the examination of titles given to Christ: we should not say that Jesus (what is not yet actually known) is Lord (known as a universal thing); it should be the other way round. The same is true to an even greater extent of God. We should not simply say that Jesus is God, as though the surprise attached to *Jesus,* but that God is what appears in Jesus of Nazareth, which attaches the surprise to what *God* is.

The fact that God is manifest in Jesus appears in all the strata of the New Testament, in the theologies of the Fathers, and, in its deepest forms of expression, in the conciliar definitions. This is what has to be remembered "perennially," corresponding to the "perennial" mystery of God, and it has to be remembered today. Only in this way can we come to know God and to avoid a great danger, perhaps the greatest danger and the specific temptation for the Christian faith: a theism without Jesus—which can come to be a theism against Jesus. As a cornerstone of our identity, we have to avoid a faith in God that—if we are honest with ourselves—has no need of Jesus and can lead to actions that blaspheme the name of God. "Jesus, fully human at the same time as perfect God, thereby makes us understand what this concept of divinity actually entails. And the answer is that God has to be understood following the key provided by Jesus' life, which is none other than the historical project of the *Kingdom of God*, with the specific contents he gave it."[5]

(b) The Central Place of the Kingdom of God

Upholding Chalcedon, remembering that we meet God essentially in Jesus, is the first and deepest thing we have to remember. But this has brought us to another reality, well known and dealt with at length in the first volume, which we also have to remember—the Kingdom of God. I come back to it now from the viewpoint of what has to be "upheld" if there is to be a Christian identity. And upholding it is not easy, for practical reasons but also for theoretical ones, which I propose to set out briefly. We saw that the christology of the New Testament developed out of two things: (1) the experience of Jesus' *resurrection,* and (2) the memory of what was fundamental in his *earthly life*. The first is obvious, but the second is less so and needs some clarification for the following reason: the synoptics present Jesus' life in a double constituent relationship, with a God who is *Abba* and with the *Kingdom* of God. In the New Testament overall *christology*—taking the resurrection as given—developed out of the relationship with the *Abba* God, so that within a period of ten or twenty years—according to Marcel Hengel—it had taken the direction that has come down to the present: *Jesus is the Son of God.*

Jesus' relationship with the Kingdom of God, however, which was just as much constituent of his life, gradually disappeared from christological thought or, at best, was reinterpreted in such a way that, although major values attaching to the Kingdom were kept, its central place was lost. The earliest formulas of faith, in Acts and Paul's letters, are centered on Jesus, to which mention of the Father and the Spirit was then added, but the *Kingdom*, the *eu-aggelion* Jesus proclaimed in order to be accepted in faith, does not appear in them. In the same way, the rite of baptism was preceded by a catechesis on Jesus, on his present state as exalted Lord and on the good news, but the latter was no longer the Kingdom of God (with the exception of Acts 8:12) but the salvation that has been worked in Christ Jesus. Later on, in the Gospel of John, the Kingdom of God and the salvation this brings were to be replaced, basically, by the Son and eternal life.

In the New Testament this was indicative of an understandable—and to an extent necessary—newness; in future centuries it was to lead to the virtual disappearance of the Kingdom from the Christian worldview, and Christian identity did not include remaking, historicizing the Kingdom of God proclaimed by Jesus. Typical of this process was the gradual appearance of three forms of devaluing, canceling, and even distorting the Kingdom of God—which, under different guises, may well still be operative.

One is the *personalization* of the Kingdom: Christ is "the Kingdom of God in person," *autobasileia tou Theou*, as Origen was to say in the third century. In this way a major change was worked in the very formal understanding of what the Kingdom of God is. It ceased to be the type of historical-social-collective reality that Jesus preached and became a different sort of reality, a personal one, which left the original concept unconsidered. The central—and utopic—place is now accorded only to the *person* of Jesus. I am obviously not denying that Jesus' person embodied Kingdom values, but, however trivial the point may appear, the reality of the Kingdom preached by Jesus (with its roots in the Old Testament) was not conceived as a person (even a collective person) but as a transformed social reality.

A second and more serious form of devaluation is the spurious *ecclesialization* of the Kingdom of God. It is true that the church is a sign of the Kingdom (as indicated by Vatican II), but under the regime of Christendom (and of the "perfect society," years later) the church came to be equated with the Kingdom of God when it effectively passed itself off as the ultimate, which led to grave errors and even aberrations.

Finally, the Kingdom is devalued by removing it to the beyond, a tendency already apparent in the sixth century, or by shifting it to the realm of a-historical and esoteric interiority, a recurrent tendency still operative today. The most serious result (varying from non-Jesuslike to downright anti-Jesus) is that in this way the relationship between the Kingdom of God and the liberation of the poor *is removed from the course of history*, as we shall see next.

This tendency—miraculously, one might say—was reversed almost two millennia after Jesus. The Kingdom of God as the central message of Jesus was recovered a century ago, but in the actual life of the church the change began to operate, timidly at first around Vatican II, and then openly at Medellín. This means that throughout virtually the whole of the church's history the Kingdom has been absent or, as I have just explained, distorted—to which has to be added the present "restoration" project, theoretical and actual. The central place in present-day teaching is not accorded to what was central to Jesus' preaching: the Kingdom of God. As a result, consciously or unconsciously, the reality of Jesus is being impaired or even distorted. And so—automatically, according to Chalcedon—the reality of God is impaired or distorted. This is why we must remember the Kingdom of God.

(c) The Theologal Status of the Poor

The most serious aspect of the disappearance of the Kingdom of God is, in my view, that with it the centrality given to the poor disappears from Christian identity. The most fundamental thing about the Kingdom of God, according to Jeremias, is that it is "*only* for the poor" (the italics being the author's and the poor understood as those for whom the minimum of a life is a heavy burden and who are marginalized and despised). Remembering the poor, however, is a difficult business. The structural difficulties, the selfishness and disdain ranged against them, are obvious: the conversion of Dives, unmoved by the sight of Lazarus (and, as Jesus said of his kind, unmovable "even though one should rise from the dead"), is virtually impossible. It is with impotence that one has to agree that "deaf ears" are being turned to "cases that should make us lose sleep" (the inhuman situation of humankind).[6]

It is also difficult to remember what matters most to the poor: their utopia, for example. Seen as a whole and not just from its islands of abundance, this world is marked more by lies, injustice, exclusion, and death than by truth, justice, free-dom, dignity, and life. What sort of utopia we need is obvious—and the poor remind us of it—but the difficulties in defining it are great. Our world tolerates "light" utopias but not one of a Kingdom for the poor and the resultant struggle against the anti-Kingdom—concepts too large for the world of today to grasp, even though, without blinking, it can devise grandiose ideas such as the global village, the end of history, globalization, and so on.

The difficulty is not merely anthropological and social in nature; it is also theological and ecclesial. Other concepts in the Christian worldview have been recovered with (relatively) greater ease at some points in history—though also sometimes with great difficulty—than the Kingdom and the poor, and this makes one think. Grace and freedom, for example, were restored by Augustine and Luther, the Jesus who came from Nazareth and his following by many holy people in the church's history. But the same has not happened to the Kingdom of God and the poor.

In my view the main problem in accepting the central place of the Kingdom lies in the fact that doing so not only leads back to Jesus of Nazareth but also gives a primary and preferential place to the poor of this world. And these poor have definite characteristics: they are in the majority (which makes other groups the exceptions); they are a necessary historical product (of various "world or-ders"); they are dialectically poor (because there are rich and oppressors); they are marginalized, despised, and excluded (because they do not fulfill the require-ments for humankind as dictated by the ruling cultures). They call the church into question, as nothing else does, which means that they have always been taken some account of by the church, but they have not been its central concern.

The most serious aspect from a theological point of view is that the poor have not come to possess the theologal status they deserve according to Jesus (Medellín, liberation theology). The New Testament contains what one might call *constella-tions,* components grouped around some central Christian concept in accordance with a logic in faith. Some of these seem to be accorded theologal status more easily than others (such as the elements of the Pauline constellation, though not, of course, exclusive to him: grace, Spirit, freedom, justification, hubris, and the like). The elements of the constellation surrounding the Kingdom—the poor, lib-eration, structural sin—are generally (with some exceptions) kept on the ethical and spiritual levels but not advanced to the theologal one. The "God who justifies the sinner" has come to be a theologal and even dogmatic statement; the "God who has compassion for the poor and the oppressed" does not generally reach this level. The "justification of sinners" has dogmatic roots; not so the "liberation of the poor." The "option for the poor" is qualified, questioned, even where it has not died the death of a thousand distinctions.

As long as they are not seen in their primary relationship with God, "the poor," "the victims," "the crucified peoples," "liberation," "society," "the social ques-tion" will always be taken into account in ethics and in spirituality, but they will not belong to theology and still less to what is theologal. (And here, indeed, lies a major difference between the social teaching of the church and liberation theol-ogy. The first—necessarily and importantly—is more ethical; the second is more theologal.) We need, then, to remember the poor, and remember them in their theologal reality: "they are God's chosen ones."

2. Journey

I have already discussed the journey aspect of Christian faith, particularly in the last chapter when dealing with the following of Jesus, a structure bequeathed by Jesus himself with the need to set it in history and bring it up to date with the power of God, the Spirit. I can therefore be briefer in this second section, but I come back to it because it seems to me an essential element of Christian identity and because it seems important at the present time. Today we speak of disillusion after the hope of past decades, which in the Christian faith began soon after the resurrection. We are told that now there are no absolutes, that everything is relative, and that it is *sauve qui peut*. At this juncture, then, there seems to be more of fluidity than of solidity, which alone would make the journey image useful. But it is not the present juncture that leads me to make use of it; it is something more theological. I am not trying to present Christianity today in such a way as to "make a virtue out of necessity"; I am, however, trying to be "honest with reality." Let me say at the start, then, that I am not proposing to take a stroll but to set out on a journey. And, as I did with memory, I begin with the theologal reality on which our journey is based.

(a) The Future of God

The Christian's journey has to be understood as, above all, the human correlation to the process within God himself. The unresolved tension, which impedes possession and imposes the journey, is theologal: it is the tension between a God of life, of liberation, of resurrection, and a crucified God. I have expressed this as the tension between a *Deus semper maior*, greater than anything, and a *Deus semper minor*, always smaller and more impoverished; the tension between a God who is Father, in whom we can trust and rest, and a Father who goes on being God, for whom we always have to be ready and who will not let us rest. And to this intra-theologal tension we have to add the struggle between the God of life and the idols of death.

If this is so, then only the future can decide the truth of this God in tension, and so futurity is proper to God, as theology has taught in the footsteps of Ernst Bloch. I am taking it up again here, not only or mainly on account of the anthropological and metaphysical importance of the future but because the tension within the very God requires it. In relation to the totality of the mystery of God, God's manifestation has been put back to the end of history, but not only because this not-yet can reveal the totality—since only the end can determine the process, as Hegel stated—or only because God has already been revealed in the resurrection but not-yet in fullness, but because the cross of history remains as a massive anti-life reality even after Jesus' resurrection. The massive permanence of the cross is not only what may rule in the short time before the parousia but what remains as an essential element throughout the course of human history.

All through history cross and resurrection, word and silence, power and weakness, showing and hiding have upheld each other and referred one to another, without any aspect of the unique revelation of God having the capacity to annul the other. This means that when I said that God reveals himself through a process and that revelation will happen at the end, "when God will be all in all," this is based on a reason intrinsic to existence itself and not just on a formal argument that only the end gives meaning to the process. The end is not merely the finish of what is provisional in temporality; it is a victory—"when all enemies will have been conquered"—over the forces of evil. This is what derives from a view of God from the victims.

(b) A Journeying Faith

The response of faith to this God can be theoretically diverse: from pure submission to the lordship of God, gratitude for the salvation God brings, and hope for the futurity there is in God to protest (and even blasphemy) at God's silence and inaction in the face of the tragedy of history and doing without God on account of the absurdity of this silence and inaction. I believe, however, that we can also respond and correspond to God by making our response include the dialectic proper to God's saving, partial, dialectical, and journeying reality. Christian faith in a journeying God can then be understood as the way we journey in history responding and corresponding to this God. By this I am not just referring to *homo viator*, which human beings are, transcendentally, owing to their historicity. Far less am I encouraging a mere wander through history as a concession to the relativization operating in many spheres of life. Faith is a journey in the sense that the apparently contrary aspects of response and correspondence to the journeying God are integrated in it.

Even if faith is defined as Micah's "walk humbly" (6:8), doing justice and loving tenderly, or as the "follow me" of Jesus' demand, proclaiming and bringing in the Kingdom of God, in faithfulness to his own fate to the end, these specific aspects seem to me to be the following: (1) incarnation in the actual situation, in the world of the victims, that is, countering the tendency to escape—roughly or subtly—from history; (2) hope of fullness in the future, despite and contrary to the omnipresence of the crosses of history; (3) journeying in action, acting with justice, building the Kingdom against the obstacles posed by persecution and death—beyond a purely expectant hope; (4) denouncing the anti-Kingdom, taking on the consequences, however onerous; (5) letting oneself be borne along by what is new, the Spirit of God that blows where it will; (6) being humble about our journey, not claiming to resolve in history what can be resolved only at the end, contrary to every kind of gnosis and dogmatism; (7) continuing on our journey in the face of all the obstacles, ideologies, and siren songs that would make it reasonable to abandon it.

Undoubtedly, faith in a God from the victims includes not abandoning the journey—or, more accurately, not being able to abandon it—as an essential element. The victims—whether they (and we) accept God, doubt God, or blaspheme against God—present us with the absolute demand to strive ceaselessly to take them down from the cross. And the victims provide us with the grace and light to see that, despite everything, it is good to go on journeying in their service. This not being able to abandon the journey, wherever it might lead, despite everything, is the translation into historical terms of letting God be God.

For many people—as I have been able to verify in El Salvador—this journey, full of darkness and suffering though it is, also produces a feeling of life and even joy. On this journey people find history and human beings giving more of themselves, thereby enabling them, despite everything, to give a name to the mystery of existence and to call it *Abba*, Father. As long as this happens, there will be people who—like Jesus—walk with God and journey toward the mystery of God.

(c) Journeying in History

The above has major implications for theology. As faith is a journey in working to bring the victims down from the cross, so theology is *intellectus amoris*. As faith is a journey in the hope that God will work justice and the executioner will not triumph over the victim, so theology is *intellectus spei*. As faith is not being able to abandon the journey because something that has been before us moves us to continue ("Within me there is something like a burning fire shut up in my bones; I am weary with holding it in, and I cannot" [Jer 20:9]), so theology is *intellectus gratiae*. But its importance lies above all in how it affects Christian identity.

The Spanish poet Antonio Machado immortalized the humility of journeying in his lines, *caminante, no hay camino, / se hace camino al andar* (Traveler, there is no road, / you make the road by walking). In Latin America the bishop/poet Pedro Casaldáliga has reinterpreted these from praxis, hope, and the poor of his people:

Camino que uno es	The road that you are
que uno hace al andar.	you make by walking.
Para que otros caminantes	So that other travelers
puedan el camino hallar.	may find their way.
Para que los atascados	So that those who are stuck
se puedan reanimar.	may find fresh heart.
Para que los ya perdidos	So that those now lost
nos puedan reencontrar.	may find us once more.
Haz del canto de tu pueblo	Make the song of your people
el ritmo de tu marchar.	the rhythm of your step.

Christianity is, I believe, if one wants to stick with this imagery, a religion of journeying through history. Such a description seems to me to go beyond the distinction between religions of *agape* and religions of *gnosis*. Christianity is certainly a religion of *agape*, but it is given hope, on the one hand, and called to account, on the other, by the very existence of victims. These also mean that its *agape* has to be historical and transforming of history. In turn, Christianity provides light for the journey, even though it certainly comes up against the opacity of the real world and its darkness. But the true *gnosis* that corresponds to God's revelation comes about only at the end. Where Christianity is indeed expert is in knowing how to walk in history, how to keep walking always and despite everything, and how to walk humanizing others, the victims and ourselves. As elders to guide the way it has Jesus of Nazareth and so many witnesses down through history: in our time Dietrich Bonhoeffer, Simone Weil, Martin Luther King Jr.; from where I write, Archbishop Romero, Ignacio Ellacuría and his companions, Celina Ramos, and most recently Juan Gerardi—a whole constellation of witnesses, martyrs who not only bear witness to Christ but who remake the life and fate of Jesus. "If every one of [their names] were written down, I suppose that the world itself could not contain the books that would be written" (Jn 21:25).

On this journey through history, not going outside history but taking flesh and delving deep into history, it can happen that reality gives more of itself, and the conviction can grow (or decrease) that the journey is a coming from, that there is an ultimate origin providing the initiative for everything good (protology), and that we are traveling to a final fulfilling destination (eschatology). This is a knowing in faith, no longer historical but transcendent: the journey is enveloped in the mystery of the beginning and the end, a mystery that antedates us, from which we come, which moves us to good and leads us to hope for eternal life.

This mystery is grace, and the victims of this world, the crucified peoples, can be, and in my view are, the mediation of this grace. The victims provide the dynamism—the quasi-physical "shove"—for carrying out the task of journeying that involves taking the crucified peoples down from their cross. And the victims provide the stubbornness of hoping against hope, hoping, in the end, that the executioner will not triumph over the victims. The victims demand a religion of journeying, but they provide directions for the journey and the grace to go on traveling.

There are many things to be said about Christian identity in our time, but perhaps these two will suffice: it means *remembering* what is important, without trivializing it, now that what's new seems to consign it to oblivion (even though history avenges itself on those who do so); it means *journeying* with the tenacity of hope that there is a goal, without trivializing this by turning it into a casual stroll.

We can, ultimately, respond to the living parable that is Jesus Christ on the personal level only. The purpose of what has been said in these two books is to provide conceptual encouragement for this response. But the greatest encouragement comes from those who inspire with their actual lives, those who today resemble Jesus by living and dying as he did. This is God's journey to this world of victims and martyrs, and it is the way to the Father and the way to human beings, above all to the poor and the victims of this world.

Abbreviations
and Short Forms

Adv. haer.	Irenaeus of Lyons, *Adversus omnes haereses.*
Adv. Marc.	Tertullian*, Adversus Marcion.*
Adv. Prax.	Tertullian, *Adversus Praxeam.*
Creeds	*Creeds, Councils, and Controversies: Documents illustrating the history of the Church AD 337–461,* ed. J. Stevenson, rev. W. H. C. Frend. London: SPCK, 1989.
De carne	Tertullian, *De carne Christi.*
De resu.	Tertullian, *De resurrectione carnis.*
DS	Denzinger-Schoenmetzer.
ECA	*Estudios centroamericanos*
Eph.	Ignatius of Antioch, *Letter to the Church of Ephesus.*
Epid.	Irenaeus of Lyons, *Eis Epideistin . . .* (The Demonstration of the Apostolic Preachings)
JL	Jon Sobrino, *Jesus the Liberator: A Historical-Theological Reading of Jesus of Nazareth.* Maryknoll, N.Y.: Orbis Books, 1993; Tunbridge Wells: Burns & Oates, 1994. Eng. trans. of *Jesucristo liberador. Lectura histórica-teológica de Jesús de Nazaret.* Madrid, 1991. The preceding volume of the present work.
Kasper	W. Kasper, *Jesus the Christ.* Tunbridge Wells: Burns & Oates; Mahwah, N.J.: Paulist Press, 1976. Eng. trans. of *Jesus der Christus.* Mainz, 1976.
LThK	*Lexikon für Theologie und Kirche.* Freiburg, 2d ed., 1957–.
Mag.	Ignatius of Antioch, *Letter to the Church of Magnesia.*
Medellín	Second General Conference of Latin American bishops, held in Medellín, Colombia, in 1968. English translation of the final documents in *The Church in the Present-day Transformation of Latin America.* Washington, D.C.: USSC, 1970.

Myst. Sal.	*Mysterium Salutis* 2/1 (Madrid, 1969). Trans. of *Mysterium Salutis. Grundriss heilesgeschichtlicher Dogmatique,* 10 vols. (Einseideln-Zurich-Cologne, 1965–70). There are corresponding French, Italian, and Spanish editions, but not English.
Puebla	Third General Conference of Latin American Bishops, held in Puebla, Mexico, in 1979. English translation of the final document in *Puebla and Beyond,* ed. J. Eagleson and P. Scharper. Maryknoll, N.Y.: Orbis, 1980; also in *Puebla.* Slough: St. Paul; London: CIIR, 1980.
RLT	*Revista Lationamericana de Teología.* San Salvador, 1974–.
Smyrn.	Ignatius of Antioch, *Letter to the Church of Smyrna.*
ThQ	*Theologische Quartalschrift.* Tübingen, 1819ff.; Stuttgart, 1946–.
Trall.	Ignatius of Antioch, *Letter to the Church of Tralles.*
ZthK	*Die Zeitschrift für Theologie und Kirche.* Tübingen, 1891– .

Notes

Introduction

1. Jon Sobrino, *Jesus the Liberator: A Historical-Theological Reading of Jesus of Nazareth* (Maryknoll, N.Y.: Orbis Books, 1993; Tunbridge Wells: Burns & Oates, 1994). Eng. trans. of *Jesucristo liberador. Lectura histórica-teológica de Jesús de Nazaret* (Madrid, 1991). (*JL*)

2. J.-B. Metz, "Teología europea y teología de la liberación," in J. Comblin, J. I. González Faus and J. Sobrino (eds.), *Cambio social y pensamiento cristiano en América Latina* (Madrid, 1993), p. 268.

3. Pedro Casaldáliga, *El cuerno del jubileo* (Madrid, 1998). p. 7.

PART I

THE RESURRECTION OF JESUS: RESURRECTION AND VICTIMS

1. Viewpoint: A "Risen" Following and the Hope of the Victims

1. The classic critique is that by Karl Rahner of the christology of the Biblioteca de Autores Cristianos (*Sacrae Theologiae Summa*, Madrid, 1956), typical of the pre–Vatican II period, in which less than a page was devoted to Jesus' resurrection.

2. Suffice to recall the impact made by the appearance of F. X. Durrwell, *Résurrection, mystère du salut* Paris, 1959). Eng. trans. *Resurrection: A Biblical Study* (London: Sheed & Ward, 1960).

3. Cf. J. Moltmann, *Jesus Christ for Today's World* (London: SCM Press; Minneapolis, Minn: Fortress Press, 1994), esp. the chapter "Resurrection in the Perspective of Nature," pp. 82–87. Eng. trans. of *Wer ist Christus für uns heute?* (Gütersloh, 1994).

4. Today the problems are greater for other reasons. Historical criticism has made it ever more difficult to read the texts covering Jesus' resurrection ingenuously. And culturally and psycho-socially, the question of the possibility of life in the beyond has widely ceased to be a central concern and does not generate the anguish to which Jesus' resurrection should give a Christian answer. We have come a long way from Unamuno's "tragic sense of life."

5. J. I. González Faus, *La humanidad nueva. Ensayo de cristología,* 6th ed. (Santander, 1984), p. 145, emphasis in the original.

6. J. Moltmann, *El camino de Jesucristo* (Salamanca, 1993), p. 308. Trans. of *Der Weg Jesu Christi* (Munich, 1989). Eng. trans. *The Way of Jesus Christ* (London: SCM Press; New York: Macmillan, 1990).

7. W. Pannenberg, *Fundamentos de cristología* (Salamanca, 1973), p. 135. Trans. of *Grundzüge der Christologie,* 3d ed. (Gütersloh, 1969). Eng. trans. *Jesus—God and Man* (London: SCM Press; Philadelphia, Pa.: Westminster Press, 1968).

8. K. Stendahl, "Jesus und das Reich Gottes," in *Junge Kirche* 3 (1969), cited in González Faus, *Humanidad*, p. 166.

9. Archbishop Romero said, "Christ risen already belongs to present history and is a source of liberty and of human dignity." Homily of 24 Feb. 1980, in *Monseñor Óscar A. Romero. Su pensamiento*, vol. 8 (San Salvador, 1980–88), p. 266.

10. Something analogous can be said of the possibility of remaking the paschal experience of the first disciples, in such a way that the paschal proclamation might be interpreted also as an invitation to relive that experience. "There is not such a difference between the way in which we reach faith in the risen crucified Christ after the death of Jesus and the way in which the first disciples came to the same faith": E. Schillebeeckx, *Jesús. La historia de un viviente* (Madrid, 2d ed. 1983), p. 319. Trans. of *Jesus, het verhaal van een levende* (Bloemendal, 1874). Eng. trans. *Jesus: An Experiment in Christology* (London: Collins; New York: Harper & Row, 1979).

11. J.-M. López Vigil, *Muerte y vida en Morazán,* 3d ed. (San Salvador, 1989), p. 119.

12. J.-M. López Vigil and J. Sobrino, *La matanza de los pobres* (Madrid, 1993), p. 249.

2. The Hermeneutical Problem (1):
The Resurrection, a Specific Problem for Hermeneutics

1. J. L. Segundo, "La opción por los pobres como clave hermenéutica para entender el evangelio," in *Sal Terrae* 6 (1986), pp. 473–82; idem, *El hombre de hoy ante Jesús de Nazaret* II/I (Madrid, 1982), p. 259. Eng. trans. *Jesus of Nazareth Yesterday and Today. Vol. III, The Humanist Christology of Paul* (Maryknoll, N. Y.: Orbis Books; London : Sheed and Ward, 1986). I shall return to this in chapter 5.

2. Succinct presentations of the authors I am going to examine may be found in H. Kessler, *La resurrección de Jesús. Aspecto bíblico, teológico y sistemático* (Salamanca, 1989), pp. 141–70; L. Boff, *Jesucristo y la liberación del hombre*, 2d ed. (Madrid, 1987), pp. 458–76. Eng. trans. *Passion of Christ, Passion of the World* (Maryknoll, N.Y.: Orbis Books, 1987); and M. Fraijó, *Jesús y los marginados. Utopía y esperanza cristiana* (Madrid, 1985), pp. 168–231.

3. I shall analyze the texts in chapter 6. Suffice it here to say that the primary formulation is the *theologal* one, and that a more *christological* one arose later: "Christ who rose from among the dead." This new formulation "accentuates the special divine power there is in him. . . . God does not act in him only from heaven but also in his person and from this" (J. Moltmann, *El camino de Jesucristo* [Salamanca, 1993], p. 307ff. Trans. of *Der Weg Jesu Christi* [Munich, 1989]. Eng. trans. *The Way of Jesus Christ* [London, SCM Press; New York: Macmillan, 1990]. This *christologization* of the resurrection culminates in the theology of John: "For this reason the Father loves me, because I lay down my life in order to take it up again. No one takes it from me, but I lay it down of my own accord: I have power to lay it down, and I have power to take it up again" (Jn 10:17–18).

4. From a systematic standpoint there is no need to understand this action of God's with regard to Jesus in complete discontinuity with what Jesus' life had been: "For him [Paul] the resurrection is not the prize God hands Jesus for having struggled and died for an impossible but beautiful cause, but the victory (invisible until the eschatology that for the rest of us will be manifest only at the end of history, but already certain) of the very values of the Kingdom and of the power of freedom placed at our service" (J. L. Segundo, *Teología abierta* III. *Reflexiones críticas* [Madrid, 1984], p. 314). The resurrection "should be viewed also as the first act of the new creation of the world" (Moltmann, *Cristo para nosotros hoy* [Madrid, 1997], p. 71ff. Sp. trans of *Wer ist Christus für uns heute?* (Gütersloh,

1994). Eng. trans. *Jesus Christ for Today's World.* London: SCM Press; Minneapolis, Minn: Fortress Press, 1994).

5. Kessler, *La resurrección*, p. 256.

6. Segundo, *The Humanist Christology of Paul*, Sp. ed. p. 265.

7. J. I. González Faus, *La humanidad nueva. Ensayo de cristología*, 6th ed. (Santander, 1984), p. 145.

8. Cf. Kessler, *La resurrección*, pp. 229–32; Moltmann, *El camino de Jesucristo*, p. 302ff. When Paul speaks of our own resurrection he also uses the language of "vivification of our mortal bodies," which implies that "the hope of the resurrection does not refer to another life but to the fact that this life has to change" (Moltmann, *Cristo para nosotros hoy*, p. 70).

9. Cf. R. Schnackenburg, "Biblische Sprachbarrieren," in *Bibel und Leben* 14 (1973), pp. 223–31. Basing himself on Schnackenburg, A. Vögtle states that "the discourse [*die Rede*] of the resurrection of Jesus from among the dead is a 'language barrier' of the first order" (A. Vögtle and R. Pesch, *Wie kam es zum Osterglauben?* [Düsseldorf, 1975], p. 12).

10. Cf. J. Delorme, "La resurrección de Jesús en el lenguaje del Nuevo Testamento," in Various, *El lenguaje de la fe en la Escritura y en el mundo actual* (Salamanca, 1973), pp. 88–183.

11. Cf. R. Bultmann, *Kerygma und Mythos* I, 5th ed. (Hamburg, 1967), p. 44ff. Eng. trans. *Kerygma and Myth* (London, SCM Press, 1953).

12. Ibid., p. 46ff.

13. Hans Küng states that, in a conversation with Bultmann, the latter denied any continuity in the body of Jesus before and after the cross but stated that there is a continuity of his "person," which refers to the permanent significance of his whole life and destiny (*On Being a Christian*; Sp. trans., p. 373).

14. Cf. Bultmann, *Kerygma und Mythos*, p. 46.

15. Ibid., p. 47.

16. Cf. M. Fraijó, *Jesús*, p. 173ff.

17. Walter Pannenberg, "Die Offenbarung Gottes in Jesus von Nazareth," in J. Robinson and J. Cobb (eds.), *Theologie als Geschichte* (Zurich, 1967), p. 163.

18. L. Boff, *Jesucristo*, p. 461.

19. "Bultmann seems to taken for granted that the eschatological meaning was something separable from the real event, not immanent in it" (González Faus, *Humanidad*, early eds., p. 158). In the sixth, revised and augmented edition (Santander, 1984), he does not cite these words but upholds the central objection: "The resurrection is, in itself, a significant event" (p. 147).

20. Cf. I. Ellacuría, "Liberación," in C. Floristán and J. J. Tamayo (eds.), *Conceptos fundamentales del cristianismo* (Madrid, 1993), pp. 690–710.

21. W. Marxsen, *La resurrección de Jesús de Nazaret* (Barcelona, 1974).

22. Cf. Fraijó, *Jesús*, p. 181; Boff, *Jesucristo*, p. 464ff.

23. *JL*, p. 87ff.

24. Moltmann, *El camino de Jesucristo*, p. 306.

25. Cf. W. Pannenberg, *Fundamentos de cristología* (Salamanca, 1973), pp. 82–142. Sp. trans. of *Grundzüge der Christologie*, 3d ed. (Gütersloh, 1969). Eng. trans. *Jesus— God and Man* (London: SCM Press; Philadelphia, Pa.: Westminster Press, 1968). Idem, "Dogmatische Erwägungen zur Auferstehung Jesu," in *Kerygma und Dogma* 14 (1986), pp. 105–18.

26. "Statements on the divine reality or divine action lend themselves to being examined in their implications for understanding finite reality, insofar as God is truly affirmed

as the reality that determines everything" (W. Pannenberg, "Wie wahr ist das reden von Gott?," in *Evangelisches Kommentar* 4 [1971], p. 631).

27. Unlike Bultmann and Marxsen, Pannenberg accepts the historicity of the appearances and also that of the empty tomb (see *Fundamentos*, pp. 110–32).

28. W. Pannenberg, *Cuestiones fundamentales de teología sistemática* (Salamanca, 1976), p. 246ff. Sp. trans. of *Grundfragen systematischer Theologie* (Göttingen, 1966). Eng. trans. *Basic Concepts in Systematic Theology* (Edinburgh: T. & T. Clark; Philadelphia, Pa.: Fortress Press, 1971).

29. Pannenberg, *Das Glaubensbekenntnis* (Hamburg, 1972), p. 122; idem., "Dogmatische Erwägungen," p. 108.

30. "Nachwort von W. Pannenberg," in I. Berten, *Geschichte, Offenbarung, Glaube* (Münster, 1970), p. 137.

31. Pannenberg, *Cuestiones fundamentales*, p. 248.

32. For analysis and discussion of this central theme in Pannenberg, see A. González, "La historia como revelación de Dios según Pannenberg. Reflexión crítica," *RLT* 25 (1992), pp. 59–81.

33. Besides Pannenberg and Moltmann, see, among others, Schillebeeckx, Rahner, Metz, González Faus, and, in Latin America, Gutiérrez, L. Boff, and J. B. Libanio.

34. We have to take account of "the possibility of a God with *futurum* as the constituent of being. . . . The power of the future, and only this, can be the object of hope and trust" (Pannenberg, *Cuestiones fundamentales*, pp. 104–5).

35. W. Pannenberg, *El hombre como problema* (Barcelona, 1976), pp. 9–80.

36. See J. Moltmann, *El Dios crucificado,* 2d ed. (Salamanca, 1977), pp. 237–40, 245ff. Trans. of *Der gekreuzigte Gott* (Munich, 1972). Eng. trans. *The Crucified God* (London: SCM Press; New York: Harper & Row, 1974).

37. Pannenberg occasionally alludes to this dialectic, as "God is the strength of hope against all hope" ("Wie kann heute glaubwürdig von Gott geredet werden?," in Various, *Gottesfrage heute* [Stuttgart, 1969], p. 55). But this dialectic is not central to his thought.

38. A. González, "La historia," p. 75.

39. Pannenberg, "Die Offenbarung Gottes," p. 145.

40. Pannenberg, *Fundamentos*, pp. 303–47.

41. Ibid., p. 139; K. Rahner, "Cuestiones dogmáticos en torno a la piedad pascual," in *Escritos de teología*, vol. 4 (Madrid, 1964), p. 167ff. Trans. of *Schriften zur Theologie*, vol. 4 (Zurich, 1962). Eng. trans. *Theological Investigations*, vol. 4 (London: Darton, Longman & Todd; Baltimore: Helicon Press, 1966).

42. Cf. K. Rahner and W. Thüsing, *Cristología. Estudio teológico y exegético* (Madrid, 1975), pp. 41–54. Sp. trans. of *Christologie—sytematisch und exegetische* (Freiburg, 1972). Eng. trans. *A New Christology* (London: Burns & Oates; New York: Crossroad, Seabury Press, 1980).

43. Ibid., p. 43.

44. Ibid., p. 46f.

45. Boff, *Jesucristo*, p. 156.

46. Ibid.

47. Boff later developed the theme more comprehensively in *La resurrección de Cristo. Nuestra resurrección en la muerte* (Salamanca, 1980), Sp. trans. of a work that originally appeared in Portuguese in 1976 and was included in *Jesucristo*, pp. 445–535.

48. Included in *Jesucristo*, pp. 283–443.

49. Ibid., p. 364.

50. Ibid., p. 366.

51. Ibid.

52. Ibid., p. 365.

3. The Hermeneutical Problem (II): Hermeneutical Principles from the Victims

1. "The act or acts of human access to God are not formally intellective ones, but those acts that physically and really take us to God as absolutely absolute reality" (X. Zubiri, *El hombre y Dios* [Madrid, 1984], p. 181).

2. Moltmann's hermeneutics are developed in the replies to these questions, as he recalls in *Cristo para nosotros hoy* (Madrid, 1997), p. 69. Trans. of *Wer ist Christus für uns heute?* (Gütersloh, 1994). Eng. trans. *Jesus Christ for Today's World* (London: SCM Press; Minneapolis, Minn.: Fortress Press, 1994). From this point of view it could be said that Pannenberg, in developing his hermeneutics, takes account of *what I can know* and *what I may be allowed to hope* but not of *what I must do*.

3. Matthew 28:18–20 makes this plainer: The risen Christ charges them not only to baptize but to convert everyone into disciples of Christ, teaching them to obey all that he has taught—the Sermon on the Mount, solidarity with the poor, and so on. On the multidimensional resurrection message, see B. Klappert, *Diskussion um Kreuz und Auferstehung* (Wuppertal, 1968), pp. 9–52.

4. Celebration is one of the basic ways in which the Apocalypse, in its hymns, actualizes the resurrection of the slain lamb and keeps alive the hope of those persecuted for their faith (see X. Alegre, "El Apocalipsis, memoria subversiva y fuente de esperanza para los pueblos crucificados," *RLT* 26 [1992], pp. 220f.; P. Pringent, *Apocalypse et liturgie* [Paris, 1964]).

5. The return of hope to a central place in theology is due largely to Bloch's *Das Prinzip Hoffnung* and Moltmann's *Theology of Hope* (London: SCM Press; New York: Harper & Row, 1977). Eng. trans. of *Theologie der Hoffnung* (Munich, 1964). In his introduction, Moltmann goes so far as to suggest that theology should view itself as *intellectus spei*, corresponding to *spes quaerens intellectum*.

6. This section is based on H. Kessler, *La resurrección de Jesús. Aspecto bíblico, teológico y sistemático* (Salamanca, 1989), pp. 30–52, for his exhaustive analysis and his focus on the problem of hope, life, and death from the theologal aspect: the relationship between God and life, as it appears in the Bible.

7. Ibid., p. 31.

8. Ibid., p. 32.

9. Ibid., p. 51. J. L. Segundo speaks of the divine pedagogy of revelation, in which God reveals himself a little at a time. On the resurrection he states: "Premature information about the next life would have propelled Israel into a disorientated quest for Yahweh outside history"; this is why life beyond death is one of the last things to be revealed in the Old Testament: ("Revelación, fe, signos de los tiempos," *RLT* 14 [1988], p. 132). See also E. Schweizer, "La resurrección, ¿realidad o ilusión?," *Selecciones de Teología* 31 (1982), pp. 3–5.

10. Kessler, *La resurrección*, p. 48.

11. See the reflections on this change of view by J. I. González Faus in "Una tarea histórica: de la liberación a la apocalíptica," *Sal Terrae* 16 (1995), p. 719.

12. J. Moignt, *El hombre que venía de Dios* (Bilbao, 1995), p. 23. Trans. of *L'homme qui venait de Dieu* (Paris, 1993).

13. J. Moltmann, *El Dios crucificado*, 2d ed. (Salamanca, 1977), pp. 242f. Trans. of *Der gekreuzigte Gott* (Munich, 1972). Eng. trans. *The Crucified God* (London: SCM Press; New York: Harper & Row, 1974).

14. Ibid. p. 241: "Only by facing up to the question of justice in suffering as a result of the evil and misery of the human world do we, in my judgment, meet the permanent and

insoluble question of apocalyptic and Jesus' reply and his unresolved history in the scandal it implies" (p. 246). González Faus also stresses the dimension of comfort and hope in apocalyptic literature ("Una tarea histórica," p. 270).

15. At present theology is reincorporating the cosmic perspective, the *nature* dimension, into its concerns and trying to unify it with the paradigm of modernity, *history*. For present purposes, a few words from Moltmann indicate this: "If we look at the resurrection of Christ from this standpoint, we shall see that we need to replace modern 'historical christology' with a new ecological christology" (*Cristo para nosotros hoy*, Sp. trans., p. 71).

16. Moltmann, *El Dios crucificado*, p. 244.

17. When these deaths take the form of martyrdom, they become the Christian death *par excellence*. Karl Rahner lamented some years ago that theology should have reflected so little on martyrdom (see *Sentido teológico de la muerte* [Barcelona, 1965], p. 89). Today, theology tackles it because martyrdom cannot be hidden (see *JL,* pp. 264–71).

18. Kessler seems to see it like this (*La resurrección*, p. 303).

19. Moltmann, *Umkehr zur Zukunft* (Hamburg, 1970), p. 76.

20. Moltmann, *Teología de la esperanza*, p. 247.

21. Ibid., p. 256.

22. Moltmann, *Esperanza y planificación del futuro* (Salamanca, 1975), p. 234. Trans. of *Perspektiven der Theologie. Gesammelte Aufsätze* (Munich/Mainz, 1971). Eng. trans. *Hope and Planning* (London: SCM Press, 1971).

23. Ibid.

24. Moltmann, *Teología de la esperanza,* p. 368.

25. The text was originally published in *30 Giorni* 3/3 (1984), pp. 48–55. I have taken it from *Il Regno: Documenti* 21 (1984), pp. 220–23. Many of the criticisms made here of Latin American liberation theologians appeared since the first Vatican *Instruction on Liberation Theology*, though this did not mention names of theologians.

26. I. Ellacuría, "Las Iglesias latinoamericanas interpelan a la Iglesia de España," *Sal Terrae* 3 (1982), p. 230.

27. R. Bultmann, *Geschichte und Eschatologie* (Tübingen, 1964). In other texts, however, Bultmann relates event and future: "Every historical phenomenon has a corresponding future in which what it is is revealed for the first time; more exactly: in which what it already is is shown *even more*. For what it is will be shown definitively only when history has reached its end" (*Glauben und Verstehen*, vol. 3 [Tübingen, 1965], p. 113).

28. Moltmann, *El Dios crucificado*, p. 114.

29. Moltmann, *Esperanza y planificación*, p. 181.

30. A. González, "La historia como revelación de Dios según Pannenberg. Reflexión crítica," *RLT* 25 (1992), p. 80.

31. Moltmann, *Teología de la esperanza*, p. 415; see also 143, 282.

32. Pannenberg, *Cuestiones fundamentales de teología sistemática* (Salamanca, 1976), p. 55. Trans. of *Grundfragen systematischer Theologie* (Göttingen, 1966). Eng. trans. *Basic Concepts in Systematic Theology* (Edinburgh: T. & T. Clark; Philadelphia, Pa.: Fortress Press, 1971).

33. Pannenberg, *Teología y reino de Dios* (Salamanca, 1974), p. 125. Trans. of *Theologie und Reich Gottes* (Göttingen, 1972). Eng. trans. *Theology and the Kingdom of God* (Philadelphia, Pa.: Westminster Press; London: Search Press, 1974).

34. This decisive precision is what marks the jump from *Theology of Hope* to *The Crucified God*.

35. Moltmann, *Teología de la esperanza*, pp. 133–36.

36. Moltmann, *Cristo para nosotros hoy*, p. 70.

37. Cf. Moltmann, "Antwort auf die Kritik der 'Theologie der Hoffnung,'" in *Diskussion über der "Theologie der Hoffnung,"* ed. W.–D. Marsch (Munich, 1967), p. 210ff.

38. See J. Sobrino, "La teología y el 'principio liberación,'" *RLT* 35 (1995), p. 138f.

4. The Historical Problem (1): The Reality of Jesus' Resurrection

1. We have seen the differences, often irreconcilable, between the theologies of Bultmann, Marxsen, Pannenberg, and Moltmann. A recent doctoral thesis by R. W. Scholla, *Recent Anglican Contributions on the Resurrection of Jesus (1945–1987)* (Rome, 1992), in which the author analyzes the positions of four contemporary Anglican theologians (A. M. Ramsey, C. F. Evans, R. H. Fuller, and P. F. Carnley), reveals the same variations and differences.

2. Besides the works cited in previous chapters, by Kessler, Delorme, González Faus and Moltmann, I have also consulted works (cited individually below) by U. Wilckens, X. Léon-Dufour, E. Charpentier, E. Schillebeeckx, L. Boff, and J. L. Segundo.

3. "The Gospel of Peter," 10, 1–9.

4. J. L. Segundo, *El hombre de hoy ante Jesús de Nazaret* 2/1 (Madrid, 1982), p. 266. Eng. trans. *The Humanist Christology of Paul*, vol. 3 of *Jesus Christ Yesterday and Today* (Maryknoll, N.Y.: Orbis Books; London: Sheed & Ward, 1986).

5. Ibid., p. 264.

6. As to the date when the formula was fixed, Paul is known to have written his first letter to the Corinthians around 56–57 at the latest, probably around 54. In it he reminds them of what he told them when he was in the city in the year 50 (cf. Acts 18:11). Paul himself must have received it as catechesis when he visited Peter and James in Jerusalem between 35 and 37 (cf. Gal. 1:18f.), or he could have heard it still earlier in Antioch. This means that the formula was forged very early, as little as three to six years after Jesus' death.

7. The introductory formula in v. 3a, "For I handed on to you . . . what I in turn had received," is a rabbinic expression for handing on teaching, a settled form of words (see the same formula in 1 Cor. 11:23, referring to the Last Supper), and its literary style is clearly pre-Pauline, since he never mentions "sins" (v. 4) in the plural, nor does he use the words *eggertai* (was raised) or *ofthe* (appeared, or let himself be seen), or the expression "the twelve" (v. 5).

8. See X. Léon-Dufour, *Resurrección de Jesús y mensaje pascual,* 5th ed. (Salamanca, 1992), p. 46, where he is following K. Lehmann, *Auferweckt am dritten Tag nach der Schrift* (Freiburg, 1968).

9. H. Kessler, *La resurrección de Jesús: aspecto bíblico, teológico y sistemático* (Salamanca, 1989), p. 123f.

10. Cf. J. Kremer, "El testimonio de la resurrección de Cristo en forma de narraciones históricas," *Selecciones de Teología* 28 (1989), pp. 323–29.

11. The physicality of the presentation may also be due, particularly in Luke, to the need to combat Platonist dualism, which excluded matter from any possible salvation by God.

12. Kessler, *La resurrección*, p. 102. U. Wilckens, *La resurrección de Jesús* (Salamanca, 1981), p. 137. Wilckens does not deny that there would have been various visions corresponding to the appearances, but the most historical of these accounts would be the appearance to Peter, probably in Galilee, the nucleus of which consisted in this: "In this vision Jesus would have appeared to him as the risen Christ and would have required

him to gather his disciples as the eschatological community chosen to share in God's salvation (cf. Luke 24:34). In this sense, Peter becomes the 'rock on which I will build my church' (Matt. 16:18). Also, in the command, 'feed my lambs,' we should hear a late echo of the early function of governing entrusted to Peter" (p. 136).

13. Kessler, *La resurrección*, p. 96ff.

14. X. Alegre, "Nota complementaria," *Selecciones de Teología* 86 (1983), p. 110.

15. Léon-Dufour, *Resurrección de Jesús y mensaje pascual*, p. 182.

16. J. Delorme, "Resurrección y tumba de Jesús," *Selecciones de Teología* 33 (1970), p. 128.

17. Kessler, *La resurrección*, p. 120. For this section see also pp. 179–93.

18. Ibid., p. 191. The quotation is from W. Kasper, "Der Glaube an die Auferstehung Jesu vor den Forum historischer Kritik," *ThQ* 153 (1973), p. 239.

19. Kessler, *La resurrección*, p. 122.

20. Perhaps the choice of the word *ofthe* is due to the fact that the Old Testament used this word to describe apparitions by God that showed his presence as salvific (ibid., p. 189).

21. Cf. G. Lohfink, "Der Ablauf der Osterereignisse und die Anfänge der Urgemeinde," *ThQ* 160 (1980), pp. 162–76, summarized in *Selecciones de Teología* 81 (1982), pp. 17–25.

22. Cf. M. Kehl, "Eucharistie und Auferstehung. Zur Deutung der Ostererscheinungen beim Mahl," *Geist und Leben* 43 (1970), pp. 90–125, also published as, "Eucaristía y Resurrección. Una interpretación de las apariciones pascuales durante la comida" in *Selecciones de Teología* 43 (1971), pp. 238–48.

23. Cf. R. Aguirre, *La mesa compartida* (Santander, 1994), especially pp. 58–133.

24. Kehl, "Eucharistie und Auferstehung," p. 243.

25. Moltmann, *Cristo para nosotros hoy*, p. 66.

26. Paul's case is the exception.

27. Segundo, *El hombre de hoy*, pp. 257–58. I take up in chapter 7 the problem of whether or not faith existed before the resurrection.

28. Ibid., p. 258f.

29. R. Aguirre, *Del movimiento de Jesús a la Iglesia cristiana* (Bilbao, 1987), p. 175. He summarizes the problem on this and following pages. See also his "La mujer en el cristianismo primitivo," *Iglesia viva* 126 (1986), pp. 513–45.

30. K. Osborne, *The Resurrection of Jesus* (New York, 1997), p. 38f. He analyzes the role of women in five traditions: Mark (pp. 36–39); the appendix to Mark (p. 43); Matthew (pp. 50–52); Luke (p. 65); John (pp. 79–82).

31. Cf. E. A. Johnson, *She Who Is* (New York, 1994), pp. 157–60.

32. Osborne, *The Resurrection of Jesus*, p. 38; X. Alegre, "Marcos o la corrección de una ideología triunfalista," *RLT* 6 (1985), p. 249.

33. G. Lohfink, *La iglesia que Jesús quería* (Bilbao, 1986), p. 102. Eng. trans. *Jesus and Community: The Social Dimensions of Christian Faith* (Philadelphia, Pa.: Fortress Press; London: SPCK, 1985). See also A. M. Tepedino and M. L. Ribeiro Brandão, "Women and the Theology of Liberation," in *Mysterium Liberationis: Fundamental Concepts of Liberation Theology*, ed. I. Ellacuría and J. Sobrino (Maryknoll, N.Y.: Orbis Books, 1993), pp. 222–31. On the situation of women in Jesus' society see E. Schüssler Fiorenza, *In Memory of Her* (New York: Crossroad, 1983); J. Jeremias, *Jerusalem in the Time of Jesus* (London: SCM Press; New York: Macmillan, 1973), p. 34.

34. According to Schüssler Fiorenza, however, Luke 8:1-3 "changes the Markan tradition by distinguishing clearly between the circle of the Twelve and the women who follow [Jesus]. . . . They are not counted as disciples (*akalouthein*) but motivated by gratitude for

having been healed by Jesus" (*But She Said: Feminist Practices of Biblical Interpretation* [Boston: Beacon Press, 1992]; Sp. trans., p. 91).

35. Schüssler Fiorenza, *In Memory of Her* (Sp. trans., p. 186).

36. See J. Sobrino, "Monseñor Romero: diez años de tradición," *RLT* 19 (1990), pp. 17–39.

37. "When the disciples say that they are *witnesses* to the risen Jesus (or to God having raised Jesus), as in Peter's preaching (cf. Acts 2:32; 3:15; 5:32) and that of his companions, they are trying to tell us: we love Jesus, or we remember him as he was when he was alive, or he is living in our memory" (Segundo, *El hombre de hoy*, p. 259ff).

38. Moltmann, *El camino de Jesucristo*, p. 299.

39. See E. Schillebeeckx, *Jesús. La historia de un viviente*, 2d ed. (Madrid, 1983), pp. 293–302. Trans. of *Jesus, het verhaal van een levende* (Bloemendal, 1874). Eng. trans. *Jesus: An Experiment in Christology* (London: Collins; New York: Harper & Row, 1979).

40. Kessler, *La resurrección.*, p. 85ff.

41. J. I. González Faus, *La humanidad nueva. Ensayo de cristología*, 6th ed. (Santander, 1984), p. 138.

5. The Historical Problem (2): The Analogy of "Easter Experiences" throughout History

1. J. I. González Faus, *La humanidad nueva. Ensayo de cristología*, 6th ed. (Santander, 1984), p. 138.

2. U. Wilckens, *La resurrección de Jesús* (Salamanca, 1981), p. 147.

3. P. Carnley, *The Structure of Resurrection Belief* (Oxford, 1987), pp. 26–27. M. Kehl stresses the similarity between our faith and that of the disciples and boldly states that "it is obvious that this faith made the same demands on the first witnesses as it does on us; it does not seem plausible to say that the faith of the first was easier than ours" ("Eucharistie und Auferstehung. Zur Deutung der Ostererscheingungen beim Mahl," *Geist und Leben* 43 [1970], p.248).

4. K. Rahner and W. Thüsing, *A New Christology* (London: Burns & Oates, 1980), pp. 46, 47.

5. Wilckens, *La resurrección de Jesús*, pp. 148, 149.

6. Carnley, *Structure*, p. 258f.

7. E. Schillebeeckx, *Jesús. La historia de un viviente*, 2d ed. (Madrid, 1983), p. 362. Trans. of *Jesus, het verhaal van een levende* (Bloemendal, 1874). Eng. trans. *Jesus: An Experiment in Christology* (London: Collins; New York: Harper & Row, 1979).

8. Ibid., p. 319.

9. H. Kessler, *La resurrección de Jesús* (Salamanca, 1989), p. 151f. For his critique of Schillebeeckx, see pp. 152–56.

10. Ibid., p. 111f.

11. Ibid., p. 210f.

12. Ibid., p. 212.

13. Ibid., p. 210f.

14. Ibid., p. 186. Cf. K. Rahner, *Visiones y profecías* (San Sebastián, 1956). Eng. trans. *Visions and Prophecies* (London: Burns & Oates; New York: Herder & Herder, 1964).

15. P. W. Gyves, "Carta de agradecimiento y solidaridad desde Estados Unidos," *Carta a las Iglesias* 291 (1993), p. 10.

16. Letter by Ann Manganaro, U.S. religious who died in May 1993. The complete text can be seen in *Carta a las Iglesia* 283 (1993), p. 9.

17. Paul says it in a more theologized form in the context of Baptism: "Offer your-selves to God as dead people returned to life." See González Faus, *Proyecto de hermano* (Santander, 1987), pp. 532–37.

18. G. Gutiérrez, *Beber en su propio pozo* (Lima, 1983), p. 172. Eng. trans. *We Drink from Our Own Wells* (Maryknoll, N.Y.: Orbis Books; Melbourne: Dove Communica-tions, 1984). In El Salvador I have often been able to observe how peasants, experts in endless suffering, do not give in to sadness but are capable of celebrating.

19. Archbishop Oscar Romero, Homily of 18 Nov. 1978, in J. Sobrino, I. Martín-Baró, and R. Cardenal (eds.), *La voz de los sin voz. La palabra viva de monseñor Romero* (San Salvador, 1980), p. 457.

20. K. Rahner and K. H. Weger, *¿Qué debemos creer todavía?* (Santander, 1980), p. 190. Trans. of *Was sollen wir noch glauben?* (Freiburg, 1980). Eng. trans. *Our Christian Faith: Answers for the Future* (London: Burns & Oates, 1980).

21. I. Ellacuría, "Quinto centenario. ¿Descubrimiento o encubrimiento?" *RLT* 21 (1990), p. 281ff.

22. J. Moltmann, *Teología de la esperanza*, 5th ed. (Salamanca, 1989), p. 237. Eng. trans. *The Theology of Hope* (London: SCM Press; New York: Harper & Row, 1977).

6.   The Theological Problem (1): The Revelation of God

1. H. Kessler, *La resurrección de Jesús: aspecto bíblico, teológico y sistemático* (Salamanca, 1989), p. 256.

2. J. Moltmann, *El Dios crucificado*, 2d ed. (Salamanca, 1977), p. 175. Trans. of *Der gekreuztige Gott* (Munich, 1972). Eng. trans. *The Crucified God* (London: SCM Press; New York: Harper & Row, 1974).

3. 1 Thess. 1:10; Gal. 1:1; 1 Cor. 6:14; 15:15; 2 Cor. 4:14; Rom. 4:24; 8:11; 10:7, 9; Col. 2:12f.; Eph. 2:5; Heb. 11:19; Acts 2:24, 32; 13:33f.; 17:31. For an analysis of the formulas see Kessler, *La resurrección*, pp. 88–93.

4. "The revelation of God himself, according to the biblical witnesses, was not made directly, as a theophany, but indirectly, through God's actions in history" (W. Pannenberg, *La revelación como historia* [Salamanca, 1977], p. 117).

5. *Dodecapropheten* I, 304, cited in J. P. Miranda, *Marx y la Biblia* (Salamanca, 1972), p. 74. Eng. trans. *Marx and the Bible* (Maryknoll, N.Y.: Orbis Books, 1974); H. Wolf, *La hora de Amós* (Salamanca, 1984), p. 44.

6. See Various, *La lucha de los dioses* (San José, 1980), especially the articles by P. Richard, S. Croatto and J. Pixley. Eng. trans. *The Idols of Death and the God of Life* (Maryknoll, N.Y.: Orbis Books, 1983).

7. J. L. Segundo, *Teología de la liberación. Respuesta al Cardenal Ratzinger* (Madrid, 1985), p. 62f. Eng. trans. *Theology and the Church* (San Francisco: Harper & Row, 1985); I. Ellacuría, "The Historicity of Christian Salvation," in *Mysterium Liberationis*, ed. I. Ellacuría and J. Sobrino (Maryknoll, N.Y.: Orbis Books, 1993), p. 264.

8. See J. Sobrino, *El principio misericordia* (San Salvador, 1993), pp. 31–45. Eng. trans. *The Principle of Mercy* (Maryknoll, N.Y.: Orbis Books, 1994). The reaction against the Egyptians is undoubtedly colored by the warlike tenor of the gods of the time.

9. See Miranda, *Marx and the Bible*; J. L. Sicre, *"Con los pobres de la tierra." La justicia social en los profetas de Israel* (Madrid, 1984); R. de Sivatte, "La práctica de la justicia, criterio de discernimiento de la verdadera experiencia de la fe, según el Antiguo Testamento," in Various, *La justicia que brota de la fe* (Santander, 1982); "La lectura del Antiguo Testamento como un todo," *RLT* 36 (1995), pp. 235–68.

10. Cf. G. M. Soares-Prabhu, "Clase social en la Biblia: los pobres, ¿una clase social?," *RLT* 12 (1987), p. 28.

11. M. Horkheimer, "La añoranza de lo completamente Otro," in H. Marcuse *et al.*, *A la búsqueda del Sentido* (Salamanca, 1976), pp. 65–125.

12. I have tried to show this from experience in El Salvador in "La fe en el Dios crucificado. Reflexiones desde El Salvador," *RLT* 31 (1994), pp. 49–75, esp. 53–59.

13. K. Rahner, "Los jesuitas y el futuro. Con ocasión de una fecha histórica," in *Anuario de la Compañía de Jesús* (Rome, 1975), p. 32.

14. W. Pannenberg, "Die Offenbarung Gottes in Jesus von Nazareth," in J. Robinson and J. Cobb (eds.), *Theologie als Geschichte* (Zurich, 1967), p. 141. Trans. of *Theology and History* (New York: Harper & Row, 1967).

15. Greek thought too, even in its form of natural theology, is still mythical for Pannenberg, because in concept, if not in language, it expresses the two essential characteristics of myth: (1) narrating an event that occurred in earliest times and which (2), because of this has a foundational character for all orders of life. See Pannenberg, *Christentum und Mythos* (Gütersloh, 1972), p. 9.

16. Pannenberg, *Cuestiones fundamentales de teología sistemática* (Salamanca, 1976), p. 204. Trans. of *Grundfragen systematischer Theologie* (Göttingen, 1967). Eng. trans. *Basic Questions in Theology* (Edinburgh: T. & T. Clark; Philadelphia, Pa.: Fortress Press, 1971).

17. Ibid. Pannenberg systematically analyzes the relationship between unity, sovereignty, and God's being as it as appears in Jesus' preaching of the Kingdom of God, which allows him to speak of God from the future (see *Theology and the Kingdom of God* [Philadelphia, Pa.: Fortress Press; London: Search Press, 1974), p. 17.

18. Ibid., p. 18.

19. Pannenberg, *Cuestiones fundamentales*, p. 204.

20. K. Rahner, *Escritos de teología*, vol. 6 (Madrid, 1969), pp. 76–8. Trans. of *Schriften zur Theologie*, vol. 6 (Einseideln, 1966).

21. Rahner, *Schriften zur Theologie*, vol. 9 (Einsiedeln, 1970), p. 525.

22. Ibid., p. 113.

23. See *Ich glaube an Jesus Christus* (Einsiedeln, 1968), pp. 16–23; "Wir bist du eigentlich Jesus," in *Geist und Leben* (1970), pp. 404–8; *Sacramentum mundi,* vol. 2 (German ed.), p. 925ff.

24. E. Schillebeeckx, *Dios, futuro del hombre*, 3d ed. (Salamanca, 1970), p. 185; see also p. 193ff. Eng. trans. *God, the Future of Man* (New York: Sheed and Ward, 1968).

25. Ibid., p. 204.

26. J. Moltmann, *Teología de la esperanza*, 5th ed. (Salamanca, 1989), p. 21. Trans. of *Theologie der Hoffnung* (Munich, 1964). Eng. trans. *Theology of Hope* (London: SCM Press; New York: Harper & Row, 19977).

27. Moltmann, *Umkehr zur Zukunft* (Hamburg, 1970), p. 156.

28. Moltmann, *El Dios crucificado*, p. 263.

29. Moltmann, *Umkehr zur Zukunft*, p. 154.

30. Various, *Gott vor uns*, pp. 235, 236.

31. Metz, "Politische Theologie in der Diskussion," in H. Peukert (ed.), *Diskussion zur "politischen Theologie"* (Munich-Mainz, 1969), p. 284.

32. Ibid., pp. 286, 287.

33. As shown by Gustavo Gutiérrez's frequent references to Pannenberg, Moltmann, Metz and Bloch in his *A Theology of Liberation* (Maryknoll, N.Y.: Orbis Books, 1973).

34. See K. Rahner, "Sobre el concepto de misterio en la teología católica," in *Escritos de teología*, vol. 4 (Madrid, 1964), pp. 53–101.

35. *Escritos de teología*, vol. 5 (Madrid, 1964), p. 14; see K. Rahner and K. H. Weger, *¿Qué debemos creer todavía?*, p. 210. Trans. of *Was sollen wir noch glauben?* (Freiburg, 1980). Eng. trans. *Our Christian Faith. Questions for the Future* (London: Burns & Oates, 1980).

36. The following analysis is based on Pannenberg, *Grundfragen systematischer Theologie* (Göttingen, 1967), pp. 181–201; *Fundamentos de cristología* (Salamanca, 1973), pp. 227–32. Trans. of *Grundzüge der Christologie*, 3d ed. (Gütersloh, 1969). Eng. trans. *Jesus—God and Man* (London: SCM Press; Philadelphia, Pa.: Westminster Press, 1968). Pannenberg acknowledges his debt to E. Schlink, " Die Struktur der dogmatischen Aussage als ökumenisches Problem," *Kerygma und Dogma* 3 (1957), pp. 251–306.

37. Pannenberg, *Grundfragen*, p. 184.

38. Pannenberg, *Fundamentos de cristología*, p. 227; *Grundfragen*, pp. 174f., 181.

39. Pannenberg, *Fundamentos*, p. 227; *Grundfragen*, pp. 171f., 198.

40. See Pannenberg, *Grundfragen*, p. 188; *Fundamentos*, p. 228. "In the doxology, the I is offered in sacrifice" (E. Schlink, "Die Struktur," p. 256).

41. Pannenberg, *Grundfragen*, p. 190.

42. Ibid., p. 186.

43. Ibid., p. 188.

44. E. Schillebeeckx, *Glaubensinterpretation*, pp. 17, 18. Eng. trans. *Understanding of Faith* (London: Sheed & Ward, 1974).

7.   The Theological Problem (2): The Revelation of Jesus

1. E. Schillebeeckx, *Jesús, la historia de un viviente* (Madrid, 1981), pp. 293–302, 351–67. Trans. of *Jesus, het verhaal van een levende* (Bloemendal, 1974). Eng. trans. *Jesus: An Experiment in Christology* (London: Collins; New York: Harper & Row, 1979).

2. Ibid., pp. 294, 300.

3. J. L. Segundo, *El hombre de hoy ante Jesús de Nazaret* 2/1 (Madrid, 1982), p. 266. Eng. trans. *The Humanist Christology of Paul*, vol. 3 of *Jesus of Nazareth Yesterday and Today* (Maryknoll, N.Y.: Orbis Books; London : Sheed and Ward, 1986).

4. R. Pesch, "Zur Entstehung des Glaubens an die Auferstehung Jesu," *ThQ* 153 (1973), p. 226.

5. H. Kessler, *La resurrección de Jesús: aspecto bíblico, teológico y sistemático* (Salamanca, 1989), pp. 148–56; see also G. Lohfink, *La Iglesia que Jesús quería* (Bilbao, 1986), p. 18ff. Eng. trans. *Jesus and Community: The Social Dimensions of Christian Faith* (Philadelphia, Pa.: Fortress Press; London: SPCK, 1985).

6. Ibid., p. 85f.

7. Segundo, *El hombre de hoy*, p. 252.

8. As interpreted by J. Gnilka, *El evangelio según san Marcos*, vol. 1 (Salamanca, 1986), p. 314. Trans. of *Das Evangelium nach Markus*, vol. 1 (Zurich, 1978).

9. Already in Matthew 6:10 and Luke 11:2 the petition of the Our Father implies a future aspect.

10. F. Mussner, *Die Kraft der Wurzel. Judentum–Jesus–Kirche* (Freiburg, 1987), pp. 122–24; J. Gnilka, *Jesús de Nazaret. Mensaje e historia* (Barcelona, 1993), pp. 313f. On Jesus' claim and the opposition his words and actions aroused see R. Pesch, "La pretensión de Jesús," in *Selecciones de Teología* 11 (1972), pp. 106–20; F. Hahn, "Methodologische Überlegungen zur Rückfrage nach Jesus," in K. Kertelge, *Rückfrage nach Jesus* (Freiburg, 1974), pp. 40–51.

11. See Gnilka, *Jesús de Nazaret,* vol. 1, pp. 266–74.

12. Mussner, *Die Kraft der Wurzel*, pp. 110–13.

13. Gnilka, *Jesús de Nazaret*, vol. 1, pp. 262–66.

14. Mussner, *Die Kraft der Wurzel*, pp. 105–7.

15. Gnilka, *Jesús de Nazaret*, p. 315.

16. Ibid., pp. 316–21.

17. Thus P. Bonard in his commentary on the Gospel of St. Matthew (Sp. ed. Madrid, 1976).

18. See Gnilka, *Jesús de Nazaret*, pp. 204–13; M. Hengel, *Seguimiento y carisma. La radicalidad de la llamada de Jesús* (Santander, 1981). Eng. trans. *The Charismatic Leader and His Followers* (Edinburgh: T. &. Clark; New York: Crossroad, 1981).

19. K. Rahner, "Líneas fundamentales de una cristología sistemática," K. Rahner and W. Thusing, *Cristología. Estudio teológico y exegético* (Madrid, 1975), p. 21. Trans. of *Christologie—Systematisch und Exegetisch* (Freiburg, 1972). Eng. trans. *A New Christology* (London: Burns & Oates; New York: Crossroad, 1980)

20. J. Jeremias, *Teología del Nuevo Testamento*, vol. 1, 6th ed. (Salamanca, 1984), p. 86. Eng. trans. *New Testament Theology* (London: SCM Press).

21. Segundo, *El hombre de hoy*, p. 266, n. 13.

22. D. Bonhoeffer, *El precio de la gracia*, 4th ed. (Salamanca, 1995), p. 20ff. Trans. of *Nachfolge* (Munich, 1937). Eng. trans. *The Cost of Discipleship*, 6th ed. (London, SCM Press, 1959).

23. M. Hengel, *Seguimiento y carisma,* pp. 88, 106, 110.

24. J. Schnackenburg, *The Moral Teaching of the New Testament* (London: Burns & Oates, 1967/1975), p. 36.

25. Hengel, *Seguimiento y carisma*, p. 128.

26. For a historical analysis of the first persecutions see R. Aguirre, "La persecución en el cristianismo primitivo," *RLT* 37 (1996), pp. 11–14.

27. Cf. P. Richard, "El movimiento de Jesús después de su resurrección y antes de la Iglesia," *RLT* 39 (1996), p. 278ff; R. Aguirre, *La Iglesia de Jerusalén* (Bilbao, 1989), pp. 49–52.

28. M. Hengel, *El Hijo de Dios* (Salamanca, 1978), p. 83. Trans. of *Der Sohn Gottes* (Tübingen, 1975). Eng. trans. *The Son of God* (London: SCM Press, 1976). The sonship of Jesus may already be implicit in Jesus' *Abba*. The expression "the Son" appears in Jesus' mouth in Mark 12:6 in the parable of the workers in the vineyard, linked to the key word "the last," and in Mark 13:32, which some see as unlikely to derive from the post-Easter community.

29. Hengel calls this "the apology of the Crucified." *El Hijo de Dios*, p. 12.

30. H. Kessler, *La resurrección*, p. 281.

31. See Schillebeeckx, *Jesús*, pp. 407–80; Aguirre, *La reflexión de las primeras comunidades cristianas sobre la persona de Jesús* (Madrid, 1982), pp. 15–19.

32. See R. Schnackenburg, "Problemática de la cristología más antigua," in *Mysterium Salutis* 3/1 (Madrid, 1971), pp. 268–76.

33. Cf. F. Hahn, "Methodologische Überlegungen zur Rückfrage nach Jesus," p. 115ff.

PART II

CHRISTOLOGICAL TITLES IN THE NEW TESTAMENT

8. The Titles and Their Problems

1. Kasper, p. 197.

2. Ibid., p. 163.

3. The only text in which some writers state that Jesus was being called God before the fall of Jerusalem is Rom. 9:5b, although the acclamation could apply to God rather than to the Messiah, as others claim. The arguments for it applying to God can be found in U. Wilckens, *La carta a los Romanos* II (Salamanca, 1992), pp. 232f.

4. See W. Pannenberg, *Fundamentos de cristología* (Salamanca, 1973), pp. 165ff. Sp. trans. of *Grundzüge der Christologie*, 3d ed. (Gütersloh, 1969). Eng. trans. *Jesus—God and Man* (London: SCM Press; Philadelphia, Pa.: Westminster Press, 1968).

5. See K. Rahner, "Wer bist du eigentlich Jesus Christus?," *Geist und Leben* 44 (1971), pp. 404–8.

6. M. Hengel, *El Hijo de Dios* (Salamanca, 1978), p. 82. Trans. of *Der Sohn Gottes* (Tübingen, 1975). Eng. trans. *The Son of God* (London: SCM Press, 1976).

7. See R. Aguirre, "Sociología de la cruz en el Nuevo Testamento," *RLT* 29 (1994), pp. 127–42.

8. See F. J. Shierse, "La revelación de la trinidad en el Nuevo Testamento," in *Myst. Sal.*, pp. 136–37. "The historical Jesus as he appears in the Gospel account is the criterion of interpretation" (Ch. Duquoc, *Mesianismo de Jesús y discreción de Dios. Ensayo sobre los límites de la cristología* [Madrid, 1985], p. 175).

9. Cf. the outline study by A. Vanhoye, *El mensaje de la carta a los Hebreos* (Estella, 1978). Trans. of *Le structure littéraire de l'épître aux Hébreux* (Paris, 1963).

9. High Priest: The Mediator

1. J.-M. Castillo, "Sacerdocio," in *Conceptos fundamentales de pastoral* (Madrid, 1983), p. 888.

2. My analysis of the Letter to the Hebrews is based on the now classic study by A. Vanhoye, *El mensaje de la carta a los Hebreos* (Estella, 1978), pp. 11–18, the true high priest as distinct from that of the Old Testament (pp. 43–51), not based on a cultic system of separations (pp. 54–57). Trans. of *Le structure littéraire de l'épître aux Hébreux* (Paris, 1963). See idem, *Le Christ est notre prêtre* (Paris, 1969) and *Sacerdotes antiguos, sacerdotes nuevos según el Nuevo Testamento* (Salamanca, 1984).

3. See Vanhoye, *Le Christ*, pp. 19f.

4. Ibid., p. 33.

5. G. Baena, "El sacerdocio de Cristo," *Diakonía* 26 (1983), p. 133.

6. See O. Tuñi, "'Jesús' en la carta a los Hebreos," *RLT* 9 (1986), pp. 284–86.

7. O. Cullmann, *Cristología del Nuevo Testamento* (Buenos Aires, 1965), pp. 113, 114. Trans. of *Die Christologie des Neuen Testaments* (Tübingen, 1957). Eng. trans. *Christology of the New Testament* (London, SCM Press, 1959).

8. See "Jesus and God (1): Jesus and a God-Father," in *JL*, pp. 160–79.

9. In my "'Conllevaos mutuamente.' Análisis teológico de la solidaridad," published in *El principio misericordia* (San Salvador, 1993), pp. 211–48, I made a theoretical analysis of the concept of solidarity from the mutual remit human beings have for giving and receiving to and from one another. Eng. trans. "Bearing with One Another in Faith," *The Principle of Mercy* (Maryknoll, N.Y.: Orbis Books, 1994), pp. 144–72.

10. The Messiah: Keeping Alive the Hope of the Poor

1. F. Hahn, *Christologische Hoheitstitel* (Göttingen, 1963), pp. 179–89.

2. The 1997/4 volume of *Concilium* is devoted to analysis of religion's potential for aggression. (W. Beuken and K.-J. Kuschel [eds.], *Religion as a Source of Violence?* [London: SCM Press; Maryknoll, N.Y.: Orbis Books, 1997).

3. J.-B. Metz, "Teología europea y teología de la liberación," in *Cambio social y pensamiento cristiano en América Latina*, ed. J. Comblin, J. I. González Faus, and J. Sobrino (Madrid, 1993), p. 268.

4. A. Salas, *El mesianismo: promesas y esperanzas* (Madrid, 1990), p. 77.

5. "The confession of Jesus Christ as the Son of God represents the core of the Christian tradition" (Kasper, p. 163).

6. J. Imbach, *¿De quién es Jesús?* (Barcelona, 1991), p. 96.

7. J. I. González Faus,*La humanidad nueva. Ensayo de cristología*, 6th ed. (Santander, 1984), p. 256.

8. J. I. González Faus, "'We Proclaim a Crucified Messiah,'" in *Concilium* 1992/4, pp. 83–94. (Christian Duquoc and C. Floristán [eds.], *Where Is God? A Cry of Human Distress* [London: SCM Press]).

9. X. Alegre, "Marcos o la corrección de una ideología triunfalista," *RLT* 6 (1985), pp. 229–63.

10. Christian Duquoc, "El mesianismo reinterpretado," in *Mesianismo de Jesús y discreción de Dios. Ensayo sobre los límites de la cristología* (Madrid, 1985), p. 159ff.

11. I. Ellacuría, "El desafío de las mayorías populares,"*ECA* 493–94 (1989), p. 1078.

11. The Lord: The Lordship of Christ, Hope, and Theodicy

1. O. Cullmann, *Cristología del Nuevo Testamento* (Buenos Aires, 1965), p. 273. Trans. of*Die Christologie des Neuen Testaments*(Tübingen, 1957). Eng. trans.*Christology of the New Testament* (London: SCM Press, 1959).

2. Ibid., pp. 237–55; F. Hahn, *Christologische Hoheitstitel* (Göttingen, 1963), pp. 74–125; J. I. González Faus, *La humanidad nueva. Ensayo de cristología*, 6th ed. (Santander, 1984), pp. 259–82.

3. Hahn, *Christologische Hoheitstitel*, pp. 74–79.

4. See J. Ernst, *Anfänge der Christologie* (Stuttgart, 1972), pp. 15–21.

5. J.-B. Bossuet, *Kyrios Christos. Geschichte des christlichen Glaubens von den Anfängen des Christentums bis Ireneus* (Göttingen, 1913), pp. 90–101.

6. E. Lohmeyer, "Kyrios Jesus," *Sitzungsberichte der Heidelberger Akademie der Wissenschaften* (1927–28).

7. Cullmann, *Cristología del Nuevo Testamento*, pp. 240–47.

8. See W. Kramer, *Christos Kyrios Gottessohn* (Zürich, 1963).

9. See Hahn, *Christologische Hoheitstitel*, pp. 95–125.

10. E. Schweizer, *Jesus Christus im vielfächtigen Zeugnis des Neuen Testaments* (Munich-Hamburg, 1968).

11. This is one of the most radical texts on following. Cf. M. Hengel, *Seguimiento y carisma* (Santander, 1981), p. 29. Eng. trans. *The Charismatic Leader and His Followers* (Edinburgh: T. & T. Clark; New York: Crossroad, 1981). González Faus, *La humanidad nueva*, p. 260.

12. J. L. Segundo, *El dogma que libera* (Santander, 1989), p. 194. Eng. trans. *The Liberation of Dogma* (Maryknoll, N.Y.: Orbis Books, 1992).

13. Cullmann, *Cristología del Nuevo Testamento*, p. 254.

14. Bartolomé de Las Casas, in *Obra indigenista* (Madrid, 1985), p. 179.

15. See the texts in O. Tuñí, "Pablo y Jesús. La vida de Jesús y la vida de Pablo," *RLT* 15 (1988), pp. 285–305.

16. M. López Vigil, *Muerte y vida en Morazán*, 3d ed. (San Salvador, 1989), p. 119.

17. I. Ellacuría, "Pobres," in C. Floristán and J. J. Tamayo (eds.), *Conceptos fundamentales del cristianismo* (Madrid, 1993), p. 1046.

18. D. Hollenbach, "Ética social bajo el signo de la cruz," *RLT* 37 (1996), p. 51.

19. I. Ellacuría, *Conversión de la Iglesia al reino de Dios para anunciarlo y realizarlo en la historia* (San Salvador, 1985), p. 183.

20. R. Mate, Prologue, in J. B. Metz and E. Wiesel, *Esperar a pesar de todo* (Madrid, 1996), p. 16.

21. International Theological Commission, "Quaestiones selectae de Christologia," *Gregorianum* 61/4 (1980), p. 632.

22. On this, see O. Cullmann, *El Estado en el Nuevo Testamento* (Madrid, 1961); K. Wengst, *Pax Romana. Anspruch und Wirklichkeit* (Munich, 1986); X. Alegre, "Violencia y Nuevo Testamento," *RLT* 23 (1991), pp. 149–67.

23. H. Braun, *Jesús, el hombre de Nazaret y su tiempo* (Salamanca, 1974), p. 65.

24. R. Aguirre, "La persecución en el cristianismo primitivo," *RLT* 37 (1996), p. 29.

25. Taken from S. Carranza, *Romero–Rutilio. Vidas encontradas* (San Salvador, 1992), pp. 124, 126.

12. Son of God/Son of Man/Servant of Yahweh: The Man Who Came from God and the God Who Came in Man

1. M. Hengel, *El Hijo de Dios* (Salamanca, 1977), p. 123. Trans. of *Der Sohn Gottes* (Tübingen, 1975). Eng. trans. *The Son of God* (London: SCM Press, 1976).

2. K. Rahner, *Escritos de teología* V (Madrid, 1964), p. 209. (Eng. *Theological Investigations*, vol. 5.)

3. Cf. O. Cullmann, *Cristología del Nuevo Testamento* (Buenos Aires, 1965), pp. 333–50. Trans. of *Die Christologie des Neuen Testaments* (Tübingen, 1957). Eng. trans. *Christology of the New Testament* (London, SCM Press, 1959). F. Hahn, *Christologische Hoheitstitel* (Göttingen, 1963), pp. 287–333; Hengel, *El Hijo de Dios*. See also *Concilium* 1982/4, especially the article by B. van Iersel, "Son of God in the New Testament."

4. Hengel, *El Hijo de Dios*, p. 62.

5. Ibid., p. 67.

6. Ibid., pp. 62–80.

7. Hahn, *Christologische Hoheitstitel*, pp. 287–319.

8. Hengel, *El Hijo de Dios*, p. 30.

9. Ibid., p. 31.

10. Ibid., p. 88.

11. Ibid., pp. 89–93.

12. J. Moignt, *El hombre que venía de Dios* (Bilbao, 1995), p. 42. Trans. of *L'homme qui venait de Dieu* (Paris, 1993).

13. J. I. González Faus, *La humanidad nueva. Ensayo de cristología* (Santander, 6th ed. 1984), pp. 241–50; see also A. Vögtle, *Die "Gretchenfrage" des Menschensohnproblems. Bilanz und Perspective* (Freiburg, 1994).

14. See J. Ernst, *Anfänge der Christologie* (Stuttgart, 1972), pp. 45–46.

15. John Paul II, *Ecclesia* 2191 (1985), p. 1189.

16. The idea that the poor and the victims are open to accepting and pardoning is one that we have developed phenomenologically in "Personal Sin, Forgiveness, and Liberation," *The Principle of Mercy* (Maryknoll, N.Y.: Orbis Books, 1994).

17. See Ernst, *Anfänge der Christologie*, p. 50.

18. Hengel, *El Hijo de Dios*, p. 119.

19. González Faus, *La humanidad nueva*, p. 192ff.

20. See R. Schnackenburg, "Cristología del Nuevo Testamento," in *Myst.Sal.* 3/1, pp. 323–46.

21. See González Faus, *La humanidad nueva*, pp. 192–95.

22. Schnackenburg, "Cristología del Nuevo Testamento," pp. 337–38.

23. See I. Ellacuría, *Conversión de la Iglesia al reino de Dios* (San Salvador, 1985), pp. 25–63.

24. Kasper, p. 166.

25. See J. Barreto, "Señales y discernimiento en el evangelio de Juan," *RLT* 40 (1997), p. 42, whom I follow in the reflections below.

26. Ibid., p. 50.

27. Ibid., p. 46.

28. Ibid., p. 33.

29. S. Freud, *Totem and Taboo* (various editions). See C. Domínguez, *Creer después de Freud* (Madrid, 1992). René Girard has reformulated the thesis theoretically: society needs an expiatory victim to establish itself, though this victim does not need to be God (see *La violencia y o sagrado* [Salamanca, 1976]; *El misterio de nuestro mundo* [Salamanca, 1982]).

30. F. Hinkelammert, *La fe de Abraham y el Edipo occidental* (San José, 1989).

31. See González Faus, *La humanidad nueva.*

32. E. Johnson, *She Who Is. The Mystery of God in Feminist Theological Discourse* (New York: Crossroad, 1992), p. 36. See also the critique of *kyrio-centrism* in E. Schüssler Fiorenza, *But She Said: Feminist Practices of Biblical Interpretation* (Boston: Beacon Press, 1992), p. 251: "The gender asymmetry of the grammatically androcentric western languages hides or confuses the kyriocentric or patriarchal character of the constructs of its social word insofar as this asymmetry does not permit the 'naming' of persons doubly marked by gender and race or class if they are not masculine."

33. Johnson, *She Who Is*, pp. 47–48.

34. I. Gebara, "Presencia de lo feminino en el pensamiento cristiano latinoamericano," in *Cambio social y pensamiento cristiano en América Latina*, ed. J. Comblin, J. I. González Faus and J. Sobrino (Madrid, 1993), p. 210.

35. F. Hinkelammert (ed.), *La crisis del socialismo en el Tercer Mundo* (San José, 1991), p. 6.

36. X. Gorostiaga, "La mediación de las ciencias sociales y los cambios internacionales," in Hinkelammert, *La crisis*, p. 131.

37. H. Assmann, *Teología desde la praxis de la liberación* (Salamanca, 1976), p. 40. Eng. trans. *Theology for a Nomad Church* (Maryknoll, N.Y.: Orbis Books, 1975); *Practical Theology of Liberation* (London: Search Press, 1975).

38. M. Novak and J. W. Cooper (eds.), *The Corporation: A Theological Inquiry* (Washington, D.C., 1981), p. 203.

39. C. Vallejo, cited in G. Gutiérrez, *El Dios de la Vida*, 2d ed. (Salamanca, 1994), p. 174.

13. Word: Truth and Good News

1. Cf. O. Cullmann, *Cristología del Nuevo Testamento* (Buenos Aires, 1965), pp. 289–97; Trans. of *Die Christologie des Neuen Testaments* (Tübingen, 1957). Eng. trans. *Christology of the New Testament* (London, SCM Press, 1959). R. Schnackenburg, *The Gospel According to St John*, I (Sp. trans., Salamanca, 1980), pp. 254–56; X. Léon-Dufour, *Lectura del evangelio de Juan,* I (Salamanca, 1989), pp. 41–51, 55–65; J. I. González Faus, *La humanidad nueva. Ensayo de cristología*, 6th ed. (Santander, 1984), pp. 316–25.

2. See Cullmann, *Cristología del Nuevo Testamento*, p. 296.

3. J. P. Miranda, *Marx y la Biblia* (Salamanca, 1972), pp. 62f. Eng. trans. *Marx and the Bible* (Maryknoll, N.Y.: Orbis Books, 1974).

4. "The Word of God" appears in Rv 19:13, and "the word of life" in 1 Jn 1:1. According to Léon-Dufour, *Lectura del evangelio de Juan*, p. 44, whether this "word" has a personal and absolute sense can be debated in the first case, but it certainly does not in the second.

5. J. Barreto, "Señales y discernimiento en el evangelio de Juan," *RLT* 40 (1997), p. 54.

6. Ibid., p. 54f.

7. See Cullmann, *Cristología del Nuevo Testamento*, p. 303f.

8. Barreto, "Señales y discernimiento en el evangelio de Juan," p. 54. In other words, "because their deeds were evil" (Jn 3:19).

9. Cf. J. L. Segundo, *El hombre de hoy ante Jesús de Nazaret*, vol. 1 (Madrid, 1982), pp. 45–73. Eng. trans. *Jesus Christ Yesterday and Today*, vol. 1 (Maryknoll, N.Y.: Orbis Books; London: Sheed & Ward, 1984).

10. Barreto explains this priority thus: "'The life was the light of all people' (1:4), in which life is the substantive concept and light (truth) the adjective: that is, the truth is nothing other than the evidence of life. ("Señales y discernimiento en el evangelio de Juan," p. 55, n. 21). Léon-Dufour upholds the contrary thesis: "Of what is Jesus 'full'? Of the truth, that is, of the knowledge of God. This is the 'gift' he can hand on: communicating the Father's truth" *(Lectura del evangelio de Juan*, p. 99).

11. The translation given in parentheses is that of the *Biblia española*.

12. Barreto, "Señales y discernimiento en el evangelio de Juan," p. 56.

13. See J. O. Tuñí, "Personajes veterotestamentarios en el Evangelio de Juan," *RLT* 30 (1993), pp. 279–92.

14. Among the specialists who question whether "God" here refers to Christ or the Father, see U. Wilckens, *La carta a los Romanos*, vol. 2 (Salamanca, 1992), pp. 232–33.

15. Barreto, "Señales y discernimiento en el evangelio de Juan," p. 57.

16. Cf. J. L. Segundo, "Revelation, Faith, Signs of the Times," in *Mysterium Liberationis* (Maryknoll, N.Y.: Orbis Books, 1993), pp. 328–49.

17. Ibid., p. 338.

18. See J. O. Tuñí, *Jesús y el evangelio de la comunidad juánica* (Salamanca, 1987), pp. 63–68.

19. See J. Sobrino, "El seguimiento de Jesús como discernimiento cristiano," in *Jesús en América Latina* (San Salvador and Santander, 1981/2), pp. 209–21. Eng. trans. *Jesus in Latin America* (Maryknoll, N.Y.: Orbis Books, 1987).

20. J. Sobrino, " Los signos de los tiempos en la teología de la liberación," *Estudios Eclesiásticos* (Jan.–June 1989), pp. 249–69.

21. J. Ratzinger, *LThK. Das Zweite Vaticanische Konzil*, vol. 3 (Freiburg, 1968), pp. 313–14.

22. See the article by X. Alegre, "Los responsables de la muerte de Jesús," *RLT* 41 (1997), pp. 139–72.

23. K. Rahner, *Curso fundamental de la fe* (Barcleona, 1984), pp. 149–56; ibid., p. 357: the German original speaks of *Selbsausstage*. See the commentary by A. González, "La novedad teológica de la filosofía de Zubiri," *RLT* 30 (1993), p. 242f.

24. X. Zubiri, *El problema teologal del hombre* (Madrid, 1997), p. 458f.

25. González, "La novedad teológica de la filosofía de Zubiri," p. 251.

26. P. Miranda, *El ser y el mesías* (Salamanca, 1973), p. 144; González Faus, *La humanidad nueva*, p. 330; M. E. Boismard, *Le prologue de saint-Jean* (Paris, 1953), pp. 89–95.

27. The distinction between *intellectus fidei* and *intellectus amoris* would also correspond to that between truth and good news. On theology as *intellectus amoris* see J. Sobrino, "Teología en un mundo sufriente. La teología de la liberación como *intellectus amoris*," *RLT* 15 (1988), pp. 243–66. Eng. trans. *The Principle of Mercy*, pp. 27–46.

28. Ch. Duquoc, *Lumière et Vie* 119 (1990), p. 91, cited in González Faus, *La autoridad de la verdad* (Barcelona, 1996), p. 101.

29. See Ellacuría, "Liberación," in *Conceptos fundamentales del cristianismo*, ed. C. Floristán and J. J. Tamayo (Madrid, 1993), p. 795ff.

30. Segundo, *El hombre de hoy*, p. 444f.

31. Augustine, *In Iohannis Evangelium Tractatus*, XIX, 14.

32. Sobrino, "La honradez con lo real," *Sal Terrae* (May 1992), pp. 377ff.

33. Barreto, "Señales y discernimiento en el evangelio de Juan," p. 55.

34. Ibid., p. 58.

35. Ibid., p. 57.

14. Jesus as *Eu-Aggelion*

1. Cf. E. Schillebeeckx, *Jesús. La historia de un viviente*, 2d ed. (Madrid, 1983), pp. 97–103. Trans. of *Jesus, het verhaal van een levende* (Bloemendal, 1974). Eng. trans. *Jesus: An Experiment in Christology* (London: Collins; New York: Harper & Row, 1979). *JL*, pp. 67–70.

2. Schillebeeckx, *Jesús*, p. 101.

3. J. Moingt, *El hombre que venía de Dios* (Bilbao, 1995), p. 35f. Trans. of *L'homme qui venait de Dieu* (Paris, 1993).

4. L. Boff, *Jesuscristo y la liberación del hombre*, 2d ed. (Madrid, 1987), p. 122.

5. L. Boff, *Una espiritualidad liberadora* (Estella, 1992), p. 15.

6. K. Rahner, *Palabras al silencio*, 9th ed. (Salamanca, 1991), p. 29. Trans. of *Hörer des Wortes* (Munich, 1963). Eng. trans. *Hearers of the Word* (London: Sheed & Ward, 1969).

7. I. Ellacuría, *Carta a las Iglesias* 245 (1991), p. 10.

8. Schillebeeckx, *Jesús*, p. 103.

9. R. Aguirre, *Del movimiento de Jesús a la Iglesia cristiana* (Bilbao, 1987), p. 51.

10. R. Aguirre, "La mesa compartida," *RLT* 35 (1995), p. 154.

11. Taken from S. Carranza, *Romero–Rutilio. Vidas encontradas* (San Salvador, 1992), p. 120.

PART III

CONCILIAR CHRISTOLOGY

15. Introduction: Concentration on the Mediator, Jesus Christ, to the Detriment of the Mediation, the Kingdom of God

1. I have consulted the following works on the history of dogmas: P. Smulders, "Desarollo de la cristología en la historia de los dogmas y en el magisterio eclesiástico," in *Myst.Sal.* 3/1 (Madrid, 1971), pp. 417–504; A. Grillmeier, *Jesus der Christus im Glauben der Kirche* (Freiburg, 1—1979, 2/1—1986, 2/2—1989, 2/4—1990); G. Alberigo (ed.), *Historia de los concilios ecuménicos* (Salamanca, 1993), pp. 19—125; B. Suder, *Dios salvador en los Padres de la Iglesia. Trinidad-cristología-soterología* (Salamanca, 1993);

J. Moingt, *El hombre que venía de Dios* (Bilbao, 1995), trans. of *L'homme qui venait de Dieu* (Paris, 1993); D. Sesbouë (ed.), *El Dios de la salvación* (Salamanca, 1995).

2. It may be surprising, but it is a fact that both I. Ellacuría and J. L. Segundo, two of the most pioneering exponents of liberation theology, valued conciliar christology—without ignoring its limitations and dangers—for what I have called its formal elements, above all the relationship between history and transcendence.

3. O. Romero, "Homily of 24 December 1978," in *Monseñor Oscar A. Romero. Su pensamiento* VI (San Salvador, 1981), p. 76.

4. I. Ellacuría, *Conversión de la Iglesia al reino de Dios* (San Salvador, 1985), p. 168.

5. A. Pieris, "¿Universalidad del cristianismo?," in *El rostro asiático de Cristo* (Salamanca, 1991), p. 164.

6. Ibid., p. 166f.

7. E. Schweizer, "Die theologische Leistung des Markus," *Evangelische Theologie* 24 (1964), pp. 337–55.

8. E. Käsemann, *Ensayos exegéticos* (Salamanca, 1978), pp. 159–89. Trans. of "Das Problem des historischen Jesus," *ZthK* 51 (1954), pp. 125–53.

9. J. Moingt, *El hombre que venía de Dios*, p. 77.

10. Ibid., p. 78.

11. Ibid., p. 87.

12. Ibid., p. 123.

13. I. Ellacuría in *Teología política* (San Salvador, 1973), p. 22; see also Ch. Schütz, "Los misterios de la vida y activided pública de Jesús," in *Myst.Sal.* 3/2 (Madrid, 1971), pp. 72–134; J. I. González Faus, *La humanidad nueva. Ensayo de cristología*, 6th ed. (Santander, 1984), pp. 53–214.

14. Moingt, *El hombre que venía de Dios*, p. 125.

15. Ibid.

16. M. Hengel, *Seguimiento y carisma. La radicalidad de la llamada de Jesús* (Santander, 1981), p. 128.

17. J. O. Tuñí, "Jesús de Nazaret, criterio de identidad cristiana en el Nuevo Testamento," *Todos Uno* 82 (1985), p. 12.

18. R. Aguirre, *La Iglesia de Jerusalén* (Bilbao, 1989), p. 48.

19. J. L. Segundo, "Revelation, Faith, Signs of the Times," in *Mysterium Liberationis*, ed. I. Ellacuría and J. Sobrino (Maryknoll, N.Y.: Orbis Books, 1993), p. 456f.

20. Moingt, *El hombre que venía de Dios*, p. 82.

21. J. I. González Faus, "Dogmática cristológica y lucha por la justicia," in *Fe en Dios y construcción de la historia* (Madrid, 1998), pp. 91–111.

22. Moingt, *El hombre que venía de Dios*, p. 80f.

23. O. Romero, "La dimensión política de la fe desde la opción por los pobres. Discurso con motivo del doctorado Honoris Causa conferido por la Universidad de Lovaina el día 2 de febrero de 1980," in *La voz de los sin voz. La palabra viva de monseñor Romero*, ed. J. Sobrino, I. Martín Baró, and R. Cardenal (San Salvador, 1980), p. 193. Eng. trans. *The Voice of the Voiceless: The Four Pastoral Letters and Other Statements* (Maryknoll, N.Y.: Orbis Books, 1984; London: CIIR, 1985).

24. H. Bettenson (trans. and ed.), *The Early Christian Fathers* (Oxford and New York: Oxford University Press, 1969), p. 87.

25. Athanasius, *Orations against Arians* III, 26.

26. Gregory Nazianzen, *Epist.* 101, 87.

27. Ireneaus, in Bettenson, *The Early Christian Fathers*, p. 82.

28. Moingt, *El hombre que venía de Dios*, pp. 83, 87.

29. See Ellacuría, *Teología política*, pp. 1–10.

30. J. L. Segundo, *Teología abierta*, vol. 3 (Madrid, 1984).

31. K.-H. Ohlig, "Zum Verständnis der Christologie. Die Rezeption Jesu auf der Basis der Sinnfrage," *Diakonia: Internationale Zeitschrift für die Praxis der Kirche* 26/5 (1995), pp. 294–304, summarized in "What Is Christology?," *Theology Digest* 43/1 (1996), p. 20.

32. Ibid., p. 16.

Excursus. Christianity in the Greco-Roman World

1. J. Moingt, *El hombre que venía de Dios* I (Bilbao, 1995), p. 50. Trans. of *L'homme qui venait de Dieu* (Paris, 1993).

2. J. Moignt, "The Christology of the Primitive Church: The Price of a Cultural Mediation," *Concilium* 1997/1, p. 91.

3. Moingt, *El hombre que venía de Dios*, p. 69.

4. Justin, *Dialogue with Trypho*, 50, 1.

5. As quoted by Origen in his *Contra Celsum* IV, 18.

6. P. van Buren, *The Secular Meaning of the Gospel* (London, 1966), p. 38.

7. On understanding the theological task as being "to raise reality to concept" see J. Sobrino, "Teología y el 'principio liberación,'" *RLT* 35 (1995), p. 122f.

8. On the meaning of "dogma" at the time see, e.g., J. Crimbont, "Intransigencia e irenismo en san Basilio," *Estudios Trinitarios* 9 (1975), pp. 227–43. On the development of the notion of dogma see W. Kasper, *Dogma y palabra de Dios* (Bilbao, 1968); J. Finkenzeller, *¿Fe sin dogma? Dogma, desarrollo de los dogmas y magisterio eclesiástico* (Estella, 1973).

9. J. I. González Faus, *La humanidad nueva. Ensayo de cristología*, 6th ed. (Santander, 1984), p. 455.

10. I. Ellacuría, *Teología política* (San Salvador, 1973), pp. 5, 7.

11. J. L. Segundo, *El hombre de hoy ante Jesús de Nazaret* 2/1 (Madrid, 1982), p. 241. Eng. trans. *The Humanist Christology of Paul*, vol. 3 of *Jesus of Nazareth Yesterday and Today* (Maryknoll, N.Y.: Orbis Books; London : Sheed and Ward, 1986).

12. J. Martínez Gordo, "La anticipación del futuro: la teología fundamental de W. Pannenberg," *RLT* 38 (1996), p. 172.

13. Moingt, *El hombre que venía de Dios*, p. 120.

14. "Common Declaration by the Pope of Rome and the Syrio-Orthodox Patriarch of Antioch," 24 June 1984. Sp. Text in *Ecclesia* 2182 (1984), p. 861.

15. Moingt, *El hombre que venía de Dios*, p. 102.

16. K. Rahner, *Escritos de teología*, vol. 4 (Madrid, 1964), p. 383. Trans. of *Schriften zur Theologie*, vol. 4 (Zurich, 1962). Eng. trans. *Theological Investigations*, vol. 4 (London: Darton, Longman & Todd; Baltimore, Md.: Helicon Press, 1966).

17. Ibid., p. 384.

18. K. Rahner, *Escritos de teología*, vol. 1 (Madrid, 1963), pp. 169–222.

19. Moingt, "The Christology of the Primitive Church," p. 93.

20. L. Boff, *Jesucristo y la liberación del hombre*, 2d ed. (Madrid, 1987), p. 193.

21. G. Gutiérrez, "Lenguaje teológico: plenitud del silencio," *RLT* 38 (1996), p. 161. Eng. trans. "Theological Language: Fullness of Silence," in *The Density of the Present* (Maryknoll, N.Y.: Orbis Books, 1999).

22. Ibid., p. 160.

23. A. Pieris, *El rostro asiático de Cristo* (Salamanca, 1991), p. 166.

24. J. Vitoria, "La soteriología histórica: un modelo a partir de la teología salvadoreña," *RLT* 34 (1995), p. 67.

25. Ibid., pp. 66–69.

26. Gutiérrez, "Lenguaje teológico," p. 161.

27. On concern for justice and the poor in the church Fathers see R. Sierra Bravo, *Doctrina social y económica de los Padres de la Iglesia* (Madrid, 1975); idem, *Mensaje social de los Padres de la Iglesia* (Madrid, 1989); J. I. González Faus, *Vicarios de Cristo. Los pobres en la teología y la espiritualidad cristianas* (Madrid, 1991), pp. 13–19.

28. *Smyrn.* 6, 2. In *The Early Christian Fathers*, trans. and ed. H. Bettenson (Oxford and New York: Oxford University Press, 1969), p. 49.

29. Which, rather than the Hellenization of dogma, perhaps constituted the greatest danger to faith.

30. J. Moltmann, *Crítica teológica de la religión política* (Salamanca, 1973), p. 20. Trans. of J. B. Metz, J. Moltmann and W. Oelmüller, *Kirche im Prozess der Aufklärung* (Munich/Mainz, 1970); also in Moltmann, *Politische Theologie—Politische Ethik* (Munich/Mainz, 1984). Eng. trans. "The Cross and Civil Religion," in *Religion and Political Society* (New York: Harper & Row, 1974), pp. 9–48.

31. X. Alegre, "El Apocalipsis, memoria subversiva y fuente de esperanza para los pueblos crucificados," *RLT* 26, 27 (1992), pp. 201–29, 293–323; P. Richard, *El Apocalipsis* (San José, 1994); R. Aguirre, "La persecución en el cristianismo primitivo," *RLT* 37 (1986), pp. 11–42.

32. H. Mühlen, *Entsakralisierung* (Paderborn, 1970), p. 200.

33. E. Käsemann, *La llamada a la libertad*, 2d ed. (Salamanca, 1985), p. 175.

34. P. Stockmeier, *Glaube und Religion in der frühen Kirche* (Freiburg, 1973), p. 81.

35. Ibid., pp. 81f.

36. H. Mühlen, *Entsakralisierung*, p. 207.

37. P. Stockmeier, *Glaube und Religion in der frühen Kirche,* p. 101.

38. J. L. Segundo, *El dogma que libera* (Santander, 1989), p. 224. Eng. trans. *The Liberation of Dogma* (Maryknoll, N.Y.: Orbis Books, 1992).

39. Stockmeier, *Glaube und Religion in der frühen Kirche,* p. 101.

40. Segundo, *El dogma que libera*, p. 223.

41. Ibid., pp. 222, 223.

42. Aguirre, "La persecución en el cristianismo primitivo," p. 239.

43. Moingt, *El hombre que venía de Dios*, p. 76.

44. Segundo, *El dogma que libera*, p. 213.

45. J. I. González Faus, *La autoridad de la verdad: Momentos oscuros del magisterio eclesiástico* (Barcelona, 1996), p. 21.

16. A God Who Can Suffer: The Pathos of Audacity and Honesty

1. Ch. Duquoc, *Jesús, hombre libre*, 10th ed. (Salamanca, 1996), p. 114.

2. Kasper, p. 164.

3. Justin, *Apologies*, 23, 2, in *The Early Christian Fathers*, trans. and ed. H. Bettenson (Oxford and New York: Oxford University Press, 1969), p. 60.

4. J. Moingt, *El hombre que venía de Dios* I (Bilbao, 1995), p. 109. Sp. trans. of *L'homme qui venait de Dieu* (Paris, 1993).

5. Ibid., p. 113f.

6. Ibid., p. 117.

7. Ibid., p. 118.

8. Kasper, p. 176.

9. Moingt, *El hombre que venía de Dios*, p. 115.

10. Athanasius, *Orations against Arians*, II, 70.

11. B. Sesboüé, "La divinidad del Hijo y del Espíritu Santo," in B. Sesboüé and J. Wolinski, *El Dios de la salvación* (Salamanca, 1995), p. 198.

12. Moingt, *El hombre que venía de Dios*, p. 112.

13. Ibid., p. 125.

14. Ibid.

15. J. I. González Faus, *La humanidad nueva. Ensayo de cristología*, 6th ed. (Santander, 1984), p. 447.

16. J. Moltmann, *El Dios crucificado*, 2d ed. (Salamanca, 1977), p. 348. Sp. trans. of *Der gekreuztige Gott* (Göttingen, 1972). Eng. trans. *The Crucified God* (London: SCM Press; New York: Harper & Row, 1974).

17. D. Bonhoeffer, *Resistencia y sumisión*, 2d ed. (Barcelona, 1971), pp. 210f. Trans. of *Widerstand und Ergebung*, 3d ed. (Munich and Hamburg, 1966). Eng. trans. *Letters and Papers from Prison*, 3d ed. (London: SCM Press; New York: Macmillan, 1971).

18. Aristotle, *Magna Moralia*, II, 1208B.

19. See the last two chapters of Aristotle's *Nicomachean Ethics*.

20. Aristotle, *Eth. Eud.*, VII, 1244bff. On this, see J. Vives, "Dios ¿principio de necesidad o interpelación absoluta a la libertad?," *RLT* 11 (1987), p. 189ff.

21. I. Ellacuría, "Pobres," in *Conceptos fundamentales del Cristianismo*, ed. C. Floristán and J. J. Tamayo (Madrid, 1993), p. 791.

22. J. I. González Faus, "Veinticinco años de teología de la liberación: Teología y opción por los pobres," *RLT* 42 (1997), p. 224, citing important texts from Domingo Soto and Bishop Bossuet.

23. See J.-B. Metz and E. Wiesel, *Esperar a pesar de todo* (Madrid, 1996). Eng. trans. *Hope against Hope* (New York: Paulist Press, 1999).

24. See J.-B. Metz, "Un hablar de Dios, sensible a la teodicea," in *El clamor de la tierra*, ed. J.-B. Metz (Estella, 1996), pp. 7–28.

25. Metz and Wiesel, *Esperar a pesar de todo*, p. 62.

26. Ibid., p. 61.

27. J. Sobrino, "El conocimiento teológico en la teología europea y latinoamericana," *ECA* 322–23 (1975), p. 440. Eng. trans. in *The True Church and the Poor* (Maryknoll, N.Y.: Orbis Books, 1984).

28. Metz, "Un hablar de Dios," pp. 23–28.

29. Metz, *Espera a pesar de todo*, p. 51.

30. J.-M. Castillo, "Teología de las comunidades eclesiales de base en América Latina," *RLT* 39 (1996), pp. 205–31.

31. J. Sobrino, "La fe en el Dios crucificado. Reflexiones desde El Salvador" *RLT* 31 (1997), pp. 49–75.

32. J.-M. López Vigil, *Muerte y vida en Morazán*, 3d ed. (San Salvador, 1989), p. 119.

33. Ibid., p. 94f.

34. Ibid., p. 119.

35. O. Romero, cited in *La voz de los sin voz. La palabra viva de monseñor Romero*, ed. J. Sobrino, I. Martín-Baró and R. Cardenal (San Salvador, 1980), p. 454. Eng. trans. *The Voice of the Voiceless: The Four Pastoral Letters and Other Statements* (Maryknoll, N.Y.: Orbis Books, 1984; London: CIIR, 1985).

17. A Human Christ: The Pathos of Reality

1. International Theological Commission, "Quaestiones selectae de Theologia," *Gregorianum* 61/4 (1980), p. 619.

2. See Puebla, no. 178, which cites the words of John Paul II in his opening address to the conference.

3. Cited in Tertullian, *De carne*, III.

4. J. Moingt, *El hombre que venía de Dios*, vol. 1 (Bilbao, 1995), p. 129. Trans. of *L'homme qui venait de Dieu* (Paris, 1993).

5. For more detailed accounts see J. I. González Faus, *La humanidad nueva. Ensayo de cristología*, 6th ed. (Santander, 1984), pp. 398–426; P. Smulders, "Desarrollo de la Christología en la historia de los dogmas y en el magisterio eclesiástico," in *Myst. Sal.* 3/1, pp. 451–502.

6. Epiphanius, *Ancoratus*, 75.

7. Smulders, "Desarrollo de la cristología," p. 497.

8. Ibid., p. 501.

9. International Theological Commission, "Quaestiones selectae de Theologia," p. 691; González Faus, *La humanidad nueva*, p. 472ff.

10. Ch. Duquoc, *Cristología. Ensayo dogmático sobre Jesús de Nazaret el Mesías*, 6th ed. (Salamanca, 1992), p. 268.

11. Smulders, "Desarrollo de la cristología," p. 501.

12. I. Ellacuría, "Función liberadora de la filosofía," *ECA* 435–36 (1985), p. 50.

13. I. Ellacuría, "Discernir el signo de los tiempos," *Diakonía* 17 (1981), p. 58.

14. See L. Boff, "San Francisco, *repetitor Christi*," in *Jesucristo y la liberación del hombre*, 2d ed. (Madrid, 1987), pp. 539–43.

15. The essentials of the *Spiritual Exercises* are structured on the meditations on the life, death, and resurrection of Jesus.

16. J. P. Miranda, *El ser y el mesías* (Salamanca, 1973), p. 9. Eng. trans. *Being and the Messiah* (Maryknoll, N.Y.: Orbis Books, 1977).

17. J.-B. Metz, "¿Qué pasó con Dios? ¿Qué pasó con el hombre? Sobre la situación del cristianismo en la Europa secularizada," *RLT* 14 (1988), p. 215ff.

18. God in History: The Pathos of the Whole

1. Ch. Duquoc, *Cristología. Ensayo dogmático sobre Jesús de Nazaret el Mesías*, 6th ed. (Salamanca, 1992), p. 267.

2. J. I. González Faus, "Dogmática cristológica y lucha por la justicia," *Revista Latinoamericana de Teología* 34 (1995), p. 53.

3. See Archbishop Romero's third pastoral letter, "La Iglesia y las organizaciones políticas populares," in *La voz de los sin voz*, ed. J. Sobrino, I. Martín-Baró and R. Cardenal (San Salvador, 1980), pp. 91–121. Eng. trans. *The Voice of the Voiceless: The Four Pastoral Letters and Other Statements* (Maryknoll, N.Y.: Orbis Books; London: CIIR, 1985), pp. 85–161. The third pastoral letter is also available separately: *Christians, Political Organizations and Violence* (London: CIIR, 1985). See also I. Ellacuría, "El verdadero pueblo de Dios," in *Conversión de la Iglesia al pueblo de Dios* (San Salvador, 1985), pp. 81–125; J. Sobrino, "Espiritualidad y liberación," in *Liberación con espíritu* (San Salvador, 1985), pp. 35–58. Eng. trans. *Spirituality of Liberation* (Maryknoll, N.Y.: Orbis Books, 1988).

4. Ellacuría, "La Iglesia de los pobres, sacramento histórico de liberación," *ECA* (Oct.–Nov. 1997), p. 717. Eng. trans. in I. Ellacuría and J. Sobrino, eds., *Mysterium Liberationis* (Maryknoll, N.Y.: Orbis Books, 1993), pp. 543–64.

5. Nestorius, *Sermo* VIII. The documents in the controversy can be found in *Creeds*, pp. 291–321.

6. Around the time of Vatican II there was an abundance of christological publications analyzing and interpreting Chalcedon. The following have become classics: K. Rahner and W. Thüsing, *Christologie—Systematisch und Exegetisch* (Freiburg, 1972)—Eng. trans. *A New Christology* (London: Burns & Oates, 1980); W. Pannenberg, *Grundzüge der Christologie* (Gütersloh, 1964)—Eng. trans. *Jesus—God and Man* (Philadelphia, Pa.: Westminster Press, 1968); J. Moltmann, *Der gekreuzigte Gott* (Göttingen, 1972)—Eng. trans. *The Crucified God* (London: SCM Press; New York: Harper & Row, 1974). Other classics include works by P. Schoonenberg, O. González de Cardedal, J. I. González Faus, P. Faynel and D. Wiederkehr.

7. International Theological Commission, "Quaestiones selectae de Christologia," *Gregorianum* 61/4 (1980), p. 618.

8. Duquoc, *Christologia*, p. 272.

9. B. Sesböué, "Le procès contemporain de Chalcédoine. Bilan et perspectives," in *Colectivo RSR* (1977), pp. 45–54. Other classic critiques are those by Rahner and the other authors named in note 6 above.

10. See K. Rahner, *Escritos de teología*, vol. 1 (Madrid, 1961), pp. 202ff. Trans. of *Schriften zur Theologie*, vol. 1 (Zurich, 1960). Eng. trans. *Theological Investigations*, vol. 1 (London: Darton, Longman & Todd; Baltimore, Md: Helicon Press, 1962).

11. Rahner, *Escritos de teología*, vol. 3 (Madrid, 1963), p. 42; B. Welte, *Auf der Spur des Ewigen* (Freiburg, 1965), pp. 424–58.

12. D. Wiederkehr, "Esbozo de cristología sistemática," in *Myst. Sal.*, 3/1 (Madrid, 1971), p. 517.

13. See K. Rahner, "Líneas fundamentales de una cristología sístematica," in K. Rahner and W. Thüsing, *Cristología. Estudio teológico y exegético* (Madrid, 1975), p. 34. Trans. of *Christologie—Sytematisch und Exegetisch*—Eng. trans. "Christology Today," pp.3–17, in *A New Christology* (London: Burns & Oates, 1980).

14. Cf. Pannenberg, "Person," in *Religion in Geschichte und Gegenwart* V, cols. 230–35.

15. Pannenberg, *Grunzüge der Christologie*, 416.

16. Ibid., 415–19.

17. Wiederkehr, "Esbozo de cristología sistemática," p. 581ff.

18. Ibid., p. 519.

19. I. Ellacuría, "Aporte de la teología de la liberación a las religiones abrahámicas en la superación del individualismo y del positivismo," *RLT* 10 (1987), p. 9. See also *JL*, pp. 121–34.

20. X. Zubiri, *La estructura dinámica de la realidad* (Madrid, 1989), p. 209; A. González, "La novedad teológica de la filosofía de Zubiri," *RLT* 30 (1993), p. 252.

21. G. Gutiérrez, *El Dios de la Vida* (Lima, 1981), p. 6. Eng. trans. *The God of Life* (Maryknoll, N.Y.: Orbis Books, 1991).

19. Formal and Doxological Readings of Chalcedon: Following Jesus as an Epistemological Principle

1. See. J. I. González Faus, "Dogmática cristológica y lucha por la justicia," in *Fe en Dios y construcción de la historia* (Madrid, 1998), pp. 91–111.

2. I. Ellacuría, "Aporte de la teología de la liberación a las religiones abrahámicas en la superación del individualismo y del positivismo," *RLT* 10 (1987), p. 9.

3. K. Rahner, *Escritos de teología*, vol. 4 (Madrid, 1964), p. 302. (Corresponding vols. in English as *Theological Investigations*.)

4. Ibid., p. 150.

5. Ibid., 5:203.

6. Ibid., 4:151; cf. ibid., 3:43.

7. Ibid. 1:205.

8. Ibid. 4:151; cf. 4:302.

9. *Myst. Sal.,* vol. 2, p. 384, n. 21.

10. Rahner, *Escritos de teología*, 1:204; 4:151, 301f.

11. Ibid., 4:153, 303; 3:40f.

12. Ibid., 4:311ff; see also 303f., 154; 3:47.

13. Ibid., 4:153, 142; 3:42.

14. Ibid., 5:209.

15. O. Romero, *La voz de los sin voz,* ed. J. Sobrino, I. Martín-Baró and R. Cardenal (San Salvador, 1980), p. 366. Eng. trans. *The Voice of the Voiceless: The Four Pastoral Letters and Other Statements* (Maryknoll, N.Y.: Orbis Books, 1984; London: CIIR, 1985).

16. K. Rahner and W. Weger, *¿Qué debemos creer todvía?* (Santander, 1980), p. 110. Trans. of *Was sollen wir noch glauben?* (Freiburg, 1980)—Eng. trans. *Our Christian Faith: Answers for the Future* (London: Burns & Oates, 1980). See also K. Rahner and W. Thüsing, *Cristología: Estudio teológico y exegético* (Madrid, 1975). Trans. of *Christologie—sytematisch und exegetisch* (Freiburg, 1972)—Eng. trans. *A New Christlogy* (London: Burns & Oates; New York: Crossroad, Seabury Press, 1980). Also K. Rahner, *Curso fundamental sobre la fe,* 3d ed. (Barcelona, 1984), p. 340.

17. D. Wiederkehr, "Esbozo de cristología sistemática," in *Myst. Sal.* 3/1 (Madrid, 1971), p. 560.

18. Rahner, *¿Qué debemos creer todavía?*, p. 105.

19. On the correlation between the act and the object of faith see K. Rahner, *Ich glaube an Jesus Christus* (Einsiedeln, 1968), pp. 11–15.

20. Rahner, *¿Qué debemos creer todavía?*, p. 111.

21. Ibid., p. 111f.

22. Cf. J. I. González Faus, *Acceso a Jesús* (Salamanca, 1983), p. 206ff.

23. Rahner, *¿Qué debemos creer todavía?*, p. 111.

Epilogue: Memory and Journey

1. J. L. Segundo, "El significado de la divinidad de Jesús," in *Teología abierta*, vol. 3, *Reflexiones críticas* (Madrid, 1984), p. 314f.

2. Ibid., pp. 306–14; see also J. L. Segundo, "Disquisición sobre el misterio absoluto," *RLT* 6 (1985), pp. 209–27.

3. Ibid., p. 307.

4. Ibid., p. 313.

5. Ibid., p. 314.

6. See J. I. González Faus' detailed analysis of both things in "Veinticinco años de la teología de la liberación: teología y opción por los pobres," *RLT* 42 (1997), pp. 236, 238.

Index